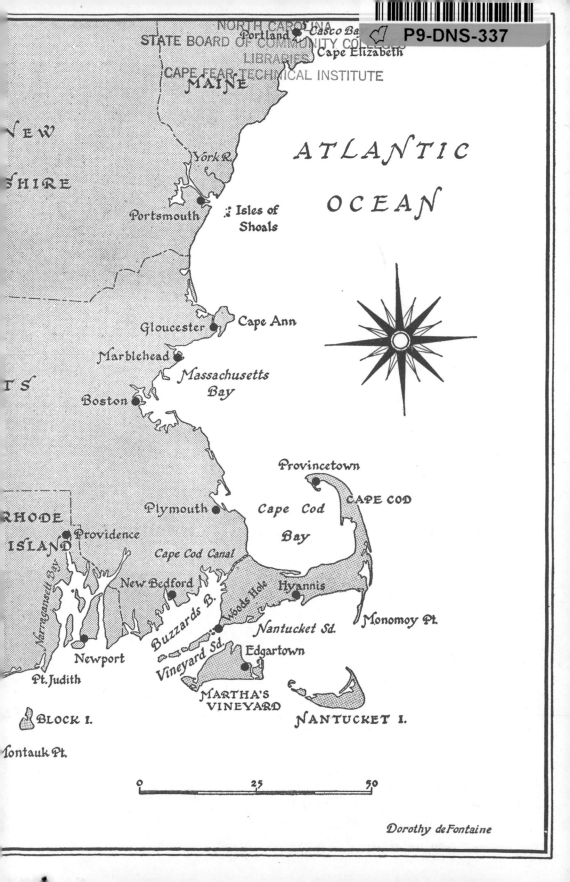

ATLANTIC

OCEAN

MAINE

Portland

Casco Bay

Cape Elizabeth

York R.

Portsmouth

Isles of
Shoals

NEW

SHIRE

Gloucester

Cape Ann

Marblehead

Massachusetts
Bay

Boston

Provincetown

CAPE COD

Plymouth

Cape Cod

Bay

RHODE

Providence

ISLAND

Cape Cod Canal

New Bedford

Woods Hole

Hyannis

Buzzards B.

Monomoy Pt.

Nantucket Sd.

Newport

Vineyard Sd.

Edgartown

Narragansett Bay

Pt. Judith

MARTHA'S
VINEYARD

NANTUCKET I.

BLOCK I.

Montauk Pt.

0   25   50

Dorothy de Fontaine

A CRUISING GUIDE TO THE

NEW ENGLAND COAST

Including the Hudson River, Long Island Sound,

and

the Coast of New Brunswick

OTHER DODD, MEAD CRUISING GUIDES

A Cruising Guide to the Chesapeake
A Cruising Guide to the Southern Coast
A Cruising Guide to the Caribbean and the Bahamas

A Cruising Guide

to the

NEW ENGLAND COAST

INCLUDING THE HUDSON RIVER,
LONG ISLAND SOUND, AND
THE COAST OF NEW BRUNSWICK

By

ROGER F. DUNCAN
AND
JOHN P. WARE

WITH ILLUSTRATIONS AND CHARTS

1979 EDITION

Dodd, Mead & Company

The poem "Offshore" from *Weathers and Edges* by
Philip Booth, copyright © 1963 by Philip Booth, reprinted by permission of The Viking Press, Inc.

The quotation from *The Wind in the Willows* by Kenneth
Grahame, copyright 1933, reprinted with permission
of Charles Scribner's Sons, New York.

Selections from *Carter's Coast of New England* reprinted
by permission of New Hampshire Publishing Company, Somersworth, N.H.

Library of Congress Cataloging in Publication Data

Duncan, Roger F
   A cruising guide to the New England coast.

   Includes index.
   1. Pilot guides—New England. 2. Pilot guides—
Long Island Sound. 3. Harbors—New England.
4. Harbors—Long Island Sound. I. Ware, John P.,
joint author. II. Title.
VK982.N43D86   1979   623.89′29′74   78-31094
   ISBN 0-396-07629-7

This book is dedicated with gratitude and respect to our wives, Mary C. Duncan and Molly P. Ware. They have served as crew aboard our boats, helped immeasurably in the collection of information, kept straight the letters, cards, pictures, and nondescript notes from which this book is compiled, fed us, protected us, and encouraged us.

Foreword

The purpose of this *Guide* is to contribute to the safety and enjoyment of the cruising man. In no way is it intended to supersede such necessary aids as the *U.S. Coast Pilot,* National Ocean Survey charts, or tables of tides and currents. We have tried to supplement them by adding information of navigational importance where we can and also by supplying information they do not include about facilities ashore. Also, we hope to make the coast more interesting by adding such notes from history, tradition, and folklore as will give character and color to what otherwise might be mere harbors, capes, and islands.

We have visited personally at some time almost every harbor described in this book and have supplemented our experience from books and magazines. More importantly, we have been assisted by literally hundreds of yachtsmen, fishermen, town officials, and local residents. We have made strenuous efforts to be accurate, but we warn readers that **the information contained herein cannot be guaranteed and must be used with caution. Charts reproduced as illustrations are not for navigational purposes but are printed through the cooperation of the National Ocean Survey as aids to following the text.**

In some cases we have mentioned names of specific people or businesses because we believed this information to be of value to the cruising man. In doing so, we intend no slight whatever to those left unmentioned. This *Guide* is not intended as an advertising medium and has never been permitted to be used in that way.

The continued value of the book depends heavily on the cooperation of its readers. Because each edition is necessarily to a large extent a subjective work, limited by the experiences and judgments of the authors, we urge cruising men to contribute to future editions and revisions any information and reflections that will improve the *Guide.*

The astute reader will note that a few harbors of a remote and secluded nature have been omitted, in the spirit of Descartes, who wrote in the introduction to his *Geometry:*

"I hope that posterity will judge me kindly, not only for those things which I have included; but also for those which I have purposely omitted that others may share in the joy of discovery."

ROGER F. DUNCAN
Box 66
East Boothbay, Maine 04544

The Origin and History of This Guide

Robert F. Duncan had first cruised the New England coast as a boy with a Casco Bay partyboat skipper and had been afloat in one vessel or another almost every summer since then. In 1934 he prepared some notes on New England harbors for his friend, Fessenden S. Blanchard, who planned a cruise from Woods Hole, Massachusetts, to North Haven, Maine. Mr. Blanchard used the notes and added his own observations and commentary.

During the ensuing winter, members of the Coastwise Cruising Club of Scarsdale, New York, of which both men were members, augmented the original notes with their own experiences and expanded them westward to Larchmont, New York, and eastward to Saint Andrews, New Brunswick. During the summer of 1935 much of the information was verified and brought up to date. In May 1936 a mimeographed volume of 169 pages and limited to 50 copies, was published by Mr. Duncan and distributed among friends with a request for additions and corrections. This edition, however, included only the harbors between Larchmont and Bar Harbor.

In response to this request for information, the book was again revised and an edition of 1,000 copies was published by David Kemp & Company in 1937. It was extended eastward from Bar Harbor to Passamaquoddy Bay. Another printing with revisions followed in 1938. In 1946 a third edition was published, this time by Dodd, Mead & Company. Mr. Blanchard joined Mr. Duncan as co-author and the book was enlarged to include the Hudson River and the Saint John River. The volume included, exclusive of appendixes, only 282 pages. A revised printing followed in 1952 and a fourth edition in 1954, with another revision in 1959. By this time the book had grown to 434 pages.

In 1961 the present writer took over the book from his father, the original author, and with Mr. Blanchard as co-author and with the able assistance of Mr. Blanchard's son-in-law, John P. Ware, published a fifth edition, entirely revised and somewhat enlarged. A sixth followed in 1968, this time by the second generation of authors alone, and a seventh edition was published in 1972. As a result of the contributions of many cruising men, of a desire on the part of the authors to make the volume as complete as possible, and of a reluctance to leave out interesting anecdotes from earlier editions, the book had grown to 697 pages and is still growing.

A comparison of the current edition with its predecessors of forty years ago reflects tremendous changes in the coastal communities and in the yachts and yachtsmen who visit them. In the thirties we saw commercial sailing vessels on the coast still carrying cargoes more or less profitably and the few yachts we saw were usually over 30 feet and often much bigger. The 100-foot schooner *Constellation,* carrying main and fore gaff topsails, sparkling in brass, varnish, and black paint, passed us off Rockland, her paid crew standing by in the lee of the foresail. Today our harbors are crowded with scores of cruising boats under 30 feet, requiring the construction of marinas and stimulating a tremendous service industry. Much of this change has come, in eastern waters at least, since the last edition.

In the current edition, the eighth, we reflect this change, but much remains unchanged. The islands stand firm, the ledges are unmoved, the tides run as they always have, and the brave west wind still blows.

ROGER F. DUNCAN
JOHN P. WARE

Acknowledgments

The authors cannot thank everyone who has helped with this *Guide.* It is a truly cooperative enterprise. The following, however, deserve our special gratitude: Dorothy Dubuque, Membership Secretary, who updated the information on the Mystic Seaport; Gerard Boardman of the South Street Seaport Museum; Russell C. Mt. Pleasant of the New York State Department of Environmental Conservation; and George S. Fox of Northeast Utilities for contributing the section on Millstone Point, Connecticut.

Our appreciation also goes to Philip A. Davis, Jr., for much of the material used from Newburyport to York; Antoine du Bourg for extensive local knowledge contributed on ports south of Cape Cod; Robert C. Duncan for gathering a good deal of the information between Boothbay Harbor and Mt. Desert; Gardner Lane and Mark Jordan for piloting the author in aircraft to take many of the air photos; Hartley Lord for much material on the coast between Portsmouth and Portland; Gerald Peer for recent information on the New Brunswick coast and the Saint John River; Nancy Taylor for painstaking typing and helpful criticism; and Hugh G. Williams for a great deal of information on the Maine and New Brunswick coasts and for much helpful criticism.

In addition to those mentioned above, there are a great many others with whom the authors talked in ship chandleries, marinas, and waterfront coffee shops—faithful correspondents, fishermen, harbor masters, postmasters, and residents of coastal towns, of which the following are representative: Jerry Abel, Bruce Angus, William Ashbaugh, Chris and Warren Bayreuther, Eric Berkander, Bill Bickley, Mary Blanchard, John Bogart, Robert Boyle, Charles Bradford, Wright Britton, Ted Brown, Charles Burt, Edward Burt, Farnham Butler, Robert Butman, George Cadwalader, David Campbell, Arthur F. Chace, Jr., Percy Chubb, Jr., Prentice Claflin, T. Clements, Stephen Cluett, Blake Cooley, Henry Cooper, Ted Cooper, Chester Crosby, Jr., John Crowell, Hunt Curtis, Bob Davidoff, Christopher Douglas, Donald C. Duncan, Jacqueline Evans, William Fisher, Peter Ford, Fraser Forsythe, Charles Gallagher, Eugene Gardner, Kathy Gill, Arthur Gray, Martin Haase, William Hadlock, George Hall, Warren and Mary Jane Hayes, John

Hallowell, Warren Harrington, Gordon Henderson, G. P. Hevenor, H. Sherman Holcomb, Henry Horner, Peter Howe, John Hughes, Stuart Ingersoll, Robert Ireland, Howland and Betsy Jones, Jill Jones, Thomas Josten, Frederick Kanders, John Kingsbury, Wilfred Kluss, Carl Koch, Charles J. Koch, Bruce Lanning, Sharon Lawrence, Lance Lee, Richard Lent, Richard Leonard, Lawrence Lewis, Robert Linberg, Louis Linquata, Bertram Lippincott, Jr., Dwight Little, Andrew Locke, Edward Madeira, Jr., Kenneth McCann, Glenn McLaughlin, Richard Meisenbach, Red and Ann Miller, Muzzie Molina, Duryea Morton, Jean Moseley, Edward Myers, Gunnar Myrbeck, Robert Nichols, Edward Noessel, Henry Norweb, Alfred Olcott, Jr., Raz Parker, Mrs. Hadley Parrot, Robert Peacock, Beau Pearson, Bradley Perry, Francis Pierce, Lawrence Pinkham, Richard Preston, Andre Rheault, Thornton Ring, Al and Betty Roberts, John Rockwell, John Roslansky, D. W. Ross, Robert Russell, Jr., William Saltonstall, Manny Sargeant, Max Scholz, Frazier Scott, Philip Sharpe, Joseph Snider, Anne Stowell, Perry Sturges, Edward Taylor, A. P. Tilton, Robert Truesdale, Robert Vaughan, Charles Vilas, Arthur Walker, Jennifer and Leslie Ware, Moses Ware, John Watson, Jr., Roberta Wells, Russell Wheaton, Samuel Whinery, H. Bowen White, Peter Willauer, Herbert Willett, Robert and Dorothy Williams, C. P. Williamson, Eric Wolman, and Al Zink.

Contents

Illustrations

The Rat said nothing, but stooped and unfastened a rope and hauled on it; then lightly stepped into a little boat which the Mole had not observed. It was painted blue outside and white within, and was just the size for two animals; and the Mole's whole heart went out to it at once, even though he did not yet fully understand its uses.

The Rat sculled smartly across and made fast. Then he held up his forepaw as the Mole stepped gingerly down. "Lean on that!" he said. "Now then, step lively!" and the Mole to his surprise and rapture found himself actually seated in the stern of a real boat.

"This has been a wonderful day!" said he, as the Rat shoved off and took to the sculls again. "Do you know, I've never been in a boat before in all my life."

"What?" cried the Rat, open-mouthed. "Never been in a—you—never—well I—what have you been doing, then?"

"Is it so nice as all that?" asked the Mole shyly, though he was quite prepared to believe it as he leant back in his seat and surveyed the cushions, the oars, the rowlocks, and all the fascinating fittings, and felt the boat sway lightly under him.

"Nice? It's the *only* thing," said the Water Rat solemnly as he leant forward for his stroke. "Believe me, my young friend, there is *nothing* —absolutely nothing—half so much worth doing as simply messing about in boats. Simply messing," he went on dreamily, "messing—about—in—boats; messing—"

"Look ahead, Rat!" cried the Mole suddenly.

It was too late. The boat struck the bank full tilt. The dreamer, the joyous oarsman, lay on his back at the bottom of the boat, his heels in the air.

"—about in boats—or *with* boats," the Rat went on composedly, picking himself up with a pleasant laugh. "In or out of 'em, it doesn't matter. Nothing seems really to matter, that's the charm of it. Whether you get away, or whether you don't; whether you arrive at your destination or whether you reach somewhere else, or whether you never get anywhere at all, you're always busy, and you never do anything in particular; and when you've done it there's always something else to do, and you can do it if you like, but you'd much better not. Look here! If you've really nothing else on hand this morning, supposing we drop down the river together, and have a long day of it?"

The Mole waggled his toes from sheer happiness, spread his chest with a sigh of full contentment, and leaned back blissfully into the soft cushions. "*What* a day I'm having!" he said. "Let us start at once!"

The Wind in the Willows—by Kenneth Grahame

OFFSHORE

The bay was anchor, sky,
and island: a land's end
sail, and the world tidal,
that day of blue and boat.

The island swam in the wind
all noon, a seal until
the sun furled down. Orion
loomed, that night, from unfathomed

tides; the flooding sky
was Baltic with thick stars.
On watch for whatever catch,
we coursed that open sea

as if by stars sailed off
the chart; we crewed with Arc-
turus, Vega, Polaris,
tacking into the dark.

PHILIP BOOTH

What I wanted in this poem were highly compressed images, images stressed—almost like
standing rigging—toward the surreal quality of a
perfect cruising day. The images aren't specifically localized; they mean to distill the almost
abstract essense of heading through islands—say
Penobscot Bay islands—and *out:* to that further
perfection where navigational stars have a specific reality of their own.

PART ONE

INTRODUCTORY

Important Notes

1. The **United States government charts** from which sections are reproduced in this book are for illustrations of the text only, and are not to be used for navigation purposes.

2. The **use of the charts** for illustration of the text is by courtesy of the National Ocean Survey.

3. "B.Y." indicated on the charts refers to a boatyard; "Y.C." to a yacht club; "B.C." to a boat club.

4. **Prices** given for dockage, etc., are the prices in effect at the time of writing and are subject to change.

5. **Distances** are in nautical miles (approximately 6 nautical miles equals 7 statute miles).

CHAPTER I

Introduction to the Coast

Fortunate indeed is the man or woman, boy or girl, who can cruise the waters covered by this volume. Nowhere else in the United States are greater and more lovely contrasts to be found so close together. Spread on the table before you the upper half of a National Ocean Survey chart 13003. Within a few hundred miles lie the protected waters of the Hudson River, the lively racing activities of Long Island Sound, the sport fishing grounds from Montauk to Cape Cod, the sand dunes of the Cape. From the Cape it is but a day's sail to rocky Cape Ann and an overnight run to the Maine Coast, where granite islands form sheltered and uninhabited harbors. The gray and tide-churned waters of the Bay of Fundy run over the Reversing Falls at Saint John into the placid Saint John River, where channels are said to be marked by black cows grazing to port and red cows to starboard.

Along this coast the strong and colorful traditions of our seagoing ancestors were firmly established. High-pooped, square-ended seventeenth-century vessels cautiously sailed up the rivers and explored the sounds, commanded by Hudson, Gosnold, Waymouth, Captain John Smith, and "merry brown Champlain, the King's geographer." Fishermen, whalers, coasters, clippers, and the fast, tough frigates of 1812 sailed these seas. The first steamers ploughed these waters and the giant North Atlantic liners of the early twentieth century moved grandly down New York Harbor, hailed by the arching jets of fireboats. Naval vessels and convoys of two world wars are still remembered by cruising men today, and you may see an atomic submarine off New London. Most of us now are just summertime sailors, but the long seas rolling into Penobscot Bay come out of the same Atlantic that Champlain sailed, and the same northeaster that sends us running for shelter drove *Mayflower* into Provincetown.

The old charts showed in the margins vignettes of the coast from off shore, little steel engravings showing church steeples rising from wooded hills or a lighthouse on the end of a point to help the mariner recognize the landmarks of a harbor entrance. A few sketches from different parts of the coast may help to suggest which regions the yachtsman may choose to explore.

The Hudson River flows between low, rounded mountains forested with hardwoods and rising quite sharply from the water. Along the edge of the stream runs a road and a railroad. A tug with several barges in tow comes down the middle, taking advantage of the current. Against the shore a little beacon on the end of a breakwater signals an anchorage in the mouth of a creek out of the tide. A power cruiser spreads a wide V on the smooth surface. Perhaps *Clearwater,* the replica of an old Hudson River sloop, rounds a distant headland, her enormous mainsail using all of the light air she can catch.

Shift the scene to Long Island Sound on a July Sunday. There must be over a hundred sailing craft in sight. Here is a class of Stars racing, everyone keyed up, getting every bit out of the boat and alert to the tactics of the competition. Over on the Connecticut shore a cruising ketch slides along before the gentle westerly, her crew sunning on top of the cabin house, the helmsman with the tiller in one hand and a cool can in the other. Ahead is an ocean racing yawl—you have seen her picture in *Yachting*—exercising the crew. A great yellow-and-blue spinnaker blossoms ahead of her. The low line of the Connecticut shore is hazy with smoke, but the harbors are clearly marked by white lighthouses or beacons and by throngs of anchored yachts. The Long Island shore looks much the same, but our contemplation of it is distracted by an airplane gliding in toward LaGuardia and then by a gleaming power cruiser, all white enamel, gold leaf, and varnish. From a flying bridge shaded by a striped awning, two men in swimming trunks wave down at us. If we put into one of the harbors tonight, we will find moorings crowded closely together, and at the marina, tiers of boats in finger piers.

Passing inside of Block Island in a fresh southerly we feel the heave of the open Atlantic and see around us fishermen with pulpits manned for the sight of a fin or with baits on long outriggers, the fisherman lounging in the fighting chair. Yonder is a party boat from Montauk, anchored and rolling heavily in the tide while the customers catch ground fish or mackerel. Passing a commercial dragger, perhaps we are lucky enough to see off Newport a great crowd of sails, dominated by the tall spars of 12-meter Cup defenders. Milling about watching are schooners, little sloops with outboards, cruisers, steamers crowded with sightseers, even a seagoing automobile complete with horn and windshield wiper! After the race, the whole fleet will run up into Newport, filling Brenton Cove, lining the wharves, and thronging Newport's bars and restaurants.

With East Chop astern, we find a very different scene. Last night we lay in Hadley Harbor, lucky to find a quiet berth. Some who came too late had to lie outside. We shot through Woods Hole this morning and with a fair wind and 2 knots of tide, we are running down Nantucket Sound for the Cross Rip horn buoy. The water is a light greenish color, for it is shallow here. The sea is short and choppy, the wind quite fresh all of a sudden. There is no land in sight, although we aren't far from the low shore. Cape Poge Light is a pencil on the southern horizon, and several water towers on the south shore of Cape Cod show above the skyline to port. As it breezes up rapidly, we overtake a small sloop lugging a Genoa jib too big for the breeze, burying her bow, yawing wildly and leaving a wide wake. Coming toward us is a power cruiser leaping half out of the water on almost every sea, being driven hard against the steepening chop. Astern, a steamer bound for Nantucket is overtaking us, her high decks crowded with vacationers. We have called ahead for a slip in the Nantucket Marina. The old whaling town is profoundly changed but in many ways we will find much to remind us of the early days. The cobbled streets lead up the hill past the whale-oil mansions of Coffins and Macys and Starbucks, and on across the bleak moors and barren beaches the whalemen knew.

Far to port are the sandy little harbors of the south shore, protected by jetties and constantly dredged—crowded, quiet little places, the shores teeming with refugees from metropolitan heat and humidity.

Look again and see us off Plymouth, north of Cape Cod. The water is dark green and much colder. The shore is a long yellow ribbon of sand, backed by yellow dunes sparsely grown over with grass. Astern is the high hill of Manomet. Abeam is Gurnet Point with the light on top, and just visible behind it is the dark cylinder of Duxbury Pier Light. The low hills inland are quite distant, but on Captains Hill in Duxbury is the unmistakable Pilgrim Monument. Far off to starboard another Pilgrim Monument rises over the dunes of Provincetown. We are running under power, for it is calm and, short of Scituate, nearly 15 miles ahead, there is no harbor fit for a vessel of our draft. Inshore is a fleet of small powerboats fishing. One of them, a light aluminum outboard, circles us. Like an advertisement in a magazine, a girl in a bikini waves. Astern are several power cruisers drumming steadily up the shore for the suburban ports of Cohasset and Hingham. Ahead lies a sloop becalmed, rolling in the uneven wash, her skipper preferring to sail all night rather than use the power. The air is vibrant with internal combustion.

Off Cape Ann we see the Marblehead racing fleet, and late in the afternoon the procession of heavy draggers heading for Gloucester after several days' fishing. A steamer out of Boston passes astern on a course for Cape Sable and European ports. Inshore are the first high rocky shores we have seen, with elaborate summer homes at intervals along the cliffs. Thacher Island with its tall twin towers keeps us clear of the wicked ledges ahead, now gently washing in the easy swell. A whale may startle us here with his hoarse blow and the majestic roll of back and fin. Fifteen feet high go the flukes and he sounds, leaving only a slick in the water and our incredulous eyes and quickened pulse.

Eastward we sail, past miles of exposed beach, here and there speck-led with summer cottages or broken by river mouths. At Isles of Shoals, the first uncrowded offshore harbor, we spend the night, scarcely aware of the easy offshore swell.

The next day we are into Casco Bay; and with the fair southwest breeze astern we find a new world of islands and ledges between long points of mainland until the Maine fog shuts down, cold and gray. Our world is a circle, two waves wide. We listen carefully for the distant roll of surf. We hear Halfway Rock bleating regularly astern and far ahead the diaphone on Seguin—otherwise only the swash of water along the lee side. The navigator, alert for pot buoys to judge the tide, watches the fathometer, listens to the peeping of the RDF, keeps an eye on clock and compass. The radar reflector swings in the rigging and drops of fog dew patter on deck. But with the powerful foghorns on Seguin and the Cuckolds, with bells, whistles, and bold shores to run for, there is no need for worry. Snug anchorages lie ahead.

Across Penobscot Bay we catch a brisk northwester. The Camden Hills stand sharply behind us. The water is cold and a bright blue-green, whitecaps and dark puffs rushing across it. A lobster fisherman hauling a trap waves as we rush by, our lee rail awash. In Deer Island Thorofare we thread our way among islands wooded to the water's edge and fragrant with the sun on raspberry, sweetfern, wild rose, and spruce. Crossing Jericho Bay we meet the three-masted schooner *Victory Chimes* close-hauled and leaning to the puffs. We count fifteen sails, some running east with us for Mt. Desert, others beating up for Eggemoggin, and three working up under Isle au Haut. A motor yacht slashes by, throwing clean spray from her bow and dragging a turbid wake, which only for a moment interrupts the rhythm of our running. A gull swings under our stern and an eider duck hustles her fleet of ducklings off Long Ledge. As the wind eases late in the afternoon, we have a wide choice of harbors. We can run up Blue Hill Bay toward Prettymarsh and tuck in under Western Mountain for the night. Ahead is Swans Island with a quiet spruce-ringed anchorage at Buckle Harbor. Or we can go down to Burnt Coat, where we will find a store, and a telephone, and a wharf where we can buy gas and lobsters. Or we can press on for Mt. Desert, where we will arrive after dark, the mountains black against the sky and the harbors starred with anchor lights.

East of Mt. Desert the character of the coast changes again. Off Petit Manan, everything is far away. To the westward is the low profile of Mt. Desert. Schoodic, left astern two hours ago, shows blue already. Petit Manan lighthouse abeam is a lonesome shaft, gray and forbidding above the bleak dwelling, the shore behind it scarcely showing in the distance. Far up Narraguagus Bay is Cape Split and the white spot of Nash Island light. Ahead the great cliffs of Crumple Island, Great Wass Island, and Mistake Island have not yet risen above the horizon. The tide is running hard as we pass the bell, and the sea is lumpy and irregular. It is a bare and lonely spot with not a lobsterman or yacht anywhere in sight. Porpoises roll and a guillemot skitters off, the white patches on his wings flashing. But we are by 'Tit Manan, and a libation to the gods of wind and tide is due. They have favored us thus far, but they may test us at any time.

From the blue Passamaquoddy we are shot out through Letite Passage on a swirling tide into the icy gray Bay of Fundy and a mighty tidal stream funneling up toward Saint John. A puffin may burst out of water nearby and splash into flight. To port are cliffs, flat topped and sheer, with the rolling hills of New Brunswick behind them. Harbors are few and exposed, protected by massive government wharves. Few yachtsmen ever see this coast, usually shrouded in fog.

But if we make it through busy Saint John Harbor and up the Reversing Falls, we find the hospitable Canadian yachtsmen sailing the long reaches of the river in clear, warm sunshine. Salmon roll, the water is clean enough to swim in, and even, in places, clean enough to drink. Pleasant farms, gentle hills, green islands grazed by cows and sheep make this a paradise after the fog and chill outside.

Start where you will. Go as far as you want and as fast. Run offshore from one big lighthouse and fog signal to another or work your way among the islands, anchoring in quiet coves, yarning with fishermen, or visiting country stores. Sail with the racing fraternity from yacht club to marina or fish the rips and ledges. The coast is to be enjoyed by each in his own way and at his own pace. By virtue of no authority whatsoever, the authors welcome you to the coast and hope that this *Guide* will add to the safety and pleasure of your cruise.

CHAPTER II

General Conditions,
Suggestions, and Advice
to the Eastward-bound Mariner

1. Weather. I have often asked a fisherman about the safety of some harbor or the advisability of an offshore run and been told, "Take *summertime,* they ain't nothin' to hurt ya." In relation to winter weather, this is true. Nevertheless, a few observations on coastal summer weather may be helpful.

Throughout the whole coastal area covered by this book, the prevailing summer wind is southwest. This is due partly to the presence of a large high-pressure area between the Azores and Bermuda and partly to the effect of the heated land close to water cooled by a branch of the Labrador Current.

In midsummer, day after day will repeat the following pattern: In the morning it will be warm and quiet. Not a ripple will break the surface. The sky will be cloudless or thinly veiled with high cirrus. Later in the morning, as the land heats up, small, puffy clouds will appear over the land. Soon zephyrs from south or even southeast will come in, hauling soon to south-southwest or southwest. Then on the glassy water will appear cat's-paws and the ripples of the daily southwester. The southwester may come at any time from shortly after dawn until noon, often coming earlier when the flood tide makes in the morning. Meteorologists deny the connection between wind and tide, but the writers are backed by local fishermen in believing that a phenomenon so frequently observed has some foundation. The arrival of this breeze is often dramatic. You may lie becalmed, sweltering in the heat and slow roll for an hour. Then in the space of five minutes the sails fill, the temperature drops comfortably, and you are under way doing 3 or 4 knots with the calm forgotten. Close astern may lie another vessel still becalmed. This breeze may increase to as much as 25 knots in some places. Buzzards Bay is notorious for its vigorous afternoon southwesters, which, with a strong ebb tide, can become dangerous for small craft and "high-charged" power boats.

Many cruising men have noticed that, contrary to what we might expect, the southwest wind is stronger under the lee of an island or point and is likely to have a bit more westerly in it than offshore. Conversely, off a point or close to windward of the land the breeze is sometimes quite feeble.

The late Dr. Charles F. Brooks of the Blue Hill Observatory in Milton explained the phenomenon thus: The southwest wind as it blows over the open sea has vertical stability. That is, it is flowing like a great river of air with the air on the bottom staying on the bottom. This lower air is somewhat slowed by friction with the water, so the upper air is traveling considerably faster. When this air approaches an island warmed by the sun, the rising currents of warm air and the interference of the land itself stir up the air, and the speed of the upper air is imparted to the whole mass. Hence Massachusetts Bay, Ipswich Bay, upper Penobscot Bay, and the northeast sides of Mt. Desert and Isle au Haut are renowned for having plenty of wind even when it is much quieter offshore. It is often better to beat to the westward through the Maine islands, where one finds a good breeze and smooth water, than it is to slat about offshore in a light air.

As the sun drops in the afternoon and the land cools, the breeze moderates. Sometimes it just quits, cut off as though someone had turned a celestial switch. The evening is likely to be calm, although sometimes the land may cool enough to produce a light northerly drawing down a harbor. By dawn, conditions will have become stable again and the pattern may repeat itself.

This schedule, however, may be interrupted by a cyclonic disturbance. This is often heralded by a murky afternoon and the southwester continuing into the evening. When this happens, the next day is usually showery and sometimes is followed by a northwester.

These northwest days are the ones we wait for all winter. Usually the early morning will be crystal clear, with a gentle northerly breeze increasing in dark little puffs. As the sun get up and the day develops, the breeze increases. By noontime it may be blowing a reefing breeze, with the puffs rushing out to sea, dark green and silvery. Still there are no clouds, and houses ten miles away still stand out sharply. As one runs offshore, the puffs become more moderate and the wind steadies. The presence of cumulus clouds over the land usually indicates that the breeze will moderate and even shift to the southwest or west-southwest later in the day. However, toward sunset the northerly will often reassert itself and provide a fine chance to make a harbor well to the westward. These are great days to travel, especially for the westward-bound vessel. Such a vessel should ease sheets and stand offshore to make all the westing and southing possible if the glass is rising rapidly. Otherwise it is well to hang under the shore, where there is more wind and where it is likely to last longer.

One cruising skipper turned his crew out and got under way before breakfast when he awoke at dawn in Camden Harbor and saw an easterly breeze and a clear sky. "A bird's nest in the grass" he termed it as he made long legs of it to the westward. Occasionally during the summer these dry easterlies come in and are indeed a gift to the westward-bound skipper. Later in the day the sky usually clouds up, visibility shortens, and the day may end in rain or fog, but 40 or 50 miles of beating up toward Boston may have been saved.

Fog. The entire area covered by this book is subject to summertime fog. In general, the farther east you go, the more likely and more lasting is the fog. However, even in the worst places, the odds based on climatological records are about two to one that you will not encounter fog on any particular day. In general, an August day is a little more likely to be clear than a July day. June and September have only about half as much fog as July and August.

If one understands the cause of coastal fog, its vagaries are more easily predicted. Imagine far off shore a southerly breeze blowing gently toward the coast. The surface of the sea is warm and the air is warm. Consequently the air close to the water soon becomes saturated with water vapor. As long as it remains vapor, it is invisible. However, when this warm saturated air approaches the coast where the water is churned up by the tides, the air is chilled, the vapor condenses into droplets, and it is thick o' fog. If the temperature is raised again, the fog will evaporate.

One can anticipate fog whenever the humidity is high and the temperature is falling. If you can see your breath, expect fog before night. Sometimes you can see a fogbank approach with a cold southerly breeze, and sometimes fog simply shuts down. That is, the vapor condenses all at once as the temperature drops below the point of condensation.

Conversely, fog will lift or dry up when the temperature rises. If the sun is shining above the fog, you can expect it to burn off or scale up as the morning advances. It will dry up first over the land and to leeward of large islands where the air is heated. It will lie thickest and longest in the middle of a bay or river where the water is colder.

Once the weather pattern is established, fog will continue until it changes. It may burn off during the day and shut down at night, but it will not disappear. This often happens during the dog days in the last of July and the first of August. Under such circumstances, do your cruising in Buzzards Bay, north of Cape Cod, up the Maine bays and through the reaches. Avoid the offshore islands.

Eventually a cold front will sweep through. The cool, dry air from the land will dry up the whole fog mull in an hour, and you will find it hard to believe in low visibility. You should be able to count on two or three days of clear weather before the gentle southerly is reestablished.

If you must move in the fog, run for bold shores, whistles, bells or horns, or the lee sides of large islands. Avoid the windward sides of islands or promontories, for it will pack in thicker than tar. Sail when you can, for your ears are more valuable than your eyes in the fog and a motor masks more important noises. If you must travel a considerable distance, get offshore and run for the big buoys and the lights with horns. Plan to get in early, for fog and dark make a combination in which it is foolhardy to grope about for the mouth of a harbor. It is better to stay at sea.

Fog seems to affect the transmission of sound. A horn clearly audible ten miles away may fade out at three miles and nearly blow you out of your shirt at half a mile. Bearings taken on sounds may be unreliable, too, but they are a lot better than no bearings.

Thunderstorms. These storms in eastern New England are seldom severe offshore and always provide adequate warning. Occasionally, however, a really heavy one will cause considerable damage. Long Island Sound and Salem Bay are renowned "hot spots" for thunderstorms.

A thunderstorm first shows as a thunderhead, a heavy, towering, cumulus cloud with a dark base. If it is north of northwest, it will usually pass over the land, but the ones to the west or west-northwest will probably come aboard.

As the cloud builds up, the top flattens and becomes anvil shaped. The bottom is blue black. As it approaches, flickers and grumbles come out of it and a veil of rain appears. The cautious skipper will shorten sail, be sure he has sea room to leeward, and jog along. If the clouds are not violently agitated, probably there is only a capful of wind, a dash of rain, and some thunder and lightning. But the dangerous ones will be boiling inside. There will be a hard roll of white cloud across the front that forms an arch. Tie up all canvas when you see this, and prepare to take what comes. A white line of wind and rain rushes across the water out of the northwest and you are on your own. These squalls can blow really hard for a short time.

Usually you will soon see light under the clouds, a rainbow will appear in the east, the sky will blow clear, and it may come off a lovely northwest evening.

Hurricanes. Occasionally a tropical hurricane will leave the usual course and run north along the New England coast. This happens seldom, but when it does, the results are so devastating that it is only good judgment to be prepared. The unannounced hurricane of September 21, 1938, dealt New England's seacoast a heavy blow indeed, wrecking boats and houses, flooding cities, and even depositing an oceangoing steamer on the bridge at New London. Again in 1944 and twice in 1954 hurricanes came through this area, the latter pair, Carol and Edna, nearly wiping out the Portland Yacht Club fleet. Hurricane Donna, in 1960, was so well advertised that much less damage was done.

The earliest warning of the approach of one of these storms, quixotically named after girls, is the radio. The Weather Bureau keeps constant watch on their formation and progress and even flies aircraft through them to explore their vitals.

The presence of a hurricane off Puerto Rico, Florida, or even Carolina need give the skipper no cause for alarm. A great percentage of them swing eastward off Hatteras. But if the lady reaches New Jersey, it is well to seek a landlocked anchorage and look to one's ground tackle.

These storms do not conform to many hard-and-fast rules, but the section in *The American Practical Navigator* about cyclonic storms and the section in the *Coast Pilot I* are well worth reading and studying closely. In the writer's experience, these storms are heralded by oppressive weather, often with light easterlies and very clear atmosphere. A heavy roll makes in from the southeast as the sky thickens. The storm itself begins with rain squalls and increasing wind. If the storm center is to pass out to sea, the wind will work easterly and northerly into the northwest. If the storm is to pass inland, the wind will work the other way and may increase beyond belief. A sheltered anchorage, good anchors, plenty of scope, and an engine that can be run slowly in the gusts to take some of the strain off the anchors are necessary. Avoid anchoring close to other vessels, especially if they are large or unattended. Against a dragging barge, little you can do is of any help . Seldom do these storms last six hours, and few well-prepared and skillfully handled vessels are lost, so one need not despair. Nevertheless, a hurricane is a severe test of boat and crew, even if one is anchored in a good harbor.

2. Tides. The moon, assisted by the sun at new and full moon, picks up a wave and carries it westward along the shore from the Bay of Fundy. High water is one-half to one hour before the moon crosses the meridian. The water, released by each previous wave, runs east to join the next one coming, so the tidal current, in general, runs *east on the flood and west on the ebb*. This rule is subject to many exceptions caused by configurations of land. For instance, the tide ebbing out of Blue Hill Bay runs east across Bass Harbor Bar. There seems to be a constant westerly set of current off Two Bush at the entrance to Penobscot Bay, and the tide seems to set almost northwest into Saco Bay on both ebb and flood. (See notes in the text under these places.)

In general, the farther east one goes, the higher the tide rises and the more vigorous the current. The exceptions to this generality are so many that one need call attention only to Hell Gate in the East River, The Race in Long Island Sound, and Cape Cod Canal, by way of illustration. But these are "tide holes," and the generality still stands.

West of Cape Elizabeth the tidal current nearly parallels the course of the coastwise cruiser, but on the Maine coast the tide sets in and out of the bays, running nearly across one's course. The current is strong enough to make a considerable difference to a sailing yacht or slow auxiliary. The writer's experience has been that for the bays west of Schoodic Point about one-quarter mile should be allowed for tide for every hour one will be in the current. At the full strength of a moon tide, however, this will not be enough. Watch the tide running by lobster buoys and remember that your first guess at the velocity of the current should be divided in half. Most people overestimate the speeds of both wind and tide.

The draggers and sardiners move so fast that they make very little if any allowance for tide.

If you keep a record in your log book at the time of high water and the way the tide sets at different times and places relative to it, you will doubtless become badly confused because you will find through the years considerable inconsistency in your evidence. Tides are often influenced by winds, a tide running against the wind often turning early and one running to leeward turning late. In some places the tide works around in a circle, running east, for instance, at three hours before high water but east-southeast an hour later and perhaps south at low-water slack. This seems to be the situation in Jericho Bay. The writer started across one foggy day and allowed for a flood tide we supposed to be running north into Eggemoggin Reach and Blue Hill Bay. Between Egg Rock and Long Ledge the tide must have been running east, for we sailed across Potato Ledge and made Shabby Island far to the south.

Careful observation, good luck, and a habit of hedging every bet with log, lead, and lookout—these you need for successful thick weather navigation anywhere on the New England coast.

3. Navigating Equipment. *Compass and clock.* The first and single most important instrument to be provided is a first-class compass in good condition. It should be permanently mounted in a solid binnacle where it is easily read from the wheel and where it can be used to take bearings. Secondly, it must be properly compensated and frequently checked in clear weather. Not only must iron and steel be kept away from it, but instruments like light meters and transistor radios must be kept away from it, for they have powerful little magnets in them.

Almost as important as the compass is a clock firmly mounted where it is visible from chart table and wheel. In the fog, your runs are made in terms of time at a known—or estimated—speed. Obviously you must use the same timepiece at all times. When you run out your time, don't just keep going in the hope something will turn up. Stop and listen, take a sounding, or make a square.

Charts. An old and reliable friend of the writer's was anchored in Rockland Harbor one foggy morning, cleaning up after breakfast and waiting for the fog to scale up, when he heard the motors of a power cruiser approaching. Presently a large varnished and bechromed cruiser churned out of the fog, threw both motors into reverse, and came to a stop close by. The owner, clad picturesquely in a yachting cap and uniform, appeared from the wheelhouse and hailed.

"Hey, which way to Bar Harbor?"

Somewhat startled by the apparition and by the question, he was tempted to reply "First left," but instead invited the "captain" aboard. As the visitor squeezed down the hatch, the downeaster unrolled chart 1203 on the bunk.

"Say," ejaculated the motorboater "that's a swell map. Where do you get those? And what's all the numbers?"

It appeared later that he had come up from Marblehead in his new boat navigating from the map in a railroad timetable.

If you have not been born with this kind of luck, you will need charts. These are published by the National Ocean Survey and are available in almost any city with significant maritime business and in a great many of the smaller harbors frequented by yachts. However, the skipper is well advised to make up his chart order in advance of his cruise and purchase charts all at once, because later in the season there may be local shortages. The Hammond Map Store (10 East 41st St., New York,

N.Y. 10017, or Hub Nautical Supply Company, 127 Broad St., Boston, Mass. 02110) will be able to fill your needs and both will respond to mail and telephone orders.

First you will need a small-scale chart covering the whole region you plan to cruise in. 1106, 70, or 1000 will do very well. You can use it for planning your trip, for orienting your guests, and for offshore runs. Then you will need the charts on a 1-80,000 scale, formerly numbered in the 1200s. These are for long courses outside and for seeing your day's run on a single sheet or two. For detailed piloting the 1–40,000 series, formerly numbered in the 200s and 300s are indispensable. There are larger-scale charts than these on a 1–20,000 scale, which are most useful for entering harbors and piloting in narrow passages like Casco Passage, York Narrows, and the Annisquam Canal.

Unfortunately for the navigator accustomed to the old chart numbers, the National Ocean Survey has renumbered the charts, using five-digit numbers and what is apparently a more or less geographical code without reference to scale. However, the old chart numbers are still printed in parentheses next to the new numbers and most suppliers are familiar with the old numbers. The appendix to this book contains a table of corresponding numbers to help the old-timer when the old numbers are completely phased out.

Charts, formerly available at the nominal price of $1.00, have now been escalated to $3.50 apiece. Thus a chart inventory involves considerable expense, one too great to repeat each year. The careful navigator will subscribe to *Notice to Mariners,* available at no cost by writing the district commander of the local Coast Guard District, and will keep his charts up to date. However, it is easy to get behind.

One solution is to purchase a *Chart-Kit Atlas* published by Better Boating Association, Box 407, Needham, Mass. 02192. Volume I covers from Portsmouth to the Canadian border and Volume II from Block Island to Portsmouth. Other volumes are in preparation. Volume I, for instance, has 41 pages of charts, each about 17" × 22". These are reproductions of National Ocean Survey charts; some are sections of small-scale charts to show general regions and some are significant sections of large-scale charts, enlarged to show details clearly. The aids to navigation are clearly shown and are up to date as of the spring of the year of publication. Each year the association will print new pages to bring up to date those pages that have become obsolete. A card in the back of the atlas can be mailed in to order these. The cost of this atlas in 1977 was $14.95. While the charts are intended for planning and are declared to be not for navigational purposes, they are sources from which to correct one's portfolio of NOS charts and they make a most useful collection for reference.

Those planning to cruise in Canadian waters can obtain a Canadian chart and publication catalogue from the Department of Mines and Transport, Ottawa, Canada. Canadian charts are also available from Hammond, 10 East 41st St., New York, N.Y. and Hub Nautical Supply, 127 Broad St., Boston, Mass. Chase-Leavitt at 10 Dana Street, Portland, Me. 04112, and S. L. Wadsworth & Son in Eastport, Me., also carry Canadian charts.

Publications. The navigator's shelf should include among others the following reference books:

United States Coast Pilot. Volume I covers the coast from Eastport to Cape Cod and Volume II from Cape Cod to Sandy Hook. The books are corrected and republished annually and contain many details not included in this *Guide.* The first two chapters are particularly valuable for specific information on drawbridges, anchorage areas, radiotelephone rules, pollution regulations, and emergency Coast Guard procedures.

Eldridge Tide and Pilot Book. This almost-indispensable compendium of valuable information is published annually by Robert Eldridge White, 51 Commercial Wharf, Boston, Mass. 02110, and is available at many marine stores along shore. It contains tide tables for the region covered by this *Guide* and, most importantly, tidal current charts for each hour of the tide for Buzzards Bay, Vineyard and Nantucket sounds, Boston Harbor, Narragansett Bay, Long Island Sound, and New York Harbor. There are also current tables for the Cape Cod Canal, Woods Hole, Pollock Rip, Newport, The Race, Bridgeport, Willets Point, Hell Gate, the Narrows, and the Battery.

Other useful and interesting information fills the book's more than 250 pages. It is wise to purchase the book early in the season and to become familiar with what it contains. It has been constructed by an experienced navigator and is constantly being improved.

Light List, Volume I. Published by the Department of Transportation, U.S. Coast Guard, this book contains all lights, fog signals, buoys, day beacons, lightships, radio beacons, racons, and loran stations between the St. Croix River in Maine and Little River, South Carolina. It is published annually and contains more information about each aid to navigation than can be shown on the chart.

Rules of the Road. Because in 1977 the United States adopted the new international rules of the road and changed the boundaries of inland waters to put under international rules almost the entire coast, except for major commercial harbors used by foreign vessels, it would be well to have a copy of the new rules aboard and to become familiar with them. They differ in some significant details from the old inland rules, particularly as they concern sailing vessels, whistle signals, and fog signals.

Logbook. While this is scarcely a publication, it deserves a prominent place on the navigator's bookshelf. Do not buy a fancy yacht log, all ruled in columns, at vast expense. Get a hardbound blank book such as law students use.

If kept up to date, the logbook is a legal document concerning the vessel's operation should a "regrettable incident" occur. The skipper should enter in it the time of arrival and departure at various buoys and landmarks, and his course and speed. Especially on a run in the fog he should record every detail of the run, including set of the tide, sounds of surf or gulls, soundings, or whatever may be useful. If he fails to find a buoy or mark, he can rework his course and make a good guess as to his location.

Record in the back of the logbook the serial numbers of engine, radio, and other expensive equipment. Include the capacity of tanks; height of mast above the water; amount of copper paint needed to cover the bottom; location of the heel of the rudder relative to something on deck, in case it is necessary to go on a strange railway; size, pitch, and rotation of the propeller; radio call letters; name, address, and telephone numbers of the yacht's insurance agent and of all people aboard; in short, whatever vital statistics are likely to be needed in short order.

Most importantly, however, the logbook should contain the things you want to remember about the trip. Names of people, vessels, and places that you want to remember you will, of course, include. Also write about your crew—what they did and said, how they felt, what they particularly enjoyed. Have a good time writing the book and you will enjoy reading it.

4. Electronic Equipment. For centuries men have sailed the New England coast without the aid of electronics, and some people still do. Nevertheless, there are a few relatively inexpensive aids that may be of great help.

The fathometer is the first of these. The instrument saves the picturesque but cold, wet, and slow operation of sounding with a lead. The fathometer is especially useful in fog navigation. The chart indicates contour lines at 18, 30, 60, and 120 feet. One can follow one of these with the fathometer, often right into a harbor. In Maine, especially, ends of points make off a long way underwater. And on the back of Cape

Cod, the bottom slopes evenly off the beach. You can often locate your position from the depth.

The fathometer is not as useful in shallow water as one might think, for it gives the depth under the boat only and gives no hint of what is ahead.

A radio direction finder is a useful instrument, if not so precise as the most expensive radar and loran machines. You can use it to "home in" on a station, but remember in approaching a lightship that you may be on a converging course with a 100,000-ton tanker. Be alert to sounds from astern as well as from both sides. For a station abeam, RDF is less accurate. To get the most out of it, be sure it is firmly mounted and then calibrate it on a clear day from a known source, thus compensating for any "bending" of the radio impulses due to local conditions aboard. *Eldridge* gives the frequencies of the RDF stations and so does the *Light List.* If not dead accurate, at least the machine gives a useful indication.

Most yachts carry a VHF radiotelephone and therefore it has become a valuable means of communication. The Coast Guard monitors Channel 16 and will usually respond quickly to a distress call. Other vessels will relay your call if the Coast Guard is out of range. Channels 26 and 28 will put you in touch with a marine operator who can connect you with the telephone system ashore. Also, the marine operators, if not too busy, will sometimes relay a call to another vessel that is out of range of your set. Channel 6 is for ship-to-ship communication and Channel 9 for ship-to-shore stations. You are expected to call on Channel 16 and shift at once to a working channel. The rules and procedures are summarized in *How to Use Your Marine Radiotelephone,* a pamphlet prepared for the Federal Communications Commission and available at $2.50 from Radio Technical Commission for Marine Services, Box 19087, Washington, D.C. 20036.

Many vessels, cars, and trucks carry citizens band sets. These have a short range but are very widely used. A great many fishermen have them and keep them turned up to maximum volume to keep in touch with each other and with a home base. A call for help on CB may be the quickest way to get assistance.

Ocean-going vessels carry an EPIRB, an Emergency Position Indicating Radio Beacon. This little long-range radio will utter a call for help when activated and is entirely independent of the vessel's power supply or antenna. Therefore it can be used in case of fire, dismasting, stranding, or collision and can be thrown into the dinghy or life raft if one must abandon the vessel. It broadcasts on frequencies monitored by commercial airplanes, by larger Coast Guard vessels, and by some shore stations. Search planes can home in on it and find a distressed vessel quickly. It is an expensive gadget, but it may make all the difference.

Radar has become increasingly popular with yachtsmen and no doubt adds greatly to the safety of the vessel and the confidence of the skipper in conditions of low visibility. However, he who waits to use it until the fog shuts down is in trouble, for learning to interpret the blips, lines, and flickers on the screen takes a good deal of practice. Note, too, that the blip produced by an approaching yacht with a radar reflector is easily mistaken for that of the buoy you seek. You may be setting up a collision for yourself.

Loran is incredibly expensive and incredibly accurate. Commercial fishermen find it very useful, but the ordinary yachtsman cruising for a month in the summer may find it an unjustifiable expense.

In considering expensive and complicated instruments, one might ask whether the advantages to be gained would make up for losing a good sailing day lying alongside a float while a technician repairs the maladjusted instrument.

5. Safety Equipment. Anyone taking command of a vessel is responsible for the safety of those aboard. This is a legal and a moral obligation sanctioned by long tradition. The skipper, before he drops the mooring, should be sure that he has the required government equipment, consisting of a life preserver for each person aboard, adequate fire extinguishers, bell, horn, and proper running lights in working order. The provident skipper will add an efficient bilge pump, at least two good anchors with 200 feet of anchor rode for each, a complete first aid kit and a copy of Dr. Paul Sheldon's *First Aid Afloat,* a ring buoy or horseshoe buoy carried loosely on deck with a strobe light attached, and a tall pole weighted to float upright. A pole in the water is much easier to see from the yacht than a man, and the man too can see the pole and perhaps make his way to it to await rescue. The yacht should be provided with a dinghy and a quickly inflatable rescue raft big enough to accommodate all hands. Next to fire, the greatest danger to a cruising yacht is a steamer. In a locker handy to the helmsman should be a powerful electric light that will bring the mate out on the bridge of a tanker at a range of a mile. Some yachts carry strobe lights at the masthead. It may not be legal, but it may save your life. Flares are also useful steamer scarers. Probably the best defense in all weather, however, is a good radar reflector. Some skippers keep one aloft at all times. One can be improvised by hanging up a pie plate or frying pan, but one composed of three planes intersecting at right angles is better.

Seldom is a well-equipped cruising boat lost, and seldom are yachts-men injured. Compared to driving a car, sailing is the epitome of safety. Nevertheless, accidents do happen at sea; and if the proper equipment is on hand, serious loss or injury may be averted.

6. Pollution. The major issues on this topic are enormously impor-tant and affect the entire population of the world. Jacques Cousteau, who ought to know, gives the oceans only forty years to live. If life in the ocean is seriously damaged, yachting won't be a problem. In this volume we cannot hope to deal with the major issues of pollution, but we might consider what yachtsmen can do to keep their own environ-ment clean and improve coastal conditions as much as possible.

In the last five years considerable progress has been made in cleaning up the waters on which we sail. In the old days, you could throw over-board a paper bag or a paper plate, knowing that in half an hour it would disintegrate. Now, however, with the wide use of plastics, most things you throw overboard will float forever. Most of us know this, and while we have been distressed to see plastic-foam drinking cups floating jauntily thirty miles offshore and beer cans bobbing in the Fundy tide rips, in general there is nothing like the mess afloat there used to be. The trash cans ashore are stuffed and running over. Two little boys came alongside one night in a skiff and offered to carry ashore our garbage and sold us some of their mother's blueberry tarts instead of asking payment, in an effort to make cleanliness both attractive and profitable.

Sewage from yachts has become a sufficient problem to attract federal attention. All yachts as of 1980 will be required to carry some sort of sewage treatment system—either a holding tank or a macerator-chlorinator system. Due to the continuing shortage of pump-out sta-tions, one would do well to have a means of flushing out the holding tank independent of shore facilities. A voyage twelve miles offshore may be far preferable to waiting in line at a marina. A list of pump-out stations as of 1978 appears in the appendix.

More serious than sewage is the problem of municipal and industrial pollution, including the danger of oil from tankers and refineries.

As far as Maine is concerned, the root of the pollution problem goes far deeper than the question of oil or no oil. Maine—eastern Maine in particular—is a disaster area. There is almost no productive work avail-able. Some go lobstering or clamming. Some cut pulp. There are a few summer people but not many, for Washington County is a long way from centers of population. There is a little subsistence farming and there are a few retired people with independent incomes. But there is not enough work to support the small population. Therefore oil or anything else that will bring in jobs and money is attractive. The man who can find a clean industry that can be operated economically in eastern Maine will deserve undying thanks.

Until such a solution is found, about all the yachtsman can do to save the coast is to cooperate with the organizations that are defending it against polluters. The Machias project is dead, the Sears Island project expired in hearing, and Portland is now embattled. Both moral and financial help are badly needed.

7. Conservation. Various groups, including Friends of Nature, the Audubon Society, and the Nature Conservancy in particular, are raising money by subscription to buy and preserve wild areas of the coast. It is not our purpose to list these places, for the list would be out of date in a month. Rather, we call on all those who love the coast to do three things:

First, whenever you land, especially on an island, be sure to leave nothing there but your footprints. Be especially careful with fire. The soil on some islands is composed of rotted vegetation built slowly through centuries. The soil is thin, and in late summer it dries out right down to the bedrock. In this condition it is inflammable. A fire that gets into the soil will smolder, flaring up perhaps when the wind fans it, and will in a week reduce the island to an ash heap. Build any fire below high-water mark and be certain it is out.

Secondly, be careful of wildlife. The ecological balances are very delicately adjusted. To walk through a meadow where terns are nesting may destroy some eggs and chicks, however careful you are, and also may drive mothers away from the nests either permanently or for so long as to damage the young. Petrels nest in holes. Tread on the ground over the hole and you may cave it in. Rats will multiply rapidly and wipe out a bird colony. Your pet dog, glad of a run ashore, may do serious damage to sheep or small animals.

Lastly, consider devoting 10 percent of your fitting-out bills to one of the organizations mentioned above.

Those interested in a nationwide analysis of conservation problems and progress and their solution should read *Islands of America,* published by the U.S. Department of the Interior, Bureau of Outdoor Recreation, Washington, D.C. 20240.

The Authors' Prejudices. Should anyone have the hardihood to read this book through, he will doubtless become aware of some of the writers' prejudices. Even with the best intentions, it is impossible to comment helpfully on so many places without occasionally making judgments with which others disagree. We admit to preferring sail to power and have made various comments about prevailing winds that powerboat men may find irrelevant. However, we hold no hard feelings toward those who prefer to motor and indeed have noted places that they may find uncomfortable or even dangerous and other places accessible to them alone.

Perhaps our most violent prejudice we would do well to air at once. We are strongly prejudiced in favor of the people who live in coastal communities the year round. The towns are theirs. They pay the taxes, provide the facilities, do the work. Yachtsmen are at best uninvited guests and should behave themselves accordingly. The local people, I suppose, are "natives" in that we all are natives of some town, but we should not speak of them as if they lived in grass huts. Local people, in this standardized age, still have a characteristic manner of speech, still use colloquialisms that we consider picturesque, still dress in a way different from ours. Nevertheless, they are not living isolated lives in a part of the world little known to city people. They listen to the same radio programs, see the same TV shows, hear the same weather reports, go to the same movies that yachtsmen do. They also deposit their money in the same banks and own shares of the same stocks. In some cases they are far ahead of their visitors.

I am reminded of the story about the city man who accosted a resident of Cape Cod and asked him the way to West Dennis. The old gentleman eyed the young city man thoughtfully, pondered a moment, and admitted that he didn't know the way to West Dennis. The city man, said, patronizingly,

"You don't get around much, do you, Grampa?"

"Well," answered the old gentleman, "I've been to Hong Kong, Singapore, and Manila, but I never had any reason to go to West Dennis."

One proud moment in the life of one writer came when a Maine lady said, "You aren't a summer fellow; you're a local resident who goes away winters."

Most of these people, at least the ones who make their living afloat, have poured more salt water out of their boots than we have ever sailed over. They know what is dangerous, and their advice is worth taking. Although you may not know it, they are watching out for one another and for you. If you ever get into trouble, you may be amazed at how fast help comes. My father and I in a skiff were run down by a seiner. Before the seiner could circle back to us, a lobsterman was alongside helping us out of the water. If a fisherman gives you advice, take it and thank him. If he helps you in a difficult crisis, thank him and offer him a drink in the cockpit; and if he has spent time, gasoline, or gear in your behalf, you can offer to pay for it. You can pay most effectively, however, with your affection and respect.

One more piece of gratuitous and prejudiced advice will conclude this introductory chapter. Don't ruin a cruise by hurrying. Early starts can be delightful. Anchoring by starlight can be magical. But to start early and run late, using the engine whenever the wind drops or hauls ahead, can be grueling. You will ruin your own disposition and your crew's. Vary your activities. Get in early and take a walk ashore. Anchor and try the codfish, or dig a bucket of clams at low water. If the breeze falls off, ghost along for a while, or lie becalmed for a while. You will appreciate the breeze when it comes in. If you find it thick or raining when you put your head out the hatch in the morning, pull it in again and lay over for a half a day or a day. Read a book or play cards or go up to the store and see who's there. Those who like to cook can profitably be encouraged.

On a cruise with my son and my new daughter-in-law I nearly ruined her cruising life by running all day in the fog from Cutler outside Moose Peak and up to Trafton Island. It was no fun, there was no need of it, and had the lady been anything less than saintly, she never would have gone to sea again. Don't let it happen to you.

PART TWO

HARBORS

WHITEHALL, N.Y., TO THE HEADWATERS OF THE SAINT JOHN RIVER, N.B.

CHAPTER III

The Hudson River
and the Passage from Long Island Sound

Introduction to the Hudson

If asked to name the writer most closely associated with the Hudson River, one would be likely to select Washington Irving. His love and enthusiasm for the river's beauty and majesty are clearly reflected in this brief diary of his first voyage up the Hudson in 1800:

What a time of intense delight was that first sail through the Highlands! I sat on the deck as we slowly tided along at the foot of those stern mountains, and gazed with wonder and admiration at cliffs impending far above me, crowned with forests, with eagles sailing and screaming around them; or listened to the unseen stream dashing down precipices or beheld rock, and tree, and cloud, and sky reflected in the glassy stream of the river. And then how solemn and thrilling the scene as we anchored at night at the foot of these mountains, clothed with overhanging forests; and everything grew dark and mysterious; and I heard the plaintive note of the whippoorwill from the mountain-side, or was startled now and then by the sudden leap and heavy splash of the sturgeon.

The Hudson River with all its delights for us still flows along majestically at the very back door of Long Island Sound. It is only 18 miles to the Hudson from City Island by way of the East and Harlem Rivers, through Hell Gate. And don't let the name of that gate discourage you from leaving the Sound by the back door. Because, if it does, you will miss one of the most beautiful river cruises on the Atlantic Coast, perhaps *the* most beautiful.

From the point where the Harlem River enters the Hudson (which is 12 miles above the Battery) to the Federal Dam and Lock at Troy, New York, is a distance of about 120 nautical miles. From the Battery at the south end of Manhattan to what is generally called the head of navigation on the Hudson, it is 132 miles. But for cruising yachts who want to explore further, perhaps go to lovely Lake Champlain, the Troy Lock is not the head of navigation but the beginning of a further cruise of 54 miles to Whitehall at the foot of Lake Champlain. Beckoning further, above Lake Champlain, is the Richelieu River leading into the St. Lawrence; but that is another story. Still another story is a cruise along the Mohawk River and the subsequent canals, westward from the Hudson starting just above Troy at Waterford. This leads to lakes Ontario and Erie, and our chapter is about the Hudson River.

While, except in the vicinity of Albany, almost all of the Hudson River is attractive, the most beautiful part, in our opinion, is below Catskill, which is 85 miles north of the Harlem River and 97 miles from the Battery. But include Catskill in this, for Catskill Creek is our favorite port on the entire Hudson. The parts of the Hudson that are most impressive are: (1) *along Manhattan Island,* where the grandeur is man-made; (2) *along the Palisades,* which begin in New Jersey, opposite New York City, and continue a short distance north of the New York State line; and (3) most beautiful of all, the section of the river that lies *between Stony Point* (where there is a first-class yacht basin at Grassy Point, 22½ miles above the Harlem River) *and Newburgh,* 41 miles above the Harlem. Along this last stretch of 18½ miles are such famous landmarks as Bear Mountain (1305 feet) and St. Anthony's Nose (900 feet) on the other side; the United States Military Academy at West Point, part of it perched on a high cliff; Storm King Mountain (1355 feet), and Bull Hill (1425 feet), on the east shore, less well known but higher.

If you can't make the whole Hudson trip, go as far as Newburgh anyway; but we'd hate to have you miss Catskill, where the steep hills are reflected in the still water. It is only 85 miles above the Harlem, as we noted. We shan't soon forget a night spent there in October, 1954, with our boat lying quietly at the dock and the moon reflected on the glassy water. This was the time of year when the banks of the Hudson were of red, yellow, and gold, as well as green, adding a new beauty to the scene as we went "Cruising down the river on a Sunday afternoon."

Through James Fenimore Cooper's writings, we can receive an impression of what a Hudson River cruise was all about more than 150 years ago:

In 1803, the celebrated river we were navigating, though it had all the natural features it possesses today [1844], was by no means the same picture of moving life. The steamboat did not appear on its surface until four years later. . . . In that day, the passenger did not hurry on board . . . he passed his morning saying adieu, and when he repaired to the vessel it was with gentlemanlike leisure, often to pass hours on board previously to sailing. . . . There was no jostling of each other . . . no impertinence manifested, no swearing about missing the eastern or southern boats, or Schenectady, or Saratoga, or Boston trains, on account of a screw being loose. . . . On the contrary, wine and fruit were provided, as if the travellers intended to enjoy themselves; and a journey in that day was a *festa*. . . . The vessel usually got aground once at least, and frequently several times a trip; and often a day or two were thus delightfully lost, giving the stranger an opportunity of visiting the surrounding country.

The Hudson River rises in Tear of the Clouds, a small lake in the Adirondack Mountains, in the northeastern section of New York State. It flows in a general southerly direction and empties into New York Bay, about 300 miles from its source. Most of it is deep, though there are some shoals to avoid. Navigation is not at all difficult, for the river is extremely well buoyed. But above Kingston it is more challenging because of the numerous steep-to shoals and middle grounds. River barges usually follow the shoreline that is most favorable with regard to wind and current; with a strong northwest wind, they will favor the west shore plying either north or south. While tide water extends to Albany, the river is generally fresh above Poughkeepsie. The mean range of tide is 4½ feet at the Battery, 3½ feet at Yonkers, 2¾ feet at West Point, 4 feet at Hudson, and 4½ feet at Albany. Currents for different parts of the river are given in the Current Tables and range from 0.6 knot average velocity at strength of current to 2.0, the strongest currents being in the lower Hudson off Manhattan (where it runs 1.9 to 2 knots) and at Catskill and vicinity (1.8). Around the entrance to Spuyten Duyvil and the Harlem River currents are swift and erratic. Numerous fish traps are planted each spring in the lower Hudson, usually from about the middle of March to the middle of May, during the seasonal running of shad to the spawning grounds in the upper Hudson. In general, the traps extend from one-fourth to two-thirds the distance across the river from the west side of the channel to the New Jersey shore. Your charts also show the fish-trap areas in the 30-mile stretch beginning about 5 miles above the Battery and extending upriver to Stony Point. Outer limits of the nets usually are marked by flags during the day and by lights at night. Caution is advised when navigating a fish-trap area, since broken-off poles from previous traps may remain under the surface.*

*Data in this paragraph from the *Coast Pilot*.

"From the point of its southward turn into the old glacial channel the Hudson flows through a gorge within an old valley. The floor of the gorge from almost as far north as Albany to its mouth lies below the level of the sea, creating a fiord or estuary where the fresh waters are ever subject to the invasion of salty ocean tides. . . . For thousands of years the great stream ran, constantly lowering its level and digging one of the deepest canyons the world has ever known. From a shallow beginning, as scientists have discovered by soundings, the floor of the gorge dropped steeply until in some places it reached a depth of 3600 feet, a thousand feet deeper than the Royal Gorge of the Colorado. Had there been human life then, a traveler in a boat on the Hudson might have looked up to the blue sky between walls more than two miles high."* But the sea came back and buried the canyon.

Once many great private estates lined the Hudson. Some still do, but now a considerable number of them have been taken over by various institutions: Catholic colleges and monasteries, Protestant organizations, museums, sanitaria, schools, etc.

There have been many changes since Giovanni da Verrazano, Florentine explorer, wrote to his employer, Francis I of France, in July 1524: "We have found," he said, "a pleasant place below steep little hills. And from those hills a mighty deep-mouthed river ran into the sea." Eighty-five years later, on September 2, 1609, an English sea captain, employed by the Dutch East India Company to find the Northwest Passage to China, sailed his *Half Moon* into the river that bears his name and came to anchor near the mouth.

There are many good docks or sheltered anchorages in the 132 miles of the Hudson River from the Battery to the Troy Lock. In the pages that follow we have described the ones that we consider the most important, thirty-one in all to Troy. We don't pretend to have covered all of them, and even if we did, we should soon be out of date, for new ones are constantly being developed, as the Hudson becomes more and more popular among cruising yachtsmen. Evidence of the size of the boating population traversing these waters comes from the Office of Canal Operations, New York Department of Public Works. In 1976, a total of 90,951 pleasure boats were lifted or lowered within the 57 locks interspersed throughout the New York State Barge Canal system.

Here is a table of the distances in nautical miles, most of them upriver from the point where the Harlem River joins the Hudson. Distances are

---

*From *The Hudson*, by Carl Carmer, in "The Rivers of America" series (Rinehart & Co., Inc.)—a very interesting book for those who cruise the Hudson.

given to a spot on the Hudson opposite each port. It may take ½ mile to a mile or so to reach the dock.

	Distance Above the Battery
Seventy-ninth Street Boat Basin (east shore)	6.
Edgewater Yacht Basin (west shore)	8.5
Englewood Boat Basin (west shore, across from Harlem River)	12.
Harlem River (enters from east shore)	12.
	Distance Above Harlem River
Alpine Boat Basin (west shore)	4.
Hastings-on-Hudson (east shore, Tower Ridge Yacht Club)	7.
Tarrytown Harbor (east shore)	12.
Upper Nyack (west shore, Julius Petersen Inc., boatyard)	13.
Ossining (east shore)	16.5
Haverstraw (west shore)	20.5
Grassy Point (town Stony Point—west shore)	22.5
Montrose (east shore)	23.5
Peekskill (east shore, Peekskill Yacht Club)	26.
Garrison (east shore)	33.
Cornwall-on-Hudson (west shore)	37.5
Newburgh (west shore, Newburgh Yacht Club)	41.
New Hamburg (east shore)	46.5
Poughkeepsie (east shore)	53.5
Maritje Kill (east shore)	56.
Staatsburg, Indian Kill (east shore, Norrie Park Boat Basin)	61.5
Kingston, Rondout Creek (west shore, 2 miles to dock)	67.
Saugerties, Esopus Creek (west shore)	76.
Catskill, Catskill Creek (west shore)	85.
Athens (west shore)	89.
Coxsackie (west shore)	95.5
Schodack Creek (east shore)	99.
New Baltimore (west shore)	100.5
Coeymans (west shore)	102.
Castleton-on-Hudson (east shore)	105.5
Rensselaer (east shore, Albany Yacht Club)	112.5
Watervliet (west shore)	118.
Troy (east shore, Federal Lock)	120.

Hudson River looking north from West Point. Storm King Mountain on left.

	From (Federal Troy) Lock
North Troy	2.
Lock 1. Canalized, Upper Hudson	2.5
Mechanicsville	10.
Schuylerville	24.
Fort Edwards (beginning of Champlain Barge Canal)	34.
Smith Basin	41.
Whitehall (lower end of Lake Champlain)	54.
Total—the Battery to Lake Champlain	186.

We are hoping that the fellow who asked us if there were any good stopping places on the Hudson will read the above and then study our descriptions of these ports below. But first we must get to the Hudson.

City Island to the Hudson River, N.Y.
(12366   223) (12339   226) (12342   274) (12335   745) (12341 746) (12345   747)

1. The Current. The important thing about the passage through the East River and its famous Hell Gate is to pick the current right. Unlike Long Island Sound, the ebb current here sets westward, the flood eastward. A good plan is to start from City Island about an hour before the ebb turns westward at Rikers Island (6 miles from City Island) and then carry the ebb through the East River and Hell Gate. From Whitestone Bridge to North Brother Island the current at mean velocity is 1½ knots. In Hell Gate, off Mill Rock, the mean velocity at strength of current is about 3½ knots for the eastward current and 4½ knots for the westward (ebb current). In the Harlem River the *north* current toward the Hudson from Hell Gate flows while the *west* or ebb current is flowing through East River and Hell Gate—and vice versa. Thus, if you carry a favorable ebb current from Long Island Sound to Hell Gate (westward), you will also carry a favorable current (northward) through the Harlem River. The northerly current in the Harlem is considered the ebb, for after passing under the bridge at Hell Gate, on its way to New York Bay, it swings around Ward and Randall islands into the Harlem River and later joins the ebb current on the Hudson at Spuyten Duyvil. This is an added reason for picking the current right if you are headed for the Hudson from City Island. Currents in the Harlem River range from 2.8 opposite Little Hell Gate to 1.1 in other parts.

The authors are indebted to James Gordon Gilkey, Jr., who, as an experienced Hudson River skipper, provides us here with additional information on tidal currents. His description has been approved by the Chief of Currents Section, Oceanography Division of the U.S. Department of Commerce.

Because the Hudson River between Manhattan Island and Troy, below the Federal Lock, for a distance of approximately 120 miles, is influenced both by the flow of tidal currents and by the downstream flow of the river, taking advantage of the current when cruising on the Hudson is a somewhat tricky business. Particularly going upstream, however, the alert cruising man can save both time and fuel by giving a little consideration to the flow of the current.

Under ordinary summer conditions, when most pleasure cruisers will be making the trip, the downstream flow of the Hudson River, eliminating the effect of tidal action, is approximately one half a knot. There is, of course, considerable local variation, depending upon the width of the river at a given point, the fresh water flowing into the Hudson from tributary streams, and the location of the navigation channel with respect to the channel the current of the river follows.

Because of the flow of the river current downstream, the tidal current floods upstream for only a bit over five hours between slack waters, while the ebb current flows downstream for approximately seven hours. This discrepancy will puzzle a skipper the first time he travels up or down the Hudson River. Table #1 of the *Tidal Current Tables for the Atlantic Coast of North America,* published by the National Ocean Survey, gives the times of slack water and the times and velocities of maximum current for a calendar year at various points along the coast. From this Table of Daily Current Predictions, giving the time when slack water occurs at The Narrows, New York Harbor, the cruising navigator can calculate, by using Table #2 in the same publication, the difference in the time slack water occurs at thirty different points along the Hudson between the Battery and Troy Lock. For every twenty miles traveled up the Hudson, slack water occurs at approximately an hour later than downstream. This rough generalization means that slack water at the Battery comes an hour and a half later than slack water in the Narrows; at the Thruway Bridge over the Tappan Zee just below Tarrytown slack water comes two and a half hours later than at the Narrows; at Poughkeepsie it comes four and a half hours later; at Catskill about six hours later; and at Albany seven and a half hours later.

Cruising *up* the Hudson, if the time of departure can be scheduled for a couple of hours *after* the time of maximum *ebb* current, as given in Table #1 for the Narrows, and corrected in Table #2 for the point of departure on the Hudson, the current the cruiser will have to buck going upstream will diminish and after slack water will then for about five hours be in his favor before once again turning against him. The buoys marking the channel in the Hudson will quickly show whether or not his calculations are accurate. Since the ebb current flows at an average rate of 1 to 2 knots, and the average flood current flows between .8 and 1.6 knots, the advantage of going with the current is considerable. During times of spring tides (new and full moon) the velocities will be about 20 percent stronger; and at certain periods of the year (around October 15) the velocity of flood could be up to 2 knots, while the ebb might run as strong as 3 knots. The effect upon fuel consumption of such currents, obviously, becomes a significant factor in any trip up or down the Hudson River.

It frequently happens that the difference of a few hours in departure time, in cruisers moving along at a speed of about 10 knots (which is maximum speed in any case in the canals for which the trip is planned), makes the difference between bucking the current or having a favorable current for much of the day. Since there are plenty of sights to see all along the Hudson while waiting for a favorable current, and since pleasure cruising is intended to be just that, adjusting the hour of departure to take advantage of the current is a game well worth the candle, and the price of fuel.

2. Distances. From City Island, the distances toward the Hudson are about as follows:

To Rikers Island, east end	6.
To Mill Rock, Hell Gate, where Harlem River comes in	11.
Via Harlem River	
To the Harlem River entrance on the Hudson	18.
Around Manhattan Island	
To the Battery	17.
To the Harlem River entrance on the Hudson	29.

Thus, it is about eleven miles further if you go around Manhattan Island. But if you have time, it is an entrancing trip, which can also be made exciting by tides, traffic, and floating debris. Don't try it at night, when the driftwood may be invisible.

3. Bridges. Should you decide to reach the Hudson via the Harlem River, however, be advised that of the fifteen fixed and movable bridges that span the Harlem, separating the Bronx and Manhattan, nine have a clearance under 35 feet.

Also be advised that boat owners requiring a bridge opening to pass through the Harlem River should realize that all movable bridges will open on signal only between 10:00 A.M. and 5:00 P.M., except for the 103rd Street, Triborough, Macombs Dam, and University Heights bridges, which require a six-hour advance notice and except for the Park Avenue and Spuyten Duyvil bridges, which open on signal on demand.

Requests for openings of any of the bridges requiring six-hour notice should be directed to the City of New York Highway Department's Hot Line: (212) 566–3406. Of course, all bridges must open on demand for United States Government and City of New York vessels.

Entering the Harlem River, having passed through Hell Gate or up the East River, the first bridge you will reach is a foot bridge at 103rd Street (55 feet, lift). After the 103rd Street Bridge come, in order, the Triborough Bridge (54 feet, lift), Willis Avenue Bridge (25 feet, swing), Third Avenue Bridge (26 feet, swing), Park Avenue Bridge (35 feet, lift), Madison Avenue Bridge (25 feet, swing), 145th Street Bridge (25 feet, swing), Macombs Dam Bridge (29 feet, swing), High Bridge (102 feet, fixed), Alexander Hamilton Bridge (103 feet, fixed), Washington Bridge (134 feet, fixed), University Heights Bridge (25 feet, swing), and then the Broadway Bridge, which is a lift bridge (24 feet high).

Now let Parton Keese describe the Harlem as he did in *The New York Times* (June 23, 1968):

The Broadway Bridge operator, as all operators are required to do, keeps a record of the vessels passing through, as well as the time, and if he cannot make out the name on the hull (many times it is on the stern and impossible to see), he will shout for the skipper to tell him. . . .

The Broadway Bridge is followed by a fixed bridge, the Henry Hudson (141 feet high), and then at last comes a railroad bridge of the swing type, only 5 feet high but usually left in an open position, as trains seldom run on its tracks.

There are three types of bridges in the metropolitan waterways system that open for tall vessels: a swing bridge, which rotates on a mechanized turntable; a bascule, or draw, bridge, which breaks in the center and raises upward; and a lift bridge, which goes up like an elevator.

On the Harlem, however, there are only the swing and lift types, besides the fixed bridges, which are all more than 100 feet above water level.

Bridges are governed by federal law, which states that each skipper shall signify his request to have a bridge opened for him by signaling with three blasts of his horn or whistle.

Also, boat owners with vessels having appurtenances unessential to navigation, such as fishing outriggers; radio and television antennas; false stacks; and masts that are hinged, adjustable, or collapsible, are expected by the Coast Guard to lower such appurtenances, so as to avoid requests for bridge openings.

Here's a final word of caution to the boat owner planning a cruise through the Harlem River: Make sure you plan your trip in accordance with the tide schedules and bridge operating hours so that you don't get stranded between bridges.

4. Anchorages: *City Island to Hudson River.* After passing between Throgs Neck and Willets Point there are several places to anchor, of which we'll mention the only two we consider fairly good. However, the anchorages or docks in the Hudson may be considered better and we'd recommend keeping on if there is still daylight.

a. Flushing Bay—World's Fair Marina **(12339 226)**. As you approach College Point to port, you head in a southwesterly direction into Flushing Bay. Note that Rikers Island channel's eastern entrance is completely obstructed by a lighted runway approach at LaGuardia Field and that just beyond, to the west, a bridge spans across this channel from the mainland to the island. The main channel into the bay is very clearly marked, and from bell buoy 3 it is a straight run to the special anchorage and facilities at the World's Fair Marina. Here is a moderately good anchorage, though somewhat exposed to the north and distant from the main passage. There are 450 deep-water slips. At the time of writing there was a minimum charge of $7.50, according to manager Pete Webster. Channel 16 is monitored for reservations. A courtesy car will go for local purchases during office hours and hauling for repairs runs even on weekends and holidays. Gas, Diesel fuel, ice, water, showers, laundromat, a ship's store, a restaurant, full-time mechanics, and a tight security system can all be found here. Subways to New York pass nearby but so does the noisy air traffic to and from the airport. Run by Nichols Yacht Yards, this is one of the largest permanent facilities in the area and as such can probably serve your boat's every need.

b. East River—New York Skyports Marina **(12335 745)**. This marina, overwater parking garage, and seaplane base, jutting out 350 feet from the west bank of the East River at 23rd Street, is easily identified by a large blue building. This is the river's only marina. The Dock Master, Guilio Paties, who is on duty from May 1 to October 31, offers gas, Diesel fuel, ice, water, and electricity at the slips. Since this is a unique spot, which is handy to the center of Manhattan, we suggest reserving your slip in advance by phoning MU 6-4548.

Just to the north, along the riverfront, stands the United Nations International School. Further up rises the attractive Waterside Plaza, on the third floor of which is a large open patio bordered by a bank, a liquor store, a hair stylist, a cleaner, and a general food store where supplies may be purchased. The intimate 23rd Marina Restaurant, with a bar and a reasonably priced menu, is also right off this patio. Other food stores and restaurants may be found on nearby First and Third avenues.

   c. *East River—South Street Seaport* (**12335 745**). Although there is extensive dockage space here, *no private boats* of any size are permitted to tie up without the seaport's specific permission. This continual restoration, in the style and tradition of Williamsburg, Mystic Seaport, and other notable havens of history, is open free to the public. It is a short and most rewarding trip to its site via the Second Avenue bus or by taxi for yachtsmen moored at the New York Skyports Marina.

South Street Seaport Museum, chartered by the New York State Board of Regents in 1967, set as its goal the restoration of this area officially designated as a State Historic Trust Preservation Site. The museum is now restoring five blocks of Old New York waterfront in Lower Manhattan, known as the Street of Ships. Buildings of the early 1800s still survive and are being saved in the old Fulton Fish Market area.

During the last century, South Street was a lively place, a home of packet ships, fishing schooners, clippers, and Long Island Sound steamers. It swarmed with seamen, merchants, travelers, and people bustling their way to market.

Today, six ships of the Seaport Museum are berthed at Pier 16, foot of Fulton Street: *Wavertree,* a large sailing vessel of 1885, now undergoing restoration; the first *Ambrose* lightship of 1907; *Pioneer,* a cargo schooner of 1885, still actively cruising; *Lettie Howard,* a Gloucester fishing schooner of 1893; the red-and-white Fulton ferryboat, *Major General William H. Hart*; and one of the seaport's main attractions, the 321-foot, four-masted bark, *Peking,* which joined the rest of this fleet in 1975.

Ashore on Water Street is found the Seaport Bookshop and Art Gallery, which sells nautical books, prints, charts, and instruments.

Nearby is the Titanic Memorial Lighthouse, which for years rose atop the Seamen's Church Institute in New York. It dropped a time ball every day precisely at noon so that mariners ten miles at sea on watch could set their chronometers accurately. Over at 16 Fulton Street there's a museum display open daily from 11 A.M. to 6 P.M. Nearby Sweet's Restaurant has the distinction of being New York's oldest seafood restaurant, whose doors first opened on Schermerhorn Row in 1845. Serving meals from 11:30 A.M. to 8:30 P.M. weekdays, it accepts no reservations; be prepared to line up!

After ten years of controversy, false starts, and near bankruptcy, South Street Seaport's $7 million restoration program got underway in early 1978 with the rebuilding of its piers. At the same time, work began on refurbishing the Seaport Museum's block, occupied by the Museum Art Gallery, bookstore, administrative offices, Bowne printing shop and the model ship store. Restoration is planned also for the buildings along Schermerhorn Row, including those of the famous restaurants, Sweets and Sloppy Louie's. Establishing a marina near the museum is even being considered. It's "something we've wanted for our boating enthusiasts for a long time," reports one Seaport official.

Nearly a million tourists come yearly to South Street, almost as many as visit the Statue of Liberty. "Our function," says the Seaport president, John Hightower, "is to give New York a sense of the past, particularly as a commercial port during the era of sail. We're really different from any other museum in the country." Certainly a tour of fascinating South Street Seaport is a must for any follower, young or old, of our American maritime heritage.

Hudson River Ports Below the Harlem River
(Going upriver, leave black buoys to port, red to starboard.)

Before cruising men embark on a trip up the Hudson, it may be wise, though regrettable, for us to warn them that this "great river of the mountains" is becoming a "cesspool," according to *The New York Times.* Native fishermen tell the story that a nail dropped into the river near Albany or New York City won't rust because there is no oxygen left in the water. And New York State studies prove more conclusively that there is now six times as much pollution in the Hudson as there was at the turn of the century. Gross pollution exists from New York City up to Tarrytown. From that point the river water is slightly contaminated to a point just north of Peekskill. The cleanest water to be found flows along the stretch from Peekskill to Kingston, but the rest of the Hudson is heavily polluted as it meets the Mohawk River above Troy. A Health Department doctor reports that he would not dare drink any of this water, much less swim in it. Yet these very waters afford you one of the loveliest river trips in America.

Robert H. Boyle, author of the now-classic book *The Hudson—A Natural and Unnatural History,** is "an outspoken friend of this great but manhandled river." In considering the Hudson's future, he presents these two alternatives:

The first is that of a clean and wholesome river from the Adirondacks down to the harbor; a wild unfettered stream in its forested mountain headwaters; productive tidewater from Troy south. Useful for both navigation and drinking water, the Hudson will be a river toward which millions of people can turn with pride and expectation. In recreation alone, the Hudson will be worth billions to the communities along its banks.

The second vision is not pleasant. Dammed and strangled in the Adirondacks to serve as a draw-down reservoir, the upper river trickles to the estuary. Overloaded with sewage and industrial wastes and cooked by cooling water from power plants, the lower Hudson is bereft of the large forms of life except for a few stray catfish or carp in isolated "zones of recovery." At night, the mountains of the Highlands thrum to the noise of pumped storage plants sucking part of the river uphill. Discovery of a dead sturgeon or a striped bass along the shore is cause for excitement and a front-page story in the *Times* on the wonder of it all. Here and there, between the transmission towers and stacks, a few breathtaking views of the valley landscape are still to be seen, if you look quickly while speeding behind a truck over a six-lane highway built on filled-in river bottom. In essence, the valley is jammed with senseless sprawl, and the river is a gutted ditch, an aquatic Appalachia, a squalid monument to greed.

The future of our "American Rhine," however, may appear to be brighter than its present waters, which Henry Hudson once found "clear, blue, and wonderful to taste." The state and federal governments, with special assigned funds, are now committed to a major effort toward reducing pollution in the Hudson. True, it will take years to clean up the river and remove many of the eyesores along its waterfront, but the Scenic Hudson Preservation Conference located in New York

*Published in 1969 by W.W. Norton & Co.

City, the Hudson River Sloop Restoration, Inc. in Poughkeepsie, and other dedicated conservation groups have taken united action toward maintaining its heritage and majestic scenery.

River people all up and down the Hudson agree with the writer that the water looks and smells better than it did in 1964, this being the result of years of effort to provide adequate wastewater treatment facilities near industrial and sewage discharges under the 1965 New York Pure Waters Program. A letter written to us in early 1978 from the Director, Bureau of Monitoring & Surveillance, New York State Department of Environmental Conservation, tells some of the latest steps being taken in continuing to clean up the river.

Conditions in the Lower Hudson River Basin, particularly below the Capital District, i.e. Albany, are noticeably improving. The Albany County Sewer District has placed two major plants in operation which replace many of the individual untreated discharges from surrounding communities and industries. The Rensselaer County Sewer District has recently been placed in operation, intercepts most of the remaining discharges, and has further contributed to improved river quality in the Capital District. Quality of the mid-Hudson region is and has been traditionally good, but quality does deteriorate in the New York City–New Jersey metropolitan area.

Federal, State and Local construction grant funds have been committed to projects totaling in excess of $1.5 billion of eligible project costs, which have either been built, are under construction or are in operation in the Hudson River Basin. In addition, 34 projects with an eligible cost of $178 million are included in the State's accelerated construction program. These figures include the $850 million North River Plant in Manhattan which will be completed in the early 1980's.

Additional expenditures estimated at over $85 million have been made by industrial facilities where separate wastewater discharges occur within the basin. Considerable emphasis has also been placed on permit issuance and monitoring of the large power plants in the Hudson Valley which pose the major thermal pollution threat.

The progress of local environmentalists was dealt a setback in 1975 when polychlorinated biphenyls (PCBs) were discovered to be a problem in the Hudson River. The General Electric Co. was found to be the principal source of PCB pollution, having used this toxic chemical in the manufacture of its capacitors and transformers at its plants in Fort Edward and Hudson Falls. This material's manufacture by the Monsanto Chemical Company was halted in late 1977.

The PCB chemical has been found in Hudson River fish in quantities tens of times greater than federal regulations permit, and it is also located in sediment on the floor of the river along the entire 200-mile stretch, from the G.E. plants to New York Harbor. This potential cancer-causing agent is so prevalent that it led to a ban on the commercial sale of any fish from the river, with the exceptions of shad and Atlantic sturgeon. And although General Electric has now switched to a different chemical for capacitor production, PCBs already discharged into the river during the past two decades still are washing downstream at a rate of about 5,700 pounds a year.

Now the Department of Environmental Conservation reports that "remedial action for the removal of PCB contaminated sediments from the Upper Hudson River by dredging has been taken." Meanwhile, a 1977 PCB study poses this thought-provoking question. "If dredging is the proper action to be taken, how, when, and where should it be done to provide the greatest removal with the least environmental impact and least cost? If dredging is to be seriously considered, the dredged materials must be treated and/or placed somewhere. Leaching could return much of the PCBs back to the river unless adequate precautions are taken." A host of scientists are now seeking answers to these problems of our own making.

While we continue to read and hear that this mighty river is "going to the dogs," perhaps we can take heart in learning that at least one devoted dog is going to the river. On our last trip to Albany, we met the yacht club's mascot, a healthy-looking, obviously intelligent black poodle, who apparently couldn't care less about PCBs. Would you believe that in summer he's known to drink *nothing* but good old Hudson River water?

One must also be encouraged to discover that an extinct type of sailboat, which plied the Hudson by the hundreds during the nineteenth century, has made a comeback. The Hudson River sloop, with a length of 75 feet, a beam of 24½ feet, an 80-foot mast with gaff rig, and 100-ton displacement, was the major workhorse for commerce between New York and Albany, making the trip in less than a day. An exact replica, designed and constructed by Hudson River Sloop Restoration, Inc., may now be seen in the form of a traveling exhibit in various ports up and down the river. The *Clearwater* promises to be just one of the many surprises in store for you as you set sail upon this unique highway of history.

1. Hudson Harbor—79th Street Boat Basin, N.Y. (east shore— 12341 746). This is the first good yacht dock you will reach on the way up the Hudson from the Battery. It is now operated by Nichols Yacht Yards, which runs five other well-located marinas in the New York area at Flushing Bay, Rye, Staten Island, Mamaroneck, and Bayside. After dredging in 1977, the slips here registered 13 feet at low water. Gas,* Diesel fuel, ice, electric connections, and nearby shower, laundry, and restaurant services are all available. Food and supplies will be delivered if you order by dock phone. At times you may feel like a goldfish in a bowl. If you desire more privacy, with less convenience but more of a roll, use an outer guest mooring.

Each of the 200 slips is available at a minimum charge of $15.00. A small ship's store is in the house at the head of the basin. This marina also provides off-season limited dockage, but no winter moorings, and is open twenty-four hours a day with a watchman on duty. Its docks are well lighted at night, just one of the several security measures taken by Nichols. Full service is available from March 15 to November 30.

This accessible basin has become very popular with boats both large and small. Majestic Diesel yachts with such exotic names as *Argo, Highlander, Interlude,* and *Mademoiselle Chanel* often put in here to the wonderment of all eyes. A wise move is to reserve space in advance of your arrival by phoning (212) 362-0909.

In 1971, the basin received considerable publicity as the scene of a $3.5 million hashish smuggling, undertaken by a yacht sailed all the way from Morocco by a four-man crew. Although much of the hashish was rapidly unloaded, the *Beaver* was soon impounded by the United States Customs and the culprits were seized.

2. Edgewater, N.J. (west shore—12341 746). As you come abeam of the range lights on each side of the river, you will spot a large white building marking the location of the Richmond Marina. Water and electricity are at the 110 slips for boats from 14 feet to 50 feet in a fully bulkheaded area dredged to 8 feet, MLW. Here is one of the few marinas we've seen with its own dredge. A gas dock supplies Diesel fuel, ice, and complete repair work seven days a week. A travelift can handle boats up to 25 tons and 55 feet in length. A snack bar, a marine store with charts, and a cocktail lounge with sundeck add to the facilities here. Nearby are a laundromat and the Pleasant Valley Deli, a good source for supplies. Recommended restaurants include the Waterfront and Tess & Joe, which specialize in Italian food. The shoreline you see is not very picturesque but it presents a panoramic view of the impressive Manhattan skyline.

---

*"Gas" is used throughout as an abbreviation for gasoline.

3. Englewood Boat Basin, N.J. (west shore—12345 747). This is slightly below the point where the Harlem River joins the Hudson and is one of the best yacht basins on the river. Located under the shadow of the Palisades as the sun goes down in the west, the surroundings are pleasant, and a wooden breakwater supplemented by sunken barges gives good protection in 5 feet at MLW from the confused waters of the much-traveled Hudson. This large and well-kept marina opens annually on May 1 and is operated by the Palisades Interstate Park Commission, which made a charge, at the time of this writing, of $8.00 per night for slips and somewhat less for moorings. A steward is on duty daily from 9 A.M. to 5 P.M. While most of the slips are rented for the season, several are reserved for transients, and there may also be vacancies while boats are away. Gas, Diesel fuel, water, ice, and electricity are provided, but supplies are available only by phoning a taxi and no repair work is undertaken. Make sure of your depths in this basin and in the one at Alpine for although there is a 4½-foot rise and fall of tide here, the bottom tends to silt up, requiring frequent dredging.

Hudson River Above the Harlem River
(12345 747, 12346 748, 12343 282, 12347 283, 12348 284).

4. Alpine Boat Basin, N.J. (west shore—12345 747). Like the Englewood Boat Basin, this is run by the Palisades Interstate Park Commission and has similar facilities and prices, except that there is no adequate breakwater and yachts are subject to almost continuous motion. Gas, water, and electricity are available, with two slips reserved for transients. We prefer the basin at Englewood, where the Palisades also rise up steeply behind in a totally uncommercial setting.

5. Hastings-on-Hudson, N.Y. (east shore—12346 748). Here is the first yacht club you will reach on the way up the river. Just above some oil tanks, the battered and ancient remnants of a once-active brigantine serve as a breakwater for an oil company loading dock and also give partial protection to the float of the small, unpretentious, and friendly Tower Ridge Yacht Club, opposite the bow of the old vessel. The club has constructed a stone breakwater to give it much-needed protection from the north. Gas and ice may be purchased at the outer dock, but don't attempt to enter the basin, where there is only 3 feet at MLW. The club may have an extra mooring available north of the breakwater. For overnight slip space, the Hastings Yacht Club, a few hundred yards downriver, is also a possibility.

The wooden breakwater was once the brigantine *City of Beaumont,* which carried lumber by sail during World War I and then roosted for years at a New York City pier. When Prohibition came she was renamed the *Buccaneer,* anchored off Tarrytown, where she functioned as a floating speakeasy and showboat, until the authorities interceded. The late Mayor Jimmy Walker is said to have entertained his friends there. Now her task is more prosaic and her keel rests firmly on the ground.

6. Tarrytown, N.Y. (east shore—12343 282). With the availability of the Tappan Zee Bridge and dredging to 12 feet in its channel, Tarrytown Harbor has become extremely convenient as a rendezvous from either side of the Hudson. Tarrytown Marina is located on a narrow point, north of a T-shaped breakwater shown on the chart. It has a $150,000 section, the westernmost walkway of which contains its own built-in breakwater. Leave red nun 6 to starboard before heading for the main dock to the north of the point. You will approach a large basin with 230 slips located offshore of the Tarrytown Boat Club. There is 4 to 5 feet of water at the slips but 6 feet at the gas dock, where the Dock Master, Ralph Viviano, will assign you a slip and give you the marina's rules. They offer ice, water, electricity, showers, marine charts, and marine supplies, and arrangements can be made for you to obtain groceries nearby. The bar and restaurant belong to the Tarrytown Boat Club; there are a theater and a hospital in the vicinity. Close by is the Tarrytown railroad station, with trains to New York, while the convenient Tarrytown Hilton offers limousine service to all local airports. Slip reservations for weekends and holidays should be made by phoning (914) 631–1300.

The Washington Irving Boat Club, which is located just to the south, is best suited for boats under 30 feet but is less comfortable due to its close proximity to the railroad.

In leaving this harbor heading north, be sure to follow closely the buoys marking the north connecting channel. You'll pass the Tarrytown Lighthouse. Constructed in 1883, it guided boats past these shores until the mid-1950s, when the completion of the Tappan Zee Bridge made it obsolete. Further up, close along the river's eastern shoreline, keep a sharp eye out and note on your chart a rock marked just south of Scarborough and approximately 1000 yards ENE of flashing buoy 5. This is infamous Bishop's Rock. Without any navigational marker, submerged at high water, it has over the years staved in many a hull, bent many a prop.

A short distance south of the junction of the bridge and the New York Thruway stands "one of the great houses of America—uniting in its walls the beginning and culmination of Hudson River Gothic." Here is

Lyndhurst, a huge baronial castle of dazzling beauty, built in 1838 and for a time the home of Jay Gould. Visiting hours at this historic preservation are from 10 A.M. to 5 P.M. daily.

Settled as a Dutch trading post in the seventeenth century, Tarrytown was developed as farmland with the rest of the rich Hudson Valley by Dutch and English manor lords. Of historic interest in this "Sleepy Hollow" country is Philipse Castle, the seventeenth-century home of Frederick Philipse, First Lord of the Manor, who once owned most of Westchester. Recently, his old gristmill was rebuilt by Sleepy Hollow Restoration, offering visitors a good opportunity to see what a center of commerce looked like over two hundred years ago. One can also pay a visit to Sunnyside, the gabled and turreted home of Washington Irving, who peopled these slumbering hills with gnomes, trolls, and comic Dutchmen.

7. Nyack, N.Y. (west shore—12343 282). At Upper Nyack is Julius Petersen, Inc., where visiting yachts up to 120 feet can find about everything they need: slips, gas, Diesel fuel, water, propane gas, marine railways, indoor and outdoor storage, a splendidly equipped marine supply store complete with charts, experienced repairmen, deep-water dockside, but unfortunately no showers. There's a functional look about the place, obviously not as attractive as the Lighthouse Yacht Center, giving one an impression of what old traditional yacht yards should resemble. However, Petersen's rates are comparatively low and they promise "We'll guarantee you a quiet night's sleep."

Its dock is located at Upper Nyack, north of the new Lighthouse Yacht Center, and is easy to identify by a number of large gray boat sheds. The small Powell Boat Yard and the Nyack Boat Club are above the old ferry. The club is said to have only 3½ feet at the dock.

Next to the Nyack Boat Club rises perhaps the most ambitious marina on the Hudson—a 10-acre, multimillion-dollar riverside complex known as the Lighthouse Yacht Center. Its protected basin, with 6-foot depth, is identified from a distance by spotting a prominent white lighthouse, formerly a four-story oil tank.

The facilities here are numerous but include no repair work. The basin accommodates 63 boats, with the usual supplies on tap including Diesel fuel. There's an adjoining cabana and swimming pool including an impressive restaurant seating 250 guests. Visiting yachtsmen using these are credited toward their dockage fee, found to be far from moderate. Of interest to the distaff side, perhaps less to the skippers, is a colorful art gallery and a boutique in the lighthouse offering fine clothes from the fashion centers. Another attraction is Richard Frank's shop, the Out of Hand, where one can admire and purchase the striking handcrafted jewelry of a master silversmith.

Jim Downey is the manager who runs a tight ship here. By following the Center's sensible rules, everybody seems to have a pleasant stay. Reservations are suggested; phone (914) 358–5200.

Nyack is the hometown of America's First Lady of the Theater, Helen Hayes, so it is fitting that the Tappan Zee Playhouse up on nearby Main Street has a first-class repertoire. Famous artists such as Faye Dunaway, Eli Wallach, Barbara Britton, Maureen O'Sullivan, and Hume Cronyn appear on stage here from time to time in major Broadway hits. The season runs from late June to early September.

Dowe Harmensen Tallman first settled in this hamlet of the Nyack Indians in 1684. Now it's known as the Art, Antiques, and Handcrafts Village of the Hudson Valley, with a hodgepodge of quaint little shops offering collectibles from the nineteenth century. Here also, on South Broadway in the center of town, is the Old Fashion Chop House Tavern whose splendid table draws people from miles around. This section of town is mapped in a free descriptive brochure, *Discover Nyack,* available at any of the stores.

Perhaps some night off Nyack's shore you'll also discover the Unresting Oarsman. A young Dutchman, he stayed too long at a Saturday party on the shore of the Tappan Zee and, though warned, he recklessly started rowing home after midnight, breaking the Sabbath. He rows there yet. Listen . . .

8. Ossining, N.Y. (east shore—12343 282). "The sunsets are still out of this world," repeated Dave Narr, Dock Master of the Shattemuc Yacht Club, as we looked westward across the panorama of mountains and hills. The club property is located on the northernmost projection of land on the Ossining waterfront, where an L-shaped pier shows on the chart. The old clubhouse burned down in 1973 and has been replaced, with the members' inspiration and imagination, by a white ferryboat formerly run by the Circle Line. There are gas, water, ice, showers, and electricity—in season—at the slips, which have 6 feet at low water on both sides. Members of other recognized yacht clubs are welcome, and the club facilities include a bar, a snack bar, and a swimming pool. You may phone Gristede's for grocery delivery. There are inland slips, complete hull work, and good engine repair at the Westerly Marina just to the south.

The club usually has spare dock space for guests. At night the signal is a yellow light at the end of a barge just to the south of the entrance to the basin. The takeoff point for the club is from Hudson red lighted buoy 8. If coming from the north, give Tellers Point a wide berth of at least ¼ mile, as the gravel-bottomed shoal projects southward further than the chart indicates. In approaching from the south, be sure to stay well outside of the dolphins; and as you enter the basin keep the stake marking a sunken barge in the channel well to starboard.

On our latest visit here, we were generously hosted by Commodore Alan Hochman and a member of his afterguard, Homer Fay. We learned of the club's growing reputation as a major sailing center on the Hudson, evidenced, in part, by the fine fleet of cruising auxiliaries and one-design racing classes tied up snugly behind a 300-foot breakwater of steel barges.

If you look westward across the river, this spot is attractive, but it is wide open, except from the southeast to northwest, in one of the widest parts of the Hudson.

The famous Sing Sing Prison was established at Ossining in 1824 with the intention of using convict labor on marble quarries. Once a prison in which severe repression was practiced, Sing Sing has now become known for its enlightened penal practices.

9. Haverstraw, N.Y. (west shore—12343 282). Nestled below the craggy cliffs of High Tor, Little Tor, and Pnygyp (so named because it resembles a Dutch loaf of bread) lies a little cove shown on the chart just southwest of black can 15. Hug this can close to port in heading into the shallow cove entrance marked by a prominent concrete plant at its southern end. Two markers to be kept to starboard will guide you by a low concrete breakwater into depths of 4½ feet at MLW.

There is not much to commend this tight little haven. The Rockland-Bergen Boat Club, nicknamed Skunk Hollow, has a shabby, ramshackle appearance, offering no facilities, so you probably won't even want to venture ashore. We mention it for one reason: The cove provides shoal draft boats excellent shelter in all winds except northeasters.

A far superior and even more sheltered basin, however, lies just 1½ miles upriver with its narrow entrance located almost due east of red lighted buoy 16. Here is housed the biggest boating installation on the Hudson, destined to become one of the most impressive of its kind on the east coast—the Haverstraw Marina, which became operational during the summer of 1978. The basin's depth varies from 10 to 30 feet at low water and can accommodate craft up to 75 feet. A peninsula jutting out from the mainland between the basin and the river like a protecting arm helps to keep the marina waters as calm as a millpond.

One of the managers, Ralph Ambrosio, may be found at the 230-foot gas and Diesel dock running along the basin's northern shore. A 30-ton

Travelift is on hand as well as pumpout facilities. There are plans for this 60-acre complex to include by 1982 a major hotel with pool, restaurants, boat shops and even a heliport. Certainly the Haverstraw Marina may turn out to be the greatest boon in years to voyagers along the Hudson.

Here it was, on September 22, 1780, that Benedict Arnold met Major John André to plot the betrayal of West Point. James Wood later discovered the modern process of making brick, establishing an industry that at one time included here forty brickyards producing over 325,000 bricks a year.

Robert H. Boyle, author of *The Hudson—A Natural and Unnatural History,* describes Haverstraw Bay's wealth of marine life in the March 1971 issue of *Audubon Magazine:*

From my point of view, Haverstraw Bay, the widest part of the Hudson—more than three miles across—is the richest exploring ground in the whole river. Changing salinities and temperatures bring an amazingly wide variety and abundance of both saltwater and freshwater life. It is the only body of water that I know of which has yielded codfish, largemouth bass, sunfish, herring, mackerel, yellow perch, sand sharks, seals, muskrats, bluefish, damselfly larvae, blue crabs, jack crevalles, needlefish, stripers, anchovies, silver hake, menhaden, Johnny darters, sea sturgeon probably up to 500 pounds, and the "endangered" short-nosed sturgeon. Biologists who have been on the bay with me have gone away flabbergasted. My main prize has been a mangrove snapper, which ranges in this hemisphere from Florida south to Brazil. It is also found on the West African coast. So far as I can determine, the mangrove snapper is now the only species of fish which has been found in both the Hudson and the Congo.

10. Grassy Point—at town of Stony Point (west shore—12343 282). This is one of the best ports on the Hudson River and certainly the most attractive in the area. Its location can be spotted from the river by a prominent church spire and the U.S. Gypsum watertower nearby. One can enter by following a 6-foot channel about 150 feet off the shore of Grassy Point until red and black buoys are reached opposite the entrance between the breakwaters. Go in between the buoys, keeping about 10 feet away from the eastern bulkhead. Here is a dredged-out clay hole with a 20-foot depth running almost to the shore. Opposite the entrance is the attractive Minisceongo Yacht Club, which was founded by the High Tor Sailing Fleet and whose name is derived from an Indian phrase, "winding waters."

The clubhouse was built entirely by the members "with their own hands." Visiting yachtsmen from other recognized yacht clubs may use the floats and facilities "as long as they behave themselves." Upon entering the basin, all boats should go to the gas dock. You may tie there temporarily until you are assigned a slip. Dropping your anchor is not permitted. Water, ice, electricity, gas, showers, and a snack bar open on weekends are all available, with food supplies delivered to you if ordered by phone. Minor repair work can be done and there is one small marine railway.

We enjoyed tremendously this snug, quiet little harbor with its friendliness and rather rustic atmosphere. We have cruised here in June and October from Newburgh through some of the most magnificent scenery on the Hudson, and the coloring along the shores left us hunting for appropriate adjectives.

For major repair work and marine supplies we suggest Grassy Point Marina next door to the east. They have 4 feet dockside but no fuel. However, they do offer showers, ice, a launching ramp, 10-ton Travelift, and an attractive picnic area for the family. The docks at the Seaweed Yacht Club, located to the north, have the same depths but the approach is shoal and wide open to the east. Bell Harbor Marina, further to the west, sells gas, provides dockage, and runs a small restaurant.

The village of Stony Point, and the rocky bluff on the shore of the Hudson, bear a name familiar to American schoolboys. Be sure to visit the Stony Point Battlefield Reservation. Here, on July 16, 1779, 1200 Continentals under General "Mad" Anthony Wayne stormed and captured a fort held by British forces. In the daring charge, General Wayne was wounded and borne forward over the rampart to victory on the shoulders of his men. A story is told that during the discussion of Hudson River tactics, Washington asked Wayne if he thought he could storm Stony Point. The General replied: "I'll storm hell, sir, if you'll make the plans!" Washington looked at him meditatively for a moment, then replied: "Better try Stony Point first." On one of the highest points on the promontory is the Stony Point Museum.

The huge "mothball fleet" of 189 ships, known as the National Defense Reserve Fleet, is no longer anchored above Stony Point. Most of these Liberty ships were mothballed from World War II to the Korean war, after the Korean war to the Suez crisis, and then again for the Vietnam war. Now they rest in some foreign port as floating warehouses or upon some rusty scrap pile to serve a newer purpose. The final sixteen ships were sold in 1971 to a Pakistani concern for $1.7 million, and the last of these slipped proudly down the Hudson towed by a tug flying the German flag.

11. Montrose, N.Y. (east shore—12343 282). On the eastern shore opposite Stony Point Bay, Georges Island juts out in the Hudson as an unspoiled peninsula, ideal for hiking, picnicking, and nature study. The 175 acres that comprise this Westchester County-owned park have been carefully preserved for the recreation and enjoyment of boatmen and local residents. A popular launching ramp located on the peninsula's southern shore has been built to accommodate boats up to 20 feet overall and leads directly to a 60-foot-wide channel dredged to a depth of 4 feet below mean low water extending some 430 feet into the river. Do not attempt to tie up to the many buoys you will see in this area. We poked along this sylvan shore in our boat of 3-foot draft, finding the best anchorage with the most beautiful setting in the bight on the peninsula's north side. If you enjoy visiting places that are different, you will not be disappointed here. The park closes at sunset.

Almost a mile northward along the innermost part of Greens Cove lies the Montrose Marina, home of the Cortlandt Yacht Club and the Montrose Cabana Club, sheltered behind a small but prominent island and a line of barges forming a breakwater protecting an inner basin. It is further identified by a line of colorful cabanas. An outer line of white buoys marks the entrance to the channel, 75 feet in width and dredged all the way into the slips where there is 6 feet of water at MLW. The narrow entrance to the basin can also be located by spotting a red flashing light placed at the end of the centermost barge. Here you can be supplied with gas, the only Diesel fuel in the area, water, electricity, slip space, and taxi service on call. The marina can handle engine repairs. A snack bar is next to one of the few swimming pools on the Hudson. Free swims are included in the dockage fee. Restaurants and a motel are nearby.

A Mr. Van Winkle, the general factotum at Montrose, has won, through his good services, lots of boating devotees, some of whom are regular visitors down from Canada. Slip reservations can be made in advance by phoning (914) 737–9540.

12. Peekskill, N.Y. (east shore—12343 282). "Everybody is welcome" is always the greeting we receive when we stop at the Peekskill Yacht Club, founded in 1908 as the Peekskill Motorboat Club. The best way to get there is to go in from the Hudson River beacon 18, whose flashing light is white. The beacon itself is red and black with its number unpainted. Leave this to port and the red nun channel buoy 2 to starboard. Round red nun 4, further in, and head for the club dock on Travis Point. The chart indicates 6½ feet in the channel, and we were informed that there is 6 feet at the dock. Enter on the north end of the barges, which form a breakwater. Unless the space is already occupied, yachts may be permitted to tie up on the north side of the dock, where they are out of the way of boats coming in for gas there, and can take lengthwise any wash that comes in from the river. Water, electricity, and gas are supplied, as well as a possible mooring if the dock space is occupied.

While the Peekskill waterfront is what might be expected in a good-sized commercial city, the view across the river to Dunderberg (930 feet) is pleasant. The Peekskill Motor Inn nearby is an excellent spot for meals, and shops are not far away. In ordinary quiet summer weather this port is O.K., but it is open to the river for some distance to the northwest and southwest.

To the south on Indian Point, you will see Consolidated Edison's nuclear power plant #1, with a generating capacity of 265,000 kilowatts, and its power plant #2, which energizes an impressive 873,000 kilowatts. Indian Point #3 adds another 965,000 kilowatts to Con Edison's capacity to meet the energy needs of New York and Westchester. Special guided tours of these plants are available to the public at the Nuclear Information Center from 1 P.M. to 5 P.M., Wednesday through Sunday, including most holidays. Visitors can also enjoy the scenic nature walks, picnic grounds, and lake surrounding the plants' property.

13. Garrison, N.Y. (east shore—12343 282). As you proceed north to Garrison you will behold the magnificent Gothic spectacle that is West Point rising from the west bank of the river. Since there is limited docking space at the academy, with reservation by permit only, we suggest you phone well ahead to make your plans by calling the West Point harbor master at (914) 938–3011.

Across the river is the basin of the Highland Yacht Club, identified by two red-lighted bulkheads. There is 13 feet at the gas dock and sufficient water in the protected basin for boats of 3-foot draft. The mean range of tide here is about 3 feet. The price for overnight dockage runs 20¢ a foot, with water and electricity thrown in. An old-style country store in back of the marina may help you "replenish the larder, or pick up that item that was forgotten." Here we learned from a native fisherman that leaping carp, so often seen on the Hudson, usually designate shallow water of 2- to 3-foot depths.

The film *Hello Dolly* was shot at Garrison, since its surroundings so closely resemble the Yonkers of the 1890s. Art fans from miles around come here annually in late August to attend the colorful Garrison art festival.

If you can obtain transportation, a memorable experience may be had by a visit to nearby Boscobel, a beautiful eighteenth-century restored mansion originally built by States Morris Dyckman for his beloved wife.

Railroad buffs may be interested to learn that Garrison has restored its antique depot, where railroad tycoons used to wait for their private cars in style.

14. Cold Spring, N.Y. (east shore—12343 282). The village of Cold Spring is included in this edition for it offers its visitors a certain uniqueness among Hudson River ports. Having just passed Constitution Island, one cannot miss the sight of a picturesque bandstand and village green set behind a prominent dock. From here, the magnificent views of West Point, Cro'nest, Storm King, and Constitution Island have probably been painted and photographed more frequently than any other scenes along the Hudson Valley.

The Cold Spring Boat Club just to the south has facilities for shoal-draft boats to tie up for a visit, or there is a possibility of a temporary mooring at the dock already mentioned, but tie up "at your own risk." If you can arrange to get ashore, an anchorage just off of it can be made in deeper water, but you'll be exposed to the river's wash.

A few hundred yards upstream lies the Dockside Marina and Restaurant, housed in a red two-story building set in attractive surroundings, which include a swimming pool. You'll find gas here and about 5 feet at MLW dockside. In easterly and southerly winds this facility will offer you adequate protection.

Next to the bandstand rises the former Hudson View Hotel, which used to be the third oldest hostelry in New York State—only the Beekman Arms in Rhinebeck and the Canoe Place Inn on Long Island predated it. Built in 1837, it housed the famous Gus's Antique Bar, filled with the pungent atmosphere of a German ale house and a wild display of steins, military insignia, and weapons of the American past. One hundred and forty years later it sold out to new owners, who have proposed for it the nondescript name of the Prime Cut Restaurant.

Although history doesn't record that George Washington slept at Cold Spring, it is a fact that in frequent visits to his American Revolutionary troops encamped nearby, he often drank from a local spring that gives the village its present name.

15. Cornwall-on-the-Hudson, N.Y. (west shore—12343 282). As you proceed north to Cornwall, you will behold some impressive wonders both natural and historic. Just above West Point there is a sharp bend in the river named Worlds End with depth exceeding 150 feet. At this point, through which you should move cautiously, the colonials strung a wrought-iron chain during the Revolution to prevent British advance upriver. Then you may see from the river the old battlements of Fort Constitution peeking out from the jagged cliffs on the north-western side of Constitution Island. Further along on the western shore rises magnificent 1400-foot Storm King Mountain, which natives years ago believed to be the haunt of hobgoblins and elves.

On the western shore across from Pollepel Island, on which Banner-man's Castle rises in medieval splendor, lies the Cornwall Yacht Club, identified by a small white building flanked by a string of barges form-ing a very protected basin. The stern of the prominent black barge marks the entrance, which should be approached from due east. Keep the fixed marker to port on entering the basin. Sound your horn as you enter and check with the steward to be assigned a slip with 8-foot depth at MLW along the outer face. Gas, water, ice, and electrical connections are all available. The warm reception we received here, with its quiet anchorage, makes Cornwall a recommended spot.

Bannerman, who began as a munitions dealer at the end of the Civil War, built his Rhine-type castle in 1900 as a storehouse for his supply of guns, armor, and ammunition. After his death in 1918, the arsenal was abandoned, with the business moving to Long Island. A fire raged through this castle in 1971, gutting the interior but fortunately leaving its "ramparts" intact.

16. Newburgh, N.Y. (west shore—12343 282). At the upper end of what we consider the most spectacular passage on the Hudson is the well-equipped and hospitable Newburgh Yacht Club, where there is a basin with many slips protected by sunken barges. It is located just below the Newburgh fixed bridge, at the foot of a steep hill. The en-trance to the basin is at the southern end of a line of barges. Slips are usually available for visiting yachts, and gas, Diesel fuel, water, ice, and electricity are on tap. There is an average of about 6 feet in the basin. Besides the lift, there is a marine railway and a modest restaurant including showers in the clubhouse. Use of the swimming pool is in-cluded in the dockage fee.

While the immediate surroundings are not beautiful, this is a very convenient and well-protected place to stop, and if you have the climb-ing ability of a mountain goat or the cash for a taxi, you can reach some movies and good stores in the city. The Hanaford Boating Center (telephone 2771) has all sorts of marine supplies and will deliver them at the yacht club on call.

17. New Hamburg, N.Y. (east shore—12347 283). To enter White's Hudson River Marina basin from the south, turn sharply to starboard at the midchannel light marking Diamond Reef and run a course close and parallel to the barges forming the basin's southern edge. With only 4 feet of water at the basin's western side, this place is best suited for power boats under 30 feet. The owner, John White, offers marine supplies, some food supplies, repair work specializing on outboards, a mobile lift, gas, and ice, but limited transient space. John is a very personable marina owner "of the old school" who goes out of his way to please his customers.

Although the surroundings are far from scenic and the whole place has a topsy-turvy look, there is excellent protection, especially from the north, and we were told that boats here have been safe even in storms of hurricane strength. Light sleepers beware, however. You may not appreciate the trains that rumble by only a few hundred yards away.

18. Poughkeepsie, N.Y. (east shore—12347 283). About halfway between New York and Albany, Poughkeepsie is well known as the location of Vassar College and also for the Intercollegiate rowing championships formerly held here. Huge college letters painted on boulders and now barely visible are the only trace of these regattas, first held in 1895.

Just above Hudson River at Highland Landing on the west shore lies the Mariner's Harbor Marina with limited dock facilities in deep water. Ice, gas, Diesel fuel, water, and showers are furnished here. The main attraction is its nautical-looking restaurant, patio, and bar, claiming "gracious riverside dining." It's fairly peaceful here except for an occasional passing train and considerable wake from the river's traffic.

Poughkeepsie's urban renewal project forced the Poughkeepsie Yacht Club to move from its former location in the shadow of the Mid-Hudson Bridge. This turn of events has been fortunate for all concerned. Now the club is enjoying a rebirth at its appealing new location on the east shore off Blunts Island one mile below Indian Kill. We were greeted by one of the club's officers, George Lyons, who told us how the members had pitched in to improve the new layout, including filling in the land on which has arisen a splendid-looking clubhouse complete with bar, restaurant, and showers.

The club's facilities also include gas, Diesel fuel, water, electricity, ice, repair work, a launching ramp, and all the depth you'll need off its outer slips. Although this location lies near the railroad and is exposed to river wake, it offers fair protection and a breathtaking view of the Hudson from the clubhouse porch. A special anchorage area has been established off the club's shore to the north.

Here you'll find an active social and junior program; it's also a choice spot for a night's layover. Look up the club's steward, Einar Reves.

19. Maritje Kill (east shore—12347 283). Two miles above the Mid-Hudson Bridge the mouth of Maritje Kill on the eastern shore marks the location of Captains Three, formerly the Riverdale Marina and Boat Basin. Sunken, dilapidated barges mark the narrow entrance to a congested basin, which has shoaled badly to a depth of 3½ feet at low water. "It's a shame," exclaimed one of the boat owners here, "how this place has run down and it sure needs some dredging." Perhaps some future entrepreneur will exploit the full potential of this isolated basin to provide us with a first-class marina. For now, it at least serves the needs of the local sailor, but it is no place for the cruising yachtsman.

20. Indian Kill, Staatsburg (east shore—12347 283). In our opinion, this is one of the two best overnight stopping places on the Hudson —the other being Catskill Creek. The Margaret Lewis Norrie State Park Boat Basin, dredged to a depth of 8 feet, is one of the most beautiful basins we have seen and is located at the mouth of Indian Kill, where two lights are shown on the chart a short distance north of Esopus Island. You come in between two lighted spars, red and green, on the north side of the inlet, and the dock master will show you where to tie up, giving you a docking permit. Water and electric current for lights only are included in the dockage fee with gas, Diesel fuel, and ice on tap at the outer end of the dock. At the inner end are showers, a laundromat, and a small store where soft drinks and snacks are served. Here, also, you'll find one of the few pump-out stations on the Hudson. The Norrie Inn Restaurant is now closed, but a pleasant alternative is serving up a meal from your own galley with the crew feasting at one of the many scenic picnic tables.

For those who might prefer a round of golf, there is a public eighteen-hole course only a mile distant. The Port Captain, Mr. Bob Garrett, pointed out a fine concrete launching ramp and presented us with some of the regulations established and strictly enforced by the Taconic State Park Commission administering the marina. We have abbreviated them somewhat:

(1) The dock master assigns slips.
(2) Don't waste water.
(3) Unnecessary noise, loud talking, playing of musical instruments

or radios between the hours of 11 P.M. and 8 A.M. are prohibited.

(4) Storage on dock is prohibited.

(5) Fitting-out or major repair work in berths is prohibited.

(6) Disposal of garbage or trash must be in receptacles provided for the purpose.

(7) Laundry shall not be exposed to public view at any time.

(8) No beer drinking is permitted in the park.

(9) Since this boat basin is run by New York, all visiting craft must be equipped with state-approved holding tanks. There are pump-out facilities here similar to those at Catskill, Hudson, and Coeymans-on-Hudson.

On all sides and across the river the surroundings and view are lovely. Some of the most lordly estates along the Hudson are within easy reach of Indian Kill. Just to the south, one of them with its own dock is the Vanderbilt Mansion National Historic Site, commanding a magnificent view of the river. The fifty-room dwelling contains many masterpieces of Italian art and is open to the public daily. In nearby Hyde Park is the home of Franklin D. Roosevelt, another National Historic Site with many fascinating collections and relics acquired by the late President. Roosevelt's grave in the rose garden is marked by a simple and impressive white marble monument. Adjacent is the Roosevelt Library, with much material of historic interest and also some unusual gifts sent to the White House. About 1 mile north of Indian Kill at Dinsmore, you will note the Ogden Mills and Ruth Livingston Mills Memorial State Park—the 200-acre estate of the former Secretary of the Treasury. The sixty-five-room Mills mansion in French Renaissance style is open daily Monday through Friday from 10:30 A.M. to 4:00 P.M. If your boat does not draw over 3 feet, you may tie up at the gray stone boathouse located at the foot of the mansion while you pay your visit.

21. Kingston, Rondout Creek, N.Y. (west shore—12347 283). On entering Kingston, be sure to keep the lighthouse marking the channel entrance well to starboard, since shoal water extends for a considerable distance from the northern shore. Maximum speed permitted throughout the entire channel is 5 mph and the tide range is 3½ feet.

Anyone cruising up Rondout Creek for the first time may be bewildered by the contrasting views it reveals round each bend. The lower part is commercial, its shoreline dotted with sunken barges, storage tanks, and dingy piers. Further up to starboard, however, across from Sleightsburg, an urban renewal project has given downtown Kingston a long-needed face-lifting. Here, also, another fixed bridge arching the

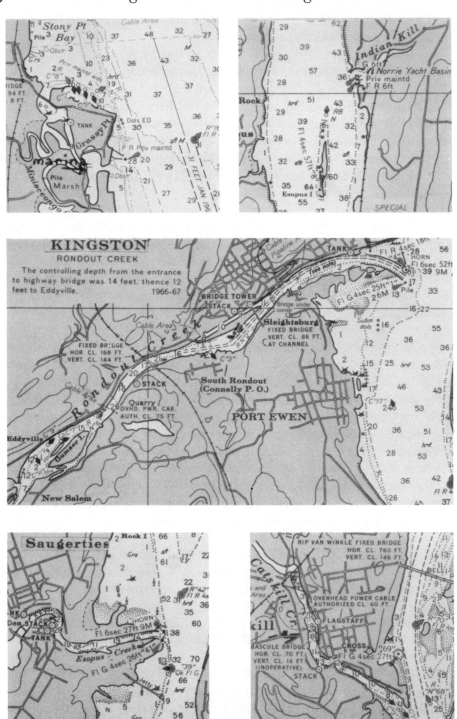

Some ports along the Hudson River. Upper left, refer to Chart 282; others,
refer to Chart 283.

creek was built in 1977 just east of the old one shown on the chart. Sailors are alerted that the vertical clearance of this new bridge is only 54 feet at high water.

About ½ mile beyond the upper bridge along the north or starboard shore lies the well-situated clubhouse and dock of the friendly and active Kingston Power Boat Association. The water is deep and gas, water, and electricity are available at the dock. The club gives reciprocal privileges to members of other recognized clubs and, as we know from experience, visitors are sure to get a hospitable welcome. Across the creek, Rondout Marine has not fared so well; it has gone out of business.

The loveliest view of the shoreline is provided during the short passage from Kingston Power until you come upon a unique structure right out of the Hudson's past. Built in 1847, this is a beautifully restored Gothic-style canal tollhouse. How ironic that it now signals the beginning of a section of Rondout defiled by commercial interests—traprock excavation to port and an ugly recycling junkyard to starboard.

But a comparatively pleasant rustic anchorage finally awaits you at creek's end at Eddyville. Make sure to hug closely to the starboard bank on the way. You'll have good water in the marked channel as far as Anchorage Rest, located just as you reach the fourth and final bridge at Eddyville. About 500 yards beyond Gumaer Island, you will reach Dock 'N Dine, set forward on a small peninsula amidst a grove of willow trees. At the time of writing, this marina had just been refurbished for the comfort and pleasure of cruising yachtsmen. Its services include an extensive bar and restaurant, showers, ice, water, and electricity at the slips. And, in its backdoor lagoon, one can spot a colorful Mississippi showboat named the Driftwood Floating Theater, which presents Off Broadway shows throughout the summer season. Nearby Certified Marine Service has a 16-ton Travelift to handle boats up to 40 feet. It's reported tops for general repairs. Next door, Lou's Boat Basin, specializing in outboard repairs, is the only local source for gas.

The best anchorage may be found along the shore across from Dock 'N Dine. Here there is 8 feet of water, literally alive with bass, perch, pickerel, stripers, and carp. You may not enjoy some of the outboard noise here and the rumblings from rock excavations, but once darkness falls you will find it peaceful. If Dock 'N Dine is filled, a slip might be open at Anchorage Rest beyond. There is a small general store nearby. The swimming is reported fine just below the dam, and nearby one can see the ruins of the first lock of the abandoned Delaware and Hudson Canal, on whose waters barges used to be drawn from the Pennsylvania coal mines. The mountains surrounding Eddyville have furnished much of the stone toward the construction of some of New York's highest skyscrapers.

22. Saugerties, Esopus Creek (west shore—12347 283). This is one of the best natural anchorages on the Hudson, and boats entering the creek should stay in mid-channel and not exceed a speed of 5 mph. A few years ago, the channel was dredged to a depth of 12 feet as far as the Coast Guard station a short distance up on the starboard shore. Across from this station lies the white clubhouse of the Saugerties Power Boat Association. We have always enjoyed our many visits here. Electricity, ice, and water are at the slips. The clubhouse provides showers and a weekend bar. One small example of this club's conviviality is the special ceremony of launching any member's boat in return for two pitchers of beer to wet the whistle of the workers. We were cautioned to stay well clear of the dam situated at the head of the creek.

We put into Saugerties Marine next to the club for gas and marine supplies, then looked over Lynch's Marina just beyond the port bank. Here you'll find equally pleasant surroundings, a bit more privacy, good water, and a capability to handle larger crafts. No repair work is available at Saugerties.

Although attractive homes border the channel, some ruins of old docks are reminders that once there was a Saugerties Night Line that maintained daily passenger service to New York. Saugerties was once a haven for the swiftest steamboats on the Hudson, such as the *Mary Powell.* Saugerties is Dutch for "sawyer's town."

23. Catskill, Catskill Creek (west shore—12347 283). Along the entire Hudson, this is still one of our favorite spots. It was first visited by Hendrick Hudson and his crew on September 15, 1609, in his vain search for a northwest passage to the Indies. "Now," according to a Catskill native, "if the river could be cleaned up, we would have to string a velvet rope across the channel and let boats in two at a time." With a large shallow mud bank covering much of the southern part of the creek entrance, it is wise to swing wide to the east and north of black can 1 as you make your approach. The creek is reported to have been dredged in 1975 to a point 100 yards above the highway bridge. Once inside, the best water is in midcreek, keeping the channel stakes to port. Halfway up, you may spot to starboard the plant of the Wright Yacht Co., which has leased the yard from the Allied Boat Co. and is now constructing auxiliaries formerly built by them. One Allied class boat, a Seawind 30, claims to be the first fiberglass vessel to circumnavigate the world several years ago.

Just beyond, you can tie up at Catskill Marina nestled on the edge of the northern shore, where the hills rise steeply on both sides and are mirrored in the glassy water. The location is delightful; at the dock are telephones, gas, Diesel fuel, ice, water, and electric connections along the floats. There's a small swimming pool for the kids but no repair service for your boat. Showers, a laundromat, and free car service to nearby restaurants complete the services here. You may walk several blocks away to the churches, stores, and theater on Main Street in Catskill. Certainly it would be hard to find a more picturesque, safe, and friendly anchorage. The swanky Skyline Restaurant is 1½ miles away, should you feel inclined to "step out on the town."

Across the creek on the south shore is Hop-O-Nose Marina, with gas, Diesel fuel, water, ice, showers, a marine railway, cookout facilities, a ship's store offering nautical charts and limited groceries, a mast-stepping rig, and the claim to be tops in engine repair work. Both Catskill Marina and Hop-O-Nose are designated pump-out stations. Motel arrangements can be made for you, and transportation to town for supplies is available; people come from miles around to enjoy the restaurant's very palatable pizzas. Since Catskill is an extremely popular port of call during the summer season, it is advisable to phone ahead for slip space reservations. Speaking of making advance reservations reminds us of the conversation between two dolls at a large marina on the Hudson. As they traipsed alongside we overheard one ask the other, "Well, which boat are you sleeping on tonight, dearie?"

Once known as Catskill Landing and before then called Kaatskill by the Dutch in the days of river and turnpike transportation, this port was a busy and prosperous shipping point. "Early tavernkeepers in this community were known as 'retailers of liquid damnation.'" Catskill mountain-brewed applejack was a staple during the prohibition era, and shady characters once established hideouts in the hills. And it was at a spot near Catskill that Rip Van Winkle is supposed to have indulged in his legendary sleep. Things are different now, for in summer many vacationists descend on Catskill and yachts come and go. But so far, nothing seems to have spoiled the quiet charm of this snug harbor, except possibly occasional lively freshets in the spring.*

24. Athens, N.Y. (west shore—12347 283). As you approach Hudson, you will pick up the Hudson Island Lighthouse, one of the two remaining midstream lighthouses on the Hudson. The other is at Esopus Flats. Leaving the lighthouse to starboard, you will leave the

*From *New York*—American Guide Series (Oxford University Press).

main channel and pass by the town of Athens, making sure to keep well off of Middle Ground Flats. Near the mouth of Murderers Creek, approximately 1½ miles beyond Hudson Island Lighthouse, you can make out Hagar's Harbor, identified by a gray-and-white stone building. This location is extremely well protected from the main channel, although open to winds from the north and southwest. The owners have gone out of their way in providing visiting yachtsmen with a modest-sized marina that is spanking clean and set in peaceful surroundings. Their attractive restaurant alone offers a refreshing change. Food and ice for your galley will be delivered to your slip on call. Don't count on having major repair work performed here, but you'll find gas and sufficient dockage space in good water with electricity provided.

Few of us may know that the town of Hudson, across the river from Athens, thrived as an important whaling center in the early 1800s. The War of Independence had disastrous effects on the highly vulnerable Nantucket whaling fleet, and, according to *Surveyor,* a periodical of the American Bureau of Shipping, Seth Jenkins left Nantucket and in 1784 led a parade of whaling ships to Claverack Landing, renamed Hudson in 1785. Situated 100 miles from New York City, this deepwater port became a safe haven from marauders during the American and French Revolutions and the War of 1812. By 1830 the Hudson Whaling Company, comprised of 20 ships, was formed. In 1831–32, the Poughkeepsie and Newburgh Whaling companies added their 10 ships to the river's fleet; whaling fever was running high. A reminder of those halcyon days may be rekindled in us today on viewing the tall, stately Nantucket-style houses in Hudson and nearby towns.

By the 1840s, the wars with Britain had ended and the need for special protection of the whaling fleets was no longer required. New Bedford, with ships twice as large as those on the river, began to usurp the place of the Hudson River whalers. The Hudson Whaling Company was forced to sell the last of its ships in 1845.

25. Coxsackie, N.Y. (west shore—12348 284). There is a good anchorage in 12 feet of water off the main channel to the west of Coxsackie Island. Stay well clear of the sandbar that stretches out from the southern tip of the island. It is well sheltered here along the former main channel except from directly south. The pretty surroundings promise you pleasant picnicking or walking tours. On the shore is the Coxsackie Yacht Club, with floats, ice, water, electricity, gas, and moorings, about a third of the way above the lower end of the island. When we put in here early one morning, the club's founder, Mr. James Carroll, invited us for breakfast and told us about their special Sunday dinner at 1 P.M.

—all one can eat at reasonable prices. These dinners are still going strong at the time of this writing. He warned us against venturing through the treacherous water behind Rattlesnake Island and to keep well clear of the sandbar stretching out from the southern tip of the island. This bar has been moving westward in recent years. Groceries will be delivered every day of the week; phone 731–8047. There is no charge for overnight dockage, but a "little brown jug" at the club's bar invites volunteer contributions both large and small.

Coxsackie is an Indian name meaning "hoot of an owl," and tribes from miles around used to gather here to make arrowheads. It is no wonder, therefore, that the club's burgee is identified by a red arrowhead on a field of white. The surrounding countryside has been one of the largest mushroom-growing centers in the world—an industry that was first developed in huge icehouses formerly supplying natural ice to New York City.

26. Schodack Creek, N.Y. (east shore—12348 284). As you approach the entrance to Schodack Creek, you will note mid-channel light 36, marking the southern tip of Houghtaling Island. Remember that a dike connects this light with the island and keep all to port on moving up the middle of the creek. The channel is unmarked but you will be safe in following mid-channel leading to the dock and clubhouse of the private Hook Boat Club. Here you may dock or anchor in deep water in the most rural, attractive, and calm spot one can find before reaching Troy. Although we were tempted to venture further up Schodack Creek, we were advised of uncharted rocks and urged not to do so without complete local knowledge. The protection at the Hook Boat Club more than makes up for its lack of supplies and facilities.

27. New Baltimore, N.Y. (west shore—12348 284). When we put into the Shady Harbor Marina just north of flashing buoy 41, the manager, Walter Stansfield, stretched out his hand in greeting and declared, "We're the friendly people. When we built this marina in 1970, we had some definite goals in mind. We thought that it was high time this part of the Hudson had a facility that you could call modern, clean, and efficiently run. We wanted to offer our cruising customers, mostly family groups, a sense of security during their visits plus some old-fashioned peace and quiet to be enjoyed in a natural setting."

A tour around this well-manicured marina, the home of the Awenke Yacht Club, convinced this writer that Stansfield had achieved his objectives. At the floating docks, gas, Diesel fuel, ice, and water are supplied, while ashore there are a fine marine store, showers, a launching ramp, and a 20-ton Travelift. There's a sizable demand here for propeller repair and orders for mast unstepping on sailing craft heading for the canals. Shady Harbor may well offer you the most carefree stopover you'll experience until you and your boat have passed northward through Troy Lock.

28. Coeymans, N.Y. (west shore—12348 284). Hug the west shore until you pick up flashing-light marker 43 marking the southernmost extension of a treacherous 1500-foot dike facing the harbor. If you do not wish to join the disreputable "Coeyman's Dike Club," be sure to leave this lighted marker 43 well to starboard, keeping off the dike at least 100 feet at all times. The five Coeyman's Dike day beacons, A through E, are equipped with diamond-shaped white day marks with orange reflective borders in whose center read the words, "Danger—Submerged Jetty." If you decide to stop at Gerry Finke's Marine docks, keep inside of any line of moorings ahead and you'll arrive safely before a large white concrete building. On our last visit, Finke's presented a tired, rundown appearance, with limited dock space and the supply of gas apparently its major service to transient yachts.

Perhaps an explanation is that the entire area inside the dike has shoaled up alarmingly in recent years. We spotted a small sloop drawing 4 feet firmly aground on her beam's end in mud just inside the dike; we're sure there'll be many more hapless craft to follow until this channel is completely dredged to its former depths.

Boats stopping over at Ravena Coeyman's Yacht Club face the same dilemma in attempting a safe, dockside approach. This club, situated just to the north of Finke's, offers reciprocal privileges and similar protection, but limited docking space and no gas. If you don't need supplies and you are lucky enough to obtain a slip, a stop here will be found enjoyable.

The Tri-City Yacht Club formerly located at Cedar Hill has moved to a new location on the west shore almost 2 miles north of Ravena Coeyman's Yacht Club and just south of the fixed highway bridge. Its entrance is marked by two upright marked poles forming a break in a low stone breakwater running north-south. Favor the starboard pole as you enter the basin with your bow on line with the top of the clubhouse roof and watch for shoaling inside the breakwater, although the basin proper has a depth of about 6 feet. The clubhouse, which one might consider chalet style but which is termed a "flustered synagogue" by some of its membership, offers showers, water, and overnight dockage, if available, to members of other recognized yacht clubs. If you must anchor, pick a spot about 50 yards above the northernmost dock, making sure not to proceed as far as the bridge. We found this haven and the people there equally delightful.

29. Castleton-on-Hudson, N.Y. (east shore—12348 284). Just above red nun 54 lies the progressive Castleton Boat Club and Auxiliary. There are a fine concrete launching ramp, floats with gas, ice, a picnic table, moorings, a restaurant and bar, a laundromat, showers, and a nearby grocery store. The club is housed in a small, well-located white building. Though there is a considerable stretch of open Hudson to the north and south, the river is narrow enough here to get little opportunity for waves to make up in stiff winds from the west. The wash from the passing boats may not trouble you half so much as the noise from the trains nearby.

30. Rensselaer, N.Y. (east shore—12348 284). Here, just below the fixed bridge to Albany at Mill Creek, is located the one-story clubhouse of the Albany Yacht Club. In 1970 the club moved to its present site, making way for new bridge construction. Mr. Art Walsh, the Dock Master, informed us that they have gas, ice, water, and electricity at dockside. There is usually room for two or three transient boats along the gas dock in deep water. The clubhouse offers as complete facilities inside as you will find along the upper Hudson. Behind the club are many stores and eating places in the city of Rensselaer. Across the new bridge is the capital of the state, with fine hotels and shops, but with a waterfront to be expected of most large cities. This is a better place for shopping and meeting friends than it is for spending the night on your boat—that is, if you like quiet and good scenery.

Two blocks south of the club is restored Fort Crailo, a museum and national landmark, where the famous song *Yankee Doodle* was written in 1758. A visit here any time between 9 A.M. and 5 P.M. is well worthwhile.

31. Watervliet, N.Y. (west shore—12348 284). The shoreline along Watervliet is almost unrecognizable to one who has not recently cruised these waters. Gone are the Tri-City Yacht Basin and the Boating Center where we used to stop—all replaced by a new riverfront highway bordering the western banks.

Troy and Watervliet are both important industrial centers, and the latter has a large arsenal. According to our historical source of information:

The War of 1812 brought the settlement one of the largest arsenals in the United States, now the Watervliet Arsenal, and immortalized

Samuel Wilson, who supplied the soldiers quartered nearby with what they called "Uncle Sam's beef," as the original "Uncle Sam."

In 1825 Mrs. Hannah Lord Montague, a Troy housewife, developed a detachable collar for men's shirts; according to tradition, she cut the dirty collars off her husband's shirts to save herself the trouble of washing the entire garment, and thereby created a new industry.*

The Federal Lock, Troy (east shore—12348 284)

Hug the east shore to avoid shoal water below the dam. You will notice a mooring wall installed in 1970 for use by boats awaiting the opening of the lock. Proceed to the lock's entrance when the green light shows, while avoiding being swept westward by the current. No permit is required for this lock, and like the other locks above, there is no charge for transit. This is the biggest lock in the system, but the lift is only 14 feet. At the time we were there the schedule called for opening the lock for pleasure craft on the hour, but should a lockage for commercial vessels be made at any other time, it is possible to follow along provided there is sufficient room.

The Canalized Hudson and the Champlain Barge Canal
("Book of Charts of New York Canals")

Above the Troy Lock, as previously noted, the "road" forks. One fork begins with the Mohawk River and leads westward through canal, river, and lake into lakes Ontario and Erie. The other fork begins as a continuation of the Hudson River—called the Canalized Hudson—and leads northward for about 34 miles. It then becomes the Champlain Barge Canal and continues northward for 20 more miles (making 54 in all) until it reaches Whitehall, at the southern end of Lake Champlain. While the westward fork is beyond the scope of this *Guide,* and involves a long trip, the northern passage offers the possibility of reaching beautiful Lake Champlain from the Troy Lock in about a day. For those who want to cruise farther than Lake Champlain, there is the possibility of continuing northward by way of the Richelieu River into the St. Lawrence and thence eastward into the Gulf of St. Lawrence; then around (or through) Cape Breton; then south and west around Nova Scotia and across the Bay of Fundy to the New England Coast.

*New York—American Guide Series (Oxford University Press).

Between the Troy Lock and Lake Champlain are several stopping places that we can only mention here, with their approximate distances from the Troy Lock (in parentheses): Mechanicville (10); Schuylerville (24); Fort Edward, beginning of the Champlain Barge Canal (34); Smith Basin (41). There are undoubtedly other places for overnight tie-up and supplies, but these are also beyond the range of our explorations for this *Guide.*

The upper Canalized Hudson is pretty and pastoral but lacking in the spectacular beauty found in the Hudson below Albany. Progress is slow on the voyage to Lake Champlain, because of the eleven locks (numbered to 12 with 10 omitted), each of which may cause delay, and also because of the speed limit between the locks: 10 miles an hour in the Canalized Hudson and 6 in the Champlain Barge Canal. The route is well marked and covered to Lake Champlain by Chart No. 180, *New York State Barge Canal System,* obtainable at a cost of $2.00 from National Ocean Survey, Distribution Division C-44, Riverdale, Md. 20840, or through its local chart agencies. There is no official chart covering the Erie Canal from Lyons to Tonawanda, since this section is a land-cut for which charts are not necessary.

A few basic rules and regulations for pleasure boaters are outlined in the free pamphlet *Cruising the Canals,* obtained by writing to the Director, Waterways Maintenance Subdivision, New York State Department of Transportation, 1220 Washington Ave., Albany, N.Y. 12232. An important leaflet entitled *Your Key to the Lock,* describing the operation of the Federal Lock and Dam at Troy, is available from District Engineer, U.S. Army Engineer, District-New York, 26 Federal Plaza, New York, N.Y. 10007. There is no charge for this.

The canal is toll-free, and pleasure boats *are no longer required to obtain permits to pass the locks and lift bridges.* However, the lock permit should not be confused with boat registration, which is still required by law. Motorboats and sailboats with auxiliary power, which are used principally in New York State, must be registered with the Department of Motor Vehicles, Empire State Plaza, Albany, N.Y. 12228.

Also useful and obtainable from Charts, N.Y.S. Parks and Recreation, Albany, N.Y. 12238 are three "Cruise 'N Chart Kits" priced at $7.50 each. Kit No. 1 covers the Northwest Passage (Hudson River and Lake Champlain). Kit No. 2 covers the Grand Canal (Erie, Oswego, and Cayuga Canals). Kit No. 3 covers the Inland Seaway (Welland Canal, Lake Ontario, and the St. Lawrence). Each kit contains a complete chart book and illustrated guide.

CHAPTER IV

North Shore of Long Island Sound
Throgs Neck, New York, to New London, Connecticut

Throgs Neck, N.Y. (12366 223). At the western end of Long Island Sound a long and narrow peninsula, known as Throgs Neck, marks the place where the sound ends and the East River begins. On the east side of this peninsula between the northern end of the Neck and Locust Point is one of the snuggest harbors on Long Island Sound—a fine overnight stopping place for cruising boats on their way to or from Manhattan or the Hudson River. The Locust Point Yacht Club, around "the corner" to starboard as one enters, is hospitable to visiting yachtsmen and will help them to find a mooring if one is available. A club burgee, one of the friendly members told us, is all the introduction needed. Ice and water are obtainable at the club during the season.

At the end of the harbor is the Locust Point Marine Service, where gas, oil, ice, water, etc., as well as small repairs, are available. From the club, buses connect with the Manhattan subway at Westchester Square.

As the chart shows, there is plenty of water inside the harbor, but one must use care in getting past several outlying rocks off Locust Point at the entrance. However, during the summer the yacht club has a pole on the outermost rock, which must be left to starboard going in.

While the inner harbor beyond the yacht club is congested with moored powerboats, it is over ¼ mile long and usually some room can be found somewhere. The Throgs Neck Bridge from the Bronx to Long Island passes over the entrance between Locust Point and Throgs Neck, but all except auxiliaries with fairly tall masts will have no difficulty in getting through. Yachts inside the harbor, we were told, rode out Hurricane Donna without difficulty.

At the end of Throgs Neck is Fort Schuyler, erected over a hundred years ago, with Fort Totten on the opposite shore, to protect New York City from enemy attack from the Sound. Now it is the home of the Maritime College, part of the State University of New York. Those standing at the end of Throgs Neck on a fateful day in October, 1776, might have watched the passage of a flotilla loaded with redcoats on their way to land on the northern shore of Eastchester Bay. The British attempt to cut off the retreat of General Washington and his army from Manhattan to White Plains failed, thanks in part to a withering cross fire from Colonel John Glover and his fishermen of Marblehead.

Little Neck Bay, N.Y. (12366 223). The fetch of water between Fort Totten on the west and the U.S. Merchant Marine Academy on Kings Point to the east forms the mouth of Little Neck Bay, where there is plenty of deep water due to dredging, as illustrated on the latest chart. However, as you pull up on the west shore to the docks of the Nichols Bayside Marina, identified on the chart and seaward by a prominent flagpole, depths decrease to less than 4 feet at MLW. This marina shares its limited facilities with the Bayside Yacht Club whose main clubhouse is within walking distance across the highway to the west. It is cordial in welcoming visiting yachtsmen from other recognized yacht clubs. Nichols has gas, ice, water, showers, marine supplies, sailing lessons, and overnight moorings with 24-hour launch service on the weekends.

In 1969, 350 acres of mud were dredged out of much of the bay to attain controlling depths of 7 feet for anchoring. Such depths can be found now in mid-channel to a point where you come abeam the south-eastern tip of Willett's Neck marked by black-and-white can LN. From that point, 7 feet can be safely carried to starboard into a sector forming almost 2/3 of the western part of the lower bay. But, also from that point, only about 3 feet can be carried to port into another sector forming approximately 1/3 of the lower bay's eastern part. This sector lies immediately east as well as south of nun A. At low ebb, no boat of 3-foot draft or greater should venture closer than 300 yards from the bay's shoreline. A popular anchorage for boats of fairly shoal draft is in the bight formed on the chart near Udalls Mill Pond on the eastern shore.

It is estimated that 500 recreational boats are moored in Little Neck Bay, and the figure is growing. Although there are limited facilities and it's wide open to the north, yachtsmen often use the bay as a convenient jumping-off point for cruising east or west. The unusual tidal currents here form a continual flushing action, which many believe gives this bay the cleanest water in western Long Island Sound.

City Island, N.Y. (12366 223). City Island is New York headquarters for yacht building and repair. Rimmed from end to end with more than a dozen shipyards, it is a forest of masts and a beehive of nautical activity in the spring. The island is about a mile long, connected with the mainland by a swing bridge, and accessible to New York by bus or taxi, and subway.

No yachtsman should miss a visit to City Island; but it is not the place for a quiet, secure anchorage. The best anchorage for large boats is to the east, approximately off the middle of the island. The holding ground, however, is reported to be only fair, and the anchorage is exposed to northeasterly and southeasterly blows. In such storms, it is well to run over to the shore of Hart Island and anchor off the upper half of that island, where the holding ground is said to be good. There is also a possibility of tying up at a slip at one of the large docks that run along the eastern shore of City Island.

For boats drawing less than 7 feet, the western side of the island is preferred, though it is exposed to southerly winds. The yacht clubs are on this side and as a rule have moorings and launch service available to members of other recognized clubs. The Morris Yacht and Beach Club is on the southerly point, near the dock used by the pilots and Coast Guard.

The City Island Yacht Club is in a white building with a green roof a short distance to the north along the westerly shore. It has a long dock with shear legs, and over 6 feet of water at low tide. The club is especially popular among the sailing fraternity and maintains a few guest moorings. The Stuyvesant Yacht Club is a little farther north, and the Harlem Yacht Club, the oldest on City Island, is in a cove on the northwest side of the island.

There are also a number of good yards and marinas on the western shore, most of them catering to smaller craft and located at the northern end. Some of the popular ones on this side of the island from south to north are Sagman's Marine, Inc. (specializing in the care and sale of smaller craft—hauling, storage, repair, slips, moorings, etc.), Kretzer Boat Works (which can take care of fairly large boats, does welding and rigging work, and has been favorably known for many years), Ray's Chris-Craft, and Thwaites Marina, marked by long floating slips with arch-forming pilings and run by R.J. Borchers. He also manages the Thwaite's Inn across the main street and provides a laundromat, but none of these facilities provide fuel. However, they are very accessible to all types of stores, including Anna's Harbor Inn, which is an appealing spot serving good meals at fairly expensive prices. Borchers wanted to transform his former Hudson River Day Line steamer, the S.S. *Keansburg,* now hanging off his docks, into a similar dining spot, but may be finding the price of restoration too costly.

On the east shore, among the leading yards are Triboro Shipyard, Minneford Yacht Yard (builders of *Intrepid, Enterprise,* and *Constellation*),

Clipper Marina, and Consolidated Yachts, run by Wesley Rodstrom for over twenty years. At these yards, you'll find all the fuel you need but don't count on finding a slip or mooring for the night. These people specialize in major professional repair work on large yachts, both sail and power; their transient trade is of secondary importance. Observing their craftsmanship today is a constant reminder of how much Scandinavian immigrants have contributed to the marine industry on City Island.

Unfortunately, few yachts are being built here now. High costs and foreign competition have taken care of that. But few ports have as much to offer in maintenance, repair, storage, marine equipment of all kinds. For instance, the Ship's Tender at 344 City Island Avenue sells many fascinating gadgets that a yachtsman will find difficult to resist.

Several leading sailmakers have their offices on City Island, including Ratsey and Lapthorn, whose reputation among yachtsmen is worldwide, Charles Ulmer, also highly regarded, and Hild Sails, who also do good work. This doesn't pretend to be a list of *all* of the good boat yards, services, and sailmakers on City Island—just a few of the ones that we know. The mean range of tide at City Island is 7¼ feet.

The island got its name in 1761, when some early settlers devised a plan to develop the area into a booming seaport that would some day outrival New York. Now many of the island's permanent residents, all very community minded, but linked to the Bronx by a bridge and taxes, are more interested in keeping the island the way it is than in competing with any other place. It's so geographically isolated that one can believe the remark recently made by a native islander: "You daren't say anything to anybody about somebody here because the chances are they're somebody's cousin."

In the early summer of 1614, Captain Adriaen Block, Dutch fur trader, sailed past City Island in his 44½-foot "jacht" *Onrust* (Restless) and thus began the first cruise on Long Island Sound ever made by white men. Many thousands of yachts have followed the path of the *Onrust* and on a weekend in summer the waters to the south of that famous island are in a perpetual state of confusion from conflicting wakes.

What Block might have observed with fearful eye as he entered the channel between Sands Point, L.I., and New Rochelle, has since become a familiar and respected beacon to thousands of seamen approaching New York harbor from the sound. Yet no light was erected upon the perilous shoals of Execution Rocks until 1850. Ed Hine of Sea Cliff, a Corinthian yachtsman, adds this interesting bit of historical lore:

With such a forbidding name, several speculations have been made about the origin of Execution Rocks. Probably no one now knows why the place got that name, but one good reason is shown on a chart in the Raynham Hall Museum in Oyster Bay, L.I. It is called the "Chart of Oyster Bay, Published in London in 1777 for His Majesty's Ships of War."

This chart shows the north shore of Long Island from Cow Bay (now Manhasset Bay) to Eatons Neck. What we call Execution Rocks has neither light nor beacon and is named bluntly "The Executioners." Certainly no name could be more apt for an unmarked hazard practically in the fairway, and this origin seems more likely than the stories of pirate hangings or other mass executions.

Execution Rocks is one of the six remaining manned lighthouses in Long Island Sound but is slated to lose its attendants and become automated in May 1979. Nevertheless, as a key navigational aid, this 62-foot structure, with its 600,000 candlepower light flashing every 10 seconds, is visible for 13 miles along the sound, can emit a foghorn blast in thick weather every 15 seconds, and issues a radio signal every 6 minutes to help the modern navigator.

New Rochelle, N.Y. (12366 223). This is one of two harbors serving the New Rochelle area. The other is Echo Bay. The two do not connect. There is a well-protected anchorage in attractive surroundings inside of Glen Island to the southwest of the bascule bridge connecting Glen Island Park to the mainland. With three blasts of your horn the bridge will open promptly. Here on the northwest shore just inside the bridge is located the excellent Huguenot Yacht Club, which extends the use of its facilities to members of other recognized yacht clubs offering reciprocal privileges. In 1965 this third-oldest yacht club on the sound was swept by fire but, like a phoenix, it has sprung anew from its own ashes with a clubhouse that once belonged to Lillian Gish, over 1200 feet of new docks, and improved depths at dockside to 8 feet. There is a fine bar in the clubhouse, and a dining terrace has been built overlooking the sound. On our last visit, we chatted with Ken Bonesteel, an officer of the club and a most agreeable fellow. From his remark that "we go out of our way to please transients" and from what we observed, it is quite obvious that they do so. Their facilities include launch service, guest moorings, water, ice, gas, Diesel fuel, showers, a laundromat, and supplies when requested of the dock master. Don't tie up on the outside of the front floats; these are reserved for the club launches.

Across the channel on Glen Island is a conversation piece—the remains of John Starin's "Rhine castle" built in 1880. Starin, a shipping magnate, ran excursions from New York City to the beer garden he operated on what is now the site of the casino built by the Westchester Park Commission in 1924. The comparative prices paid for the island by Starin in 1880 and by the county in 1924 offer an interesting footnote —from $18,000 the price jumped to $500,000. Westchester County's Department of Parks has built a fine launching ramp next to the picturesque castle on the northern perimeter of the island. It is limited to boats up to 21 feet overall and requires that their owners have a Westchester County resident permit.

Still further to the southwest is the large and well-equipped N.Y. Athletic Club Yacht Club and service center belonging to the famous New York Athletic Club. Members of other recognized clubs are welcome, and usually slips or moorings are available. Gas is sold here, and it is not so crowded as further to the east. Launch service and other facilities are offered. Beyond the N.Y.A.C. the channel is tricky and should not be attempted without a local pilot. Speed limit in the harbor is 4 knots.

While Glen Island Park is reserved for residents of Westchester County, it provides a pleasant outlook for visiting yachts anchored in the harbor. From the other side, access to the heart of the City of New Rochelle is obtained by bus from the Fort Slocum Dock.

There are two main channels into New Rochelle Harbor, one between Glen and Davids islands and the other north of Davids Island. They are both well marked, but don't skip any of the buoys; there are many outlying rocks.

Davids Island has been returned to the City of New Rochelle by the Consolidated Edison Company. Mayor Vincent Rippa has announced that the 80-acre tract's future "will be determined by the use we find for the island—residential, commercial, perhaps a convention center or even a casino if the state gambling laws are changed."

Beside the harbor behind Glen Island there is also a Northeast Channel behind Davenport Neck. Caution is necessary here as there are no markers inside the harbor entrance. Just to port on entering this channel with its 8-foot depth, you will note the docks of North Atlantic Marine Enterprises, which specializes in powerboats, gives fairly complete services to transients and presents to the eye a rather commercial image. As a contrast, up the channel to starboard you may reach the new, alluring Imperial Yacht Club, whose many facilities are open to cruising people. It claims to be "the most luxurious, largest and modern marina in the New York metropolitan area." This is evidenced perhaps by its offerings not only of all basic fueling and repair services but of a completely manicured layout, including laundromat, toilets and showers, a snack bar, and the major attraction—a 75-foot heated swimming pool. For all this, including overnight dockage, be prepared to pay a premium price. Reservations are suggested by phoning (914) 636–1122. The Castaways, just beyond, is also a new but smaller marina complex, which apparently is trying with some success to emulate its competitor next door.

If the anchorages of the Huguenot Yacht Club or the N.Y.A.C. are crowded or hot and moorings are unavailable, the best place to anchor is in the stretch of water between Goose and Glen islands. This spot offers fair protection in all but northeast storms and is apt to be cooler than inside.

First settled by Huguenot refugees in 1689, New Rochelle is said to have been the scene of George M. Cohan's *Forty-five Minutes from Broadway.*

Echo Bay, New Rochelle, N.Y. (12367 222). This harbor behind Beaufort Point is too commercial and crowded to be appealing for an overnight stop, though it is well protected from all winds. On entering this harbor at night, carefully note that the extreme left limit of the outer channel is on a line straight between green flasher 3BR, northeast of Bailey Rock, and a flashing green light on a flagpole set near the southeastern end of Beaufort Point.

As you enter the inner harbor, you will come up to the large Municipal Marina on the starboard shore. In 1971, this facility was completely modernized at a cost of $2.3 million, borne by New Rochelle and New York State under the Harbor and Refuge Act. Concessions here include boat and engine repair shops, showers, a laundromat, snack bar, and a gas dock with Diesel fuel. Docking is available for 600 boats, including 145 slips with electrical connections for those over 18 feet overall. However, slips are usually reserved for local residents. The Harbor Master at this dock will assign you one if it is available. In 1976, there was 7 feet at low water in the basin except for shoaling to 6 feet along its southern shore. Groceries are located nearby to the south on Pelham Road. At the time of writing, a new restaurant was being planned for installation on the roof of the marina office.

There are several special anchorage areas for yachtsmen to use in Echo Bay. One mooring area, for large craft, is in the western part of the bay inside of a line from can 5 off Duck Point to the flashing buoy Bailey Rock. This is open from northeast to south. The other one, for smaller yachts, is northeast of a line running between nun buoys 4, 6, 8, and 10. Other space for anchoring, which is much used, is between

Beaufort Point and Echo Island to the east of the channel. This anchorage is, however, wide open to the southeast, and any wind between east and south may make it uncomfortable for a small boat.

The Harrison Island Yacht Club has its clubhouse on the south side of Harrison Island, and a shore station at Beaufort Point. Moorings are sometimes available for members of accredited yacht clubs on inquiry at the Harrison Island float, and launch service is also available.

Echo Bay is a convenient anchorage, because it is only a short distance from the center of New Rochelle, which is about thirty minutes from Grand Central station, New York. Except for shoal-draft boats, it does not provide a comfortable or safe anchorage in northeasterly to southerly winds, and is much less secure than New Rochelle or Mamaroneck harbors nearby. However, in a storm, shelter can be found in the inner harbor.

Larchmont, N.Y. (12367 222). Like Marblehead, Massachusetts, this is one of the most important yacht racing centers on the coast; it is attractive for that reason, rather than for the excellence of its harbor. During Race Week several hundred boats are anchored off Larchmont or race from there. The harbor is protected from easterlies by a breakwater but is open from approximately southeast through south. The breakwater has a flashing red light but, being rather dimly lit, may be difficult to pick up against a confusing background of lights ashore. The beacons on North Ledge and on Umbrella Rock are lighted by the club from May 10 to September 10.

The large and well-equipped Larchmont Yacht Club is on the westerly shore. The club float and launch service are available to members of recognized yacht clubs. There's a Cruising Club mooring and guest moorings are also occasionally obtainable. Anchor in the southern part of the harbor, or fairly close to the breakwater if moorings are unavailable. There is no public gas dock in the harbor, though the yacht club supplies gas and Diesel fuel to its members at the work float. The nearest boatyards are in Rye and Mamaroneck. Several good restaurants are available on the Post Road, a short distance from the harbor.

A tour of Larchmont's clubhouse will soon reveal how highly established it has become as a hub of our yachting heritage. Interclub dinghy racing first began here in 1946. Another contribution was Larchmont's convincing demonstration that the Marconi rig was a more efficient racing rig than the old gaff. In 1917, in a series of ten informal regattas, the Marconi-rigged *Varuna* won eight out of ten races against four gaff-rigged one-design competitors in the O boat class, designed by William Gardner. The S class and the Victory class, still seen on the sound today, are said to be the two first one-design Marconi-rigged yacht classes to be built.*

Larchmont is famous for its frostbite dinghy racing carried on all winter by the yacht club, which remains active the year round. It is said that more than half of the total adult population of Larchmont commutes daily to New York.

Mamaroneck, N.Y. (12367 222). Mamaroneck (Indian for "he assembles the people") was first settled in 1650, by English farmers. Apparently some of the neighboring cities did not always approve of what went on there later, for in 1704, Colonel Caleb Heathcote, Lord of the Manor of nearby Scarsdale, wrote as follows: "The most rude and heathenish country I ever saw in my life, which call themselves Christian; there being not so much as the least marks or footsteps of religion of any sort; Sundays being the only time set apart by them for all manner of vain sports and lewd diversion."**

We are afraid that Mamaroneck must plead guilty, not to the absence of churches, for there are many, but to being—even on Sunday—a very active center for many sports and diversions, though neither vain nor lewd—especially yachting. Believe it or not, in this small harbor, we have located seven yacht clubs and seven boatyards, and we may have missed a few. Hank Sheridan, the Harbor Master, reports that the more than 1,400 boats moored in Mamaroneck Harbor contribute over $40,000 a year to the village in mooring permit fees and slip rentals. This makes the harbor practically self-sustaining in helping to pay for the maintenance of its facilities and the salaries of the police patrol and Sheridan's staff.

Mamaroneck is a splendid example of what a community can do to increase the attractiveness and value of its harbor and waterfront. The West Basin, formerly flats at low tide, showed a controlled depth of 5 feet in a 1975 survey, and Harbor Island (which isn't really an island) between East and West basins has been converted into an attractive park with beach facilities and a village dock. The dock is on the westerly shore of Harbor Island about halfway up the Basin, and the Harbor Master will assign a guest mooring to a visiting yacht if one is available. Mr. Sheridan is on duty daily from 8 A.M. to 5 P.M. in the large brick building at the dock. Just beyond, Flotilla 63 of the Coast Guard is housed in a small white headquarters. We learned from the officials here that all incoming vessels should use engine power from the time

*From *Long Island Sound,* by Fessenden S. Blanchard (D. Van Nostrand Co., 1958).
**Quoted in the section on Mamaroneck from *New York*—American Guide Series (Oxford University Press).

they reach lighted buoy 5, at Outer Steamboat Rock, until they make their final mooring.

Mamaroneck offers much better protection from wind and sea than its neighbors, Milton Harbor at Rye, or Larchmont Harbor. There are two snug, if crowded, landlocked basins, fully protected from all directions. However, the other two harbors mentioned offer considerably more privacy, and have their own particular assets. There is also an outer harbor at Mamaroneck where many boats are moored during the summer months but which is open from southeast to southwest. During the winter, boating continues at Mamaroneck—now active in "frostbiting."

The entrance to the inner harbor is narrow and a speed-limit sign outside warns boats to slow down on entering. The place where the channel forks is marked by a red-and-black buoy. Follow the channel carefully, whichever way you go, as there are closely bordering shoals.

The West Basin is prettier and quieter than the East Basin, and not close to the Boston Post Road and its heavy traffic, as is the other basin. At the same time, however, it is less convenient to the city center with its many fine stores.

For overnight, we much prefer the West Basin, the best tie-up being to port halfway up the basin at the dock of the Nichols Yacht Yard headed up by Gerald Berton, who also supervises other Nichols branch marinas at Rye, Great Kills Park on Staten Island, Bayside, Hudson Harbor 79th St. Boat Basin, and the World's Fair Marina in Flushing Bay. There is 6 feet of water at the main dock, and gas and Diesel fuel may be obtained there as well as fresh water, electric connections, ice, and telephones. It is safer to arrange for dock space by placing an advance reservation, phone (914) 698–6065 or try Channel 16 VHF. The yard, as we know from experience, has good repair service, including engine, electronics, and sail. In 1978, they are planning on expanding the number of their moorings and starting launch service in catering more to transients.

At the entrance to the West Basin, just beyond the small dock of Total Yacht Sales, a fine assortment of small craft is on display and for sale, from dinghies to outboard cruisers, boat trailers, and marine hardware. Both dock and yard are operated by Mamaroneck Boats and Motors and run by a most accommodating and competent marina manager, Guy Deutermann. He is an Evinrude dealer and knows outboards from top to bottom. Gas is sold at the M.B. and M. float where there is 4 feet at low tide.

In 1975, a survey in the East Branch channel showed a controlled depth of 6 feet at low water for a midwidth of 80 feet. The branch

Mamaroneck Harbor from the air, looking about northwest.

channel to the north of this basin also recorded a depth of 7½ feet for a midwidth of 65 feet. Be careful to avoid a dangerous rock, covered at high water, which is located right off nun 16 and is marked by a prominent stake. The branch channel to the north of this basin now records a depth of 7½ feet for a midwidth of 65 feet. At the basin's north end are gathered over half of the boat yards and yacht clubs in Mamaroneck, all crowded together. From west to east they are the popular Post Road Boat Yard managed by Jack Brewer, offering 6 feet at its gas dock plus Diesel fuel, ice, water, electricity, showers, slips, and a laundromat nearby. It is open daily from 8 A.M. to 8 P.M. Then comes the R.E. Derecktor Shipyard, the recent birthplace of many a 12-meter contender. Next comes the Orienta Yacht Club, which has two guest moorings, and finally McMichael Yacht Yard #1. Nearby on the Post Road is Brewers', established over eighty years ago and a first-rate marine hardware emporium, sometimes open on Sundays in summer. Next door to Brewers', the atmosphere is informal at Jonathan Seagull, where entrees posted on a blackboard rarely exceed $8.00. Seafood is their specialty. All these are fine facilities, but our advice to visiting yachtsmen is still to spend the night in the West Basin, on an assigned mooring, not on your hook!

James Fenimore Cooper married a Mamaroneck girl in 1811 and lived in his wife's ancestral home for a while after the wedding. The original building was eventually sold at auction for $11 and then moved. Today, this black-and-white gabled house overlooks the harbor near the corner of the Post Road and Fenimore Road. It's called the Fenimore Cooper Inn but serves mostly as a restaurant. And over in Harbor Island Park a small outdoor stage forms the scene for free cultural events in the opera, dance, and theater during the summer.

Rye (Milton Harbor), N.Y. (12367 222). In coming from the direction of Lloyd Harbor, a tall office building in New Rochelle with a square knob on the top is a good guide for the Scotch Caps buoys and the entrance to Rye. On entering at night, it is important to give the Scotch Caps a wide berth, as the entrance is deceptive, the lighted buoy being much farther to the west than the contour of the coast would seem to require. After leaving the Scotch Caps lighted bell buoy to starboard, run toward the north until the two red range lights on the club grounds are in sight, and then run in. Note that on West Rock at the south end of the Caps, there's an orange-white day beacon considerably difficult to spot both from seaward and from the chart. This is privately maintained from April 1 to November 1 and should be kept well to starboard on entering the harbor.

The anchorage, to the west and southwest of the American Yacht Club, is fair except in a southwester when, if desired, one can quickly run over to Mamaroneck. It is frequently rough in the harbor, and uncomfortable when the tide is against the wind. If drawing more than 5 feet, anchor in the deep water between the southern end of Hen Island and the end of Milton Point, if possible, either to the north or to the south of the gut that runs between the clubhouse point and the first of three islets forming the Scotch Caps chain. A tide rip runs through this gut, and in a storm the sea comes through. The bottom is soft, sticky mud.

Over on Hen Island, thirty-four families enjoy the isolation of spartan island living surrounded by many species of bird and marine life. This little Shangri-La was first occupied by Indians of the Apaqquaminis tribe, whose sachem sold Rye to John Budd in 1662.

The American Yacht Club float, with Diesel fuel, gas, ice, and water, and a depth of 5½ feet at low tide, is available to visitors from accredited yacht clubs, as is the club launch service running on weekdays from 8 A.M. to 10 P.M. and on weekends from 8 A.M. to midnight. Your signal should be three blasts of the horn while displaying code flag T during daylight hours and turning on spreader lights at night. All guests must register with the dock master. The club has three guest moorings with vacant moorings sometimes available; contact the launch man. American has an excellent restaurant in its clubhouse overlooking the sound as well as a swimming pool as fine as you'll see at any yacht club.

Supplies can be obtained from the Harbor Delicatessen almost a mile down the road on Milton Point; it is open evenings and part of the time on Sunday. Near there is the closest formal restaurant, The White Elephant.

Proceeding up the harbor, one can see the Shenorock Yacht Club just beyond the stone town dock to starboard. At the harbor's head are two boatyards in a basin, all reached by a narrow, 1-mile-long channel marked by #5 class buoys and dredged in 1976 to 6 feet at MLW. The mean range of tide here is about 7 feet. On the west fork at the northern end of the channel is Nichols Yacht Yard–Rye, with about 6 feet at the dock at low water. The writer has used this small yard over the years and has found it very satisfactory. On the east fork is Shongut Boat and Engine, the only spot for gas and possible overnight dockage, and beyond that the Municipal Boat Basin, open only to residents of Rye and not set up to handle transients.

The American Yacht Club is reportedly the fourth-oldest yacht club in the United States, founded in May 1883 by a small group of steam-yacht enthusiasts headed by Jay Gould. It became one of the leaders in the middle 1920s in establishing a Junior Yacht Club and instructional program that is now one of the most active on the sound. Over the years, it has hosted scores of national and regional sailing championship competitions; many of its members have distinguished themselves often in winning racing honors on Long Island Sound and in international events. *Thunderbird,* a Cal-40 owned and skippered by T. Vincent Learson, won the Newport-to-Bermuda race in 1966, sailing against a record fleet of 167 yachts. In 1977, members of the JAYC won the Long Island Midget Championship. At the same time, Bob Hutton sailed his 47-foot blue racing sloop, *Tatoosh,* to a winning campaign in the Annapolis–Newport Race, the Vineyard Race and the Whittmore Series, as well as an unprecedented four major trophies on the 1977 New York Yacht Club Cruise.

The remarkable recovery of the American Yacht Club from a fire on July 27, 1951, which resulted in the destruction of its three-story clubhouse built in 1887, is a credit to the resourcefulness of its officers and the loyalty of its members. The annual Club Cruise started on the date planned, two days after the fire. The neighboring Apawamis and Shenorock Shore clubs made their facilities available, so that most of the club services could continue. The first meal was served one year, to a day, after the fire, in a new and modern clubhouse. With the old flagpole still a white landmark, the present home of the American Yacht Club now looks out from Milton Point on one of the busiest scenes on Long Island Sound.

Playland, Rye, N.Y. (12367 222). This is an artificial harbor made by two converging breakwaters at Rye Beach. The narrow entrance is open to the southeast, but the harbor offers a good shelter from all other winds. The jetty lights are operated by the Westchester County Playland Commission. Playland is a summer harbor, so if one is entering out of season, a careful check on the neighboring buoys and lights should be made in advance. There is from 6 to 10 feet of water in the anchorage at low tide, with 10 feet at the pier.

The park, which is well worth a visit as an outstanding example of a community enterprise, is operated efficiently and like Spotless Town by the commission. There is an excellent beach of imported sand, and plenty of music, expansive picnic grounds, and restaurants—a complete change for people on a cruise, except possibly for the roller coasters. However, one's privacy is about equal to that of a goldfish, as in summer the beach is crowded and swimmers are apt to line the log boom nearby. Don't try to drink soup, for it may land in your lap from the waves of a passing speedboat. A beautiful 80-acre salt-water lake lying behind the amusement area offers a wildlife sanctuary that attracts bird-watchers and boating enthusiasts from seven to seventy. A main attraction is the famous *Showboat,* a small replica of a Mississippi riverboat, which gives its riders a twenty-minute tour of the islands. Both electric- and rowboats are rented by the hour there.

In entering at night, watch for a line of heavy log booms parallel with the beach and well out from it. The nearest boat yard is at Rye. Supplies and gas can be obtained about 4 blocks away. The Rye railroad station is about 2 miles away, reached by bus from Playland.

Playland is the largest, and one of the finest, municipally owned amusement parks in the world, with over 270 acres. If you want an evening of fun, go there.

Port Chester, N.Y. (12367 222). The best place here for overnight anchorage or tie-up is not in the crowded and commercial Byram River, where oil barges and tankers come and go. There are two better choices: one is an anchorage (if there is room) in the deep water south of the black beacon with the flashing green light, and to the west of the main channel. Another possibility is to tie up in a slip (if one is available) in a yard the existence of which you might never suspect from looking at the chart. This is the Tide Mill Yacht Basin in the bight at the edge of Kirby Pond and behind Manursing Island. The basin there has been dredged to a depth of 6 feet and is reached by following private black and red cans marking a 6-foot dredged channel. The approach is through the charted deep water south and southwest of the black beacon mentioned earlier. This marina is identified by a prominent red dockhouse offering gas, Diesel fuel, ice, showers, telephone, slips with electrical connections, a mechanic, various marine supplies, and arrangements for grocery delivery. The dockhouse is part of the original Old Tide Mill built in 1770 by Wright Frost and owned and operated for 50 years by a David Kirby. With the basin protected from all winds and seas, an overnight tie-up here is desirable.

The Port Chester Yacht Club is on the north shore at the entrance of the Byram River and will let you tie up at their float for a while if you want to get supplies.

Port Chester has improved its name as well as its harbor. It was once known as Saw Log Swamp and later as Saw Pit.

Byram Harbor, Port Chester, N.Y. (12367 222). Byram Harbor is attractive mainly if the tide is high enough for boats to go into the shallow cove to the west of Huckleberry Island. Byram Park is a pretty place and the Byram Shore Boat Club in the cove is most hospitable.

The best place to anchor is to the east of the line between Huckleberry Island and Wilson Head, but this is only for shoal-draft boats and is open from east to south.

The depth in the cove is about 3 feet at mean low water. There is a guest mooring just outside of the narrow channel to the cove, but no gas or supplies are available at the club. Check in with the Harbor Master before picking up this mooring. Slips in the cove are reserved only for local residents.

For deeper-draft craft, the best anchorage is north of Calf Islands between the tower and the flashing red-lighted buoy south of Otter Rocks. Enter between this buoy and black can 1 north of Bowers Island. A reef, bare at low water, connects the two islands. Southern Calf, owned by the Greenwich YMCA, has become, partly because of its natural charm, a favorite rendezvous spot for many local yacht club fleets, including the Westchester Power Squadron. Groups wishing to go ashore for a picnic game should first place their reservations with the YMCA officials. Another possibly quiet anchorage, except in southerlies, can be found in the bight formed by the western shore of Calf Island and the small private island to the northwest on which is located the stone tower.

Greenwich, Conn. (12367 222). Captain Harbor, north of Great and Little Captain islands, affords fair shelter for large boats in the open area east of Field Point and the channel. Small craft, allowing for ample swinging room, should anchor across the channel west of the attractive and well-equipped Indian Harbor Yacht Club, which stands on the point to the east of the main channel, whose depth all the way to the head of the harbor is reported to be 12 feet at the time of writing. The Captain Harbor anchorage is exposed to the south and southeast, although the islands afford some protection. It is comfortable only for large yachts or in calm weather.

In bad weather the best entrance is the easterly one, as a direct course can be laid from the light on the bell to the end of the channel off Field Point. Give at least 50 yards' berth to the beacon on Hen and Chickens. From there to the yacht club the harbor is filled with boats in summer, and a visitor can pick an anchorage in the vicinity of boats about his own size. The outer or larger yachts all carry mooring lights and one should have no trouble.

In a storm, a moderate-draft boat can find a snug anchorage in Chimney Corner north of Tweed Island, though it may be crowded.

There is seldom any weather to which the inner harbor is exposed. The Indian Harbor Yacht Club float, launch service, and guest moorings are open to members of recognized yacht clubs. Before you do anything, make sure to check in with Dock Master Tom Clark, who will assign you a mooring if one is available. Depth at the float is about 6 feet, but you'll find no gas on tap here. Above the yacht club stretches the 600-foot bulkhead of the smart-looking Showboat Inn whose Showboat on the Water serves up fine food and music whether you're dressed in boating denims or a Dior. Dockage is free for those making a stay here. You might also try the widely acclaimed Italian cuisine found at Manero's Restaurant inshore to starboard halfway up the channel.

Across the channel on the east side of Grass Island ferries leave from the town dock for trips to Great Captain Island and Island Beach. Here, too, is Grass Island Marine, whose fuel supply and services are available only to Greenwich residents.

Greenwich is a convenient place to meet people coming from New York as the Indian Harbor Yacht Club is only ½ mile from the railroad station and ¾ mile from the post office. It is a less convenient harbor to obtain fuel and supplies.

The town, just north of the depot, offers excellent shops and restaurants. The country back of Greenwich, with many large estates on high land enjoying wide views of the sound, is most attractive and well worth a motor ride. It was at Greenwich that General Putnam of Revolutionary War fame escaped the British by riding down the face of a cliff.

Cos Cob or Riverside, Conn. (12367 222). Many yachtsmen prefer this harbor to Greenwich. The buoys should be watched carefully on entering, as there are numerous rocks and shoal spots. The beginning of the 50-foot entrance channel appears to be even narrower between can 1 and nun 2 to make sure you give ample berth to ominous Hitchcock Rock. The best anchorage is on the western side of the channel, northeast of Goose Island. Once past nun 8, mud flats rise sharply on both sides.

The Riverside Yacht Club is one of the most attractive and hospitable clubs on the sound and is glad to welcome yachtsmen from other clubs with whom reciprocal privileges are exchanged. It is on the point to the starboard (just before reaching nun 10), and has a long pier, with 5 feet of water along its edge, reaching to the channel. Gas, ice, water, and guest moorings are available, as well as showers. Launch service runs from 8 A.M. to 11 P.M. on weekends, to 10 P.M. on weekdays. Both the Yardarm Bar, with its nautical ambience, and the club's dining room command a splendid view of the harbor.

Soundings in the channel running north from nun 10 reflect considerable shoaling to 4 feet at MLW all the way to the head of navigation, so this part of the Mianus River is used primarily by powerboats. A bar is forming just south of the bascule bridge, which will open on your signal of three blasts from 5 A.M. to 9 P.M.

Boat yards and marine services concentrated beyond the bridge along the west shore include, in order: Palmer Point Marina, with the most complete facilities and repair services; McMichael Yacht Yard No. 3, with no gas or setup for transients; Harbor Marine Center; and Drenckhahn Boat Basin. Some of these have slips available for overnight; some do repair work on inboards, some on outboards. They are all close together, so if you can't find what you want, try another.

They are also not far from a new Sheraton Motel on U.S. Route 1 and a fine shopping center where fresh supplies can be gathered. Try Salt Water Farms should you wish to prepare a fresh seafood dinner aboard. The Clam Box and the Parsley Restaurant, both within walking distance, come highly recommended.

Riverside, like Larchmont, Manhasset Bay, and other yacht clubs on Long Island Sound, has become active in frostbiting and has a large fleet of dinghies.

Greenwich Cove, Riverside, Conn. (12367 222). Here is an attractive, cool anchorage with plenty of room, though without shore facilities or supplies for cruising yachtsmen. The swimming is first rate. There is fairly good protection from all sides if you anchor northeast of Pelican Island; another anchorage is further up the harbor opposite Greenwich Island. The bottom is mud, providing poor holding ground.

Come in toward Cove Rock and its nun, numbered 2, keeping south of the line between this buoy and the red flasher on Newfoundland Reef in order to avoid Finch Rock, marked by a privately maintained can buoy.

The Old Greenwich Boat Club has a dock with 6 feet of water just to the east of the northern tip of Greenwich Point, south of Pelican Island. The club also occupies the tower nearby, and, if our experience is any guide, is hospitable to visiting yachtsmen from other clubs. Overnight moorings may be available, but the launch service is primarily reserved for Boat Club members.

Julius Wilensky, author of the very useful guide *Where To Go; What To Do; How To Do It on Long Island Sound,* gives us some background on this area:

The whole of Greenwich Point, Flat Neck Point, and the narrow neck north of Greenwich Point is a public park, much of it left wild. Ducks and swans are at home here. It is known locally as Tod's Point, not to be confused with the point of the same name at the south end of Riverside. The Tod family had a huge three-story Victorian mansion on the point, which wasn't torn down until 1961. Greenwich had bought the peninsula for $550,000 early in World War II, and used the mansion to house returning veterans. The park includes an arboretum.*

Don't get caught outside the park after dark, for everything locks up at 8 P.M. We tried every password in the book to get past the guard at the front gate. One of them finally worked, and we were faced with a long trudge in pitch blackness back to our anchorage.

Stamford, Conn. (12368 221). Thanks to considerable development and improvement in recent years, the facilities and opportunities at Stamford Harbor available to visiting yachtsmen are among the best on the sound. Along the eastern shore of the upper harbor, on the East Branch, there are now at least five boat yards and marinas, including one of the finest marinas on the coast—Yacht Haven. On Shippan Point, well up the harbor, the Stamford Yacht Club, one of the sound's leading clubs and host of the annual Vineyard Race, is very active in both the yachting and social life of the community.

Stamford Harbor is easy to enter and the channel inside the breakwaters is simple to follow. But outside of the channel there are a few rocks, in inconvenient places, to be avoided in looking for an anchorage. The two breakwaters have greatly improved the harbor as a place of refuge, though it is still large enough in the outer harbor for many "local" whitecaps, and boats may drag in a southwester. The Stamford Yacht Club is noted on the chart and is about halfway up Shippan Point, an attractive residential section of Stamford. In case you approach the channel in poor visibility, as we did on one visit, we might note that the fog signal at the west breakwater light has been changed from a siren to a horn sounding one blast for a two-second duration every twenty seconds. The light itself is now a green flasher, equal interval, 6 seconds.

For boats not wishing to land, a convenient and easy anchorage is just behind the western breakwater, east of the rocks shown on the chart. Further up the channel, a course taken from red nun 8 directly for the end of the Stamford Yacht Club dock will give at least 5 feet of depth all the way in; but don't stray from this "straight and narrow path," for

*From *Where To Go; What To Do; How To Do It on Long Island Sound*, by Julius M. Wilensky (Snug Harbor Publishing Co., 1968).

there are some rocks close to the north side of the channel and on the south side, too. Head in for the club dock by passing through the fleet slowly and then between the private red-and-white spar buoys; the white one to port marks a hidden rock and the red marker to starboard identifies a dangerous reef extending southward.

There is a depth of about 5 feet at mean low water at the outer end of the Stamford Yacht Club dock. Gas, water, and ice are available. The club facilities, including guest moorings when not in use, are available to members of recognized yacht clubs who come there by boat. On a summer weekend the swimming pool and tennis courts are very active, while in the harbor one has to keep a watchful eye to avoid water-skiers, "sailfish," as well as the many attractive yachts that make up the fleet. Supplies can be ordered at the club from the city, which is 2 or 3 miles distant.

The boat yards and marinas along the East Branch, to starboard as one enters, are as follows: Yacht Haven East, which you come to first, is a subsidiary of Marina America and has about everything a yachtsman could want in ranking as one of the largest marinas on the east coast. It also runs a sizable yacht brokerage and chartering service. A breakwater offering good protection has been constructed from Jack Island eastward to the mainland. Dredging has taken place just above this breakwater to provide fill for the building up of the southern shore of Ware Island, permitting the formation of additional piers. There are now twelve piers with a total of about 500 slips having depths of 9 feet, and a daily rate of $7.00 minimum. This includes water, electricity, and use of showers. Gas, Diesel fuel, ice, telephones, a marine store with charts, a laundromat, electronic repair service, and Travelifts to haul up to 40 tons are among the many facilities. But boats requiring all hull and engine work are sent across the harbor to a joint subsidiary, Yacht Haven West, which is set up to handle repairs efficiently. Yacht Haven East, on the other hand, is preferable for an overnight stop. It's quiet after dark, a bit more residential, and boasts 24-hour security—the Stamford Marine Police dock is here. Ship to Shore on Shippan Point will deliver liquor and groceries. But the future of the Admiral Benbow Restaurant is questionable at the time of writing. In 1978, a new hotel-office building is being constructed nearby on Ware Island.

Further up-channel lies Yankee Harbor Marine, the former Doane Harbor Marina, recently renovated by the Snyder family, and beyond that is Schooner Cove, followed by the large and well-equipped Scofield Boat Yard, which hauls and repairs boats of all sizes, especially sailing craft and their inboards. Dockage is usually cheaper at any one of these marinas, all of which have comparable facilities. During a visit here we witnessed and were told about a rather strange marine phenomenon: The channel water, though acceptably clean to the eye, contains so much sediment build-up that it acts as a persistent antifouling agent. No marine growth was apparent below the waterlines of the Stamford boats we saw dockside.

In 1967 a hurricane barrier was constructed across the East Branch channel between Yacht Haven East and Doanes. Its 90-foot-wide gate is equipped with lights. This dike gives the upper channel added protection, but boatmen along the shore have viewed the performance of the "contraption" with dubious eyes. From this point, 6½ feet can be carried to a point 800 feet north of East Branch Light 2.

The Southfield Park and Marina, located to port just beyond the entrance to the West Branch, is open only to local residents. In entering at night, note the two range lights where the channel separates. This is the wider and deeper of the two branches but it is generally less attractive. Depths in this channel run as deep as 12 feet at MLW, with average readings of 8 feet MLW up in the turning basin. Halfway up to starboard looms the prominent dockhouse of Yacht Haven West, managed by Bill Morris and home of both the annual North Atlantic All Sailboat Show and a Coast Guard station. It is situated on land formerly occupied by the Luders Marine Construction Co., builders of the 12-meter contenders, *Weatherly* and *American Eagle.* Here you can obtain about everything but food supplies and a steak dinner. Experienced ship builders and mechanics, fiberglass craftsmen and MacDonald Yacht Rigging are all available the full year. Nearby Ramada Inn will send its courtesy car for your dining or arrange for car rentals. And next to the marina, the Ponus Yacht Club reportedly serves good meals.

Express trains run between Stamford and New York City, making it a convenient place for picking up crews or reaching Manhattan.

It was a Stamford resident, Abraham Davenport, member of the Connecticut House of Representatives in 1780, whose high sense of duty enabled him to stand firm before his fellow members of the legislature during Connecticut's "Dark Day" of May 19 in that year. As the sky became darker and darker, the Solons, at the State Capital, fearing that Judgment Day had come, carried a motion to adjourn. When this motion came before the Council, Davenport rose to his feet, and spoke as follows: "I am against adjournment. The Day of Judgment is either approaching or it is not. If it is not, there is no cause for adjournment; if it is, I choose to be found doing my duty. I wish therefore that candles may be brought."*

*From *Connecticut*—American Guide Series (Houghton Mifflin Co.).

Westcott Cove, Stamford, Conn. (12368 221). Westcott Cove has a completely sheltered "lagoon," as it is called locally. It has a well-marked channel of 50-foot width and a surveyed depth in 1976 of 7 feet at mean low water to can 9, thence 5 feet to the basin. But follow the channel carefully; it is very shoal on either side, especially to port entering, near the end of the jetty. Thus favor the nuns all the way and, once inside, hug the Muzzio docks to port.

Muzzio Bros. Yacht Yard supplies gas and Diesel fuel and is well staffed with riggers, joiners, sailmakers, and mechanics, but does not encourage overnight transients. Marine Diesel of New England specializes in servicing major engine makes such as Westerbeke, Perkins, and Volvo. John Alden, long-time yacht brokers, has its dock and office at Muzzio's yard. At the northwest corner of the lagoon, in Cummings Park, is the Halloween Yacht Club, which offers its facilities to yachtsmen from recognized clubs with whom reciprocal privileges are exchanged. The club, we were told, usually has a spare slip or berth for visiting yachtsmen. Tie-up is fore and aft, as the harbor is too small and busy to allow swinging at anchor.

The water averages about 6 feet at MLW over most of the inner lagoon. There are several good grocery stores about ¼ mile from the club and restaurants are nearby. On the point to the south of the lagoon is an excellent bathhouse. The vicinity is apt to be crowded and busy on weekends, and there is less privacy than in a larger, more isolated harbor.

Darien River, Noroton, Conn. (12368 221). This is one of the numerous "made" harbors on Long Island Sound, located off the Noroton Yacht Club on the western shore of Long Neck Point. Be sure to keep nun 2 well to starboard in entering. About midway between this nun and the end of the yacht club pier there is a bar across the channel, as the chart indicates, but it is reported to have been partially eliminated. This may be troublesome, however, only at low water for most small cruising craft, though it can be rough on the bar in strong southwest to southeast winds. There are range lights at the club from Memorial Day to Labor Day. One of these is located at the end of the dock and the other stands at the right edge of the attractive clubhouse. There is 6 feet of water at dockside.

In entering, head from nun 2 to the yacht-club dock. Once past the bar, there is plenty of water to the pier, where a guest mooring is sometimes obtainable. Beyond the pier also there is good water to the gut opposite Peartree Point, but not beyond the Darien Boat Club docks to starboard where it has shoaled considerably. Not shown on the chart is some fairly deep water, reported at 10 feet, in the dredged but congested basin to the west of the pier, where it is well protected; but space may be hard to find. Large boats anchor close to Pratt Island or in the anchorage area, where it is deeper, less crowded, though more open. In 1968, this special anchorage area, as shown on the chart, was established off the southwesterly side of Long Neck Point.

There is a large and impressive-looking residence at the end of Long Neck Point. Once the estate of Anson Phelps Stokes, it was until recently occupied by the Convent of the Sacred Heart. Now it has been split up to make separate private residences.

The Noroton Yacht Club has a large, active fleet of Blue Jays, Lasers, Fireballs, Solings, Tempests, and Ensigns and the anchorage is often full. The weekend racing is hotly contested. The club has an outstanding reputation in yachting circles, largely due to its philosophy that there is nothing more important than sailing. Its excellent junior program has produced some great sailors, such as Bob Bavier, helmsman of the winning America's Cup defender, *Constellation,* and Bill Cox, skipper of the almost-defender, *American Eagle.* In addition, to his credit, Cox has the Sears Cup, International Class championships, and two Lightning National titles. And, if that is not enough, there's Bob Smith, the top catamaran sailor, who challenged for the Little America's Cup; Bob Shiels, winner of the nationals in the Tiger Cats; and the Linville brothers, Jim and John, world champions in the Tempest Class. The ladies enjoyed their share of glory, too, when Sue Sinclair won the Women's National Championship in 1962.

The club is most hospitable to members of recognized yacht clubs and has a snack bar but no bar, and water but no gasoline. Pumping of heads within the harbor is forbidden. Repair facilities are available at nearby Fivemile River or at Stamford. It is about 1 mile to the village of Noroton. There is a good beach at Peartree Point, open only to local residents. However, a small, pleasant beach spreads out in front of the clubhouse. This harbor is a good destination in normal summer weather and provides a most appealing natural setting.

Hay Island, Noroton, Conn. (12368 221). North of Hay Island, on the east side of Long Neck Point, is one of the lesser-known and most attractive harbors on the sound, well protected from all but strong winds from northeast to southeast, when an unpleasant roll penetrates. Shallow-draft yachts, however, can escape most of this by going south behind the island. This delightful inlet with its low rocky cliffs and lush foliage is known locally as Ziegler's Cove. How it earned the name, no one seems to know.

Hay Island Harbor, also called Ziegler's Cove, as seen looking to the northwest.

In entering, pick up nun 28 off Long Neck Point and then head for the exposed rock, formerly marked with a spindle, just east of Hay Island. Pass this close to port and, having left it well astern, head over for the steep shore on Great Island. Follow this in, and anchor, preferably, near the 8-foot spot. The harbor is surrounded by private estates and no supplies or public landing facilities are available. You'll think you are in Maine until you go swimming, and then you'll be glad you aren't.

The harbor is apt to be crowded on weekends, so get in early if you want to find plenty of swinging room. Fortunately, some boats come there to fish—and often do very well at it—but leave in the early evening, so the overnight flotilla is reduced considerably. The writer has been there at least ten times and has never failed to find satisfactory anchorage. It is one of his favorite ports on the sound.

Fivemile River, Rowayton, Conn. (12368 221). This anchorage between Roton Point and Darien, rates high on the following counts: (1) convenience; (2) protection from all winds; (3) docks from which groceries, gasoline, ice, and water can be obtained; (4) boat yards and machine shops. The nun (Number 26) off Greens Ledge Light is a good guide to the entrance, about 1 mile distant. The entrance is well buoyed, though narrow. There is a 5-foot spot just outside the outer twin buoys.

This harbor is attractive, with perfect shelter from all winds, but crowded. Butler Island, at the left of the entrance, is wooded and high, and marked by a flagpole. There is a dredged basin on the westerly shore opposite red nun 6 beyond Butler Island. This is a possible anchorage, but the crowded harbor makes a tie-up preferable, if you can find one. The Federal government has designated Fivemile River as a special anchorage area insuring that the 8 feet at MLW within the dredged 100-foot channel currently reported will be controlled up to the river's head, as shown on the chart. It may be hard to believe, but a recent Federal survey of this harbor showed it to be the second cleanest river on the east coast. Moorings must be on line with other boats.

The first dock you reach to starboard is the Town Dock at Fivemile Landing, where you can pick up gas, ice, and water and which offers the best possibility for overnight transient yachts. The dock master is on duty here from 8 A.M. to 6:30 P.M. At the nearby Boat Works, where you'll find Diesel fuel, there rises a large gray building devoted to the service and repair of Hood Sails.

The main dock of the Rowayton Marine Works just to the north provides all types of repair work on boats up to 25 tons and houses a fine little marine store. Mr. R.G. Ely is the owner of this facility, which in turn is affiliated with The Boatworks (the South Yard) and the North Yard, formerly Bounty-Smith Marine. Yachts of greater tonnage can be hauled at this North Yard. Grove Ely, a very personable and experienced boating man, recently arranged for the building of his racer-cruiser, *Nimble,* the prototype for a fast new one-design class entitled the New York Forty.

Next to Rowayton Marine, the Bait Shop specializes in the sale and repair of outboard motors; Rowayton Lobster at Ely's dock dishes out fresh clams and lobsters. For first-class repair work on all types of electronic gear, you might try Connecticut Marine Electronics up at the head of the harbor. The main street, which runs behind the docks, displays antique stores, a general market, an art center, a package store, and Higgins' Restaurant specializing in the "freshest of the fresh" seafood served in a cheerful publike atmosphere.

Fivemile River is a friendly and intimate place, and the writer has rarely been in there without finding friends along the boat-lined water front. Though there is no yacht club on the river, the clubby mood makes one seem unnecessary. However, the Norwalk Yacht Club is just across the point.

Rowayton has well been called "a delicious and crazy hodgepodge of boat yards, lobster fishermen, artists, writers, boating enthusiasts and just plain local people."*

South and East Norwalk, Conn. (12368 221). Like Stamford, here is another case where man has stepped in to improve yachting facilities. There are now seven possible anchorages or tie-ups but the snuggest and, in our opinion, the most desirable of all is the man-made dredged harbor behind Calfpasture Point, across the river from the conspicuous stacks of the Connecticut Light and Power Company on Manrissa Island.

A number of yachtsmen have reported that the entrance channel to Norwalk through Sheffield Harbor is narrow, increasingly busy with boating traffic, and tending to shoal along its edges. The approach from the east through Cockenoe Harbor may be found less formidable, though a sharp lookout and helmsman are still required. But moving in a more or less easterly direction, as we are in this book, the seven anchorages or tie-ups are as follows:

1. *Off the Norwalk Yacht Club* in what is locally known as Wilson Cove,

---

*From *The Exurbanites*, by A.C. Spectorsky (J.B. Lippincott Company, 1955).

located roughly between Noroton Point, Tavern Island, and Wilson Point. The club landing, located on the east shore on Wilson Point, has 6 feet at low water, and there are club moorings usually available with tender service. Hug the eastern side of the cove as you enter. The club, organized in 1894, boasts a large fleet of good-looking cruising boats and is very active in dinghy and frostbite racing. Its launch service runs from 8 A.M. to 9 P.M. on weekdays and from 8 A.M. to 10 P.M. weekends. Ice, water, and gasoline may be had at the landing. The protection is not good in a hard blow from south to west, but in normal summer weather this is a most attractive and convenient stopping place. The modern one-story clubhouse is made available to members of other recognized yacht clubs. Continuing northward following the markers lining a 5-foot-deep channel, one can reach the dock of the Wilson Cove Yacht Club, which was constructed in 1960 and offers slips for an overnight stay, gas, water, and ice. Just to the east is nestled the Wilson Cove Marina. A quieter or more secluded place than this would be hard to find. Unfortunately, its entrance channel is tending to silt in.

2. Those who want to "get away from it all" can anchor off the *north shore of Sheffield Island,* where there is good holding ground. Usually the anchorage is safe in summer and the island is a good place for a picnic. The usual anchorage is off a stone pier at the northerly point of the island. However, this is open to the southwest. The small bight at the western end of Sheffield Island, near the lighthouse attracts a number of yachts. Although this island is privately owned, no one seems to mind a moderate amount of exploring, especially around the remains of a large burnt-out home on the northern shore. Beware the poison ivy!

3. *Between Calfpasture Point and Peach Island,* on the eastern side of the dredged channel and off the pier shown on the chart. This is exposed to the south for some distance, though partly protected by the Norwalk Islands. It is also close to the traffic along a busy channel.

4. In the *anchorage triangle above Gregory Point.* This, however, is on the edge of Norwalk River traffic, somewhat less than private, and unattractive.

5. *South Norwalk Boat Club* on the west side of the river just above the anchorage triangle and *McMichael Yacht Yard #4.* This hospitable club, founded in 1900, has a loyal and remarkably large-size membership of 800 members, who come from hither and yon. It started out in an old barge afloat in the channel, then moved into a horse barn situated on its present location. They still laugh about the "hay falls" sprinkling down from the musty loft above onto the heads of the Saturday night jitterbugs. A new clubhouse, with an impressive bar and restaurant, including showers, was built in 1960. On our latest trip here we fol-

lowed protocol and reported in at the bar where "Happy" Combis and Past Commodore Johnny Rogers signed us in while renting us overnight dock space for a nominal fee. They couldn't have been more accommodating. You'll find 6 feet off the club's slips.

6. *Rex Marine Center,* on the west side of the river just above the Boat Club. Here are berths for transients, a well-stocked marine store, gas, Diesel fuel, ice, water, electricity at slips, the renowned Pier Restaurant on the water front, and one of the most complete marine repair yards around. A shopping center is nearby. This boat center is run by Gardella, father of the fellow running the Cove Marina described below.

7. *Norwalk Cove Marina,* behind Calfpasture Point. This is the best of all, if you enjoy a snug anchorage and don't mind a tie-up or its cost. Just beyond black can 17 to the northeastward a sign (to be left to port) and a wooden breakwater indicate a 10-foot dredged entrance channel between Calfpasture and Gregory Point leading into a protected basin of 8- to 10-foot depths throughout with piers and slips. Black buoys indicate the port side of the channel. A gas dock is on the starboard side of the entrance and there dockage is assigned. Besides gas, Diesel fuel is available, as are ice, water, electricity, telephone, showers, a marine supply store, mopeds for rent, laundromat, and a 40-ton Travelift. Dockage is 40¢ a foot. We have often seen some fine-looking deep-draft auxiliaries there as well as distinctive power cruisers. The nearby Skipper's Restaurant, specializing in seafood, offers temporary free dockage to its patrons, and visiting yachtsmen can use the park swimming pool, with adjoining snackbar, on weekdays for a small fee.

Cruisers who prefer anchoring out will find suitable crannies here and there in the harbor. Unfortunately, most of the anchorages are both well known and prone to surge. Some boats anchor between Grassy and Goose Islands, and exploring on Grassy, which is town property, is fine. Goose Island is a bird sanctuary and it, like all the outer islands, is a major nesting place for such northeastern shorebirds as herons, egrets, Canadian geese, and pheasant. Be sure to tread lightly if you venture ashore during nesting season.

Shea Island is also publicly owned, so many Norwalkers camp here on summer weekends. The landing place, for small boats only, is on the southeastern corner. It's the only Norwalk island with a warden, Alice Cingolani. Each summer she "hosts" about 1,500 visitors, who enjoy the wild strawberries, blackberries, and raspberries that abound on the island, as well as the red, pink, and white roses, the daisies, honeysuckle, beach peas, and the yellow cactus blossoms.

To the northeast lies Chimon Island, the largest of the Norwalk Island group. Its 70 unspoiled acres make it a unique sanctuary for many forms of marine life and numerous kinds of land and water birds. To lie off this island, many shoal draft boats anchor due north of Copps Island but are aware of the poor holding ground.

Another way to view these islands is to board the *Long Island Queen* departing Norwalk Cove Marina daily for Northport. Or, for a shorter trip, take the *Lady Joan* from the same dock for a 1½-hour tour to witness by sea some of Long Island Sound's most beautiful resources.

On July 11, 1779, Calfpasture Point was used as a landing place for 2,500 British troops carried by twenty-six vessels. Both Congregational and Episcopalian churches were burned, as well as many houses and barns. The Indians used the point as a pasture. Norwalk was formerly one of the largest transatlantic oyster-shipping ports in the country.

Saugatuck, Conn. (12368 221). Compo Yacht Basin has been dredged in the lee of Cedar Point at the east of the entrance to the Saugatuck River. Its entrance can be located easily from seaward by sighting a tall, round water tower located inland and plotted on the chart.

The channel to the yacht basin (also known as the Cedar Beach Yacht Basin, run by the town) is well marked on both sides by a string of red-and-black privately maintained buoys. It has range lights also for entrance after dark. To enter this harbor, do not attempt the channel passage that leads from the west from Peck Ledge Light northward around Cockenoe Island to the Saugatuck River. It is not marked, and at low tide the best draft obtainable is not more than 2 feet. Instead, enter this harbor from the east, carrying the black can off Georges Rock and the lighted buoy off Cedar Point on your port. Having just passed Saugatuck River nun 8, you will spot the channel to the yacht basin. Be sure to carry nun 8 on your starboard when entering this narrow channel.

The 50-foot channel has been dredged to a 10-foot depth, except where it has begun to shoal along the small sandspit to starboard almost at channel's end. Just before reaching this point, stay well to the port. "If the *Clearwater* can come in here, so can you," hailed the Harbor Master as we came alongside. Protection from all winds may be found in the oval basin, 400 yards long by 100 yards wide, with a depth of about 9 feet, but extremely shallow along its entire southern shore. The basin is very congested, over 180 boats, large and small, being moored there on any summer weekend. Anchoring is impossible, so it is necessary to obtain a mooring, usually fore-and-aft. As a rule, two guest moorings are vacant, but if they are occupied, the dock master can usually provide an alternate. A depth of 8 feet at low water can be carried to the float, where gasoline and water may be obtained. There is no overnight dockage. The dock master is on duty seven days of the week from 9 A.M. to 8 P.M. and is usually spotted in the clubhouse formerly held by the Cedar Point Yacht Club, which has moved westward to Bluff Point. We found nearby Compo Beach active with bathers.

In approaching the Cedar Point Yacht Club, located on the northeastern shore of Saugatuck Shores, follow the buoys leading to the west but don't become beguiled by the fleet of boats moored beside the channel. They have left little space and depth in which you can anchor. Beware, too, of a nasty shoal, which for some time has been building up insidiously to port between cans 9 and 11. Give it a wide berth.

In 1966 the very impressive-looking two-story clubhouse of the Cedar Point Yacht Club was erected on the point south of can 15. "It's 'Cedar Point modern,' " exclaimed Rear Commodore George Morris, whose congeniality made us feel right at home. Standing on this beautiful site, we were treated to a panoramic view of the region while listening to his story of a yacht club on the move. A narrow channel, running southeast from nun 16, cuts through the peninsula on Bluff Point and leads into a freshly dredged basin approximately 150 yards wide by 250 yards long with 10-foot depth throughout. No anchoring is permitted in the basin, but this is no drawback since the new slips are among the finest we have seen with electrical outlets. Unfortunately, these are available only if temporarily vacated by a cruising member of the club. The club's facilities include gas, ice, water, showers, and a neat snack bar open daily from 11 A.M. to 6 P.M. Facing open water, a 600-foot beach invites bathing. We always see a preponderance of sailboats here, since the club has a rich sailing heritage; it has hosted the National Atlantic Class Championships for several years and runs an active Junior Program. Cedar Point extends reciprocal privileges to members of other recognized clubs with the understandable request that visiting yachts please not lay over longer than twenty-four hours or discharge their heads into the basin. Pick up a copy of the club's guest rules on registering.

Further up the Saugatuck River channel on the western shore lies the Saugatuck Harbor Yacht Club's dock at the head of Duck Creek, affording a quiet, unspoiled, but crowded shelter. Keep the black marker in the center of the entrance to port coming in. As you pass the gas dock to port, pick up the range lights help guiding you further in. The only facilities here are gas, water, ice, use of the swimming pool for a modest fee, and electricity at the docks with reported 8-foot depths. This private club had its beginning in 1960 in an old, attractive carriage club. If you are a member of a recognized yacht club, it is suggested you phone ahead for a reservation. Whenever leaving the creek, make sure to stand off until incoming boats have cleared the "narrows" at the entrance.

The nearest inns are 2½ miles to the north at Westport.

The channel up the Saugatuck River to the railroad bridge is now marked but subject to shoaling with a 3-foot depth at low water reported just beyond nun 26. Above the bridge the channel is not marked and strangers are advised not to attempt it. However, just above the railroad bridge on the west bank is Coastwise Marine. If you want to go there for any reason, tie up temporarily at the Yacht Basin, telephone the yard, and they will send a man to pilot you to their dock. At high tide the yard can haul out boats up to 45 feet with a draft of 6 feet.

Southport, Conn. (12369 220). Here is another instance of a community's improving its water front to form a perfect shelter, under any conditions. By means of a breakwater and dredging, the entrance to Mill River has become an appealing, fully protected though narrow, harbor. The channel has a width of 50 feet and a depth of 7 feet at low water all the way to the very head of the harbor where the depth becomes limited to 4 feet in the anchorage area.

Though the channel is marked by two flashing lights and eight can and nun buoys, it is somewhat tricky. For instance, on our latest visit, we were advised by a local authority not to go too close to the outer nun buoys but to favor the black cans until the last red nun, number 10, was reached; that nun should be favored closely. Like many offshore channels with shoal water on each side, this one has a tendency to silt up at times. So enter with caution if the tide is low. We don't advise strangers to enter after dark. Watch for oyster stakes off the entrance.

The town dock is on the west side of the entrance channel near where the chart shows White Rock. Gas and water are available there or a possible tie-up or mooring. Beyond, also to port, where the harbor widens, is the well-known Pequot Yacht Club, one of the leading clubs on the sound. The club offers a helpful visiting yachtsmen's guide and reciprocal privileges to members of other recognized yacht clubs and may be able to provide a mooring on a first-come-first-served basis. It is necessary to tie up fore and aft, as the river is crowded and narrow, with no room to swing at anchor. Launch service runs from 8 A.M. to 9 P.M. There's no charge for one-night layovers, but extended visits run $5.00 per night.

Gasoline, Diesel fuel, ice, and water can also be procured at Pequot's float, where there is 7 feet at low tide. Showers and daily luncheons are available in the clubhouse. It's just a five-minute walk to the small village center located inland from the fountain outside the club entrance. Here you will find such stores as a pharmacy, a coffee shop, and a grocery, as well as hardware, gift, and liquor stores. A newspaper store supplying limited groceries is open Sundays. The best meal in town is reportedly served at the Pepper Mill Steakhouse, reached by taxi.

Southport is one of the most delightful harbors on the Connecticut shore. In Revolutionary times, crews were organized here to protect the town from numerous Tory depredations suffered by settlements along the sound. Southport was once a famous onion-shipping point. It is part of the town of Fairfield.

On October 21, 1799, the town voted that it was willing to allow the General Assembly to grant a lottery to raise money for "Sinking the channel of Mill River harbor."

Black Rock Harbor, Bridgeport, Conn. (12369 220). This harbor, west of Bridgeport, is easy to make both day and night, on account of the lights and buoys at the north and south of the entrance. A white tower on the sandspit to the east of the entrance is a good guide in the daytime from far out in the sound. Penfield Reef Light, converted to automatic operation, is a sure guide to the entrance at night.

The Black Rock Yacht Club is in a white building to the west, inside of Grover Hill, where a pier is indicated on the chart. In approaching this pier through the deeper water, take the course that will keep directly on your stern the lone house on Fayerweather Island. The best anchorage for all but small and shoal-draft boats is across the channel from this yacht club north of nun 8. This, however, is exposed from southeast to southwest. In a blow it is possible to run for shelter into Cedar Creek, where complete protection is available in the dredged channel.

The Black Rock Yacht Club is both a lively social club and a yacht club. Beside its pier in 5-foot depth, it has a swimming pool, tennis courts, a fine restaurant, and a handsome clubhouse, all open during the summer months. Across the channel an impressive fleet of yachts may be seen anchored or moored. An overnight mooring is available at $4.00, with launch service provided. Members of other recognized yacht clubs are warmly welcomed by this club, whose Sunday night buffet we have found delectable.

Further up the harbor on the west shore of Cedar Creek, across from Fayerweather Island and on the point where Black Rock is indicated on the chart, is the Fayerweather Yacht Club, with a large membership and open the year round. Its large barroom was bustling with activity during our latest stopover. Unlike many of the other yacht clubs visited, in this club more men of our own age were around than younger people, and the convivial aspects of the club were much in evidence among the hospitable members who were on hand. There is 7 feet of water at the dock, and the club usually has spare moorings for visitors, and provides gas, ice, and water. But if there's space, boats up to 40 feet can tie up to a floating club dock across the channel in 7-foot depth. Visiting yachtsmen are always welcome, the commodore told us, whether members of other clubs or not. "We aren't fussy," said one of the members. "We like to be friendly to everyone." And they certainly have been to us.

Should you happen to get caught in a blow and don't carry too deep a draft, you'll find a protected spot in Burr Creek, north of can 13. Hug the eastern shore of the creek where the water runs deepest. There is 5 feet of water at the slips. The Bridgeport Municipal Marina does not have many facilities nor is it a very pretty place but, according to the dock master, "everybody seems to find us whenever a three-day nor-'easter strikes."

Black Rock is less commercial than Bridgeport Harbor and much to be preferred by yachtsmen.

Bridgeport, Conn. (12369 220). The best anchorage is up Johnson's Creek just beyond the large gas tanks on the western point as one enters the creek. The Miamogue Yacht Club is here with increased dockage space and will advise yachtsmen as to moorings and where to get gasoline and supplies.

While this is a fully protected anchorage, it is very unattractive and commercial, with tankers coming and going nearby. Not much can be said for going up the long channel into Bridgeport. One will probably meet barges and collect much coal dust and soot. Bridgeport is useful to cruisers chiefly as a protection in a storm.

Stratford, Conn. (12370 219). Here is another river entrance cutting into the Connecticut shore that is no place to enter at night if it can be avoided. There is a strong current in the river, and sometimes, when the wind is against an outgoing tide, a short, hard sea breaks in the channel and the buoys are dragged under. However, dredging of the channel to a 100-foot width and an approximate depth of 18 feet, at least as far north as can 29 below Popes Island, has helped to minimize the current and make river navigation easier. The mean range of tide at Stratford is 5.5 feet.

Two tall black chimneys at Devon, up the Housatonic, stand out prominently as a good guide in clear weather from far out in the sound for both Milford and the entrance of the Housatonic River. The ebb tide swirls and eddies about, so that power is a necessity.

The Pootatuck Yacht Club, in its red building with two rows of piazzas, is located west of what appears on the chart as black can 19 opposite where the river channel turns northeastward, about 2½ miles from the entrance of the river. The club sometimes has slips, and also has gas, water, ice, and usually spare moorings for visiting yachtsmen.

Just below the yacht club is Stratford Marina, formerly Fladd & Kahle's, with one hundred and forty deep-water slips and the most complete facilities around. Should you need any repair work on your boat, have it done here, with special attention given to inboards at Fred's Marine Engine Service and to electronic gear at Maritronics. In addition to these services, you'll find about everything you and your boat could wish. The dockage charge is 40¢ per foot and Dock Master Ralph Fladd obviously caters to the theatergoers. You'll find you are within easy walking distance of a laundromat, a liquor and drug store, such fine restaurants as Fagan's and Spada's Blue Goose. A well-stocked ships store with charts and a scuba store are on the premises. A courtesy car can take you to these and other stores, including the Mermaid Tavern at the Stratford Motor Inn. Phone Ralph at (203) 377-2111 for an advance slip reservation.

We have stayed also at the hospitable Housatonic Boat Club, which is just above nun 16 on the west shore; they offer no gas or ice, but they do have guest moorings and launch service until 9 P.M. If you decide to anchor and dinghy in, make sure you are set firmly while paying out plenty of scope and allowing for swinging room within the swift current. This club is near the impressive American Shakespeare Theater, Connecticut Center for the Performing Arts.

At the time of writing, this debt-plagued theater announced plans calling for a wider range of activities and year-round use of the playhouse. William W. Goodman, chairman of the board, said that he foresees "a minimum" of 20 weeks of Shakespeare, including the traditional spring season for schoolchildren. He also mentioned a period of about 10 or 12 weeks when the theater would be turned over to Connecticut-based ballet and opera companies. The rest of the year, he explained, would be filled with popular commercial attractions, such as *Godspell,* *Wonderful Town,* and *South Pacific* which would share their profits with the theater. If you are in the mood for gaining an unforgettable theatrical experience, "follow your spirit" and call for ticket information at (203) 375-4457.

The anchorage off the Pootatuck Yacht Club is exposed to the southward and northeast for some distance along the river, and most of the nearby land is low and marshy. While the yacht facilities, stores, and other conveniences are at Stratford, the beauty of the Housatonic is up the river where little dredging has occurred recently and depths shift mysteriously.

If you decide to explore further, it is a run of about 9 miles from the yacht club, along a well-marked channel, to the head of navigation at Derby and Shelton. Beyond Culver Bar at can 31, the controlling depth in the channel is about 3 feet at MLW. These minimum depths are found in the channel between cans 31 and 37, and occur again along Drews Bar at nun 62. Along the shores as you approach Derby, the scenery is impressive, and hills of 200 to 300 feet in height come down to the shores. The two bascule bridges at Devon demand our attention. They usually open on signal daily from 5 A.M. to 9 P.M. but on Monday through Friday from 7 A.M. to 9 A.M. and from 4 P.M. to 5:45 P.M., these draws need not open for vessels. The opening signal for the first US 1 Bridge is one long blast followed by one short blast. The bridge will comply by repeating this signal. Opening signal for the second Penn Central Railroad Bridge is one long blast followed by two shorts. One long blast from this bridge will confirm its opening for you.

While Adriaen Block, the Dutch fur trader, stopped at Stratford in 1614, the first settlers were English. They came there in 1639 and named it for Stratford-on-Avon. Today it is well known for its summer Shakespearean festivals.

Milford, Conn. (12370 219). Should you put in to this well-protected but crowded port of Milford on one of its interclub race days, you will probably find a busy yachting center swarming with attractive young boys and girls who have gathered from far and near. Some of the boats will be on trailers getting a final going-over, others will be in the water or on the way in. Blue Jays, Lightnings, 210s, Thistles, 420s, and Lasers will be teeming with youngsters aboard. Such liveliness confirms a Milford Yacht Club officer's comment that "We're probably the most active sailing club on the sound."

Across the Wepawaug River, above the yacht club, are the docks and oyster boats of the Cedar Island Corporation, for oysters and clams have been important Milford products since the earliest days of the settlement. Under the name of the Northern Oyster Company, the oyster business continues. The National Marine Fisheries Service has a laboratory at Milford to advise oyster "farmers." Plans were being made in 1978 to dredge the river channel to a depth of 10 feet up to the oyster dock and thence 8 feet to the head of the harbor just above the Milford Boat Works.

The harbor is formed by two jetties at the mouth of the Wepawaug River, completing the protection of the anchorage from all winds. In 1977, the 75-foot channel, lined by buoys with reflectors, carried about 7 feet all the way to the Milford Yacht Club on the west side of the entrance, on Burns Point to port. Members of other recognized yacht clubs who register in the clubhouse are welcomed hospitably; Dock Master Malcolm Dymkoski, located in his office next to the club's swimming pool, will assign, if available, a free guest mooring or a slip at $15.00 minimum. The pool is open only to members and their registered guests. On a previous visit, past Commodore Charles Stokesbury, Jr. had helped bring us up-to-date on his club and on Milford, the sixth-oldest town in Connecticut. Gas, water, ice, telephones, a bar, afternoon tea, and meals are all available at the club, and there are stores, including a laundromat, fairly nearby. Regular launch service is provided.

Congestion is the chief difficulty at this otherwise splendid harbor. The outgoing tide sweeps in under a bridge from the east, making it unwise to anchor behind the eastern jetty, where it is also shoal. On a warm summer day even the beach at the club is crowded. There is 8 feet at the club float at low tide. Milford is a good place to visit, but it is quieter on weekdays or nights than on weekends. The late Captain Bradley, a local authority, told us, "The ducks may wake you up if you are fool enough to feed them." And don't be foolish enough to try to anchor along the river.

The channel upriver from a point 250 yards above Burns Point had a reported depth in 1977 of about 6 feet at low water all the way to the town dock (convenient to supplies) shown to port on the chart, near the end of the dredged part of the river. At the time of writing there were 3 marinas and a boatyard on the Wepawaug River, all providing slips and other facilities, thus helping to lessen the congestion in the lower river; Commodore Marina (in yellow buildings to port just below the first creek that runs among the marshes); Spencer's (housed in a barn-red building to starboard at the prominent pier a short distance up); and just beyond to port can be found a unique boating complex composed of Milford Harbor Marina, Milford Boat Works, and Milford Yacht Sales.

We have often laid over at Jim Allen's Spencer's Marina, where local authorities confirm that it renders complete and efficient service to boats of all types. If you need Diesel fuel, put in at Commodore Marina, which has the only supply in Milford but reportedly delivers rather ordinary service to overnight transients. Flourishing Milford Harbor Marina, on the other hand, has much going for it. Their facilities include fuel and ice, heads and showers, and their marine, the "Chandlery," is one of the best on the Connecticut shore. Close by are a laundromat, restaurant, town shops, and Taled Electronics, serving both power and sail. They are knowledgeable about boats here, including the needs of boating people.

At the turn of the century, Milford was, strangely, a center for the manufacture of straw hats. Now it's a popular and attractive summer resort with pleasantly shaded streets and lovely homes. There is a railway station on the main line of Amtrak, with express trains to New York or Boston stopping at nearby New Haven.

"On a quiet night a pleasant place to anchor if bound east or west," writes a yachtsman, "is just to the north of Charles Island. The bottom is sand and good-holding. At low water a bar connecting Charles Island with the mainland is dry, so don't anchor to the northwest of the island. This, also, is a good spot to duck into for a quick bite if the going is rugged on the sound."

Charles Island, now owned by the state of Connecticut, is rich in historic lore and was originally purchased in 1639 by Milford settlers from Ansantawae, chief of the local Paugusset tribe, for 6 coats, 10 blankets, 1 kettle, 12 hatchets, 12 hoes, 24 knives, and 12 small mirrors. Its peaceful, rustic appearance is deceptive, for down through the years it has borne three mysterious curses, harbored the secret hiding place of two unfound treasures (one of them Captain Kidd's), and served as the proving ground for America's first submarine, *The Turtle,* which served conspicuously in an American Revolutionary naval battle. At various times in its history, it has housed a mansion, a hotel, a factory, and a Dominican retreat, whose foundations may still be seen. If you enjoy exploring ashore, don't miss a stop here.

New Haven, Conn. (12371 218). This harbor, the third-busiest commercial port in New England, is accordingly of moderate interest to yachtsmen except as a refuge or a place to secure supplies. As the chief carrying trade of the port is coal and oil, and as New Haven is a manufacturing town, coal dust abounds. Despite three outer breakwaters, small boats usually have a restless time. The entrance, outside of which stand numerous oyster stakes, is well lighted and easy to make at night or in fog or storm.

New Haven officials have recently been investigating new ways to lure boatmen to their waterfront. In 1977, the city was accepting bids for the development of Gateway Landing, a key 8.6-acre site at the head of the harbor. If and when completed, Gateway Landing will include a marina, a public park, and restaurants. "It will give you someplace to go in the harbor," they claim.

But the usual anchorage for yachts is still at Morris Cove, where we have seen that the New Haven Yacht Club is "alive and well and visiting yachtsmen are welcome." First chartered in 1882, it held a prominent place in yachting circles for many years, until damage by the 1938 hurricane forced the closing of its doors. A group of sailing buffs in 1967 came upon the old clubhouse and leased a portion of it while restoring the original charter. It is now housed in a white building set behind a long pier jutting out from the cove's southwestern shore. What this modest "do-it-ourselves," all-sailing club lacks in facilities, it makes up in the dedication and enthusiasm of its members.

Just to the west, the New Haven Marina does engine and hull repairs and has a gas dock in a tiny basin behind a prominent stone jetty. At the time of writing, plans were being made to dredge the depths dockside to 5 feet MLW.

The anchorage at Morris Cove is not a quiet one. A sea roll from the southwest frequently makes in by the breakwaters, and the anchorage is rough in westerly winds. A sheltered spot can be found at the head of the harbor, but the distance is so great and the environment so unattractive that few yachts go north to the wharves. Anchorages are described in the *Coast Pilot*. The harbors 5 miles to the west at Milford or to the east at Branford, Pine Orchard, or the Thimble Islands are ordinarily much to be preferred.

About the best facility in New Haven Harbor is Trader's Dock, identified on the chart as two peninsulas reaching out from the southern shore of City Point just north of can 11. It is further identified by the stylish-looking Chart House Restaurant. Make your approach passing the buoys marking the West River channel. Trader's Dock has space for over one hundred boats, most of which tie up in 10 feet of water in the twin basins formed between the peninsulas. Deep-draft boats usually lie outside along the bulkhead, which is completely open to the northeast. You'll find gas, Diesel fuel, ice, water, electricity, showers, marine supplies, and twenty-four-hour repair service here, but don't bank on getting any supplies. The surroundings are not overly commercial looking, since there is a residential district to the north. Boats are widely exposed to winds from the east and south, but apparently this spot is good enough for the New Haven Harbor police, who make it their "headquarters." The Chart House is quite an attraction, providing a premium fare at premium prices.

In 1977, West River channel recorded a depth of 12 feet at low water up to a point 630 feet north of nun 18, thence a depth of 8 feet to 80 feet south of the Connecticut Turnpike crossover. The bascule bridge is closed during the morning and late afternoon rush hours and also at noon. Kimberly Harbor and the City Point Yacht Club lie just above the bridge, promising good protection in case of a blow. But this is a good example of a place with simply too many power boats and not enough space.

Branford, Conn. (12373 217). Chart 12373 shows a large shallow bay 4 miles east of New Haven, fully exposed to the south. But, like so many other places on the Connecticut shore, the farther in one goes, the better the anchorage for small boats.

In 1976 the 100-foot-wide channel was vastly improved by being dredged to a controlling depth of 8 feet from Little Mermaid all the way to the bridge at the upper end of the river. The entrance must be made under power by all except very small boats. Don't attempt it at night. If you must enter by night, we would like to advise that the flashing green light on Big Mermaid's pipe tower is difficult to pick up. A good anchorage offering a bottom of mud and rock can be found in the charted 7-foot depth area between Big Mermaid and Lamphier Cove to the north.

With dredging and filling, and new docks at the yacht club located on the north shore, this harbor was transformed prior to "Branford Day," which came on August 18, 1954. Now Branford has become, in its facilities for yachtsmen, one of the finest ports on Long Island Sound. Yachting activities revolve around the Branford Yacht Club, which was organized in 1909 and is now equipped with a first-class marina containing many slips. Members of recognized yacht clubs offering reciprocal privileges are welcomed there. Report when you come in to Dock Master Dick Krewsky at the long gas dock to your port after you have kept well clear of the nearby mud flats running along the northern edge of the channel. He will assign you a slip or a tie-up between mooring stakes across the channel, if one is available.

Beside gas, Diesel fuel, ice, and a telephone at the main dock, electricity and fresh water are provided at the slips. At the large piers, depths of up to 10 feet are available. Supplies may be purchased at a store about ¼ mile away.

Not only has the Branford Yacht Club concentrated on maintaining its fine dockage, its clubhouse is spic and span and its manicured grounds with numerous picnic tables afford a splendid view of the river.

The channel, marked in part by stakes on both sides as one proceeds upriver, winds its way among the marshes. Hug these stakes closely. In the middle of the bend on the east shore, on now-filled land, is Bruce & Johnson's Marina, with slips, ice, water, gas, and Diesel fuel, a ships store, full repair work, showers, and a restaurant. This place is popular with sailing men. After rounding the bend and heading westward beyond the stakes, keep in the middle. Below some large buildings on the west shore is the Dutch Wharf Boat Yard Marina. Here are slips and moorings, a supply store, but no gas. Hauling and repair work are done here, and we saw some fine-looking yachts tied up. A package and grocery store may be found nearby.

Pier 66, just beyond the yacht club, is an enterprising marina run by Armand Williams, Jr., who knows the harbor like the back of his hand and built up this facility from a mountain of mud to a facility that includes 350 floating slips, a ship's store, gas dock, and a snack bar featuring home-style Italian cooking. While it has apparent appeal for powerboat people, we still prefer the setup at Bruce & Johnson's.

Branford is an attractive residential community, deservedly popular among cruising men. There are many fine old houses. Yankee traders were once very active there. When West Indies rum didn't pay, some took up slave trading and on occasions procured slaves for some very pious people. One of the pious was Reverend Ezra Stiles, president of Yale, who asked for a fine specimen and got him.*

Pine Orchard, Conn. (12373 217). Pine Orchard is an attractive summer resort between Branford and the Thimble Islands. In making your approach at night, line up on the club's range lights marking the outer end of a breakwater. East of Brown Point and behind this breakwater lies a dredged basin with depths that vary from time to time according to the dredging. This basin inside of St. Helena Island was dredged in 1964 to a depth of 7 feet at MLW with considerable shoaling reported in 1977. On entering, make a sharp turn to port just after passing the eastern end of the breakwater that marks the short channel to the basin. Stay well off of a chain of rocks that extends southward from St. Helena Island.

On the west shore of the basin is Pine Orchard Club, with a fine clubhouse, docks, tennis courts, a nine-hole golf course, a fresh-water swimming pool, dining room, and yacht facilities that include slips, guest moorings, water, ice, electric connections, gas, telephone, etc. An enthusiastic member once told us that this was the "only club on Long Island Sound that has everything." Judging from what we have seen, he wasn't far off. Guest privileges, we were told, are granted to yachtsmen who are members of recognized clubs that accord reciprocal privileges.

Anchoring in the basin is not permitted, because of very limited

*From *The Yankees of Connecticut*, by W. Storrs Lee (Henry Holt & Co.).

swinging room. The club has floats for mooring, for which it charges $6.00 per night. The inner moorings lie in 5-foot depths but there's 7 feet further out. You'll pay 35¢ a foot at the slips, with an extra fee for use of the swimming pool and tennis courts. The Pine Orchard Market, ½ mile distant, has been recommended as a good source for supplies.

Large yachts can anchor outside the island, but with little protection from south to east winds and from the frequent crying of the seagulls nesting. The charted channel running northeastward by St. Helena leads to a cove just east of Juniper Point. This is busily used by traprock barges so you'll find no suitable anchorage here.

During the summer months an active group of attractive people of all ages keep the club and nearby waters very busy.

Pine Orchard, in spite of its tendency to shoal up, has become one of the more appealing ports of call on the sound except in easterlies.

Little Harbor, Leetes Island, Conn. (12373 217). For yachts drawing under 4 feet here is a very pretty "little harbor," protected by jetties on both sides of the entrance of Harrison and Clark points. While no depths are given on the chart, our soundings indicated depths of 7 feet or more leading up to the entrance, 6 feet at the entrance, 5 feet just inside, and 4 feet at mean low water in most of that section of the harbor that is south and west of the point that separates the two inner branches. Most of the bottom is fairly hard, and we would expect the holding ground to be only fair. If you are so lucky as to find enough free-swinging room, an anchorage here is satisfactory in ordinary summer weather, though likely to be uncomfortable in strong southerlies.

For those who don't need supplies or want to land, this is a pleasant variation from the usual, better-known anchorages, and appealing especially to those who like poking into new places. The surrounding land and docks are privately owned, so there are no landing facilities for visiting yachts, except possibly in dinghies on the beach at the head of the east fork.

Thimble Islands, Stony Creek, Conn. (12373 217). "Like a section of the Maine Coast, drifted into Long Island Sound,"* the Thimbles offer a good, picturesque anchorage between Money Island and West Crib Island.

Despite the red lines on the chart warning about cables, this anchorage is clear. It is preferable to that at Sachem Head, being larger and much better protected. But it is a difficult place to enter at night or in

*Quotation from *Connecticut*—American Guide Series (Houghton Mifflin Co.).

the fog. In the daytime a shoal boat under power can approach through the narrow passage from the east, but it is not recommended without power. The anchorage is apt to be rough in a storm or strong sou' wester, and a roll frequently comes in from the sound. We have found the most scenic spots to anchor, offering good holding ground, are either northwest of Money Island just to the south of the Cribs, or along the shore southeast of High Island.

The village of Stony Creek lies about 1 mile north of the anchorage. With caution, a draft of 4 feet can be carried at low tide to the public dock, which is on the point east of Burr Island. Gas and supplies can be had here.

A supply "Islands Service" motorboat runs frequently between the islands in summer and will transport one to the public landing at Stony Creek. At our most recent visit to Stony Creek, we were told by the obliging Captain Dwight Carter, the ferry skipper, that the boat leaves Stony Creek during the summer at a quarter before the hour, from 7 A.M. to 9 P.M. and will pick up passengers from yachts for the return trip if signaled or on call from the phone at the public dock harborside (telephone 488-9978). The pick-up would be about on the hour, as it is a fifteen-minute trip each way. Thus, it is possible for visiting yachtsmen without power dinghies to obtain supplies or a shore meal at Stony Creek while their boat lies at anchor among the islands. Aside from the inconvenience of obtaining supplies, the Thimble Islands afford one of the most appealing anchorages on the sound.

The Thimble Islands anchorage is a good stopping place for the first night on the way east from the various yachting centers at the western end of Long Island Sound. In good weather and during the daytime it is easy to enter and very little off the direct course eastward.

Wayne Allen Hall, in his article in *The New York Times,* presents us here with an interesting story about the Thimbles:

Named by the Stony Creek Indians for the lowly thimble berry, second cousin to the gooseberry, the Thimble Islands consist of 365 islands, 32 of them habitable, the largest being Horse Island, 17 acres, and the smallest, Dogfish Island, three-quarters of an acre.

The islands are glacial deposits of pink granite, which was quarried at the turn of the century to make sturdy foundations for the Statue of Liberty and the Brooklyn Bridge. Even the Indians discovered that the rocks made excellent arrowheads.

Captain Kidd had his observation headquarters on High Island, providing him with a semilandlocked cove, where he hid from American sloops of war. Across the narrow channel on Pot Island, he found a cavern, reachable only from under the water.

It is rumored that Kidd left a substantial amount of gold in the cavern, but to this day no one has been able to find the underwater entrance. High Island still flies the Jolly Roger, has black cottages and black motorboats and is the summer residence of a semisecret club of businessmen who call themselves the Buccaneers.

Pot Island gained fame in the 1880's when a fat men's club used the island's glacially formed potholes for a drinking rite. The club filled one pothole 30 feet deep with their punch and didn't leave the island until the hole had been drained.

Sachem Head, Conn. (12373 217). This is a small harbor open to the west and southwest, at the outer end of Sachem Head, with 6 to 10 feet of water at low tide. In entering, keep well off the southerly side of the point. The anchorage is difficult for strangers at night, but in the morning they will be won over by the charming scene of a rock-ribbed shoreline on which lovely residences are perched.

The Thimble Islands anchorage is less crowded, larger, and better protected. Sachem Head is highly recommended for shelter in easterlies. In northwesters it can be very unpleasant, and in hard southwesters a correspondent warns, "It is a regular saucer bowl and is apt to roll the sticks out of you."

The Sachem Head Yacht Club, with three well-marked guest moorings, maintains a well-sheltered float at the shore end of the lighted breakwater extending northwestward from the small island to the south of the entrance. A flashing red light is on the breakwater's outer end, and across the harbor below Joshua Point there's a privately maintained flashing white beacon. Consult the steward regarding moorings reserved for guests from accredited yacht clubs. After two nights of free use of club moorings, visitors are required to pay a charge of $2.00 a night, the limit on such mooring to be a total of one week. Boats should not remain at the club docks for any reason other than to load or unload. Gas and ice are unavailable but a snack bar and showers can be found within the clubhouse.

The nearest boat yard is at Branford. The town of Guilford, where there are good restaurants and all manner of supplies can be purchased, is only three miles distant. A house built in 1639 is extant.

On Sachem Head a bloody battle of the Pequot War was fought in 1637. Tradition says that the head of an Indian, slain in combat, was placed by Uncas in the fork of a tree, where the skull remained for many years, giving the point its present name.*

Guilford, Conn. (12373 217). Interestingly, Guilford is considered a harbor of refuge. Of course, this is provided you can enter safely in the first place, assuming you are blessed with a skillful skipper at the helm of a boat of fairly shoal draft. The entrance acts as a delta, taking the mud silt coming down from East River and Sluice Creek and building up currents of at least 3 knots in the channel. Last dredged in 1981, it is subject to continual shoaling. A major hurdle in entering can be found between nun 10 and can 9. During 1977, four powerboats, on separate occasions, struck a rock just inside of nun 10. On the other hand, be advised that depths close to can 9 record only 4 feet at MLW. Nevertheless, the Town Marina dock master, Don Lowell, told us to favor the black cans all the way up East River. In 1981, the main channel was reportedly dredged to a depth of 6 feet at MLW and a width of 100 feet all the way up to the head of the harbor.

Up to starboard in the creek, the Town Marina's slips are all rented to local boaters—there is no transient or refueling dock. But the dock master may be able to rent you a slip at $5.00 a night, or an East River mooring for $2.50 if the regular occupant is out cruising.

Another alternative is to anchor up the East River between cans 7 and 9 in 4-foot depths with lines out fore and aft to cope with the current. On the way upriver you will note to port a launching ramp and float. Here you can leave your dinghy while eating at either the Captain's Table Restaurant or the Little Stone House nearby.

You can wear your sailing duds to Captain's Table, which specializes in seafood. The Little Stone House, where you can select your own lobster for dinner or to take out, requires more formal attire and is considered one of the finest dining spots on the Connecticut shore. Everything along the creek shuts down on Mondays. To obtain all kinds of supplies or to visit the charming, historic Guilford Town Green, a mile away, you can phone Guilford Taxi at 453-2264. Or you may prefer to explore the extensive marshland and its birdlife by dinking nearly a mile up the East or Neck rivers—both ecologically intriguing. Jacobs Public Beach, which stretches to port at the harbor's entrance, is reported to have good clean water and always looks extremely inviting to us.

Although the Guilford Yacht Club stands along the West River, we were strongly advised not to attempt this passage.

*From *Connecticut*—American Guide Series (Houghton Mifflin Co.).

Clinton, Conn. (12374 216). The shifting channel depths in this protected harbor demand a watchful eye of the helmsman. Although the latest chart shows a channel depth of 7 feet at MLW, there is reportedly only 5 feet at its first turn, where unchartered buoys 8 and 9 are located. These are often moved to mark the deepest water. Also note that the 100-foot channel narrows to just 50 feet at this spot, sometimes creating a traffic bottleneck. Follow the middle carefully and stay within the channel around Cedar Island until you see the Holiday Dock Bait Shop on the starboard shore, a short distance beyond nun 16. The outer channel was dredged in 1981 to a depth of 8 feet at MLW.

Here you may find the town dock master, who may assign you a fore-and-aft mooring along the opposite side of the channel or will place you at the dock if space is open. Just to the east is the modest-looking Clinton Harbor Marina, which specializes in all types of engine-repair work.

We recommend the attractive Cedar Island Marina seen spread out beyond Holiday Dock. They have protected floating docks berthing boats up to 95 feet, with complete services including refueling, hauling and repairs, showers, swimming pool, a general and ship's store, laundromat, and the popular Top-of-the-Dock Restaurant. Their rates at the time of writing were 50¢ per foot. For a meal change aboard, pick up a freshly cooked lobster from Ward Hadley at the Bait Shop.

Since the Hammonasset River begins to shoal beyond these marinas, boats of deep draft are advised not to proceed further upriver without local knowledge. Also, we were told that the anchorage area marked on the chart just west of nun 16 is no place for an overnighter to swing at anchor.

Among the old dwellings in Clinton is Stanton House, built in 1789 and now a Colonial museum. In the center of the green is a monument commemorating the early years of the Collegiate School, later Yale. The first Yale students attended classes at this school until the opening of the college of Saybrook.

Duck Island Roads, Clinton, Conn. (12374 216). To some yachtsmen (not including the writers) this is the most appealing harbor on Long Island Sound, although designated by the *Coast Pilot* as a harbor of refuge. It is formed by two long breakwaters extending north and west from Duck Island. Another breakwater to the westward offers additional protection from the southwest.

One determined yachtsman, who is obviously on our side, presents his impression of this questionable retreat:

Who has not chilled, at least once, to the aubade of a wifely voice saying, "Goodness, I didn't think we had anchored that close to the breakwater!" For me, this summarizes this place. Avoid it. Either your anchor drags or it fouls among the lobster pots and it's a damn tide hole. If caught here, look up the Patchogue River for a berth.

There is a strong run of tide off Kelsey Point Breakwater. When you are making Duck Island Roads from midsound, with no direct bearings, the cottages on Hammonasset Beach and the elevated tank shown well to the east are helpful. An experienced cruising man writes as follows (consult chart 12374 in reading these directions):

If approaching from the west at night with a slight to medium haze, and sailing fairly close in along the Connecticut shore, having left Falkner Island well astern (roughly 4 miles) and bearing about east a quarter north to gong 8 (roughly 2½ miles ahead), it is then well to know of certain confusion which has been experienced by others under similar circumstances because of the varying intensity of the lights on the three breakwaters.

As one approaches closer, with the white light appearing to be very close at hand, one should also begin to pick up the flashing (every four seconds) red light on the west end of the longer breakwater on Duck Island proper (one half of the intensity of the white light). It is then wise to note that the new, white Kelsey Point Breakwater light is probably dead ahead, mingled in the background of shore lights running all the way eastward from Hammock Point to the Patchogue River entrance. Don't fear that this 2½ sec. white light is past or lies well to port, but hold on, bearing off somewhat to starboard (south), and await your approach close aboard the Kelsey Point Breakwater until this white light comes into distinct view.

The danger lies in attempting to go farther inshore in the hope of running in closer to, and thus picking up, this white light, which in reality has little brilliance and is probably dead ahead clouded by the shore lights. To run in may present the danger of entering the foul waters surrounding Stone Island Reef.

Having held on, picked up the white light, and passed it close abeam on the port hand, one will find the entrance simple. Swing the bow to port (north) and run close past the red light of the longer Duck Island Breakwater to starboard.

It might be appropriate here to remind the reader that changes in aids to navigation are constantly being made on the sound as well as along our entire coast. To cite an example, Kelsey Point Breakwater Light, Branford Reef Light, and Seaflower Reef Light have all been given a new daytime appearance. They have been "changed to pipe towers and equipped with diamond-shaped daymarks divided into four diamond shapes which are colored so that the horizontal diamonds are white and the vertical diamonds are black with a white reflective border."

Good anchorage will be found in the V of the breakwater, with only fair holding ground. But don't get so near to the breakwater that you haven't plenty of room to swing and let out more scope on your anchor in case of a northwester or a northwest squall. The lights on the breakwater make Duck Island Roads extremely easy of access at night, with no particular dangers. However, lobster pots sprinkled throughout the area have become an annoyance to many a skipper.

A large fleet can be accommodated, and everything is lovely if it doesn't start blowing from the northwest. There is some privacy, and the very desolateness of the place has a charm.

On the northeast end of the shorter breakwater on Duck Island proper there is a brilliant flashing (every four seconds) white light. This has four times the intensity of one of the other breakwater lights, and can under most conditions be picked up long before the flashing (every two and one-half seconds) white light on the sound end of Kelsey Point Breakwater. In midsummer this condition is aggravated by the mass of lights in the background, at Kelsey Point and along the beaches to the north. This white light is well out to sea and some 2 miles nearer a vessel approaching from the west than the aforementioned white light that flashes at four-second intervals.

There has been considerable shoaling in the last few years, and the chart at the time of writing showed depths of 6 or 7 feet, even 4-foot spots, in the angle between the breakwaters, where 15 to 19 feet were shown in 1948.

Patchogue River, Westbrook, Conn. (12374 216). Here is another developed man-made channel and harbor, the most convenient alternative to Duck Island Roads. For those who prefer to anchor in the Roads for the night it is a nearby place for gassing up or obtaining supplies. The 75-foot channel, beginning just south of can 3, was dredged in 1976 to 8 feet at MLW all the way up to the Route 1 highway bridge, the head of navigation. However, in 1977 two shoal spots began to appear. The first is at uncharted can 5 marking the entrance to the Menunketsesuck River. In entering this river, favor can 5 closely and then hug the starboard shore proceeding upriver. The second localized trouble spot is in the Patchogue River channel just beyond nun 6, where we sounded 3 feet at MLW at the time of writing. So stick to the "straight and narrow path" while observing the "Leave No Wake" signs.

The Pilots Point Marina South is on the main channel just beyond nun 6. The first two of the three east basins shown on the chart have been dredged to 8 feet, and substantial bulkheads have been erected. The overnight minimum charge is $5.50, a reasonable price for the services provided. These include gas, Diesel fuel, water, ice, electricity, showers, and a ship's store, with charts available. A 50-ton Travelift, a nearby market, and a full-time mechanic and canvas-maker complete the facilities. We can promise you a secure berth for a week or perhaps more here, in case your cruise plans include some layover time.

To the east and up on the starboard shore of the Menunketesuck River can be found Pilots Point Marina North, with similar facilities in pleasant surroundings and restaurants nearby. Its only drawback is that although its river approach carries about 5 feet, there tends to be bad shoaling at its entrance off the Patchogue River channel, as mentioned earlier. Proceed cautiously through this very narrow entrance, favoring the docks in making your approach. Finding good restaurants, easily accessible, even a miniature golf course, may come as a welcome surprise. Frankies Restaurant and Dick's Clam Barn both set a good table and are within easy walking distance. The Hungry Lion is a bit more plush and expensive. And upstairs in the marina's building, you'll find the home of the convivial Menunketesuck Yacht Club, founded in 1968.

Far up the Patchogue River you'll first come upon Rackliffe Marina on the port shore, lined with small sailing craft belonging to the local residents. Just below the bridge are gas dock and slips belonging to Lawson's Marina, where there's an excellent lobster pound and a market for supplies ½ mile away. But this area is congested and not nearly as attractive as downstream.

Connecticut River, Conn. (12375 215, 12377 266 & 267).

Entrance: Saybrook (12375 215). Yachtsmen with a love for exploring rivers and creeks and poking their way into fascinating byways should not miss the Connecticut River. Some of its byways between Essex and Middletown have a beauty and charm reminiscent of the Upper Hudson or the coast of Maine. While long a mecca for motorboats, the depths of some of its coves and creeks and the speed with which the drawbridges are opened make the Connecticut attractive for sailing craft also. It is not recommended, however, for boats without power, except for purposes of refuge near the entrance and with favoring tides. The Connecticut state boating law restricts speed limits to 6 mph within 100 feet of anchored boats, docks, or marinas.

We might advise those who are planning a cruise up the Quinnehtqut, the Indian term for "long tidal water," that the Connecticut River Watershed Council has updated its eighty-six-page river-guide booklet. It covers the entire 410-mile stretch of the river from Canada to Long Island Sound. Useful information on boating, fishing, and camping is provided, with particular emphasis on canoeing. In addition to the booklet, the guide "package" includes maps of the three major sections of the river. All of this may be obtained for $4.50 by writing to the Connecticut River Watershed Council, Inc., 125 Combs Rd., Easthampton, Mass. 01027.

Charles A. Goodwin, in his very interesting *Connecticut River Pilot* (1944), explains that, while Adrian Block discovered the river, it was King Charles and his bishops who forced the first settlement at Saybrook. Lord Say and Lord Brook got together with Pym and decided to resist the King and to prepare in the wilderness a place of refuge for the conspirators, in case their plans miscarried.

In 1797, Timothy Dwight, president of Yale College, looked upon the land bordering the Connecticut River and wrote this description: "In its extent, it is magnificent. In its form, it is beautiful. Its banks possess uncommon elegance, almost universally handsome, with a margin entirely neat and commonly ornamented with a fine fringe of shrubs and trees." At the same time, he reported the river's water to be "remarkably pure and light . . . everywhere pure, potable, perfectly salubrious," —quite the reverse to what it is today.

Rising in the extreme northern part of New Hampshire, 375 miles from the entrance, the Connecticut River is one of the most important rivers in New England. Hartford, 45 miles upriver, is the head of navigation for all but very shoal draft boats, except in times of high water, though the most beautiful part of the river is below Middletown. At Deep Water, 10½ miles from the sound, and above, the water is fresh. High water occurs at Hartford four and three-quarter hours after it does at the entrance at Saybrook, and low water six and one-quarter hours later. Some of the principal towns or entrances to the best anchorages are at the following distances from the Saybrook Breakwater Light:

	Nautical Miles
Saybrook Point	1.4
Essex	6.0

Hamburg Cove entrance	7.5
Selden Creek entrance	9.0
Salmon River entrance	15.0
Middletown	28.0
Wethersfield	42.0
Hartford	45.2

With 4 or 5 knots of power, there is no difficulty in entering for shelter or to explore. Any smart sailing boat can negotiate the river without power with favorable winds. Tidal current is a factor as far as Middletown, and the combination of river current and ebb tide can be strong, occasionally 3.5 knots. The mean rise and fall of tides in the Connecticut varies from 3½ feet at Saybrook to 1¾ feet at Hartford.

The entrance is clearly marked by Saybrook Light and a pair of stone jetties. The entire river is well marked by buoys, but reference to charts is essential, as the buoys are not always self-explanatory.

In entering between the jetties, watch for the sweep of the current across the entrance and note the shoals inside the jetties, particularly the one to starboard.

There has been a striking extension in the ports, marinas, and facilities along the Connecticut River in the last few years. It is now possible to find overnight dockage or anchorage to suit almost any taste or purse, from the clublike atmosphere of Terra Mar to the privacy of Selden Creek or Salmon Cove, from the active sailing community at Essex to the motorboat haven in landlocked Wethersfield Cove. In discussing the many ports and tie-ups along the river, we shall "cruise" northward from Long Island Sound. We should remind those proceeding upriver to give three toots of the horn on approaching the railroad bridge.

While we have made every effort to spot the principal docks and marinas offering tie-ups or other facilities along the way, we won't guarantee that we have mentioned them all. In fact, we are sure that by the time you get there after reading this book, there will be some unmentioned new ones. But we think we have suggested enough possibilities to take care of any requirements. Where prices are given it is at the time of writing and they are, of course, subject to change.

One final note: Due to the wake from heavy traffic along the lower Connecticut River, it is hazardous for masted vessels to lie alongside some of the higher wharves—such a tie-up can roll your boat's spars right up against the pilings with unfortunate results.

1. Hull Harbor One, Saybrook Point (west shore—12375 215). Located right below conspicuous Terra Mar, this marina is most convenient for those yachtsmen cruising Long Island Sound who wish to find an accessible haven closest to the Connecticut River entrance. There is 8 feet of water at the 84 slips, where gas, Diesel fuel, water, electricity, ice, showers, a laundromat, crank-case service (in fifteen minutes), an emergency pump, and a reputable mechanic are all available.

The grounds are spacious and manicured with the swimming pool a popular attraction. Paul Barton, the experienced owner, encouraged us to welcome all cruising craft, large or small, power or sail—no reservations necessary. Shelter from all winds, except perhaps strong easterlies coming across the river, is provided by a breakwater on the south side and outlying bulkheads.

Look up Charlie Miller for the best in engine service and repairs.

*2. Saybrook Point Marina, Saybrook Point (west shore—12375 215). In the past few years, this marina has come upon hard times. It has undergone several changes of ownership and has even been closed from time to time. Once billed as among the plushest of marinas on Long Island Sound, its buildings and docks fell into disrepair. But, in 1977, Terra Mar began to "turn the corner." It was purchased by a three-man corporation, Ramarret Enterprises, Inc., of Jericho, N.Y., for $640,000; new docks were built and the motel, restaurant, and coffee shop renovated. All this should do much toward helping the facility overcome its tarnished image. In 1981, Terra Mar became Saybrook Point Marina.

Although 7 feet of water is reported at the slips, most deep-draft keel auxiliaries prefer to tie up at the outer dock. This is primarily a motorboat haven, and almost every yacht we have seen there belongs to that class. However, it is convenient to any cruising boat whose crew wishes to gas up or stop for a meal. There is free, short-term docking for all restaurant customers.

Bob Leavitt, the dock master, pointed out to us the usual marina services, including showers and a laundromat. We learned that they were making plans to hold live entertainment nightly, barbecue festivals, and to establish a new recreation center for the family. But the marina does not undertake repairs and mechanical service; that is left to the boat yards further upriver.

North Cove and its channel, lying just northward, were first dredged in 1965 to provide a new harbor of refuge for cruising yachtsmen. But

---

*The new owners of Saybrook Point Marina have decided to concentrate on building up the marina part of the business.

the 100-foot channel tends to silt up. The greatest amount of shoaling occurs between can 15 at the entrance and can 1, located 400 yards to the west and on the southern edge of the channel. Steer dead center as you run westward from can 15 through the middle of the narrow mouth of the cove between nun 2 and can 3. Be sure to compensate for the river's strong current abeam so as to avoid being swept up on the channel's shallow edges. Although the chart may show a 4-foot depth in the channel and in the cove itself, new dredging has taken place and a 1977 survey reported a depth of 8 feet MLW throughout the channel. The eastern one-third section of the cove offers 11 feet at low water; soundings in the remaining two-thirds to the west reveal 6 feet at low water. Nevertheless, the stakes marking the rectangular dredged area must be observed carefully, as the remainder of this popular basin, especially along the northern and southwestern edges, is only a foot or so deep at low water. As you approach the basin's western end, you will spot two markers—between these lies a rock to be avoided. But most of the bottom here is ooze, not good holding ground for a light anchor, yet the good shelter provided by the cove reduces your chances of dragging. We were warned by local residents to protect ourselves against the mosquitoes, which breed rather abundantly in the neighboring marshes.

The North Cove Yacht Club, founded in 1968, owns an attractive clubhouse, built in 1975, standing on the western shore of the cove. This is a friendly, active place boasting a fleet of 82 boats and offering reciprocal privileges to members of other recognized yacht clubs. The clubhouse, which offers showers, is open Wednesdays, Fridays, and on weekends. Although there are just two assigned guest moorings, the club steward may assign you one vacated by a boat that is off cruising. At the dedication of the clubhouse, the Fleet Chaplain expressed this thoughtful wish: "May our burgee become a standard and hallmark for kindness and charity, for friendship and hospitality, for trust and thoughtfulness, and above all for good seamanship."

The town is a ¼-mile walk up the road from the club. There you'll find sources for supplies and the Village Restaurant, serving good food at reasonable prices. North Cove is a fine protected spot where one can "get away from it all."

3. Chimney Point Marina, Old Saybrook (west shore—12375 215). This new marina lies in a dredged basin at the western end of a narrow charted creek whose entrance is just beyond the bascule railroad bridge near the location of the old ferry slip. It is named after the prominent stack of the nearby Saybrook Marine. Proceed up the middle of the creek, which has been dredged to 4 feet, MLW. The deep-water basin, nestled midst marshland, offers excellent security and practically no current. The marina's staff, including a mechanic, is on duty 7 days a week. Here you'll find gas, Diesel fuel, marine supplies, slips with electricity, water, ice, and showers. We were assured by the management that the depths both in the creek and the mooring basin will be maintained. This is an interesting haven.

4. Saybrook Marine Limited, Old Saybrook (west shore—12375 215). Just above Chimney Point and the railroad bridge, this long-established marina caters especially to sailboats and has the dealership for Santana Yachts and Westerbeke marine engines. It is run by the personable Mr. David Green, who has gained a good reputation for fast repair work. Most of the boats stored here for the winter are sailing craft, and they come in all sizes. There is 8 feet at the dock at mean low water; gas, Diesel fuel, water, ice, electric connections, and showers are available, and usually a slip or dock space for transients. A 30-ton Travelift and a 2-ton derrick can handle almost any hauling job.

*5. Black Swan Marina, Old Saybrook (west shore—12375 215). Just beyond Saybrook and before reaching the fixed highway bridge, you will come upon one of the newer full-service marinas on the river. One glance at this manicured facility, with its concrete piers and modern-styled wooden buildings of many angular shapes, levels, and sizes, and you may understand why Black Swan is promoted as the stopping place for "discriminating yachtsmen." The inner basin, which has been dredged to 6 feet at low water, offers complete protection, while the outer slips provide as much as a 13-foot depth. Report to the Texaco gas dock to receive their information brochure and to be assigned a slip. While the overnight rates are not modest, they do include water and electricity at each slip as well as swimming pool privileges. Much is also to be said for the many conveniences at hand. The facilities on the premises run the gamut from restaurant to gift shops, from a clothing store to a "spirit shop," from showers to washers and dryers. At the time of writing, even a nightclub is being planned. Boats can be given emergency repairs and there is haul-out capability.

6. Oak Leaf Marina, Old Saybrook (west shore—12375 215). This is just beyond the fixed bridge. Here we have seen boats of all types, since, for

---

*Black Swan Marina unfortunately closed operations in 1980.

total services, this is one of the best stopping places before one reaches Essex. At their dock, with a 7-foot depth, MLW, gas is sold and there are guest moorings and slips. Other services include a ship's store, showers, ice, and a snack bar—all available 7 days a week. Hauling and repair work is also undertaken.

7. Ferry Point Marina, Old Saybrook (west shore—12375 215). Unless you happen to be a native of the Connecticut or an avid reader of such cruising guides as this one, you might pass right by this charming marina tucked away in a secluded basin on the southwestern shore of Ferry Point. The narrow dredged channel, with 10 feet at MLW, runs south from a point just beyond some old stone piers located along the point's northern shore. On entering this channel you will pass between some piles and note a sunken barge that marks its starboard edge. Gas, Diesel fuel, water, showers, ice, a 25-ton Travelift, and a ship's store are here, plus electricity at the slips, where 6 feet of water is reported at MLW. There is a flat fee of $8.00 for an overnight stay. Food supplies are located about 3 miles away in Old Saybrook. Try the Howard Johnson's just a stone's throw away should you be short of rations.

All is calm here. The loudest noise we heard came from the voices of the sports fishermen who were proudly comparing their day's catch.

8. Old Lyme Marina, Old Lyme (east shore—12375 215). Sheltered behind Calves Island and in attractive surroundings, this is one of the best ports on the river. Follow the channel behind Calves Island to a first-rate dock on the east shore of the channel, about halfway up to the point, where the channel turns to the northwest. Nun RB is left well to port. We liked this marina's owner, Len Abrahamsson, who told us that there's a good 25-feet depth at dockside. Overnight dockage at the time of writing runs 30¢ per foot, with a $6.00 minimum; the rate for a mooring is $5.00. Gas, Diesel fuel, ice, water, electricity, showers, all types of professional repair work, and even taxi service are among the facilities here. The marine store is attractively furnished and the whole place is kept "Bristol fashion," reflecting Abrahamsson's concern to offer the best in service. A shopping center with a good restaurant, a drug store, an A&P store, a bank, etc., are only five minutes away.

When Old Lyme decided it needed a police boat for patrol and rescue, but the budget said "no," a group of concerned neighbors in the community, headed up by W.E.S. Griswold, Jr., and Len Abrahamsson, gave enthusiastic financial support to the project. Now when you happen to spot Resident State Trooper Michael Rutledge patrolling the river in the powerboat, *Friendship,* you'll be witness to a shining example of the spirit of Old Lyme.

For years we have read and heard about the glories of Lord Cove as a gunk hole, beautifully sheltered beneath the steeps of Lord Hill to the north. Morten Lund records in his book, *Eastward on Five Sounds,* that he reached Lord Creek way across the unmarked cove without mishap using power and depth-sounder in a catamaran drawing 2½ feet. But we have been advised by Old Lyme natives that in a boat of any greater draft, it is unwise to venture beyond the cove's entrance between Goose Island and Quarry Hill. Use bow and stern anchors if you wish to lie to here.

9. Essex (west shore—12375 215). Six miles above the entrance to the Connecticut River, this ancient town clambers up several hills above the valley and looks down on its three coves and one of the most active yachting scenes to be found on Long Island Sound. Few harbors are as popular as Essex among real cruising men, and few have as much to offer.

Shallow-draft power boats approaching Essex from the south may find secluded shelter but no more the services and dock of the former Connecticut Yacht Service. This was found near the western end of a narrow staked channel, dredged to 4 feet at MLW and running along the northern shore of Thatchbed Island into Middle Cove.

Sailing yachts, on the other hand, often stop at the deep-water dock of the Essex Paint and Marine Co., just north of the Essex Yacht Club, where they can pick up gas, Diesel fuel, ice, water, and marine supplies. It is too congested offshore here for an easy and comfortable anchorage.

The Essex Yacht Club, founded in 1933, with adjoining dinghy dock and clubhouse, provides launch service from 8 A.M. to 9 P.M. and has overnight moorings to be rented from Essex Paint and Marine. We heard that it is "undoubtedly the first if not the only yacht club which was founded through the inspiration of frostbite dinghy sailing." The Cruising Club of America has a station at this club, with many yachts moored there belonging to members of that famous organization of cruising men. On the other side of the E.P. and M. Co. is the fenced-in Dauntless Yacht Club, with a limited and exclusive membership, said to be better known for its social activities than for its yachting. The Pettipaug Yacht Club is now stationed upriver on the western shore facing Brockway Island. It is active in small-boat racing.

The cupola identified on the chart to the north marks the location of historic Steamboat Dock, recently restored by the Connecticut River

Foundation. Few of us are aware of the role this property played in the history of the Connecticut River. During the eighteenth century more than 500 large commercial ships were built in this general location and the present dock, built in the mid-nineteenth century, was a scheduled port of call for New York-to-Hartford passenger steamers. Now, through private donations and foundation membership, Steamboat Dock has become an impressive cultural center, including a museum, a library, a meeting place, and Wolcott Park, named in memory of Frank Wolcott, an avid yachtsman and conservationist. Alongside this property lies the Town Dock, permitting boats up to 40 feet to tie up for several hours if there is space.

Northward, across the narrow channel leading to North Cove, is the attractive Colonial-style complex of the Essex Island Marina, where, according to its slogan and our experience, "it's fun in the sun and cool in the pool." For transient boats of any size, this spot is "tops" in our book. Its management appears to have anticipated practically every visitor's need and whim—for his boat and for his crew. The brochure they'll hand you proves it. This is such a popular spot that placing reservations is suggested in advance by phoning (203) 767-1267. Ask for Wally.

This marina is actually set on the southern tip of an island, so a ferry constantly runs guests across the 150-foot channel to the mainland. Numerous protective basins and floating docks frame the large administration building, swimming pool, repair shops, and "The Galley Locker." The daily charge (up to noon) for dockage runs $20.00 for boats up to 25 feet, $22.50 up to 35 feet, $25.50 from 36 to 40 feet, and $29.00 from 41 to 45 feet. Prices include use of all facilities. They offer towing service and can "quick-haul" a boat as fast as any yard we've seen.

The Essex Boat Works, headed up by Stuart Ingersoll, performs the repair work coming out of the Essex Island Marina. It is identified by a large red boat shed to port, just inside the entrance channel to North Cove. Mr. Ingersoll, who was of great help in updating this section on Essex, says "we will do our best to accommodate you." With 35 men on duty, they provide 7-day-a-week service, are especially equipped to handle emergency repairs and, although there are no slips here, a number of overnight moorings are rentable. This yard's workboat, named *Flora,* a fire boat built in 1906, might look a bit old-fashioned, but the services here, including Diesel engine repairs, are strictly up to date. They have an amazing facility for locating all types of hull fittings and engine parts quickly; they even fly to get them. Perhaps it's only natural that the Essex Harbor Master, James Francis, may be found officiating at the works.

Rather strong currents running through North Cove channel often may give the helmsman a case of the jitters. One skipper, caught in a crosscurrent here, to the amusement of several bystanders, was heard to bellow, "I know all about the current, but I don't know what in hell to do about it!" Assuming, however, you handle this current like a Josh Slocum, you'll come up to the docks of the Dauntless Shipyard Marina, which runs a yacht brokerage under the name of Lion Yachts and really accommodates their own customers. It is reported that they may be moving in the direction of a full-service marina. What is impressive about Dauntless is its complex of facilities, all easy to reach. These include Connecticut Marine Instruments for electronics; the Essex Yacht Riggers and Clark Sails for sail repair and manufacture; Yachting World of Essex, presenting an outstanding ship's chandlery; the publishers of *Soundings* magazine; and an attractive restaurant named The Gull, serving a tasteful menu at quite expensive prices.

It is reported that there are normally eight hours of ebb current at Essex and four hours of flood. Essex is a secure and most attractive anchorage though it can also be a bit uneasy on occasions when the wind blows strongly from the north or southeast, unless you are tied up at one of the boat yards. A preferred anchorage, if one must moor in the river, is in the apex of the charted anchorage area northeast of white nun D. We cannot close our report on Essex without mentioning the competence of Essex Machine Works in handling accident work, such as straightening prop shafts and reconditioning propellers.

The town of Essex is well worth a visit. "On Main Street, the interesting Griswold Inn, built in 1776, well preserves the flavor of an earlier day. Visitors are provided with the 'Rules of the Tavern,' which stipulate that bed and supper may be obtained for six pence, that no more than five may sleep in one bed, that boots may not be worn in bed, and organ-grinders must sleep in the washhouse, while razor-grinders and tinkers are not taken in at all."* We can recommend the drinks, food, and pictures at this fascinating inn, which is only a short walk from the waterfront.

If you are looking for a less expensive meal than that served at The Gull or Griswold Inn, we can recommend Tumbledowns over on Main

*From *Where To Retire and How,* by Fessenden S. Blanchard (Dodd, Mead & Co.).

Hamburg Cove, landlocked harbor on the Connecticut River. The turning basin at the village of Hamburg is shown at upper left.

Street or the nearby Lighthouse Delicatessen, which is a fast-food establishment.

There are many fine old houses along the shaded streets of Essex, and another inn, the Osage, is even older than the Griswold, though less accessible to yachtsmen. Larders can be stocked in town, about three blocks from the waterfront.

At Essex, in 1775, Uriah Hayden constructed the *Oliver Cromwell,* the first warship of the Continental Navy. A year later he built The Old Ship Tavern, a structure still in use as the headquarters of the Dauntless Yacht Club. On April 8, 1814, British marines landed near where the Steamboat Dock now stands and burned twenty-eight local ships.

10. Hamburg Cove (east shore—12375 215). Half a mile above Essex, opposite Brockway's Island, is the entrance to Hamburg Cove, which is practically a fjord, 1½-miles long. The entrance channel is well marked with government buoys, and there is a depth of at least 6 feet, but the channel is narrow and buoys should be hugged, especially the red nun at the mouth. It is also reported that these entrance buoys tend to shift from time to time, so enter the cove cautiously. Here you'll find a sheltered, idyllic anchorage but with poor holding ground and depths averaging 12 feet except at the edges. Absolute quiet reigns, with only sky, glassy water, trees, and a few houses to be seen. Few who enter for the first time realize that a tiny channel, winding to the northeast, leads to a small, picturesque basin off the village of Hamburg. This channel is marked by stakes with pointers put out during the season by the Hamburg Yacht Club, located on the eastern shore of the basin, with 3 feet at its docks.

Reynolds' Garage & Marine's docks can also be found just to the north. Gary Reynolds told us that, although there is 2 to 3 feet of tide, he would not want to navigate a boat up to Hamburg that draws more than 4 feet. Gary's father also mentioned that the cove's water is cleaner now than it was fifty years ago when he was here as a young lad. Supplies are available at the Cove Landing Store. Several good inns are at Old Lyme, about 5 miles away. The nearest railroad station is at Saybrook, about 8 miles away. If you have a chance, visit the state park 8 miles from the wharf. It is known as the Devil's Hop Yard.

The Lower Cove is the place to anchor for the night, in one of the most attractive anchorages anywhere. The many ball-shaped moorings here are privately owned, but perhaps a vacant one can be picked up if your conscience doesn't bother you. Shut in by wooded hills, the place can be hot, but, except in very warm weather, it is a delightful and beautiful spot.

11. Selden (or Shirley) Creek (east shore—12375 215, 12377 266). The entrance to Selden Creek is not impressive and does not reveal the attractiveness you discover farther up. You will find the opening on the east shore after passing the stone-walled Brockway's Landing. The entrance is in a flat, marshy area, flanked by the stumps of uprooted trees, and just upriver from a high rock cliff with two houses at its foot. Soundings by one of the authors in the spring of 1977 revealed at least 10 feet at low water in the center of the entrance, on a line running down the middle of the creek. A shoal makes out from the northern point and a smaller shoal from the south bank. There is plenty of deep water between these shoals, but it is advisable to proceed up the creek on a rising tide.

After you get inside, keep in the middle. The creek is only 50 feet wide in spots and continues for about 2 miles, with from 4 to 13 feet of water up to Selden Cove's entrance. The best anchorage for deep-draft vessels is under the first or second rock cliff almost a mile up the creek along the starboard shore. Carry a bowline to the shore and set out a stern anchor to prevent swinging across the channel here. Further up, just below the cove, you will come to two forks in the channel. Stay out of the left or western fork since it leads to a dead end and has little water in it. The right fork, giving passage to the cove, carries about 3 feet at high water, but watch out for some boulders as you enter. If you are crafty enough to get into the cove with a shallow-draft boat, don't anchor there for long or you'll get hung up. On one visit on an ebbing tide, we were surprised to see a 30-foot auxiliary sloop on her beam's end in the middle of the cove. We hailed its crew, offering assistance, to which the skipper replied nonchalantly, "We're just sitting here waiting for that old tide to shift."

The current in the creek is not strong, but anchorage fore and aft is usually necessary. The upper passage directly from the cove to the river is reported to have been nearly filled in by a hurricane.

During the Revolution, river shipping used to hide in Selden Creek to escape British raiding parties.

Further upriver, along the east shore, facing Eustasia Island, you can spot the deep water, floating docks of the Deep River Marina, which probably attracts more sailing craft than any other facility north of Essex. There are reasons. Although Diesel fuel and provisions are not available, Deep River does have gas, ice, water, electricity, outdoor grills, a marine store, inexpensive overnight rates, and repair service; and housed within its large brown office building are some of the most splendid rest rooms and showers to be seen at any marina. There's also something special here not easily found elsewhere—spacious manicured grounds, offering complete protection and solitude. Phone Doug Van Dyke at (203) 526-5560 for reservations.

About a mile north of Selden Cove is the Rhenish castle built by the actor William Gillette, who won fame for his portrayal of Sherlock Holmes. When he died in 1937, his will specified that he hoped the executors would see that the property did not get into "the possession of some blithering saphead who has no conception of where he is or with what surrounded." He need not have had any fear, for his estate is now the beautiful Gillette Castle State Park, commanding a superb view of the Connecticut River. If you want some exercise while moored in the creek, row across the cove and walk to the park, which is open from 11 A.M. to 5 P.M. every day but Monday from late May to October.

One can gain closer access to the castle by dinghy, having anchored off a small landing just above the Hadlyme ferry dock on the east shore, as shown on the chart. From here, it's a steep climb straight up the hill to meet the road leading to the castle grounds, about 400 yards to the north.

12. Connecticut River Marina, Chester (west shore—12377 266). Across river from Selden Creek's northern exit lies the mouth of Chester Creek, showing little water according to the chart. But just to the south of the creek's mouth, Bob Garthwaite has one of the larger boating facilities on the Connecticut River, with 5 feet of water at the slips. The entrance to his basin was dredged in 1977 to 5 feet at MLW. Most of your boat's needs will be filled here. This marina is also one of the few spots this far north that furnishes some food supplies with a restaurant. It has twenty-four-hour service, including towing service, should you experience engine failure (phone 526-9076). It is wise to approach this basin by heading westward from a point in the main channel that is well north of black can 37.

Just to the north of the basin a privately maintained buoy marks the entrance to sheltered Chester Creek, along which run the congested slips of Parker's Boatyard. We were advised by the people here that they are not set up to serve transient yachts.

13. Whalebone Creek (east shore—12377 266). Just above Selden Creek's northern exit, this creek is a fascinating detour for boats drawing under 2½ feet, or for dinghies or canoes. Hug the northern shore on entering to find the deepest water.

Across from Whalebone Creek to the southwest, a basin, shaped like the end of a golf club, appears on the chart a short distance north of Fort Hill. In reality, this basin, which is the home of Chrisholm Marina, is much larger than the chart has depicted. Depths here have been recorded at 5 feet MLW. Named after its congenial founder, a remarkable octogenarian, Andrew Christianson, Chrisholm is a rather new, delightful, and protected stopping place. Its services appear adequate; its snack bar is an added convenience. We received a warm reception here.

14. Middletown Yacht Club (west shore—12377 266). On the west bank opposite the lower end of Lord Island, the Middletown Yacht Club has its well-groomed headquarters. A dredged basin with bulkheads on three sides and rows of slips provides an efficient-looking modern layout. Gas is available at a float and a clubhouse on high ground overlooks the river. Yachts not in the slips are usually moored across the river near Lord Island, off the channel, with launch service furnished. The large swimming pool is a center of activity. Members of recognized yacht clubs would do well to stop at this fine, friendly club to see if a mooring is available or a slip for an overnight charge of $10.00.

15. Goodspeed's Landing, East Haddam (east shore—12377 266). A stopover here promises a rewarding experience for anyone interested in American theatrical history or who enjoys fine continental cuisine.

If there's space, you can tie up at the Opera House dock just below the bridge to starboard. A short walk will take you to the center of the charming old town, where all types of supplies may be purchased. Just north of the bridge on the west shore lies a marked channel leading to a small marina. Don't attempt entering unless your boat draws under four feet.

In 1877, William Goodspeed, a shipbuilder, created the Goodspeed Opera House. It became a rousing success, but by the late 1950s it was forsaken and ready for demolition. This triggered widespread interest in Goodspeed's value to history, and the Goodspeed Opera House Foundation was formed to refurbish it. It now has an active season from mid-June to mid-September, offering the finest in Broadway drama and musicals. In 1965, it housed the first production of *Man of La Mancha.* Performances begin at 8:30 P.M., with matinees on Wednesdays at 2:30 P.M. and on Saturdays at 5 P.M., from June to September.

The Gelston House, next door, is a charming Victorian establishment where one may enjoy a view of the river's rustic landscape and some unusual culinary delights.

The New England Steamboat Lines runs its Yankee Clipper Cruises out of Haddam. A 500-passenger excursion boat leaves daily on the

Greenport Cruise on Wednesdays through Saturdays. The cruise to Sag
Harbor departs also at 9 A.M. every Sunday, Monday, and Tuesday.
These boats are due back at Haddam at 6 P.M.

16. Salmon River (east shore—12377 266). Just above East Haddam is
the entrance to Salmon River, where a good anchorage in deep water
is to be found in the narrow part of the channel. But feel your way in
carefully as the entrance is subject to shoaling and, as is frequently the
case with tributaries leading into larger rivers, the upriver point has a
fairly long shoal, to port as you go in. A good anchorage is just opposite
the first tiny creek you will meet to starboard. The latest *Coast Pilot*
reports that Salmon Cove "is navigable for vessels of less than 6-foot
draft as far as Scovill Landing, about 1½ miles above the entrance, and
for small craft of less than 3-foot draft about 1 mile farther. Considerable grass in the channel and cover makes boat operation difficult. The
entrance to the cove is subject to shoaling." Based on our recent ardu-
ous voyage upriver, we can subscribe only to the *Pilot's* last sentence.
Depths recorded on the present chart are badly outdated. Beyond the
aforementioned creek, the unmarked channel begins to shoal along
much of its western edge to muddy, grassy depths of 2 to 3 feet, with
not much more water to starboard. We advise not to proceed farther.
The land is marshy along the shores, but to the east the heights rise to
300 feet or more.

For those of you readers who are ardent gunk-holers we offer this
fascinating tip, revealing how the Salmon River passage was safely
negotiated over twenty-five years ago. The writer was Ham deFontaine,
his boat a 33-foot sloop named *Direction,* with a draft of 6'6", and a crew
member named Fess Blanchard, the late coauthor of this guide.

You had better plan your first arrival at close to low water so you may
see from the mud banks just where the channel lies. Deep water is
obvious as far as the 15-foot sounding at the island, labeled "Grass"
on the chart. Anchor temporarily here. Then with your dinghy stake
out the channel as much further as you care to go. You can easily
carry 6'6" beyond the high tension wires to where the 8-foot sounding on the chart marks the termination of the deep channel. You can
carry 3 feet of water with care on up to where the channel deepens
again with 11-, 7-, 17-, 9- and 7-foot soundings on the chart.

You may swing to an anchor up here beneath towering pines but
lower down you must moor bow and stern. Our favorite spot for
Direction was between the 9- and 7-foot soundings just below the high
tension wires. Here you may enjoy the privacy and illusion of a lake

in Northern Maine practically within commuting distance of New York City.

The loveliest part of the Connecticut River is between Salmon River and Middletown, especially the passage through the Straits just below Middletown.

17. Portland (east [north] shore—12377 267). The Portland Boat Works is a high-class yard catering to inboards. Gas, water, electricity, ice, hauling, engine repairs, and a ship's store are all here, as well as possible overnight dockage in 8-foot depths. Supplies can be obtained within walking distance. Just above on the same shore is Riverside Marina and Yankee Boat Yard, with more modest facilities but with moorings available. We liked the rustic, traditional charm of Yankee, run by the three Meehls brothers who have an obviously loyal following among the local sailing crowd.

Middletown, across the river, is the principal shopping center of Middlesex County and the home of Wesleyan University. It was once an important shipping port for the West Indies. Its name resulted from the fact that the city is about halfway between Saybrook and Hartford.

The river between Middletown and Hartford is less settled and also less beautiful than it is below, but it is nevertheless pleasant and less crowded. Except in Wethersfield Cove, the only good anchorages are in the river itself—within the charted special anchorage areas for small craft along the northern and eastern shores between Bodkin Rock and Portland.

18. Rocky Hill (west shore—12377 267). Just below the ferry landing is a small dock with gas called Hales Landing. There is a nice anchorage in pretty surroundings across the river on the bend above the east side ferry landing. At Hales Landing runs our nation's oldest continuing operating ferry service. Its first trip across river between Rocky Hill and Glastonbury took place in 1655.

19. South Wethersfield (west shore—12377 267). The latest chart will show you that a gunk hole has been formed through the western shore of the river about 2 miles south of Wethersfield Cove. It is such a concealed place that it hasn't been given a proper name, so natives call it simply "No Name Cove."

This rectangular basin, 1000 yards long and almost as wide, was dredged out in recent years to provide fill for the construction of nearby Highway 91. Its narrow entrance is difficult to spot but lies on the west shore at the foot of Crow Point, a mile beyond nun 126. Hug the port shore very closely and carefully on entering; only 3 feet at best at low water can be carried through a constantly shoaling bottom. Inside there is good water throughout, with a bottom composed of soft ooze, and plenty of room for water skiing. You'll probably find yourself alone with no marinas to mar the natural beauty of the still water surrounded by tiny beaches, lush trees, and bushes. The cove is incomparable. Although there is no one around to tell us, it may closely resemble the Wethersfield Cove of a century or more ago.

20. Wethersfield Cove (12377 267). This is a rather unusual, completely landlocked cove with a very narrow entrance of 60 feet subject to considerable shoaling. The shallowest point is at the entrance of the channel between the black-and-red government-maintained and charted buoys. In 1977, most of the centerline of the entire channel recorded a depth of 6 feet at MLW, and this same depth may be carried throughout most of the basin's southern portion. The tidal change is about 1½ feet, so most motor cruisers have no trouble in getting in. Keep in the middle of the entrance channel and then follow the buoys to the Wethersfield Yacht Club dock on the southwest shore. Regardless of an apparent shoal spot on the channel side of the last black buoy, follow close to these markers and you will be all right—at least, that is what we were told by a local authority, Gene Holmes, steward at the yacht club.

The club has gas, water, is accessible to stores nearby, and is most hospitable to members of other yacht clubs. If there is a spare mooring, the club will make it available. The Harbor Master at the Cove Park Anchorage on the southeastern shore may also be able to provide a mooring. The bottom is soft clay, so set your anchor well in a blow.

An excellent launching ramp is located on Cove Park's shore, and inland there are picnic tables and telephones. The old stone-and-wood building is a warehouse where traders stored their loads of fish and furs during the times of the Revolution.

Two events have taken place that have stripped this cove of much of its former appeal. Extreme water pollution, an increasing problem along the Connecticut, prohibits any swimming here. And the fixed highway bridge, arching over the channel, allows only a 38-foot vertical clearance to prevent most sailing craft over 27 feet from entering.

Cruising yachts able to get in would do well to make Wethersfield Cove the end of their upriver navigation. There are no good yacht facilities in Hartford, and above Hartford the river is usually too shoal for cruiser navigation except possibly by expert pilots with local knowledge.

"The Connecticut River above Hartford," says the *Coast Pilot*, "is practically unimproved, but is navigable about 30 miles to Holyoke for boats not exceeding 3-foot draft, when the river is not low. The channel is constantly shifting. For a distance of about 10 miles above Hartford to Enfield Rapids, bars with 2½ feet at low water and many other obstructions are encountered."

Niantic River, Conn. (13211 214). Before you approach this river, note that a special anchorage area off the Niantic Bay Yacht Club on the western side of Niantic Bay has been assigned by the Coast Guard and appears on the latest charts. The club has guest moorings with launch service, but its anchorage is also wide open to winds from the east and southeast. Its basin at Crescent Beach, however, is protected on the south and east by a breakwater. Another possible anchorage selected by the Bayreuther brothers is just northeast of Wigwam Rock off McCook Point, affording good protection from northerlies and westerlies.

To go up the Niantic River, boats formerly had to cope with tidal currents of 2 knots or more, but with channel dredging in 1970 to a low water depth of 6 feet all the way north to Sandy Point, the flow is now less swift, and entry through the two narrow bridges at the entrance is not such a great challenge. However, it is still advisable to make this passage at slack water or against the current. There is a 2½-foot tide range here.

Although the first bridge may be open, unless a train is approaching, the second (swing) bridge is always closed and often slow to open. The first bridge opens on signal of one long blast and two short blasts of horn or whistle; the second, on sounding one long followed by one short blast. Acknowledgment from both bridges is the same as your own signal for them to open. When either draw cannot open or is open and must close at once, the bridge tenders will sound four blasts. In this event, back off and wait, while staying within the turning basins, which have been dredged on both sides of the bridge and marked with poles on which reflectors have been placed. Between the two bridges you may come to lie along the bulkheading there. Note, also, that from 7 A.M. to 8 A.M. and from 4 P.M. to 5 P.M., Monday through Friday, except holidays, these draws need not open for vessels.

It is heartening to learn, at the time of writing, that Amtrak and the state are planning to eliminate these hazards. Construction of a new railroad bridge is scheduled to begin in 1979, for completion by early

1981. Amtrak claims the new bridge will open more quickly, stay open longer, and increase the present clearance beneath the bridge from 45 to 100 feet. The present drawbridge is to be replaced with either a vertical lift bridge or another drawbridge. As soon as this improved bridge is completed, the state will begin construction of a new highway bridge, also expected to ease the flow of traffic both on and over the river.

Proceeding up the marked channel, you will note similar-looking marinas lined up in the following order: Niantic River Marina; Boats, Inc., catering only to outboards; Darrows Boatyard, with a marine railway and travelift; and Niantic Boatyard, also with a railway. The services here are rather complete and comparable but water at their docks runs only about 4 feet.

About ¾ of a mile above these facilities, the narrow 50-foot-wide channel will lead you to the entrance to landlocked Smith Cove on your port hand. Privately maintained stakes, with appropriately marked red-and-black arrows, have been set out to mark the 6-foot-deep channel leading to Bayreuther Boatyard & Marina, where their slips offer 8-foot depths. To enter this channel, make sure to bear off to port just before reaching Marker #27, located in the main channel. Since most of Smith Cove is 3-foot deep, with a mud bottom, a tie-up at Bayreuther is advised, although guest moorings are available for boats of under 3-foot draft.

Chris and Warren Bayreuther, who keep their establishment "Bristol fashion," obviously cater to transients, while being very successful dealers for Morgan, O'Day, and Dyer sailing craft, among others. They have about everything to suit you and your boat's needs and fancy, including excellent repairmen on duty, electronic repair, a 30-ton Travelift, a fine marine store, ice, a laundromat, and the most polished rest rooms and showers you'll ever see in any marina. Motels and a shopping center are nearby. A courtesy car is at your disposal. Yachtsmen who are between cruises often use Bayreuther as a layover preferable to New London.

The quiet cove, almost pondlike, presents the observer with a pleasant image. The water is clear, the swimming good, for all boats putting in here are not permitted to pump their heads unless equipped with a retaining tank. Fish such as flounder, stripers, and mackerel abound here and along the river.

The channel further up the river is apt to shift from time to time but is marked by privately maintained stakes that are moved to conform to the changes. Niantic River is a beautiful spot, widens into a well-sheltered lake, and offers good holding ground in about 15 feet of water south of Sandy Point's bluff.

Excellent taxi service from Niantic can take you to good restaurants in the vicinity and in Old Lyme.

Millstone Point, Conn. (13211 214). The Third Edition of this *Guide*, published in 1946, described Millstone Point Harbor as "an intriguing little cove on the southwest side of Millstone Point (east side of Niantic Bay)—a quaint, secluded place, usually unfrequented by yachts." Regretfully, the passing years have not helped preserve its natural solitude and another obsolete gunk hole has become a sacrifice, this time to our nuclear age.

Today, Millstone Harbor is marked by a 375-foot-high, red-and-white banded ventilation stack belonging to the Northeast Utilities' Millstone Nuclear Power Station. Since our federal government now requires very tight security around nuclear power plants, anyone entering Millstone Harbor would be questioned and probably asked to leave unless it was an emergency situation. From this standpoint, Millstone could be an ideal spot to summon help through the security guards on duty. For the cruising yachtsman, therefore, Millstone should be considered a harbor of refuge in emergencies only.

As for the other property at Millstone Point, including Fox Island and Bay Point beach, picnic area, and visitors' information center, the growth in construction has forced the closing of these areas to the public. George S. Fox, nuclear information manager for Northeast Utilities, is hopeful that "the U.S. Nuclear Regulatory Commission will permit us to reopen them when construction of our third and last generating unit is completed in 1982."

The U.S. Naval Underwater Sound Laboratory still occupies the big stone quarry said to be one of the oldest in southern New England. Boats are not permitted to enter here through the opening to Twotree Island Channel, where a log boom acts as a gate.

New London, Conn. (13213 293, 13212 359). This is one of the leading yacht centers on the sound, and provides virtually every requirement the cruising yachtsman may seek, except possibly a snug anchorage. New London Harbor, formed by the Thames River, is large and seldom quiet. But it is fairly well protected, and has all sorts of provisions for cruisers.

The best small-boat anchorage is within the chartered area along the west side of the lower harbor just south of Greens Harbor. Heavy repair work is done at the Electric Boat Division of General Dynamics and at the old Thames Shipyard; small repairs can be handled by a mechanic at any one of the yacht stations we will mention.

Harbor conditions are generally good except in strong southerly winds, when it is advisable to anchor in the upper harbor north of the United States Coast Guard docks on the west side, 2½ miles from Southwest Ledge. These docks are distinguishable at night by a red light at the outer end.

Burr's Yacht Haven, just below the Orient Point Ferry and about 1 mile from the entrance on the western shore in Greens Harbor, is an excellent place to leave a boat or to outfit for a trip. In entering this harbor, favor black can 5, keeping it close to port to avoid Hog Back Rocks marked by nun 4. The famous ocean racer, *Ondine,* reportedly struck this dangerous reef several years ago. Permanent moorings, in the shape of large orange, pick-up ball buoys, are available, and good care will be taken of any boat left with the management. These moorings are obtainable at $5.00 a night, with slips running at a minimum rate of $10.00 each. Moorings may be picked up after checking personally with the dock master. Many convenient slips with electrical connections have been built at the wharf for those who prefer to tie up there in 9 feet, MLW. Here you'll find "complete one-stop service." Burr's claims that, "if we haven't got it, we can get it."

Gas, Diesel fuel, ice, water, etc., are found at the dock, and up at the marine store, operated by Burr's owner, Raymond Bergamo, you can find an ample stock of hardware and charts. Complete engine/hull repair work is available. On the premises are showers, a laundromat, The Grogg Shoppe, and highly recommended Chuck's Steak House, where informal dress is permissible.

One block west of Burr's straight up the hill is a road on which buses run to New London every thirty minutes. Also located here is a small grocery store where you can pick up supplies, or they'll deliver by calling 443-9696. Their hours on weekdays are 8 A.M. to 6 P.M.; Saturdays 8 A.M. to 8 P.M.; and Sundays 7:30 A.M. to 1 P.M. Taxis can be ordered quickly by phone to provide transportation to the New London railroad station, where most through trains between Boston and New York stop. Ferries also run regularly to Fishers Island, Block Island, and Orient Point from docks located just northeast of Shaw Cove.

For protection in blows, yachts sometimes go further upriver through a drawbridge into landlocked Shaw Cove on the west side of the Thames. The bridge operates for boat traffic from 6 A.M. to 10 P.M. daily and opens on a horn signal of one long and one short blast. Established in 1881, Crocker's Boatyard has been run by five straight generations of Crockers; in 1978 it was planning to build a new marina headquarters, complete with a marine store and showers. Several coal wharves, however, tend to make this fine "hurricane hole" rather unattractive.

Just south of Burr's lies Marsters Marine Service, whose efficiency has been praised by a Corinthian yachtsman. The Thames Yacht Club is located next door. On one of our visits here, the people there couldn't have been nicer in rightfully showing off their fine new clubhouse, including immaculate showers and snack bar. Visiting yachtsmen may make use of its sandy beach and perhaps a spare mooring or two but they can obtain no gas or supplies. This active sailing club, open from 10 A.M. to 6 P.M., offers anchorage in the most attractive surroundings found on the Thames.

There is some protection for shoal-draft craft off the Shennecossett Yacht Club behind Pine Island on the east side of the river entrance, but there are limited supplies. Anchoring here saves making the trip up the river, yet it is not recommended for an overnight anchorage unless you're desperate. In westerlies you'll be exposed to both wind and rolling swells, not to mention the noisy air traffic landing and taking off from nearby Trumbull Airport. This small, crowded harbor is marked by a prominent water tower of the Coast Guard station on Avery Point. If you are still tempted to enter, make your approach through the western passage until you reach the yacht club's dock, with a reported 6-foot depth. Here you can find gas, ice, marine supplies, and perhaps a spare mooring. Spicer's Marine just beyond the yacht club has gas, water, and ice with a state launching ramp, but at this spot the water shoals rapidly to less than 3 feet at MLW.

Places of interest in New London include Connecticut College, the United States Submarine Base above the railway bridge, the Tale of the Whale Museum, and the U.S. Coast Guard Academy where band concerts are held during summer weekends and a visit aboard the training ship *Eagle* promises a treat if she happens to be in port.

It is interesting, from a mooring or slip at Burr's Landing, to see the sleek, gray submarines glide by, to watch fine-looking yachts as they come and go, to share in the conversation and activities at one of the leading ports or rendezvous for cruising men on the New England coast.

Special Note on Tides. The tide runs strongly off the southern end of Bartlett Reef, near New London, and the same is true of Black Point.

The tides are strongest at the easterly end of the sound—especially east of Faulkner Island. The tide is almost twice as strong outside Long Shoal—near the Cornfield lighted buoy—as inside the shoal. A correspondent reports finding an ebb tide of from 1½ to 2 knots off Cornfield, and making good time to New London from the Duck Island westerly breakwater by taking the slightly longer outside route. (See special government tide and current book on Long Island Sound tides.) Therefore, should you be riding a fair current along the 6-mile length of Long Sand Shoal and be heading up the sound, stay to the south and gain the extra lift. Bucking the current, however, run north of the shoal, where the velocity is weaker.

A fire in 1976 destroyed the barracks of the famous Faulkner Island lighthouse and subsequent vandalism forced the Coast Guard to close this popular haven to visitors. At the time of writing, funds were being sought to replace the temporary light with a first-class illumination, radio, and fog signal system.

CHAPTER V

South Shore of Long Island Sound Manhasset Bay to Montauk Point

Manhasset Bay and Port Washington, Long Island, N.Y. (12366 223). Manhasset Bay, though large, is one of the best harbors on Long Island Sound. It has deep water everywhere and a good holding bottom, is easy to enter by day or night, and has plenty of good anchorage space with protection from wind or sea. There are practically no tidal currents except at the entrance, and the average rise of tide is about 6 feet.

Few, if any, harbors on the Atlantic coast have as many services and facilities to offer yachtsmen as Manhasset Bay. There are so many yacht clubs—we have counted ten—that we can mention only several of the best known. Boat yards, marinas, marine supply shops, public and private docks, water-front restaurants greet the mariner whichever way he looks.

One of the two oldest yacht clubs on Long Island Sound, the North Shore Yacht Club, is now housed in a small white building in Manorhaven on the north shore. Organized as the New York Canoe Club in 1871, it has been going ever since and gives visitors a friendly reception, as we know from experience. The two luxurious marinas next to the club, the Capri Marina just to the west and the Riviera Marina to the east, have about everything to offer, including slips and moorings, restaurants, swimming pools, gas, water, electricity, showers, toilets, telephones, and repairs.

In addition, the Capri Marina has a marine store, pump-out facilities, plenty of open greensward for just lounging around, and the Barge at Capri, a first-class, floating restaurant approved by *Cue* magazine and requiring "neat attire." The premises at Riviera in 1977 were undergoing a needed face-lift evidenced by the appearance of a trim-looking, wood-shingled restaurant. But based on overall appeal and services, we admit a slight preference for Capri.

Behind Toms Point are several small marinas, but the real display of facilities is at Port Washington, along the eastern shore of Manhasset

Bay. Here, from north to south, are three large and well-known yacht clubs: the Knickerbocker Yacht Club (1874), which held the first frostbite race, on January 2, 1932; the Manhasset Bay Yacht Club (1891), which began life on a scow with a piano and a bar and now has luxurious quarters overlooking a swimming pool and the bay; and the Port Washington Yacht Club, furthest south, with a modern clubhouse flanked by a pool with a long pier in front. Manhasset Bay Yacht Club is credited with having helped launch a new type of racing in January 1932— frostbiting. The regatta's first prize, won by Colin Ratsey, was a reported "suitably engraved gallon alcohol tin—empty." All of these clubs are hospitable to yachtsmen from other recognized clubs offering reciprocal privileges. All maintain launch service.

Among the leading boat yards and marine supply houses along the Port Washington shore, from north to south, is Flagship Yachts, a dealer for Gulfstar, Pearson, and Allied boats and catering mostly to sailing craft. Having no transient slips, they can only offer emergency repairs to cruising yachtsmen. Next door is the impressive store of A & R Marshall, Inc., which has one of the most complete collections of marine supplies and charts we have seen anywhere. Should you have any money left after a visit here, it's just a few steps to the renowned Louie's Shore Restaurant where you can tie up in 5 feet MLW dockside for a dinner prepared by fourth-generation continued management.

Further to the south is Seaman's Boatyard run by the appropriately named Albertson Seaman. His place has the smell, look, and ambience of the reliable, traditional boat yard open for service seven days a week. If you arrive under sail, this is where you should go for repairs by coming up to the work dock at the end of the pier in 6 feet at low water. During our visit to Seaman's office, we saw something through his window that would have gladdened the sporting heart of the late coauthor of this *Guide,* Fessenden S. Blanchard. Only a few feet away, on the grounds of the Manhasset Bay Yacht Club, stood the deck, vertical uprights, and screens of a new platform tennis court. Blanchard invented this popular game with James K. Cogswell in 1928.

For supplies, one may be able to tie up temporarily at the North Hempstead Town Dock just north of Louie's. They'll let you stay here for 24 hours in emergencies, but there's only 4 feet at low water at the dock. Stores are just a block or so away. The harbor master advised that yachts should not try to anchor in the special anchorage area to the north and marked on the chart.

There is little commercial traffic in Manhasset Bay, just swarms of yachts, large and small. The Coast Guard has estimated that there are now about 200,000 small craft plying Long Island Sound each summer, and at certain times one might imagine they have all gathered together in Manhasset Bay. Manhasset, at the southern end of the bay, has some interesting old houses, such as the Onderdonk House, considered a fine example of Greek Revival architecture. It also has an active shopping center.

Glen Cove (Hempstead Harbor), Long Island, N.Y. (12366 223). "The old order changeth, yielding place to new." Gone is the glitter from the Glen Cove yachting scene. All that is left to remind one of the famous Station 10 of the New York Yacht Club, once located just inside of the breakwater on the east shore, is a small gray building with wide, overhanging eaves. The larger building, once the clubhouse where the "four hundred" of the yachting world were wont to gather, was rafted away in June, 1949, to become a fixture on the grounds of the Marine Historical Association at Mystic Seaport. This was the end of an era at Glen Cove, when palatial yachts belonging to such men as J. Pierpont Morgan and Cornelius Vanderbilt lay moored off Station 10.

Now, the site is called Glen Cove Landing and the anchorage area is known as Glen Cove Harbor. Behind the gas dock, the gray building with the paneled eaves now houses the Glen Cove Yacht Club. For an overnight stay, on weekends only, you may find some room dockside in 6 feet of water providing you remain aboard, or perhaps the dock master can let you borrow one of the private moorings. Launch service runs 9 A.M. to 8 P.M. weekends only. It is pretty isolated here, with added protection from the breakwater rebuilt in 1966. But this is no place to be anchored in a sou'wester! Just to the north lies the beach where Morgan used to take his morning dip after strolling down from his mansion.

Off the dock are many small sailboats and motor cruisers where once the *Corsair* lay. Most of the larger boats we found moored further up the harbor. But the best shelter from northerly winds is off the yacht club's dock behind the breakwater. It is also much cooler there on hot summer nights than it is at the landlocked Glen Cove Marina, described below.

South of Glen Cove Landing, also on the east shore, just north of the entrance to Mosquito Cove, is the Hempstead Harbor Yacht Club. We hope that the name of the cove is not suggestive, though there are marshes nearby. The dock master says that there is 4 feet at low water at the club dock and that the club offers reciprocal privileges to members of other recognized yacht clubs. There are several guest moorings in deep water, but these are open to the northward for a considerable distance and under some conditions provide an uncomfortable anchorage. The club does not supply gas, but water and ice are obtainable. Another club, the Sea Cliff Yacht Club, is on the south side of the cove. From the channel, head almost due south in making your approach to the extending pier. Not only is Sea Cliff an appealing-looking club but its members seem like a spirited group. On one visit we enjoyed watching their bricklaying party, held on the club's front patio. "We have the best bar and the cheapest drinks in Glen Cove," exclaimed one busy member with trowel in hand. Other services, depending upon one's mood or the time of day, include a fine restaurant, swimming pool, and regular launch service.

More evidence of the change at Glen Cove is observed when one glides into the 7-foot channel of Glen Cove Creek. In 1977, plans were being laid for the construction of a condominium complex on the site of the Sea Cove Marina located along the first basin to starboard. Next comes the Glen Cove Yacht Service with gas, Diesel fuel, ice, water, marine supplies, berths with electricity, and a pump-out station.

In the second basin beyond, with a mean depth of 8 feet, one may find the largest facility in Glen Cove—the Glen Cove Marina. This place may well be your best bet for the deepest water in the creek, the snuggest though perhaps the most active anchorage, and the most convenient location to stores, restaurants, and theaters. All these marinas do comparable repair work. In the summer you will not only find the creek extremely sociable but often quite hot.

The southern part of Hempstead Harbor is entered through a dredged, marked channel from the entrance at Bar Beach. The 1977 *Coast Pilot* reports that, "in 1968, the controlling depths were 4 feet to a point opposite South Glenwood Landing thence 4 feet at midchannel to a point opposite the Old Town Wharf."

At the south end of the harbor, on the east shore opposite Bar Beach, is the site of the old Fyfe Shipyard, which, from its humble beginnings in 1905, came to be known as the "Tiffany" of boat yards. Here such majestic "gold-platers" as J.P. Morgan's *Corsair* and Marjorie Merriweather Post's *Sea Cloud* came to be fitted out in times gone past. Now it is out of business, perhaps having been too wedded to wood construction in the age of fiberglass. The Long Island Lighting Company has taken over the property.

Glen Cove has exchanged much of its former glamor for modern conveniences, suited to the more modest pocketbooks of those who now use its docks and facilities.

An article by Clarence E. ("Ike") Lovejoy in *The New York Times* in the late thirties describes Glen Cove as it used to be and to some extent still is:

The curious, gingerbread-type of building used by the N. Y. Y. C. has a history of its own. It was part of the original club station provided at Weehawken by John C. Stevens, founder and first commodore. But in 1907 the building was towed from the Hudson, up the East River, through Hell Gate and to Hempstead Harbor to be located on land made available by J.P. Morgan. . . .

South of Glen Cove and the N. Y. Y. C. anchorage plenty of water is available for a night's anchorage off Bar Beach, the curious, narrow sandspit that almost—but not quite—closes the inner harbor. Bar Beach is sandy, just right for a swim, and many a yacht party up for an early Sunday breakfast has seen the congregation of some colored church on the North Shore gather here for a daybreak baptism, the preacher immersing members of his flock while standing waist-deep off the beach and the brethren and sisters singing hymns.

Passing around the point of Bar Beach, yachts of medium draft may run in a depth of 4 feet at MLW right up to the head of navigation at Roslyn and tie up along public bulkheading for a meal ashore.

Roslyn, which dates from 1636, got its present name in 1844 when William Cullen Bryant and others felt the surrounding country resembled Roslyn Castle in Scotland. Hempstead Harbor was first entered in 1640 by immigrants from Lynn, Massachusetts, and the first use of the necks of land now occupied by great estates and summer homes was for the common pasturage of cattle. Settlers worshiped on Sundays in stockades, assembling at the call of kettledrums from the ramparts.

Glen Cove was called Musketo (or Musceta) Cove until 1834. This word really meant to the Indians "cove of grassy flats"; but because it was confused with mosquito, the new name was wisely adopted.

The Long Island Lighting Company buildings dominate the upper harbor, which is less attractive than it is nearer the entrance. A small boat basin is located at Glenwood Landing.

Oyster Bay, Long Island, N.Y. (12365 224). This is an attractive, well-protected bay with several good anchorages. One is off the Seawanhaka Corinthian Yacht Club in the cove west of Plum Point, Center Island. This club, organized in 1871, is one of the two oldest yacht clubs still in business on Long Island Sound, the other being the North Shore Yacht Club of Port Washington. While the surroundings are lovely, the anchorage is inaccessible when supplies are needed, and the tide runs strongly.

Seawanhaka's services, including meals, are available only to yachts flying the burgee of a recognized yacht club. There are no designated guest moorings but moorings of members whose yachts are away are made available to guests. In making your approach, you will note three prominent piers jutting out from the club's shoreline. Launch service in season runs during the hours of 7 A.M. to 10 P.M. from the eastern-most dock where visiting yachts should first report to be assigned dockage or a guest mooring. The middle pier is reserved for swimming, while the new dock beyond is used mainly for repairs and for supplying fuel, ice, and water. Dockage there is restricted to a ½-hour tie-up per boat on Friday, Saturday, Sunday, and holidays. At the time of writing, guest charges ran $10.00 per hour after the first ½ hour, with moorings provided when available at $7.00 per night.

"At the time of Seawanhaka's organization, the group who left the handling of their yachts to professional skippers and crews, the wealthier members, were in control of the New York Yacht Club. Some of the other group, the Do-it-Yourself exponents, who skippered and sailed their own boats, decided to form a new club in which the principles of amateur or 'Corinthian' racing would prevail."* Apparently, sailing with amateur crews had long been popular in England, but it was the founding fathers of this one-hundred-year-old club who are recognized as having introduced an entirely new system in racing to American yachting.

The Cruising Club of America, which has held many a rendezvous in Oyster Bay, usually anchors either off the south shore of Centre Island or preferably, we think, in the large bight between Cove Neck and the wharf at Oyster Bay.

In 1965 the former shoal area that ran along the southern shore of the harbor from the oyster dock west to the charted dredged canal was removed, thereby making the various facilities here accessible to boats of deep draft. The first marina you will reach is Oyster Bay Yacht Service, run by Mr. Read Taylor and Mr. Park Benjamin. A very agreeable fellow, Mr. Benjamin was eager to state that he can provide yachtsmen with gas, water, and ice at dockside, and that his overnight moorings, including launch service, run $5.00 for boats under 30 feet and $10.00 for those longer. Launches operate from 6 A.M. to midnight daily. Since the slips dockside are available by reservation only, phone ahead by calling (516) 922-6331. They offer a good selection of marine hardware.

Practically next door is the Sagamore Yacht Club, housed in an attractive shingled building, which we have often enjoyed visiting. There is

*From *Long Island Sound*, by Fessenden S. Blanchard (D. Van Nostrand Co., Inc.).

7-foot depth dockside but only water is provided and only showers and a phone inside the clubhouse. CB Channel 11 is monitored for launch service, which runs 9 A.M. to 9 P.M. on weekdays and 8 A.M. to 10 P.M. on weekends. You may have to settle for a guest mooring if one is available, since slip space is hard to come by anywhere in the harbor. This very tidy club offers reciprocal guest privileges to members of other recognized yacht clubs. The Town of Oyster Bay has further developed its Roosevelt Memorial Park Boat Basin, shown on the chart as just east of a prominent flagpole. Gas may be obtained here but unfortunately the docking facilities are open only to local residents. Supplies can be obtained nearby.

Jakobson's Shipyard, well and favorably known to many Long Island Sound yachtsmen, is located in the cove to the west of the flagpole. Having been acquired by a tugboat association, it no longer caters to transient boats.

Some possible anchorages can be found just south of Brickyard Point and Moses Point, as shown on the chart. Another good anchorage, with less tide than the others and good swimming, is at the northerly end of the bay, west of Centre Island; but keep well away from Brickyard (Soper) Point to avoid some outlying rocks. This area has no official name of its own, but the local people often call it Morris Cove. Shoal-draft craft sometimes go through the drawbridge into Mill Neck Creek and anchor there, but the tide is strong at the bridge and the charted soundings unreliable. If curiosity gets the better of you, go in at high water but proceed with care.

Theodore Roosevelt's famous home, Sagamore Hill, is about 1½ miles from Oyster Bay Village. It is open seven days a week from 9:30 A.M. to 6 P.M., Memorial Day to Labor Day, and well worth a visit, especially by admirers of T.R. "After all," he once wrote, "fond as I am of the White House and much though I have appreciated these years in it, there isn't any place in the world like home—like Sagamore Hill. . . ."

Cold Spring Harbor, Long Island, N.Y. (12365 224). A hundred years ago Cold Spring Harbor was a whaling port, with a main street on which so many languages were spoken that it was called Bedlam Street. Today, so far as we know, whatever bedlam there is in the vicinity is left behind in the Sand Hole at Lloyd Point, which you pass on your way to one of the prettiest and most foolproof harbors on the sound. It has been vastly improved through recent dredging at the southern end of the channel.

It is almost impossible to get into any trouble in Cold Spring Harbor, at least in your navigating. A conspicuous lighthouse shows you the way in; once past this, there are no obstacles to avoid if you keep a reasonable distance from shore. The water front is private, lovely, and unspoiled. The only place at which gas is available is concealed from the outer harbor behind the Cold Spring Beach peninsula at the southern end of the harbor. A narrow, unbuoyed deep-water channel with well over 10 feet at MLW was dredged in 1966 through the cut between the north end of the peninsula and an island, enabling yachts to tie up at at H & M Powles Marine and obtain gas, water, ice, food supplies, repair work, etc., further up on the eastern shore. As you enter this cut, favor the peninsula's shore and once having passed through, hug the shoreline to port proceeding all the way upchannel. Near Powles are the Whaler's Inn and County Kitchen, both recommended eating spots.

Good water can be carried in the channel all the way to the delightful basin at the harbor's head. The Whaler's Cove Yacht Club to port offers only water and electricity at its slips and no showers but has become a popular visiting place. They will handle boats no longer than 45 feet overall at a $15.00 minimum dockage fee. As with many yacht clubs having reciprocal privilege arrangements, dock space is available provided a member's slip is open. The best water, 7 feet MLW, is to be found along the eastern shore. We were advised to rent an overnight mooring from Powles and to stay within the perimeter marked by the mooring floats, since there are mud flats to the west.

The Cold Spring Harbor Beach Club, on the east shore near the head of the harbor, is the only yacht club, though it is also an attractive tennis and beach club. There is at least 9 feet at the dock. In summer, the small basin, protected by a hook of land and a jetty, is filled with small sailboats and dinghies. Here, where there's a fine fleet of Atlantics, we were first introduced to the Laser Class, a new 13-feet-10-inch sleek fun-boat designed by Bruce Kirby and more sophisticated than the Sun-Fish. Visitors from other recognized yacht clubs, we were told, are given reciprocal privileges, and several guest moorings are usually available. The club has put in a new swimming pool and runs a snack bar during the day. You will find George Fonde very helpful during your stay here. Anchorage Inn, about ½ mile from the club, is said to furnish good accommodations.

Yachts can find good anchorage, except in strong northwesters, almost anywhere in the harbor. The depth is almost uniformly from 15 to 18 feet and the holding ground is good, with room for plenty of scope if necessary. But it is no place to be in nor'westers, as we once found out. In winds from this direction, perhaps the best place to be found is in the bight on Cove Neck opposite Sagamore Hill, Theodore Roosevelt's famous home.

On Cold Spring Harbor's main street its Whaling Museum Society maintains a museum open three days a week during the summer. Here you'll find a fascinating collection of whaling paraphernalia, including a whaleboat, old prints, scrimshaw, ship models, whaling irons, and log books. Mr. Leslie Peckham is in charge.

The "Sand Hole" at Lloyd Point, Long Island, N.Y. (12365 224). This popular weekend harbor is inadequately charted, so the description that follows may be helpful to the few people who haven't already been there.

The "Sand Hole," or "Sand Diggers" as it is often called by Long Islanders, was dug out of the low-lying end of Lloyd Point and is not easy to recognize at a distance until perhaps you see some tall spars apparently rising out of the sand. The high land south of the Sand Hole is visible for a long distance. As there is an often-submerged breakwater on your starboard hand, projecting northward at the harbor's mouth as well as shoals building to port, don't enter too "careless-like."

Head into the opening, giving the breakwater a fair berth but keeping clear of those shoals, which extend inward for several hundred feet from the north shore of the entrance. After that, follow the shore to port. This maneuver will involve curving north for a short stretch, as you run between parallel shoalings from each spit. It shelves fairly steeply most of the way, but don't get too close. Since the good water is between the sandspit and the dolphins, be sure to keep the latter to starboard as you make your final swing into the harbor. Visiting yachts may come there to anchor no closer than 200 feet offshore but their crews are not permitted to land. Make sure to avoid the shallow spots marked on the chart along the eastern shore as well as at the northern end of the hole. Rafting-up is forbidden.

The "Sand Hole" is popular among the weekend yachting fraternity of New York City and points east. During July and August it is apt to be crowded with motorboats of every description bearing occupants of both sexes possessed of varying musical abilities and financial resources. If you plan to spend a night there, we'd suggest avoiding midsummer weekends. It is now under the control of the New York State Park Commission and recently became a part of the Caumsett State Park, a 1426-acre tract in the center of Lloyd Neck.

No supplies or facilities of any kind are available nearer than Cold Spring Harbor. When it isn't too crowded, it is a pleasant place to anchor, though the presence of an untouchable beach can be irritating.

Lloyd Harbor, Long Island, N.Y. (12365 224). This excellent anchorage is on the southeast side of Lloyd Neck, just west of the entrance

Skyviews Survey Inc.

The "Sand Hole" at Lloyd Point looking southwest. On the upper left is Cold Spring Harbor and at the top right lies the entrance to Oyster Bay Harbor to Huntington Bay. The most popular anchorage is in the northeast corner of the harbor, in sticky mud, behind the sandspit. The holding ground here is good.

In a strong southwesterly, anchorage off the southwest shore of the harbor is to be preferred, though it is lined with private estates.

In a dinghy one can sail westward far up the harbor to the narrow strip of land that separates Lloyd Harbor from Oyster Bay to the west. This is one of the most isolated anchorages to be found within a similar distance of New York City. The shores are thickly wooded. There are no stores or facilities of any kind, but you can land on the east beach.

Yachtsmen who go ashore and roam over the sandspit will find genuine Texas cactus growing wild, a rarity in these latitudes.

While many more deep-water cruising yachts are to be seen there than in the "Sand Hole," the chief "out" about Lloyd Harbor is its popularity, especially on weekends. But, if you like to visit around or to watch some fine-looking yachts come and go, you will enjoy it there. And if you are from suburban New York you'll undoubtedly see some of your friends.

While under ordinary conditions this is a well-sheltered, landlocked harbor, in strong gales from the eastward at high tide the water from Huntington Bay may sweep in over the narrow point and make it extremely unpleasant. At times like these it is well to run up into Huntington Harbor close by. This is also the place to go for gas or supplies.

We recall the cooling breeze on hot summer evenings wafting down the long western channel that leads to Oyster Bay. Neither can we forget the sound of sailors singing to the crackling of a fire on a chilly autumn night, huddled around the ruins of the point's old light.

In September 1931, Lloyd Point was the scene of one of the most baffling murder mysteries ever to confront the police of Long Island. Two still-unknown pirates boarded a motor cruiser on which were cruising Benjamin Collings with his wife and a five-year-old daughter. Collings was bound and thrown overboard. His battered body was found on the beach a week later. The boat was left drifting off Lloyd Point with no one on board but the five-year-old girl. Mrs. Collings was found the next morning screaming for help in a moored boat in Oyster Bay. The mystery and motive were never solved. Some called it "the perfect crime."*

---

*An account in some detail of the circumstances of the Collings murder mystery is contained in *Long Island Sound*, by Fessenden S. Blanchard (D. Van Nostrand Co., Inc.).

Huntington, Long Island, N.Y. (12365 224). This is one of the best all-around harbors on Long Island and the most convenient port for gas and other supplies in the Huntington Bay area. Its major drawback is the ever-increasing congestion. The harbor is seemingly one vast fleet of wall-to-wall boats except for the narrow marked channel resembling the exit lane of a modern shopping center complex. Speed limit in the channel is 5 mph.

In entering, be prepared to find a stiff current in the narrow cut off Wincoma Point. After passing this point keep straight ahead until you have left the flashing green buoy to port. Follow the buoys southward and then east between hundreds of yachts moored on either side of the channel. A less-crowded anchorage, if you can find swinging space, may be found in the cove to starboard after having passed the lighted channel buoy inside the entrance. On the nearby hill stands a prominent red baronial building housing the Huntington Art Center and open to the public. Around the bend, also on the south side of the harbor, is the Wyncote Yacht Club where gas, ice, and electricity are on tap and a spare slip possibly available in 6 feet of water. Their minimum charge for dockage is $3.00.

A good plan is to continue up the harbor to the hospitable Huntington Yacht Club marked on the chart. This club, to port just beyond nun 12, has gas, water, and ice, and offers its facilities to yachtsmen from other recognized clubs that provide reciprocal privileges. The clubhouse, built following a fire that destroyed the old one, is a modern structure, with a dining room that has a fine outlook. It is usually closed Mondays. A marina and Olympic-size swimming pool with showers and snack bar were added here in 1970. Electrical outlets are found at over 40 slips, where the overnight charge is $17.50 minimum. Club launch service runs from 8 A.M. to 8 P.M. on weekdays and from 8 A.M. to 10 P.M. on weekends. There's a fee of $5.00 for an overnight mooring.

Beyond, on the east shore just north of the "Old Town Dock," is Knutson's Marina, which hauls, stores, and repairs large yachts. It also has gas, Diesel fuel, ice, water, and some overnight dockage space with electrical outlets. For supplies we suggest that you tie up to the Town Dock for a maximum time limit of three hours on one dockside and one hour on the other while you visit the nearby delicatessen and 7-11 Store. The Harbor Master can usually be found in a white building close to the dock. Further to the south lies the Ketewomoke Yacht Club, and then comes Sport Boats, in the southeast corner, run by Bill Knutson, offering marine supplies and reliable outboard service. Around the corner north of the bridge is the sizable Willis Marine Center with slips (at a $10.00 minimum overnight charge for boats up to 40 feet and $20.00 for those of greater length). Willis has moorings for $5.00 a night, with launch service provided. There's also electricity, gas, water, ice, showers, and some repair work is done. This place is on a five-year lease from Knutson, who runs a fine marine store here. Town Marina just to the west is used just by local residents. Try the Harbor Inn or The Salty Dog for the best meals in town. If you want to get anything done to your boat in Huntington, it would be a good idea to consult either Tom or Bill Knutson.

Beyond the bridge across the pond some fine concrete ramps and nearby parking space offer encouragement to owners of trailer-borne outboards.

The shores of the harbor are pretty and illustrate what a residential community can do with its water front. If you enjoy seeing a wide variety of boats and crowds of people of all ages having a mad whirl on the water, come to Huntington. The harbor is well protected from sea and wind, and transportation can be obtained to the town of Huntington, 2 or 3 miles away, where there are stores and a railroad station.

At Halesite in Huntington is a monument to Nathan Hale, the noted American spy, who landed there and was captured by the British in September 1776. On the monument are the famous words uttered by Captain Hale shortly before he died: "I only regret I have but one life to lose for my country."

Although in 1971 the citizenry was up in arms about harbor pollution, now the tide is beginning to turn fair for Huntington. Water quality here has improved, due to a combined program of environmental education, beach stabilization, wetland creation, and sewer and shorefront construction management. Portions of Huntington, Centerport, and Northport harbors, closed for years with badly polluted waters, were reopened in 1977 for clamming. These harbors were the first on Long Island to qualify under the state's water quality standards. Some areas of the sound and outer bays have been reopened, but no other inner harbors had been able to satisfy the New York State Department of Environmental Protection by 1977.

SPECIAL NOTE

Entrance to Northport Bay, Long Island, N.Y. (12365 224). When entering from the west in fair weather, skirt along the row of red nuns off Lloyd Neck. Then steer southward, heading just to the left of the nearest tall gray water tower that rises above the houses in the middle of the shore ahead. The flashing buoy off the tip of West Beach marks the turn to Price Bend, Northport, and Duck Island Harbor.

Price Bend, Long Island, N.Y. (12365 224). This anchorage, open to the south for some distance, used to be a favorite rendezvous for the Cruising Club of America in May and October. The entrance between buoys along the shore to the south is easy to follow. In entering, leave can 3 to port and then swing your bow in a wide arc toward the north to avoid the charted shoals. The holding ground is rather poor and in two October rendezvous a number of Cruising Club boats dragged their anchors. The area is no longer completely deserted but there are no stores nearer than Northport. The shoreline is not unattractive, with clean, coarse sand beaches left by dredging operations extending north and south. These are weed-free and offer good swimming and steep shores even at low tide. This popular sandspit, on which the foundations of an old sand and gravel company may still be seen, is now open to the public under the name of Hobart Beach, established for the town of Huntington. The north and east sides of Price's Bend are private and now all built up, including the entire shoreline between the northern end of the sandspit and the southern end of the Eaton's Neck cove.

Duck Island Harbor, Eaton's Neck, Long Island, N.Y. (12365 224). This harbor should not be confused with Duck Island Roads, 45 miles to the east on the Connecticut shore. This is a remote, unspoiled, seldom-visited, well-protected, but small and shallow anchorage on the northeast side of Northport Bay, open across the bay to the south and southwest. Note that off Winkle Point, Little Neck Point, and Duck Island Bluff, red stakes have been placed in 10 feet of water. Stay outside of these and you'll avoid grounding. In entering, go to a point about 75 feet west of the flashing red buoy off Duck Island Bluff. Then steer for the entrance, curving slightly to the west to avoid a 4-foot spot off the eastern shore. At low tide a lead is desirable.

There is 12 feet at the entrance and 8 feet a little way in, but the water shoals rapidly with a 7-foot tide range. Although the harbor is a haven for water-skiers, there is little other traffic, and hence one can safely lie in mid-channel just inside the entrance.

The chief disadvantages of the harbor are difficulty in making a landing at low tide and lack of supplies. Asharoken police boats hound these waters to prevent crews from venturing ashore. A local ordinance forbids rafting and refuse-throwing and rules that there must be at least a 150-foot berth between anchored vessels.

Duck Island is well suited to anyone desiring quiet and good protection.

Another popular anchorage offering shelter in northerlies is behind the bluff rimming the south shore of Duck Island. The water shoals rapidly northward here so anchor well offshore.

Northport, Long Island, N.Y. (12365 224). Like all the ports on Huntington Bay, this harbor is attractive. Under most conditions the shelter is fairly good, though it can be very rough there in nor'westers. The place to go, if you are a member of a recognized yacht club and present your club's personal membership card, is to the refurbished Northport Yacht Club, formerly called the Edgewater Yacht Club. This is at the first large pier to which you come, on your port hand, after passing Bluff Point. There you can obtain gas, water, showers, and launch service to and from guest moorings, for which there is an overnight charge of $5.00 entitling you to use of the club's facilities. The launch runs from 8 A.M. to 9 P.M. on weekdays and from 8 A.M. to midnight on weekends. Check first with the dock master to be assigned a color-coded space alongside, where you can tie up for a thirty-minute limit in 4 feet of water. There's an 8-foot rise and fall of tide. Dockage is not available overnight and no advance reservations are accepted.

The Northport Yacht Club is a very active sailing center with almost one hundred youngsters in its junior racing program. We found the swimming pool and the new restaurant with bar most appealing. Next door, you'll spot the guest moorings and docks of Karl's Mariners Inn. Crowds there attest to its fine cuisine.

Further south, on the same shore, is the weather-beaten Seymour Boat Shops with gas, ice, water, and marine supplies, but no slips. Don't let its appearance deceive you, for its repair work is said to be excellent; Centerport Yacht Club members are among Seymour's most loyal customers. Just beyond lies the Public Dock with an amber light and a two-hour tie-up limit. There may be space at this dock for a twenty-four-hour tie-up in 8 feet, but after 8 P.M., you'll be charged a flat rate of $10.00 for an overnight stay. A pump-out station is located next door, behind some prominent bulkheads.

Looking to the southwest, you will note that along the port shore a winding channel, shoaling to 5 feet in spots and marked with private buoys, leads to the protected basin shown due south on the chart. Keep in mid-channel close to these buoys as you make your approach to the most elaborate complex in the harbor—Northport Marine Center. There's everything here but a restaurant and even that is being planned. If you don't mind slow work, they can repair a compass, a fiberglass hull, sails, most engines, restock your galley or chart library, or haul a 60-footer. Outside the basin, the channel is beginning to shoal up as it circles to the north around and behind the prominent low-lying island. We were advised not to use this passage.

At Little Neck, or Centerport, across the town of Northport, is the Centerport Yacht Club. It offers 6 feet at low water dockside, ice, water, guest moorings with launch service, a restaurant and bar, and showers, but no gas. Supplies may be obtained on weekdays through the courtesy of the club launchman, who was Pete Coffey in 1977. We've seen how keen the competition is among the juniors here in their club races with Huntington and Northport.

Little Neck used to be occupied by the Vanderbilt estate, which had its own private golf course. The tee for the first hole was on the roof of the main building. Now it is the Vanderbilt Museum, open to the public. Seventeen thousand varieties of marine and wildlife are housed there—animals, birds, fish, shells, shields, daggers, guns—collected from many parts of the world by the adventurous William K. Vanderbilt. There are also bathtubs of solid marble and gold plumbing fixtures, reminiscent of the good old days when millionaires were millionaires and expressed themselves grandly.

Once ships built in Northport sailed around the world. Now it is a deservedly popular and attractive center of yachting activities.

Eatons Neck Basin, Long Island, N.Y. (12365 224). The very narrow entrance is clearly marked by buoys well south of the tip of the point; as you make your approach, note that the jetties on either side are under water from half to flood tide. A long, dangerous reef runs northward directly from the black lighted cans and is further identified by the appearance of a white-and-orange buoy labeled Rocks. A Coast Guard officer at the Eatons Neck station exclaims that "People try to cut inside the black can off the basin entrance and it can't be done. There is no shortcut into or out of the basin!" Unbelievably, at least thirty skippers judged otherwise in 1977 and had to pay a pretty price.

In the channel from the buoys up to an anchorage inside the western shore of the spit there is a range from 10 to 21 feet at low tide. The entrance buoys make access to this excellent harbor under power an easy matter. The swimming is as good as this section of the sound affords. The water in the lagoon is, at least in early June, much warmer than on the outer beach. A grand place to take the children for a picnic and swim!

On our latest visit we wanted to learn more about restrictions within the basin so we visited Chief W.E. Hemstock up at the station to relay them on to our fellow yachtsmen. Don't anchor anywhere in the channel. The pumping of heads is forbidden unless they are chemically treated. For safety reasons, no rafting is allowed. Boats should anchor no closer than 150 feet apart. Since all the land surrounding the basin is the private property of Mr. Henry Morgan, an Asharoken Town ordinance rules that no one can venture ashore. We gathered, however, that the law might look away benevolently providing the visitor respects

Fairchild Aerial Surveys, Inc.

Eaton Neck, with Northport and Huntington Bays. This air photo, looking southwest, shows, from left to right: the entrance to Duck Island Harbor and anchorage there; the anchorage at Price Bend and entrance to Northport Bay; anchorage at Eaton Point; and, in upper right-hand corner, Huntington River and Lloyd Harbor.

and preserves the beach area as he would his own backyard, leaving only his footsteps behind to mark his sojourn.

The most peaceful anchorage in mud bottom can be found up along the western shore, preferably in the northwestern section of the basin where the 10-foot spot appears on the chart. But once anchored, prepare for heavy wakes from mission-bound Coast Guard rescue craft, which often bolt from the basin like so many midget PT boats attacking at flank speed. On one of our visits here, a line squall, packing up to 50-knot winds, with stinging rain, came screaming across the basin, turning it into a seething caldron. But the fleet there rode it out safely in relative protection.

As a refuge during thick weather, however, this cove is impossible for rest and relaxation because of the proximity (only a few yards away) of the Eaton Point fog signal. The Electronic Remote Control and Communications Center installed here at the Eatons Neck Coast Guard Station marks the end of Long Island lighthouse keepers' lonely jobs. This center operates the lights, radio beacons, and fog horns of the following lighthouses: Eatons Neck, Penfield Reef, Stratford Point, Stratford Shoal, Greens Ledge, and Great Captain's Island. And all with a mere flick of a switch! Eatons Neck is reportedly the fourth busiest Coast Guard station in the United States, behind only Miami, Cape May, N.J., and San Francisco. Looking backward, this station was opened in 1792 by order of President George Washington.

As if to keep up with the Eatons Neck station, the 100-year-old Stratford Shoals Lighthouse, in the middle of the sound about five miles north of Port Jefferson, recently installed the nation's first solar cell-powered RAMOS weather station reporting meteorological data leading to improved weather forecasts in an area heavily used by commercial and recreational shipping.

Northport Basin, Northport, Long Island, N.Y. (12365 224). This small basin is nostalgically known as the Asharoken Beach Sand Hole. At various places on Long Island Sound sand and gravel companies are creating excellent harbors for their tugs and scows. One of the most interesting of these is the sand hole at the eastern end of Asharoken Beach, which rims the easterly shore of Eaton Point. It's identified as Northport Basin on the chart.

Unfortunately, the construction here of the Long Island Lighting Company's huge power plant with its quartet of 610-foot stacks and prominent bare buildings has stripped the harbor of much of its former appeal. The plant has erected, for transhipment purposes, an elevated mooring platform, with off-lying mooring buoys, marked by a light-and-fog signal on its western end. This is located approximately 1½ miles due north of the basin's entrance.

The entrance can be recognized from the sound by large sand cliffs, private lighted and unlighted buoys, and the tall stacks of the power plant located on the basin's east shore. There is at least 12 feet in the channel. Run in parallel to the east jetty, avoiding the dangerous rock at the end of the west jetty to starboard. Once inside, be sure to keep at least 200 feet away from the plant's concrete docks to port, where currents often swirl. Minimum depth throughout the area is 7 feet at MLW. Your best anchorage is in the small bight to starboard, well out of the narrow main channel. A fine launching ramp runs to the shore nearby. At the head of the basin may lie an old barge reminding one of former visits here when the Metropolitan Sand and Gravel Company used to work the pit.

It is still an intriguing place, much of its old charm lost by the installation of the power plant to meet the needs of an expanding population. The nearest source of supplies is at Northport, about 1½ miles away.

This harbor is the easternmost of a number of harbors on the "North Shore" of Long Island, from Manhasset Bay to the Asharoken Beach Sand Hole. From here eastward, the shore is far less hospitable to cruising men, with Port Jefferson, Mount Sinai, and Mattituck Inlet the only available harbors between the Asharoken Beach Sand Hole and Greenport.

Port Jefferson, Long Island, N.Y. (12362 361). Few yachtsmen who have cruised Long Island Sound have failed to visit "Port Jeff," and many of them have stopped there more than once. It is an ideal place for a yacht-club cruise to rendezvous. It is large and deep enough for a good-sized fleet; it is completely landlocked; all kinds of supplies are conveniently available, together with good landing docks, railway connections to New York, and ferry connections across the sound to Bridgeport. And—another important point—except for Mount Sinai Harbor, where there are few supplies, it is the last port on the Long Island shore, as you head eastward, until Mattituck is reached 25 miles away. And Mattituck has its limitations, so that for some cruising yachts the nearest good Long Island Harbor is at Greenport, 52 miles away. The chief trouble with "Port Jeff" is its size, making it far from snug when the wind blows from the wrong direction.

In approaching Port Jefferson from any direction, it is wise to keep offshore and watch the chart carefully, as there are outlying rocks and shoals. The entrance is narrow and there is apt to be a strong tidal current in or out. An experienced cruising man warns that:

Sometimes a really dangerous sea makes up outside and between the jetties on an ebb tide against strong northerly or northwesterly winds. Entering under such conditions is possible, provided proper care is taken, but leaving is attended by risk. I have seen many vessels trying to leave get completely out of control between the jetties in high seas, and strongly recommend that all vessels in harbor during a strong northwester not attempt to leave until the tide floods.

For convenience to docks and supplies the best anchorage is along the eastern shore off the piers, where there is ample protection except in a hard northwester. In that eventuality one can run toward the "Sand Hole," often called Mt. Misery Cove, just inside the harbor entrance to the east. This is protected perfectly on all sides, but is a long way from supplies. Fessenden Blanchard went in there many years ago on the brigantine *Yankee,* which drew 9 feet. To enter the Sand Hole, make southward for green flashing bell #5, leave it to port, and then head for the bluff rising from the entrance's starboard shore. Follow close along the piers south of the entrance while favoring the starboard shore until about one-third of the way in. Then you can bear off to port, anchoring in the northeastern sector of the Hole under the steep sand-bank there. One must be careful in the Hole, however, for it is filling in and offers poor holding ground. A sunken barge just below the surface at low water has been reported in the bight to the southeast. An alternative anchorage is in the lee of the outer beaches and particularly at a spot about 500 yards east of the main channel just south of the sandspit.

Although many boats like to anchor in the lee of Old Field Beach, it is wise to keep well offshore, avoiding the various shoal spots shown on the chart. The bottom here is mud. In southerlies and westerlies, a possible anchorage is off the northeast shore of Strongs Neck if one avoids the 5-foot shoal in the center of the bight. The *Coast Pilot* warns that strangers should not attempt to enter the narrow channel leading westward to Conscience Bay, for treacherous bars and rocks are there. But we are not the only ones who have enjoyed anchoring in the peaceful and pretty gunk-hole just beyond the Narrows. Favor the starboard shore going through until you approach a small sandy beach close to the 2-foot mark appearing on the chart. Then swing over to mid-channel and slightly favor the port shore going in. With lovely homes and marshes surrounding us, the only nautical neighbor we had was a 40-foot sloop, whose skipper must obviously know his way around these parts.

For those anchoring in the main harbor and wishing to go ashore for supplies or a good meal, the prominent pier furthest to the east and marked Exxon with a light at night is the one to use. At the time of writing, however, it was being sold by its owner, the Setauket Yacht Club, which recently moved to a different site just 500 yards to the east.

Setauket's new floating clubhouse is the old 200-foot ferryboat, *Newport,* which used to run regularly between Newport and Jamestown. The air-conditioned and heated cabin level is being made into a dining room, while the upper deck may provide bar service and outdoor dining with a scenic view of the harbor. It was a bargain purchase at $29,000. Established in 1959, the Setauket Yacht Club is dedicated to the needs of the sailor. It has launch service and guest moorings for transient yachts. A work program was initiated in its early days requiring every member to put in ten hours of maintenance work or pay $40. Most of the 165 members elect to work rather than pay, reports Commodore Bruce Washeim.

The next dock to the west belongs to the Bridgeport & Port Jefferson Steamboat Company, with ferries like the *Martha's Vineyard* operating across the sound several times a day during the summer season. This is the sixth in a line of ferries dating back to the 1880s when P.T. Barnum started the business. He wintered his circus animals in Port Jefferson and had to shuttle them across the sound to and from Bridgeport.

The location of the Port Jefferson Town Marina is identified on the chart and can also be sighted from seaward by lining up on two range lights—one on the outer dock and the other atop a small white observation tower inland. Here you can find showers, water, and ice, plus twelve transient slips with electricity at an overnight rate of $10.00. On the outer edge of the mariner's dock is a separate Texaco facility providing gas and Diesel fuel. You may be able to get dockage here also. Interestingly, little repair service may be found at Port Jeff.

That attractive brick building in the southwest corner of the harbor is the clubhouse of the Port Jefferson Yacht Club. It has moorings, launch service, a dock with 10-foot depth, a bar, showers, and several slips. Rates are $10.00 per slip, with a $6.00 charge for a mooring. The club can be reached on VHF, Channel 16. In coming up to its main dock, we add one note of caution to prevent possible stranding. Note the string of barges just to the northwest of the club. Since these mark the deepest water, be sure to keep them close aboard as you make your approach. More than one yachtsman has reported to us the kind reception given by the people here to visiting members of other recognized yacht clubs.

Port Jefferson was widely known as a shipbuilding center in the nineteenth and early twentieth centuries, and somewhat less known as a bootlegging center during Prohibition. It was formerly called Drowned Meadow. During the past ten years there has been a sprucing up of the business area, now offering interesting shopping for visitors. The Port Jefferson Motel is next to the ferry landing and practically next door, on West Broadway, one can find all types of nautical gear. The village has dozens of fascinating little shops, with imaginative names like Shoe Port, Swan Creek, Goodies Galore, and Remember When. A good place to start a walking tour is at the corner of West Broadway and Main Street. You'll pass Chandler's Pub; Gristede's supermarket, where all types of provisions can be gathered; Deno's Restaurant, serving seafood and Greek-style dishes; and Der Schooner, located on the waterfront and specializing in German food, which you can eat on the premises or take out to your boat. As you can see, fine restaurants abound in Port Jefferson. Probably the best place to eat in town for the least amount of money is the Elk Hotel Restaurant, which the average visitor would probably not discover for himself because there is nothing in its name or appearance to indicate its quality. But the natives know and told us so.

As you depart from Port Jefferson, take a look at the steep bluffs along Old Field Point to the west. They are being eaten up by erosion at a critical rate. A study undertaken by scientists of the Marine Sciences Center of the State University of New York at Stony Brook reveals the areas in Suffolk County where the most rapid erosion is taking place: Old Field Point receding 5.2 feet a year, Crane Neck Point with 2.6 feet, and Miller Place and an area near Orient Point each with 2 feet receding each year. Widening the protective beaches along the foot of these bluffs is the best natural barrier to this alarming cliffside erosion.

Setauket, Port Jefferson, Long Island, N.Y. (12362 361). Picturesque Setauket Harbor may be reached by following a dredged 150-foot channel winding west from red nun 2 between Tinkers Point and Strongs Neck. The latest *Coast Pilot* reports shoaling in this channel but "with local knowledge, a depth of about 4 feet can be carried." The entrance is easily identified from Port Jefferson Harbor by the high wooded bluff that marks the northeast point on Strongs Neck. Since the harbor is quite shallow and the controlling depth through the channel is about 5 feet, boats of deep draft should not attempt to enter except at high tide and under power. There is a mean range of tide of about 6½ feet, and it is wise to keep in mid-channel away from the mud flats extending from both shores.

Once well past the shoaling at Tinkers Point and heading due south, you will have good water for ½-mile length in mid-channel until you come abeam of the Setauket Harbor Boat Basin down on the port shore. This inner, very narrow channel is poorly marked by buoys or ranges, some of them uncharted and privately maintained. One often has to wend one's way among the congested boats at their private moorings, since they actually mark the deepest water. One may have difficulty in locating sufficient swinging room in which to drop the hook.

Since dredged channels have a way of filling, we'd advise caution and a flooding tide for yachts entering this harbor for the first time. If your boat doesn't draw too much, however, Setauket is worth trying.

Once you get into the deep area south of Strongs Neck you will probably be glad you came. It is much snugger than Port Jeff and attractive. There is a small boat yard on the east shore of the shallow cove to the south, which can be reached only at high tide.

Mount Sinai, Long Island, N.Y. (12362 361). This harbor, about 2½ miles east of Port Jefferson, is recommended for those who like an evening "away from it all," especially if you have a sailing tender or one with an outboard motor for exploring the shallow inner harbor. The channel entrance can be spotted at the easternmost end of a long high bluff running along the northern shore of Mt. Misery Point. Enter carefully midway between the short jetties, which are usually awash at high water. The one to the east normally has a flashing light on it but was nowhere to be seen on our last visit there. Attempting to negotiate this channel at night without this vital beacon lighting the way is risky business, as was later confirmed to us in a discussion with Mount Sinai Yacht Club officers. Brookhaven is supposedly responsible for its operation but pressure from frustrated local boat owners at the time of writing has been unable to move town officials toward any positive action. The dredged channel, in which the current runs up to 2 knots, has a controlling depth of 8 feet. And the narrow inlet that used to run behind the sandspit to starboard has completely filled in.

Mount Sinai Harbor has undergone quite a change in recent years due to sizable dredging throughout the northern sector of the harbor. Dredging has been completed on a 10-foot-deep channel with a constant width of 1200 feet running eastward all the way from the main entrance channel and passing south of Cedar Beach to the marshes bordering the harbor's eastern shore. Unlighted block buoys maintained by the town mark this channel, in which a speed limit of five mph is strictly enforced. A possible anchorage, therefore, is anywhere you can find swinging room along the southern side of this dredged trough, but most yachtsmen prefer to anchor along the prominent but small spit just southeast of the harbor's entrance.

In 1964 this harbor was blessed by the establishment of a new yacht club—the Mount Sinai Yacht Club, located on the southwestern point of Cedar Beach. It is proudly described by its members as a "working man's" organization, composed of real boating enthusiasts, who are truck drivers, doctors, lawyers, businessmen, teachers, lobstermen, and engineers. Warren Wenberg, the club's first commodore, commented that "we bought the old barge that forms the basis of our clubhouse from the Delhart Shipyard on Staten Island for $800. It had been retired by the B & O Railroad." With perspiration and inspiration, the membership hauled it ashore, converted it into a charming clubhouse, with a bar, restaurant, and fireplace, and constructed a massive concrete bulkhead out in front. We climbed "aboard" to interview the following club officers who couldn't have been more cordial: Commodore John Iberger and Vice Commodore Bruce Toole. When you stop here, you'll find gas, water, ice, perhaps some space dockside, and a few guest moorings.

"Seeing your family doctor tarring the roof alongside a truck driver is one of a hundred examples of the marvelous spirit that has made this club a success," Mr. Wenberg exclaimed. We sensed that same spirit, which we feel certain will be shared by other visiting yachtsmen.

Further up to port lies the Mount Sinai Marina, which, with its 8 floating docks, proves that power boats have at last discovered Mount Sinai. Gas, water, and electricity are all available, but the place is choked with small craft, it's brightly lighted at night, there are no supplies, and the fee for overnight dockage is $10.00. A 6-foot rise in tide is reported here.

Ardent conservationists have been active recently in preserving the beauty of the natural wetlands stretching along the southern and eastern sections of the harbor. Therefore, Davis Island Boat Yard on the southwestern shore and Ralph's Fishing Station across to the east will probably have moved by the time you read this. Check their latest locations with people at the yacht club. Ralph's is scheduled to move next door to the club.

The balance of the harbor is covered with shoal mud flats and marshes, which are often dry at low water. Despite these, Mount Sinai is crowded on weekends, for the place is picturesque and away from the lights and sounds of a town, and the swimming on Cedar Beach is excellent. The land to the west is high, wooded, with many private estates.

A delightful old fisherman with a personality as salty as his looks, who did not give us his name "less the police seek me out," warned us to avoid the uncharted rocks that lie ½ mile off Cedar Beach.

Mattituck Inlet, Long Island, N.Y. (12358 363). During World War II, this harbor was so long neglected that by 1946, a bar with only 1 foot at low water had built up between the outer jetties. Since then, the federal government has often redredged the channel, designated Mattituck as a "port of refuge" and added further improvements to help make the harbor an outstanding one. It is the only available harbor on the north shore of Long Island between Port Jefferson or Mount Sinai and Greenport, making it particularly important to yachtsmen cruising Long Island Sound. More and more boats are visiting here, since it offers excellent protection should sudden storms or foul weather arise. Once you get inside, the harbor provides absolute shelter and a chance to get supplies conveniently, and it is an interesting place withal.

The 1977 *Coast Pilot* reports that, from the 1976 survey taken in Mattituck, the depth at mean low water was 7 feet from the beginning of the entrance channel to a point 650 feet downstream. Previous additional surveys had also shown 7-foot soundings all the way to the bridge at Old Mill Road, where Ye Old Mill Inn is located. Here is recorded slightly less than 5 feet, MLW, but a 7-foot depth is picked up again once you come abeam of Mattituck Inlet Marina and Shipyard; this can be held all the way to and throughout the anchorage basin at the head of the harbor about 1.8 miles above the entrance. Privately maintained buoys string along the entire channel. The mean tide range is about 5 feet.

The entrance to Mattituck Inlet is not easy to identify from some distance away, as the breakwaters, though long, are low. The shore is a low point of white sand between fairly high hills and cliffs on both sides. A long break in the bluffs marks the inlet, further identified by a flashing beacon silhouetted against the prominent tanks of the Mattituck Petroleum Corporation. Entering is difficult should you have a northeast wind and the 3-knot tidal current running against you. Pick up black bell 3A and then head for the tower on the starboard or west jetty, which has a flashing light. An uncharted black can facing this light should be held close to port coming in, for swirling currents have built up extensive shoals stretching out into the channel from the western breakwater. Also watch for shoals further in to port, especially as you approach the first bend.

In coming up the creek, you can find dock space at the Naugles Dock a short way up on the starboard side or tie up at the Anchor Inn bulkhead dock for a meal at the Dock and Dine Restaurant. Nearby, Ye Old Mill Inn (moderately expensive and old world) is preferred by many of the natives. Mattituck Inlet Marina and Shipyard, just above the bridge, has a swimming pool, gas, Diesel fuel, ice, slips with electricity,

Mattituck Inlet on the north shore of Long Island looking southward to the town's basin. Great Peconic Bay lies beyond.

repair work, and the most complete facilities in the harbor.

The Mattituck Park District Marina at the head of the channel has a landing dock a short walk from the center of the village. The basin here lies in quite charming surroundings, with an atmosphere one could describe as homey. On a summer weekend, it attracts as many as fifty boats resting at anchor, with a dozen more at dockside, where the depths are 6 feet, MLW. Although there is considerable seaweed in the basin, the holding ground is reported to be good, providing the anchor is well set in. Use plenty of scope; then take up on the rode. Stuart MacMillan, one of the most accommodating Harbor Masters we have met, is stationed at this marina, where there's an opportunity for a shower or brief dockage. Nearby stores include Raynor & Suter, offering a complete line of nautical equipment, and Mattituck Laundromat, where laundry is done on half-day delivery (no self-service). For a meal you can try Tony's Restaurant or The Chinese Restaurant. The Coffee Pot is best for breakfast. Most of these places are open on Sundays.

Stuart, in his free time, sells Gideon bibles very successfully. Perhaps that's why we listened so intently when he gave us a local fisherman's advice, which we couldn't resist putting into verse:

> When sailing by Long Island Shore,
> A storm approaching from the nor'
> A rising tide will drive away;
> If *falling* tide, make port and pray!

Less than twenty-four hours later, the weather gave us the chance to test its veracity. After being holed up safe and sound in Mt. Sinai during a violent thunder squall, all we can say is that it works!

In 1977 we again visited Matt-A-Mar Marina, run by Frank Nowak on the northeast side of the basin. Frank thrives on business "progress," partly evidenced by the installation of his marina's Olympic-size swimming pool, surrounded by an expansive barbecue area. Almost all of Matt-A-Mar's customers are transients who have access to slips with electricity, gas, Diesel fuel, water, ice, bike rentals, and a snack bar.

A genial Mattituck native named Morrison Wines, whose personality is as appealing as his name, pointed out to us that few yachtsmen take advantage of the pleasant anchorages to be found in the several finger inlets running off of the main channel. Venture up these inlets with their 6-foot depths, keeping in mid-channel, and you will be alone and quiet. The first inlet to starboard is perhaps the choicest, but, as are the others, it is unmarked, so avoid the small island located at its entrance. Should you desire a bit more civilization, you can run all the way to the head of the creek where you will find the aforementioned basin. Mattituck claims that it is "the Village that has everything." We quite agree.

Plum Gut Harbor, Long Island, N.Y. (13209 362). This is a scooped-out puddle, nearly landlocked, with about 14 feet in the entrance and harbor, though some shoaling has occurred. Keep midway between the lighted jetties and head for the wharves, where yachts seeking shelter usually lie. Plum Gut Harbor and the island itself are under the supervision of the U.S. Department of Agriculture, which maintains its Animal Disease Laboratory, "the nation's only research center for the study of contagious foreign animal diseases." It may be used only with the permission of the local representative of that department, as suggested in the following tactful reply to our inquiry: "Ferry or government boats use the wharf daily. Harbor would be sought by yachtsmen only as a harbor of refuge."

A correspondent, writing about Potter Cove in Narragansett Bay, says, "The mosquitoes are bad but not as bad as at Plum Island."

It is reported that Plum Island got its name from early explorers who were enchanted by the beach plums growing along the shore. In 1659 the ruling Indian Chief of Long Island sold this island to the first European owner for a coat, a barrel of biscuits, and one hundred fishhooks.

Plum Gut is a vicious piece of water, where seven currents come together forming a tide rip that can run as high as 10 knots. Although larger vessels stay to the outside of Plum Island, smaller craft heading for Peconic Bay or the south shore of Long Island must transverse the gut.

Many yachtsmen are dismayed to learn that by early 1978, Plum Island Light, a beacon to mariners since 1897, is expected to become deactivated. The familiar stone house, dating back to 1869, stands 75 feet above sea level at the northwestern point of the 850-acre island. Closing of this station will reduce the number of manned lighthouses in Long Island Sound to five: New London Ledge, Race Rock, Little Gull Island, Lynde Point, and Old Saybrook breakwater.

Meanwhile, its companion, the "coffee can" Orient Point light is slated to be upgraded to serve as the prime navigational aid here. The fixed red beacon, 64 feet above sea level, with a visibility of 5 miles, will be improved to a 5-second flashing white light with a range of over 15 miles. Its candlepower will be increased from 1,665 to 11,880, and the foghorn power doubled in intensity.

Whenever the going gets rough, the only visual bearings you can now expect bracketing the Gut are the Orient Point light and, if you can pick them up, the two jetty lights at the entrance to Plum Gut Harbor. The

New London Coast Guard Station will be responsible for the automation of this newly improved aid.

Shelter Island and Shelter Island Sound, Long Island, N.Y. (12358 363). Shelter Island is best known as a delightful summer resort of wooded hills, winding roads, and snug harbors, with a year 'round population of about 2000 and a summer population several times that number. It is a connecting link between the north and south flukes of eastern Long Island. With its five harbors, each providing its own special charm, the island has long been a popular rendezvous for Long Island Sound cruising men.

Though not settled by whites until 1652, Shelter Island, which the Indians called "Ahaquatawamock," had several English owners before then, from whom it successively acquired the names of "Mr. Farrett's Island" and "Mr. Goodyear's Island." In 1651 Mr. Goodyear sold the island for "1,600 pounds of good merchantable Muscavado sugar"— which has been calculated at a valuation of 1¢ an acre, based on the price of sugar at that time. About 150 years ago ships large enough to cross the ocean with a fair-sized cargo were built on Shelter Island, on a tributary of West Neck Creek.

The principal whaling ports on the Atlantic Coast were Provincetown, Nantucket, New Bedford, Fairhaven, New London, and Sag Harbor. Many young men of Shelter Island sailed from the last of these harbors. Whales have been seen or caught between Shelter Island and Greenport.

Eventually Shelter Island became a summer resort, the new era beginning in 1871, when a group of Methodists bought Prospect for their camp meetings. A year later a hotel went up. Now sport fishing and summer visitors, or both, are leading industries.

Just before his death in 1929, Samuel H. Groser wrote a poem about Shelter Island, called "My Playland," in which (as illustrated in the second verse) he expressed his "poignant longing":

> For the wonderful view from its headlands,
> For the clear, cool, starry nights,
> For the gorgeous hues of the sunsets,
> And the harbor with myriad lights;
> For the shady roads through the woodlands,
> For the green on the Dering side,
> For Ram Head, and White Hill, and the beaches,
> For the lap of the lazy tide.*

*Historical data and verse from *History of Shelter Island*, by Ralph G. Duvall, with a Supplement by Jean L. Schladermundt (Shelter Island Heights Association).

While we found the tide anything but lazy, to the rest of these sentiments we would add a hearty assent.

There are two ferry services to and from Shelter Island: one between Greenport and Dering Harbor on the northwest shore and one from the south shore of the island at Smith Cove to North Haven Peninsula and Sag Harbor.

In discussing the harbors on, or across from, Shelter Island, we'll first go around Shelter Island via Shelter Island Sound in a counterclockwise direction. Those who want to go further, into Great and Little Peconic Bays, will find the harbors on these bays covered in the Peconic Bays Section.

1. Greenport, Long Island, N.Y. (12358 363). This is the leading port in the Shelter Island Sound area from the point of view of boat yards, gas docks, marine hardware, and general facilities of all kinds. But it is by no means the most beautiful, and it is noted more as a fishing headquarters than as a rendezvous for yacht club fleets, though the Essex Station of the Cruising Club of America has found Stirling Basin, Greenport, a more satisfactory and protected harbor for its annual cruise than Dering.

As you approach the town, the white church spire near the northern end, and the standpipe that shows up over the center, are good landmarks. The flashing red Greenport Harbor Light, on the end of the breakwater off Youngs Point, is the most obvious guide for those entering at night.

While many boats anchor southwest of the breakwater, this anchorage is frequently very uneasy, as the sound is apt to be choppy along here and there is a considerable sweep from the southwest. The best place for the night by far is in Stirling Basin, which has been dredged to a depth of 8 feet at low water. Bush stakes mark the edges of the basin's shoal areas. Since this harbor is tight for space and has considerable boating traffic, anchoring is not recommended. It is better to follow up the 100-foot-wide channel with 9-foot depth leading up to the head of the basin. In the western fork is situated the rather swanky Townsend Manor Marina, boasting an attractive colonial-style hotel and restaurant and offering weary crews a dip into the swimming pool or into a cocktail. Use of the pool is included in the dockage fee. Their services also include gas, ice, water, showers, and fifty slips with electrical connections and a mechanic on call. This marina provides peaceful protection and the opportunity to visit the center of town, only a fifteen-minute walk away. Just to the south along the basin's shore, you'll pass Pell's Fish Market, an excellent source for the freshest of seafood.

By far the most impressive marina in Stirling Basin is the Stirling By The Sea Marina, which can also claim to be one of the finest and most immaculate on the eastern coast. It assures its visitors security and tranquility within a 10-acre parklike setting at the end of the eastern fork. The facilities are just too numerous to list here; these are just a few: complete dock service including gas, Diesel fuel, and ice; showers; a sauna; washers and dryers; fixed docks and floating finger slips for yachts up to 85 feet with 10-foot depth alongside; a fresh-water swimming pool; and the elegant Boathouse Restaurant, affording a panoramic view of the harbor. All types of repair work can be undertaken; there's even a bubbling system, for the marina is open all year round. Bike rentals, and, nearby, a golf course, tennis courts, a riding stable, and picnic grounds all help make this a great spot for family fun. Slip reservations should be made at least twenty-four hours in advance of your arrival by phoning (516) 477-0828.

There are several large shipyards along the Greenport waterfront between Stirling Basin and the ferry slip. Greenport Yacht and Shipbuilding in this area is well equipped to do all kinds of work. Along the bight west of the ferry slip can be bought gas to suit every taste, as well as Diesel fuel.

Nearby, the town, resembling a slice of New England, furnishes a wide variety of everything, including marine hardware, charts, and antiques and paintings in a fascinating store run by S.T. Preston & Son since 1888. The oldest family-owned restaurant in the United States, Claudio's Restaurant and Marina at the foot of Main Street, has a fine reputation among cruising yachtsmen, due in part to its succulent seafood and ocean-fresh lobster. To the west, Mitchell's Marina & Restaurant is a bit less expensive and formal but also provides dock space to its patrons. It's close to a fishing supply store and market. At both these places we were told that "you don't have to climb into any fancy dress to eat in here." Such an open invitation reminded us of how a dedicated Greenport fisherman once admonished a roving reporter with these salty words: "You want cocktail parties, you head on over to the Southside. You wanna be yourself, you stay over here on the North Fork." So far as we know, there is no important yacht club on the Greenport water front; the nearest is across Shelter Island Sound at Dering Harbor.

Greenport has direct rail connection with New York City, while Cross Sound Ferry Services, Inc. operates a ferry daily between Orient Point and New London. First called Stirling, then Greenhill, and finally named Greenport in the early nineteenth century, this is a splendid place to meet guests, fit out, leave the boat for a while, or enjoy the bustling, boaty atmosphere. It's one of the few places left on the East Coast where you can see commercial fishing trawlers unload their catch.

You can also catch a glimpse of history, for it was at Orient Point that Benedict Arnold, after deserting the Patriot cause, launched raids on Connecticut. At the head of Village Lane, across from the monument on the corner of Route 25, the buttonwood tree under which the Patriots gathered on July 4, 1776, still stands today.

Northeast toward Orient Point lies Gull Pond, set between Youngs Point and Cleaves Point. It is a secure basin for craft drawing 3 feet or less; a launching ramp is at the entrance. Although the chart shows a depth of 6 feet in the 35-foot narrow entrance between the jetties, only about 3 feet can be carried over an outer bar at low water. Once inside, however, the controlling depth throughout most of the pond is 5 feet MLW. Be sure, however, to stay at least 40 feet off the marshes running along the port shore. The private moorings should also be given wide berth when dropping anchor here. Part of this place's charm comes from its snugness, its lack of commercialism, and the attractive appearance of the private homes gathered along the eastern shore. Two creeks running north from the pond have been dredged to good depths for further gunk-holing. The northwest channel leading to a smaller hole is preferable to the one that stretches northward.

2. Dering Harbor, Shelter Island, N.Y. (12358 363). If you want to see a fine-looking collection of sailing yachts, you will find them at Dering Harbor at almost any time during the summer months. They may be on a cruise of the Off Soundings, the Storm Trysail, a Corinthian fleet, or perhaps an American Yacht Club rendezvous, or just a lot of handsome yachts following their own inclinations. The harbor is attractive, and the Shelter Island Yacht Club, on the point to starboard of the entrance, is most hospitable to members of other recognized yacht clubs. The clubhouse has undergone a complete modernization, with the installation of a restaurant and bar accommodating 210 people.

The only objection to Dering Harbor is that it is very uncomfortable in northwesters. The Essex Station of the Cruising Club of America moved to Stirling Basin at Greenport for that reason. However, the protection is good with winds from all other directions, and we have stayed there many times in complete comfort, usually finding friends among the fleet, savoring the keen enjoyment that comes from watching yachts coming in to find anchorage while we are already well fixed for the night.

In entering, be sure to stay well off the northern tip of Shelter Island Heights, where shoaling to 4 feet has been reported. Depths throughout the harbor are ample, though behind the yacht club hook of land, the chart shows 4 feet, and the area is too small, anyway, to offer protection to many yachts in northwesters. The club offers 15 guest moorings at an overnight charge of $5.00 each, with launch service running from 8 A.M. to 9 P.M. on weekdays and from 8 A.M. to midnight on weekends. We have found the holding ground to be excellent.

Gas, Diesel fuel, water, ice, showers, a laundromat, a shore meal, and supplies, including spirits, can all be obtained near the head of the harbor at Dering Harbor Marina, located to the north of Chases Creek. This marina has 25 slips, with 12 feet at its outer dock, a swimming pool, and even tennis courts. Just to the east, the festive new Dering Harbor Inn provides a pier where you can tie up for food or sport. Its management says they will come to meet you if you're over at the yacht club. The Chequit Inn, not far from Dering Harbor, offers nightly entertainment. Good eating places include The Catch-All, serving wines and cheeses; The Dory Restaurant, dishing up tasty seafood at moderate prices; and The Cook, located up the street from the yacht club, with about the best food on the island but "it ain't cheap." Greenport is easily reached by ferry, if any of your crew want to see a movie or catch a train to New York. The ferry runs every twenty minutes, with the last trip from Greenport scheduled at 12:30 P.M.

The harbor is named for Thomas Dering, of an ancient Saxon family, who married a Shelter Island girl and took up residence there in 1760, to become a leading citizen. But if you throw a stone into a crowd on Shelter Island, you'll probably hit a Tuthill. And then you may get into trouble, for he'll probably be supervisor of the island.

3. Southold, Long Island, N.Y. (12358 363). In checking our latest charts at the time of writing, we noted that there was 6½ feet at MLW at the channel entrance to Southold, that Jockey Creek carried 6 feet for the most part down the middle, and that Town Creek showed about a foot more of depth all the way to its head. These depths are good for a width of about 75 feet except for the reported shoaling in Town Creek to 4½ feet at low water. The harbor entrance is marked not only by a prominent tower and a small red buoy but by bulkheads and sandy beaches to both port and starboard. Uncharted red-and-black vertical stakes clearly identify the channel, which is rimmed by extremely shoal water. Make your approach from due east and you will not run into trouble. At the docks, just inside to starboard, the depths are not greater than in the channel. Many good-sized motor cruisers were tied up at the slips.

These docks on Founders Landing offer you the deepest water at any

marina in Southold and belong to Goldsmith's Boat Shop, which provides gas, water, electricity, and telephone, besides repairs, hauling,
and limited dockage. While you will have plenty of neighbors and little
privacy if tied up at the dock, and the surroundings of a boat yard are
not usually ideal, this place is well protected. A suitable anchorage may
be found up Jockey Creek; or, as we did, run up to the head of Town
Creek, which is not only a pleasant spot but extremely convenient to the
Southold Town Dock.

The unpretentious Southold Yacht Club is on the northern tip of
Paradise Point.

4. West Neck Harbor, Shelter Island, N.Y. (12358 363). Based on our
latest visit here, we have three important words of advice to yachtsmen
negotiating the channel's entrance—proceed with caution! Certain natural changes are taking place here, and there are no immediate plans
for dredging. The tidal current has become swifter and the bar marked
on the chart as a 2-foot spot has extended very close to the tip end of
Shell Beach. This bar across the channel has just 4 feet over it at low
water but fortunately the clean water enables you to sight the shoaling
bottom off to starboard as you enter from the southeast. Although the
latest chart shows a green flasher on the sand spit to port, none was
observed there in 1977. However, there was a red-lighted buoy off the
entrance, which should be kept to starboard coming in. Keep the single
black marker close to your port.

After passing the inner marker, swing to port and run parallel and
fairly close to Shell Beach, making sure to avoid the middle ground to
starboard, and noting the sign that says "anchor no closer than 400 feet
offshore." After you have run along about two-thirds of the length of
Shell Beach, swing northwest toward the neck marking the entrance to
West Neck Creek. As you pass the neck be sure to give it a wide berth
while avoiding the 4-foot spot in mid-channel just beyond. The entrance can be further identified by a flagpole ahead on the port shore
and by a large harbor sign, which should be left to starboard. Having
passed all of this, keep generally in the middle. The channel into West
Neck Bay has been shoaling up in recent years, and our soundings in
1977 showed 6 feet at low water where 10 feet appear on the chart.

While in very hot weather it would probably be cooler in the wide part
of the lower harbor or in West Neck Bay at the other end, the snuggest
and prettiest anchorages are in West Neck Creek in one of the spots
where it widens out. A very good place for dropping your hook is in the
bight with 5-foot depth just before West Neck Creek turns to the west
into West Neck Bay. Here there is a deeply shelving beach for easy

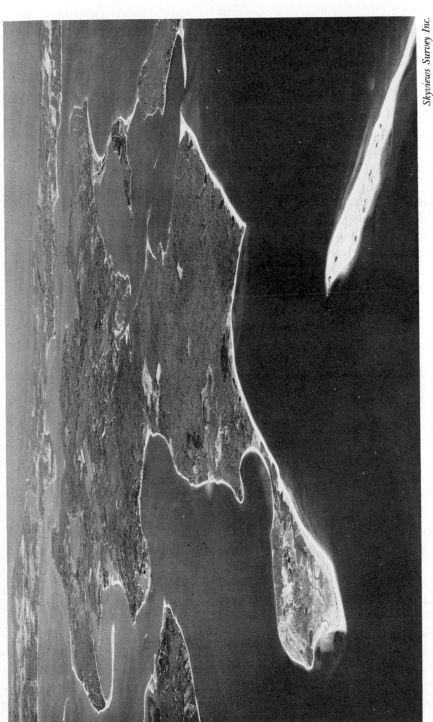

Shelter Island looking north. Clockwise from Mashomack Point in Lower left lies Majors Harbor, Smith Cove, and West Neck Harbor. At the top of the photograph Dering Harbor faces Greenport and on the right can be seen Coecles Harbor and its entrance.

landing and a road leading to a store only ¾ mile away. Further up in West Neck Bay, the best anchorages are either near the docks along the southeastern shore or to the port or starboard of the small point that juts out from the northern shore.

West Neck Harbor is one of the most attractive, unspoiled, and well-protected harbors in the entire Shelter Island-Peconic Bay area. It is unfortunate that the chart depths are so deceptive. With the prevailing tidal difference of about 2½ feet, sailing yachts drawing no more than 5 feet should have no difficulty in entering, except at low tide. Most motor cruisers will have no trouble at any time if they stick to the channel.

Supplies are obtainable at Dering Harbor a mile or so away, but if you want to cook your own clam chowder, join the clam diggers along the inside of the long sandspit.

A long-time boat yard on the northeasterly shore of the wide part of West Neck Harbor apparently was one of the many Shelter Island marinas plagued by the ravages of the record-breaking winter ice of 1976. On our last visit, we could still see evidence of how masses of ice can uproot docks and spiles. Hopefully, when you visit West Neck, this old marine landmark will again be servicing boats of under 3-foot draft.

5. Smith Cove, Shelter Island, N.Y. (12358 363). On southern Shelter Island, this cove offers an attractive anchorage amidst quiet surroundings reminiscent of the Coast of Maine. There is a nice beach under a fairly high bluff, and you will find that deep water runs surprisingly close to the shore. While it is open to the southeast, it is well protected in winds from other directions. A small marina named Shelter Island Marina & Fishing Station is installed on the west shore, so that supplies, unobtainable heretofore, can now be secured. They can furnish gas, ice, water, marine supplies, a laundromat, showers, and slip space with electricity. Transportation to town is provided, with a market and motel nearby. It is hoped that marina owner Clifford Tuttle didn't head off for Bora Bora, as he threatened to do after his docks disintegrated during the tragic ice storm of 1976.

For those boats anchoring in the harbor, no trespassing along private shore-front property is permitted. The ferry to North Haven Peninsula and Sag Harbor runs from Smith Cove.

6. Majors Harbor, Shelter Island, N.Y. (12358 363). About a mile southeast of Smith Cove, Majors Harbor provides the same kind of protection in northerly winds and exposure to the south. On entering the harbor from the north, one should keep well to starboard of the rocks lying off Majors Point and shown on the chart. Spread out before you appears a sandy crescent-shaped beach bordered by a colorful tree line and tall grass. The clear, clean water and smooth bottom will tempt your crew to take a swim in perfect solitude, while the romantic appearance of the land calls for a picnic or further adventures along the shore. We were tempted to do so until we noticed signs reading "Beware of dogs. No fishing, hunting or trespassing under penalty of the law."

7. *Sag Harbor, Long Island, N.Y.* (*12358 363*). This harbor is well protected from all seas by the breakwater, on the western end of which stands a high skeleton tower marked by a flashing white light. There is plenty of room for anchorage behind this breakwater, but the Sag Harbor Yacht Club to the starboard—or west—of the large oil tanks (which don't add to the harbor's beauty) may just have a mooring, but no launch service. Here all yachtsmen are welcomed whether or not they are affiliated with any yacht club. There is 8 feet at the outer dock and 6 feet in the slips, where gas, water, Diesel fuel, ice, and electricity are obtainable. There is a moderate charge for overnight dockage, and although there is no club restaurant, food and supplies may be purchased in the center of town nearby. An excellent launching ramp lies in the small inner basin. The club, founded in 1898, is housed in a trim little blue-and-white building, formerly a New York Yacht Club station on Shelter Island. It was slid over the ice to its new home one wintry day in 1920.

From the clubhouse, we observed to the east a large, clear-span boat shed—a practical solution to small-boat storage. This place is called Malloy Boat Yard, where hundreds of small boats can be easily "dry-landed," stacked up piggy-back fashion on racks like so many colorful cords of wood. This system serves a number of unique purposes. It is an answer to the belief that marinas and mooring areas have not been able to keep pace with the number of boats owned by Long Islanders, which is expected to double in the next decade. Indoor storage can usually double the life of a boat, and its owner, using such a "high-and-dry" marina, may use his craft year round by just picking up the phone. Malloy has moorings available, gas, Diesel fuel, a ship's store, can do engine and electronics repairs and has a sailmaker, Dave Khammers.

West of the yacht club is the steel-bulkheaded Suffolk County Long Dock, where visitors may tie up with a seventy-two-hour limit. The *Mystic Whaler* ties up at the east face of this dock during her regular visits to Sag Harbor. The windmill at the foot of this pier is a tourist information office, where you can quickly learn how to make the most of your stay.

Do not attempt to go into Sag Harbor after dark; there are too many outlying shoals and unlighted buoys, especially off the eastern shore of North Haven Peninsula. A particularly dangerous spot is Little Gull Island, formed by a cluster of rocks just south of lighted buoy 13. In daylight, the entrance presents no difficulties.

The channel up into Sag Harbor Cove just west of the main harbor has been dredged to a width of 75 feet and a depth of about 8 feet, and is marked by privately maintained buoys. If you can pass under the fixed bridge with its vertical clearance of 20 feet at mean high water, you will find first to port Whalers Marina, convenient to the center of town. Further up to port lies the red dockhouse of Baron's Marina, offering similar services to yachtsmen. There's 8 feet at low water at its outer dock and about 4 feet in the bulkheaded basin, where boats up to 60 feet can take on gas, Diesel fuel, water, electricity, and ice. For the crew there are a swimming pool, snack bar, laundromat, showers, groceries, and an excellent motel and restaurant across the road, Baron's Cove Inn. Gristede's supermarket is in a brick colonial building nearby. The only real drawback at both of these marinas is their lack of repair service. They both monitor VHF-16 for reservations.

You may wish to venture further by following the buoyed channel to the west, leading you to Long Beach, where there is excellent swimming on the Noyack Bay side. Although it appears from the chart that 7 feet can be carried around Brush Neck, the deepest water has not been marked, and all we saw were a few small powerboats. Check at Baron's before taking this passage. The area up there is pleasantly surrounded by houses tucked along the shore.

In town, a whaling museum is open to the public and some interesting old doorways can be seen. Sag Harbor came to share with New Bedford, Fair Haven, Nantucket, and New London, among a few others, the distinction of being one of America's leading whaling ports. In 1845, it had sixty-three whaling vessels. We were reminded of all this when we suddenly stumbled upon a weathered old keel alongshore the yacht club. Saltair Industries recently gave this 92-foot keel to the Mystic Seaport, where marine historians verified that the timbers belonged to the old whaleship *Thames*. The *Thames* first sailed out of Sag Harbor in 1818, ending her days as a breakwater near Conklin's Point.

8. Coecles Harbor, Shelter Island, N.Y. (*12358 363*). In 1975, the controlling depth in the entrance channel to this harbor was 7 feet, offering a first-rate place for a large fleet of yachts. Coecles, pronounced like the word "cockles," is well marked by privately maintained tripods, beacons, and buoys. The best plan is to head in from a point nearly perpendicular to the eastern shore of Ram Island to reach lighted black can 1 about ½ mile due east of Reel Point. Keep in mid-channel while passing between the red flashing beacon set on the end of the spit to starboard and black can 5 to port. Once well beyond the entrance, steer dead ahead or make a broad swing to port according to where you want to go and the anchorage that provides the best protection from the prevailing wind. Coecles Harbor is large and unfavorable in northeast winds.

The most popular anchorages are as follows: (1) in the first large bight to the south of the entrance. This is very pretty and more "away from it all" than other anchorages. Be sure to clear can 5 before turning to enter this bight; (2) in the first bight to the north after entering. Here some yachts are moored and there are a number of private docks; (3) in the second or third bights to the north; (4) at the dock or on the moorings of Coecles Harbor Marina & Boatyard located on the upper western shore of the harbor, just beyond a small island. Keep the red nuns close to starboard in making your approach. This first-class dock, which is F-shaped, has 6 feet of water at its outer end and room for fifty boats. Here you'll find most required services for boat and sailor. There are complete hauling facilities as well as full-time mechanics capable of performing practically any type of repair work. Gas, Diesel fuel, water, ice, pump-out service, and electricity are available at the berths; ashore you can find showers, a laundromat, marine store, snack bar, swimming pool, and even bike rentals. Grocery orders taken by the dock attendants will be delivered to you. Arrangements can be made for transportation to local restaurants like the Dering Harbor Inn.

Coecles Harbor is pretty and unspoiled by commercial activities, though too large to be snug, like West Neck Creek, for example. There is comparatively little traffic in the harbor, and particularly in the southern bight just beyond the entrance you may have the place almost to yourself.

Along the neck that connects Ram Island with the rest of Shelter Island are some huge osprey nests, perched on the tops of telegraph poles.

It can be rough at the entrance of Coecles Harbor when the wind blows strongly from often-turbulent Gardiners Bay, so use care in entering. Once inside, you can find protection from any wind by choosing the right bight.

Peconic Bays (Great and Little), Long Island, N.Y. (12358 363).

In discussing the harbors along the two Peconic Bays, we shall again follow a counterclockwise course, as we leave Shelter Island Sound and enter Little Peconic Bay, heading for Nassau Point. There are still no good harbors on the north shore until this point is rounded. However, those skippers whose boats are shallow draft and who are dying to discover new gunk-holes may want to poke into two dredged creeks located in the extreme northwestern end of Hog Neck Bay. There is about 6 feet of water in the channel leading into and connecting with a number of shorter finger channels inside of Corey Creek, which is shown on the chart as due east of Laughing Water. And just to the southwest, red privately maintained stakes mark the 7-foot channel running to the tip of Indian Neck and then westward into Richmond Creek. Through all these very narrow channels, one must proceed cautiously, while following the markers closely. You won't find any facilities, only enchanting surroundings. Should you decide to anchor for the night in one of the creeks, allow for the effects of current and run up your anchor light.

One of the authors will not soon forget a struggle he once had trying to bring his sloop around high and wooded Nassau Point from Hog Neck Bay, in the face of a rising easterly gale. There is a long and dangerous shoal, which we first had to weather. Never did a port look better to us than the tiny private lagoon, which we found in the lee of the point.

1. Cutchogue Harbor, Little Peconic Bay (12358 363). Across Cutchogue Harbor, which as a whole is fairly open to winds from southwest to southeast, there is a "barb" of what looks like a Nassau Point "spear." This forms a shelter (known as the Horseshoe) from southerly winds and is often used for this purpose by boats drawing 6 feet or less. There are no landing facilities except a sand beach and no supplies. A preferred anchorage is along the inner western shore of the barb.

Nassau Point is hilly and occupied by many attractive estates, several of which have their own lagoons. Channels have been dredged into Haywater and Broadwater coves, to the north, which offer good dinghy sailing. The vicinity is full of creeks and you never can tell where you will find an unexpected harbor.

There is a 2-knot flow and 6-foot depth through the main channel leading to East and Mud creeks running to the northwest and to Haywater and Broadwater coves running to the east. Follow the middle of the channel, keeping the red stakes fairly close to starboard. As you pass the sandspit to starboard, don't cut around it sharply to the east or you'll probably run aground in shallow Haywater Cove. Rather, maintain your original course as you detour around the east shore of the large grassy island located north of the entrance.

Here you'll find yourself in the middle of a waterway labyrinth, but it is an easy matter to run due north, following the red stakes leading into Mud Creek, where we sounded 8 feet all the way up. A prettier passage is promised by following the eastward, staked channel into Broadwater Cove. Favor the port side of this channel to its head in the northwest quadrant of the cove. An anchorage here offers complete seclusion in 5 feet at MLW. There are slightly greater depths in the staked channel in East Creek, which unfortunately leads into a tiny, barren mudhole. With the very limited traffic running through these marshy creeks, however, one is fairly free to select the anchorage of his choice—one which will guarantee sufficient swinging room, water under one's keel, and a view that's most pleasing to the eye.

If you do not draw over 5 feet with sail or power, you can make a delightful stop at fairly sizable, well-maintained Boatmen's Harbor, which has slips and general services with a mechanic on duty and is located off Marsh Point at the starboard entrance to Wickham Creek. A small town dock also permits two-hour docking. We might note here that there is bad shoaling off to port as you make your approach. The staked entrance channel is extremely narrow but deep along its middle. There's 7 feet off the marina's slips, which afford unusual peace, security, and a broad view of wetlands to the west. The creek has little room for an anchorage. Even the Southold Town Police can be found docking here.

2. New Suffolk, Little Peconic Bay (12358 363). On the point on the west side of the entrance of Cutchogue Harbor is an intriguing little lagoon. It is known as Schoolhouse Creek and shows on the chart as a tiny "slit" in the shore, just north of the streets of New Suffolk. Its entrance can be spotted approximately 500 yards north of the North Fork Shipyard and the adjacent fishing docks. The channel is marked by red stakes and a piling to port. As you approach, shoaling can be seen off to starboard and also along the inner bulkhead to port with its projecting rocks. Don't try it under sail, but if you have power, keep in the middle. The channel frequently fills in and then gets dredged again, so check up on dredging operations. The tide rises about 3½ feet. Depths at most ebb tides are 6 feet in the channel, most recently dredged in 1976.

Inside the entrance, the controlling depths remain at 5 feet, and you will find on both sides of two narrow forked channels rows of slips occupied by numerous motorboats, large and small—almost all equipped for taking out fishing parties. It gives perfect protection. George Moore, one of the local fishermen, rode out the 1938 hurricane here in complete security.

In May and June nearly every slip is taken by pleasure boats, for that is the big season for flounder and weakfish. Later there are a few vacant slips. New Suffolk Shipyard, between the forks of the channel where the depth is reported as about 4 feet at its gas dock, has a few slips, is a handy source for supplies, and is equipped to repair boats up to 40 feet, but for any major work, the North Fork Shipyard is preferable. School-house Creek has much of the atmosphere of a Down East fishing village. Near this basin is the site of the first submarine base in America, where the U.S.S. *Holland,* first submarine commissioned by the U.S. Navy, was based for trials between 1899 and 1905.

Just to the south of the creek entrance are two breakwaters. The one nearest to the end of the point, on the south, belongs to the town. Here's as tiny a basin as you'll find anywhere, but it affords good protection and depth. Run out both bow and stern anchors. A launching ramp can be observed ashore. Between this breakwater and the creek is another small town basin, with more than 10 feet of water, enclosed by a partly submerged breakwater and piles. You can tie up here, get gas, and, nearby, supplies, and be well protected except from strong easterlies. New Suffolk has good eating places and stores, with fishing-party signs and bait on all sides. Just one step away from North Fork Shipyard's docks, the quaint Galley Ho Restaurant has often served us the very best food this side of Greenport.

3. Mattituck, Great Peconic Bay (12358 363). On a heading west toward Mattituck, you will pass through North Race leaving can 3 to port and nun 4 to starboard to avoid the nasty bar running all the way from this nun northward to the mainland. Readers who are fascinated by the migratory habits of animals might be interested in learning of reports that deer have been spotted crossing North Race on their way to and from Robins Island. Their familiarity with the rules of the road has yet to be determined.

Although there is at present 5 feet at low water at the entrance to James Creek, there is a 3-foot rise in tide, making this inlet a possible harbor of refuge for a small craft caught in foul weather along the northern shore of Great Peconic Bay. The creek entrance can be identified by taking a bearing on the prominent flagpole just west of the entrance or on the lighted sign of the small Mattituck Marina at night. After having left the red-marked private stakes close to starboard outside the creek, favor the port side of the channel once you're past the breakwater. You will experience very little tide rip. When you swing past the first bend to starboard, you will spot the small Mattituck Marina, situated on grassy mud banks but surrounded by some attractive private estates. Mr. Strong, the manager, offered us gas and water and advised us that boats over 30 feet should not enter this inlet because of the lack of turning and anchorage space. The upper end of the narrow channel to the west has been dredged to 5 feet where the red stakes must be kept close aboard. The best way to find a peaceful refuge here is to take a slip at the marina if one is vacant or, if you must, to anchor just beyond the marina where the channel opens up.

4. South Jamesport, Flanders Bay (12358 363). The facilities of the South Jamesport Boat Marina make this small harbor the finest presently available in the entire western part of Great Peconic Bay. Its entrance is just west of Miamogue Point and can be detected at night by a flashing red light set out by the South Jamesport Boat Marina. Approach the channel entrance from the south running between flashing red buoy 4 and black can 5 until you reach three prominent striped stakes, which should be left closely to port. The two outer stakes are lighted. The channel depth is 6 feet at low water, with a 3½-foot rise and fall in tide. The harbor's entrance, further identified by a prominent wharf, is very narrow, having a width of only 40 feet. Further on to starboard you'll note the marina's basin, which has been dredged to a depth of about 6 feet and has accommodated yachts up to 55 feet in length. We have enjoyed our visits at this facility, made hospitable by its owner, Richard Ragazzi. You'll find a 45-ton Travelift, complete repair work, supplies, floating docks, and a chance for a stroll around the nearby summer colony. The Dreamers Cove Restaurant caters to visiting yachtsmen and extends cab service to them. This is a much more practical and attractive stopover than Riverhead to the west.

The Town of Riverhead has dredged and bulkheaded a well-protected basin in the lower half of East Creek just ½ mile northeast of Miamogue Point. A lighted red piling stands well off the entrance to the southeast. On our last visit, we lined up with the range reflectors located at the entrance and passed between the two prominent sandspits. Stay in the middle and swing to starboard into the basin, giving the starboard shore fairly good berth. You can anchor here, tie up to the bulkheads surrounding the basin, or run in to the modest Riverhead Town Marina on the eastern shore, where overnight slips are available.

Gas, water, ice, electricity, and a small store can be found here. This place is appealingly different and provides an excellent launching ramp. There's at least 6 feet of clear water in the basin. Everywhere you look there is sand, which has helped to form an unspoiled swimming beach to the east. We predict that this will become a popular spot.

5. Aquebogue, Flanders Bay (12358 363). Proceeding west from lighted buoy 9, near the entrance to the Peconic River, you can pick up the red-and-black private buoys marking the narrow channel leading into Meetinghouse Creek, reportedly redredged in 1975 to 10 feet throughout. Pass close to the light off the point, keeping it to starboard. Further in on the starboard shore rests the modern, clean-looking Larry's Lighthouse Marina. This is the finest overall marina to be found in Flanders Bay. Its manager, Larry Galasso, mentioned its services, which include gas, water, ice, showers, electricity, a laundromat, a minimum charge of $6.00 at the slips, complete repair work with a Travelift, a well-stocked marine store, and the Poopdeck Clam Bar and Restaurant. Food supplies may be purchased at a general store located at the head of the creek. Whether you stay at the marina or anchor in the northern end of the channel, as a port of call Meetinghouse Creek is much to be preferred over busy and commercial Riverhead. Larry monitors VHF Channel 16 and CB Channel 13. Boats can even anchor in the dredged 7-foot channels off Terrys Creek to the west of Indian Island or up into Reeves Creek to the east, but do so with caution, since markers may not be there to guide you.

6. Riverhead, Flanders Bay (12358 363). This anchorage is in the Peconic River, on the west side of the large, difficult, and shoal Flanders Bay. Unless you have some strong reason for going to Riverhead, our advice is to skip it. The channel is narrow, commercial, and unattractive. There are several small boat yards. Visiting craft tie up at piles along the shore. Riverhead is a good-sized town.

7. Red Creek Pond, Great Peconic Bay (12358 363). Red Creek Pond, lying to the east of Red Cedar Point, has been opened up to permit visits from boats of under 4-foot draft. Privately maintained buoys mark the narrow channel, in which we recorded a depth of about 5 feet at low water in 1977. Favor the lighted black buoy on entering. The pond offers privacy, and except for a few attractive summer houses, it has kept its primordial charm. There are no markers within, so it is wise to anchor in or close to the end of the dredged channel halfway down along the eastern shore. We saw a number of small auxiliary sloops anchored snugly in this area. The pond's bottom is said to be mud.

8. *Shinnecock Canal Basin, Great Peconic Bay (12358 363)*. If you wish to find shelter for the night in the southern part of Great Peconic Bay and your boat doesn't draw over 5 feet, go into the basin at the northerly entrance of the Shinnecock Canal. It is just to port as you enter, and you can tie up at the bulkhead, but not for more than 7 days. One must obtain a permit for a longer stay. This basin, in which the Shinnecock Marina is located, belongs to Suffolk County, has a dock master, water, electricity, pump-out facilities, showers, and heads. Docking fees cover from midnight to midnight or any part thereof. No swirling from the canal's current is felt here. At the basin's outer edge you'll find a rig to unstep your mast should you desire to proceed south through the canal. A fine swimming beach is located just to the north.

The mile-long canal has been dredged to a controlling depth of 5 feet above the locks and to a depth of 4½ feet below them. In 1966 it was reported that the approach to the mouth of the canal had been dredged to a depth of 10 feet.

Corrigan's Yacht Basin, which apparently caters to sports fishermen, is located on the starboard shore north of the railroad bridge. There is 8 feet of water off the slips. Gas, Diesel fuel, water, electricity, ice, marine supplies, and complete repair service can be found here. Many of the marinas along the canal have courtesy cars for use in picking up supplies.

Below Corrigan's lies the Shinnecock Yacht Yard & Marina, a division of Saltair Industries, Inc. It boasts a 40-ton hoist and complete and elaborate facilities, including the only laundromat on the canal.

If your craft is a power boat with a mast height of under 20 feet and a draft of under 4½ feet, you may go, preferably at high tide, through the Shinnecock Canal, explore the great bays along the outer Long Island shore, and poke your nose out into the Atlantic. We were told that there is some shoaling at the gates just below the first bridge, where the current runs about 1½ knots. When the gates are opened to permit the flow to set south through the canal, currents can build up to a nasty 5 knots. There is no difficulty in gaining passage through the gates if one observes their lights and signals three blasts of one's horn.

The Skipper's Motel on the starboard shore below the second bridge can guarantee the whole family a quiet night ashore in attractive surroundings at reasonable prices. Patrons can tie up at the motel's docks in 4 feet of water. Natives of Shinnecock recommend Judge's Sea Food

Restaurant near the second bridge as the place to go for the best in meals.

Cold Spring Pond, whose entrance lies a mile east of the canal, is now a possible harbor for boats of 3-foot draft and under. Enter between nun 2 and lighted buoy 1 while heading between the stakes and on a direct line with the center of the entrance's mouth. Be prepared to face a fairly strong current. The main channel inside runs east and then southward into a 4-foot dredged basin that resembles a key on the chart. Skippers should not enter the pond without local knowledge.

9. Sebonac Creek, Southampton, Great Peconic Bay (12358 363). The lowlying entrance to this very appealing creek may be spotted just to the north of the famous National Golf Links of America Course, situated on rolling hills. From lighted buoy 35, approach the channel entrance lined with red-and-black styrofoam block buoys. The depth at the entrance in 1977 was 8 feet. A white range light rises off the sandy point to port and shortly beyond stands a red-lighted range tower in midstream. Keep this to starboard as you wend your way up the marked creek, which has shoaled to a depth of 5 feet at low water all the way in.

One-half mile in on the port side, the private Bull Head Yacht Club has a first-class dock, with 4½ feet at low tide, at the end of a road leading to the northeast shore of Bullhead Bay. It provides slips, moorings, fresh water, electricity, and gas, as well as rest rooms and showers housed in a fine new clubhouse. All the docks have been built and maintained by the club's hard-working membership. The best anchorage for deep-draft boats is in 7 feet of water off the northeastern shore of Ram Island facing the club docks. The town dock next to the club has 5 feet at MLW, but watch out for a large submerged rock lying 100 feet off its outer end and further marked by a red-and-black buoy. Phone Sal's Market for food supplies.

Bull Head's members say that their neighbor, a New York lawyer named Pincus, has the perfect commute. He flies his seaplane daily from his home on Ram Island to the East River skyport.

This is one of the best ports in the Peconic Bay area, affording excellent protection in easterly winds, a 2½-foot rise and fall in tide, and most scenic surroundings.

10. North Sea Harbor, Little Peconic Bay (12358 363). This is another harbor that looks impossible for all but craft with drafts of under 2 or 3 feet and the *Coast Pilot* confirms that it is "an excellent harbor of refuge for boats with drafts not exceeding 3½ feet." Any greater draft should not attempt the channel, especially at low water, since the 6½-foot depth at MLW charted as of 1967 is misleading. Soundings within the channel in 1977 indicated much silting, with recordings of an average depth of only 5 feet at MLW. Enter the narrow channel between the light to starboard and can 1. Favor cans 3 and 5 further upchannel but don't get too close to the port shore at the first bend for you may interfere with the casting of some fisherman. Your boat will face a rather fierce current should you try to enter this harbor at ebb tide.

There is a bulkhead inside to port just beyond a bridge to Conscience Point. Don't go beyond here without local knowledge; there are some unmarked shoals. The small North Sea Marina can be found on the southwestern shore of the harbor, but use caution in getting here, for there are no markers inside. The bottom is soft, with good holding ground.

At present, this harbor is much less appealing to us than nearby Wooley Pond, which is to be preferred in almost all respects.

In 1640, colonists from Lynn, Massachusetts, landed on Conscience Point and founded Southampton, the first English settlement in New York State.

11. Wooley Pond, Little Peconic Bay (12358 363). This is a fascinating little place on the eastern shore of Little Peconic Bay, providing good protection even in northerly winds. A large and sturdy lighted black beacon and nun 2 show the well-concealed entrance through which the tide rushes fast, continually piling up sand dunes on both shores. In 1976, the entire channel was dredged to a depth of 8 feet at low water, but from examining surveys of this harbor over the years, we cannot expect this depth to hold for long without periodic maintenance. Favor the red nun on entering, then try to keep in the middle of the channel while avoiding the visible shoals on either hand, one to port, which you reach first, and then one to starboard just inside. Once past the entrance and its Scylla and Charybdis, you swing sharply to starboard and follow a fairly straight channel into Wooley Pond, favoring the nuns all the way in.

The scenery is pleasant, but the pond is restrictive; don't anchor if you draw more than 3 feet. Proceed, instead, to the foot of the marked channel and tie up to starboard at the docks of the Peconic Marina in 5 feet of water. There are no moorings, but slips are available, as well as gas, water, ice, and supplies; a mechanic is on duty. An unpretentious bar and restaurant complete the facilities. Yachts will find this a snug haven providing they stay within the markers and use care in negotiating the challenging entrance with its swirling current.

12. Mill Creek, Noyack Bay (12358 363). While beating against a strong westerly on one of our cruises in Noyack Bay, we decided to make a run for protection to Mill Creek Harbor, located on its southern shore. It turned out to be a wise decision, for this well-sheltered harbor, not often used by cruising boats, continues to expand its facilities. A prominent pointed radio tower standing inland is almost due south and on a line with the 100-foot channel. There has been no dredging here in almost ten years, but plenty of depth remains in the harbor—at least 6 feet at low water; the same can be said for depths at the channel's entrance, but shoaling was becoming evident in 1977. On entering, keep well to starboard of the black can, which marks shoaling water along the built-up sand bar. Keep between the red-and-black stakes until you make your sharp swing to port outside of the black can and stake located off the end of the spit. After you have rounded the spit to reach the inner harbor, you will pick up ahead to starboard the large shed of the Noyac Marina, nestled among a string of small private homes. The hospitable owners can supply you with gas, water, ice, and all types of fishing gear and marine equipment, and will point out the location of the general store and Noyac Motel nearby. This marina also specializes in servicing outboards. You can tie up to the bulkhead in about 5 feet of water or pick up a possible overnight mooring nestled midst a crowded fleet of small craft.

Mill Creek, only 4 miles by car and 7 miles by water from Sag Harbor, still strikes us as up and coming. The new Mill Creek Marina lies at the foot of the road along the southeastern shore of the creek. Floating docks, water, ice, gas, electricity, a marine store, and the new Lo Monaco Seafood Restaurant are all available here. The overnight docking fee is $10.00 minimum. This is a spot that will offer you delightful snugness in pleasant surroundings. Mill Creek is a small fishing center, and only 2 miles away lies Jessup Neck, reputed to be the finest fishing grounds in the area, where blues, weakfish, kings, and porgies abound. This neck is a federal preserve, open to landing parties for swimming and exploring.

13. Northwest Harbor, Long Island, N.Y. (12358 363). Heading east to Three Mile Harbor from Sag Harbor, one passes along Northwest Harbor, whose southern shore is marked by a bluff on Barcelona Point. Just to the east of this point, a navigable channel has been dredged southward through a sandbar into Northwest Creek, located to the south of Cedar Point. We made our approach to the entrance almost due south from can 5. Although the channel had a reported depth at the time of 7 feet, be sure to stay in the middle and then favor the starboard shore to avoid sand bars reaching inward from both sides. Having passed through the narrow cut, swing gradually to port and head for the dock front along the eastern shore while staying within the red markers. Don't expect to find any facilities here, just a few small cottages and outboards. There's at least 6 feet in the anchorage area, which is open a bit to the south but otherwise well sheltered. Why we were the only sizable boat there we cannot tell, for this "secret" harbor has a quiet and natural charm hardly duplicated elsewhere on Long Island. Its lovely sandy beach and wetland to the south merely help to "gild the lily."

14. Threemile Harbor, Gardiners Bay (13209 362). This is a first-class protected harbor, which is large and deep enough for a whole yacht-club fleet. In approaching its entrance from the west, be sure to keep well off the rocks marked by a red-and-black buoy, which lies 1½ miles east of the light on Cedar Point. These rocks are known locally as Hedges Bank.

The main channel has been dredged to a 150-foot width and to a controlling depth of 10 feet. A lighted bell buoy lies 800 yards due north of the red-and-black buoys marking the channel entrance. Avoid the shifting bars on either side while entering between the two privately maintained lights set at the end of each jetty at the harbor's mouth. Then follow the line of block buoys arranged to guide you in; they are all equipped with radar reflectors. Prepare to face up to 3-knot currents and be most careful not to turn too soon toward the center of the harbor for an anchorage, but be sure to pass well beyond the last buoy before swinging to starboard. The holding ground is good.

The first facility upchannel to port is the Harbor Marina, which has complete repair service, gas, Diesel fuel, ice, showers, slips with electricity for boats up to 50 feet, a laundromat, and a gourmet restaurant. It caters primarily to powerboats.

Many yachtsmen are drawn to the Maidstone Marina when they spot its staked channel just north of the Maidstone Boat Yard on the eastern shore. Its basin is marked on the chart. Here there is about 6 feet at low water with 125 slips and 400 feet of side dockage. The usual services for your boat may be obtained at the dock; for the crew there are showers, a laundromat, and good food and drink served in the Silver Seahorse Restaurant, a popular haunt with young people, especially on the weekends. It has been said that "there are larger waves in the Maidstone swimming pool than in its basin in a hurricane."

Sailing people are especially attracted to the Maidstone Boat Yard, owned and operated next door by personable Dick Sage. After all, he is an experienced sailing man himself, whose conscientiousness is reflected in his remark, "Any boat I handle here, I treat like my very own." He has transient slips with electricity behind a protected, clean water basin with an 8-foot depth. Launch service will shuttle you back and forth from the twenty moorings lying off the basin. Gas, Diesel fuel, water, ice, showers, a shed for dryland storage, marine supplies, and four competent repairmen on duty include some of the services here. There's a special sociability about the place; free newspapers are handed out and the informal Sunday breakfast encourages the usual swapping of yarns among the visiting crews.

The Boat Yard has now become a part of a larger complex, Maidstone Village. This also includes a marine store, a small barn, a carriage house, a display of unusual boats, a restored seamen's chapel, and a low-profile motel. "It's our plan to construct a Mystic Seaport atmosphere here. There will be no further expansion of the waterfront."

What Dick and Jane Sage have already created just along their waterfront is a feast in itself, for the eyes as well as the palate. The Lighthouse at Maidstone Village is a unique restaurant and architectural achievement, which took 2½ years of planning. While the walls are constructed of old brick and masonry in Tudor style, the interior is stunningly decorated with natural wood paneling. At the building's entrance appears a scale model of the cockpit of *Courageous;* nearby on a 45-foot wall is a massive marine blueprint of this famous America's Cup defender. But what really strikes the unsuspecting eye is *Jade,* a fully-rigged 5.5-meter, 1965 Olympic gold-medal winner, standing behind the bar just as she was raced then, under the name of *Webb III.* The restaurant was purposely designed to accommodate *Jade*'s 48-foot mast and 32-foot hull.

As you may gather, this is a place of taste, serving an excellent, rather expensive, cuisine. It features dance music and entertainment seven days a week during season. Proper attire is required.

Dick Sage continues to impress us as a dedicated man who truly cares —about the future of his harbor, his "Village" and his clientele. He, along with another nearby marina owner, Bob Story, have founded the progressive Association of Marine Industries, which is doing much for the protection of Long Island's waterfront interests as well as those of the cruising yachtsman. Dick and his wife, putting it in their own words, are trying successfully here to portray "in an honest way, a working statement about boating. And the *Jade* is an integral part of it all."

Yachts may also proceed up the channel to put into several small marinas along the port shore. The Shagwong Marina basin, faced by a bulkhead, has thirty-three slips in 4½ feet at low water and ample facilities situated in a natural setting. Boats belonging mostly to sports fishermen and local residents stay here. There is more water and space further up at Threemile's oldest marina, Halsey Marina. The trimmed grass lining the docks adds great appeal to this secluded spot. There is 6 feet of water in the channel leading to the cove at the southern end of the harbor, but watch out for the shoaling to port as you enter. Along the eastern fork of this cove lies a tiny basin in which is housed Gardiner's Marina, clean and attractive, offering slips and basic shipboard necessities including, as do all the marinas in this harbor, gas, Diesel fuel, ice, electricity, and showers. Here you'll be "guests" of Robert Gardiner, owner of nearby Gardiner's Island. The town dock is just to the south, while further on rests the deep-water dock of the Threemile Harbor Boat Yard run by Bob Story, who has gained an excellent reputation for service and for doing all types of repair work. There's also a well-equipped ship's store here. More dockage space may be found at the East Hampton Marina, reached by entering the other fork to the west, but this is used mostly by powerboats. While no anchoring is permitted in the cove, this is one of the few places in the entire harbor where you can pick up food supplies conveniently. The town park adjoining makes the surroundings pleasant but less private than the outer harbor.

Regular seaplane service flying to New York City is available at Threemile Harbor. If necessary, check with Dick Sage for details.

15. Acabonack Harbor, Napeague Bay (13209 362). On our first visit here many years ago, the late Captain H.R. Miller of the Devon Yacht Club gave us a guided tour of this important harbor, opened up in 1959 for cruising craft. It is the only harbor of refuge between Threemile Harbor and Montauk. The southern tip of Cape Gardner, forming a breakwater to the harbor, has been completely filled in to the mainland and a new channel cut through it due west of red nun 8. The 75-foot channel, according to our sources, was last dredged in 1976 to a depth of 5 feet MLW but this entrance, with its swift currents, tends to silt up, resulting in unpredictable depths. Take careful soundings, therefore, as you head due west from nun 8. The mean range of tide here is almost 2 feet. You will soon pick up a small, privately maintained, lighted red nun, which is kept to starboard. Note the reported submerged rock marked on the chart as being located on the channel's southern edge and keep this to port as well as the black marker further on. Having passed between the two sandspits, you have a choice of following one of two branch channels, whose depths are 7 feet at low water. The narrow channel running due south is marked with three black cans, is far more sheltered and is to be preferred. The other passage leading to the northwest is also buoyed to show the deepest water along its first 400-yard leg. Do not proceed up the charted second leg without local knowledge. The harbor bottom is clay.

You will have to anchor here, as there are no facilities, but this adds to the place's natural charm. Captain Miller, as a former president of the East Hampton Baymen's Association, a conservationist group, was largely responsible for developing, yet not spoiling, this rustic area, which has few homes, picturesque marshes, and beaches lined with multicolored shells.

The Devon Yacht Club lies 2 miles to the southeast. It has long been identified by name on government charts and its dredged basin, also designated, might serve as a possible place of refuge in an emergency. The holding ground is reported to be good off the club dock.

This *Guide* is written "to contribute to the safety and enjoyment of the cruising man." If our last visit to the Devon Yacht Club in 1977 is an example of the usual welcome accorded a visiting yachtsman, then we can promise the reader little enjoyment here. Never, during his many hundreds of personal visits to yacht clubs, marinas, and boatyards along the east coast over the last thirty years has this author been treated with less civility. In a curt interview with the club manager, we were advised that the less said in this book about her club the better. We will now try to oblige but not without a few additional comments.

Subsequent urgent attempts to reach this club's commodore to gather updated information both by letter and by phone were totally in vain. Apparently, other sailors have faced Devon's inhospitality. In early 1978, *Soundings* printed a headline that read, "Sailors Complain of Snubs." The article began with the statement that "some members of the Long Island sailing fraternity are still smarting from what they perceive was a snub last summer at the hands of the Devon Yacht Club." Little purpose will be served in amplifying this report but it certainly substantiates our own recent experience. In all fairness to Warren Woodward, club commodore, the article closes with his quote of Devon's policy: "Visiting yachtsmen are always welcome as long as they wear coats and ties in the dining room and observe the other rules of the club." He'll have to prove it to us! Meanwhile, if anyone knows anything about those "other rules," we'd surely like to know.

The Devon Yacht Club was founded in 1917, under the name of the Gardiner's Bay Boat Club, by a group of summer residents, largely from Cincinnati.

Little may one realize that Gardiners Island, perched in the bay about 4 miles north of the Devon Yacht Club, boasts the longest ownership by a continued dynasty of any piece of land in the United States. Purchased in 1639 by Lion Gardiner from the Montauk Indians for a blanket, some trinkets, a very large dog, and a bottle of rum, it is now preserved as a naturalist's paradise by the sixteenth Lord of the Manor, Robert David Lion Gardiner. Deer and wild turkeys roam the island underbrush, hundreds of different bird species make it their home, and as many as 150 majestic ospreys nest here regularly from March to September.

Such an intriguing place may tempt you to pay a visit ashore, but don't try unless you happen to be a Gardiner—just listen to an anecdote that Mitchel Levitas spun in *The New York Times.*

Among the uninvited visitors shooed off a few years ago were several brothers Rockefeller. Jock Mackay, who has worked and lived on the island since he left Scotland in 1929, spotted the group disembarking from a boat. When he asked them to leave, recalls Mackay, the visitors identified themselves, adding that they were friends of the absent proprietor. Mackay was not moved. "I'm sorry," he said, "I don't care if you're Astorbilts, you'll have to go."

A few years ago, Robert Gardiner decided to open the island on a limited basis to visitors because of his interest in helping build the scholarship trust fund of Southampton College of Long Island University. It is now possible to take a five-hour sail to Gardiner's Island, thanks to the *Rachel and Ebenezer,* a replica of a nineteenth-century coasting schooner, regularly docked next to Preston's at Greenport. The charge at the time of writing was $15.00 per person.

Lucky visitors can now observe such historic landmarks as the 1795 windmill, which still contains its original machinery; Whale Hill, commanding a view of Block Island Sound; the virgin-oak Bostwick Forest with its aged trees, many of them pre-Columbian; and the site of Captain Kidd's treasure, buried and recovered in 1699.

Approximately 3 miles east-northeast of Gardiners Island, the U.S. Navy has established a restricted anchorage area for the exclusive use of its submarines operating out of New London. It is shown on the chart as a ¾ × 2-mile rectangle. Regulations state that no vessel or person may approach or remain within 500 yards of a U.S. Navy submarine anchored in this area.

16. Napeague Harbor (13209 362). For use by cruising men, this harbor, located southeast of Gardiners Island, has a number of strikes against it. Its entrance channels are unmarked, narrow, and tend to silt, and the harbor is shoal for the most part—too large to be snug. Since this port is also being used for oyster farming, local residents frown on the appearance of cruising yachts here where no facilities exist.

There are two reasons for our mentioning Napeague: It can be a possible refuge in northeasterly weather, when the local bays are kicking up. Also, the entrance channels north and south of Hicks Island both show on the latest chart tolerable depths of 4 feet at low water. The mean range of tide here is almost 2 feet.

Enter cautiously through the northerly channel, whose unmarked entrance is approximately 400 yards due south of the red-and-black buoy west of Goff Point. Favor the eastern shore all the way in, having posted a bow lookout. Don't be tempted to head over to any moorings to the west but select an anchorage fairly close along the eastern shoreline, avoiding the three charted rocks. The low-lying dunes will not give you great protection in winds from any direction, but, once here, you may find that you've escaped those "graybeards" sweeping across from Block Island Sound.

17. Montauk (Great Pond) (13209 362). This is primarily a great sport-fishing port, which caters more to fishermen than to cruising people. But dredgings and newly constructed facilities have made Montauk an exciting port of call. The harbor currents and poor holding ground, however, still exist. In 1977, the controlling depth in the channel was 11 feet MLW to the boat basin northwestward of Star Island, with a 9-foot depth reported in the basin itself. You can also carry 11 feet in the east channel to the yacht basin east of the island. These channels are marked by privately maintained seasonal buoys. We were told by a Coast Guard duty officer at his station on Star Island that some yachtsmen entering the harbor at night overlook the fact that the bell buoy just north of the jetties is unlighted, resulting in some near collisions.

"Montauk is not a good place to spend the night riding at anchor," says the commodore of a leading Long Island Sound Yacht Club. "The currents swirl all over the place, causing anchored yachts to swing every which way." This report is still true, but with the advent of some outstanding marinas affording boats good protection dockside, many yachtsmen prefer to tie up, keeping their anchors stowed away. Furthermore, the latest chart shows changes in hydrography from a 1974 survey by the National Ocean Survey, all of which reflect improved depths for a roomier anchorage in Lake Montauk than heretofore.

In coming in, most water is to the west, and as you get to the southerly end of the lighted jetties, swing away from the day beacon on your starboard hand and over slightly to port toward the channel center where there is ample water. Only a fairly small area off the docks to starboard has deep water, with about 10 feet; and this is near the channel through which the 2½-knot tide sweeps. In the small bight on the western shore, facing the Coast Guard station, lies the Montauk Marine Basin with pump-out facilities, gas, Diesel fuel, ice, water, showers, electricity, a laundromat, countless slips, and grocery supplies. It is also reputed to provide about the best all-round repair service in the harbor. Boats of under 6-foot draft can proceed from this basin southward in a dredged and buoyed channel running along the western shore. Sports fishermen will find good refuge and service at Cove Marina, located to starboard at the end of this channel. Gas, Diesel fuel, ice, water, electricity at the slips, marine and fishing supplies, an ice locker for fish storage, groceries, and a fine machine shop are all here. Next door to the south, a fairly new boatel, the Westlake Fishing Lodge, claims complete accommodations for the cruising boatman, including motel units with a restaurant and cocktail lounge.

Over on the less-crowded western shore of Star Island, next to the Coast Guard station, lies the Star Island Yacht Club, housed in a two-story tan building of modern design. Here is one of the most recently built public marinas in Montauk, under the management of Henry Colombi. It can handle boats up to 60 feet at its floating slips, where we observed mostly power boats tied up alongside. Like so many of the newer marinas in the harbor, this one has something for everybody, including a swimming pool and tennis court, but no restaurant.

From the Coast Guard Station southeastward about ⅜ mile down the east channel, one can reach the basin of the Sea and Sky Portel. It is easily identified by a row of pilings along its northern face and by a bulkhead opposite. This modest marina came under the new management of George Kouvatsos in 1977. His docks can accommodate twenty-four boats in 6-foot MLW at the reasonable flat rate of $10.00, covering all conveniences overnight. Rooms are available; its Flying Fish Restaurant is convenient for meals. Montauk Airport is nearby, but we have been told by visiting yachtsmen here that they had not been disturbed by droning aircraft during the night.

Directly across the channel from Sea and Sky stretch out in one long line three of the largest public resort-marinas to be found anywhere. Each offers superb dockspace accommodations for visiting yachts, with lovely landscaping, restaurants, ship's stores, complete supplies dockside, and the use of swimming pools and tennis courts ashore. From north to south they are: Star Island Marina and Villas, the Deep Sea Yacht and Racquet Club, and the recently renovated Montauk Yacht

Club & Inn. The first-class service they provide requires first-class rates, so here's a sample of what you get, for instance, at the Montauk Yacht Club for a rate of 75¢ a foot at the time of writing. It will recapture for you "the priceless art of hospitality and matchless service of a bygone era." It will furnish such niceties as dockside "room" service with maids, valet, and laundry service, box lunches, on-board telephones, MATV, and complimentary transportation to golf and shopping in the village. "All the services of the hotel are available to the yachtsman," according to dockmaster Harry Clemenz, and that would include indoor heated swimming, sauna, and Jacuzzi, not to mention billiards room rights. Why, all this pampering might even make one balk at the very thought of ever returning to that self-reliant existence, that comparatively spartan world of the average cruising man.

Once you do decide to cast off, however, you can reach the southern part of Lake Montauk by going between the three sets of red-and-black privately maintained buoys marking the deep water. You may swing over to port into 8-foot depths only after having passed the last black can 7. A pier shown on the chart as jutting out from the shoreline southwest of Prospect Hill designates the location of the Captain's Marina and Inn. Behind its prominent control tower rises its headquarters, a beautiful Norman villa. Being quietly sheltered and away from it all makes this a choice spot for the cruising family. The rates are fairly modest, at 40¢ a foot; there's free bus service to nearby restaurants and, if desired, you can pick up a National Rental car. Although you'll find no repair service here, this marina offers such compensations as a good 7-foot depth at the slips, a fine salt-water swimming pool, and a congenial staff managed by Bob Cohan. Bob cautions yachtsmen against anchoring close to the western shore of Lake Montauk. Uncharted, dangerous boulders lie up to 600 feet off that shore and occasional sudden wind shifts can easily swing your anchored boat upon them.

Montauk was once the home of the Montaukett Indians, a peaceful tribe that lived well off local game, the ocean, and the land. In 1614, the Dutch explorer, Adrian Block, came ashore and according to historians was the first white man to set foot in Suffolk County. By 1686, white settlers had bought all of Montauk's 10,000 acres for 100 pounds. Descendants of the Montauketts no longer live in the hamlet, but reside in East Hampton village, just to the west of Montauk.

This seaport became one of America's first cattle- and sheep-ranching areas, then a whaling center, and finally a commercial fishing port near the turn of the century. Its year-round population is about 3000, which rises to about 18,000 during the summer season. It is now very much on the move.

Montauk Manor, built in the 1920s, closed in 1964 but is now converted into condominium apartments. Gosman's Dock, located to starboard at the harbor's entrance, has bloomed into a clean, colorful, and charming group of boutiques and restaurants near the fishing docks. Much of Montauk's past is equally colorful.

Here was the scene of the final encampment of the Spanish-American War's Rough Riders, commanded by Theodore Roosevelt. Roosevelt brought 2,800 of his Rough Riders to the Deep Hollow Ranch when the unit was to be disbanded. In his diaries, Roosevelt recalls that "galloping over the open, rolling country through the cool fall evenings made us feel we were out on the great western plains."

The Star Island Casino, now the site of the Deep Sea Marina, housed illegal gambling throughout the 1920s, and well into the 1930s, when the law finally put it out of business. It was here that Mayor Jimmy Walker of New York was "pinched" in a police raid. He hung a white towel over his arm, posed briefly as a waiter, and finally fled barefoot down the dock to the sanctuary of the nearby yacht club.

One of the most tragic boating accidents in recent years off Montauk was the capsizing of the fishing boat *Pelican* on September 1, 1952. Of the sixty-four persons aboard, forty-five lost their lives.

Montauk is the last harbor to the eastward on Long Island and thus a good "jumping-off place" for Block Island, about 18 miles away, and points east. Its famous lighthouse, constructed in 1796 by order of President George Washington, is an octagonal stone tower 108 feet high, with the light 168 feet above sea level. Henry Baker was its keeper during the first quarter of the nineteenth century. His pay was $333.33 a year.

Now this old landmark is in danger of toppling into the sea below. It stood 297 feet away from the cliff when first erected but nature's inexorable erosion has brought the edge to within only 49 feet. The Coast Guard gives the lighthouse a maximum life expectancy of two more decades.

Robert Moses, former chairman of the State Council of Parks, is reported to have said: "Everyone who loves water, wind, sky, and distance, and is not chilled by bleakness, must love Montauk."*

*From *New York*—American Guide Series (Oxford University Press).

CHAPTER VI

Fishers Island to Buzzards Bay, Including Narragansett Bay

Fishers Island, N.Y. (13214 358).

SPECIAL NOTE ON FISHERS ISLAND SOUND

All wise yachtsmen use the current whenever possible when going east or west along the shore. For that reason it is well to remember that the velocity of the currents through the Race is twice as great as through Fishers Island Sound. It may be preferable, therefore, in heading east or west, to work your way through Watch Hill Passage. Note here that in strong easterlies and westerlies cans 3 and 5 are often swept nearly underwater at times of maximum flow, although the currents in this passage run considerably weaker than at the Race. The government publication, *Tidal Current Charts, Block Island Sound and Eastern Long Island Sound Including the Thames and Connecticut Rivers,* available at $3.00 at all National Ocean Survey sales agents or from the National Ocean Survey, Distribution Division (C44), Washington, D.C. 20235, shows the direction and strength of currents each hour. This portfolio is extremely useful in these waters. There have been many navigational-aid changes recently along this section of the coast, so it is necessary for yachtsmen to refer to the latest charts.

There are often fluky winds and "soft spots" off New London Harbor and west of Dumpling Island. There is an eddy on the flood, and little current, close under the west end of Fishers Island.

1. Silver Eel Pond, Fishers Island (13214 358). This tiny harbor on the extreme western tip of the island is not reserved solely for government use. Steamers from New London dock here, instead of in West Harbor as formerly, and use a dock on the west shore next to the Fishers Island Coast Guard Station. However, there may be room for a few yachts to tie up but not for an anchorage. While the protection is very good, no gas or supplies were available when we last visited, and the place is uninviting, with government buildings all around and cars going to and from the steamers. The entrance between the lighted docks is not easy to negotiate in westerly winds, and one should be on the lookout for reported pilings that have washed into the channel. Silver Eel Pond is valuable chiefly as a convenient and safe harbor of refuge, or as a take-off point for the Race.

2. *Hay Harbor, Fishers Island (13214 358).* This harbor makes a quiet mooring for shoal-draft power boats. The channel is narrow and difficult without local knowledge and not recommended for keel boats. We poked in here in a boat drawing 3 feet and experienced little difficulty, having posted a bow watch. A local authority says that with the aid of local stakes 4 feet can be taken inside, though how this is done at low water is not evident on the chart. Once inside, there is good water in the western part of the harbor and dock.

3. *West Harbor, Fishers Island (13214 358).* Among cruising people this is by far the most popular harbor on Fishers Island, and deservedly so. It is easy to enter, provided you watch the shoal to starboard. Well protected except from the northeast, it has good holding ground and is altogether delightful. Although the channel records a depth of 12 feet at the time of writing, we were told not to hug nun 14 too closely to starboard. And deep-draft boats should be especially wary of the 5-foot spot just beyond this nun, which marks the end of the dredging.

Steamers from New London no longer use West Harbor, though the steamer dock is still available for tying up. Steamers now run between New London and Silver Eel Pond, as already pointed out. Gas, Diesel fuel, water, and ice are available in West Harbor at the Fishers Island Services dock just beyond the old steamboat wharf. The Fishers Island Yacht Club, in a small white clubhouse beyond the gas dock to starboard, is hospitable to visiting yachtsmen from other recognized clubs. It has showers and launch service. Sometimes the club has spare moorings, or possibly dockage space, for which a charge is made. Most visitors anchor well north or northeast of Goose Island. Shoal-draft boats can obtain complete shelter from all winds in the coves at the south end of the harbor.

In 1971, a channel leading into these shallow inner coves was dredged, primarily for local commercial use, to a controlled depth of 7 feet at low water. From this narrow buoyed channel's entrance, just southward of Goose Inlet, boats drawing less than 5 feet may proceed in a southeasterly direction. A pair of buoys northeast of Goose Island helps to point out this passage. Toward the end of this channel, along the port shore, lie the finger piers and marine railway of the Pirate's Cove Marina, a rather new and long-overdue facility on Fishers Island. The writer was impressed with the apparent efficiency and professional attitude of its manager, Peter Sanger, whose office is above a finely stocked marine store. And should you have engine problems, ask for his mechanic, Wes Greenleaf. The two nearby basins, recording 7-foot depths, are possible anchorage areas, since Pirate's Cove is not set up for overnight transients.

Sea Island Seafood is a store on the Fishers Island Services dock selling lobsters, cold drinks, and snacks. One can also obtain supplies at Doyen's or at Harbor Foods, up the road to the left on leaving from the dock. A drug store (with New York papers) and other stores are reached by following the main road and making one left turn; by making two left turns one finds the old Pequot Inn where boating people can eat, drink, and be merry.

West Harbor is typically high-class residential, with many fine yachts permanently moored there in summer. There is plenty to do ashore, but, as in similar communities, some things may be expensive. The swimming is very good.

Fishers Island has existed for most of a century as a summer playground for the wealthy, whose palatial estates provide the major reason for its being. Now, rising taxes, high prices, and a changing life-style are reducing its population—from 508 year-round residents in 1960 to 462 in 1970 to 350 in 1977. The main industry of these people is the summer residents who, as "the working rich," have nowadays less vacation time on the island and thus less time to spend money here. Moreover, two-thirds of the island is privately owned by the summer people. As one native islander has said, "What we need is for more people to come out here right now." But as long as there is Fishers, he may have no fear of a shortage of enthusiastic and loyal boating people.

4. East Harbor, Fishers Island (13214 358). There is considerable foul ground in East Harbor, but it is well marked with buoys. A good guide on entering is the prominent former Coast Guard station near South Beach, which is now privately owned. The long-private Fishers Island Club pier is the first one you will see to starboard. We found shoal water right off both of these docks. An excellent 18-hole golf course borders on East Harbor. The harbor is exposed to winds from northeast to northwest, but the holding ground is fairly good.

Noank, Conn. (13214 358). This village, on the west bank of the Mystic River, has docks along the waterfront, with plenty of deep water.

But don't get too close to nuns 8 or 10. The well-kept Noank Shipyard, located behind a protected bulkhead on the port shore just above nun 8, is the first facility you'll reach and as such offers as complete service as you'll find anywhere, including emergency repair work of all types. It provides its customers with gas, Diesel fuel, ice, water, an excellent marine store, showers; a laundromat and a store for supplies is nearby. The *Bill of Rights,* a deep-draft, 125-foot schooner, is a frequent visitor here.

Just beyond the shipyard stands one of Noank's major assets, Abbott's, the largest lobster pound in southern New England. Visitors come here from miles around to tie up dockside while ordering fresh clams, shrimp, or lobster for instant eating on the porch outside or to be taken aboard. These fishermen are the "Americanus Homarus" experts—"We'll tell you everything you want to know about lobsters!"

For instance, the lobster when born is the size of a mosquito and takes six years to reach approximately one pound and the reproductive stage. The largest lobster caught on record was forty-nine pounds, caught in 1890 offshore Carolina. Jumbo lobsters, which weigh from fifteen to thirty pounds, could be over fifty years old. The New England lobster ranges from Newfoundland to the north and to the Carolina coast on the south, while it is caught from inshore depths of one fathom to offshore depths of 400 fathoms.

Upriver, just beyond nun 12, you'll note the long, sturdy-looking dock of the Ram Island Yacht Club. There is a flagpole on the pier. This modest-sized club has 4½ feet at MLW off this pier, few services for transients, but does have a possible guest mooring available.

In ordinary summer weather, Noank is OK for overnight, but it is very exposed to winds from the northeast to southeast, and is close to the much-used channel to Mystic Seaport, thus a victim to the wash of many passing boats.

Mason Island, Conn. (13214 358). Progress has come to Mason Island, so far as facilities for yachtsmen are concerned. On the west shore of Mason Island, opposite black can 23, is a fine, classy, modern marina, the Mystic River Marina, with 6 feet in the slips at low water and a reported 10 or 12 feet at the end of the gas dock. Here, besides gas and Diesel fuel, are available many slips, water, ice, electricity, showers, toilets, telephone, laundromat, marine store, swimming pool, restaurant, a mechanic on duty, and a 20-ton Travelift.

A large parking space is an encouragement to amphibious cruisers. A glassed-in building, with a long sloping roof, offers an opportunity for lounging. Minimum charge for overnight dockage, we were told, is $3.00.

On the other side of the island, with less luxury and more privacy, there is an anchorage between Mason and Dodges islands off the flag-staff of the Mason Island Yacht Club, which has a pier on the east shore of Mason Island just north of Enders Island. Visiting yachtsmen from other recognized yacht clubs are welcomed at this attractive club, located on the private property of the Mason Island Company.

Ten feet can be carried 100 yards north of the flagstaff. There is excellent holding ground and plenty of room to swing, but the place is not good in a blow, as it is open to the south and has a long sweep to the north also. On the way up to this secluded, attractive anchorage, be sure to leave nun 6 well to starboard to avoid the rocks to the northwest.

In northerlies, better protection can be found by running around Enders Island into the bight between there and Mason Point.

Mystic, Conn. (13214 358). Entering the Mystic River, you see the picturesque village of Noank to port, where a floodlit church spire is a beacon after dark, and off your starboard quarter Masons Island and the Mystic River Marina. The course is nearly due north to Mystic, at the upper end of which is the Marine Historical Association's far-famed maritime museum, Mystic Seaport. A near-perfect shelter for visiting yachtsmen, amid attractive surroundings, aesthetic as well as history laden, is offered here.

The Mystic River—Mistick, which means "great tidal river," as the Indians named it—is as fascinating in history as it is in actuality. Un-doubtedly to know a little about these shores will help alleviate the sometimes frustrating delay caused by the yachtsman's necessary ad-herence to the two bridge schedules he must encounter.

The railroad bridge has a flexible schedule, governed, of course, by the flow of traffic over its rails. If a train is approaching, you must wait in the river until it passes. While waiting, look just beyond the bridge to the left of the rocky promontory, partially covered by foliage, with a few old houses strewn about its base. This was Fort Rachel, where in 1814 a hardy band of local people successfully manned an artillery battery and soundly repulsed the British, who were bent to the task of the assault and sack of the town.

Concerning your passage upriver, we add the following words of caution: The speed limit throughout the river is 6 miles per hour; this limit is posted and enforced. The average river channel depth at mean low water is about 12 feet. However, there is serious shoaling in many spots, especially at the channel turns. So beware of the pitfalls of the Mystic River channel!

Since there is little sense in going through the bascule bridge into the Mystic Seaport unless you have a confirmed reservation, and since

Aerial view of the Marine Historical Association's nineteenth-century museum, Mystic Seaport, Mystic, Connecticut.

Mystic Seaport Photograph

anchoring in the channel is obviously prohibited, the unexpected visitor must have an alternative plan. One time we put in at the floating slips of the Whit-Mar Marina, located just to the east of nun 30 on Murphy Point. Although the depth at the slips has been dredged to 5 feet at low water, this marina does not accommodate boats over 40 feet. Report to the gas dock along the face of the marina or call ahead for reservations (203) 536–2293. In approaching or leaving, be sure to stay south of the pilings standing off the north side of the dock. The services are adequate here and it is less congested than at the facilities further upriver. It's also possible to reach the Seaport by taking a 25-minute walk. Seaport Marine, just before the final highway bridge, can handle larger craft and all types of repairs.

Once through the railroad draw, you may again have to wait, this time for the highway bridge in downtown Mystic, which has a most precise schedule: one opening each hour at fifteen minutes past the hour, from 8:15 A.M. through 7:15 P.M. At other times the bridge will open at the yachtsman's signal—one long and two short blasts of a horn or whistle. This bridge monitors channels 13 and 16. Be sure to watch it in action. It's called a *bascule* bridge, which in French means *seesaw*.

Now look along the western bank of the river. There on Gravel Street are handsome houses built a hundred years ago or more. These were homes of some of the more affluent in the area: shipowners and builders, sea captains and merchants. On the eastern bank of the river you will soon see a large red building and a lift dock, which are part of the new Ships' Preservation Facility at Mystic Seaport, and which mark the south end of the museum grounds.

Advance reservations *must* be made for all visits to Mystic Seaport. These may be arranged by writing, or by telephoning (203) 536–2631 and asking for the Dock Master, William Farrell. This can be done daily in season between 8:30 A.M. and 5 P.M. All this should be done at least three weeks in advance of your planned arrival. If it is requested, your reservation confirmation will be mailed to you along with all necessary information to make your stay a pleasant one.

When you arrive at the Seaport you will be met, at least between 8 A.M. and 7 P.M., by a dock attendant who will assist in your berthing, register you, and generally be at your service. He will deliver various folders that will help orient you, explain the museum exhibits, and answer questions relative to the shower and laundry facilities at the New York Yacht Club Station 10 Annex. He will also point the way to the Galley, the delightful Seamen's Inne, and the Seaport Stores. At the dock houses adjacent to the wharves, you will find weather information, tide tables, a list of local boat yards, and the taxi number. It is handy also to know that food markets and spirit shops are within easy walking distance of the Seaport.

Here are a few important notes we have quoted from the Seaport's special brochure entitled *Welcome Yachtsmen:*

Reservations will be held only until 4:15 P.M. unless we are notified of an ETA by VHF ship-to-shore on Channel 16 or 9. The dock master monitors these channels during museum hours for this purpose. Plan to call between a quarter to the hour and a quarter after the hour.

Rafting will be allowed only with permission of the yacht owner whose boat is next to the wharf. The regular wharfage charge and admission fees are in effect.

After-dark touring of the grounds or boarding exhibit ships or craft is not permitted. We must request "all quiet" after 11:00 P.M.

A facility similar to the New York Yacht Club Station 10 Annex is also available to yachtsmen at the south end of the property.

Schedules of special daily events are available at the North and South Gates.

Ice, water, and electricity are available at the docks. No fuel is available for sale.

Sustaining members and those with higher classifications of membership in the Marine Historical Association are not required to pay dockage fees for the first twenty-four hours of their visit. However, if a second night's stay is involved, the customary fee of 50¢ per foot of overall length is levied. Permission for longer visits may be granted only through the office of the director. All nonmembers of the association who arrive by boat (except professional crew members) must pay the regular admission charges to the Seaport grounds. All fees for dockage and admission should be paid to the dock attendant upon arrival.

Frankly, you, your family and guests will need at least one full day to see Mystic Seaport properly. Go aboard the tall ships for a keener flavor of their meaning, study the Mystic River Diorama to waft yourself back properly a hundred years to Mystic's formative days, and allow plenty of time to see the formal maritime exhibits and to observe the craft shops in action. Also share the pride and fun of the Mariners on the *Conrad* or sailing in the harbor. These young people are in residence training as part of the Seaport-sponsored educational program based on the *Joseph Conrad,* a nineteenth-century training ship. In 1978, a new permanent exhibit, New England and the Sea, opened at the Seaport. This graphically shows the when, how, and why maritime trades such as fishing, sealing, whaling, and other seaborne commerce have affected New Englanders from the Colonial period through to the present.

During the summer, the Seaport Planetarium offers special programs for visiting yachtsmen and their guests. The *Yachtsmen's Special,* given several times weekly, is an hour-long program of special interest to navigators. On selected evenings, the *Family Special* presentation in the planetarium is followed, weather permitting, by outdoor observation through telescopes.

So, by all means, head for Mystic Seaport, take heed of their cheery Welcome Aboard, and linger a while to relax and to absorb a host of exciting activities and memories.

Stonington, Conn. (13214 358). Stonington makes an excellent stopping place. It is well protected, except during hurricane tides, by three breakwaters, the east one 2000-feet long. In winds from south to northwest, or in no winds at all, the prettiest, quietest, and cleanest anchorage, though the least convenient for landing or supplies, is behind the second breakwater—the long one to port off the west shore. In northwesters you can carry 9 feet close to the west shore. In southwest winds, anchorage in the angle of the breakwater is to be preferred. In northerly or easterly winds good shelter can be obtained either behind the small breakwater on the east shore or in the special anchorage area well up the harbor. This last anchorage is good under ordinary conditions. The only "out" about this area is the noise from the passing trains on the main shore line of Amtrak.

In 1970, a new, less familiar sound began to come wafting across Stonington Harbor. Natives call it the "humidity horn" or, as one shellback snarled, "Everything you can lay a tongue to!" Yachtsmen, however, attempting to enter the harbor in poor visibility will probably bless the blast. It's the foghorn established at the Stonington outer breakwater light, sounding one blast every ten seconds.

The attractive Wadawanuck Yacht Club, on the northeast shore at the head of the harbor, is part of the larger Wadawanuck Club, which engages in athletic and social activities other than yachting. As such, this yacht club is without the launch service, guest moorings, and dock space usually available at larger clubs. Its members, however, participate enthusiastically in the harbor's traditional Wednesday Night Dinghy Series, open to a variety of one-design classes. During one of these races, one can spot as many as seventy-five sailboats tacking to and fro behind the breakwaters.

On our latest visit to Dodson Boat Yard, tucked away in the northeast "special anchorage area," we heard several yachtsmen comment, "We surely miss Johnny Dodson." Leonard Beal is now the owner and has wisely kept the Dodson name, for this marina has always appealed to a clientele described by Dodson himself as "just salty boat-loving people." Paul Revere Curtis, Jr., still remains on watch, serving as greeter and general factotum. This is the one all-service facility in the harbor of prime attraction to sailing craft. The charge is $7.00 minimum at dockside, where there is a depth of 6 feet, and gas, Diesel fuel, water, ice, and electricity are available. Overnight moorings (there are about one hundred) may be obtained at $5.00, with launch service running from 8 A.M. to 8 P.M. Repair work and hauling are performed, while a marine store, showers, and a laundromat are all on hand. Although the holding ground is mud, it is choked with eel grass, which suggests mooring rather than anchoring. Experience has taught us to phone Dodson's ahead of arrival, if possible, to be guaranteed an overnight reservation. Phone (203) 535–1507.

Whenever a yacht-club fleet comes into Dodson's, it often takes over, and under such circumstances one may have trouble in finding any space without a reservation. In that event, the Stonington Boat Works, situated on the east shore, halfway up the harbor, is your best bet. You might prefer being closer to the center of town here while using the facilities of this modest-sized yard, which include gas, ice, showers, marine supplies, laundromat, and engine and hull repairs. Besides serving a limited number of transient yachts, the people here also build Cartwright 36s, a new, well-built ocean cutter designed by Jerry Cartwright. This yard, under Hank Palmer, for almost thirty years after the 1938 hurricane gained a fine reputation in building Stonington Draggers and subsequently Stonington motorsailers.

Stonington has all of the facilities a yachtsman is apt to desire in the way of supplies, repairs, and communications. The shopping district on Water Street includes gifts, art galleries, antiques, grocery stores, gourmet foods, liquor, ladies wear, and a dry cleaner. The Sugar & Spice Shop specializes in rare food delicacies, the preparation of a variety of casseroles, and Stonington's Portuguese bread. The Harbor View Restaurant, farther down Water Street toward the point, is a must for anyone who dotes on fresh seafood and famous Stonington chowder. It's housed in an old plant that used to process whale oil from the town's large whaling fleet. Natives claim that the Portside Restaurant is first-rate for all meals. Far less expensive and formal is Sandy's Restaurant and Fish Market on the waterfront behind and west of the Harbor View. It dishes up lobster, crabs, steamers, chowder, and what have you, to eat informally dockside or to spirit aboard.

Stonington helped to make history and was once called a "nursery for seamen." Captain Edmund Fanning of Stonington served as a midshipman under John Paul Jones. When he was eighteen years old (July 15, 1798), he discovered the Fanning Islands, now an important air stop on the Pacific Ocean. During the Revolution and the War of 1812, the town was twice attacked by the British and twice successfully repelled the invaders. Some British cannonballs are now valued relics.* The town has that intangible quality called "atmosphere," and it's fun to wander through its streets, perhaps on the way to view relics of bygone days in the museum of the Stonington Historical Society at the old granite lighthouse near Stonington Point.

Watch Hill, R.I. (13214 358). As the chart clearly shows, the anchorage at Stonington is nearer the east-west course through Fishers Island Sound than is the anchorage at Watch Hill. To reach the latter it is necessary to go a considerable distance to the north around Sandy Point and then southeast through a well-buoyed but narrow channel. For this reason, Watch Hill is a less frequent port of call for 'longshore cruisers than it deserves to be, as it is an attractive summer resort.

In 1977, maintenance dredging in the main channel, from its entrance just north of nun 4, located off Sandy Point, all the way up the Pawcatuck River to Avondale, helped restore this passage to its authorized depth of 10 feet at low water. In entering Little Narragansett Bay on your way to Watch Hill, keep as far off Sandy Point as the buoys allow, for the shoal off the island is moving westward. Stick close to the black buoys to port. After that, follow the entrance channel carefully, as there are rocks and shoal spots in several places just off the channel. According to local yachtsmen, at least 8 feet can be carried at low water through the short channel leading into Watch Hill Cove.

There are several good docks for visiting yachts. The first to starboard that entering yachts will reach is that of the hospitable Watch Hill Yacht Club, where the usual reciprocal privileges are given to members of other recognized yacht clubs. Launch service runs here, and you may be able to pick up a spare mooring in the 10-foot anchorage area by first checking with the club steward. If not, an anchorage is possible just to the west of the club's small boat fleet inside the breakwater; or run up the cove to the large Watch Hill Docks, operated by the local Fire District. Here one can find overnight dockage, gas, water, ice on order, and electricity, with a depth of 8 feet alongside. Check for space with the dock master, Mike Mackin. This is such a popular spot for visiting yachts, that Mackin suggests you phone his office at (401) 348-8779 at

---

*Historical data from *Connecticut*—American Guide Series (Houghton Mifflin Co.).

least a week in advance of your arrival for a slip reservation. Stores are near at hand or can be reached by telephone.

Hubbard Phelps, as commodore of the Watch Hill Yacht Club, and a local authority, continues being helpful in updating us on this harbor. He advises that no lights are required within the inner anchorage and that rafting up is limited to one boat only. He also suggests that Jim Long, who is at the Watch Hill Boat Yard up the Pawcatuck River, will service your boat at the yacht club; phone him at 348–8148.

The only "out" about Watch Hill is that it usually takes a terrible licking in hurricanes, for the protecting Napatree Beach is low, and hurricane-driven tides go right over it. Hurricane Carol (August 31, 1954) badly damaged the yacht clubhouse and docks. It is also vulnerable to winds coming in from the north to northwest. On our last visit there were two state moorings in Watch Hill Cove.

A recent correspondent writes that "more might be said about the pleasures of Napatree Point. It is most accessible by boat, offering a beautiful beach on the south side—fine for swimming and picnicking. The best anchorage is along the northern shore in the 7-foot charted area midway between the mainland and the point. There's not much protection and the tidal currents become stronger closer to the point. This spot is popular on the weekends because it also promises a pleasant walk on the beach and tempts the kids to explore the ruins of a mysterious old gun emplacement."

Westerly, R.I. (13214 358). Those who want better protection, or who like to poke their way up rivers or creeks, may find it interesting to go up the scenic Pawcatuck River for all or part of the way to Westerly. On their way they will leave to starboard the Watch Hill Boat Yard headquarters on Colonel Willie Cove. To reach there, make a heading just before reaching nun 4 toward the marshy end of Graves Neck. Having passed this point fairly close aboard, swing to the southeast to pick up the yard's buoyed channel. Depths for this approach are 5 feet. A short distance further upriver lies the Avondale Boat Yard, the only local marina that offers Diesel fuel. Both of these facilities have gas, water, ice, electricity, marine supplies, and repair service. A good market for supplies may be found near the latter's docks. The Frank Hall Boat Yard, a bit further up to starboard, has the only Travelift in the area, charts, slips, and moorings, but no gas.

Still further up, across the river from Pawcatuck Rock, is the modern marina and clubhouse of the Westerly Yacht Club, with many slips, gas, water, electricity, a snack bar, an ample parking space, no overnight moorings, but a large fleet, chiefly of motorboats. Space may be found in the anchorage area just beyond nun 16. The river bottom is mud. On our most recent visit here, we were treated to an idyllic scene of countless swans and cygnets wending their way upstream. There must have been several hundred of them at least—all feeding, as we were told later, on the green sea moss thriving so abundantly along the river coves.

Further up the dredged channel is the city of Westerly, with many stores, shops, restaurants, etc. The best place for an overnight tie-up would be at the Westerly Yacht Club, if there is room, and they extend the usual privileges to members of other recognized yacht clubs. We were told at the club that there is no great advantage in proceeding further upriver.

Block Island, R.I. (13217 269, 13215 271). Although discovered by Giovanni da Verrazano in 1524, Block Island was named for Adriaen Block, who first arrived there, nearly ninety years later, on his way to Narragansett Bay. Verrazano found the hills of the island covered with trees, most of which have long since gone, though various types of wild flowers now help to fill the aesthetic gap. The Indians called it the Isle of Manisses or Little God's Island. The clay-formed Mohegan Bluffs, which remind one of the chalk cliffs of Dover, stretch along the island's southern shore, rising to more than 200 feet above sea level. They were so named when, centuries ago, the island's Manissean Indians drove a group of invading Mohegans across the moors and over these majestic bluffs to their death.

About 5 miles long and with an elevation of 211 feet, this is the first of the outlying islands encountered on the way east from Long Island Sound. Though not so attractive as Martha's Vineyard, Nantucket, and other islands further east, it is an interesting place to visit and a convenient offshore stopping point on the way to Vineyard Sound.

There are two good harbors, one on the east and one on the west side of the island; the latter is the harbor usually preferred by yachtsmen, as the former is small and used mainly by commercial fishermen. There is a good deal of open water between Long Island, Block Island, and the mainland, so anyone who ventures to Block Island in a small boat must be prepared to go to sea. Fogs are frequent in Block Island Sound during July and August and the current information in Eldridge must be carefully determined. In 1969 the National Ocean Survey began issuing large-scale Chart 13215 (271), providing complete up-to-date detail for the continued safe navigation of busy Block Island Sound and the east entrance to Long Island Sound. It has been estimated that 500,000 recreational craft frequent this area each year.

Block Island, showing Great Salt Pond, New Harbor, and the breakwaters at Old Harbor beyond at the upper left.

In the vicinity of Montauk, on the ebb tide, there is a decided trend of the current to the eastward. If one is bound for Block Island, it is well to get away from the Long Island shore, so as to minimize the current and avoid the rips off Montauk. One correspondent writes: "I decided at the last moment, 5:30 P.M., to sail to Block Island in a light four-knot wind at full ebb tide. The course was east by north. I sailed northeast, and hit Salt Pond light on the nose at 10:15 P.M."

Approaching "Block" from east or west in clear visibility, it resembles two islands, with the northern part hilly only along its eastern shore and the southern part mostly high ground, the tallest point of which is marked by a stone castle atop Beacon Hill at a 200-foot level. Coming from Point Judith, stay well clear of Block Island North Reef, which kicks up a vicious rip when the tidal current runs strong and especially when there is an opposing wind. Should you run round the island to New Harbor from the east, or make for Old Harbor from the west, be sure to stay north of 1 B1 Bell. And going around the south end of the island in heavy weather, watch out for breaking seas on Southwest Ledge. Southeast Light, housed in a 67-foot tower, with a radio beacon and fog signal, looms high on the southeast point of the island. Its fog signal is reported difficult to hear close to but is quite audible several miles away.

1. Great Salt Pond, Block Island (13217 269). Because of two jetty lights, the fog signal on this jetty to the southwest of the entrance, and the Block Island Coast Guard station nearby, this harbor, whose southern part is called New Harbor, is quite easy to make. The 1977 edition of Chart 13217 showed the entrance channel had a 150-foot width and a depth of 16 feet at MLW. Shoaling still continues to form off the inner jetty light. As most of the bad weather at Block Island comes from the eastern quadrant, it is to be preferred to East Harbor, though it is large and can be rough, particularly in a northeast gale. The best anchorage is off Champlin's Marina on the south shore, between it and the steamer dock, or north of the yacht dock, where there is less wash and the lee of a bluff provides some protection from the prevailing afternoon southwest winds.

In a storm, go to the snug inner harbor, readily navigable and land-locked. Proceed to the steamer dock at the east side and follow in, hugging close to it. Then cut over to the 10-foot channel. This place is known as the Hog Pen or Smuggler's Cove. Payne's Dock at the ferry landing has good facilities, with dockage and electricity at $9.00 minimum, gas, Diesel fuel, ice, showers, groceries, charts, bicycles for rent, and local delicacies—clam cakes and chowder. Try the homemade potato salad at their deli. This is a favorite marina to many people and its lack of repair service is apparently no drawback. Watch out for a colorful character named Aldo the Baker, who brings freshly warm bread and pastry along the docks to sell to visiting yachts. The end of Payne's dock is left open for the ferry service from New London, but transients can berth along both sides.

Champlin's Marina, down on the western shore of the harbor, is the home base for Block Island Race Week, sponsored every other year since 1965 (non-Bermuda race years) by the Storm Trysail Club. Among the facilities or supplies obtainable here are gas, Diesel fuel, water, ice, marine supplies, charts, engine repairs, showers, a salt-water swimming pool, laundromat, bike and car rentals, boat charters, a restaurant, and basic food supplies in a shack dockside. We found Captain Murphy here very cooperative; he suggests phoning for a slip reservation: (401) 466–2641.

Additional supplies can be had at the village across the island to the east. Deadeye Dick's Restaurant, 200 yards up the road from the steamboat dock, is well recommended for its excellent service and food, particularly its swordfish and lobsters. Ballard's Inn, over at Old Harbor, has been renovated and offers room and board the year round. Champlin runs a jitney service to and from the center of town and to Ballard's every twenty minutes.

On our last visit, we discussed Great Salt Pond with Parker Black, its Harbor Master for the past several years. He pointed out the *Gar-Barge,* a special service boat, which meanders through the fleet of boats picking up their garbage. We were reminded that this harbor is deep and the bottom close to shore shelves off steeply. Since permanent moorings here are scarce, visiting yachts that must set their anchors must allow for plenty of scope. The southeast sector of the harbor is the most popular anchorage in a heavy blow. And yet we remember observing a Cruising Club fleet safely ride out a driving gale while anchored along the shore just to the northwest of Champlin's dock.

Champlin has an attractive competitor lying just to the west of the ferry landing. Block Island Marina, run by Bill Transue and open all year, has become a popular port of call of the Off Soundings fleet and appeals to family groups. It doesn't boast a swimming pool, but in other respects its services are comparable to Champlin's. In addition, it has a 25-ton lift, complete repair work, the well-stocked Windjammer Gift Store, the Oar Restaurant for cocktails and light meals, a marine store, and the Marina Deli, where food supplies may be purchased. There's even a diver on hand for underwater repair work. The rates at the time of writing were $12.00 up to 30 feet; $14.00 up to 40 feet; and after 40 feet, 40¢ a foot. Depths at the floating docks are 10 feet MLW. This place is quiet at night, perhaps due to the no-rafting rule strictly enforced.

For excellent surf bathing, take the dinghy to the shore east by north from Champlin's dock, ½ to ¾ miles. Then cross the road and take the path through a break in the fence to the ocean. Here is a 2-mile beach; once practically deserted, it now has a new State of Rhode Island Pavilion picnic area. It is sometimes hard to escape "progress."

The Interstate Navigation Co. (Point Judith, R.I.) operates steamers between Point Judith and Block Island, four times daily in summer and once a day (except Sundays) in winter. It also runs daily trips in summer from Providence and Newport, arriving and departing from Old Harbor. The Nelseco Navigation Co. (New London, Conn.) operates between New London and Block Island once a day in summer. Sailing time from Point Judith is about one and one-quarter hours; from New London, two and one-quarter hours. Get in touch with these companies if you want their latest schedules. Viking Airlines runs daily flights between Block Island and Providence, and Block Island and Westerly. Montauk-Caribbean, Inc., conducts daily flights in summer between Block Island and Flushing Airport (next to LaGuardia).

A sightseeing trip is one of the memorable pleasures a cruise to Block Island provides. Take a taxi or peddle a bike passing miles of moors, rolling hills, and magnificent sand dunes and cliffs, without a tree in sight. There are hundreds of freshwater ponds, 365 to be exact. Head north on the road to Sachem Pond and stop for a dip along the east beach on the way. Or head south from Old Harbor for two miles to reach Mohegan Bluffs, where the view is breathtaking and a trail leads down a ravine to an imposing solitary beach. For quicker trips, cabs are available at Champlin's, the ferry dock, or from town. Mrs. Melvin Rose, better known as Maizie, who was one of our drivers several years ago, wrote a fine book about her island entitled *Block Island Scrap Book.* Another book we can heartily recommend is *Block Island Lore and Legends* by Mrs. Frederick N. Ritchie.

John P. Runyon, a Corinthian yachtsman, beautifully describes just one of the many spells that Block Island casts over us in this, his description of Block Island Week.

It is a week-long gathering of yachts from the entire Atlantic seaboard from sixty-four footers to the MORCs. No one who has seen or participated in the morning parade of close to one-hundred magnificent yachts down the channel out of Great Pond, sometimes in bright early morning sunlight, often in swirling fog, can fail to be thrilled as this great fleet debouches into Block Island Sound, maneuvering around the Committee Boat for the starts of the many classes. Or at the heart-stopping sight of the forest of masts with fluttering burgees and the gleaming hulls filling every available space in Champlin's and the Block Island Marina with the overflow moored so thickly that the Block Island ferry can barely get through its slip. And there is the fun of joining in the variety of shore activities planned for the afternoons and one lay day. Everything from kite flying to trap shooting, to dancing, to the traditional band. There are the crowds waiting anxiously around the bulletin boards for the day's results to be posted, the lobster dinners ashore, the beer, the sociability, the excitement and the fun!

2. Block Island Harbor on East Harbor (13217 269). This artificial harbor on the eastern shore, shown on the chart as Old Harbor, is likely to be crowded in summer. In coming in from the east in a fog, watch for the dead spot under the cliffs; you may not hear the foghorn at Block Island Southeast Lighthouse. A member of the Cruising Club of America lost a boat here a few years ago. "Lots of others, too," writes a correspondent.

Harbor Master Gary Hall brought us up-to-date on Old Harbor on our most recent visit here. There's solid bulkheading along the eastern shore of the inner basin in front of Ballard's Inn and the Town Dock now has gas and ice. Register at Hall's office at the head of the harbor. His charge for a night's layover is $7.00 for boats up to 30 feet; $9.00 for those 30 to 40 feet overall; and for over 40 feet, $11.00. This covers water and electricity, but there are no showers, and the only rest rooms are in the inn. At low water the depths are 14 feet in the inner harbor and 12 feet in the less-protected outer basin. Should you elect to anchor in the latter, make sure to stay clear of the ferry dock to the west.

Here in the town of New Shoreham you'll find the largest market in town, Block Island Grocery. The Spring House, the largest and oldest hotel, built in 1852, is on a hill a short walk south of town. It requires jackets in the dining room. Nearby, the 1661 Inn has a reported reputation for the best gourmet dining on the island and Ernie's Old Harbor Restaurant caters to seafood gourmands.

Up until a few years ago there was a fish market on the dock at Old Harbor. A conversation was overheard there one day when a woman bought two lobsters and asked the elderly fisherman who was on duty to split them for her. As he brought his meat axe deftly right through the lobster's middle, she inquired: "Does that kill it?" "Well," he replied with typical dry Block Island understatement, "it don't help it none."

Supplies can be obtained right in the town of New Shoreham. There's a rusticated movie theater here, but if you want a picture of Block Island nightlife, try Smugglers Cove or the Block Island Inn.

Block Island was never popular as a summer resort for the very well-to-do. There are no imposing "cottages" like those to be found in Newport and on Fishers Island. There was no adequate harbor at first, so the whaling vessels didn't put in. Perhaps that's why you don't see any imposing mansions with their "captain's walks," like those found in the Vineyard. But Block Island's heyday finally arrived during the latter half of the nineteenth century, when Victorian architecture was all the rage.

The famous Ocean View Hotel was erected in 1873 and stood on that prominent knoll above Old Harbor's entrance. It had two notable features: It had the longest bar in the world (287 feet long, with one hundred bar stools), and it was the summer "White House" of President Grant. Whether there was any connection between these two facts, no one has discovered. All we know is that the bartenders wore roller skates to provide for their thirsty customers with unusual alacrity, and that this wonderful old homestead burned to the ground in 1966.

Point Judith Harbor of Refuge, R.I. (13219 268). If you are approaching Point Judith Light from the northeast, be careful to maintain a course 2 miles off of Point Judith Neck. These offshore waters are thriving with fish traps. Anchor in the southern end of the harbor—the angle of the main breakwater—in about 4 fathoms. This is almost the only good holding ground, and here the water is usually quietest. One should be aware of the heavy kelp bottom; a sandbar is building up inside the elbow of the breakwater, so give it good berth.

Care should be taken not to anchor too far southward in the V-shaped part of the breakwater. In sudden northwest squalls at night, several boats have gone ashore on the inside of the breakwater and been completely wrecked. While the water inside the breakwater is apparently calm, the surge of the sea penetrates through the rocks, making landing on all parts of the V-shaped breakwater difficult, except in the calmest weather.

Most yachts wisely prefer to go north toward Point Judith Pond, pass the improved breakwater located to starboard, and tie up or anchor in Galilee, where a Block Island Ferry dock has been built, or else go northward in the Pond for 3 or 4 miles further to the thriving city of Wakefield.

The Wilking Studio

Point Judith as seen looking south from Wakefield. The center of the photograph shows Point Judith Pond; at the top lies Galilee with the outer breakwaters beyond.

Galilee, R.I. (13219 268). Most yachts cruising alongshore find a tie-up here at the public dock on the east shore, or anchor in the dredged triangular basin shown on the chart, where it is quieter but less convenient. Go into the Texaco gas dock or tie up at the Galilee State Pier, which is in front of the Dutch Inn sign seen ashore. Then go see the accommodating Harbor Masters, Alan Gorham or Bob Brow, whose office is on the shore end of the state pier. They will either find space for you, at the pier for $5.00 overnight, with water and electricity, or suggest to you an anchorage well out of the steamer's way. Gas is available nearby. Along the shore is a long row of commercial and sport fishing docks, and on the main road are small stores, restaurants, hot dog joints, and what have you. Don't forget to visit George's Restaurant located at the foot of the main road. It's a Mecca for seafood gourmands. You'll see a mixture of all kinds of people, from genuine fishermen to tourists in search of atmosphere or a good time. The noise pollution emitted here at dawn by fishermen, gulls, and engines shouldn't upset the early riser.

This port is a good place for shelter, but you will like it better on weekdays than on weekends unless you are very gregarious by nature. The tide is strong at times, and if you are at anchor you may do some swinging. This is especially true if you attempt to anchor in the small dredged basin shown on the chart as directly south of Little Comfort Island. Fairly shoal, with a mud bottom, this place with its almost imperceptible whirlpool action caused by the tidal currents will have you swinging on your anchor and may even break it out.

To reach Snug Harbor on the west shore of Point Judith Pond just beyond Galilee, proceed northward, having left nun 2 to starboard. Favor the west side of the channel. First you'll come upon the Snug Harbor Marina, with berths, gas, Diesel fuel, ice, groceries, marine supplies, but no repair service. Next, the Rhode Island Marine Services has comparable offerings, including repair work. And, finally, you will reach Salt Pond Marine Railway, which claims to be a full service yard, including the only showers around. These are fine facilities, but once tied up at one of the slips, you are apt to get a good roll from the nearby channel traffic. Excellent quahauging is reported to be found in the pond.

Wakefield, R.I. (13219 268). If you have time and your boat draws under 4½ feet you can follow, preferably at high water, the buoyed channel for 3 or 4 miles to the attractive city of Wakefield, where there are good shopping facilities, motels, eating places, etc. Note on the chart the comment that "improved channels shown by broken lines are subject to shoaling, particularly at the edges." Most experienced boating people also know that channels dredged out of shoal and marsh can silt up quickly, especially in a storm. The passage from Snug Harbor; beginning at can 7 and extending to nun 12 south of Plato Island, is such a channel.

Making this passage on a *flood* tide, during one of our visits, we tailed a Concordia yawl of 5′8″ draft without incident. The mean range of tide is 3 feet. Consult your chart and favor the port side of the channel all the way up. Along the way, anchorage can be found in several places, one of which is Smelt Brook Cove in the northwestern part of Point Judith Pond just north of Crown Point. Stay fairly close to the port shore on entering, since a rock ledge lies along the northern mouth of the cove. Here you can lie at a quiet anchorage in about 5 feet of water lined with a gravel bottom. Another good anchorage, though exposed to the north and south, is between Gardner and Beach Islands. Between the channel's red nun 16 and black can 21 be sure to follow the buoys rather than what appears on the chart as the deeper water. A dangerous spot for strangers is what natives term "Bill's Island," a rock shelf to starboard between nuns 16 and 18. (You will find how this island got its name shortly.) Proceed cautiously throughout this area, keeping both rock and can well to port. At Wakefield's Upper Pond basin, with 6 feet of water at low tide, there are several boat yards with hauling and repair facilities, and docks well equipped for landing and providing gas, water, electricity, and other facilities. This is an interesting trip and provides anchorages or tie-ups in some ways more desirable than those at the towns with the biblical names.

At Wakefield are two small yacht clubs, the Point Judith Yacht Club and the University of Rhode Island Sailing Club, both located on the west shore. During our many visits here we have become friendly with Bill Schmid, manager of the Ram Point Marina, and can vouch for his very competent engine and electronic repair work as well as his genial hospitality. His services also include gas, Diesel fuel, water, ice, showers, and electricity at the slips. We suggest you do not anchor here at Wakefield, for the basin's mud bottom offers poor holding ground. You can hang on one of Bill's sixteen moorings for an overnight charge of $3.00, or take one of his six transient slips for 25¢ a foot. This is such a popular spot that it might be wise to phone (401) 783–4535 for an advance reservation. Ram Point's facilities are quite adequate, although you'll have to go a mile to Wakefield for restaurants or supplies. Bill's wife runs the store, which is well stocked with charts and all sorts of marine gear. She caters to female customers too. A snack bar is located at the smaller Stone Cove Marine just up the line. The following reputable restaurants can easily be reached by taxi: Larchwood Inn requires only casual dress and offers music and dancing; the Sweet Meadows Inn is located in a charming old mansion, caters to guests in more formal attire and is quite expensive; and Open Hearth Steaks, which invites its customers to "come as you are."

Narrangansett Bay, R.I., and Mass.
(13223 236, 13224 278, 13221 353).

A well-known manufacturer of small boats tells of a yachtsman who chartered a yacht from him in Narragansett Bay for a period of three weeks during World War II, and then discovered that he couldn't take the boat out of the bay. A submarine net barred his way.

"Don't keep her any longer than you want to and we'll fix the price accordingly," said the boat manufacturer.

Three weeks passed, with nothing heard from the fellow who did the chartering until the last day.

"I could have spent a month cruising in Narragansett Bay," was his enthusiastic comment.

This well-protected, well-buoyed, well-lighted bay of many good harbors affords some delightful sailing, despite the omnipresent United States Navy. The scenery is restful and pastoral, the water is generally smooth, and the wind is usually just right. At the foot of the bay is the famous yachting harbor of Newport, where the Bermuda racing fleet gathers every other June. At the head of the bay, 24 miles from the open sea, are two great cities: Providence and Fall River. In between is an almost bewildering collection of islands, peninsulas, bays, and passages, easy to navigate, lovely to sail.

As in Buzzards Bay, the prevailing summer winds are from the southwest, but they are usually less violent. A typical summer day is likely to include a light northerly in the early morning, then a calm until the early afternoon, when a moderate sou'wester will begin to stir up a few whitecaps. With evening, calm again descends upon the waters of the bay. The swimming is good in many parts of the lower bay—not so good near Providence and Fall River.

While Narragansett Bay took severe beatings from the hurricanes of September 21, 1938, and August 31, 1954 (Hurricane Carol), and also some damage from several other hurricanes, its yacht clubs and fleets have recovered, and the bay is far better equipped than ever before to take another, if it comes. For instance, the Rhode Island Yacht Club, on the Providence River, which has had two clubhouses washed away, is now perched up in the air on "stilts."

There are at least thirty-five good harbors in Rhode Island waters, including Narragansett Bay (a small part of which is in Massachusetts), and we have counted twenty-eight yacht clubs. Boat yards and marinas are well spread out over the bay. At the time of writing there are thirty state summer-guest moorings strategically placed in various harbors, as we shall note in each case. These moorings are about 2 feet in diameter and are stenciled with the words "State of R.I. Guest Mooring Buoy." They are maintained by the Rhode Island Department of Natural Resources, are marked with the weights of the anchors, and are limited to 12-hour use. Yachtsmen are also advised to keep a sharp lookout, especially at night, for fish weirs or traps, which, as shown by the dotted lines on the charts, are strung out throughout the bay.

The Rhode Island Yachting Association is active in sponsoring and stimulating racing, and the Twenty Hundred Club sponsors races by cruising craft to Cuttyhunk and elsewhere. Indeed it is a fine cruising area, as recognized by the Cruising Club of America, one of whose summer-cruise announcements contained these words: "Your Committee, having had so many wonderful reports of cruising in Narragansett Bay, has scheduled the next rendezvous at Bristol, Rhode Island."

In 1976, a *Cruising Guide to Historic Rhode Island* was issued by the University of Rhode Island's Marine Advisory Service, Narragansett Bay Campus, Narragansett, R.I. 02882, at a price of $1.00. Its purpose is to enable travelers either by boat or by car to explore those of the state's historical attractions that lie within easy reach of the coastline. It is used in conjunction with marine charts and cruising guides and even indicates the location of shellfish beds. On the back of the book is a color reproduction of a map of the bay drawn in 1777.

There are three important passages running up the bay in a northerly direction: the *West Passage,* starting between the mainland on the west side of the bay and Conanicut Island; the *East Passage,* between Conanicut and Aquidneck islands, with Newport as the usual take-off point; and the *Sakonnet River,* with the much-improved Sakonnet Harbor at its southern end. While Newport and Sakonnet harbors are convenient ports of call for longshore cruisers, we are not forgetting here that they are also starting points for cruising on Narragansett Bay.

In this book we shall follow each of the three above passages northward, stopping at each harbor on the way. The ports are all in Rhode Island, unless otherwise stated. As usual, we are giving the numbers of the largest-scale charts available. Chart 13221, however, covers very well the whole bay.

WEST PASSAGE

1. Dutch Island Harbor (13223 236). Among many Rhode Island yachtsmen this is the most popular harbor on the bay, not for its facilities, for there are almost none, but partly because of its lack of them. It is unspoiled, uncrowded even when a yacht-club fleet makes it a rendezvous; the swimming is fine; and except in blows from the north it is fairly well protected.

In 1977, the Coast Guard announced that the blinking red beacon of Dutch Island Lighthouse, which has guided boats along the west passage of Narragansett Bay since 1827, would shine no more. An official stated that "since the Navy left Newport, vandals have had a field day," and apparently the high repair costs were a major factor in the decision to close the lighthouse down. When you read this, the light will have been replaced by a lighted gong buoy on the southern side of the passage.

This new buoy should make it easy to enter the harbor at night, and there are no important outlying obstacles after leaving nun 2 to starboard. Supplies are available at Jamestown, a little over ½ mile away. The Dutch Harbor Shipyard, just north of a dilapidated wharf on the east shore, has a dock with gas, water, ice, and moorings. One authority recommends walking over to Mackerel Cove, which, with Dutch Island Harbor, almost divides Conanicut Island. There you will fine a splendid swimming beach.

At the time of writing there are, in summer, 8 state moorings in the harbor. If none is available when you get there, the best anchorage is between the wharf at the northerly end of Fox Hill and the eastern shore of the harbor. Those trailers swarming on top of Fox Hill congregate during the weekends in what is called the Fort Getty Recreation Area. An excellent launching ramp is at the foot of the hill.

2. Wickford (13223 236). Wickford was formerly Updike's Newtown, named in 1663 and platted in 1707. In contrast to Dutch Island Harbor, it has more facilities than any port on the bay. On approaching the harbor, pick up the church spire in Wickford or the prominent abandoned lighthouse on Poplar Point. While some may prefer to anchor behind the breakwaters in the outer harbor to obtain more privacy, perhaps using one of the three state moorings in that area, most visitors go into Wickford Cove, where they have much to choose from.

Along the east shore to port, as one enters this cove, sits the large marina of Wickford Shipyard, one of the most attractive and best-equipped marinas in New England. On our most recent visit, Wally

Wickford, Narragansett Bay.

Hudson, the long-time dock master here, updated us on the cove and invited us to look over several fine new Sea Sprite sloops turned out at his shipyard. Besides many slips, gas, Diesel fuel, water, electricity, telephones, ice, hauling and repair work, showers, laundromat, swimming pool, and marine supply store, Wickford Shipyard has a fine large restaurant. They charge 35¢ per foot at the slips. The Harbor Master may be found at the town dock, chiefly commercial, which lies across the shipyard at the cove's entrance. You can tie up here for a two-hour time limit.

Proceeding up the channel, dredged to a controlled depth of 7 feet MLW, one finds to port another first-class establishment, the Wickford Cove Marina, which caters primarily to power boats. For all types of supplies, one can pass westward through the marked channel in Wickford Cove to a public landing located up on the west shore. Here you can tie up temporarily, pick up supplies at nearby Ryan's Market (open Sundays), and stroll among the pleasant shops and quaint old streets of the town.

There are also two boat yards on Mill Cove, located to the north: Pleasant Street Wharf and Johnson's Boat Yard. Favor the starboard side of this cove's channel going in; its depth has been controlled to at least 6½ feet MLW throughout. On one of our visits, we had a delightful chat with Ralph Vale, one of the founders and past commodores of the Wickford Yacht Club, situated on Pleasant Street Wharf at the entrance to Mill Cove. It is a "fun club," hosting an active sailing program. The clubhouse, housed in an antique oyster house dating back to the seventeen hundreds, has been completely refurbished while maintaining much of its original charm. Wickford certainly welcomes visiting club yachtsmen, though it has limited facilities for them. If one of the club's five guest moorings, marked blue and white, is not available to you, pick up one from Pleasant Street Wharf. Mill Cove, offering 6-foot depths and good holding ground, promises a peaceful, scenic anchorage.

Wickford traces its origins to 1640, when Richard Smith, an associate of Roger Williams, established an Indian trading post on nearby Cocumscussoc Brook. He named the general area Wickford, supposedly in honor of Elizabeth Winthrop, wife of the governor of Connecticut and a native of Wickford, England. Capitalizing on its harbor, the village first developed into a shipping center for wealthy Narragansett planters and after the Revolution became a maritime community, with its economy based on fishing, boat building, and related industries.

Today, some leading yachtsmen put Wickford at the head of their list of appealing Narragansett Bay harbors, not only because of its perfect shelter and the many modern facilities and conveniences available but because it is a remarkably preserved postcolonial town, crowded with lovely Georgian period houses. As many as 850 pleasure craft have been counted here on a summer's day!

3. *Allen Harbor (13223 236).* This harbor lies on the western shore of the West Passage between Wickford and East Greenwich. The latest *Coast Pilot* says that it "is entered through a buoyed channel which has a depth of about 8 feet, m.l.w.," and this is verified on examining the current chart. However, local authorities reported to us at the time of writing that boats of 5-foot draft have touched bottom in the channel at low water. Despite this, Allen Harbor offers excellent protection midst pleasant surroundings and is used extensively by the members of the Quonset Davisville Navy Yacht Club located on the southeastern shore. With all the moorings and dolphins private, none are to be picked up, and with no facilities here for transient yachts, one is forced to drop anchor in soft bottom in good depth. The government has placed a buoy well out from Calf Pasture, since shoaling has extended further to the east than is indicated on the chart. Stay well offshore!

4. *East Greenwich (13224 278).* This harbor is attractive, and the shelter, bathing, and facilities are all good. But it is on the main line of Amtrak and trains whistle as they go by. It can be uncomfortable in a northeaster. Nevertheless, here is one of the best natural harbors on the bay.

The entrance is made from Warwick Point Light. The channel is well marked and easily entered by day, but it is narrow, and boats drawing more than 6 feet should keep close to the buoys. Take special care to stay north of can 5 marking Sally Rock; this is no channel in which to cut buoys.

In entering at night from can 5, steer southwest for the lights at Norton's Shipyard enabling you to pick up nun 6 and then can 7 beyond.

Black can 7 opposite Norton's Shipyard and Marina on the west shore indicate the entrance. There is a bad shoal from this can to Long Point on the port, so keep close to the starboard shore. With many of the moorings already occupied in this harbor, one may be obtained from the shipyard or at the East Greenwich Yacht Club on the west shore beyond. If no moorings are available, there is ample opportunity to anchor between the shipyard and the club.

There is about 12 feet of water at the marina dock and 8 feet at the club. Appropriately, there's a good marine store at the shipyard and a fine bar and showers in the clubhouse. The club's charge for an overnight slip is 25¢ a foot and a mooring is $3.00. Launch service operates from 8 A.M. to 10 P.M. daily.

The East Greenwich Yacht Club, established in 1909 and one of the leading boating centers on the bay, is pleased to offer its marina facilities to members of other recognized yacht clubs. With a hundred youngsters in its Junior sailing program and 88 percent of its three hundred fifty members boat owners, its fleet totals close to 300 boats, of which most are Sea Sprites, Lasers, 505s, Tempests, Blue Jays, and includes eighty-five Sunfish alone. The club has hosted such racing regattas as the Sears, Mallory, and Adams Cup as well as the Atlantic Coast Lightning Championship. Both Bob Broz, for twenty-three years the steward here, and past commodore Joe Lawton are delightful fellows, who can spin yarns all day long about the bay and its 400 miles of coastline.

If you like shore exercise in pleasant surroundings, take a walk in Goddard Memorial State Park located on Potowomut Neck across the harbor or climb the long steep hill to the town's main street, where all sorts of supplies can be obtained. Good food is served at Harborside, Pals, or Mama Ciello, all within three blocks of the yacht club, and Harbourside Lobstermania, a new waterfront restaurant with docks for guests, is just to the south.

Shallow-draft boats can go nearly to the head of the harbor, which is attractive. But don't proceed beyond Arnold's Boat Shop, where the mud bottom begins to shoal badly. Norton's is the place to go for competent engine, hull, and rigging repair work. In the town are a number of early American houses, including the General James Mitchell Varnum house. There is also the Naval and Military Museum, in the Varnum Armory.

5. Apponaug Cove (13224 278). In approaching this cove, make sure to stay well off of The Brothers, a cluster of dangerous rocks ¾ of a mile due west of lighted buoy GB. They have often been the nemesis of yachtsmen unfamiliar with Greenwich Bay.

Before entering the channel, you will note the rather expansive Cowesett Marina located on the western shore just southwest of can 3. This place provides full marina and repair service with good water dockside and a restaurant. Just beyond Cowesett's is the Masthead Marina with comparable facilities but no fuel available at the time of writing. Both these places appear to cater to power boats and have constructed sizable breakwaters to provide greater protection in easterlies.

The cove, which forms the northwestern arm of Greenwich Bay, is navigable through its channel with a depth of 5 feet, MLW, in 1976. However, the channel is tending to shoal in spots, and boats drawing more than 4 feet are advised to proceed with caution at low water. There is 4-foot tide range here.

The channel leading to the cove begins at nun 2 just off Cedar Tree Point. On Arnold Neck to port, you can pick up a mooring or slip space at Apponaug Harbor Marina, the home of the Apponaug Harbor Yacht Club, which has turned out some of the best sailors on the bay. Check in with the very obliging Charles Dickerson at the main dock, depth 6 feet. As the marina's manager, he'll assign you a slip for 30¢ per foot or an overnight mooring for $5.00, with electricity and water thrown in. Gas, ice, showers, and all types of repair work are on hand; the marina is popular with sailing craft, but one must go to Cowesett for Diesel repairs and fuel. Supplies can be picked up with taxi service to nearby Apponaug and the Theodore Francis Airport only six minutes away. Moorings for deep-draft vessels are found outside the harbor, south of Arnold Neck. But for better protection in a strong southerly, you can venture further into the cove while avoiding the sandbar extending from the west between cans 5 and 7. This upper channel is lined with tire moorings set out by the town. Since there is little space for anchorage, one must tie up to these fore and aft.

Ponaug Marina at the very head of this cove has only 4 feet at its docks at low water but is conveniently located for taking on supplies and gaining the opportunity to enjoy a satisfying meal ashore at a nearby popular restaurant. Here the surroundings are pleasant and quite peaceful, disturbed only by the airplane traffic and trains rumbling over the bridge to the west.

6. Warwick Cove (13224 278). A man who knows the bay says that this is a "nice harbor." With a 5-foot rise and fall of tide here, the entrance is tricky but at low water it has 5 or 6 feet both there and inside if you know where to go. A local authority urged favoring the east shore in approaching the entrance. Further in, watch out for a bad shoal, bare at low water, extending 150 yards westward from the west side of the channel between cans 5 and 7 to the southeast tip of Horse Neck. In 1976 we sounded 5 feet at MLW along much of the 150-foot-wide channel, with slight shoaling recorded in the 300-yard stretch southwest of nun 10. There are, however, two mooring basins with 6-foot depths located alongside the channel halfway up. One is across from the Warwick Cove Marina and the other is just to the north along the western shore. See Earle Steere, the marina manager, for advice on dockage and most any other service needed by cruising people. His slips have the deepest water and he can provide gas, Diesel fuel, ice, water, electricity, and a possible mooring for the night. A shopping center is conveniently located nearby. More extensive repair work is performed at the C-Lark Marina toward the head of the cove. The only drawback about Warwick Cove is that it has become a congested paradise for local craft and as such leaves precious little room for the transient yacht.

7. Bullock Cove, Providence River (east shore—13224 278). Here is a fine protected harbor whose main channel has, in 1976, unfortunately shoaled to the following depths—4½ feet MLW in the narrow entrance channel to the special mooring basin eastward of Bullock Point, except for shoaling to ½ foot on the eastern limit of the channel at the entrance to this basin, thence 5 feet in the basin, thence 4 feet to the mooring and turning basin ½ mile above Bullock Point, thence only 2 feet in the basin at the very head of the cove. Follow the buoys carefully since they and the dolphins have been shifted to signal the best water. Inside, on the west shore, are the Narragansett Terrace Yacht Club and the Narragansett Terrace Boat Yard; both places are congested with moored boats. Further up to starboard, just below the final basin, is the large Cove Haven Marina, which we have found to be most complete and cooperative. They can't provide provisions but do offer yachtsmen the opportunity to have cookouts near attractive Haines State Park. The Crescent Amusement Park, providing fun for the family, is fairly close at hand. This marina, one of the most popular facilities on the east shore of Narragansett Bay, can accommodate boats of almost 6-foot draft and up to 42 feet overall at its floating slips, where there's a 25¢ per foot charge, including water, electricity, and use of the swimming pool. The row of pilings off this dock mark the north and south channels to the slips.

Bullock Neck is a nice residential area, and the harbor is one of the snuggest and most attractive on the bay, deep enough for most cruising yachts and marred only by unsightly floating algae occasionally brought to the surface after a summer storm. It's still a wise move to post a lookout, however, whenever negotiating this channel at low tide.

8. Pawtuxet Cove, Providence River (west shore—13224 278). The construction of a prominent 800-yard dike south of Pawtuxet Neck several years ago has made the southern end of this cove a sheltered and rather fascinating place. The dike runs from Rock Island northward to a point just south of the cove's entrance. Come between can 1 and nun 2 heading westward on the range lights. Proceed up the middle of the 4½-foot dredged channel, pick up the markers to starboard, and make a wide turn around the point, making sure not to hug it too closely. From here, the narrow channel to the north records on the 1977 chart a mere 1½-foot depth at MLW all the way to the Edgewood Marine on your port and Carl's Pawtuxet Cove Marina further up to starboard. Before negotiating this shoaling passage, your boat should be of very shallow draft or you should be sure to consult local authorities concerning the latest depths.

If boats of considerable draft wish to anchor in this harbor, their best bet is to ride in the 100-yard-wide south basin, whose limits are marked by white buoys and depth is reported to be 5 feet at the time of writing. The dike makes this a very safe anchorage but it is still open a bit to the south. Should you be an apartment dweller feeling rather homesick, you may get some relief by gazing up at a string of condominium apartments rising to the west.

9. Edgewood, Cranston, Providence River (west shore—13224 278). While this section of the Providence River above the Pawtuxet River is too wide and exposed to be called a harbor, the presence on this shore of two of the leading yacht clubs on the bay makes this a rewarding port of call for visiting yachts cruising on the bay. From south to north these are the Rhode Island Yacht Club, organized in 1875 and thus one of the oldest yacht clubs in the country, and the Edgewood Yacht Club, organized in 1889 and now sometimes called "the sailingest club on the bay."

The Rhode Island Yacht Club is on the north end of Washouset Point on Pawtuxet Neck and easily recognized as the "club on stilts," resting one story up on large steel-and-concrete pillars, high enough, it is hoped, to avoid the fate of its predecessors, swept away by hurricanes. Until very recently, perhaps, this club has stressed social rather than yachting activities. But there are now signs that yachting there is coming back. North from the clubhouse is a long gas dock.

The Edgewood Yacht Club, which, though battered, has survived all hurricanes to date, is a short distance to the north. Here a very active sailing program is undertaken, with much stress on Junior activities. It boasts the first sailing school on the bay and in 1975 won the Narragansett Bay Junior Racing Championships. There are also races for Peppy Pappies, formerly called Tired Fathers, until the fathers said they weren't tired anymore. This busy club is most hospitable to visiting yachtsmen from other yacht clubs, as we know from our own experience; if a spare mooring is available, we feel sure a visitor would be accommodated. Ice and water can be picked up at the gas dock. Space at their floating slips, with 4-foot depths, is a flat $9.00, while overnight moorings rent at $6.00. The launch operates from 8:30 A.M. to 9 P.M. Unfortunately, they don't serve meals here.

That odd-looking breakwater running outside and parallel to the club's outer dock reflects the inventiveness of Dr. Tadeusz Kowalski of the Ocean Engineering Department at the University of Rhode Island. As an authority on floating breakwaters, he helped design this rather unique model. Apparently, building such an installation using old rubber tires is far cheaper than constructing a traditional barrier of wood or stone. What's more, it seems to work!

Various intercollegiate yacht races have been hosted here, and from what we have seen the club carries out well the simply stated objectives of its constitution: "To encourage the sport of yachting, to promote the science of seamanship and navigation, and to provide and maintain a suitable Club House and anchorage for the recreation and use of its members."

Above the Rhode Island and Edgewood Yacht clubs is the Narragansett Yacht Club, protected from the north by Field Point. Here, in the corner is Port Edgewood, its slips protected by a stone breakwater and further identified by a large blue-faced boatshed. Although this spot has gas, ice, a marine store with charts, and complete repair service, it remains largely a boat dealer and has no room or moorings for transient yachts. Parent's Marina just to the northeast is an obvious alternative for a layover. The nearby Cranston Hilton Inn serves excellent meals.

Since yachtsmen when cruising will generally prefer to stay away from the heart of a big city, we shall end here our voyage up the West Passage of Narragansett Bay and go back to the entrance of the East Passage.

In making your way up the East Passage, note that historic 107-year-old Rose Island Light House Station, just below the Newport suspension bridge, has been discontinued, and in 1976 the deed to its property was handed over to the University of Rhode Island whose Ocean Engineering Department will use it for teaching, research, and environmental programs. Lighted Bell R12, just off the southwest shore of the island, has replaced it.

10. Newport, Aquidneck Island, R.I. (13223 236, 13221 353). One of the principal summer resorts and yachting centers of the Atlantic Coast, Newport is not always a snug or a quiet anchorage, although its inner harbor has undergone a dramatic restoration in recent years. To confuse the waters further, it is an important commercial center. But the two harbors (inner and outer), divided by city-owned Goat Island, are protected, well marked and lighted, so that Newport is easy of access at all times. Newport is the most practical 'longshore harbor capable of holding a fleet of yachts between Stonington, Connecticut, and Padanaram in Buzzards Bay. Being near the entrance of Narragansett Bay, it is a convenient harbor for those cruising alongshore, as well as a good take-off point for bay cruising.

Most yachts anchor in Brenton Cove, the bight in the southern part of Newport Harbor, but it can be rough there in a northeaster and sometimes in a northwester. Though less convenient for supplies than the main harbor, it is noncommercial and the water is clean. The quietest spot is near the head of the cove; there are five state guest moorings on the south shore near the point at the entrance of the small inner cove. Just pick up any one that is vacant. There are no landing or other facilities here. For that purpose an anchorage off the Ida Lewis Yacht Club is the best bet.

The Ida Lewis Yacht Club, where cruising yachts are most likely to stop, also has guest moorings and, in addition, launch service is provided. There is no gas, nor are there dining facilities. This club is located in the eastern part of Brenton Cove and occupies the lighthouse, kept at one time by Ida Lewis, where she made such a reputation for the rescue of seamen in distress that several rocks were named for her. The eighteen lives she saved are represented by the eighteen stars in the club's burgee. Her rescues, some of which are recorded on the wall of the clubhouse, were made between 1859 and 1906. On one of our visits, Charles "Ted" Nelson also showed us some fascinating Cup Defender memorabilia in his salty dock-master shack. The club, organized in 1928, has a 300-foot gangway to the shore. There is a landing float on the west side, and the club is hospitable to visiting yachtsmen from other recognized yacht clubs, as we have always found. This is a club that is primarily interested in sailing, and the water is deep nearby. In June, during even-numbered years, Brenton Cove and vicinity is the rendezvous for the Bermuda Race fleet, and there, on the eve of the race, is to be seen one of the finest gatherings of cruising yachts to be

John T. Hopf

Newport Harbor and Narragansett Bay. Ida Lewis Yacht Club and Brenton Cove lie to the left center of the photograph and Goat Island to the right. Conanicut Island and the West Passage may be seen in the distance.

witnessed anywhere in the United States. On odd-numbered years, the Annapolis-Newport Race now ends at Newport and the races for the America's Cup take place off Newport. During all of these major events Newport is the hub of the yachting universe, and the Ida Lewis Yacht Club is in the middle of that hub. For the rest of the season the yachts seen in Brenton Cove are apt to be relatively few in number compared to those seen in earlier days or now moored in such ports as Padanaram or Marblehead.

For those who carry their cruisers on trailers and would like to start or end a cruise at Newport, there is a fine concrete launching ramp in King Park, adjoining the Ida Lewis Yacht Club.

The other yacht club in Newport is the Newport Yacht Club, organized in 1890, and located on Long Wharf, the town dock in the northeast corner of the harbor. The club has reserved six of its numerous floating slips for cruising yachtsmen from other recognized yacht clubs; a permanent breakwater lies to the south. Before tying up, signal the dock master to see if there's space available. Neill Gray, the club's steward and a Newport native, welcomed us on our last visit here. Although launch service, ice, and water are provided, no guest moorings or fuels are to be had. Showers and a bar are located in the attractive clubhouse.

Ashore nearby, J.T. O'Connell, ship chandlery, is the place to go for all types of marine supplies. And if you need him, Newport's Harbor Master, John Violet, when we were there, can usually be found stationed in a red wooden shack next to the club. His number is 847–6458. In the event that this is your first extended visit to Newport, it's a short walk over to the Chamber of Commerce's office at 93 Thames Street, where you can pick up such free, useful guides as the *Rhode Island Visitors' Guide,* a *Welcome to Newport* map, and an excellent reference booklet for cruising people, *Boating in Rhode Island.*

The harbor's waterfront facing the Newport Yacht Club has undergone a dramatic, faithfully styled restoration, recapturing much of the Colonial charm of old Newport. Running from north to south, the following points of interest can be seen: Long Wharf Mall, with its many shops; The Brick Market, a three-story, 1760 building on Long Wharf housing a craft shop specializing in Newport and other Colonial reproductions; the Newport Harbor Treadway Inn, including a swimming pool and the Blue Porpoise Tavern built on the exact site of its predecessor; and historic Bowen's Wharf, an eighteenth-century cobblestoned wharf, with its collection of quaint restaurants, taverns, and charming shops like the Chandlery and the Clay Pigeon.

Treadway Inn makes numerous slips and overnight moorings along its waterfront available through Oldport Marine Services. This is a convenient location for a layover or for those dining at the Blue Porpoise, from which the schooner *Black Pearl* may be viewed. Prices at the time of writing ran 45¢ a foot at the slips and $5.00 for a mooring; the inn's pool, showers, and sauna are available to its guests but there is no fuel supply. Other services provided include the rental of Bullseye daysailers and the use of launches within the harbor—even by those guests shuttling to the Ida Lewis Yacht Club. Phoning (401) 847–9109 for reservations at Oldport Marine is certainly in order.

As a matter of fact, to guarantee your boat a mooring or tie-up, we suggest that you phone or write in advance of your arrival to let any one of the following Newport marinas of your choice know your specific visit plans. These facilities, with their full range of services, run along the commercial waterfront on the east side of the harbor. Listed from north to south, here are their names and phone numbers:

Bannister's Wharf (847–0100), formerly Port O'Call, has no repair service but has two excellent eating places, the Clarke Cooke House and Black Pearl Tavern. The cup defender, *Courageous,* had its berth here. The Mooring (847–9790) at Sayers Wharf promises complete docking facilities. Marine supplies can be found at Murphy Marine (849–2010), where the engine repair service supervised by Gordon Murphy is said to be topnotch. Next in line comes Mathinos & Son Shipyard (846–7809), located on Hammetts Wharf. Christie's (847–5400) has dock space for yachts up to 100 feet and Newport's oldest waterfront restaurant, affording a spectacular view of the America's Cup 12 meters during the races. The *Bill of Rights* is now berthed here. Newport Shipyard (846–6700) is highly regarded for hauling, repair work, etc., but does not sell gas or Diesel fuel. From here or from Bannister's, there's access to a laundromat.

We still like the Williams & Manchester Shipyard (846–0725), the reason being that it obviously caters to sailing craft, including the "Twelves" during the Cup Races. It also has a dock master named Charlie Bingham. You may not find him around on a Sunday morning, as one yachtsman has reported to us, but most of the time he's very much on the job and is worth contacting. This handsome marina, equipped with excellent docks, is the first one you will reach on leaving the Ida Lewis Yacht Club and entering the main harbor. Here you'll also find the Pier Restaurant, a large and busy place, serving mostly seafood for lunch and dinner, with music nightly.

Looking to the west, one can easily observe the result of Goat Island's face-lifting. The large brick building, resembling a fancy grain elevator, is the Sheraton-Islander Inn, not connected with the Goat Island Marina, whose headquarters is housed in a prominent concrete building just to the south. This expansive marina offers sheltered dockage with 150 slips providing water and electricity. To be assigned a slip, put in at the gas dock facing the inner harbor, where fuel, ice, a laundromat, and marine supplies are available. Large power cruisers are usually tied up at the outer docks while sailing craft are assigned dockage on the north side of the marina building. The daily dockage fee, including water and electricity, for a boat under 30 feet was $12.00 at the time of writing; for over 30 feet it was 40¢ a foot. People docking here can use the Sheraton-Islander facilities, and at the end of the bridge along the causeway a convenient shuttle bus to town may be picked up. Peter Dunning, the efficient manager at Goat Island Marina (849–5655), knows his way around Newport and boats. His is the host marina for the Observer Single-Handed Transatlantic Race from Plymouth, England, every four years.

One cannot write up Newport without noting that she has possibly the world's largest sailing navy, what with her colonial sloop-of-war *Providence,* the square-rigged hermaphrodite brig, *Black Pearl,* and the British frigate HMS *Rose* over at King's Dock near the Treadway Inn. Built in 1756, *Rose* was reconstructed in 1969 using the original plans and some original wood. She boasts twenty-four guns and the distinction of not only being the only ship of the Revolutionary War in existence but of being instrumental in the founding of the American Navy. Another spectacle is *Bill of Rights,* a replica of a 125-foot gaff-topsail schooner of the 1850s. She is now being used for commercially scheduled windjammer cruises in southern New England and Chesapeake Bay waters. Her builder, the late Harvey Gamage, is considered by his fellow natives down East to be the last of the great builders of wooden ships. Concerning *Bill of Rights,* he has said, "The last time I see this ship is when it's put its tail to me and is disappearing down the harbor. I won't ever see it again, but I will know it is a good ship, because I built it." With frequent visits from the likes of *Shenandoah, Brilliant,* and other American sail-training vessels, one can admire more traditional ship design here perhaps than anywhere, with the possible exception of Mystic Seaport.

Similar to Mystic, Newport is also feeling the impact of a growing boating population. No one can deny that the increase in its harbor congestion during recent summers is creating deep concern among both Newporters and cruising people. The combination of major sailing events and lobster landings translate into hard cash for this city, which has managed to survive the Navy fleet pullout of the early 1970s by attracting tourists, boating enthusiasts, and fishermen, who have not always mixed harmoniously on the waterfront.

At present, many of the fishing boats dock at the harbor's north end and must power through a crowded anchorage and maneuver between pleasure boat slips to tie up at wharves there. More than one of us may agree with another skipper's comment that "if you're next to a lobster boat coming in, you're going to be praying to hell they don't hit you." In 1978, negotiations were underway to purchase the old Newport Shipyard complex on Thames Street for use as a docking and service facility for at least fifty-seven of the eighty to ninety inshore and off-shore fishing boats based in Newport.

Authorities say that there are three Newports: the Historic Newport, symbolized by Thames Street along the eastern shore of the harbor; the Social Newport, where once the "Four Hundred" held court; and the Navy Newport. To this we would add the Yachting Newport, which reaches its peaks intermittently when the fleets come in. All are interesting in different ways. When you are there, take a look at the Old Stone Mill in Touro Park, made memorable by Longfellow's "Skeleton in Armor":

> There for my lady's bower
> Built I the lofty tower.

While historians dispute the accuracy of the story that it was built by a Viking nearly a thousand years ago, no one knows who did build it, and no plaque or inscription describes its origin.

Like Glen Cove, Long Island, Newport is reminiscent of the bygone days of great estates, when palatial steam yachts rode at anchor. Many of the estates have since been sold to schools or other institutions and, to understate the situation, yachts are smaller now.

11. Jamestown, Conanicut Island (13223 236, 13221 353). While this is an open anchorage on the west side of the East Passage, the presence of the hospitable Conanicut Yacht Club, a short distance north of the ferry dock and just south of Bryer Point, is an incentive to drop anchor off the club and hope for a reasonably calm night, since the holding ground is rather poor and the water comparatively shallow. This yacht club, founded in 1891 originally as the Jamestown Yacht Club, has a fine clubhouse, including a 220-foot pier with a 5-foot depth at its outer end. Visiting yachtsmen are welcomed provided they are members of other recognized and accredited yacht clubs. If so qualified, one must check in at the clubhouse to register with the steward. Conanicut's services are limited to several guest moorings with launch service, showers, and ice.

In approaching Jamestown Harbor from the south, be sure to give The Dumplings a very wide berth as you swing gradually around to port heading in. This spot is a poor place to be in an easterly blow.

The Conanicut Marina, just to the south of the yacht club, lies in a protected basin next to the ferry dock and in front of the old Bay View Hotel. This full-service marina, managed by Bill Munger, monitors Channel 68 for reservations. Here you'll find gas, Diesel fuel, ice, water, electricity, slips in 10 feet, MLW, moorings, launch service, marine supplies, showers, a laundromat, general repair work, and restaurants nearby. It is also accessible to a variety of stores for supplies.

South of the ferry, on the eastern shore leading toward Bull Point and inside of some islands and outlying rocks, are the piers of the Wharton Shipyard, which takes care of yachts, while providing guest moorings, if available, and gas, water, and repairs. George and Margaret Scott have taken over and expanded this yard, operated for many years by the late Charles Wharton. The holding ground is said to be satisfactory here. Go in to the Wharton dock on either side of the small island north of Old Salt Works Beach. The Dumpling Association has a private dock just north of this beach. Also to the north, Round House Shipyard is another facility but is mainly devoted to repair work.

Entering Jamestown, one can't help but gaze up in awe at that strange-looking house perched like a giant osprey nest atop one of the rocky Dumpling Islands. Built in 1904, and christened Clingstone in true nautical tradition, it was the dream house of Joseph Wharton, a wealthy ship owner and father of Charles Wharton. The house was built with $12'' \times 14''$ white oak ship timbers from Tennessee. The present owner claims "it isn't just nailed, it is pinned and tenoned like a clipper ship." What's more, it's shingled both inside and out. Let us hope that such a spectacle will stand as permanently as the foundation upon which it is built.

To the west, between Southwest Point and Short Point, boatmen have found Mackerel Cove a most inviting place in which to venture. The entire rockbound shoreline is privately owned and unspoiled. A pebbly swimming beach stretches across the head of the cove, and although it is public, no one is permitted to build fires or to picnic there. Yachtsmen will find this harbor devoid of any facilities, a fact that adds to its charm, and they are advised to navigate slowly, reducing their boats' wash to a minimum. Although the holding ground is good, don't get caught here in a strong southerly.

While you are at Jamestown, get someone to drive you to the southern end of Conanicut Island at Beavertail Point, the site of the third-oldest lighthouse erected on the Atlantic Coast. The view looking down from the cliffs is impressive.

The Jamestown high-level bridge across the West Passage brings Conanicut Island and Jamestown in the line of traffic from the New York area to Newport and Cape Cod. The island and the community are very much worth knowing.

12. *Coasters Harbor and Coddington Cove (13223 236, 13221 353).* Just above Newport, these are very much Navy, and visiting yachts are not encouraged. Navy requirements have precedence. The Navy is also active in Melville.

However, it is reported that a full-service marina will open up in 1978 within a basin just to the north of Melville. Its location is further shown on the chart as an inlet due south of Coggeshall Point on the western shore of Rhode Island and northeast of Dyer Island. Named the Bend Boat Basin and operated by the Fales family of Bristol's Hawkins & Fales, it promises to answer the prayers of yachtsmen who have often longed for a good facility within the East Passage.

13. *Potter Cove, Prudence Island, Narragansett Bay (13224 278, 13221 353).* Here is an excellent anchorage, protected from virtually all winds, on the northeasterly end of Prudence Island. Three red nuns lead to the cove's mouth. Many yachtsmen confuse this harbor with the other Potter Cove located on the eastern shore of Conanicut Island. But there is no comparison. Our leading authority on this harbor was once a professional clam digger, who "hung out" there or in the cove on the other side of the island most of the time. Here is how he feels about it:

> One of the reasons Potter's Cove is so well thought of is that there's absolutely nothing there but a landlocked anchorage. There is a well up at the farm that has good water. Don't fail to fill a jug or two while there. There is no "most convenient wharf for visiting yachtsmen." If you want to go ashore, you either row or swim. The "best place to obtain a meal" is in your own galley, and if you are looking for a hotel, crawl into your bunk and forget it. Never go to sleep on a strange craft.
>
> Follow the buoys in entering and anchor anywhere. It is crowded on weekends but restful and quiet through the week. There is good clam digging. The mosquitoes are terrible, but other places are worse.

The five state guest moorings are marked by ball floats painted white with a blue strip and are located along the western shore of the cove. The nearest source of gas, supplies, and repairs is at Bristol, about 3 miles away by water. Potter Cove is worth visiting, but be sure your screens are working, and try not to pick a weekend. A visitor to this harbor has reported that "the mosquitoes had either departed by the time we got there or their numbers and hunger have been exaggerated." From our experience, we have learned that if the mosquitoes don't appear on the scene, the horseflies probably will; your insecticide is your best defense.

Prudence Island is about 6 miles long and is without a town.

14. Bristol (13224 278, 13221 353). If you are entering or leaving Mt. Hope Bay while passing under the Mt. Hope Bridge, you may be curious about a modern-looking complex on Bristol Point to the north. This is the new $7½ million campus of Roger Williams College.

Bristol Harbor is large and exposed for some distance to the southwest and south. However, under the conditions usually prevailing in summer it is one of the most satisfactory ports on the bay for an overnight stop and large enough to hold a club fleet without crowding. The hospitality of the Bristol Yacht Club, the facilities in the harbor, the recently opened Herreshoff Marine Museum on the site of the yard where Nathanael and his sons conjured up their yacht-building wizardry, and the many fine old houses all combine to give Bristol an especial appeal to cruising yachtsmen.

The Bristol Yacht Club moved in 1955 to its present commodious headquarters on Popasquash Neck along the west side of the harbor near its northern end. The club has come a long way since the days when dues were 5¢ a month and those in arrears for six months' dues were liable to expulsion.

On one of our visits here, former Fleet Captain Seth Paull filled us in on a bit of its history. His grandfather, Commodore William Trotter, founded the club in 1877 as The Neptune Boat Club of Bristol, with a fleet of six-oared shells. Its laudatory purpose was "for the encouragement of boating, other athletic exercises and social enjoyment, and for the promotion of physical and mental culture." The marine architect, Halsey Herreshoff, who operates his firm in Bristol, is presently one of the yacht club's most distinguished members.

It is now rated among the leading clubs on the bay and, as such, hosted in 1970 the National Ensign Championship and the Atlantic Coast 110 Championship. When we were there, it boasted an active Junior Sailing Program of seventy boys and girls. We were greeted by Vice Commodore Herb Browne who reminded us that members of other recognized yacht clubs are made welcome. The clubhouse provides a snack bar, barroom, and showers. There are three state moorings at the extreme head of the harbor, but if these are not available, signal the launchman for a possibly vacant club mooring. Launch service runs from 8 A.M. to 9 P.M. Gas, water, and ice can be drawn at the club dock where there is 5 feet at low water.

Just north of the club lies the Bristol Marine Co., offering hauling service and full repair work. New Bristol class auxiliaries are fitted out here. They also may have a few spare moorings.

Two Bristol Harbor police boats, under the control of the Harbor Master, patrol nightly the harbor and adjacent waters.

Southeast of the yacht club and on the east shore a State Pier is located and appears on the chart. You will find the Harbor Master, Manny Sousa, at this landing. See him for a possible tie-up at one of the public moorings or at one of his slips. Here you'll find a launching ramp and parking area, a public telephone, and you'll be close to the center of town where all types of supplies may be purchased.

Just north of Walker Island to the south, you can pick up the small entrance channel to Hawkins and Fales, which has a few slips in just 4 feet at low water. Here you may find a marine store and general repair work but no fuel, ice, or showers. As the top distributor of Pearson Yachts, their primary business is as a yacht broker, not as a full-service marina.

Further to the south, it is a fascinating experience to visit the old buildings that once comprised the Herreshoff Boatyard and have been purchased by Sidney and Halsey Herreshoff, Captain Nat's son and grandson. There has been some new construction, but the buildings look as they did over a half century ago. If you are lucky, Halsey will show you around the workshop and museum where are displayed photographs and half models of classic yachts built here, including such America's Cup defenders as *Vigilant* (1893) to *Rainbow* (1934).

Bristol does it up red, white, and blue in celebrating the Fourth of July. Actually, the Fourth starts on the third—by early afternoon the demonstrative patriots are in the pubs and on the streets. All over town sharp explosions startle the poor townspeople and things get rowdier and louder as evening approaches. But the morning of the Fourth is another matter entirely. Responsible planning and precise organization produce such a glorious parade that the celebration draws sixty thousand to eighty thousand visitors each year. It should be a pretty good show. After all, it's the oldest, annually run Fourth of July parade in the nation.

Toward the head of the harbor at 119 Hope Street, The Lobster Pot is a recommended waterside eating place. Very popular Balzano's Restaurant in town specializes in delicious Italian food and seafood.

We were advised by a local authority to warn visiting yachts to keep well off the Castle Island light, as there are some uncharted rocks, with only 6 feet at low water over them, a short distance to the west of the light.

15. Warren and Barrington Rivers (13224 278, 13221 353). This anchorage, about 2 miles up the Warren River, is practically landlocked. The approach is narrow and tortuous, but well buoyed and easy to negotiate under power. Some yachts often find a pleasant anchorage in northerly and westerly winds in the middle of Smith Cove away from the river's current. Upriver to starboard, just before you turn into the Barrington River, is the late Bill Dyer's Anchorage, Inc., where the famous "Dyer dinks" are made. Be sure to pay this interesting place a visit, whether or not you are contemplating a new dinghy; you may get some ideas, as we did. Next to Dyer's, you can tie up in good water at the dock of the Wharf Tavern. They'll give you a good meal and don't require formal attire.

Most yachts continue into Barrington River to the attractive Barrington Yacht Club, located below the bridge to Barrington on the west shore of Tyler Point. Just before reaching the club, you will pass the new Barrington Marina on the point's southern tip. This is the yacht club's facility, providing slip space for twenty-five boats belonging to members and transients. Red range markers on both ends of the clubhouse help you determine the limits of the dredged channel. There is 6 feet of water at the dock of this active club, and since a 3- to 4-knot current runs in the river, it is preferable not to anchor but to pick up one of their moorings if available. On leaving the club dock, make sure to keep the marked obstruction buoy to port. Gas, Diesel fuel, water, and ice are on tap at the dock. A new clubhouse extension was built in 1976 providing a bar, showers, snack bar, and assembly hall, all available to members of recognized clubs that offer reciprocal privileges. The launch runs from 8 A.M. to 9 P.M.; the mooring charge for nonguests is $3.00 at the time of writing. However, if a slip is open, all visitors are charged at 20¢ a foot. The Stanley Boat Yard is nearby with very competent repair service and well-stocked marine supplies. The office of Thurston Sails is also near at hand. Supplies can be bought in Warren across the bridge, or in Barrington.

One of the outstanding clubs on Narragansett Bay, the Barrington Yacht Club, is the headquarters of a fine-looking fleet of cruising yachts, as well as the home of many one-design racing boats. It boasts one of the larger Blue Jay and 420 fleets in the country. In 1976 it hosted the World Championship 420 Cup with 75 boats competing.

We shall now go back to the entrance of the third passage up Narragansett Bay—the Sakonnet River and Mount Hope Bay.

The Sakonnet River and Mount Hope Bay

The Sakonnet River is the third and most easterly of the three passages leading northward up Narragansett Bay. Some bay yachtsmen call it the most beautiful of the three, especially in the fall, when the leaves are turning color.

16. Sakonnet Harbor (13221 353). Sakonnet is a good example of what man has done to turn a rather poor harbor into a snug harbor of refuge. To attain this, the basin was dredged to 8 feet, a dangerous rock in the middle removed, and the breakwater extended to 800 feet in length, thus providing some protection from northwesterlies, which was sorely needed. It still has its drawbacks. You can practically walk across the harbor on boats in the summer, it's so small. The holding ground is found to be poor, especially along the inside of the breakwater. Special care is required in setting anchors, since the bottom is foul in spots. No wonder it is preferable to pick up a mooring, if one is available, from the yacht club or obtain a possible slip at the Fo'c'sle.

The Sakonnet Yacht Club, organized by John Alden, Edward Brayton, and others, is near the head of the harbor and has a long pier on the east side with 5 feet at MLW at its outer end. Few facilities may be found at this club. Look up Harbor Master Jim Blades, who lives near the club, or phone him at 635–4428. At the fishermen's dock, near the end of Breakwater Point on the west side, gas, water, and ice are on tap. You'll find only 5 feet at low water here. The Fo'c'sle serves good meals and packs chowder "to take out." An old general store next door which used to be a source for supplies has unfortunately closed down.

In approaching Sakonnet Harbor, keep well off Sakonnet Point and watch for long lines of fish weirs, sometimes poorly marked. The best plan is to pick up whistle SR, head from there to red bell 2A, and from there to the breakwater marked by a flashing light and a set of triangle markers at its outer end. Be sure to keep well off the harbor's eastern shore. Off Sakonnet Point, the old lighthouse tower is abandoned. Three bells and a whistler, less appealing but less expensive, now guide yachtsmen into the Sakonnet River.

17. Sachuest Cove (13221 353). Behind (north of) Flint Point, on the western side of the entrance to the Sakonnet River, is an anchorage that is better than any to be found in Sakonnet Harbor from the point of view of accessibility, room, and privacy. Except in winds from north to east it offers good shelter and has been highly recommended by several yachtsmen as having excellent holding ground.

18. Fogland Harbor (13221 353). This is also easy of access and roomy. If you don't need supplies, you may prefer it to Sakonnet. It is open from northwest to north-northeast, but the holding ground is good.

A yachtsman advises: "In entering the harbor, follow the channel north in Sakonnet River until 100 yards past the point. Then turn and go straight into the middle of the bight. Swing south to a line between the point and two flat-topped modern bungalows on the east shore. There is 12 feet of water here at low tide. If you row ashore and phone from a nearby farmhouse, the garage at Tiverton will send down a taxi for the 4-mile trip to Tiverton."

19. Tiverton (13221 353). Between the old Stone Bridge, which used to connect Almy Point on Aquidneck Island with the mainland, and the Tiverton fixed bridge, is a section of the Sakonnet River that has become an active yachting center. The channel span of the Stone Bridge has been removed and the tide rushes through. Go through this bridge and obtain an anchorage or dockage at Tiverton on the east shore. Above, the new bridge, with a vertical clearance of 57 to 70 feet, gives access to Mount Hope Bay and the mill city of Fall River in Massachusetts.

The homey Tiverton Yacht Club has a dock on the eastern waterfront, though its clubhouse is across the main street, a three-story house with a cupola. The club is very active in small one-design class racing, in which older members, known as the "Dashing Daddies," also participate. As the house rules of the club state, "Privileges of the club will be extended to visiting yachtsmen at all times." They may be able to use the deep-water dock space if any is open; showers are in the clubhouse, as well as a snack bar.

Gas is available at several places along the waterfront, including the dock at the Stone Bridge Boat Yard just above that bridge on the west shore. The Standish Boat Yard, identified by the large white building further to the north on the opposite shore, does hauling, repair work on engines, hulls, sails, compass and electronic gear, supplies marine charts in a well-equipped store, and provides gas, Diesel fuel, water, and ice at its main dock, recording 15 feet at low water. Taking a fifteen-minute walk south along the main road will lead you to a grocery, a bank, a post office, and a package store. Jack Brimicombe, who obviously caters to cruising people, has moorings at $5.00 a night, slips at 30¢ per foot. And he can sell boats about as well as he services them. Standish, we understand, is the nation's largest Cape Dory and East-ward-Ho dealer.

The Pirate Cove Marina, directed by the appropriately named Donald Kidd, is across the river from Standish, protected behind a stone break-water. The facilities are newer here, you'll lie away from the current, and although the basin is often crowded with local craft, this marina is set up for transients, providing a good 10-foot depth at its slips. They monitor Channel 16. One can pick up gas, Diesel fuel, water, ice, and marine supplies; showers can be taken and there's a courtesy car available for obtaining food supplies. For a meal we suggest the Porthole Restaurant, just a five-minute walk away, and The Sportsman, serving good food and drinks at reasonable prices.

The tidy S'konnet Marina may also be found on the west shore, just north of the swing bridge. It is housed in a deep-water basin, first dredged in 1965, and marked on the chart just west of can 13. You'll also find good protection here and since it's family operated, with few frills, the dockage fees are apt to be comparatively modest. Their engine-repair work is reportedly quite competent. Phoning 683–3551 will guarantee you a reservation.

We do not suggest anchoring in Tiverton Harbor, for the river current runs from 4 to 5 knots at times between the bridges.

Tiverton, originally the home of the Pocasset Indians, is an interesting place for a visit, though too near Fall River, it would appear, for good swimming. Unfortunately, we can no longer recommend the food served at the Stone Bridge Inn, since reports we have received from recent visitors have been less than favorable.

20. Kickamuit River, Mt. Hope Bay (13221 353). An attractive anchorage, though too large to be snug, lies in the river to the east of Bristol Neck. Keep close to the red nuns in the narrow entrance channel, as outlying rocks line along the shore. Your best shelter can be found along the eastern shore beyond black can 1. The small community of Coggeshall on the point is residential. For facilities and supplies, one must go to Fall River, since none can be found here.

21. Cole River, Mass., Mt. Hope Bay (13221 353). This anchorage is not snug, being wide open to the south until you get into the narrow part of the river, where it is marshy and too shallow for cruising boats. The modest Swansea Marina is on the east shore of the wide part of the river, at South Swansea on Gardners Neck. Gasoline, Diesel fuel, water, ice, electricity, repairs, showers, and a snack bar are available. There is a reported 6 feet of water at one pump, 4 at the other. The yard has moorings, transient slips, a marine railway, and supplies are not far away. We found the best anchorage in the deep-water area southwest of the marina.

With Cole River we end our cruise on the Sakonnet River and Mount Hope Bay. Yacht clubs and docks abound on the Taunton River, but most of us cruising Narragansett Bay will not want to go that far— unless, of course, it's our home port.

Our cruise on Narragansett Bay ends here and we now go back to Sakonnet Point and head eastward from there toward Buzzards Bay.

Westport, Mass. (13228 237). Don't be confused by the two West-ports, Westport Harbor at Acoaxet and Westport Point upriver. The yacht club and the facilities are at the latter Westport. The entrance is a bit tricky, and there is a 3- or 4-knot current. A local authority advises as follows: "Pick up the bell southeast of Twomile Rock and stand toward the Knubble (a conspicuous high rock) until Dogfish Ledge is abeam to port. Then head for nun 4 off Halfmile Rock and leave it close to starboard. After that swing around the Knubble and follow the buoys." Don't attempt to enter in strong southerly winds, when the sea breaks on the bar at the entrance. This hidden entrance made Westport a perfect hideout for rumrunners during prohibition days.

The dock that appears to port opposite nun 10 is not a public wharf, as it seems to be, but privately owned. Just beyond, about opposite can 13, is a dock and boathouse that looks like a yacht club but isn't. Instead, it belongs to a nonagenarian, Richard K. Hawes, who likes to watch the yachts come and go. He calls his lookout Cockeast Boathouse. While the tide is strong in the lower harbor and the dockage, facilities, and best anchorages are off Westport Point, if you do prefer to anchor below, pick a spot just above can 13 and about southwest of nun 14. This spot offers one advantage. Supplies are difficult to obtain up the harbor, but here at Acoaxet you'll find a small general store located within a stone's throw of the water tank marked on the chart and standing visibly to the south.

Most cruising yachts will prefer to go on further to Tripps Boat Yard & Marina or to the nearby Westport Yacht Club on the south shore on Horseneck Point, south of can 23. This long-established and reliable facility is run by Mrs. Fred Tripp and her sons, one of whom is named Bill and is always out to greet us. In producing the popular Compleat Angler, a line of trim 22-foot fiberglass fishing boats, they proudly claim to be "builders for those who care a little more." Tripp has transient slips and spare moorings. At the time of writing, an overnight mooring was $3.00 and dockage was 25¢ a foot. It also supplies gas, Diesel fuel, water, ice, electricity, marine hardware and charts, toilets, a Travelift, and offers complete repair work. There's a public wharf, used chiefly by fishermen, at the end of Westport Point.

On one of our visits, we picked up a deep-water mooring at the yacht club next door and came in on the launch to have a friendly chat with Commodore Emile Durand. "Visitors love this place," he exclaimed enthusiastically, and from what we saw of the general area we could understand the reasons for his remark. In 1976, it hosted a 28-boat fleet from the Boston Yacht Club. Westport Yacht Club, offering reciprocal club privileges, has a snack bar, showers, a nice sandy beach, and runs a jitney service to town. Its dock facilities providing 8-foot depths were greatly expanded in 1977. Mr. Durand suggested that we take a nature walk down the road to the west, leading into the Cherry & Webb Conservation Area. Here we found a secluded bird sanctuary, wonderfully shaped pieces of driftwood, and a dune affording us a fine panoramic view of the coast and harbor channel.

The Westport Market, where groceries can be obtained, is 1/3 mile north of the bridge in the village. Excellent surf swimming is found on Horse Neck Beach on the seaward side of the neck that forms the harbor. The eastern half of this beach is state owned and is open to the public for swimming.

William Whipple, that very ingenious, enterprising lobsterman, whose offshore harvesting operation we described in this *Guide*'s last edition, has since sold out his Prelude Corporation, which is now relocated in Wickford. Needless to say, only the lobsters are happy about this news.

The town of Westport, some distance up the river and beyond its navigable part, is an old town, part of which was purchased from the Indians by Miles Standish in 1652. Later on in the whaling era, during the first half of the nineteenth century, Westport Point became an active whaling port. The village westward of the Knubble is named Acoaxet. For those of you who, like Professor Henry Higgins, are sticklers for precise enunciation, the natives here call it *A-cokes-et*.

CHAPTER VII

Buzzards Bay, the Elizabeth Islands, and the Cape Cod Canal

As a cruising ground, Buzzards Bay has much to recommend it. Calms are few, for the southwest wind blows up the bay nearly every afternoon, sometimes strongly enough to become a reefing breeze. Fogs are few, seldom as "choking thick" as the down-east specimens, and usually of short duration. The summer sun will usually burn off the fog before noon. Aids to navigation are frequent, large, and noisy. There is a lane of lighted buoys from Penikese to the canal. There is plenty of company, for the bay is scoured daily by hundreds of yachts—outboards, Beetle Cats, power cruisers, and some of the largest, fastest, and handsomest ocean racers on the east coast. Add the possibility of meeting a square-rigged topsail schooner and a replica of a down-east coaster with a gaff topsail set from hoops aloft. Harbors in the bay range from the busy fishing port of New Bedford to yachty Padanaram and picturesque Cuttyhunk. But no harbor in this area—within easy reach of Boston, New York, and Providence—is deserted.

Tidal Currents. An almost indispensable guide to tidal currents in Buzzards Bay, Nantucket, and Vineyard sounds, and through the "holes" between the Elizabeth Islands is *Eldridge Tide and Pilot Book,* published by Robert E. White on Commercial Wharf in Boston. By means of a series of current diagrams, one for each hour of the tide, the book comes as close to predicting tidal conditions as the mind of man can do it. *The Tidal Current Charts, Narragansett Bay to Nantucket Sound* (consisting of two sets of charts at $3.00 each) are very useful and may be obtained from National Ocean Survey sales agents or from the National Ocean Survey, Distribution Division (C44), Riverdale, Maryland 20840.

The problem centers around the difference in water level between Buzzards Bay and Vineyard Sound. Whenever the water is higher in the bay, the current will flow southeastward into the sound, and *vice versa.* Because the times of high water are radically different in the bay, Vineyard Sound and Nantucket Sound, the tidal currents, while predictable, are irregular.

Because the tidal currents run with inspiring velocity, particularly in the "holes," careful attention should be paid to their direction. Note that if one must buck the tide, it is better to do so in Buzzards Bay than in Vineyard Sound.

Included annually in *Eldridge* is a letter the original publisher wrote to skippers and mates navigating Vineyard Sound, pointing out that vessels entering Vineyard Sound from the south will experience a strong set to the northwest on both flood and ebb, thus giving the shores of Cuttyhunk and Nashawena the title of "The Graveyard," because of the number of vessels wrecked there. The letter is interesting not only for its information but for the pleasant and personal touch it imparts to an otherwise arid volume of tables and factual information.

Around the Cape or Through the Canal? As he approaches the Texas Tower at the entrance to Buzzards Bay, the eastward-bound skipper must decide whether to sail up Buzzards Bay and pass through the Cape Cod Canal or to sail up Vineyard Sound, east through Nantucket Sound, and then up the outside of the Cape.

The route through the canal is shorter. On a voyage from Woods Hole to Gloucester, the canal saves 36 miles. There are several excellent harbors in Buzzards Bay and beyond the canal in Massachusetts Bay. The route is through protected waters all the way; and, except between the eastern end of the canal and Plymouth, buoys are noisy and close together. The waters of Buzzards Bay and Cape Cod Bay are crowded with commercial craft, fishermen, fine yachts, and big steamers. Should you decide on this course, see page 262 for specific advice on the canal.

The route through the sounds and around the Cape, however, is a good deal more challenging. Once committed to this route, one must be prepared to keep going. From West Chop to Pollock Rip the course lies among shoals and through tide rips. From there one faces open ocean and apparently endless beach, with no practical shelter whatever before Provincetown, 45 miles away.

But there is something about the long, seemingly endless dunes of the Cape that has a peculiar fascination to many yachtsmen. What appears to be a point, which you never seem to pass, keeps always ahead of you as you go on for mile after mile. The gradual convex curve of the Cape gives this illusion. Were it not for the famous lighthouses, Chatham, Nauset, and Cape Cod (or Highland), Race Point, Wood End, and Long Point, you might wonder if you were holding your own.

Until the Cape Cod Canal was opened in 1914 the route around the Cape was crowded with sailing vessels and steamers. Whalers, fishermen, and square-rigged cargo vessels ran down the line of light ships or lay at anchor in Vineyard Haven or Menemsha Bight awaiting a fair wind. Almost every winter gale caught several vessels on the dangerous shoals, parted their ground tackle, and drove them ashore. Coast Guardsmen at life-saving stations manned surfboats to the rescue with courage, strength, and skill now legendary. The great five- and six-masted coal schooners of the first quarter of this century were the last; now only an occasional tanker or fisherman and an infrequent yacht make the passage. However, anyone who undertakes the lonely voyage can take a good deal of satisfaction in having made successfully a difficult passage.

Harbors on the Buzzards Bay Mainland, Mass.

Padanaram, South Dartmouth (13229 252). We are now back on the northwest shore of Buzzards Bay, opposite the Elizabeth Islands. Padanaram is the next good mainland harbor going east after Westport.

On the chart it is called Apponaganset Bay; the town is South Dartmouth; and yet to all yachtsmen and many others, it is known as Padanaram. The only recognition the chart gives to that name is at Padanaram Breakwater. Authorities differ as to how the name "Padanaram" came to be applied to that port. One explanation, told to an interested cruising man by a member of the New Bedford Yacht Club, is as follows:

A man named Laban once lived in South Dartmouth. He thought that if he ran water over a mill wheel he would get enough power to raise the water up again, with something left over for other purposes. He built a mill to test the idea, which was dubbed Laban's Folly. Then, as the Biblical Laban lived in Padanaram, the locality was unofficially given the name. The biblical reference is Genesis 28:1, 2, which reads:

"And Isaac called Jacob and blessed him, and charged him, and said unto him, Thou shalt not take a wife of the daughters of Canaan. Arise, go to Padan-aram, to the house of Bethuel thy mother's father; and take thee a wife from thence of the daughters of Laban thy mother's brother."

A student of local history discounts the story, placing the first use of the name for this community much earlier than Laban's Folly, and says that the term "Padanaram" was first applied to Howland's house, there almost a century before. Anyway, we'll join everybody else and call it Padanaram. Padan-aram was one of the original names of Mesopotamia and lay between the Tigris and Euphrates rivers in Assyria.

There is an excellent and lively anchorage in the Apponaganset River off the South Dartmouth headquarters of the New Bedford Yacht Club, at the head of the harbor to starboard. Heading toward Padanaram from the south, your initial landfall will be a prominent radar installation on Round Hill Point off of which rise Dumpling Rocks. Strangers approaching the harbor from the west should make the sandspit red flashing bell and then proceed to West Passage lighted buoy 9, which is in a northerly direction and is a lighted gong. They are then able to lay a course directly from there to the Padanaram breakwater off Ricketsons Point. This gives an excellent entrance in either darkness or fog. It gives better than 18-foot draft right to the breakwater, eliminating all possibility of getting into any trouble with the numerous rocks in that part of the bay.

A breakwater at Ricketsons Point, with a flashing red light on its western end, protects the anchorage from the east except in abnormally high tides. Only south and southeast gales and hurricanes cause any trouble at the anchorage, and the breakwater breaks all but the worst of these seas. For a quiet spot, especially desirable for one entering after sundown, swerve in toward shore to starboard immediately after passing the breakwater and anchor just inside the breakwater. It is quiet and calm, and there is no disturbance from the town and automobiles, or from the numerous craft plying about in the large fleet usually anchored in the inner reaches of the harbor. Also the water is cleaner here, and an early morning dip will be enjoyed.

There are landing facilities at the club, however, and it is more convenient. Depth at the main dock is 7 to 10 feet with 4 feet at its newer dock to the south. Visiting yachtsmen must register at the clubhouse to be granted reciprocal guest privileges. Two club tenders run from 8 A.M. to 10 P.M. daily. It is often possible to obtain a mooring from the steward at a $5.00 charge. Slip space, if available, runs $5.00 up to 30 feet and 25¢ a foot if longer. This includes electricity and water. The steward will issue you a guest card good for seventy-two hours. Gas, Diesel fuel, and ice are available at the dock from 8 A.M. to sunset. Showers can be found in the clubhouse, and stores, where all kinds of supplies may be purchased, are only a short walk away. A cab can take you to a laundromat located 3 miles away toward New Bedford.

The New Bedford Yacht Club, founded in 1877 and originally located on Popes Island in New Bedford Harbor, was hit hard by Hurricane Carol in 1954. The fine old clubhouse survived, and its shore property offers a protective bulkhead, a cement boat-launching ramp, and extensive dockage.

There is much yachting life in the harbor, the New Bedford Yacht Club starting many boats each Wednesday and Saturday in July and August. In the latter month, the club holds the three-day Buzzards Bay Regatta. There are several dinner-dances held throughout the season at the clubhouse, at which all visiting yachtsmen are welcome. During recent years the New York Yacht Club has paid Padanaram squadron visits during its annual cruise in late July or early August. New Bedford's racing tradition is epitomized in its annual Whaler's Race around the whistler off No Mans Land, thence either way around Block Island, and homeward to Padanaram.

The village boasts no hotel, but there is no shortage of good eating places. The Whale's Tale is a quaint little spot for drinks and sandwiches, The Sail Loft and The Landing serve excellent seafood, while some of the natives claim that Dugdale's has the best cuisine in town.

Padanaram is only a short run by automobile or bus from New Bedford, and is much to be preferred to that port. There are two marine yards located on the Apponaganset River. One is the Concordia Company, which is famous for Concordia yawls and Beetle Cats and is located directly north on property adjoining the yacht club. Here you may obtain marine services. They also have a marine railway that can handle boats up to 50 feet in length. There is 6 or 7 feet of water at the ways at low tide. Mechanical service and riggers are available. On adjoining property is a shop called The Concordia Packet, which has a fine supply of government charts, sports clothes, and many other things of interest to the boating set, including postal service. The White brothers here are good sources for local information. Norman Fortier, one of the country's leading marine photographers, occupies a fascinating studio next door. Many a skipper has arranged here to have Fortier "shoot" his vessel hard on the wind off Padanaram. Nearby is Manchester Yacht Sails, Inc., a renowned sail loft. You will find them very obliging when it comes to repairs or a new set.

Down the main street there's a package store right next to Gulbranson's Market specializing in the sale of fresh meats and fish.

Davis and Trip, located close to the bridge, has gas, Diesel fuel, and water as well as some dock space with electricity. And up the river above the drawbridge lies Marshall Marine, famous for building Marshall Cats.

Yachts over 50 feet in length requiring yard facilities will find several in New Bedford and Fairhaven.

New Bedford and Fairhaven (13229 252). Once famous as a whaling port, New Bedford later became an important textile center. It also has managed over the years to get in the way of at least two devastating hurricanes, one in September 1944, which finished off the clubhouse of the New Bedford Yacht Club on the Fairhaven Bridge, and another, Hurricane Carol, on August 31, 1954, which badly damaged some of the harbor's boat yards and docks—to say nothing of its fleet.

Finally, New Bedford-Fairhaven and the federal government decided to take action in preventing such future storm devastation, and in 1965 a huge $18-million hurricane dike was completed. This 4600-foot barrier, located at the mouth of the Acushnet River, runs west from Ft. Phoenix to the southern tip of Palmer Island, thence all the way to the western shore. At the location of the present channel, there are two gates, one on each side of a 150-foot opening. These massive hinged gates may be swung shut to close off the harbor in case of storms. In entering through these gates, we spotted a high green light to port and a red to starboard. The current through this opening reaches a maximum of 2.4 knots and the tide has a tendency to set you to the east as you pass through. A diaphragm horn has been installed on the west gate, sounding one blast every ten seconds for a two-second blast. This beautifully constructed barrier, having a maximum clearance of only 2 inches between all its rocks, has now helped to make New Bedford a major harbor of refuge for cruising yachtsmen.

The former yacht club station on Popes Island is now a small marina, known as the Outdoorsman, which specializes in fishing tackle, marine equipment, etc. They have docking facilities for cruising yachts and also supply gas, Diesel fuel, water, ice, etc. There's just 5 feet dockside here with no hauling or repair work conducted.

On the Fairhaven shore just beyond nun 12 is Fairhaven Marine, equipped with new dockage and complete services such as gas, Diesel fuel, water, ice, a marine store, showers, and a laundromat. Go up to the gas dock to be assigned a slip for a minimum charge of $7.50 at the time of writing. This yard's main function is hauling, repairs, and storage, and it is reported they can take care of yachts up to 135 feet in length and 16-foot draft. D.N. Kelley & Son also has deep water at its yard further north and duplicates most of the services found at Fairhaven Marine. Stores and a restaurant are nearby and it is only a short walk to town. Davy's Locker over on the western shore of the harbor has the best food around but the prices are high.

Padanaram has taken the place of New Bedford as the important yachting center of the vicinity, and what was once a branch station of the New Bedford Yacht Club is now the headquarters of that outstanding club. There is no station in New Bedford.

C.E. Beckman still has its well-equipped marine hardware store in New Bedford.

In 1959, a plaque honoring Captain Joshua Slocum was dedicated at Fairhaven's Poverty Point. For it was here on the bank of the Acushnet River that Slocum had rebuilt and launched in 1894 his 36-foot cutter, *Spray,* in which he became the first man to circumnavigate the world alone.

New Bedford and Fairhaven have many attractions for yachtsmen, this center being the best for nautical supplies between Boston and Narragansett Bay. The Whaling Museum in New Bedford and the Rogers Unitarian Church in Fairhaven are especially worth visits. Cape Island Express runs steamers from New Bedford to Martha's Vineyard (Vineyard Haven) and Cuttyhunk Boat Lines operates a ferry to Cuttyhunk. Both trips take 1½ hours each way.

In 1924 there were only two of the old whaling vessels left: *Charles W. Morgan* and *Wanderer,* built in Mattapoisett in 1878. Today only the former remains, lovingly preserved by the Marine Historical Association, Inc., at Mystic Seaport, Mystic, Connecticut, a place that every lover of boats should visit.

As for *Wanderer,* she set out from New Bedford in August 1924, on her last whaling voyage. On the night of the twenty-sixth she anchored in lower Buzzards Bay. That night the tail end of a West Indies hurricane came up the coast. While her captain was ashore, she dragged anchor, drifted across the lower bay, and was completely wrecked on the reef southwest of Cuttyhunk Island. There are at least two excellent models of her, one at the New York Historical Society, 170 Central Park West, New York City, the gift of George A. Zabriskie in 1939, and another in the H.H. Kynett Collection at Mystic Seaport.

Mattapoisett (13229 252). Large and easy to enter, with few outlying obstacles, Mattapoisett Harbor serves as a popular rendezvous for club fleets, particularly for that of the New York Yacht Club, which meets there from time to time. Its disadvantage from a cruising man's viewpoint is its size and the fact that it is wide open to the southeast. Nevertheless, in ordinary summer weather it is usually satisfactory, with plenty of room for everyone and depths about right for all concerned. Good anchorage is obtainable right up to the town wharf with the amber light. Even the *Shenandoah,* a beautiful 120-foot topsail rigged schooner, makes Mattapoisett a regular port of call.

But the harbor has surprisingly limited dock space. Mattapoisett Boat Yard has a yard and short dock located not far beyond the lighthouse on the northeast shore. Moorings are provided for visiting yachts. There is 5 feet of water at their float at low tide and the yard does engine servicing and repairs and has a marine railway. Gas and water are on tap, and there's a marine store, ice, a Travelift, and a launch for transporting passengers. Carl Collyer, the Mattapoisett Harbor Master, can usually be found at this boatyard.

The Mattapoisett Yacht Club sits right next door. Small, most unpretentious, it is hospitable to visiting yachtsmen from other yacht clubs. Its founding in 1889, according to Lloyds Register, makes it the third oldest yacht club on the bay; only Beverly Yacht Club at Marion (1871) and New Bedford Yacht Club (1877) predate it. There are no slips here, but launch service is provided with a possible few guest moorings.

A small public dock offering a 4-foot depth at mean low water is located just above nun 8 at the northern end of the harbor, where gas, Diesel fuel, ice, and supplies can be picked up. There are four piers, with many boats tied up between them; Norman Soares is the wharfinger here. The model of a swordfish on a pole rises above one of these piers with a sign bidding "Welcome to Mattapoisett." A fine concrete launching ramp makes it possible to launch boats from trailers, and there is ample parking space for all. Four well-marked guest moorings are put out by the town just off the main wharf.

The shopping area is nearby. Why not try dinner at the rare old Mattapoisett Inn right across from Shipyard Park, where band concerts are held on Tuesdays and square dances run on Saturdays? Cannon Street offers the sightseer a fine opportunity to view a line of charming colonial homes shaded by majestic old trees.

Mattapoisett meant to the Indians "Place of Rest," a name that did not seem particularly appropriate when we visited the town docks early on a Sunday morning in August. Later, the town became a shipbuilding, whaling, and salt-manufacturing port. Many of the New Bedford whaling vessels were built here. Its famous tradition of master boat-building is still being carried on today at New England Boat Builders, formerly the Allan Vaitses Yard. Allan Vaitses remains manager. Here, "we still make a good honest boat," including the Cartwright 40, a blue-water cutter, and a modified reproduction of the classic Herreshoff Meadowlark. Most hospitable to visitors, they claim that "we have half of the marine architects in the country drop in to see us each year."

But a "good honest boat" wasn't always built in this harbor. Anne Stowell from Mattapoisett has unearthed another account from earlier days:

The late Wilson Barstow, who lived to be over 90 and died in 1891, said in a communication to the press about 30 years ago, that vessels were built here as early as 1740 or 1750, sloops and small schooners. There was no science, they were built by sight of the eye and good judgment! . . . There were no models.

Queer results were sometimes produced by this method. "Mr. Hastings," says Wilson Barstow, "was put in a towering passion by being told that his starboard bow was all on one side, and one sloop was nicknamed *Bowline* because she was so crooked." The old whaler *Trident,* of 448 tons, built in 1828, was so much out of true that she carried one hundred and fifty barrels more oil on one side of the keel than the other. Sailors said she was "sure logy on one tack, but sailed like the very mischief on the other."*

Today, over at the Brownell Boat Yard, new fishing craft are being turned out. Even that flagpole in the park, the mizzenmast of the *Wanderer,* helps retain some of Mattapoisett's nautical heritage.

Marion (Sippican) (13236 251). Here is one of the best all-round harbors on the coast. To the east of the entrance is Bird Island Lighthouse. Totally dark for the past forty-three years, it was relit on July 9, 1976, after a community financial effort restored the light to its six-second cycle, on for one second and off for six. Built in 1819, Bird Island Light was part of the Coast Guard Navigational Service for one hundred eighteen years, until it was terminated in 1933. It is now maintained by the Sippican Historical Society.

To the west is Blake Point, marked by Converse Point on the chart, occupied by summer homes and marked by a tall flagpole. This western shore should be given a wide berth, as there are many outlying rocks. The red Sippican Harbor Lighted Buoy 8, showing a flashing red light every four seconds, at the entrance off Ram Island, though close to the westerly shore, must be left to starboard, as its color indicates. In off-season, this light is replaced by a nun. The black can and the little island beyond are then left to port. At night it is important to note that there are no range lights in the harbor. Like Mattapoisett, Sippican can easily be entered under sail.

The harbor's popularity, especially on weekends, affords limited space for anchoring; permanent moorings are everywhere. One possible anchorage lies to the north of Little Island (which is just west of can 9) in 9 feet. A more protected and preferable choice is to moor north of Ram Island in the deeper water there while making sure to keep well clear of those five charted rocks. Other possible anchorages are in the good water to the south of Allens Point or further to the north along this point's western shore. These two areas, however, are apt to be rough in strong southerlies.

*From *Mattapoisett & Old Rochester* (Grafton Press, 1907).

It is more convenient, of course, off the Beverly Yacht Club or Barden's Boat Yard on the west shore beyond. This club used to have its clubhouse on Butler Point but lost it in the hurricane of 1938. A new clubhouse was erected at Barden's Yard next to the Town Dock. But Hurricane Carol dealt the club another severe blow. The club has fully recovered and is now well established in a clubhouse converted from a former residence and located just to the south of Barden's Boat Yard and the town dock where there is 5 feet MLW. Do not come up alongside the yacht club float at the end of the pier; it's a busy place and the water is shallow. Members of other recognized yacht clubs granting reciprocal privileges are welcomed here. The launchman, once hailed, may be fortunate in spotting a vacant mooring for you. His service runs from 8 A.M. to sunset and he should be signalled with three blasts and a display of your T-flag or a call on channel 68 VHF. Beverly has no gas or slips, but does provide showers, ice, as well as a bar and small grill, both of which are open from 11:30 A.M. to 5 P.M. Many yachts stop here before or after passing through the Cape Cod Canal, as Marion is neither too near nor too far from the canal entrance.

The Beverly Yacht Club, the oldest on Buzzards Bay and one of the oldest in the country, was organized, according to Lloyds Register, in 1871. However, as the *New Bedford Standard Times* reports, it was formally launched in February 1872, at a supper party held by Edward and Walter Burgess in their Boston home. This was the family, specifically Edward and subsequently W. Starling, who designed so many successful defenders of the America's Cup. The club name came from the fact that the founders had their summer residence in Beverly, on "The North Shore" of Massachusetts Bay, and the early activities took place there. According to James R. Fraser, the club historian: "Three things emerge from the history of the Beverly Yacht Club. The first is the interesting evolution of its present location, the second is its unsurpassed tradition in small-boat racing, and the third is a characteristic of family participation that has become stronger over the years." Following a trial race on August 3, 1912, land at the end of Butler Point was purchased and the club finally moved to Marion.*

Bill Coulson runs Barden's Boat Yard just to the north of the yacht club, operates a fine marine hardware store named The Locker, and is also Harbor Master at the time of writing. See him for a possible mooring, but be reminded that there are only three designated guest moorings in the entire harbor. We suggest that you reserve a mooring from him in advance by phoning (617) 748–0250. Gas, Diesel fuel, water, and

---

*From *Block Island to Nantucket*, by Fessenden S. Blanchard (D. Van Nostrand Co., Inc.).

ice are to be had at the stone pier where there is 4½ feet at MLW. Sperry Sails has a loft nearby. Bill Coulson and his men are unexcelled for prompt service and repairs, as we know from our own experience. Both Barden's and Burr Brothers close down tighter than a drum on Sunday afternoons at 4 P.M.

After Fessenden Blanchard's death in 1963, his friends wished to express their affection through an appropriate memorial. After contact with the officers of the Cruising Club of America, of which he was a member, it was decided to establish through voluntary contributions a "Blanchard Memorial Guest Mooring" for member yachtsmen putting into Marion Harbor. Therefore, in the spring of 1965, a 600-pound mushroom anchor was set out in 10 feet of water located well to the east of the Beverly Yacht Club, where we hope it will be for many years to come. It can be identified by the blue-and-white burgee of the Cruising Club. See the club's launchman for its use, remembering that Cruising Club members have mooring priority.

North of can 13, the winding channel is marked by orange-on-black cans, all the way to Burr Brothers Boatyard. This channel records 5 feet to the Old Town Landing Wharf, then 3½ feet at MLW to Burr's. Toward the northern end of this channel, favor the left side and note that the black striped buoy is a midchannel marker. Burr's has transient slips at finger piers in 4 feet at low water, moorings, gas, Diesel fuel, ice, electricity, and all types of repair work. Harding Sail Loft is also here.

Marion is also a good supply port. A local tradition, Petersen's Ice Cream, has sadly gone out of business, but across from the town dock is Jenkins (closed on Mondays), which serves excellent light meals and provides a gift shop and dairy products. Marion General Store is almost next door, with a wide selection of supplies including liquor. If necessary, they'll even transport you back to shore with your provisions. The post office is up the street. For fresh baked goods of many varieties, try the Crust and Crumb Bakery. The main restaurant in town, L'Auberge, is recommended, as is the food and drinks at the Colonial Coach, accessible by cab on nearby Route 6.

There is little nightlife in Marion, but concerts are given at the bandstand next to Barden's every Friday night in summer. A visit to the Marion Art Center, housed in a converted church, and to the Sippican Historical Society is well worth while.

Here, too, is the home port of the lovely dark-blue hull, two-master *Tabor Boy,* the training ship of Tabor Academy, whose trim campus can be seen just above Barden's. Many homes of Boston summer residents are on wooded slopes on both shores. Some of the finest sailing on the coast is near at hand, and many of the best harbors are within a day's sail. The town has a large summer weekend population, as it is accessible from Boston or New York via New Bedford or Providence.

Marion was the home of Captain Benjamin S. Briggs, master of the doomed half-brig, *Mary Celeste,* whose complete disappearance of crew off the Azores in 1872 still remains the world's greatest sea mystery.

Though settled in 1679, Marion was named for a famous Revolutionary hero, Francis Marion, the "Swamp Fox," about whom the "Song of Marion's Men" was written.* On May 14, 1852, the town became officially Marion, though the harbor is still Sippican. Cruising yachtsmen, however, speak of it fondly as Marion Harbor.

Wareham (13236 251). Once a whaling and shipbuilding port, Wareham has become an important cranberry center, though on the Wareham River the number of boats being built is probably greater than ever before. These are the products of the Cape Cod Shipbuilding Company, well known for such small sailboats as Raven, Mercury, and Bull's Eye.

While somewhat off the main track toward the Cape Cod Canal, Wareham River offers several possible anchorages or tie-ups for yachts drawing under 6 feet. One of these is under the partial lee of Long Beach Point, and the other in the narrow part of the river off Wareham Neck below the bridge. The latter is convenient to the town of Wareham and supplies, but it takes quite a jaunt upriver to get there. Long Beach Point, much of which is under water at high tide, is about 1½ miles from nun 4 off Great Hill and an equal distance to the docks up at Wareham.

The buoyed channel to Wareham is crooked and twisting, with the most difficult part at Quahaug Bar, where depths cannot always be counted on. The mean range of the tide here is 4 feet. Going up-channel, hug can 21 close to port, don't be lured into Broad Marsh River no matter how inviting looking, and keep nun 32 well to starboard further up. Warr's Marine, located on the port shore just above nun 30, has 4½ feet at its main dock at low water. Here you have access to moorings, slips, electricity, gas, Diesel fuel, water, showers, ice, and all types of repair and marine supply service. Since a 3-knot current runs along this upper part of the narrow channel, we were definitely advised not to attempt anchoring. At the wharves at Wareham depths are from 5 to 11 feet, according to the *Coast Pilot,* and 9 feet according to the chart. The *Coast Pilot* advises strangers to obtain local information about channel depths before attempting to navigate the river.

---

*As reported in *Massachusetts,* American Guide Series (Houghton Mifflin Co.).

Onset (13236 251). This popular harbor is a valuable asset to the cruising man who may want to make an early start through the Canal, or who, heading the other way, may find the going too rough on Buzzards Bay and would like to hang over awhile.

There are two anchorages here: (1) off the Onset Town Wharf at the end of the channel, and (2) the special anchorage area off Point Independence, this latter place being larger and less noisy, with depths of 5 to 12 feet; riding lights are not required. Of the approaches to them, a local authority writes as follows:

> When approaching from the Cape Cod Canal or from Buzzards Bay, turn westerly into the 100-foot Onset Bay Channel, keeping about 75 feet to the southwest of flashing white light 11 on a steel-pile dolphin. Expect to fight a violent crosscurrent going at 90 degrees to the channel entering Onset and often towing under the entrance buoys. The Onset Bay Channel has a minimum depth of 12 to 15 feet to Wickets Island and thence 15 feet to the 200-foot Onset Town Wharf. There is 7 to 15 feet in this basin. The channel is well marked with nine black and eight red buoys. Coming into the inner harbor at night, use the high wide arc light on the town wharf as a range light, after making the turns at Wickets Island. Both the Onset and Point Independence anchorages are well sheltered, offering safe anchorage and excellent holding ground.

The proximity of the business section offers an unusual convenience for purchasing supplies of every kind and having repairs made by competent and experienced mechanics. Water is furnished pleasure craft without charge on application to the Harbor Master at the town wharf. He is on duty there from May to October. To insure greater comforts for yachtsmen, speed regulations will be strictly enforced in the vicinity of both anchorage basins. There is 13 feet at MLW along the face of the town wharf, where boats are permitted to tie up for one hour to stock up on provisions.

Craft drawing less than 7 feet can also use the Point Independence anchorage basin. Swing northeasterly after passing red buoy 10, giving both Onset Island to starboard and Wickets Island to port a good berth until off the large marine railway on the mainland. Then veer west to an anchorage.

The best anchorage in this basin is off the Point Independence Yacht Club dock. The club people are obliging and will supply gas, Diesel fuel, and water, and order ice for you. The club has showers and usually guest moorings but only about 6 feet at its docks. Just to the east, the

Onset Bay Marina has gas, Diesel fuel, water, ice, electricity, a railway, showers, laundromat, shuttle service, and 6 feet at its slips. Other facilities include a marine store and a cocktail and sandwich bar called The Shallow Draft.

Stores for supplies are a short walk west from the yacht club. Onset Cash Market will deliver groceries to the club Monday through Saturday from 9 A.M. to 4:30 P.M. The best restaurant in town is reportedly Sorrento by the Sea, just across the bridge to the west. It specializes in Italian cuisine and seafood, all reasonably priced.

All yachtsmen are asked to cooperate to keep Onset Bay and adjacent waters free of pollution. Complete information of interest to yachtsmen and tourists can be obtained from the Onset Bay Chamber of Commerce. Onset is not an exclusive place, but everyone we have found there, while cruising, is very friendly.

Through the Cape Cod Canal (13236   251). The trip through the Canal is easy for a small vessel and usually involves no formality whatever. The most important consideration is a fair tide. As the current runs at something like four knots, a trip against the tide can be tedious for a low-powered auxiliary. Consult the *Eldridge Tide and Pilot Book* and lay over at Monument Beach, Pocasset, Marion, or Onset to await a favorable current.

Regulations governing the Canal, promulgated by the U.S. Army Corps of Engineers, are published in *United States Coast Pilot 2,* section 207. Those that pertain to yachts under 65 feet are substantially these:

1. Vessels must proceed directly through the Canal. Stopping or anchoring is prohibited.

2. Vessels must use power through the land cut. Sailing is prohibited. Power must also be used from Cleveland Ledge to the land cut if it is necessary in order to keep the vessel under control.

3. Fishing from boats is not permitted in the land cut.

4. Speed must be moderate.

5. Vessels moving with the current have right of way over those moving against it, *except* that vessels under 65 feet must not interfere with navigation of vessels of greater length. The Canal and Buzzards Bay is under Inland Rules, not International Rules. Therefore these rules govern except for the above regulation. Presumably this includes meeting and passing signals.

6. One can communicate with the Canal officer via radio on 2350 Mhz (WUA-21) or by telephone (PL 9-4431 or 4432). Also, one can call the U.S. Coast Guard at the east end of the Canal on Channel 16, VHF, for the latest information.

7. No refuse or oil may be thrown overboard or left on the shore.

8. Anchoring is permitted in the East Boat Basin, but not so as to obstruct the Coast Guard or Engineers' floats. No anchoring is permitted in the West Boat Basin. Go in to Onset or Monument Beach.

9. Traffic lights are shown at Wings Neck and Sandwich. They do not apply ordinarily to vessels under 65 feet. However, if you enter against a red light, you will probably be hailed from the shore or from a patrol boat and granted clearance or required to wait. Yachts over 65 feet should consult the rules printed in the *Coast Pilot.*

10. The railroad bridge is usually kept raised but is lowered on the approach of a train. If the bridge is about to be lowered, the bridge tender will blow two blasts. When it is about to be raised, he will blow one blast. When the bridge is lowered in thick weather, the tender will blow four blasts every two minutes. The danger signal is five blasts.

East Boat Basin, Sandwich, Mass. (13246, 1208). This is a useful if not very attractive place for the westbound vessel to anchor and wait for a fair tide. An eastbound vessel may find it a good place to spend the night following a late afternoon passage through the Canal. Coming from the eastward the entrance is easy to find in clear weather. The 300-foot stack on the power plant can be seen from Provincetown and it is distinguished by brightly flashing strobe lights, which work day and night. From closer in, the jetties and the light on the northern one are easily picked out. In thick weather a radio beacon and fog signal make entrance easy, especially as the fog is likely to scale up along the south shore of Cape Cod Bay.

If one is beating down Cape Cod Bay against the southwest wind and chop, a good tactic is to stay on the starboard tack until well in under the Cape shore. Then on the other tack one can romp to the Canal with a good breeze and smooth water.

If approaching on a weekend or at what may be a busy time, the cautious skipper can call the Coast Guard by radio at the East Boat Basin to find out if there is room to anchor. If not, the best course is probably to anchor north of the north jetty.

The anchorage is small and has about 20 feet of water in the middle. Protection is perfect and holding ground good, but room to swing is limited. Rafting up can be hard on topsides when traffic is heavy in the Canal outside. At the west end of the Basin is a marina with a few slips for transients. A hard-top launching ramp for trailer craft is at the head of the cove. Gasoline, ice, water, and Diesel fuel are available at a float east of the marina and there is a public telephone at the head of the wharf.

Less than ½ mile from the shore is an excellent supermarket. Head

The Boat Basin at the east end of the Cape Cod Canal.

west along the road from the gasoline wharf, cross the parking lot and railroad track, take the first road to the right, and you will see it immediately. There are a laundromat, a restaurant, and a bus station in Sandwich, ¾ of a mile away. The bus runs to Boston in an hour and a quarter.

Pocasset, Mass. (13236   251). There are several snug and secure anchorages in the bay between Wings Neck and Scraggy Neck around Bassetts Island. Any one of these makes good shelter should one have to lie over to wait for a fair tide through the canal. In the event of a heavy blow or a hurricane, you can scarcely do better than to hole up in one of these anchorages. With two anchors down and plenty of scope, one cannot be safer anywhere in Buzzards Bay.

In approaching Pocasset from the south, be very careful to locate and identify correctly the two nuns on Southwest Ledge. In 1977 neither buoy displayed a discernible number. The author, searching for the other nun in shore, suddenly found it outside him to the westward. An all-standing gybe and the powers responsible for guarding the careless preserved him from losing his boat. Note that not only is there foul ground between the buoys but there is another rock, "reported in 1971" but unquestionably there, to the NNE of the outer nun.

Once by this peril, follow the shore of Wings Neck, leaving nun 2 to starboard and favoring the Wings Neck shore slightly to avoid a bar making out from Bassetts Island. The late Mr. Blanchard, a coauthor of earlier editions of this book, warned against being pooped by the short steep seas generated when a Buzzards Bay southwester meets an ebb tide outside Bassetts Island. For a small boat, the rip could be uncomfortable if not actually dangerous. Anchor between Bassetts Island and the shore north of it, working up to the southward to keep out of the tide. There are numerous moorings here, all private. However, some of them are seldom used. If you are going to stay aboard, you might take a chance and pick one up, but leaving your boat unattended on another man's mooring is a singularly discourteous infringement of his rights.

This anchorage is quiet, clean, and at least on weekdays, usually uncrowded. Even on weekends it is not as noisy as some places, for those who come here do so in search of peace and quiet.

There is little point in landing on Bassetts Island, as it is private property, and it is said to be infested with wood ticks and poison ivy.

The Buzzards is the name of a yacht club located on Wings Neck in the cove to port just inside of the narrow entrance to the inner harbor. This is a small club with no facilities except a dock and, we have heard,

Looking east into Pocasset Harbor with Bassetts Island on the right.

a telephone. It is reported "by sources that we believe to be reliable" that the women members thought that the club name was insufficiently dignified. They were outtalked and outvoted. The name remains.

Anyone in search of stores, repairs, or other boatyard services can continue through the channel north of Bassetts Island to Red Brook Harbor. The charted buoys are supplemented by a series of cones used ashore as traffic markers. Each of these floats on a little raft. Their colors are sufficient guide. There are several anchorages:

Barlows Landing is a possible anchorage for shoal-draft boats. There is a small yard and a launching ramp here. The owner of the yard is almost unique. He does not want to expand. He does not seek to do more work on boats than necessary. One skipper asked him to make a minor repair and he replied, "Why don't you just do that yourself?"

Hen Cove is a large shallow cove suitable for shoal-draft boats. There is no store and no landing.

Red Brook Harbor. This is a large, secure, and well-buoyed harbor, the busiest in the region. There are likely to be guest moorings available and room for transients in the slips at Kingman's, the largest and northernmost of the two boat yards. Kingman's has everything. The yard can haul the largest yacht that can enter Red Brook Harbor. Carpenters, mechanics, and riggers await your orders. The yard will take damaged sails to a nearby sail loft for quick repair. A marine electronics expert in the vicinity will fix your radio, fathometer, or radar. There is a well-equipped marine supply store at the yard. Gasoline, Diesel oil, water, and ice are available at the floats, and a laundromat is on the wharf. There are plug-in facilities and water hoses at the slips. The Chart Room, a well-appointed bar, lounge, and restaurant, can provide a meal ashore in pleasant surroundings; and you can look over an assortment of gifts in Pearli Mae's little shop, whimsically named The Boom Dock-Ltd. She has gifts, nautical gadgetry, and a very few supplies. You can even rent a Moped and ride to the grocery store in Pocasset. Kingman's yard listens to Channel 16, so you can arrange for service or reserve slips and moorings in advance.

"Raz" Parker's yard to the south is an entirely different kind of place. On a hot July afternoon he told the writer, "Parker's Boat Yard is 95 percent sailboats. Able, work-type powerboats are welcome; all others keep to hell out." The yard, however, is well-equipped to handle repairs for the types of yachts mentioned. Mr. Parker has guest moorings and a launch, which responds to three blasts of the horn. In 1977 the charge for moorings was $5.00 for one night and $4.00 for each subsequent

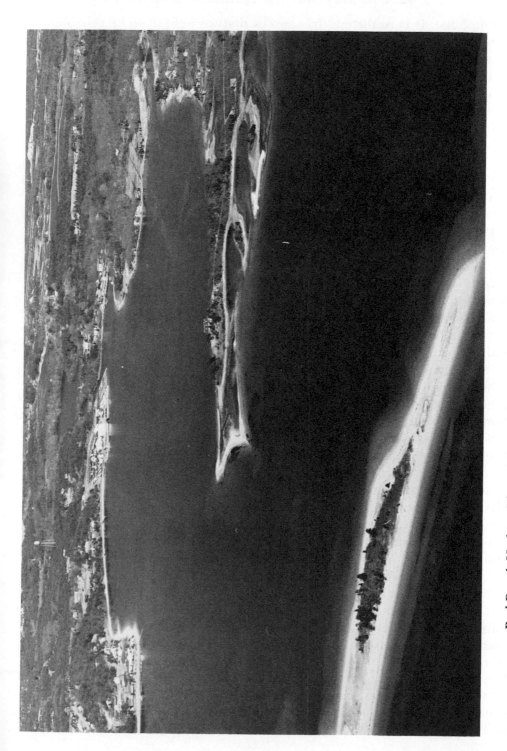

Red Brook Harbor. Kingman's and Parker's marinas at top left. South end of Bassetts Island below.

night. The launch service is free if you are on one of Parker's moorings. No one listens to the radio at Parker's but the writer found people friendly, helpful, and communicative face to face. The proprietor likes to call his establishment "the boat yard with a yacht club atmosphere."

Hospital Cove. The money had been appropriated and the preliminary work had been started in 1977 for dredging the entrance to Hospital Cove and the channel south and west of Bassetts Island. It is expected that vessels of at least 6-foot draft can use the new channel. Prior to the dredging, Hospital Cove was a quiet cove used mostly by local people and little frequented by cruising yachts. It remains to be seen if the dredging will attract crowds in search of solitude.

There is a quiet anchorage with no facilities whatever but adequate depth of water along the east shore of Bassetts Island.

Megansett (13236   251). In ordinary weather Megansett Harbor is entirely satisfactory, although large and subject to some motion from a sea running up the bay. There is better protection off the Megansett Yacht Club behind the jetty at the head of the harbor. The town wharf is used by the club, which maintains a guest mooring in the cove. There is no gas at the float, but this can be obtained at Fiddler's Cove. In a hard northwester the anchorage can be uncomfortable. One correspondent recommends following the dredged channel into Squeteague Harbor. Another writes:

> The channel is only marked toward the end, and by red floating wooden poles either painted black at the top or left red. These are hard to see, especially at night, and to the unwary boatman, appear more of a hazard than the shoal water.

While the author is confident that a skillful and alert skipper can take his yacht into Squeteague, to approach the entrance with a brisk northwester astern requires a confidence bred of extensive local knowledge.

On the southern shore of Megansett Harbor is *Rands Harbor,* which looks like an inverted Y on the chart. A local resident writes: "The entrance is virtually impossible at low tide and features a large poorly marked rock in dead center. The rock is not on the chart."

Fiddler's Cove. This secure spot is crowded with powerboats and affords no anchorage, but there may be a slip available at the marina. Gasoline, Diesel oil, water, ice, and a laundromat are available here. It is described by a salty correspondent as "a powerboat hole," not the

Fiddler's Cove

place for a cruising auxiliary but entirely satisfactory for a maneuverable motor yacht seeking the facilities of a slip. The basin has a good 5 feet, running up the curved channel to port. This is to be lined with rocks. The starboard or western shore is a sandy beach.

The marina on the eastern part of the harbor has slips with water and electricity for visitors. Gas, Diesel oil, water, ice, laundry service, and groceries are available here. The hospitable Balentines are in charge.

Silver Beach, Wild Harbor, Mass. (13236   251). In the northeast corner of Wild Harbor is snug and often-crowded Silver Beach Harbor. To enter, pass between a pair of privately maintained white and orange buoys outside the jetty and come in cautiously. The dredged channel is subject to silting. As there is no room to anchor, tie up to the bulkhead to starboard and inquire of the Harbor Master for a mooring or slip. The Wild Harbor Yacht Club sponsors an active racing program and plans a clubhouse in the near future.

No gas or water is available here, but there is a small store nearby.

If no berth is available in Silver Beach Harbor, a shoal-draft boat can anchor north of Crow Point.

West Falmouth, Mass. (13230   249). This harbor, well marked by a lighted bell, a can, and a nun outside, and protected by a breakwater, is easy to enter and is well protected for boats drawing 6 feet or less. Enter carefully and anchor at the edge of the channel about 150 yards inside the breakwater. The tide runs about 1 knot here but is not a serious problem. Shoal-draft vessels may continue up the channel, well buoyed with privately maintained cans and nuns on a miniature scale, to the basin, where chart 249 shows 6 feet. There is a wharf here where a telephone and gas are available. From here it is a short walk to a well-equipped store.

This is a clean and quiet harbor with attractive estates on the shores and no commercial interests except the unobtrusive gasoline wharf at the head of the inner harbor. The lovely summer morning the writer spent in West Falmouth was made lively by schooling mackerel, diving terns, and vigorous activity in Beetle Cats by the younger members of the Chappaquoit Yacht Club.

Quissett (Quamquissett), Mass. (13230   249). Marked by a lighted bell outside and distinguished by a large standpipe on the hill behind it, Quissett is easy to find by day or night. It is a secure and convenient anchorage. The entrance is clearly marked by cans and nuns. Despite their confusing appearance, there is no difficulty in proceeding directly

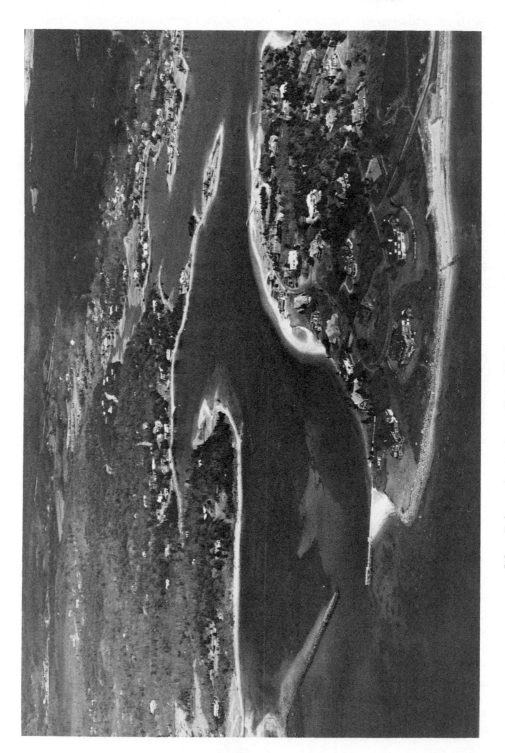

West Falmouth. Anchor off the big houses on the south side.

from one to the next, as they are numbered on the chart.

In ordinary summer weather, anchorage in the outer harbor is entirely satisfactory. In the event of a smoky sou'wester, one can move under the southern shore for excellent protection, but if the wind shifts to the northwest—a likely development—this berth might be uneasy.

The inner harbor is secure against all winds. In entering, respect the privately maintained buoys and carefully avoid the rock shown as a tiny island on chart 249. Once inside, you will find scant room to anchor. The boat yard at the head of the harbor on the eastern side had a few moorings to rent in 1977, but in future years it may not be able to maintain them. Location of all moorings is now under the direction of the Harbor Master. Local taxpayers who are told that no space is available for them to moor their boats in "their own harbor" rather resent the boatyard's maintaining moorings to rent at a profit to transients. The Harbor Master is an officer of the town, hence responsible to his constituency. In any case, do not try to anchor in the inner harbor.

The place to land is at the boat yard wharf. Here there is a public telephone. There is no store, no marina, no laundry machine. The yard provides gasoline, Diesel fuel, ice, and water and can make ordinary repairs. The town consists mostly of private homes, some of them well worthy of the name of estates, and is little concerned with cruising people.

There used to be a large hotel on the point west of the inner harbor. This has now been torn down, although some of the lesser buildings remain. The entire point, formerly the property of the late Miss Cornelia Carey, was left by her to the Salt Pond Areas and Bird Sanctuaries, Inc. There is a pleasant walk around the point starting at the wharf in the northwest corner of the harbor.

The Quisset Yacht Club has the use of the wharf, but the club owns no land, no buildings, and has no facilities whatever for visitors.

Woods Hole, Mass. (13229   114SC). Before you enter Woods Hole, consult carefully the large-scale chart and be sure of the layout. Once you get into the tide, things are likely to appear confusing, and a great many vessels go aground because their skippers become disoriented.

Entering from the Buzzards Bay side, notice that the passage is buoyed on the basis of entering from the eastward. Therefore red buoys are to be left to *port*. It is not necessary for most yachts to go out to the bell. Leave the red flashing buoy to port and continue by the two big nuns, leaving them to port. Between the second nun, 6, and the lighted beacon, 5, you must decide whether to follow the cans to starboard down Broadway and out into Vineyard Sound or to follow the nuns to port into Woods Hole Harbor. Both courses are clearly marked by big buoys. Nevertheless, at times when the tide is running hard, even these buoys are pulled under.

It is of the greatest importance to keep a sharp eye astern as well as ahead in order to notice to what extent the vessel is being set sideways by meeting the current at an angle. The turn at can 3 is particularly dangerous, for one rounds the can and heads up Broadway, feeling that the worst is over, and finds himself set sideways on to Middle Ledge. The same is true coming in the other direction, between nun 4 and the green flasher off Nonamesset.

The tide may reach 6 knots at its greatest strength and seldom runs less than 4 knots at full flood or ebb, so even though the distance through the hole is short, it is worth planning the passage for slack water or a fair tide, particularly on one's first trip. However, in ordinary weather most yachts can make it against the tide. The writer negotiated the hole under sail, single reefed, against the tide, although he does not recommend the practice as a usual thing.

In making the passage from Vineyard Sound westward, be wary of Great Ledge. Pass between black flasher 1 and nun 2 or go all the way up to the flashing red bell 2. Note that the beacon inside nun 4 is very small and low. It barely shows its red triangle above high water.

The steamers running from Woods Hole to Martha's Vineyard normally use the southerly passage to the west of Great Ledge. In the writer's observation, their skippers are careful of yachts and are ready to give the right-of-way where they are required to do so. However, the cautious and considerate yachtsman will remember the note in the Inland Rules, which gives the right-of-way to a large vessel under power in a narrow channel. He will also remember that a steamer constructed on the lines of a warehouse must maintain considerable headway in order to keep control in strong winds and tides. Whether he has the right-of-way or not, the yachtsman will take clear and definite action to avoid these monsters in sufficient time to make his intentions clear to them. In thick weather, he will display his biggest radar reflector, blow his horn vigorously, and use the channel east of Great Ledge.

There are three anchorages in Woods Hole:

1. *Great Harbor.* Enter from Buzzards Bay by following the line of nuns around to port at flashing beacon 5. Leave flashing beacon 4 and nun 2 to port and then leave can 9 to *port.* The best anchorage is well up in the northwest part of the harbor in about two fathoms.

In entering from Vineyard Sound, note that there is a range of green lights, the southerly one flashing, which lead in from red flashing bell 2.

The Woods Hole Yacht Club, whose landing and small building is below the northern range light, has one guest mooring, which is likely to be occupied. There was an orange balloon in 1977 labeled WHYC in the middle of the harbor. This is *not* a mooring but marks one end of the starting line for small boats that race in the harbor.

There are two floats at the Yacht Club, the westerly one for dinghies, with a depth of 4 feet and the easterly one with a depth of 8 feet. There is a pay telephone in the clubhouse, which is open and in charge of a steward from 8 A.M. to sunset. It is a pleasant walk up the road to the right from the club to town. However, should you have bundles to carry, row over to the beach inside the stone jetty on which stands the southerly range light and land right in town.

2. *Eel Pond.* The entrance to this bottle-tight pond lies between the ships of the Oceanographic Institute and the steamer wharf. It is a narrow cut and looks rather perilous in a brisk southwester. However, enter the cut cautiously, blow two long blasts and two short—the bridge tender responds to no other signal—and watch for a response from the bridge. If the traffic continues to pour across the bridge and nothing happens, tie up to the side of the cut, go ashore, and inquire. The bridge does not open around noontime and at morning and evening rush hours.

Inside to port are the wharf, float, and boatyard of Harbor Master Sumner Hilton. He will assign you to a rental mooring if one is available. He also can provide gasoline, Diesel fuel, water, and ice and effect minor repairs to hull, spars, and engine. The head of his wharf is right on the main street, where grocery stores, restaurants, laundromat, and telephone are easily found.

The steamers for Martha's Vineyard leave from the wharf just east of the bridge and connect at the wharf with buses for Boston. There is no longer a regular passenger steamer to New Bedford, but a freight steamer makes the run several times a day and it may be possible to get passage on this. The boat for Nantucket now leaves from Hyannis.

3. *Little Harbor.* Formerly considered too exposed for an anchorage, Little Harbor now is home port for a considerable fleet of moored yachts, as well as a base for the Coast Guard. It would be an acceptable anchorage except in a strong southerly but, as it is exposed to the length of Vineyard Sound, would seldom be a quiet one. Large vessels sometimes occupy the Coast Guard moorings, so allow plenty of swinging room for them. There is a landing on the western shore. Under most circumstances Great Harbor is to be preferred.

Three famous institutions make Woods Hole a center for study of the ocean and marine life: Woods Hole Oceanographic Institution, Marine

Woods Hole looking west. Little Harbor is in the foreground with Eel Pond at the far right.

Biological Laboratory, and United States Fish and Wildlife Service, now known as Bureau of Commercial Fisheries. The latter maintains an aquarium and a number of exhibits of commercial fishing methods that are well worth a visit. The harbor is busy with Coast Guard vessels, steamers, and research vessels.

Hadley Harbor (13229   114 SC). This is one of the best protected and most attractive anchorages in the cruising ground south of Cape Cod. It is easy of access and the dangers are clearly marked. The tide does not run hard by Cape Cod standards and there is deep water right up to the shores of Nonamessett Island. Bull Island deserves a little more respect, but the half-tide rocks indicated are within fifty yards of high-water mark. Given a working breeze, there should be no great difficulty in entering under sail. Respect the buoys and keep your bowsprit out of the bushes.

Anchor clear of the channel which runs along the west side of the inner harbor. It should be kept open for the freight boat, which supplies the inhabitants of Naushon.

Like most "unspoiled" places near centers of population, Hadley Harbor is likely to be crowded on weekends. If you come late, you may not be able to find swinging room. Rather than anchor on too-short scope or bump your neighbors in the night, anchor either north of Bull Island or north of Goats Neck. Both these coves are shallow but are adequate for most small cruising boats in search of swinging room.

Naushon Island is owned by the Naushon Trust and has been in the Forbes family for a great many years. They have built on the island but have preserved most of it in its natural state. It is inhabited by deer, sheep, and many species of birds. In order to keep it unspoiled, the trust asks that no visitors come ashore except on Bulls Island, where a float is provided in summer. Picnics, fires under careful control, and dogs are allowed here. Bring your own fuel. Because the island has been so carefully protected, one may sit in one's cockpit at sunset and watch deer come unafraid to the shore to browse.

Robinsons Hole (13230   249). This is the next passage south of Woods Hole between Buzzards Bay and Vineyard Sound. The tide does not run as hard here as it does through Woods Hole and presents no serious obstacle in ordinary circumstances to a yacht under power. It is buoyed on the basis of entering from Vineyard Sound. Red buoys should be left to *port* on entering from Buzzards Bay. It appears from the chart that a direct course from nun 6 to nun 8 runs right over a half-tide rock. However, the writer, proceeding with great caution against the tide, did not find this to be the case, since he did not actually see bottom.

There is no good anchorage here, as the shores are rocky and the tide runs hard. Both Naushon and Pasque are privately owned and off limits to visitors in the interests of preserving them in their wild state. Both islands are regularly patrolled.

Quicks Hole (13230 249). This hole, between Nashawena and Pasque, is much more easily negotiated than Robinsons Hole. North Rock and South Rock are both prominent at all tides. Felix Ledge, with sixteen feet of water, marked by a can, is of no concern to most yachts, and the ledge on the eastern side is marked by a flasher. The tide runs hard but presents no insuperable problem, although beating against it in a moderate breeze is quite a challenge. There is good anchorage in summer weather off the beach on the Nashawena side. This beach of fine white sand is very popular with visitors and, while seldom crowded by city standards, is likely to be well populated on weekends. However, the crowd melts away rapidly in the late afternoon, leaving the beach to the few who are willing to wait for it.

Landing on Pasque is prohibited. One can land on the Nashawena beach but should not venture inland and should not bring dogs ashore, as the island is inhabited mainly by sheep.

Flounders have been caught on the sandy bottom off the beach and striped bass are said to frequent the hole. Many eager fishermen patrol these waters, but the writer has dragged a lure from North Rock to South Rock many times with no response whatever from bass or bluefish. However, you will never catch a fish if you don't go fishing. It may be worth a try.

One should remember that all of the Elizabeth Islands except Cuttyhunk and Penikese are privately owned by people who are trying to keep them in their original wild state. With a few disgraceful exceptions, yachtsmen honor this public-spirited intention, confine their visits to the beaches, and help to save for all of us a few small islands of solitude untrampled by the feet of megalopolis.

Canapitsit Channel (13230 249). Despite a grim write-up in the *Coast Pilot*, Canapitsit Channel is passable for shoal-draft boats. Local knowledge at Cuttyhunk declared there was "plenty of water," but declined to express the idea in feet or fathoms. It is "shallow on the edges" and the first can, 5, should be given a good berth. Strangers are urged to try it for the first time on a coming tide. It should be avoided entirely if a heavy sea is running.

Penikese Island, Mass. (13230 249). The waters around this island are shoal and tide-scoured. Any approach must be made with the greatest caution.

The island was the site of one of the first marine biology laboratories in the world. Louis Agassiz worked on the island for a number of years. Later it became a leper colony and then was abandoned to the gulls and terns. In 1973, George Cadwalader established the Penikese Island School, a project that he describes in his own words:

Penikese Island School is a nonprofit Massachusetts corporation founded in 1973 to provide a program of character-building activities and vocational training for sixteen to eighteen-year-old boys referred to the school by the Massachusetts Department of Youth Services. We began on an otherwise uninhabited island, fourteen miles from Woods Hole in Buzzards Bay, and our curriculum on the island is organized around teaching the skills and attitudes necessary to establishing a self-sufficient community in a remote and inhospitable environment. Students have built a house, barn, and shop; raise and cook much of their own food, and operate the boat, which provides the only link to the mainland. We have tried to make Penikese a place where honesty, cooperation, and loyalty pay off in terms of the obvious happiness of the community. More concretely, we emphasize attitudes such as pride in workmanship, tolerance to frustration, and the ability to accept criticism, without which none of our students can hope to compete successfully on the job market.

Visiting yachtsmen are welcome to come up to the house for a cup of coffee. The best approach to the island is north from the Cuttyhunk bell, keeping the Gull Island shoal well to starboard, and heading directly for the salt-box building. There's about 3 feet of water at the end of the stone jetty at high tide. The harbor is apt to be filled with eel grass in late summer, which makes anchoring difficult. Penikese is wide open to the southeast and should be avoided when the wind is in that quarter.

Cuttyhunk, Mass. (13230 249). Cuttyhunk is a favorite weekend goal for the many yachtsmen sailing out of Buzzards Bay and Martha's Vineyard ports. It is well to windward, presents no difficult navigational problems, and is picturesque and unspoiled. Also, the anchorage is secure from all winds. The result of this idyllic situation is that the small anchorage soon becomes crowded. On a pleasant July day there may be a dozen yachts anchored in the pond at noon. By four o'clock others will begin to pour in, anchoring on reasonably long scope. The influx continues until by drink time those entering will find few holes in which to anchor and they will be on short scope or rafted up. By seven, the anchorage will be overcrowded, the slips at the marina filled, and there will be a dozen yachts lying outside, the shoal draft ones north of the jetty and others along the beach stretching out towards Nashawena. Summer nights are usually quiet; but should the wind come off hard northwest or northeast, considerable tumult ensues in the crowded anchorage.

In approaching Cuttyhunk in thick weather, be especially careful of the shoals around Penikese. They are extensive and low lying, but they are really there. From bell 6, pass between the beacon to port and the light on the jetty. The beacon is not easy to find from a distance and may give the stranger an anxious moment. Stay in the middle of the dredged channel. In the winter of 1977 the part by the elbow about halfway in was being dredged out again to a depth of 10 feet. The channel is narrow, but the shores are abrupt. A man standing waist deep in water can almost touch a passing vessel.

The dredged mooring basin inside is more or less square. The southeast side is open to the entrance channel. The southwest side extends roughly from a prominent pile in the southern corner toward a modern-looking, brown, flat-roofed house on the northern shore. The northwest side lies on a range established by an old wharf and a little gray house more than halfway up the hill to the west. The west side of the Coast Guard wharf lines up more or less with the northeast side of the anchorage. The edges have a tendency to silt in, so should be approached with caution, but everyone approaches with such caution that there is often room to swing near the edge. Shoal-draft boats tie up to the pilings on the west side of the anchorage or anchor among them, but this is no place for a yacht drawing 5 feet. If you get in early, inquire at the marina for one of the few rental moorings or just pick one up. Someone will appear to collect the necessary fee.

There are four wharves on the southwest side of the entrance channel. The first on entering is the steamer wharf, where the ferry *Alert* lands from New Bedford. Gasoline is available here until six P.M. The next is the Coast Guard wharf. Then comes the marina with slips for visitors and a few rental moorings. Gasoline, Diesel fuel, ice, and water are available here. The beacon with the square top is left to port by those approaching the marina. The last wharf is the "fish dock," used as a base by the local fishermen, lobstermen, and charter skippers, and is presided over by wharfinger John Rockwell. He is an officer of the town of Gosnold and is responsible for whatever takes place on the wharf and in the anchorage. He can be found on the wharf almost any

Canapitsit Channel looking southeast.

time between seven A.M. and six P.M. and is a pleasant and accommodating source of local information. The 10-foot dredged channel runs to the front of the fish dock, where there is deep water at any tide. There is a fresh water hose on the wharf. Because there is considerable traffic here, one cannot lie alongside this wharf for more than a few minutes, but there are a few deep-water slips available for transients. Consult Mr. Rockwell.

Reservations for slip space can be made at either the marina or the fish dock by writing ahead and sending a deposit, but no one listens to the radio for reservations.

In leaving the fish dock or the marina, note that one must leave to port the pile at the corner of the dredged area. The sketch and the following paragraph written by a summer resident of Cuttyhunk make clear the extent of the danger:

> Visitors keep running aground. And they do it every day in summer. And, of course, in exactly the same place—or two places. Our windows look over the harbor and never a day goes past that a glance out doesn't spot a keel sailboat heeling awkwardly in the mud just beyond the south corner of the dredged basin. Usually they get there by trying to go from the fish dock to the basin, or vice versa, without due regard for the north-south line that marks the dredged area. I will attempt a crude drawing and attach it to this letter, and you can see for yourself. The second spot for habitual groundings is just inside (to the southeast) of a line running from the old Coast Guard dock to the marina. Anything inside that line is fit only for small outboards except for a few feet out from the slips along the easternmost finger pier.

At the head of the harbor in the shoal water is the Cuttyhunk Yacht Club, with an active program for Juniors but no facilities for visitors.

Land on the beach by the fish dock or on a float behind the marina. There is a public telephone beside the road just above the fish dock and a clump of several more booths 100 yards up the hill. Turn right at these booths for Thompson's general store, well equipped to supply ordinary needs. When one considers the vast number of strangers besieging the place daily, their multiple desires from ice cream to laundry soap, and their interminable questions, it is little short of a minor miracle to find Mr. Thompson and his staff so relaxed, friendly, and willing to go out of the way to meet the needs of off-island customers.

Continue up the hill for a magnificent view of the island, Gay Head, Vineyard Sound, and Buzzards Bay. On a clear day you can see from

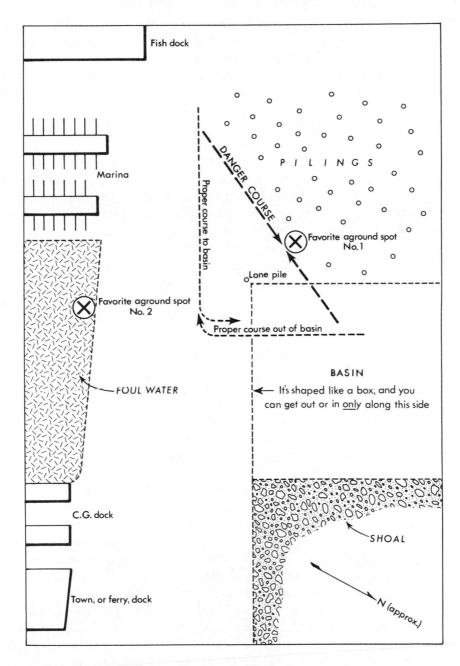

Fish dock

Marina

DANGER COURSE

PILINGS

Proper course to basin

⊗ Favorite aground spot
No. 1

Lone pile

Proper course out of basin

⊗ Favorite aground spot
No. 2

FOUL WATER

BASIN

← It's shaped like a box, and you
can get out or in only along this side

C.G. dock

SHOAL

Town, or ferry, dock

N (approx.)

Cuttyhunk Harbor

the bridges at the canal to the beaches below Westport and from No-mans Land north to the south shore of the cape. Looking down on the peaceful anchorage, it is hard to believe that winter gales sometimes drive seas right over the narrow beach protecting its western side. The road to the summit, lined with well-constructed stone walls, appears rather surprising on a bleak hill. It was built by the late William M. Wood of the American Woolen Company as the approach to a pro-jected mansion on top of the island. The mansion never materialized.

Bushwhacking across lots on Cuttyhunk is out. The land is all pri-vately owned and the owners look on trespassers without enthusiasm. There is a path around the southern shore, to which anyone will direct you, and a road out the spit toward Canapitsit Channel. Otherwise, visitors should keep to paved roads and the beaches.

Weather permitting, Roman Catholic services are held in the Cut-tyhunk church on Sunday mornings and Protestant services on Sunday evenings. Aside from informal socializing around the telephone booths, the fish dock, the marina, and aboard yachts, there is no night life on Cuttyhunk, and early in the evening the anchorage usually quiets down.

Meals and rooms can be arranged at the Allen House and the Bos-worth House, both to the left of the road up the hill. It is well to make a reservation if you plan to dine ashore. There is an attractive gift shop at the Allen House. Both places are of long standing at Cuttyhunk and retain much of the traditional atmosphere but have recently been ex-panded and modernized. Note that Gosnold is a dry town.

If you must return to the States in a hurry, call Norman Gingrass, who operates the Island Air Service. He can land you in New Bedford in ten minutes and in Boston in half an hour.

An interesting reminder of old times are the remains of a railway across the sand spit on the starboard hand as you enter the anchorage. Before the pond was dredged and the channel cut, there was enough water in the pond for the big catboats used by Cuttyhunk fishermen, but not enough water in the channel. Ordinarily the boats lay outside, but in threatening weather they were floated onto a cradle mounted on a car and hauled over the spit to a safe berth in the pond.

From a great distance, a huge windmill on the top of Cuttyhunk is a prominent landmark, culturally and scientifically as well as physically. It represents a determined effort to provide energy for the island by wind power. The three 40-foot blades are of an advanced airfoil design developed in Holland. With a breeze anywhere between 8 and 50 knots, they will turn at 30 rpm and generate 200 kw, more current than the 138 kw that the island requires at peak load. In 1977, the windmill was being completed and there was a question among the conservative as to whether it would work as advertised. One of the selectmen expressed some skepticism as to whether the town would buy it, as it was said that $800,000 had been put into it at that time. Another resident objected to the use of direct current, which the machine produces. Nevertheless, proponents argue that when oil supplies dwindle and become much more expensive, Cuttyhunk will be grateful for an abundant source of energy. By that time they expect the difficulties to have been worked out.

The builders regard the project as a prototype, claim that other installations can be built much more cheaply, and see the wind as an abundant and economical source of power.

On the plain in the southeast part of Cuttyhunk rises a tower in memory of Bartholomew Gosnold, who tried to establish a trading colony on Cuttyhunk in 1602. His biography, entitled *Bartholomew Gosnold, Discoverer and Planter,* was written by Warner F. Gookin, completed after Gookin's death by Philip L. Barbour, and published in 1963 by Archon Books, Hamden, Connecticut. It traces, in detail fascinating to the modern navigator, Gosnold's exploration from his landfall near Cape Neddick to Cape Cod Bay and at last to Cuttyhunk. Gosnold, embayed by Cape Cod, climbed a hill near Barnstable, saw Nantucket Sound, and got the lay of the land. Then he rounded the Cape, entered Nantucket Sound through Muskeget Channel, and explored Martha's Vineyard, the Elizabeth Islands, and Buzzards Bay. The first he named after his daughter and the second name he applied to Cuttyhunk and Nashawena, then one island, in honor of his sister. Gosnold built a house on an island in the pond on Cuttyhunk, established contact with local Indians, and made a good beginning at a trade in fur and "copper," a name given loosely to metal in general. However, the half of his crew who had agreed to stay in America with him changed their minds. Disappointed, he loaded his ship principally with sassafras and cedar, realizing enough for a break-even voyage, and returned to England. He never returned to Cuttyhunk, but was a leader in the Jamestown colony of 1607, and died in Virginia on August 22, 1607, a serious loss to that colony.

Mr. Gookin's enthusiasm for Gosnold is unmeasured and he romanticizes both Gosnold and the Indians. The claim that Gosnold was the first Englishman to see Cape Cod and the waters of Nantucket Sound and Buzzards Bay can scarcely be supported by evidence, as the first Indians he met were wearing European clothes. However, Gosnold well deserves his monument and a pilgrimage to it is a rite the historically minded will not neglect.

Cuttyhunk, situated as it is within half a day's sail of many yacht

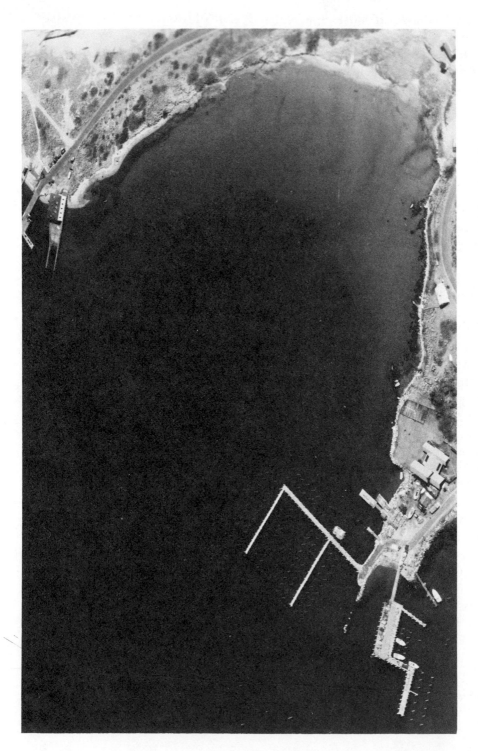

Cuttyhunk Harbor. The Fish Dock is at the lower left. The edges of the dredging are shown clearly.

anchorages, is a fragile place, easily destroyed by its admirers. It bears a remote-island quality composed of simplicity, bleakness, and independence, its moors, wild roses, ducks, rabbits, deer and the surrounding sea. Its inhabitants and its visitors sense this fragility and for the most part treat it with the respect accorded a museum piece.

CHAPTER VIII

Vineyard and Nantucket Sounds, and the Voyage Around Cape Cod

General Conditions: Vineyard Sound presents few difficulties. Its entrance from the west is clearly marked by the Buzzards Bay tower, a lighted whistle off Sow and Pigs, a lighted gong on Devils Bridge, and Gay Head light. The only obstruction to a yacht is Middle Ground Shoal, clearly marked on its western end by a flashing bell. There are excellent harbors at Menemsha Pond, Quicks Hole, Woods Hole, and Vineyard Haven. Overnight anchorage in quiet weather can be found in Menemsha Bight and Tarpaulin Cove, shelters once frequented by coasting schooners waiting out a foul tide.

Pay particular attention to George W. Eldridge's letter to skippers and mates in the *Eldridge Tide and Pilot Book.* The gist of it is that the first of the flood tide, instead of setting northeast up the Sound, sets north toward the shores of Nashawena and Pasque. A vessel bucking an ebb tide running southwest out of the Sound, is set heavily to the north, especially on the starboard tack. Consequently in thick weather, keep a sharp eye on the fathometer and tack to the south in a depth of less than 10 fathoms. In the event of a head tide, it might be better to lie over in Menemsha, Quicks Hole, or Tarpaulin Cove and enjoy those picturesque anchorages than to buck the tide up the Sound.

With an ebb tide running against a hard southwest wind, Vineyard Sound can be a lumpy spot, particularly off West Chop, where the current often reaches 2 knots.

The voyage through Nantucket Sound presents no serious problems by day or night in clear weather with good visibility. It is only about 30 miles from West Chop to Monomoy, and with a 1- or 2-knot tide running under you, it should be no more than a half-day's sail. The land on both sides is so low that it soon drops out of sight from the deck of a small yacht, leaving water towers peering over the horizon at odd intervals. One runs compass courses from bell to whistle to gong, surrounded by unseen shoals and moved by unpredictable currents. It is a weird sensation for the navigator unaccustomed to it. In the event of a head tide, light airs, or poor visibility, there are a number of picturesque little harbors on the south side of the Cape for shoal-draft yachts. Woods Hole, Falmouth, Hyannis, and Stage Harbor are deep-water harbors, as the term is understood on the Cape. The harbors on Martha's Vineyard and Nantucket are good stopping places as well as worthwhile objectives in themselves.

If you must navigate this channel in thick weather, do so with extreme caution. The following account of the loss of a well-found yawl under the command of an experienced skipper should emphasize the possible dangers. Read it with chart 1209 before you, and bear in mind that it was written in the thirties, when Handkerchief Shoal and Stone Horse Shoal were marked by lightships with powerful horns. The nun mentioned has now been replaced by a bell.

The yawl left Nantucket on a clear day with clear weather reported ahead. The Handkerchief Lightship south of Handkerchief Shoal to the southwest of Monomoy was picked up without difficulty in clear weather. From there the course is NE by E ½ E to the Stone Horse Lightship with its diaphone, 5 miles away and about ⅝ mile off the Monomoy beach. The wind was light southwest, almost dead astern.

According to the current tables there would be slack water on that day (August 5, 1938) at the time when the yawl might expect to arrive at Stone Horse. Then a flood tide would have carried her on her way. To allow for a possible set toward the shore during the last of the ebb, the skipper headed half a point to the eastward of the course to Stone Horse toward the flashing white bell 9. This buoy is nearly 1 mile off Monomoy and more than ½ mile outside nun 12, which marks the edge of the shoal southeast of Monomoy. So it seemed as if the margin of safety were sufficient, especially with slack water supposed to be due.

After a mile or two of the five-mile course had been completed, the fog came in thick and from then on the lead was in constant use. The sound of the horn on Handkerchief continued to come down clearly on the following wind. But still no sound was heard either of the diaphone on Stone Horse to leeward, or the bell. In fact, neither the diaphone nor the bell ever was heard, even from less than a mile away.

When the log indicated that the bell should have been picked up or Stone Horse heard, the skipper decided to anchor until he could determine his position.

As the vessel swung toward the shore for heading into the wind, she struck. All efforts to get her off failed, for despite the prediction of the current table, a strong northwesterly ebb continued for two hours to drive the yawl more firmly into the sand. Being a keel boat, she heeled far over on her side. Waves and current combined to fill her gradually with sand and water.

A rift in the fog soon disclosed the fact that the boat had struck on the shoal off Monomoy Point near nun 12. Despite the efforts of the nearby Coast Guard, the yawl, being embedded in the sand, could not be hauled off and was a total loss.

The Coast Guard reported that fishing craft had gone ashore almost every day for a week at the same place and for the same reasons.

What are the lessons to be drawn for cruising men from this experience? The opinions expressed by the skipper of the lost yawl can be summed up as follows:

1. Off Monomoy, the direction, velocity, and time of change of the current are unpredictable. This is confirmed by the experience of the Coast Guard. In this case, the tide continued to ebb two hours after predicted slack water. Instead of ebbing in a westerly direction as expected, the direction of the current was rotary, swinging around Monomoy in a clockwise direction, being northwesterly off the point.

(*Note:* The *Coast Pilot* reports that the average velocity of the current at Stone Horse Shoal Lightship at strength of flood is about 2 knots and at strength of ebb 1¾ knots. The greatest observed velocity was 3.6 knots. Flood current there sets about NE ½ E and ebb about SW by W ½ W. Such a direction would not have set the yawl on Monomoy Point, but a northwesterly current with the strength indicated above might and evidently did.)

2. Don't rely on hearing fog signals against the wind.

3. Don't sail through this area in thick weather on a dead reckoning basis, though you may have no trouble even in a fog with an accurate radio direction finder, fathometer, and other modern improvements.

To the above, the authors would like to add this warning: If you want to go through what are considered by many the most dangerous waters on the New England coast, pick your weather. If caught off Monomoy in fog, anchor and await favorable conditions.

Cruising men have contributed several other suggestions about the navigation of Nantucket Sound.

Fog is much more frequent in Nantucket Sound than it is at Race Point or even outside Pollock Rip. Southerly breezes are likely to bring it in, and although it may burn off in the middle of a hot day, only a change of wind to a northerly quadrant will dry it up.

Winds are subject to sudden changes in direction and velocity. A strong breeze kicks up a short, sharp chop, not very high, but enough to swamp a tender or soak down the sunbathers in short order. When the breeze drops, however, the sea subsides quickly.

In warm summer weather the southwest breeze may continue day and night, but outside Pollock Rip it usually dies away in the late afternoon. Yachts often sail right out of the wind in coming out of Pollock Rip.

There is an intricate shortcut between Handkerchief Shoal and Monomoy that may save a small boat many miles in a passage from one of the south shore harbors. It is to be attempted only on a clear day with a moderate breeze or with local knowledge, as it is not well marked.

The water in Nantucket Sound is warm enough for pleasant swimming. The fishing is usually good. There are many yachts traversing these waters from the humblest of backyard boats to the most elegant schooners, ocean-racing yawls, and motor yachts.

The smaller ports are often picturesque—sometimes pointedly so—and in spite of the crowds of people that press in upon places like Hyannis, there are secluded backwaters, coves, and tidal rivers inhabited by birds, fish, and muskrats.

Occasionally, however, Nantucket Sound gets a bit gritty. A hard easterly with a flood tide, for example, can raise a short, violent sea against which few auxiliaries can make progress. If one is set onto a shoal under these conditions, he is in serious trouble. Yet when the wind subsides, the sea quickly flattens out.

Although traveling the main ship channel bound either east or west is easy, use extreme caution in crossing the shoals from north to south. The buoyage is not calculated to make navigation easy. Cans and nuns become of the greatest significance, so clear weather is a necessity. The tide will be running across your course rather than with you or against you. Landmarks are of very little help for, in the hardest part of the trip, the low-lying land is below the horizon, and one water tank looks much like another to the stranger. Furthermore, it is well to call ahead on the radio and be sure the harbor you are approaching can accommodate you.

Menemsha, Martha's Vineyard, Mass. (13233   264). This is the first shelter available to a vessel bound east up Vineyard Sound. Coasting schooners used to anchor outside in Menemsha Bight waiting for a fair tide up the Sound, but it is an uneasy anchorage for a small boat.

Make the bell off the jetty and run in, lying either in the basin just outside or continuing into the pond. Conditions in the basin have been much expanded if not improved in recent years. Now there are marina slips nearly all the way around the shore except on the east side where the original wharf and the picturesque fish houses still stand. Anchoring in the basin is impossible and auxiliaries are not permitted to be alongside among the power boats. Consult the Harbor Master about a slip.

Gas, Diesel oil, water, and ice are available at the wharf in the basin. There is a store, Dutcher's, carrying marine hardware and fishing gear a short distance up the road and a grocery store about ¼ mile away at the wharf on the pond.

Menemsha Basin is a center for sport-fishing activity on the shoals to the southwest of Martha's Vineyard. Large motor yachts with high flying bridges and long outriggers crowd the harbor and the gasoline wharf at night and early in the morning, their enthusiasm making for an early start even by the casual cruising man.

Anchoring in Menemsha Pond is discouraged. The entrance is constantly shoaling up, and although frequently dredged, may not be exactly as the chart indicates. It would be well to check on conditions in the channel before entering. Also, because the pond is being used for the rearing of shellfish, use of the head is prohibited. However, the pond is a beautiful, quiet, and picturesque anchorage. It is said to be a pleasant 3-mile walk from the west side of the pond to the colored sand cliffs of Gay Head, where there is an inspiring view over the waters to the south and west. The surf here after a storm is worth the trip.

A correspondent who visited Menemsha in 1977 adds: "On August 26, 1977, we carried 6-foot draft through the channel at mid-tide, touching bottom once but not stopping progress. Heads were not sealed in the Pond but I am told heads are sealed in the Basin. . . . Climbing on the cliffs at Gay Head is forbidden. We discovered this after climbing them."

After just a quick look at the Basin, one can understand the necessity for sealing heads there.

The channel into the Pond is constantly shifting and is frequently dredged. Many have reported that the shoalest place is close to can 5, where a bar is said to build out by the buoy very quickly.

The walk to Gay Head is reported to be more of a hike than a stroll.

Tarpaulin Cove, Mass. (13230   249). This delightful anchorage on the eastern side of Naushon Island is much frequented by picnic parties on weekends, but during the week there seems to be plenty of room. The best place to anchor is off the southwest end of the beach under the light. Chart and lead are safe guides, as the water shoals gradually.

The beach is of fine, soft sand, delightful for swimming, although

The entrance to Menemsha looking northwest. The Basin is on the far right.

there is little shelter from the sun on a hot day. Late in the afternoon, however, many of the visitors depart and on a quiet evening the beach and anchorage are peaceful and sometimes almost deserted. A correspondent suggests: "Repeated nights spent at Tarpaulin Cove have taught me that the stern anchor, enabling one to lie with the swell regardless of the wind, makes life much more pleasant when the steamer wash swells come in, as they always do during the night."

Camping ashore is forbidden, but fires below high-water mark are permitted.

Naushon abounds in sheep, deer, and ducks, which the owners are trying to preserve. Therefore, no dogs or guns should be brought ashore, and visitors are asked not to venture inland from the beach.

Mr. David Forbes of the Naushon Trust writes:

At Tarpaulin Cove all driftwood has long since been burned up. Most people now bring self-contained fires which burn briquettes. As these do not send off sparks into the woods, and as they are carried off after the picnic, any words of encouragement for that type of fire would be welcome. Fires burning wood or paper should be attempted, if at all, only when the wind is offshore.

A correspondent adds:

I adventured along the entire rim of the cove to enjoy one of the most pleasant moments of our cruise—outstaring a beautiful fawn nestled in a groove of beech trees and at only a 30-foot distance.

Mr. Warren Ford maintains the mounted patrol on Naushon. You may be fortunate enough to meet him at Tarpaulin Cove. After a boyhood on the coast of Massachusetts, he became a successful rancher in Montana. In 1967, at the age of sixty-three, he returned to Massachusetts and in a 30-foot Tahiti ketch set out on an eventful circumnavigation, from which he returned two years later. He now combines ranching with the salt water on Naushon.

Lake Tashmoo, Martha's Vineyard, Mass. (13233   264). This is a landlocked and attractive anchorage for those who can get into it. Although it is reportedly dredged occasionally, the bottom in the entrance is shifting sand and responsive to tidal currents. Inside there is a depth of 10 feet in the anchorage. The problem lies in getting to it. The following account was written by a yachtsman entering in June 1974.

Drawing 6 feet, we entered cautiously using lead line and depth finder and had no water less than 6½ feet at one hour before high water. At 1300 on a sunny day we had no difficulty seeing the sandbars.

We came in on 155° magnetic for a point just to the east of the east breakwater, swung up to it, and strongly favored the east side of the channel. We had 8 feet all the way into the lake. The first markers in the lake seem to have suffered the most shoaling, but we crept through just to the left of center channel without touching. After the second marks, all was clear with 8 to 12 feet. We did not seek or find the 6-foot spot shown on the chart. There is good water all along the east shore.

The cluster of docks is said to be private, but the southernmost of them belongs to Lester Baptist, who has a small boat yard. He hauls and paints small local boats and rents moorings. Further along the shore is the town dock, which is guarded by a 3-foot spot. The head of the harbor where the charts show 11 feet is a beautiful little cove.

There is an effort being made by some local landowners to prevent fuel pumps in Lake Tashmoo for fear these would bring crowds of customers.

Inquiries in 1977 substantially support the experience of our 1974 correspondent. Favor the east jetty sharply. The shoalest place is between the can and nun inside the entrance. Make it by here and you are home free. The best water is said to be very close to the can.

Strangers would be wise to enter on a rising tide and to proceed very slowly, for there is only about a foot of tide here to float you off if you guess wrong.

Vineyard Haven, Mass. (13233   264). This is a large and busy harbor, well sheltered, easy of access, and consequently crowded in summer. It was once much used as an anchorage by coasting schooners waiting for a fair wind and tide through Nantucket or Vineyard sounds. It was then known as Holmes's Hole.

Enter between East Chop and West Chop. The name refers neither to the state of the waters off these points nor to a rib of pork or lamb. It is an eighteenth-century English word meaning "jaw" or "cheek."

Once up to the breakwater, you have several choices. If you seek a mooring, approach the town wharf north of the steamer wharf beyond a short beach. The Harbor Master, Don King, may be able to assign you to one of the few town moorings or to the mooring of an absent owner in the area sheltered by the breakwater. If he cannot help, one of the

The entrance to Lake Tashmoo. Notice the deep water close to the east jetty.

two marinas south of the steamer wharf may have a vacant mooring. If none is available, anchor along the southerly side of the harbor opposite the breakwater. Stay well clear of the main steamer channel. One look at *Uncatena* or *Islander* passing the breakwater at 7 knots with a bone in her teeth will convince you of the wisdom of this advice. If you anchor in any real danger, you will probably be hailed from the shore and advised to move.

It is important, too, to avoid the channel close to the oil wharves, as tankers land here and the freight boat from New Bedford noses up to the shore next to the wharf inside the oil wharves. The anchorage outside the breakwater is perfectly satisfactory if you do not need supplies. It is likely to be cooler and quieter than a berth inside.

If you like to lie in a slip, choose one of the two marinas. The Coastwise Wharf Co. maintains the northerly one. Gasoline, Diesel oil, water, and ice are available here and the slips provide 110- or 220-volt current and water. Yachts are not permitted to raft up at this marina. There is a laundromat on the wharf. At the head of the wharf is the Black Dog Tavern, said to have an excellent reputation. Reservations are not accepted, so go early to avoid waiting in line.

The Pilot House, operated by Machine and Marine Service, Inc., is the southerly of the two marinas. This, too, provides the usual services, although yachts do raft up here.

Bill Chase, an independent mechanic, has a shop at the head of this wharf. He is an expert at outboard-motor repairs.

Neither marina monitors the radio, but either can be called by telephone to reserve slip space.

A short walk up the street is an A&P. Three quarters of a mile up South Main Street is John's Fish Market, a source of fresh fish and local information.

The Martha's Vineyard Shipyard on the southeast shore of the inner harbor has several marine railways and docks and is well equipped to make repairs. They also have a first-class store for marine supplies and gadgets. This yard has a fine reputation. Another boat yard, which is much smaller but also does first-class work, is located at the end of the short westerly arm of Lagoon Pond. It is run by Erford Burt. If you want Burt to do some work, call him up and get him to pilot you in. Burt specializes in smaller boats.

Those who seek a quieter anchorage than Vineyard Haven harbor may want to lie in the Lagoon behind the drawbridge to the east of the breakwater. A 10-foot channel has been dredged, and the draw is manned from 9 A.M. to 5 P.M. except on Sundays. At other times a phone call to the Highway Department brings quick action. There was, in

Vineyard Haven. This picture was taken in March when the harbor was uncrowded.

1977, a "loosely enforced" prohibition against the use of the head in the Lagoon, Lake Tashmoo, and Vineyard Haven harbor. It is the writer's guess that it is likely to be taken more seriously in the future.

Vineyard Haven is a good spot from which to visit the northwestern part of the island. Automobiles and bicycles can be had in the village. The Vineyard Haven Yacht Club is an active racing organization and has a small pier and station but no regular launch service, well north (outside) of the breakwater.

Vineyard Haven was famous for a long time as the home of Captain George W. ("Yours for a Fair Tide") Eldridge, son of the Captain George Eldridge of Chatham, who made the first accurate large-scale charts of important fishing grounds.

The story goes that in the early seventies the elder George was publishing a book well known to mariners of that time, the *Compass Test. Eldridge Tide and Pilot Book,* referred to in chapter II, continues the story:

> He told his son, George W., who was at the time in poor health, that if he would go to Vineyard Haven and take charge of selling the book there he might have the gross receipts. This offer was accepted and George began his work. As the ships came into the harbor he would go out to them in his sailboat and offer his book for sale. While engaged in this work he was constantly being asked by mariners as to what time the tide TURNED to run east or west in the Sound. This set him to thinking whether or not some sort of a table might be prepared which would give mariners this important information. So with this in mind he began making observations, and one day, while in the famous ship chandlery store of Charles Holmes, he picked up one of the Holmes business cards and made the first rough draft of a current table on the back of it. This was in August of 1874. Shortly after, with the help of his father, he worked out the tables for the places, other than Vineyard Sound, which were of the most importance, and in 1875 the first "Tide Book" was published. It did not take long for mariners to realize the help that this sort of a work could be to them, and it soon became an almost indispensable book to all who sailed the Atlantic Coast from New York east. From time to time the captain added important information for seamen, one of the most important things being the explanation of the action of the currents, which caused so many vessels to founder in the "Graveyard." The book has even been referred to as the Mariners' Bible, so constantly is it used and so helpful has it been in making navigation safer.

One Saturday night in July the writer beat up Vineyard Haven harbor and anchored in the southerly part of the harbor long after dark. Sunday morning he was startled to find himself lying close under the quarter of a nineteenth-century topsail schooner, Captain Robert S. Douglas's *Shenandoah*. Built by Harvey Gamage in 1964 in South Bristol, Maine, for the passenger trade, she had some difficulty weathering the Coast Guard regulations. Since then she has been a great addition to waters formerly crowded with coasting schooners, fishermen, whalers, and naval vessels, all under sail.

Oak Bluffs, Martha's Vineyard, Mass. (13238   261). The harbor at Oak Bluffs, 4 miles eastward of Vineyard Haven, is formed by Lake Anthony, entered by a cut in the beach. Two jetties, with a light on the northerly one, protect the entrance. The entrance is somewhat narrow for craft without a motor, but it is possible to approach the jetties closely on either side. There is a depth of 7 or 8 feet in the pond, which is usually crowded in July and August.

The Harbor Master in 1977 claimed a depth of 8 feet in the channel.

The small "made" harbor is so crowded that anchoring is forbidden. Ask at the Harbor Master's office at the southwest end of the harbor for a town mooring. If none is available, local rule and custom sanctions tying alongside another moored boat with as many as three boats permitted on one mooring.

The usual supplies of gasoline, Diesel oil, water, and ice are available at the wharves. The main street borders the anchorage, whence groceries are easily obtained.

Oak Bluffs in the nineteenth century was famous as a camp-meeting center for religious groups. The old Methodist campground with its gingerbread cottages and main building with a prominent cupola is but a short distance from the harbor. The town is now heavily crowded with campers, craftsmen, artists, and musicians. Supplemented by literally hundreds of day visitors disgorged by the frequent steamers, these people provided a lively and noisy atmosphere. Weekends are said to be "something else again!"

Edgartown, Mass. (13238 261). This is a lively and picturesque town in which all kinds of supplies and repairs are available. In the busy anchorage you will be surrounded by some of the most elegant yachts on the Atlantic coast.

Entrance is easy in clear weather. The Squash Meadow and Middle Flats are clearly marked, although the can at the west end of the Squash Meadow is too small to look as menacing as it should. If you can make

Laurence Lowry

Martha's Vineyard and Nantucket. Lake Tashmoo, Vineyard Haven, Oak Bluffs, and Edgartown can be clearly distinguished.

the bell 2 on Middle Flats, even in thick weather, you can make your way into the harbor by following the line of the bell, the nun, and the flasher on the east edge of the shoal.

Many yachts enter Edgartown under sail. The shores are quite steep and the wind is usually brisk as it comes off the warm land in summer. However, make due allowance for a strong run of tide and watch for the ferry carrying cars from Edgartown to Chappaquiddick. It crosses at the sharp bend inside the lighthouse.

Anchoring along the northeast side of the channel is possible, although the bottom is gravelly and the tide is likely to foul or trip an anchor. Look for a pink mooring labeled Ruddy Duck or EM, followed by numbers and no name. In due course a launch will appear to charge you $7.00 (in 1977) for the use of the mooring and launch service. You can radio for a mooring in advance by calling Ruddy Duck on channel 68 VHF.

Ruddy Duck, Edgartown Marine, and the Edgartown Market are entwined in complex ways, but for the visitor it works out thus: There are three launches: *Market Boat, Nor'East* and *Nor'West.* Any one of the three may respond to three blasts of the horn and a T flag. Anyone cruising these waters should have a T flag as big as a bedsheet to help the launch driver identify the yacht whence come the blasts of the horn. The service operates from 8 A.M. to 12 midnight. If you are on a Ruddy Duck or Edgartown Marine mooring, the service is free. Otherwise it is 75¢ per person each way. It is wise to use the launch service as there are few satisfactory places to tie a dinghy. At a wharf inside the yacht club a number of them jostle each other in the harbor chop.

Should you wish supplies, hail *Market Boat* or call "Market Base" on channel 16 and prepare to switch to channel 68. You can give your order and have it delivered aboard. Or you can go uptown to the Edgartown Market and have it sent off in *Market Boat.* The boat will also deliver newspapers and messages. The skipper in 1977 was most accommodating. He will even arrange to have your boat watched if you have to leave her untended for a few days. Or you can make the same arrangements through Edgartown Marine.

Edgartown Marine, formerly Norton and Esterbrook, provides every kind of service a yachtsman could ask for. Gasoline, Diesel fuel, water, and ice are available at the float just inside the harbor. They have an elevator capable of hauling most yachts. Their carpenters, mechanics, sailmakers, and electronics men can make almost any repair you may require. On the wharf is an extensive marine hardware and clothing store. A laundry machine and showers are on the wharf. If you need

Edgartown. The Yacht Club, which bears a flagpole, is on the end of the long wharf closest to the point of Chappaquiddick.

anything else, see Bob Morgan, the manager, or John Edwards, the Harbor Master.

The Edgartown Yacht Club, whose dignified nineteenth-century clubhouse stands on the starboard hand as you enter the harbor, finds itself not quite up to coping with the twentieth-century yachting scene. The club is hospitable by inclination and seeks to do its best for cruising people, but there are too many of them. It maintains a launch service, which responds to four blasts of the horn and the code flag "L" from 8 A.M. to 10 P.M. Sunday through Thursday and until midnight on Friday and Saturday. The fare is 75¢ per person each way. Club facilities are open to members of those yacht clubs with reciprocal arrangements with Edgartown Yacht Club or to those who are introduced by a member of the Edgartown Yacht Club. The club maintains a bar and serves dinners by reservation each night except Monday. Lunches are available Wednesday through Sunday. The club is still experimenting with different solutions to its problems, but this is how matters stood in 1977. An A&P and an excellent fish market, Lowry's, are a long twenty-minute walk to the west on the tar road. The walk alone is worth the trip, for the first part is through shady streets lined with the eighteenth- and nineteenth-century mansions of Edgartown whalers, traders, privateers, and shipbuilders. The second half of the trip reflects the income tax, the automobile civilization, and the twentieth-century influence of suburbia.

Old buildings and narrow streets give Edgartown an antique flavor somewhat modified by boutiques, gift shops, and modern restaurants. The summer population has a heavy accent on youth, some quite picturesquely dressed and adorned, but, to the casual visitor at least, very pleasantly disposed. Their grandparents, living in the antebellum yachting tradition, are almost equally evident.

First settled in 1642, the town, when incorporated in 1671, was named for Edgar, the son of James II. In the eighteenth and nineteenth centuries, Edgartown was a successful whaling port. Men ashore were active in refining whale oil and making candles, while the women turned out socks, mittens, and wigs. In the Edgartown Cemetery there are headstones dating as far back as 1670, many with curious epitaphs.

Nantucket, Mass. (13242 343), (13241 265). Nantucket Island, objective of many a Cape Cod cruise, is well worth a visit of several days. The island is far enough offshore to have an atmosphere of its own despite frequent visits of large steamers bearing heavy cargoes of tourists. Its history, dating from the Vikings' visit about A.D. 1000 (if we accept Pohl's deduction) to the decline of its whaling industry at the time of the Civil War, is a romantic and exciting one. Populated by what Herman Melville calls "fighting Quakers," it was the home port of a hardy, enterprising, audacious people who sailed wherever there was water to float their square-ended vessels. Many a South Sea Island native knew of Nantucket before he ever heard of Boston, New York, or London. Names of Nantucket skippers and vessels still cling to Pacific islands.

The approach to Nantucket from the west is clearly marked by a row of lighted buoys ending with the horn buoy at Cross Rip. Note that this buoy does not groan like a whistle buoy but bleats like a sheep. That is, the pitch is constant and does not go from low to high as does a whistle.

In clear weather, one can cut Cross Rip, pass between can 5 and nun 4, leave can 3 to port, and turn around the end of Tuckernuck Shoal at bell 1. It is easy to be set to the south of this course by a flood tide. Keep the bell bearing about southeast as you approach it. Local yachts treat Tuckernuck Shoal rather lightly and are seen sailing about in what the writer considered rather perilous circumstances. The answer to his query on the matter was "There is plenty of water there. Quite big boats go right across it." Still, soundings of 10 feet or less on a shoal 4 miles off shore are worthy of some attention.

Your first sign of the island on a clear day will be a tower well to the west of the town. Then the gilded dome of a church and the tops of other buildings in town will gradually appear. You will not see land from the deck of a yacht until well inside bell 1.

In approaching Nantucket, be prepared for a change in weather. In 1971, the writer passed can 5 with a pleasant gentle WNW breeze and charged past Brant Point shortly afterwards, single reefed, soaking wet, with the dinghy half full of water. In 1977, a pleasant gentle SW breeze off can 5 expired completely and only the tide, errant zephyrs, and a constitutional indolence saved him from use of the "iron topsail."

Once by Tuckernuck, run down to the black-and-white bell off the entrance and follow the buoys in. Notice that the tide follows the channel in general and runs with a considerable velocity. If you are bucking it, you can easily be set to one side or the other. The writer saw a large ketch on the flats to the east of the channel, all sail set, well heeled over, and motionless.

There is a light on the end of the east jetty and this jetty shows above high water for most of its length. The end of the west jetty is marked only by a nun and is often submerged at high water.

Brant Point Light and the range lights can be of help at night. A low-power radio direction-finder station was established at Brant Point in 1977 with the characteristic BP (-... -.-.). The steamers from Hyannis use this channel and deserve the greatest respect and the largest radar reflector you can obtain.

If you wish to lie in a slip at the Boat Basin, call ahead on your radio (channel 16) for a reservation. Approach the stockade of yellow-topped piles and follow the outside of it to the southerly side. Here you will be hailed through a bull horn from the dock master's office and handed a slip assignment impaled on the end of a long pole. Only then can you enter the stockade. There are well over one hundred slips, each with electric current, water, a telephone jack, and a powerful fire-extinguishing system. Use the head on the wharf. In 1977 the minimum charge was $15.00 per night. Gasoline, Diesel fuel, ice, and water can be obtained by nonresidents of the Basin alongside the southern side, although on a busy morning you may have to wait for dock space. Supplies of all kinds are available nearby in the town.

If you prefer more privacy than the Boat Basin affords, anchor off the town. Keep clear of the turning basin used by the steamers. Ordinarily the anchorage is not crowded and there is ample swinging room. Under ordinary conditions, the anchorage is well protected, although it may be choppy at times. However, in a hard easterly or northeaster, when every wave has a 5-mile running start down the harbor, it can be dangerous. The late Mr. Fessenden Blanchard, a former coauthor of this *Guide,* wrote:

> In a September gale Nantucket can be very bad. Once, in such a gale, one of the authors was lucky enough to have a shoal-draft auxiliary sloop and managed early enough to get up into Polpis Harbor to the east of the bay leading to Head Harbor. It blew from 60 to 70 mph for twenty-four hours. We rode it out in Polpis, but in Nantucket Harbor yachts were strewn along the western shore.

Land at a small float at the head of the wharf forming the south side of the Boat Basin. If you prefer, you may blow your horn three times, display a T flag, and be taken ashore in a launch for 75¢ per passenger each way.

The area around the heads of the wharves has been "restored." The streets are cobbled and the buildings are finished with gray-stained shingles and white trim. Even the A&P conforms, its large front window made to look small-paned with strips of white plastic. The streets are crowded with little shops purveying craft work—some of it artistically conceived and skillfully executed—and lunches to tempt the crowds coming off the steamers from Hyannis.

If you are in need of repairs, consult Joe Lopez, dock master at the Boat Basin. Chuck Butler, an independent mechanic, was prepared in

Nantucket Harbor looking northerly.

1977 to make repairs on gasoline and Diesel engines, outboard motors, and electronic gear. He would also do underwater work, such as clearing fouled propellers. The Radio Shack in town can make repairs to electronic gear.

Beyond the Boat Basin is the Nantucket Shipyard, reactivated in 1977 under the management of Prentice Claflin and Christopher Fay. As sailors themselves, experienced in local waters, and as working owners who will be continually at the yard themselves, they seek to establish here a yard capable of repairing or rebuilding any vessel that can enter Nantucket harbor. They had a 20-ton lift in 1977 and had assembled a crew of capable mechanics, carpenters, and riggers. They intend to install a 100-ton railway to handle the big draggers working the offshore fishing grounds, and wharf space for unloading and transporting fish is being made by the town. Thus it may be possible to base part of the fleet much closer to the fish than Boston, New Bedford, or Woods Hole.

All this will be supplemented by a yacht-construction and charter program built around a school like the Apprenticeshop in Bath, Maine, where young people can learn the crafts involved in building boats.

At present, in the fall of 1977, most of this project is on paper, but Mr. Claflin declares that definite progress has been made and that the summer of 1978 will see significant changes.

The Nantucket Yacht Club is located in the northwesterly corner of the harbor. Tremendous pressure from its own increased membership has forced it to suspend use of its facilities and services to cruising people. It maintains a limited launch service for its members only; and the club, while not inhospitable, is so busy with its own programs and so crowded with its own members that visitors cannot be encouraged.

An experienced explorer of the shoal and sandy channels south of Cape Cod contributes the following directions for getting to Head of the Harbor and Wauwinet:

I have taken the liberty of including a transparency of the Nantucket buoyage system I wrote you of. This is a delightful sail. I think that I've got all of the buoys straight, but continued refinement over a few years may still leave a few degrees error in my locations. (You know small boats!) Here is a set of directions to the "Head of the harbor," Nantucket—a good number of boats of decent size (up to 5 ft. draft) do this trip and it is delightful and the mark of an adventuresome spirit. If you make it to Wauwinet (and you've a sailboat!), everyone in that small resort community will know that you have arrived and will happily greet you.

As you leave the general anchorage, look for the black and white cylinder (can?) just off First Point. Observe it well, as you'll be hunting for the next half dozen. They are unnumbered—the numbers are only for my chart reference. Typically you skirt the shore finding the deepest water. The points are confusing and similar, so here are a few uncharted landmarks: There's a broken-down wooden pier off Second Point. The "Sherbourne Yacht Club," a grounded large red barge (belonging to some friends), is located at X next to Third Point. Buoy 5 has been difficult to locate recently and is perhaps intended only as a guide to the entrance of Polpis Harbor (which has its own red-and-black crossstick floats). So I have given course directions from 4 directly to 6—aiming directly for the middle of the very tall Pocono bluff. The hairiest negotiation comes at 7 where one turns some 130° to get around the shoal off Pocono sharply enough not to hit Bass Point. (Prepare to touch bottom!) Finally, after coming to buoy 8 (and these are all vertical striped center-of-the-channel), head for the middle of the Head. A number of boats stop at many places along the way. The current can run up to 1 knot near buoys 1 through 3, but is less nearer the Head, I believe.

If you get this far and feel like a land-based meal, Wauwinet House can include you for dinner. The atmosphere is one of relaxed gentility.

In the 1890s there used to be a sailing ferry that made the run from Wauwinet to Nantucket for the hotel guests.

Nantucket offers something for almost every taste. There are, of course, the usual food, clothing, and hardware stores. Then there are a great many little shops purveying all manner of craftwork and souvenirs. There are excellent restaurants, among the best being The Mad Hatter, Captain Tobey's, and the Languedoc.

The Whaling Museum, to which anyone can direct you, is worth several hours of time for anyone interested in American maritime history. In the basement are excellent representations of the different trades involved in fitting out for a whaling voyage. Tools actually used by riggers, coopers, shipwrights, and sailmakers and samples of their workmanship are displayed. Upstairs there is a whaleboat completely fitted out and ready to lower. Pictures, charts, and whaling gear are attractively displayed with excellent explanatory placards. The writer and his crew found this museum in itself worth the whole trip.

Parts of town retain the variety and individuality of old Nantucket. The mansions built by Coffins, Macys, and Starbucks still stand among shingled cottages and brick houses.

Nantucket beyond the town bears its own characteristic atmosphere. Rent a bicycle at one of the many waterfront shops and ride over to Surf

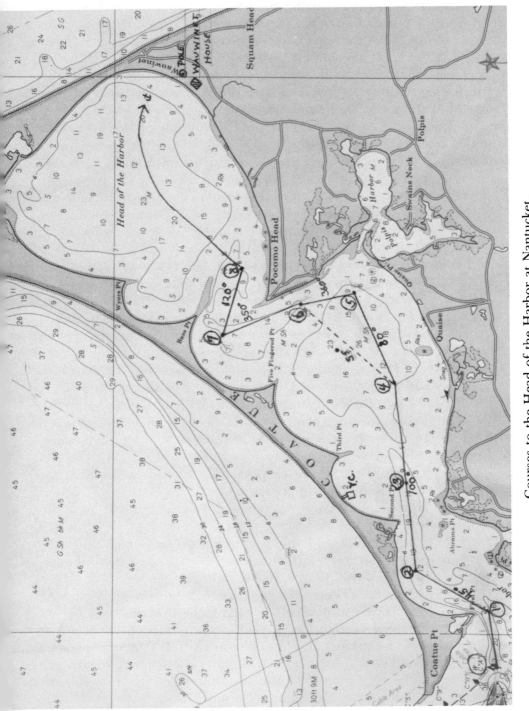

Courses to the Head of the Harbor at Nantucket.

Side. Outside the town, on the moors, you feel the bleak offshore quality of the place, despite the cars whizzing by your left ear. Scrubby pines, waving grass, thickets of bayberry and beach plum remind you that this is no continent but an island, which, if not actually afloat, at least stands up to ocean winds and ocean seas. The great South Beach confirms this. A steep sandy beach faces you with savage shoals offshore and a blank horizon. There is a refreshment stand, a lifeguard's tower, and perhaps a throng of bathers, but walk a half mile east or west along the beach and you are at sea.

Continue eastward to Siasconset, an attractive town of gray cottages and roses, on to Sankaty Head, and return to town by the back road.

Lengthy as this account is, the writer cannot forbear to include the following extract from the *Sailor's Magazine* of November, 1848. The article is entitled "A Cruise Along Shore in the Seventeenth Century":

I shall never forget that homeward passage. It was late in November, and we judged ourselves seven leagues southeast of Nantucket. The old man was below, on his beam ends, with a cruel rheumatism, when the wind, which had been blowing hard from the north, hauled to the east. The mate, whose name was Salter, had no thought of running under circumstances so unfavorable, and went below.

"Captain Phillips," said he, "the wind has canted to the eastward, but it is awful foggy—so thick that you can't see across the deck."

"Sound!" said the old man, "and pass the lead below."

They did so, and after a glance at it, he turned to the mate, and said, "Shake out all the reefs, keep her northwest two hours, then sound again, and let me see the lead."

"Yes sir," said the mate, and he passed up the companion-way, not particularly pleased with the prospect.

In two hours, soundings were again had, and the lead passed to the skipper.

"Five fathoms, with sand, and a cracking breeze," said Salter.

"Don't you mean seven fathoms, Mr. Salter?" asked the old man, scraping the sand with the nail of his right-fore finger.

"There might have been *about* seven sir," said the mate, "I allowed pretty largely for the drift: but it is best to be the safe side."

"Right, Mr. Salter, right. I am glad to find you so particular. We are close in with the land, and can't be too careful. You may keep her northwest, half west; I don't expect you can *see* much, but if you don't *hear* anything in the course of fifteen minutes, let me know it.—An open ear for breakers, Mr. Salter! We must be cautious—very cautious, sir."

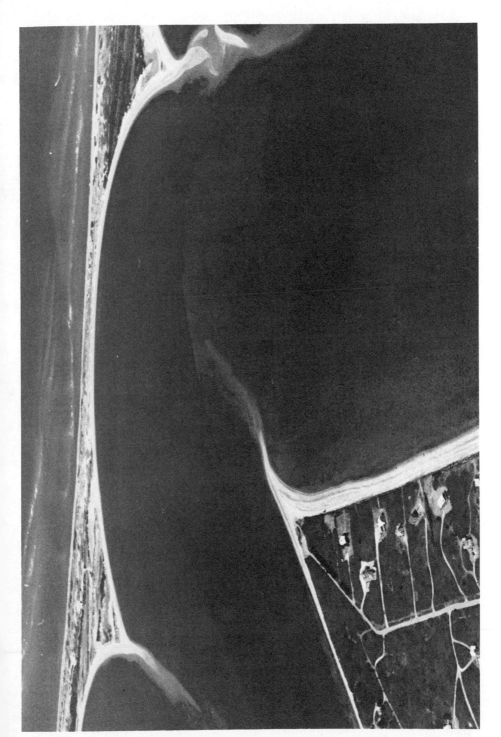

The Head of the Harbor at Nantucket

The mate, although a fellow of considerable grit, was somewhat staggered at the last orders. He, however, nodded a respectful assent, and made his way to the forward part of the vessel. The wind had freshened, and the *Little Mary* (as the schooner was called) was doing her prettiest. Salter leaned over the larboard bow, and was pondering upon the folly of running before a gale of wind through a fog, to make the land, with no other guide than a few particles of gray sand, in which he had no more confidence than he would have had in a piece of drift seaweed.

Eight or nine minutes only had passed, when the roar of breakers struck the ear of the mate. "Luff, Luff, and shake her!" cried he. The schooner was brought to the wind in an instant. The foam from the receding waves was visible under her lee; but in a moment the dark line of Seconset head, in the southwest, told the mate that everything was right.

"We are clear of the scrape, so far," growled Salter, "but I don't think a handful of sand is a thing to run by in a time like this. I'll *know* if there *is* any difference between the bottom here, and the last we had, Sam, heave the lead, while I keep her steady."

The lead came up, and the mate declared not only the bottom, but the depth of the water to be the same. "I think," continued he, "all the sand within forty miles of this spot is alike. Sam, pass me some of that which the cook brought on board to clean his things with, while we were lying in Seconset. There," said he, comparing the two, "there is no difference, even in this, except what the water makes"; and he proceeded to prove his position by putting fresh tallow on the lead, and covering it with the sand which had been brought from the uplands of Seconset.

"Sam," said Salter, "you may wet that lead. I'll try it on the old man."

The lead was washed in the sea for a moment, and the mate took it below chuckling at the thought of snaring the old veteran.

"Captain Phillips," said he, with counterfeit anxiety, "the fifteen minutes are gone—it blows spitefully in flaws, and spits thick."

"Mr. Salter," returned the old man, raising himself in his berth to take the lead, "north west, half west, should have brought you within ear-shot of the breakers some minutes ago. I am afraid you have not kept her straight."

He raised the lead, and the first glance at the soundings seemed to shake his very soul—but the flush on his high, pale forehead passed away in an instant. Ordering the skylight to be removed, he placed the lead in a better position, and riveted his clear blue eye upon it for a full minute, when he turned to the mate, with the utmost coolness, and said, "Mr. Salter, I am glad to say that there has been no fault in your steering; the schooner *has* run north west, half west, as straight as a gun-barrel; at the same time I am very sorry to tell you that Nantucket is sunk, and that we are just over Seconset ridge!"

The South Shore of Cape Cod—
Falmouth to Stage Harbor, Chatham

This stretch of coast is a frightful sight through the eyes of the skipper of a long-legged, narrow-beamed craft, but through the eyes of the skipper of a shoal-draft boat with hard bilges, it is worth at least a week's exploration. The low, barren beach with lagoons or ponds behind it is pierced at intervals by dredged channels, making shoal but secure harbors and giving access to the shallow marshy headwaters of the inlets. Off the beach lies an area of navigable water and beyond that are shifting shoals, often with soundings in single digits. To the shoal-draft boat all this shallow water offers no peril. A grounding means simply shoving with an oar or jumping into warm, waist-deep water to push off. Getting ashore on the windward side of an outer shoal in heavy weather, though, is another story. The sand can be as hard as concrete, and there is no pushing off.

The towns that have grown up near the dredged channels are predominantly populous summer communities strung along the main road. They offer necessary supplies but are not otherwise particularly attractive, although certainly Chatham has retained a unique character in spite of its many visitors.

Woods Hole, Falmouth, and Hyannis are deep-water harbors, as the Cape uses the term, with accommodations for most yachts, but if you want to explore the smaller places it is well to call ahead for the latest information on the state of the channel and to be sure that you can be accommodated with a mooring or slip. Plan to enter on a rising tide.

The *Eldridge Tide and Pilot Book* is a most helpful volume in this area as it shows the hour-by-hour change in tidal currents. These are quite worth considering, running from 1 to 3 knots in some places.

Falmouth, Mass. (13230 249.) Falmouth provides whatever services a yachtsman may require. It is easy of access by day or night and public transportation is available to Boston and New York.

To enter, simply make bell 16 and run for the green flashing light on the west jetty. Do not be disturbed by the *Coast Pilot*'s estimate of a controlling depth of 4 feet. In July 1977 there was ample water for a large ocean-racing yawl to beat down the harbor.

Just inside the entrance is the Coast Guard base. Beyond that, the sides of the harbor are lined with marinas and boat yards. There are a few moorings available for visitors. Ask at any of the marinas.

There are several boat yards capable of making repairs to hull, spars, engine, sails, and electronic gear. One of the best known is Mac-Dougall's, located about halfway up the east side of the harbor and prominently labeled. Not only does this yard have capable carpenters, riggers, mechanics, and electronic technicians, but it has a complete sail loft capable of building you a new sail if the old one is too far gone to repair. There is a marine store at the yard carrying the usual assortment of hardware, both the necessities and the frills. Falmouth Marine Service provides many of the same facilities and has a sound reputation. Gasoline, Diesel oil, ice, and water are available at the boat yards and marinas. There is a supermarket, Angelo's, a healthy walk from the shore near the head of the harbor. The Flying Bridge, a restaurant on the west side, is well spoken of and commands an interesting view of harbor traffic.

With steamers coming and going to Martha's Vineyard and a number of yachts coming into the boat yards seeking remedies for their ills "right away yesterday," Falmouth is a busy harbor. It is a good place to get into when you need help or want to change crews or to lie over during a gale of wind, but it is also a great place to get out of in quest of quieter and more picturesque anchorages to the eastward.

If you have time to spend in Falmouth, organize a ride to the New Alchemy Institute. Here a number of thoughtful and original people are actually trying what many of us merely talk about when mention of the approaching oil shortage rises to the surface of a conversation. They have built a house to use solar heat. It is banked with earth on the north side. The south side consists of plastic half-cylinders laid like roof tiles. Each is double, with an air space between, sealed at the top and plugged at the bottom with a spongelike caulking, which lets condensation run out but prevents a free flow of air. When the sun shines through the roof, even in winter, it heats the air inside. This warm air collects under the peak of the roof, whence it is blown through ducts under the floor to a bin full of loosely piled rocks. On a sunny day these get almost too hot to touch. When the sun is not shining, the rocks give off heat and warm the building for as much as three days. Tomatoes and other vegetables grow in the building all winter, needing only very occasional help from a small wood stove. Experiments continue in search of a better way than rocks to store the heat.

Outside are several plastic cylinders about 6 feet high, each full of water. They stand in front of semicircular walls painted white. The cylinders are planted with algae and warmed by the sun. Fish feed on the algae and grow almost while you watch them.

Other projects are constantly being developed and tried out on an experimental basis. As funds are limited, materials are inexpensive and ready to hand and workmanship is simple and ingenious. The New Alchemy Institute is well worth a morning's exploration.

Waquoit Bay, Mass. (13229 114 SC). This large shallow bay is what a shoal-draft boat is built for. Its upper reaches are secluded and quiet. There are several channels leading into it and communicating with other backwaters.

Entrance from Nantucket Sound is marked by a flashing red bell 2 and a light on the east jetty. A beacon marks the west jetty. The jetties are hard to find from offshore. However, during the summer, campers congregate on the beach at Dead Neck just east of the east jetty. They look like "funny little houses." Head for them and you will find the jetties.

In 1977 the channel was reported to have a depth of 5 feet at low water and a vigorous current. One local yachtsman estimated it at 6 knots, which is practically a waterfall.

The beaches on both sides of the entrance are clean and pleasant places to swim. Inside, the channel is marked by a series of cans, each marking the end of a sandspit. Local reports in 1977 gave depths of 12 feet all the way to the head of the Bay and the Waquoit Yacht Club. The eastern part of the lower bay is popular with water skiers but there is quieter anchorage on the west side above the prominent spit south of the Seapit River. There are no landing facilities here. Above the mouth of the Seapit River is a town landing and above this is the Waquoit Yacht Club, with a fleet of small boats and occasionally a mooring to be had. There is not water enough at the float for a cruising boat. About a mile to the west, on the main road, is a store, but there are better and more convenient sources of supplies than Waquoit.

It is possible to follow the local buoys through the Seapit River and up the Childs River to the Edwards Boat Yard operated by Ollie and Pete Swain. For this trip count on no more than 4 feet at low water. The yard has facilities for repair of any boat that can reach it, and can provide gasoline, Diesel oil, ice, and water. There is also a well-stocked marine store. Yachts lie in slips here, as the river is narrow. This is the head of navigation on the Childs River for masted vessels, as a highway crosses the river just above the yard and electric wires overhang the channel.

Great River and Little River join and flow together into the east side of Waquoit Bay. Each of these flows out of a large pond with islands and coves worth exploring in a sailing dinghy or rowboat. There are local buoys to guide you, and there is said to be a small boat yard on the west shore of the pond. Local yachtsmen declared Great River to be not navigable in 1977.

The fishing at the entrance to the Bay is said to be sporty.

In sailing along the south shore of Cape Cod, many skippers stand offshore around Succonesset Shoal and Wreck Shoal, but there is a navigable channel for shoal-draft boats along the shore inside the shoals. Be sure to find and pass close to the tall red-and-black spindle flasher marking the west end of the shoal. This is locally described as a "cardiac-arrest area," as it is shallow and the tide runs hard. However, once by the buoy, proceed by careful use of the depth finder to keep in the "deep" water between the shore and the shoal. Note that your course will diverge from the land down to the flashing green bell off Cotuit.

It is likely to be smoother in here than it is outside in the main ship channel, yet even in here, with a strong wind against the tide, a very short steep chop will build up, which in a small boat can be wet and unpleasant. One yachtsman reports that his dinghy was swamped in here.

Eel Pond (13229   114 SC). This pond, with a cut through the beach, will be of little use to cruising boats until it is dredged out. In 1977 there was a depth of only 3 feet in the very narrow channel at the entrance and the tide runs very swiftly across the bar.

Popponesset Bay (13229   114 SC). This is a very shallow bay, with depths of as little as 2 feet reported in the entrance. However, the *Coast Pilot* reports a small marina on Daniels Island, so the Bay must be navigable for small boats.

Cotuit and Osterville, Mass. (13229 114 SC). There is a large and lovely area of shoal and protected water around Osterville Grand Island, easily navigable by a boat drawing 4 feet in the hands of a skipper who doesn't mind touching the sand.

The entrance to Cotuit has recently shoaled up considerably and until it is dredged should be avoided by any but the most shoal-draft boats. Enter at Osterville, passing between a black flasher 1 and can 3. At the entrance to the dredged channel is a privately maintained lighted buoy to be left to starboard. Our correspondent notes: "I've wandered out of the channel and noticed no difference in depth until a few hundred yards from the jetty. These privately maintained aids would appear simply to keep you 'on the straight and narrow.' I'm suggesting that the first few can be cut, and that there is gradual shoaling without surprises. This entrance is somewhat hard to find. The cue: a dozen houses to the right of the jetty, relatively unpopulated to the left. This is the Audubon Bird Sanctuary: 'Take only photographs; leave only footprints.'

"Just inside the jetty, the Seapuit River leaves the channel on the western side, a delightful mile of narrow sand on the left, nice homes and lovely boats on the right." He adds, "Boats over 26 feet may not anchor in the river."

The channel up West Bay is locally buoyed and has a depth of 5 feet at low water. There is limited anchorage in the cove to the east as one approaches the narrows between Little Island and the shore.

Just above the bridge are two large boat yards with a few moorings, numerous slips, and all facilities for cruising people. The first is that of Chester A. Crosby & Son, run now by Chester Crosby, Jr. The Crosby family has been building sound wooden boats here for well over a century. Horace S. Crosby and his brother Worthington built *Little Eva,* traditionally recognized as the first "Crosby Cat." These famous vessels, used as commercial fishing boats in Nantucket Sound before the days of gasoline engines, were wide, flat boats with a centerboard, square stern, and an outboard rudder. The sail plan consisted simply of a huge gaff-headed mainsail hoisted on a short heavy mast stepped as far forward as possible and often existing without visible means of support from standing rigging. The boom was longer than the boat and the gaff nearly as long. They were fine, able boats for the conditions they were designed to meet, although more than a mite hard-headed off the wind in a breeze. Recently a number of replicas have been built, and at least one fiberglass model is being marketed—not, however, by the Crosby yard. Mr. Crosby is a most obliging person, well acquainted with local history and local conditions and with an eye for a good boat. When the writer visited the yard, he found an ancient catboat being restored plank by plank. "It is a labor of love," said Mr. Crosby. The yard appears to be efficient and well maintained and ready to effect any repairs one may find necessary. It is one of the few yards on the coast still building wooden boats. Recently several small stock "Curlew" sloops have been built, boats admirably adapted to Cape Cod waters. Gas, Diesel oil, water, ice, and a few moorings are available.

The yard to the north is Crosby Yacht, identified by a characteristic symbol well known to readers of yachting magazines. This yard, too, provides gas, Diesel oil, water, ice, and can perform necessary repairs. There are slips in which to lie alongside and several moorings in North

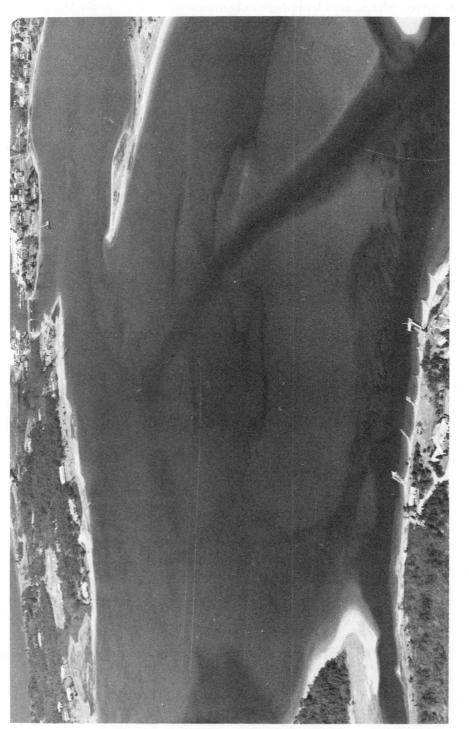

The entrance to West Bay and Osterville. The mouth of the Seapuit River is at the lower left. Crosby's yard is at the bridge near the top of the picture.

Bay. Also there is an elegant marine store and snack bar at the head of the wharf. Grocery stores are located in the village of Osterville to the east of the bridge. It is a walk long enough to raise an appetite—about a mile.

One can continue above the boat yards into North Bay and all the way to Prince Cove by a very narrow channel. The Oyster Harbor Yacht Club stands on Osterville Grand Island at Tims Cove, and the Cotuit Yacht Club, merely a landing without a clubhouse, is across the bay from it.

Hyannis, Mass. (13229 114 SC). Hyannis is a busy summer resort town—hot, crowded with automobiles, and redolent of all that we go cruising to avoid. However, it is one of the few deep-water harbors on the south shore of the Cape and has facilities for repairs of all sorts. Communication with Boston and New York by bus and air is easily arranged. Steamers run to Martha's Vineyard and Nantucket.

If you contemplate running before a brisk southwest breeze for the entrance to Hyannis, you are likely to have no trouble avoiding the well-marked dangers. However, as you get into the shoal water and fast tidal current west of Point Gammon, you will encounter a short steep chop, which could swamp your dinghy, soak you down, and which would be dangerous in a small open boat. Once inside the breakwater at Hyannis Port, you should have no trouble making the flashing buoy at the entrance to the dredged channel. Thence follow the buoys into Hyannis.

The inner harbor is likely to be crowded and room must be left for the steamers to turn. Therefore, you will probably have to lie at a slip.

Hyannis Marine, the large marina on your starboard hand, has all the facilities you could ask for and more, too. Slips with electric-power connections and water are reserved for transients. Gas, Diesel fuel, and ice are sold on the wharf. At the head of the wharf is a well-equipped marine store, with everything from oilclothes, to hardware, charts, books, and natty little knick-knacks to pretty up the cabin. Repair facilities include a 25-ton lift, a sail loft, an electronics shop, an engine shop, and a rigging loft. There is also an engine-parts shop, which just may have exactly the set of points or the little spring you have been looking for all summer. Ashore, either at the yard or close by, are a shower, a head, a laundromat, a restaurant and a car-rental agency. Less than a mile away is a small combination liquor and grocery store, which will keep your crew from starving to death. The supermarket is near the western end of the main street, a long, hot walk. Hospital, bus depot, and airport are within an easy taxi ride. The Nantucket and Martha's

Vineyard steamers leave from the other side of the harbor.

Across the harbor, in the western end of it, is Bradbury Marine. A correspondent writes of it:

> My report would not be complete if I failed to mention and recommend Bradbury Marine, Inc. They have served my boat faithfully for twenty years and Captain Klimm's yard is now in its third generation of the Bradbury family. Jim Bradbury runs this yard very competently and rather independently. He likes cruising people, dislikes outboards, and is very knowledgeable. Specialties: rigging, electronics (does it himself), hauling (40-foot maximum), transient slips. He has one of those modern hydraulic trailers that he backs into the water so that he can move under a boat, adjust it, haul it right out, and trail it anywhere, or deposit it in the yard. If you have a special boating problem, he is the one to see. He was also the Harbor Master in 1977. (tel. 775–1707).

Up the street from Bradbury Marine and a large restaurant is the town of Hyannis. It consists principally of one long, long main street, lined with smart clothing stores, a Howard Johnson restaurant, various notion-and-pottery establishments, and indeed, everything but a grocery store. After a long trek to the westward, the hungry mariner will find an enormous brick-and-glass supermarket, providing for all his needs. On his journey along this hot, cement-paved sidewalk, he will see every type of summer costume, every kind of vacation-bound automobile, every aspect of the summer trade on Cape Cod. It is a far cry, indeed, from a down-east general store, with its confused aroma of oilclothes, codline, and cheese.

About a mile out of town is a great shopping center with every conceivable type of store from Sears and Filene's to a boutique and a restaurant. Hyannis, indeed, has much to recommend it.

If you do not require the services of a metropolis, there are pleasanter places to spend the night than in Hyannis. The first is behind the breakwater at Hyannis Port. Seek the best lee you can find. The anchorage is seldom so crowded as to limit your choice. There is a small yacht club at which you can land if you want to, but unless you want to swim on the beach, there is little to land for. There is no store near by, no facilities whatever for repair, and no public transportation. Ashore you will find large estates in unbroken rows along streets as suburban as Chestnut Hill and Wellesley. One of these, to the northeast of the clubhouse, is inhabited by the Kennedy family.

Another anchorage much favored by cruising men is under Harbor

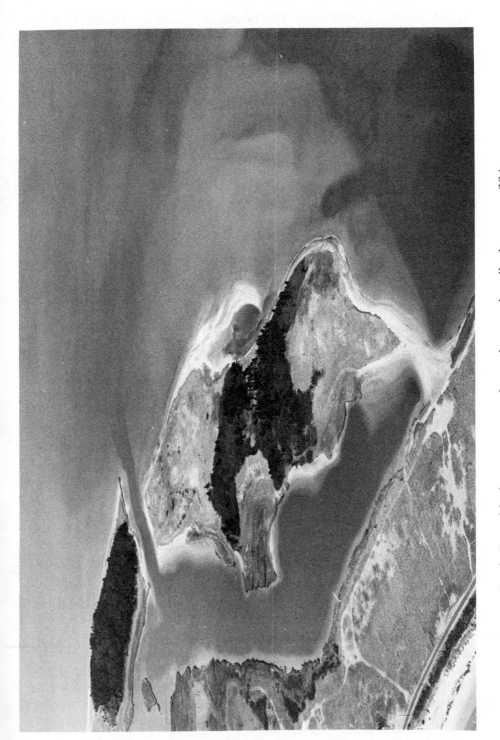

Lewis Bay with the entrance to the anchorage described on page 324.

Bluff to the west of the channel. The headquarters of the Hyannis Yacht Club is here and there may be a vacant mooring. Inquire of the steward.

One can anchor anywhere in Lewis Bay on a quiet night. Usually the wind dies with the sun and of course no roll from outside can penetrate here. If you seek snugger anchorage, follow the directions generously contributed by an explorer willing to share his discoveries:

Proceed up the channel to lighted buoy 18 and run 150 degrees magnetic, thus avoiding Egg Island. Now you might ask why a small boat would go all the way to #18 instead of turning to starboard at, say, #14. I've been aground so many times on the various flats, Egg Island, etc., at night that it seems better to go up to more protected waters and a known point before heading out of the channel. Keep an eye out for Fiddle Head Rock beacon and buoy off to starboard. You will have 5 feet of water all the way. This will bring you to a small stone jetty on the starboard side of a small cut. This cut is to the left of some tall trees. Beware of a shoal off the jetty and of one to the left of the cut. Go right down the middle of the cut. There is deep water right up to the beach at the right, but no place to stay overnight because of the current. Proceed around to port and anchor anywhere in the small bay. You'll be the only boat there on *any* night. If you proceed farther to the head of the harbor, you will find deeper anchorage and occasional company.

I have also had occasion to explore Uncle Roberts Cove. This one is *tough!* Egg Island is lined with poles at the south end, so that one can skirt along it and turn to port at the appropriate point. The rock labelled X on the accompanying chart is usually marked by a Clorox bottle. Proceed dead slow. The two rocks marked on the chart appear to be another small jetty, and one should pass fairly close to it. I sailed in, sailed off in the dinghy for an hour or two, leaving two students on board. The wind shifted and I returned to find them high and drying. (They hadn't noticed.) To make a long story short, the natives were *most* hospitable. A nice cove, but harder to get into than the first because of the nasty rocks all around.

Parker River, South Yarmouth, Mass. (13229 114 SC). There is a marina here providing the usual services, but the entrance is very shoal and, until it is dredged again, will be of use only to small powerboats. If it is dredged out, it is easy to find, as it is right beside a huge drive-in movie screen, marked on the chart and prominent from offshore.

Bass River, Mass. (13229   114 SC). This river, like Parker River, has silted up in recent years, but local authorities claim 4 feet at low water on the bar in 1977. The entrance is well marked by local buoys.

Inside, on the west shore, is Ship Shops, a marina with slips and "full service." Their office monitors Channel 16 VHF, so you can call ahead.

Above the highway bridge, which has a vertical clearance of 15 feet, is the Bass River Marina. Gas, water, and ice, but no Diesel fuel, are available and there is the usual marine store. A public telephone, showers, and a head are near the wharf. The marina provides "in and out" storage and has slips for visitors. There is a mechanic in attendance for engine repair and the marina can send out for repairs to electronic equipment. There are a grocery store and laundromat in town, close to the bridge. The marina listens to Channels 16 and 68 on VHF and 9 on CB.

Although the lower part of Bass River is not particularly attractive to the long-legged deep-water cruising boat, it is interesting because of the controversy over Leif Ericson's alleged visit.

On June 9, 1951, Bass River became one of the most widely talked about ports on the New England coast, at least among readers of the *Saturday Evening Post.* On that date the *Post* published an article by Morton H. Hunt called "The Secret of the Vanished Explorer." In the article, Hunt told of the studies and explorations of a schoolteacher-become-archaeologist named Frederick J. Pohl, which led Pohl to believe that Follins Pond, 6 miles upriver, was the site of the Vinland of Leif Ericson and of his Viking encampment in A.D. 1003. Descriptions in ancient Norse sagas seemed to point to the south of the Cape, with Bass River as a likely possibility. But how was Dr. Pohl to find evidence in support of his theory?

He and his wife went to Bass River, and, first near the shore of Follins Pond and later at points on the river, they discovered mooring holes, of the type used by the Vikings, drilled in several rocks. The Vikings used to put spikes in such holes at an angle that would enable them to put ropes around the spikes to hold their craft without danger of the ropes' slipping off. Dr. Pohl became convinced that these holes were not the drill holes used for blasting, but could be nothing else but holes drilled by the Vikings. He told his story to Hunt. Hunt wrote the article and started a controversy. Some archaeologists raised objections to his theory, while others came to his support.

One of the criticisms pointed to the shoal water. How could a Viking ship have got that far? But Dr. Pohl adduced evidence to show that the sea level 1000 years ago was 2 or 3 feet higher than it is today. In 1952 Dr. Pohl wrote *The Lost Discovery,* in which he traced in detail the travels

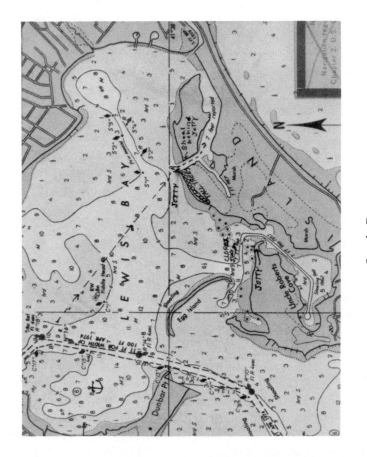

Lewis Bay.

of the Vikings in North America, backing his conclusions with most convincing evidence. Unlike many historians, Dr. Pohl took the trouble to visit the places he described.

Admiral Morison, in his scholarly and colorful *European Discovery of America, Northern Voyages* (1971), locates the Viking colony at L'Anse aux Meadows on the northeast peninsula of Newfoundland. He scorns all efforts to locate it in New England. He writes:

> These [mooring holes] were made by the English natives of New England to receive iron eye-bolts through which to reeve a line to a boat mooring or fish trap. I could have shown him some made for me! It is true that Scandinavians then, as now, liked to moor fore and aft, both to an anchor and to a ring-bolt or tree ashore. But in New England there were plenty of stout trees near shore and no need to drill holes in granite rocks.

Allen Harbor, Harwich Port, Mass. (13229   114 SC). There is about 7 feet of water in the channel into Allen Harbor. The harbor itself is completely landlocked, very crowded, and devoted mostly to powerboats. It does have excellent facilities, however. There are many well-equipped slips, about ninety belonging to the Allen Harbor Yacht Club, fifty to the Allen Harbor Marine Service, and sixteen to the town of Harwich. Most of these are seasonally rented, although Allen Harbor Marine Service is most hospitable and will, if at all possible, take care of any transients. Allen Harbor Marine Service is operated by Rupert Nichols and is a very well run operation, with gasoline, Diesel oil, outboard and inboard mechanics, and ship carpenters available during the season, seven days a week. There is a very nice gift and marine store here. The harbor is about ten minutes' walk from a shopping center where groceries and other supplies are available.

Wychmere Harbor, Harwich Port, Mass. (13229 114 SC). Entrance to this tight little harbor is made clear by the drawing on page 328. The dredged channel is straight and has been marked at times by local buoys not shown on the chart. However, a direct course from one can to the next should keep you on the straight and narrow path. Inside the harbor, the best water is said to favor the port side—about 5 feet at low water.

The Stone Horse Yacht Club is prominent on the west side, and just beyond it is the Harwich Port Boat Works, owned by Arthur Coté. Inquire here about moorings or slips, as there is no room to anchor in

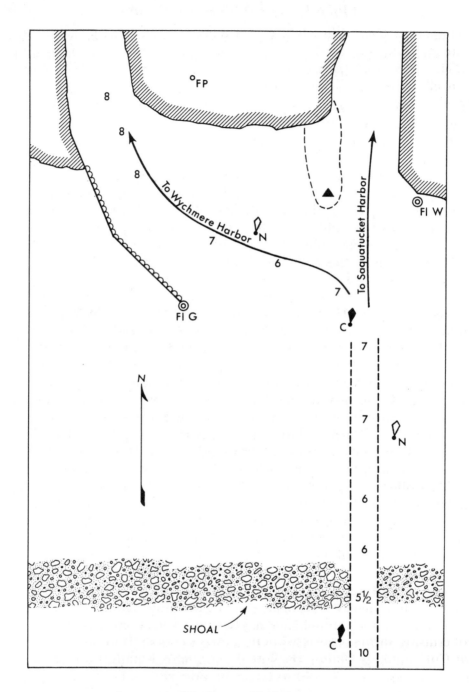

Wychmere Harbor

Wychmere. The Yacht Club has six guest moorings, marked by posts with white tops.

The Boat Works can haul any boat that can get into Wychmere and can effect most repairs. George Luscomb is said to be an excellent mechanic. Gasoline, Diesel oil, and water are available here, but no ice. If you make 5 knots through the water, leave Woods Hole bound east at low water and you will carry 2 knots of fair tide all the way to Wychmere. The reverse is true, too, of course. Leave Wychmere at high water bound west.

Saquatucket, Mass. (13229 114 SC). This is a tiny bottle of a dredged harbor, just east of Wychmere. It is crowded with slips, leaving room for a few moorings and no room whatever to swing at anchor. There is 5 feet in the dredged channel at low water. Because the harbor is so small and crowded, yachtsmen are asked to use the heads on the wharf and not pollute the harbor with their own heads. Gas, Diesel oil, water, and ice are available at the fuel wharf. Showers, laundry, and public telephones are located at the landing.

Because space is at a premium, it is wise to call ahead before planning to spend the night at Saquatucket. Thomas Leach is the Harbor Master. He can be reached by telephone, on Channel 16 VHF, or Channel 7 CB.

Groceries are available at an A&P to the west of the harbor on the main road, but there are no repair facilities.

Saquatucket is good shelter and a good fuel stop, but it is not much to look at. There are more interesting harbors both east and west of it.

Stage Harbor, Chatham, Mass. (13229 114 SC). Chatham is less submerged by the flood of summer visitors than most ports on the south shore of the Cape. There are still commercial fishing vessels based here. They are reminiscent of the husky catboats used in the days of sail—broad, shallow, with square stern and stubby bow. They are heavily powered and employed in dragging for quahogs and scallops as well as in fishing. In the outer harbor there are a fish wharf and a small boat yard. The yacht club is not dominant. Such yachting as is based here is largely day sailing in small boats. There are increasing numbers of cruising yachts reported, but nothing like the pressure that builds up at Cuttyhunk or Hadley Harbor on a summer weekend.

Chatham is off the path of cruising yachts "doing" Nantucket Sound, most of whom find it far to leeward when bound either for Nantucket or Woods Hole, and to get out through Pollock Rip calls for a 12-mile beat around Handkerchief Shoal against the prevailing southwest wind. There is a channel between Handkerchief Shoal and Monomoy, which a local authority regards as perfectly practicable. In this author's opinion, a stranger should view it with great caution.

Entrance to Stage Harbor from Chatham Roads is clearly marked by a black-and-white lighted bell, a green flasher nun at the entrance to the dredged channel through Harding Beach, and a flasher opposite the jetty. Shoaling to 8 feet is reported in the channel from the entrance to nun 8. On a southwest breeze a steep, confused chop is likely to build up outside the jetty because the south shore of the Cape and the shoals of Monomoy act like the sides of a funnel.

While this may occasion surprise and distress on running in before the wind, it can be frightening to the skipper beating out against it. The worst of it, however, is near the channel entrance. A mile or more outside, the sea is not nearly so bad.

The principal anchorage at Chatham is in the basin east of nun 12 off the wharves. There is said to be a depth of 10 feet here. A quiet and possibly less-frequented anchorage is southeast of nun 6 in what used to be the entrance channel before the cut was made through Harding Beach. There is a small marina in the Mitchell River just below the bridge, and next to it the Mitchell River Marina maintains several guest moorings and slips for transient yachts. About 6 feet can be carried to the bridge at low water. The channel is marked with local buoys.

Gas, Diesel oil, water, and ice can be obtained at the Old Mill Boat Yard in the outer harbor or at the bridge. The bridge has a vertical clearance of 8 feet. Yachts that can pass under it will find quiet, clean anchorage in Mill Pond and can even penetrate to Little Mill Pond, where there is a town wharf close to the shopping center of Chatham. The trip is worthwhile in the dinghy, anyway, and affords a pleasant way to visit the store.

The most convenient place for repairs to hull, spars, or rigging is the Old Mill Boat Yard, operated by Tom Ennis on the north shore of the outer harbor. He has a railway that can haul yachts drawing up to 5 feet. Also, at the Mitchell River Marina, run by Houyd Meincke, is a crane capable of lifting a small boat or stepping a spar.

The bridge giving access to the Mill Pond was out of commission in 1977 but is scheduled to reopen. Inside the Pond is the yard of Robert Walch, who builds small boats here. The owner is F. Spaulding Dunbar, a yacht designer and a reliable source of local information.

Repairs to electronic equipment can be made at Chatham Marine Electronics Laboratory.

There is a great deal to see and do in Chatham. There are the well-known Chatham Murals, painted by Mrs. Carol Wight and now housed in a barn at the old Autward house. There is the Railroad

The entrance to Chatham looking east.

Museum in the no-longer-used railroad station. There is the view of the open Atlantic from Chatham Light. A summer theater is operated by Ohio University. Some people might enjoy boating on Pleasant Bay and Chatham Harbor, the large body of shallow water between the Chatham —South Orleans shore and Nauset Beach.

Peter Ford, Harbor Master of Chatham, reports that there is no channel south of Morris Island. A sandbar runs from Monomoy Island to Morris Island with a few feet of water over it at low water. Currents are strong, and this area should be avoided. No buoys are located here.

Mr. Ford also warns mariners that no person, regardless of his experience, should attempt to use the passage into Chatham Harbor between Monomoy Beach and the southern tip of Nauset Beach. It is an area subject to shifting shoals and heavy, breaking seas. Although he maintains some buoys here, they cannot be shifted to conform with changes in the channel for several days after a storm because of sea conditions. We strongly recommend that all yachtsmen heed his advice.

In front of Chatham Lighthouse on a bluff is a sign reading:

About nine miles SE of this place are the shoals of Pollock Rip which turned the *Mayflower* back to Provincetown Harbor and caused the Pilgrim Fathers to settle in Plymouth instead of on the Jersey Coast, their original destination.

It might be noted also that the shoals off nearby Nantucket turned Henry Hudson back from Cape Cod and in the direction of the river that bears his name.

How those shoals made history!

Monomoy Point, really an island, extends south about 6 miles from the town of Chatham and includes about 3500 acres. It is presently in the possession of the Fish and Wildlife Service of the Department of the Interior, with the exception of a small area that is privately owned in the vicinity of the abandoned lighthouse. This unspoiled and beautiful expanse of dunes is a habitat of much wildlife, and a stop for migratory birds.

Another attraction on the Cape, especially when one is weathered in, is the Cape Cod National Seashore. This comprises a sizable portion of the total area of Cape Cod, from Chatham to Provincetown, and will preserve the natural beauty of the dune land. Many interesting exhibits and restored historical sites are on display. To take advantage of this project, enter the Seashore at Eastham, where the Visitor's Center is established.

As we go to press in 1978, we hear that the winter storms of this

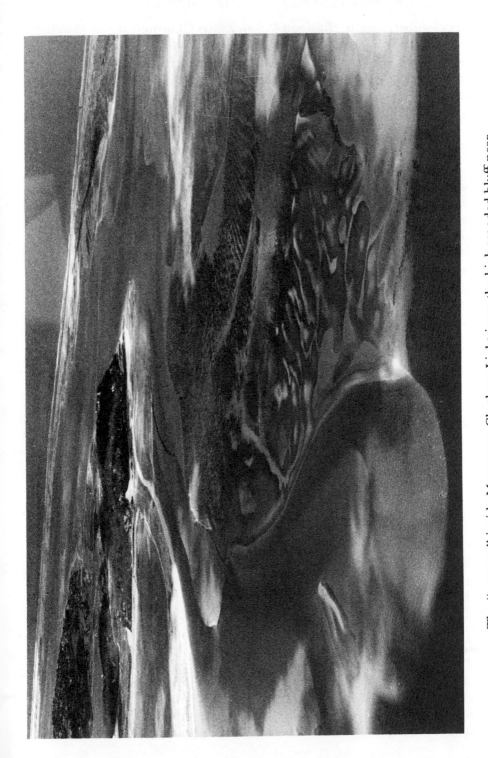

The "passage" inside Monomoy. Chatham Light is on the high wooded bluff near the center of the picture. The tip of Monomoy appears at the right.

year have substantially changed Pollock Rip Channel. It has shoaled up considerably and the Coast Guard has removed several of the buoys. Consult the latest charts, seek local information, and proceed with the greatest caution. It may be wise to go the longer way around through Great Round Shoal Channel.

Monomoy and Beyond

Cape Cod is the most conspicuous outpost of the mainland on the New England coast. Geologically, it is unusual, and there is nothing like it anywhere on the coast of the United States. It is a narrow glacial peninsula, constantly being modified through the action of wind and sea, but based on a rock-and-preglacial-clay foundation that is called by geologists one of the ancient drainage divides of the country. Much of it is terminal moraine, with its few large rocks brought by the glacier from far to the north and scattered around the Cape, conspicuous in the sandy soil.

The first part of the Cape to be seen by the early voyagers from overseas was its Great Beach, running from Provincetown on the north to the southern tip—a long and narrow spit of sand and marsh known as Monomoy Island. Between Monomoy and Nantucket and beyond to the southward are some of the most dangerous waters on our Atlantic Coast—with shoals, variable currents, and frequent fogs that have challenged the courage and seamanship of cruising men since the days of Bartholomew Gosnold and Samuel de Champlain. As we have seen, these shoals affected the whole history of the Yankee coast.

While Bartholomew Gosnold, the English explorer, gave the Cape its present name in 1602, there is little doubt that other Europeans had sighted the Cape in the preceding century, and the Norsemen may have been there six centuries earlier.

From then until now, the sea continued to take its toll, and the timbers of thousands of wrecks lie buried in the sands of the Outer Beach.

One of the Cape's occupations that has passed away is "moon-cussing": cursing at the moon when it came out from behind a bank of clouds in time to show the beach to a ship that had sailed too close to the shore. According to a story related by Dr. Morison, a certain Reverend Mr. Lewis of Wellfleet saw through the window of his church a vessel going ashore. The congregation was nearer to the door, but apparently had their backs turned to the sea. Stopping his sermon, the pastor descended the pulpit stairs and with a shout of "Start fair" led his congregation pell-mell out of the meeting-house door.

Ralph Waldo Emerson wrote in 1854: "Went to Orleans Monday, to Nauset Light on the back of Cape Cod. The keeper Collins told us that he found obstinate resistance on the Cape to the project of building a lighthouse on this coast as it would injure the wrecking business."

Sometimes life-saving and the plundering of wrecks were combined. But, compared to the splendid record of heroism of Cape Codders in saving shipwrecked men and women, the unsavory cases of mooncussing were few indeed.

Edward Rowe Snow, author of *Romance of Boston Bay, Storms and Shipwrecks of New England,* and other books, was taking a crowd of school children through an old house on Outer Brewster. There he found an old book; as it happened, a rare first edition. He took it to the Boston Public Library and there someone noticed certain letters were pricked with a pin. She listed the letters pricked, cracked the code, and got a lot of bearings on Nauset Beach.

Snow rushed down and dug here and there without result and gave up. His brother, a radar expert, rigged up a device like a mine detector to detect the presence of metal in the ground. They tried it, got a click, dug 8 feet down, and pulled out an iron box of gold coins worth $2,700. The whole place is now sanded over several feet deep again. Alton Hall Blackington told the yarn at a lecture in Concord, Massachusetts, and showed movies of the whole business.

This may suggest an addition to your cruising equipment.

Before attempting Pollock Rip Channel, consult the *Eldridge Tide and Pilot Book* on the time of the fair current and plan to have it in your favor. If bound east, especially if there is a sea running outside, prepare for a rough passage, for a strong current meeting the sea roll can produce a rough and even dangerous rip. One can anchor and await slack water if the situation looks too dangerous to proceed; but once committed to the channel with a fair tide, retreat can be difficult.

Beyond Monomoy, the navigator faces 35 miles of practically unbroken beach to Peaked Hill Bar at the tip of the Cape, and another long 10 miles to the first shelter at Provincetown. In an easterly storm, this beach can be a dangerous lee shore, but on an ordinary summer day, the trip is a pleasant sail. The bottom shoals gradually toward the shore, so that a sounding determines one's distance from the beach, a very hard thing to judge by eye. The beach is deserted for the most part— an occasional dune buggy breaking the monotony. At intervals, roads penetrate the dunes from towns on the other side, and there will be a flowering of beach umbrellas and a few bathers, but these are soon left astern. Progress is marked by an occasional tower, tank, or flagpole, by the light at Nauset, and by the great tower and radio mast at Highland Light. Offshore, beyond the 20-fathom curve, is a line of lighted whistles. Approaching darkness poses no great problem, for with the radio-direction station, the powerful beam at Highland Light, and the whistle off Peaked Hill Bar, one's position off the tip of the Cape is easily determined. From here, one can take off for Cape Ann, the Maine coast, or points east, or one can work around to Provincetown.

The approach to Provincetown can be long and slow, for the tide runs hard—up to 2 knots—and there can be an unpleasant rip off Race Point where the flood runs south, swinging around to the southeast between Race Point and Wood End. The ebb runs in the opposite direction.

Beware of Peaked Hill Bar and of Shank Painter Bar. The tendency is to close with the beach in anticipation of the next point, and it is almost impossible to judge accurately one's distance from a featureless beach. Rely on soundings and the line of buoys offshore.

There is considerable activity by draggers out of Provincetown. Some of them are very big, and they proceed with speed and determination.

Steamers bound in and out of Boston are no problem for a yacht bound for Provincetown, but anyone heading north of Race Point should display a radar reflector and keep a sharp lookout, particularly at night. These vessels travel at high speeds and are unwieldy to steer. Under conditions of limited visibility one can be run down with very little time to maneuver. The route around the Cape is interesting in its length and loneliness, especially when one remembers the *Mayflower* turning back from Pollock Rip's "shoals and roaring breakers." Along this beach moved the homeward-bound clippers and whalers in the 1850s, and later in the century racing fishermen and the fleets of four-, five-, and six-masted coal schooners, winged out and heavily loaded, bound east and beating westward in ballast through the shoals. The beaches, then patrolled by Coast Guardsmen, battered wrecks into the sand, from which they occasionally emerge. If one has never made this trip, it is worth doing at least once.

CHAPTER IX

Cape Cod Canal, Massachusetts, to Cape Elizabeth, Maine

Barnstable, Mass. (13251   339). This is the closest shelter to the Cape Cod Canal, but if there is a northerly breeze and any sea is running, stay in the Boat Basin at the Canal. Barnstable has a channel dredged to a nominal depth of 8 feet, but the actual depth depends on how recently it has been dredged. The entrance is marked by a lighted bell outside, Black Point Light, and a series of buoys and brush stakes leading into a narrow appendix of a harbor, too narrow for anchoring but dredged to 8 feet in 1977.

On the starboard side are a cranberry freezer, several private wharves, and Barnstable Marine Service. Slips may be available here for transients. On the port side is the town landing, where one can tie up briefly, and the Millway Marina. Although there are no slips for transients here, one can come alongside for gas, water, and ice. Diesel oil is not available. At the head of the wharf is a marine store and an outboard repair shop—a very busy place. Across the parking lot are a fish market and a restaurant, Mattakeese Wharf. An interesting line of shoal-draft, lap-streak, dory-type yachts, rigged as ketches or ketch cats, was on display in the parking lot in 1977.

There is a conviction at large that the town will build a marina in the southwest corner of the harbor and that the state will build a facility at the beach just east of the entrance to the inner harbor.

Note that Barnstable and other harbors in Cape Cod Bay have a 9-foot range of tide, while harbors south of the Cape have but 2 or 3 feet range of tide.

Sesuit, Mass. (13250 581). This small harbor, a base for fishing party boats and small local craft, is the only shelter for a cruising boat between Wellfleet and Barnstable, and neither Sesuit nor Barnstable is possible if any considerable sea is running.

The depth of water on the bar at Sesuit depends on how recently it was dredged. Call Sesuit Marine Services on channel 16 VHF for the

337

latest advice on depth of channel and availability of slips. At over half tide, there is almost certain to be water enough for most cruising boats. Enter between the jetties, favoring the east side only slightly, and follow the channel, which runs close to the anchored sailboats. Do not anchor. The bottom is "scultch" and poor holding ground.

On the west shore is Sesuit Marine Service, run by Richard W. Lent. He offers slips for transients, water, ice, gasoline and Diesel fuel, moorings, and launch service. With a 15-ton Travelift, he can make minor repairs to hull and engines. At the yard is a store selling marine supplies, fishing gear, and NOS charts. Nearby is an electronics repair shop and a shop selling diving gear. A restaurant and shopping center are ¾ of a mile away.

There is a town wharf with a few slips and the wharf of the East Dennis Yacht Club, which has very little in the way of facilities for cruising people.

Wellfleet, Mass. (13250   581). In recent years the approach to Wellfleet has silted up badly, and political conflict between local and federal governments over marshlands stands in the way of dredging. In 1977, one could carry 5 feet to the outer wharf but at low water there was said to be less inside and the holding ground is poor. Fishermen lie at the outer wharf, exposed to southerly winds. If the conflicts are resolved, the channel and harbor will be dredged to 10 feet.

Wellfleet Marine on the west side of the anchorage has several moorings. Also Bay Sails, which maintains a launch in the harbor, and rents moorings, can effect repairs by hauling you on a hydraulic trailer. Several people in town monitor Channel 16 VHF and Channel 9 CB and will be glad to call the Harbor Master for you by telephone. One of the busiest radio enthusiasts is "Muriel Sturgeon," Mrs. Stocker of Dennis. She listens to CB and is extremely helpful in finding out information, sending help, or answering questions. She has several rescues to her credit.

Do not go behind the long jetty to the town slips. There is no space for visitors and some of the local boats sit in the mud at low water. Gas is available at Wellfleet Marine, but the pump is on the inside of the jetty, available to visitors only at high tide. Diesel oil must be brought down in a truck.

Both Wellfleet Marine and Bay Sails have good stores selling yacht equipment and fishing gear and making minor repairs. Bay Sails, situated, inconveniently for the yachtsman, on the main road, has an excellent store and good repair service, hauling boats on a hydraulic trailer. They specialize in electronic equipment and service.

There are several restaurants along the road to the right of Wellfleet Marine. There is a grocery store uptown at no great distance.

Wellfleet used to be a good harbor and may be so again when it is dredged, but now its usefulness to the cruising auxiliary is much reduced.

Buses run to Hyannis, connecting with bus and plane transportation to Boston and elsewhere.

The Pilgrims, exploring for a place to settle near Wellfleet, were driven off by Indians in 1620 and moved on to Plymouth.

The lower spar of the flagpole in front of the Town Hall was made from the main boom of the Boston fishing schooner *Quannapowitt,* wrecked on the outside shore of the Cape in November 1913. It is an impressive spar!

A number of interesting excursions are available for a lay day at Wellfleet. Ask the Harbor Master for a brochure on the region supplied by the town.

Provincetown, Mass. (13249   580). Governor Bradford of the Plymouth Colony described Provincetown in 1620 as "an harboure wherein a hundred saile of ships may safely ride." Three hundred and fifty years later, the recommendation is still sound, but in other respects the Pilgrim governor would find Provincetown vastly changed.

The leading mark for the harbor is the Pilgrim Monument, 255-feet high. It can be seen from the east end of the canal and from Plymouth on a clear day. As you approach, you will raise the dunes and the yellow, sandy shore. The Coast Guard station, Race Point Light, and Wood End Light are prominent marks.

In approaching from the west and north, the navigator can cut lighted bell RP and the bell off Wood End; but if he does, he must be careful of Shank Painter Bar, rising abruptly from over 150 feet to less than 20 feet. The fathometer is not very helpful and it is difficult to judge one's distance from a featureless beach, with no man or house to give it scale.

Fortunately the beach between Wood End and Long Point is very steep and unlikely to cause trouble. From the bell off Long Point, run for the light on the end of the breakwater. There are several moorings off the boat yards south of the town, which provide shelter in a hard southwester. Otherwise, unless you have boat yard business, you are well off behind the breakwater. It is seldom crowded.

There are two principal wharves. The northerly one, by far the most substantial, is devoted to shipping fish brought in by draggers, which berth alongside. The Coast Guard keeps a boat along the southerly side and further in are berths for party boats taking fishing and sailing expeditions. There is seldom a place to tie up even a skiff at this wharf. The other one is a series of floats tied to piles with finger piers. A few of these slips are occupied by local boats, but most are available for transients. In approaching this wharf, beware of a number of old piles outside the end of the outer float and to the left of it. One of the piles shows above high water. All of the others are said to be to the left, south, of the one that shows and inside, west, of it. Between the inner ends of the wharves is a small town wharf and float where one may tie a dinghy. Gasoline and Diesel fuel are available here. It is planned to have water piped to it soon.

The first thing one meets ashore is a vast parking lot. Somewhat diagonally to the right, across this waste of asphalt, is a group of telephone booths. The main street parallels the rear of the parking lot and, while not as wild a place as it appeared in 1971, it is still a study in sociology on a warm summer evening. The product most heavily advertised is a "foot-long hot dog to go," but there are also formal restaurants. Artists and craftsmen of all ages and degrees of skill offer for sale paintings, jewelry, hand-woven cloth, pottery, and leather goods. The narrow main street is jammed with them, their customers, and those who have come to see the show. Costumes range from peasant to suburban to the wildly exotic. Record-player rhythms from the shops mingle in the streets, and through the press creep automobiles in single file.

In the morning, however, the scene is more conventional. Grocery stores, located back from the main street, are open. One can easily make his way along the sidewalks, and the inhabitants who appear in daylight are as friendly to the cruising man in search of oranges or a lamp chimney as those anywhere. If the latter is your problem, try Lands End Marine between the main street and the shore to the north of the parking lot. The part fronting the street is an ordinary hardware store, but up the alley behind it is one of the best-supplied marine stores in the commonwealth. They supply commercial vessels as well as yachts. You can buy a galvanized shackle so big you cannot lift it or a shiny little fitting to go on the clew of a sailing dinghy's jib. Rope, electrical and electronic gear, charts, ground tackle, fishing gear, or whatever you may need, will doubtless be there. In the back shop, mechanics repair outboard motors—Evinrude and Johnson for choice—and others if they have time.

South of the town are two boat yards, Flyer's and Taves's. They have a few moorings and railways that can haul most yachts. They can repair damage to hull, spars, and engines.

If you seek shelter only and have no need to go ashore, anchor in the deep hole behind Wood End. A diver who has explored the bottom in Provincetown Harbor reports "sand tides." The current near the bottom is so heavily loaded with sand that it is like drifting snow and comes and goes in sufficient volume to change the shape of the bottom radically between high water and low.

It is worthwhile to spend a little time in Provincetown, once you arrive. The Pilgrim Monument, built in 1910 to commemorate the first landing of the Pilgrims in America, affords a magnificent view of the harbor, the town, the hook of the Cape, and the back shore. The cliffs across at Plymouth are often visible, and on a clear day the Blue Hills in Milton and the tall buildings of Boston show on the horizon. The monument is open from nine to five at a nominal cost.

At the foot of the tower is a museum with a number of relics of the town's history, most of it built around the fishing industry.

One can walk across to the dunes or ride a rented bicycle on a paved bicycle path or, for a price, join a tour in a "beach buggy." The dunes are ecologically very fragile, for they are held down by sparse tough beach grass and a scattering of scrubby bushes. If these are damaged, even over a small area, the dune will begin to move as the wind drifts sand up one side and down another, thus uprooting more grass. Be careful to walk where directed.

The view from the back shore is bleak and dramatic, well worth the trip. The following account of a visit to the dunes comes from W.S. Carter's classic account of a cruise in a chartered fishing sloop in 1858.

As the Professor desired to examine a beach four or five miles distant, on which the Atlantic rolls its waves unchecked by any land nearer than the "far-off bright azores," we hired a wagon, a span of horses, and a queer little urchin of a driver, to conduct us thither over the sand-hills. In a few minutes we had left behind us the single street of the village and merged into a desert of white sand, that looked as if it had been rolled into high waves by a raging tempest, and then suddenly arrested and fixed before it had time to subside to a level. Here and there in the dells and hollows were patches of vegetation, alders, huckleberry-bushes, low pitch-pines, scrub-oaks, and clumps of wild roses, glowing with the brilliant hues which the sea air gives to flowers. But outside of the village there were no houses, fences, paths, or any traces whatever of man or beast. It was a wilderness, as it was when it first met the eyes of the Mayflower pilgrims. The horses that tugged us onward had the muscles of their rumps unusually developed from working always fetlock deep in sand.

At length we gained the shore and stood by the sea. A prodigious multitude of terns flew up at our approach, and wheeled around in the air clanging their wild and piercing cries. No other signs of life were visible, save a few white sails far away on the horizon. Signs of death were around us in the shape of fragments of wrecks thrown high on the beach by storms. I picked up a piece of bamboo which perhaps had floated from some vessel returning from India or China, or the isles of the East.

Provincetown is a good place from which to take a departure for the Maine coast or Nova Scotia or for the voyage around the Cape. It provides an interesting variation in a cruise east from the canal. Bound west for the canal against the southwest wind, one may be tempted to reach across to Provincetown from Cape Ann; but if the wind continues southwest, you will face a dead beat of many miles to the canal. The shoal waters of Cape Cod Bay can kick up a violent short sea, which makes for a most unpleasant passage. It is preferable to hug the western shore of Cape Cod Bay, where the wind draws off the land and the water is likely to be smooth.

Plymouth, Mass. (245). Plymouth Bay provides the only deep-draft shelter between Scituate and the canal, so is a popular refuge for cruising yachtsmen. Most vessels follow the well-buoyed channel south from Duxbury Pier Light to the dredged anchorage basin at Plymouth. However, this can be a tedious trip for a low-powered auxiliary motoring against the tide. If just seeking shelter for the night, one can anchor under Clark's Island or behind the Nummet to the westward of Duxbury Pier Light.

After leaving Manomet, yachts bound east will have no difficulty in picking out the light on the prominent knob of the Gurnet. Those bound west on a hazy day will be surprised at the interminable length of Duxbury Beach. The nun on High Pines Ledge is difficult to locate in the afternoon sun. There is a clump of pine trees on the shore roughly abreast the ledge from which, no doubt, it is named.

Note that the tide runs as much as a half knot northwesterly parallel to the shore outside Duxbury Beach.

In taking bearings on the high monuments back of Plymouth and Duxbury, note that the highest and most northerly one is on Captain's Hill in South Duxbury and is *not* the monument shown in Plymouth.

A local resident of extensive yachting experience writes:

Formerly the basin at Plymouth was small and crowded. Now, however, there is a 60-acre area behind a 1000-yard breakwater with a depth of 10 to 12 feet. There is good water to the town and state piers. For going alongside the yacht club and Plymouth Marine floats you will have to do it on the tide. There are ample gas, Diesel, water, ice, and repair facilities. All necessaries can be procured at stores in the town. There is good bus service to Boston and the Cape. The inner harbor is patrolled by the Harbor Master, who does a good job keeping speeds down. The outer channel, which is narrow, is not made any more attractive by the big and heavy fishing-party boats that charge out in the morning and in at night.

Plymouth Cordage Co. and Plymouth Marine Railway maintain several guest moorings. Consult the Harbor Master on the wharf at the north end of the anchorage if you do not find him patrolling the anchorage.

Plymouth Marine Railways in the southwest corner of the anchorage is a well-equipped yard capable of hauling vessels up to 65-feet long, drawing up to 8 feet. The yard maintains showers for visitors and a well-supplied marine hardware store. Access for deep-draft vessels is limited to high water, however.

There are excellent restaurants and grocery stores not far from the yard.

Prominent on the west shore of the harbor is *Mayflower II,* a replica of a seventeenth-century vessel of the same type as that on which the Pilgrims crossed the Atlantic in the fall of 1620. If she looks a bit high and cranky, it is because her 'tween decks were raised up a foot so tourists would not bump their heads on the deck beams. She was designed by George Baker, after extensive research into seventeenth-century shipbuilding practices, and built in England in 1957. She was sailed across the Atlantic in the summer of that year by Captain Alan Villiers in fifty-three days. The *National Geographic Magazine* for November 1957 carried the story of the voyage. Exhibits and wax figures aboard help you to imagine what life was like in 1620 with one-hundred-two passengers and about twenty-five seamen on a winter crossing of the Atlantic. Alongside lies a reproduction of the shallop used to explore the coast of the Cape in search of a place to settle. A visit to the *Mayflower II* is well worth the modest price of a ticket.

In Plymouth there are other museums and exhibits of colonial life, the most elaborate being Plimoth Plantation, a reconstruction of the Pilgrim settlement as it was in 1627. Guides costumed as Pilgrims explain the tools and household equipment of the early inhabitants and go on to discuss the customs, laws, religion, and economy of the village. It is well worth a half day's thoughtful attention.

Duxbury, Mass. (245). Follow the same course as though going to Plymouth as far as Duxbury Pier Light, where the dredged channel to Duxbury turns northward. This channel has been dredged to a depth of 8 feet but it is reported to have filled in some. The basin at Duxbury may also be a little shallower than the 9 feet to which it was dredged.

Although the anchorage may be crowded during July and August, the hospitable Duxbury Yacht Club often can provide moorings for visitors. Duxbury Marine Railway, Bayside Marine, and Long Point Marine provide some tie-up facilities and fuel, ice, and water. Winsor's offers meals and accommodations. There is a well-equipped grocery store in town.

Two Rock Channel, running northeast from nun 12, is a quiet anchorage on a summer night, although far from facilities. The flats prevent any great sea from building up.

Green Harbor, Mass. (245). This is a narrow channel running up behind Brant Rock. In 1971 it was dredged to a depth of 6 feet. It is subject to shoaling, especially at the entrance, and should be viewed as an adventure for a coming tide. In a heavy sea, or conditions of doubtful visibility, either Scituate or Plymouth is to be preferred.

Of North River, Cohasset, Hull, Allerton, and Hingham a local observer writes:

"These are fishing ports for both amateur and professional fishermen; thanks to the bounty of bass, bluefish, groundfish, and the high market price for fresh fish and lobster. The seaside entrepreneurs beckon the compressed suburbanites to escape through their facilities. Their attention to coasting yachtsmen is minimal. The torrent of casual pleasure-boaters emanating thence creates constant traffic congestion except in bad weather and in the magic moments between dawn and sunrise.

"The picturesque remnants of bygone marine enterprise have been overwhelmed by convenient facilities for weekend trailer craft and quick food, fuel, and bait service for their passengers. The Coast Guard stations at Scituate and Pemberton provide comprehensive monitoring service both afloat and aloft. This is complemented by Harbor Masters' and Coast Guard auxiliary craft. This dynamic scene is a stimulating diversion to passengers and crew, but a constant strain on responsible skippers and helmsmen.

"Only blasé adventurers should enter these ports without auxiliary power. The summer zephyrs are coy enough at best. This is attributed to the vertical thermal drafts generated by the neighboring areas of black roofing and paving. This gloomy advice may be ignored if you are in the company of an experienced local hand."

New Inlet, North River, Mass. (13267 1207). The great storm of November 1898 broke through the beach between Third Cliff and Fourth Cliff, about two miles south of Scituate, making a new mouth for the North River, which used to come out about three miles further south near Rexham.

The entrance is now a rather shoal estuary, marked by a white bell and a series of five nuns. If there is much of any sea running, especially on an ebb tide, do not attempt the entrance. However, on a reasonably smooth summer day, with the wind out to the southward or southwest, one should have no trouble.

Hug the nuns closely, as there are said to be boulders on the southern side of the channel, and keep the fathometer going. After a summer northeaster in 1977 nun 4 went adrift. A sports fisherman bound out rounded nun 6 and got onto the shoal to the north. He ran into two heavy breaking seas, was stove up, swamped, and sunk in a very short time. The crew was rescued.

After passing nun 10, go close to the sand spit and the shore to starboard. Here begins a series of black cans and bank markers leading up the Herring River. Despite several 3-foot soundings shown on the chart, one can carry a draft 5 feet up to the Simms Yacht Yard. Favor the northerly shore and, in general, keep to the outside of the bends.

After a straight stretch of about half a mile, you will find the disused bulkhead and wharf of the Boston Sand and Gravel Co. Go in close to the bulkhead, follow close to the southeastern side of the wharf, turn sharply around the nun off the end of the wharf, proceed to the next nun, and continue more or less in the middle of the very narrow channel to the turning basin at the yard.

Here are slips for ninety yachts, a Travelift with a capacity of twenty-five tons, a crane to set spars, complete repair facilities for wooden and fiberglass hulls, and for spars, rigging, and electronic gear. Mechanics skilled in working on both inboard and outboard motors are on duty. Gasoline, Diesel oil, water, and ice can be purchased at the float. A marine store is near the head of the float. If you need groceries, it is likely that a man from the yard can give you a ride to Angelo's Market about half a mile up the road. The yard is open seven days a week from 8 A.M. to 6 P.M. in the summer.

If you do not care to push up the Herring River, anchor behind the sand spit by the first can and explore in the outboard. The tide does not run heavily in the Herring River but is quite swift at the turn between nuns 8 and 10.

One can go up the North River as far as the markers on the sides of the channel. Those to starboard are maintained by Scituate and those to port by Marshfield. Proceed with caution, as the channel is intricate and in some places quite shoal. Furthermore, ice sometimes carries markers away. A recent visitor to the North River writes:

The salt meadows bordering the North River from New Inlet to the first highway drawbridge have yielded little of their beauty to civilization and from the first drawbridge to Hanover present delightful vistas of salt meadows against occasional groves of venerable pine trees and the square white mansions built by the early inhabitants who converted the virgin forest into ships. At one time twenty-three shipyards operated on the river, eleven of them visible from the Hanover bridge, all seven or eight miles from the sea. Plaques along the river bank tell where some of the principal yards were located. How those builders launched their ships into the shallow river and got them down stream and over the bar is one of the many interesting corners of New England history.

One can arrange to have the first drawbridge opened by calling A.F. O'Toole at (617) 947-0664 or 9001. Just above this bridge is Mary's Boat Livery, a source of gas, water, and local information.

"The Plymouth County Commissioners were determined to repair the second drawbridge," writes the 1977 visitor, "but I suspect the work was never done, because the vandalism on the highway signal lights and hydraulic control panel, from which the two lift pistons are actuated, is eloquent testimony to the sentiments of some local inhabitants. Clearance under the draw is about 6 feet at high water."

South River is also narrow and shoal but it, too, is marked by stakes and local buoys. There is said to be good anchorage just south of its mouth, where the channel turns abruptly to the east.

With care, one can continue all the way to Humarock, where there is a considerable settlement with slips, moorings, landing floats, fuel; and the stores, restaurants, and snack shops incident to the summer trade.

New Inlet, with its tributaries, is used principally by local fishermen, both amateur and professional, and by them it is navigated with confidence. The stranger with a taste for the unusual will find the salt meadows and quiet streams abundant with the life of the marshes, a pleasant change from Cape Cod Bay.

Scituate, Mass.   (13269 244). This is probably the best harbor of refuge between Marblehead and the Cape Cod Canal. It has an easy, short approach, turning WNW from the S/L flashing black-and-white

SA bell buoy to the buoyed channel running in south of the breakwater, which has a tower on its end with a flashing red light. The harbor anchorage area is all along the north and west of the channel, once inside. To the south is the Scituate Coast Guard's boathouse, with two large white government emergency anchor buoys. The Scituate radio beacon is on the Coast Guard's dock, transmitting continuously on 305 KCs the characteristics S H (... ....). However, do not home on it from outside, as you will be led to the southwest of the buoyed channel and onto the rocks.

Scituate Harbor Yacht Club is prominent on the point to the NW upon entering. Cruising yacht-club members will find water, showers, and directions to a mooring from their docks. Just beyond, on the NW rim of the harbor, is the smaller, but salty Satuit Boat Club, with a fine dock carrying 6 feet at MLW and offering water, showers, and a couple of guest moorings. The SHYC launch runs daily, answering to three blasts and the SBC launch runs weekends only, responding to two blasts.

Further to the west, beyond the public launching ramp, is the Pier 44 Marina and Restaurant, providing ice, water, a few transient slips, and Texaco gas and Diesel fuel. Further around the western rim is the large Scituate town pier, where a small fishing fleet ties up and where Harbor Master John Fenton holds forth with several transient slips (stern-to mooring) and a dink dock inside. In a compact half mile, starting at the end of the town pier, Scituate's Front Street is a complete shopping area. Opposite the pier is the Ship's Locker Marine Store and just a bit south, behind the Gulf station, an excellent fish market. Further down the block is a large supermarket, open six days, and all along Front Street are scattered specialty shops, a twin cinema, package stores, and several fine restaurants. Vessels can carry 6 feet at low water on to the SE from the town pier to the inner harbor, where more moorings are clustered, along with two small boat marinas and Maxwell's Esso Fuel docks. At the eastern extremity of the inner harbor is John Young's Boat Yard with a large Travelift. Also, seven days a week, by phoning 545-3000, the nearby Simms Yacht Yard will send over a qualified mechanic to solve any engine problems you may have. Scituate is indeed the complete port for the cruising yachtsman.

The town was attacked in the War of 1812 by the British. The story of how the attack was repulsed was told to the late Farnham Smith in 1879 by the two old ladies who as girls had been the heroines of the affair. *The Boston Evening Transcript* printed Mr. Smith's account, as follows:

Rebecca . . . proceeds to tell us how happily their childhood was passed down by the lighthouse; that they all had to help work in those days, and when the war came they had hard work to make both ends meet, food, especially, was so high, and a meal was only got by long hard work; how mad the people got when they heard of vessels being burned by the British, especially if the vessels had grain or flour on board. That here in Scituate the men formed themselves into a guard to look out for the British ships, warn the people of their approach, and if possible protect their property; how one day when two of our ships were in the harbor laden with precious flour, two British ships appeared, and the guard, not knowing they were then off the coast, had gone inland to help harvest grain, or something, she forgot just what. Rebecca looked out from the window and saw the boats being lowered to come into the harbor, and knew their object was to set fire to the American ships. What could she do to save them? Something *must* be done, so she called Abby and asked her advice. There was no time to lose. Couldn't they make believe the guard were coming—how? "Why, by playing on the fife and drum behind the barn out of sight of the 'Britishers.' " Fortunately both girls—in their teens then —were able to play, and fife and drum were in the house, and with a determination to do their duty they began; Rebecca played the fife, Abby beat the drum, the men in the boats heard the sound, looked about, stopped rowing, fearful of running into danger; then to the joy and relief of the girls, they saw the signal hoisted for the boats to return to the vessel. Tired as they were they give "Britishers" a parting tune, "Yankee Doodle."

Mr. Smith received from each lady a personal note. The letters are now in the possession of Eric Parkman Smith of Concord, Massachusetts:

Abbie the Drummer one of the American army of two in the War of 1812, Drove from our shore two British barges, saved two Vessels laden with Flour from Capture, and, even from prison with fife and, Drum, Abbie Bates.

> age, 82, Scituate Harbor, Mass.

Rebecca W. Bates, born 1793, aged 86 years—one of the American army of two in the war of 1812 who with her Sister aged 15 years saved two large vessels laden with flour and their Crew from imprisonment with fife and drum from being taken by the British off Scituate Harbor Mass.

> Rebecca the fifer.

The Salvage of the *Etrusco*

On the evening of March 16, 1956, in a howling northeast snow-storm, the 7000-ton *Etrusco,* trying to make Boston Harbor, ran ashore on Cedar Point outside Scituate. She had neither cargo nor ballast so could not be lightened.

Unable to get her off, her owners sold her to Global Shipping Co. of Panama for a reported $125,000, a fraction of her value. Global obtained the services of Admiral Curtis, USN retired, who had been responsible for much of the salvage work at Pearl Harbor.

The admiral found *Etrusco* hard aground, sitting on her bottom on a stony beach only 100 yards from high-water mark. The insurance companies declared her a "total loss." Everyone who knew anything about it said she would stay there until she rusted away. However, the admiral employed dynamite and bulldozers to dig a channel around her and astern to deep water. He ran heavy anchors out astern, then cables led to *Etrusco*'s winches. A few days after Thanksgiving a high run of tides was expected, and a great effort was to be made with tugs and kedges to get her off.

On the day before Thanksgiving, with an easterly breeze piling the water on the South shore, *Etrusco* began to move in her berth. Hastily, tugs were called, steam got on the winches, pumps started, and just before high water the vessel ground over the boulders, lifted and bumped a bit, and floated into the channel Admiral Curtis had prepared for her. She was carefully maneuvered into deep water and towed safely to Boston. A pile of scrap became a ship again, a challenge met and mastered.

Cohasset, Mass. (13269 244). At first glance, Cohasset looks like the first good shelter south of Boston and a convenient stop for a vessel bound from Gloucester or Marblehead to the Canal. However, there are several considerations against it.

While the approach is marked by Minots Light, a very prominent structure with a good fog signal, the course from there into Cohasset in thick weather is intricate and shoal. At low water, or with a heavy sea at any tide, it is dangerous. Second, the harbor is small and, during the yachting season, crowded with local boats. No moorings are available for visitors. Third, no fuel is available in Cohasset, because the oil companies insist on delivering a certain minimum amount, which is more than the town will permit the wharf owners to keep in storage tanks. Local people lug gasoline in cans or go to Scituate. They are so out of the habit of buying gasoline locally that when a pump was finally put in operation, no one patronized it.

If, however, you decide to visit Cohasset in spite of these difficulties, it would be well to call the Harbor Master on VHF Channel 9 or on the CB to inform him of your approach. He may be able to find a mooring or slip temporarily vacant. There are three channels into the harbor:

1. The easiest channel into Cohasset is from Davis Ledge bell westward, leaving Minots Light to port, to the black flashing bell 1 off Hogshead Rock. Leave the bell close to port to avoid a 10-foot spot about west-southwest of the buoy and run for nun 4. Leave the nun to starboard and run for Sutton Hole, a white 4-second flasher on a skeleton tower. This course should leave can 1 to port. From Sutton Hole, follow the series of red flashers up the harbor.

A Cohasset yachtsman suggests the following plan for entering at night. After passing the black flashing bell 1, line up the three red range lights and run in by nun 4, which you will find close to starboard shortly after the water shoals to under 2 fathoms (at low water). Then head for the flashing white light. You should find can 1 just to starboard. Leave it to port and continue for the white light until the red lights line up again. Then run in on the range.

2. The eastern course, according to the commodore, is "one which, like matrimony, should only be entered upon 'discreetly, advisedly, soberly, and in the fear of God.' " Before reaching Davis Ledge bell on a course from the south, swing in a westerly direction between can 1 off West Willies and nun 2EL on Enos Ledge. Leave can 3 close to port and run for Sutton Hole light. Your success on this course is absolutely dependent on being able to see the buoys.

3. The western course is found by leaving can 1 on Chittenden Rock to port and nun 4 on Buckthorn Rock to starboard. Pass either side of Barrel Rock beacon, but note that a 6-foot shoal extends to the south and east of the ledge. Leave nun 6 to starboard and head between Sutton Hole light and can 1 as before.

Of Cohasset, a recent visitor writes, "The anchorage in Cohasset harbor is 'drove up' all summer. The Cohasset Yacht Club still retains a puritan simplicity. There are two public landings: one to the east of the entrance to the Gulf, the other just west of Hugo's seafood emporium on the south side of the harbor. John Smith is supposed to have landed at the latter spot. The head of Cohasset harbor is now embraced by a motel. It appears to be well patronized the year round."

One can land at a float off a hot-topped wharf east of a boat yard on the south side bearing a sign "Gaffey's Yachts." The Harbor Master operates from a little white building with windowboxes and radio antennae on the knoll above the landing. He can advise you on where to tie up for the night.

The boat yard can take care of repair work of all kinds and has a well-equipped marine store, which is the east-coast outlet for Gibb-Henderson pumps and parts. They are not easily obtainable elsewhere.

On the high land behind the Harbor Master's office are two circular granite platforms, which served as the test assembly platform in the construction of Minots Light many years ago. At the easterly corner of the "island" is the headquarters of a sailing-instruction school for children who do their sailing in 10-foot Sprites.

Cohasset has many beautiful estates and an attractive year-round colony, many of whose members commute to Boston. On half-a-dozen weekend nights during the summer, the Cohasset Yacht Club holds dances for members and guests. There is a first-class golf club between Cohasset and Hingham. The beaches are all private, except for the town beach. That is for residents only. Minots Light is now unwatched, so you probably cannot climb it. But try to imagine what it is like when great waves break on the 114-foot tower and shoot up above the light. This has actually happened. If you want local color and anecdotes, read Edward Rowe Snow's *History of Minot's Light.* A romantic significance is attached locally to the flashes of this light—one-four-three, meaning "I love you."

Boston Harbor, Mass. (13270 246). Although vigorous efforts have been made in recent years to render Boston Harbor more attractive as a recreation area and although the improvement is dramatic, there are more attractive places for the cruising yachtsman. The harbor is traversed by big steamers, particularly by tankers. These obviously must be avoided by yachts, as such big vessels cannot maneuver smartly. The powerful tugs in attendance on the steamers are busy and pay no heed to yachts. Fishing vessels, numerous party boats bound for Provincetown and the Boston harbor islands, Coast Guard vessels, and innumerable small motorboats keep the waters agitated.

Nevertheless, a great deal of sailing is done right up in the inner harbor, and there are anchorages and marinas for small craft. If you want to visit a historic harbor, sail under the guns of USS *Constitution,* see steamers, tugs, and pilot boats in action, and lie more or less in the shadow of city buildings, a sail up the harbor is worthwhile. Following are notes on some of the anchorages:

Hull. This harbor, like all the others in Hingham Bay and Hull Bay, must be approached through either Hull Gut east of Peddocks Island or West Gut at the other end of the island. Hull Gut is the worst, but the tide rushes through both these narrow passages at an inspiring rate.

When it sets against a heavy southwesterly or northeasterly wind, the passages can be dangerous for small craft. The harbor at Hull is a rather open bight, desirable principally for its convenience. It is a short walk to Telegraph Hill and Fort Revere, which has been converted to a park, and from which a dramatic view of Boston harbor extends from the Blue Hills and the tall buildings in the city all the way to Cape Ann. There is an active Coast Guard Station at Hull, which keeps a careful eye on Boston harbor traffic.

Allerton, behind Hog Island, is a better harbor than Hull; and if plans for dredging it in the winter of 1977–78 go through, it will be quite snug. The Hull Yacht Club is at the northernmost margin of Allerton Harbor, between Telegraph Hill on the west, topped with a water tower and Fort Revere, and Allerton Hill on the east, topped with a concrete artillery triangulation lookout. Plummer's Marina is located on the east shore of Allerton Harbor and Waveland Marina is about a quarter mile to the south.

Worlds End. East of Worlds End and Planters Hill and west of an extensive mudbank in the Weir River is a favorite anchorage. A dozen or so large moorings lie along the edge of the channel, on which as many as fifty large yachts are said to raft up on weekends. Worlds End is a park and a pleasant place to go ashore. Bass fishing is said to be good off the shore on the west side of the peninsula. The head of the Weir River, right under the back of Nantasket Beach, affords anchorage not far from a popular amusement park. Excursion boats from Boston land here.

Hingham. One who threads the shoals of Hingham Bay will find the Hingham Yacht Club on the end of Crow Point. The club would like to be hospitable to all cruising men, but it is overwhelmed by weight of numbers, numbers of its own members as well as of visitors. Members of other yacht clubs should hail the float and inquire about moorings. The club fleet is moored not only in the dredged area south of Crow Point but even outside to the north and west of the point, the owners evidently thinking that the horrors of being confined ashore without a boat are less than the perils of a northeast storm. There was a snack bar at the club in 1977. Gasoline and water, but no Diesel fuel, were reported to be available at the yacht club in 1977.

For supplies, follow the buoyed channel to the head of the bay between Langlie Island and Sarah Island (misnamed Sailor Island on the chart). The late Mr. Blanchard, a former coauthor of this *Guide* and a summer resident of Hingham, claimed that the three islands just inside the yacht club were named for a Hingham girl know as "Ragged Sarah Langlie." She later became Madame Derby, from whom Derby Academy got its name.

At the head of the harbor, just east of an equestrian war memorial statue, known irreverently as the iron horse, is Kehoe's Boat Livery. Here is a float with 8 feet of water alongside and a marine store carrying an extensive inventory of fishing gear. Kehoe's rents boats, moorings, and fishing gear. East of Kehoe's is Bare Cove Marina, with a number of slips. Gasoline, Diesel oil, ice, and water are available at both places. West of Kehoe's is the town landing float. Robert Bouvé has a small yard on the west shore at the mouth of Broad Cove, where he sells marine supplies, but no fuel. He serves as Harbor Master.

Close to Kehoe's is the Fruit Center, a well-supplied fruit and grocery store. Two restaurants are nearby.

Weymouth, Quincy, and Dorchester Bay afford adequate protection, but are crowded and not very attractive to cruising boats. Many small local craft, both sail and power, moor in these places and swarm out during late afternoons and weekends, somewhat to the dismay of those used to less crowded waters.

Boston Inner Harbor. There is, of course, no place to anchor in Boston's inner harbor. However, slips for transients are sometimes available.

The wharves along the waterfront beginning at the Aquarium and going north are: Long Wharf, Commercial Wharf, Lewis Wharf, Sargent Wharf and Union Wharf. Constitution Wharf is next to the Coast Guard base farther around to the north and west. Most of the yacht berths are occupied for the season; but if you call a week ahead, you may be able to reserve a slip. Try Commercial Wharf (491-9640) or the dock master (582-0235), Lewis Wharf (723-3460), Yacht Haven (523-7352). These marinas provide security safeguards, and it is said to be safe enough to walk ashore at night on lighted streets. For further information, call Boston Redevelopment Authority or Boston Educational Marine Exchange.

The exchange, under the vigorous leadership of Carl Koch, is developing plans for a public landing on the waterfront, for mooring a large vessel alongside a wharf as a museum and educational center, and for improvement of harbor transportation by improved docking facilities. Plans are also afoot for the development of Peddocks Island as a marine research and educational facility for use by schools and colleges. The next few years should see dramatic changes along the shore.

If you follow the ship channel around to the north, you come to the Coast Guard base and then to the bridges and the lock at the entrance to the Charles River. It is well to inquire about the bridge schedules before pushing in here. Highway bridges are reluctant to open during rush hours and the railroad bridge serves trains before it serves yachts. In 1977, the Charles River lock is being rebuilt. The schedule for its future operation has not yet been determined. However, if you press on, and have no spar, you can go up the Charles all the way to Watertown, past Massachusetts Institute of Technology, Boston University, Harvard University, and the Perkins Institute for the Blind. The river is busy with small sailing craft and racing shells, as well as the inevitable assortment of outboards. The water and adjacent land is under the control of the Metropolitan District Commission, which is rather particular about slow speeds and low wakes.

Tankers and freighters use the Mystic River to approach the warehouses and tank farms above the Mystic Bridge. There is little up here to attract yachtsmen. On the Charlestown shore is the old Boston Navy Yard, where the USS *Constitution* is kept afloat. She has been fully restored as a frigate of the War of 1812. Built to outgun any vessel of her size and outsail anything she could not fight, she was the pocket battleship of her time. For a nominal fee, one can inspect her from stem to stern, and then go through the excellent museum ashore. It is an experience not to be missed.

Tie up at the 150-slip Constitution Marina on the Charlestown side of the entrance to the Charles River. It is in the shadow of Bunker Hill and next door to the USS *Constitution.* Next to it and on the Marina grounds is an interesting museum, which reenacts the battle of Bunker Hill. If you plan to spend a weekend, it is a bit like going foreign. Within walking distance of the marina the Italian community has a festival with parades and native delicacies every Friday, Saturday, and Sunday of the summer. Provisioning can be an adventure, with scores of pushcarts selling produce, fish and meat adjacent to historic Faneuil Hall. The New England Aquarium is a must for the kids. A dinghy trip through the Charles River locks with a tie-up at the Science Museum will please all hands. A visit to the Tea Party Shop in Fort Point Channel is well worthwhile.

Be sure to see the ultra-smart shopping and dining areas at Quincy Market, the former warehouse and counting rooms for Boston's clipper-ship fleet. As a contrast, many harbor islands are unspoiled. Fort Warren or George's Island is a good lunch stop.

Boston Harbor Islands. A number of the larger islands in Boston Harbor have landing facilities and either slips or anchorages for the use of visitors. These include George's, Gallops, Lovell, Bumpkin, Slate, and Grape. Landing is permitted on Peddocks with a special permit. Castle Island, now connected to South Boston by filled land, is notable for a monument to Donald McKay, designer and builder of American clipper ships, and for Fort Independence, where Edgar Allan Poe served as a soldier in the coast artillery. A skeleton found in the walled-up end of a corridor prompted him to write *A Cask of Amontillado.* Georges Island, Lovell Island, the Brewsters, and Peddocks Island also have forts built to protect the harbor in early wars. One can land on Little Brewster and see Boston Light, one of the first lighthouses built in the United States. Great Brewster and Outer Brewster still bear signs of military occupation. The emplacements for 16-inch coast defense guns remain on Great Brewster and the barracks used by those who tended antisubmarine nets stand on Outer Brewster.

While it is conceivable that a cruising man will enter Boston Harbor with eager curiosity, it is certain that he will leave the North Channel, bound east, with enthusiasm.

Marblehead, Mass. (13276 241). This harbor is described as the "yachting capital of the world." Of course, this is an overstatement, but few indeed are the harbors with a longer history of yachting, a more distinguished roster of famous yachts, and a more crowded calendar of present-day racing.

Note that while the new International Rules of the Road apply to most of the coast east of Cape Ann, the line defining the boundary of Inland Rules of the Road runs from Bakers Island to Marblehead Light. Fog and whistle signals and rules of the road governing sailing vessels are different under the different sets of rules.

The visitor cannot help but be impressed, as he approaches Marblehead harbor, by the close-packed spars of the racing fleet, varying from the smallest of day sailers to elegant ocean-racing yachts, whose names are familiar to every reader of yachting periodicals.

The first stop by the visiting cruising man must be the float of the Marblehead Transportation Company, just above Graves's yard, about halfway up the west side of the harbor. Inquire here about a mooring. Anchoring in Marblehead is now next to impossible. The water is deep and its surface is crowded. The bottom is said to consist largely of bottles and cans, the detritus of one-hundred years of yachting. Whether this is true or not is irrelevant, for one must either anchor on

Marblehead, Manchester, and the South Shore of Cape Ann.

such a long scope as to swing into his neighbors, or shorten up and drag.

If you must leave your boat in Marblehead while you are away, be sure you have a clear understanding with someone ashore about what is to be done in the event of a northeaster's sweeping the whole fleet onto the causeway at the head of the harbor. Some yachtsmen whose boats were saved by intrepid and capable young men ashore have expressed something less than genuine gratitude.

Launch service is supplied by Eastern Yacht Club (3 blasts), Boston Yacht Club (2 long, 1 short), and Corinthian (2 blasts). Marblehead Rental Boat Co. has a water taxi that responds to 4 blasts. All these launches listen to channels 11 and 13 on CB. After you blow your horn, hoist as big a T flag as you can provide. Something about the size of a counterpane is suggested. At night, turn on spreader lights. It is advisable to use the launch service, as the facilities for tying dinghies are limited.

The Transportation Company sells gasoline, Diesel fuel, water, ice, stove fuel, limited hardware and marine supplies. The manager, John Veesy, is a reliable source of local information and his crew is always ready to be of help. More specialized marine items may be purchased from the store at Graves's yard.

It is a short and pleasant walk to the main street through narrow byways, past small shingled houses and fragrant rose gardens. On the main street are several grocery stores, among them the Marblehead Supermarket, which can supply all your grocery needs. There are also clothing stores, gift shops, art-supply stores, and almost any other kind of emporium you might seek. Pay especial attention to Fred Woods's shop. He carries such hard-to-find items as wicks and chimneys for various sizes of kerosene cabin lamps, 3-arm protractors, yacht-club burgees, charts, books, and navigational instruments.

There is frequent bus service to Boston.

Restaurants in various degrees of elegance abound both in Marblehead and nearby Swampscott and Salem.

Repairs to hull, spars, sails, engines, and electronic equipment can be made at Graves's yard or at Fred Hood's yard at Little Harbor, on the northwest point of Marblehead Harbor. There are various other well-known sailmakers in Marblehead, among them Cloutman, Fred E. Hood, Wilson & Silsbee, and Norman Cressy. Ralph Hulsman at Oakum Bay specializes in dodgers and covers.

The principal yacht clubs in Marblehead are Eastern, Corinthian, and Pleon on the east side, and Boston, Dolphin, and Marblehead on the west side. Of these, Eastern, Corinthian, and Boston are the largest and best known. Traditionally they have always been hospitable to cruising men from other clubs and would like to continue. However, increasing pressure from their own membership, as well as increasing numbers of cruising people, sometimes puts the management under undue pressure. Surely the visitor will understand. If opportunity offers, however, visit one of these clubs, which were founded in the preincome-tax days of 100-foot schooners, steam yachts, and racing sloops with jack-yard topsails of outrageous acreage. To preserve the tradition, observe the request of proper attire, including coat and tie at dinner.

It is impossible to step ashore on the town side of the harbor without finding yourself in streets right out of the seventeenth or eighteenth century. There are lovely Colonial and Georgian mansions at Bank and Washington squares and elsewhere throughout the town, with the Lee Mansion (Marblehead Historical Society) and the King Hooper Mansion (Marblehead Arts Association) the most famous, and open to the public for a small fee.

In addition, there are many less pretentious, dating from the time when this town was one of America's leading fishing and overseas trading ports. Josiah Cressy, master of the famous clipper *Flying Cloud,* was a Marblehead native, as were General John Glover, who commanded the amphibious regiment that rowed Washington across the Delaware; Elbridge Gerry, a signer of the Declaration of Independence and Vice President of the United States under President Madison; Captain James Mugford, Revolutionary War hero; and Captain Nicholas Broughton, who commanded the first American naval vessel, the schooner *Hannah.*

The town lays claim to being the birthplace of the American Navy. The homes of these distinguished settlers still survive, although most are not open to the public except on special occasions. The original of the famous painting, *The Spirit of '76,* hangs in Abbot Hall, where the town offices are located; and whose red-brick tower may be seen for many miles at sea. The old Town House at the lower center of town (head of State Street); St. Michael's Church, oldest Episcopal edifice in New England; the Old North Church, with a Bulfinch tower; the Eagle House, locale of the best seller, *The Hearth and the Eagle;* and Burial Hill, one of several cemeteries containing stones with quaint epitaphs, are other interesting sights.

Flanking the entrance of Marblehead Harbor, which was the home port of the America's Cup defenders *Mayflower, Puritan,* and *Volunteer, Nefertiti,* and many other historic racing yachts, are two interesting parks. On the starboard hand entering the port is old Fort Sewall, now a town park, whose guns saved the *Constitution* during the War of 1812, when Old Ironsides was pursued by a superior British force. At Lighthouse Point is Chandler Hovey Park, given by a former commodore of the Eastern Yacht Club, which provides a superb yachting grandstand during the yachting season, and especially during Marblehead Race Week.

No discussion of Marblehead would be complete without mention of Race Week, usually the last week in July, but now expanded by several days. By day, astronomical numbers of boats race in many classes and over many courses. At night, they all moor in Marblehead somehow, along with a much-augmented fleet of visitors. The evenings are spent in socializing. It is the biggest assembly of sailing craft to be met with anywhere in the world, and no place for the casual cruising man.

In 1965, and again in 1966, the federal government offered to build a breakwater at Marblehead to protect the harbor from northeasters. The town was to put up $357,000 and the government $2,600,000. However, the town meeting turned down the proposition in several successive votes. The principal argument against the breakwater was that it would make possible and profitable the construction of marinas at which hundreds of powerboats could berth. Not only would the concentration of power cruisers, with their noisome fumes and irritating wakes, be increased, but it would also narrow the entrance, increase the tidal current, and interfere with the race courses, which have been traditional for generations.

The Marblehead Town Meeting voted a resounding *No.*

Beverly, Mass. (13276   241). The next harbor after Salem is Beverly. The harbor is deep and offers good protection in all but a roaring northeaster. Gas, water, and ice are available at the Jubilee Yacht Club floats located to starboard as you enter. The floats have plenty of water with 6 feet the minimum at dead low water. Anchoring is difficult due to the congestion, but moorings are generally available from the dock master or launch operators for yachts up to 40 feet. The club is hospitable and offers its launch, showers, and club privileges to members of other clubs.

Entering the harbor is straightforward. Just follow the channel buoys and resist the urge to cut across monument bar. Leave the granite monument to port when entering.

Manchester, Mass. (13275 240). This is the pleasantest and most secure harbor on the south side of Cape Ann and consequently is heavily crowded. Permits for 600 moorings have been issued. Although there is no room to anchor, it is usually possible to find a vacant mooring or a place to lie alongside one of the wharves or floats.

Vessels over 55 feet long are not permitted to moor in the inner harbor, but lie outside can 5 in Manchester Bay. This is fair enough protection, unless it blows hard from the south.

In 1968, extensive dredging opened up a 10-foot channel all the way into the anchorage basin, and a program of maintenance-dredging has maintained a good 6 or 7 feet. The pairs of red-and-black buoys indicate a channel about 175 feet wide, sufficient in its whole width at low water for vessels with a draft of 5 feet. The middle 100 feet is deeper, reduced to a width of 50 feet in the outer 500 feet of the channel because of a shortage of funds. A depth of 7 feet at low water may be carried between buoys 6 and 7 and can 5. Vessels drawing over 7 feet are advised not to enter within two hours of low water. Note that at moon low tides, which occur at the times of full and new moons, the extreme low water may be as much as 2 feet below charted low-water depths.

Approaching the harbor from can 5, steer 60° magnetic for can 7 in the first pair of buoys. Favor the black (port) side of the channel, passing about 20 feet from can 7, for the deep dredging is only about 50 feet wide from here for the next 500 feet. Continue to can 9, still favoring the port side. After this, the 7-foot channel widens to 100 feet and the moored boats will keep you in it.

Inquire for a mooring from any of the Harbor Masters, whose boats are marked Police. Robert McDiarmid was Harbor Master in 1978 and had several deputies. Carl Magee, at the Manchester Yacht Club, prominently located on the western shore, may know of a member absent on a cruise whose mooring may be available. Inquire, too, at the Manchester Marine Corp. and the Crocker yard for rental moorings or slip space. Small power boats may continue under the railway bridge to the inner basin.

Gasoline, Diesel fuel, water, and ice are available at the float of the Manchester Marine Corp. and inside the bridge at the Trysail Marina. The Marine Corps also maintains a marine store stocking rope, hardware, charts, and other necessaries. Next to this yard is that of Sturgis Crocker, son of the late S. S. Crocker, designer of fast and comfortable yachts, many of which were built in this yard. Either Crocker or Manchester Marine can attend to any necessary repairs.

Visiting yachtsmen may land at Morse Pier in the northeast corner of the harbor, at Seaside Float or the float of Manchester Harbor Boat Club. Stores and two ice machines are a short walk away. The Historical Society is well worth a visit. The town, while graced with many buildings in the best style of late Colonial and Federal architecture, strikes a suburban note. It is something of a surprise to step into the suburbs from the salt water.

The harbor is mostly surrounded by handsome houses and well-kept shores, and one of its most attractive features is the multitude of fine yachts. A leisurely dinghy trip through the anchorage is an education in elegance. However, when a real northeaster is forecast and the fleet comes over from Marblehead to lie three-deep along floats and wharves, one can view as fine an assemblage of yachts as is gathered anywhere on the east coast.

Gloucester, Mass. (13281 233). This is a well-protected harbor and easy of access at any time, with lights on Eastern Point breakwater and Ten Pound Island. In heavy weather, enter west of Round Rock. Notice on the western shore a bell on Norman's Woe, where Henry Wadsworth Longfellow wrecked the schooner *Hesperus* in verse. The wreck the poem describes was actually on the ledges off Cape Ann, but the romance of the name Norman's Woe was irresistible to the poet.

Gloucester is interesting as the scene of some of the earliest settlements on this coast. English fishermen were operating successfully from here before the Pilgrims landed at Plymouth. Here were drying stages and camps ashore for the crews who cured the fish. As there was always a rush in the spring for the best sites, it is probable that at an early date fishermen wintered here. Later, recognizing the economic possibilities of the saltfish trade, Gloucester became one of the leading Massachusetts ports and the headquarters of the Atlantic fishery. With the growth of railroads, Boston became the center for the fresh-fish market, but for many years, through the early part of the century, the long main booms of Gloucester schooners swung past Eastern Point to fish on the Grand Banks. *Captains Courageous* took place on one of these vessels.

As a memorial to the fishermen who have been lost from Gloucester, there has been erected, on the boulevard on the west side of the harbor, a stirring bronze statue of a fisherman at the wheel of a schooner. It is well worth seeing. To realize what fishing under sail was like, read James B. Connolly's *Out of Gloucester*.

There are three anchorages at Gloucester.

Smith Cove. This anchorage is perfectly protected and easy of access by day or night. Simply follow the buoyed channel and keep a sharp eye out for harbor traffic. After rounding Rocky Neck, you will notice a clear channel up the west side of the cove, with moorings thickly scattered to the east. Many of these are rental moorings, owned by Bickford's marina. Pick one up; the attendant will come out to collect. In 1977 the fee was $5.00 per night. One can lie alongside Bickford's float, or in a slip, for 50¢ a foot. For an additional dollar, electric service is available. For $1.50 one can fill up with fresh water. The marina is guarded by a watchman. There is a telephone on the wharf and a laundromat is nearby. Gasoline, Diesel oil, ice, and water are available on the wharf. Inquire for Steve Cluett, a very capable young man, who is in a position of increasing responsibility at Bickford's. His mother is the proprietor. A mechanic is usually available here and Bickford's railway can haul yachts up to 50 feet long, with as much as 9 feet of draft. In 1977, the owner could work on his own boat, bring in outside help, or employ yard labor.

Major repairs can be made at Beacon Marine on the east shore or Rocky Neck Yacht & Vessel on the point, where many big draggers are hauled.

There are several restaurants in different modes along the western shore of Smith Cove, ranging from lunch counter to a candles-and-checkered-tablecloth dining room, with musical accompaniment.

A grocery store adequate for all ordinary needs stands at the corner where the road down Rocky Neck joins the main road at the head of the cove.

Buses run to Boston at fairly frequent intervals.

Smith Cove is a mixed blessing. It is a secure anchorage in any storm, although somewhat crowded. Facilities of all kinds are available. The cove has been cleaned up recently and no longer smells of oil and sewage. However, it is certainly a city harbor, busy with commercial fishermen, big sport fishermen, and party boats. The writer enters it with relief at getting in out of the weather and leaves it with enthusiasm.

Gloucester Harbor. On the west side of the inner harbor is Old Harbor Cove, much frequented by fishermen, especially by the smaller in-shore boats. There are a few slips at the head of the cove. If one can find a vacant one, access to the principal stores and restaurants in Gloucester is easy. A short distance to the right (north), on the street bordering the shore, is the Building Center, an excellent marine hardware store.

There is no anchorage in Old Harbor Cove, and most of the slips are reserved for individual fishermen. The scenery is far from attractive and the place not good for a protracted stay.

Near the head of Gloucester Harbor, dockage, marine service, and the usual supplies are available at Burnham and Thomas and at Gloucester Yankee Marine Service. Markets are within easy walking distance, and repairs can be made here, too. For engine problems, Brown's Gloucester Yacht Yard is well recommended. On the western side of the harbor is the Seven Seas Wharf, with the Gloucester House Restaurant at its inshore end. The restaurant maintains a float where you can leave your boat while you dine. Stores are only a block and a

Laurence Lowry

Cape Ann, looking north, with Gloucester Harbor in the center. The Isles of Shoals, Cape Porpoise, and Cape Elizabeth are just visible to the north.

half away. On the west side, also, is a new Coast Guard station, complete with helicopter.

Eastern Point. Behind the breakwater at the entrance to the outer harbor is the Eastern Point Yacht Club. The club maintains a float and moorings, well enough sheltered in anything but a westerly or northwest wind, which gets quite a rake across the harbor. At low water there is said to be 8 feet alongside the float; but there is a rock south of it, with only about 3 feet over it. Water is piped to the float, but there is no gasoline or Diesel oil. There is no store nearby, although for a substantial order it is likely that a grocery store in Gloucester would make a delivery. The club has a bar and serves meals in rather formal style. It has been customary to extend hospitality to members of other yacht clubs, but with the greatly increased number of cruising men on the coast, this may have become impossible. However, even in the event that the club must restrict the use of its grounds, float, and moorings to its own members, the anchorage behind the breakwater is still the best in Gloucester on a quiet night, for it is clean, cool, quiet except for the wash of passing fishermen, and provides a far more pleasant vista in any direction than does Smith Cove.

Sandy Bay, Mass. (13279 243). This is a triangular bay between Straitsmouth and Andrews Point, more or less protected by an unfinished breakwater and the ledges outside it. The original idea was to provide a large and easily accessible harbor of refuge for the Navy, but the project remains unfinished, with most of the breakwater submerged. According to the *Coast Pilot,* "it extends 1200 yards northward from Avery Ledge, then 830 yards northwestward toward Andrews Point." It is buoyed and can be avoided easily.

This is a dangerous place to be in a heavy easterly. The ledges off Cape Ann are mostly low and hard to see. Thacher Island with its twin towers is an excellent mark, but the Salvages and the Londoner extend to the north and east of it, with shoal water all around them. Keeping clear of Thacher is no guarantee of safety. The shoals are well buoyed with bells, gongs, and a lighted whistle, but in heavy weather, especially with poor visibility, they might be hard to find. There is a radio direction-finder station on Eastern Point, which can be very helpful, but the skipper is warned to be suspicious of radio bearings when the signal passes over the land.

It was on the ledges off Cape Ann that Longfellow's *Hesperus* was wrecked. The poem is an imaginative account of an actual incident. The skipper who wishes to impress his crew with the perils of a winter northeaster can read the poem aloud. However, in ordinary summer weather and with ordinary seamanlike caution, Cape Ann presents no great danger.

In Sandy Bay there are three harbors: Rockport, Granite Company Cove, and Pigeon Cove.

Rockport, Mass. (13279   243). Unless the visitor has friends here who can arrange with the Harbor Master for a mooring, or a chance to lie alongside one of the few wharves, Rockport is too crowded for the cruising man. It may be a foreshadowing of what we are coming to elsewhere. Yachts are moored fore and aft; an air view looks a little like a freshly opened sardine can. With boats rafted alongside those moored, it is almost literally possible to walk across the harbor. A channel is kept open for party boats and fishermen, most of whom have moorings in the inner harbor.

In an effort to discourage visitors, a town ordinance prohibits the sale of gasoline and Diesel oil from the wharves. Fishermen lug fuel in cans and the party boats fuel from tank trucks, which come down early in the morning. Water and ice are available at the yacht club, but you will not be allowed to lie at the float. Tie up alongside the pilings on the end of the wharf.

Rockport is not inhospitable, just crowded.

On a quiet night, yachts anchor north of the breakwater off the beach. The holding ground is said to be good, and there is usually ample room to swing. Land on the beach or row up to the yacht club. If there is any likelihood of the wind's coming off to the east, keep away from Sandy Bay. Gloucester is the nearest safe refuge.

Ashore, Rockport is unusual. It is an old fishing town, which has been so "appreciated" that the appreciators and those who feed on them have submerged the town they came to appreciate. Bearskin Neck, which extends to the base of the breakwater on the north side of the harbor, used to support a nondescript collection of fish houses and camps. Some of the fish houses are still there and replicas fill the spaces of those that have fallen down. Each is now the site of a gift shop, an artist's studio, or a craft shop. The street is crowded with sightseers and shoppers, most of whom will not be there tomorrow. The main street has a number of restaurants and coffee shops. Back from the shore a discreet three-quarters of a mile is a shopping center where the usual groceries are available.

A bus runs to Gloucester and Annisquam.

A quaint town of old houses and winding streets, Rockport has a year-round population of 3500. Settled in the late 1600s, it was a part of Gloucester until 1840. During the War of 1812, a British man-of-war bombarded the settlement, lobbing one cannonball into the steeple of the Congregational Church, where it still remains. In the latter half of the 1800s, Rockport was famous for its granite quarries, and the stone for many a public building and the paving blocks of streets in many an eastern city came from Rockport—hewn out of the quarries by Finnish and Swedish quarrymen.

Just west of T-wharf is an old stone pier surmounted by a red fishhouse. Paintings and drawings of it have appeared in countless exhibitions, and it is known to artists as Rockport's Motif Number One. It was at least partly destroyed in the great gale of February 1978.

Rockport attracts to it in the summer busloads and carloads of visitors. Dressed in the most unconventional attire, they crowd the sidewalks and stores. They spill out into the streets. One frustrated resident writes a letter in which he declares that a helicopter is necessary to get from one place to another. The student of sociology need simply visit Rockport and take his degree. To the yachtsman, Rockport is a good shelter, but it is a crowded harbor and a very busy town.

Granite Company Cove, Mass. (13279   243). This is a possible anchorage behind a breakwater of "grout" (quarry waste), just north of Rockport. It is likely to be crowded, is not nearly so interesting or picturesque as Rockport, and is exposed to a heavy surge in easterly weather. The bottom is rough and the holding ground a little chancy.

A correspondent adds:

A yacht should pass to the north of a rock at the entrance because there are 4-foot spots south of it. There is deep water at the landing where many years ago three- and four-masters would lie alongside and take on half their cargo. Then they would anchor off and be loaded by lighters.

Pigeon Cove (13279   243). This is a very small cove, with room for about one yacht to swing at an anchor. There are no facilities for yachtsmen, but ashore there is a market and a small variety store.

Lanes Cove, Mass. (13279   243). This is a small shelter with a foul bottom and a poor chance to lie alongside, but it is a possibility, if one must wait for the tide up the Annisquam River. A local authority writes: "If it's too hubbly to enter Annisquam, go around to Eastern Point. I've seen it breaking over the breakwater at Lane's when it was OK to go upriver." There is a small grocery store at Lanesville. Buses run to Annisquam and Gloucester.

Hodgkins Cove, Mass. (13279 243). This is no place for a yacht, except in an emergency. There is about 20 feet of water. The cove is open to northwest winds. On a hill overlooking the cove is the mansion of General Butler, renowned as the military governor of New Orleans during the Civil War. This is said to be the only estate in Massachusetts with a deed granting ownership to low-water mark.

Annisquam, Mass. (13281   233). For the westbound skipper, Annisquam offers several advantages over the outside passage around Thacher. In thick weather, especially if the sun shines over the fog, there is almost certain to be a scale-up under the high land of Cape Ann. There are three bells, spaced about a mile apart, on the edge of the shoal water in the area of an expected landfall. On a summer afternoon, when the breeze offshore is gentle, there is often a good draft off the high land and through the valley of the Annisquam River.

Do not try for the entrance to the Annisquam River, however, in an easterly or northeasterly. The bar is shoal and the shoal water extends for nearly a mile off the beach. In December 1975 a stout powerboat, *Aquarius,* was lost off this shore. After riding out a northeast snowstorm all night in Ipswich Bay and extinguishing a fire aboard, she sighted the green flasher off Essex. Running over to identify it, she got into shoal water, and in a matter of minutes her house was smashed in, she was swamped and sank. Two of her crew were lost; the other three got ashore on the beach through the surf. The skipper found an inhabited house among the cottages, whose people found the other two survivors, nearly frozen to death.

The eastbound skipper can save considerable distance on his run down east by spending the night in Annisquam rather than Gloucester, particularly if the ebb tide will be running in the morning. From the bell off Annisquam he can head directly for Isles of Shoals, the Portland "Monster Buoy," or Seguin. Once outside the river, the tide is negligible, yet it runs briskly down the shore from Thacher to Eastern Point.

Entering Annisquam from the north, move with great caution, for the bar is shoal and the sand shifts. In 1977, a shoal made out on the east side of the channel opposite the lighthouse. Until it is dredged again, keep away from can 5 and stay close to the line between nun 4 and nun 6.

Inside nun 8, off Wingaersheek Beach, the edge of the channel is very abrupt. Bathers waistdeep can nearly touch passing vessels. Early in the morning and late in the afternoon inshore draggers from Gloucester use the Annisquam River to get to and from the fishing grounds near the Isles of Shoals. The skippers are likely to be short tempered with yachts that carelessly obstruct the channel. There is a possible anchorage opposite Lobster Cove off the beach, but the holding ground is poor and the traffic is disturbing, although the swimming is good. A better plan is to call the Annisquam Yacht Club on channel 16 VHF and ask about moorings in Lobster Cove. Mr. Eric Berkander, the manager, is most accommodating, and someone will be in attendance at the club from 8 A.M. until midnight. There is 10 feet of water alongside the float on the outside, but the edge of the bank is very steep. Dinner is served at the club by reservation every night during the summer except Mondays and Tuesdays. There is a snack bar open from 11 A.M. to 2 P.M. The Annisquam Yacht Club has a busy program of racing and social events for its own members, and however hospitable it may wish to be to members of visiting clubs, it is only reasonable to remember that its moorings, dock space, and shore facilities are limited.

If you cannot be accommodated at the yacht club, leave can 13 and the beacon behind it close to port and follow the west side of Lobster Cove to the Lobster Cove Market Marina. The marina maintains a few moorings, or may perhaps allow you to lie alongside the float overnight. Gasoline, Diesel oil, ice, and water are available here.

The Market is a complete grocery store at which you could fit out for an arctic voyage. As it is right on the wharf, it is most convenient. There is also a small restaurant and snack bar here. A short distance up the street, which comes in at a right angle to the shore road, are a marine store and a garage whose mechanics are well acquainted with the ordinary diseases of the marine engine. From the east end of the bridge across the cove, buses run frequently to Gloucester, where almost anything for a boat may be found.

Annisquam, although a hot and crowded harbor, is sheltered from all winds and is an excellent place in which to fit out for a voyage to the eastward. However, once outside the bar, you are at sea and must take what comes, for there is little shelter in hard weather short of the Isles of Shoals or Portsmouth.

Annisquam River and Blynman Canal (13281   233). This marine version of the Southeast Expressway is one of the busiest stretches of water in New England, constantly agitated by commercial fishermen, party boats, fast motorboats, and cruising yachts, both sail and power. One should not even approach the passage without chart 13281 and an effective horn. The motor must be in reliable condition, especially as regards the reverse gear, for the tide, flooding in from both ends and meeting more or less in the middle, runs very hard at times under the bridges near the Gloucester end. If a bridge tender is slow, or if a train is coming so the railroad bridge must be closed, it may take all the reverse that a low-powered auxiliary can muster to hold back against the current. There is scant room to turn, and no sailing vessel maneuvers well when going backwards. This problem may arise unexpectedly if you are bound north, for the flood tide can set you down very hard on the first bridge, as you enter from Gloucester Harbor. You may not be expecting it.

When a bridge does open, proceed cautiously. Heedless motorboats, familiar with the canal, sometimes come through at excessive speeds and with little concern for the cautious. Yet note that the bridges are narrow and the current often swift, so that to maintain positive control of your vessel, considerable speed may be necessary.

The buoyage seemed reliable in 1977, but the channel is dredged through sand and mud, so bars build up and points make out. In general, favor the outside of a curve, especially at can 29, where people ashore waved the writer to the west side of the channel. At least that is what he thought they meant, and disaster was averted.

Gateway Marina, Rust Island. On a little river just north of the high fixed bridge, carrying route 128, is the Gateway Marina. A buoyed channel with a depth of 4 feet at low water leads to the wharf. Boats up to 40 feet long can lie at a float or a mooring over night. Gasoline, water, ice, and oil are available at the float and Diesel fuel can be brought in by truck. Mr. Richard Daniels, the proprietor, can make minor repairs. A restaurant is a short walk away on the Rust Island overpass over Route 128. Beyond the restaurant is the sales office of Gloucester Yankee Marine Service, where sail- and powerboats and related equipment and supplies are on display.

Cape Ann Marina. Just south of the Route 128 bridge, which has an advertised vertical clearance of 65 feet, is the Cape Ann Marina, an enormous complex with literally hundreds of slips and every service the yachtsman could ask for except peace and quiet. There is little of that commodity on Cape Ann and none on the Annisquam River.

Gasoline, Diesel oil, water, and ice are available on the outer float, where brief tie-up is permitted. From June to September the float is manned from 8 A.M. to 8 P.M., on Friday and Saturday nights until 10 P.M. Hours are shorter during off seasons. Slips were available for transients at 50¢ a foot in 1977. The price includes electricity (220 v. or 110 v.), water, and 24-hour security. Showers and toilets are located at the head of the wharf and an overworked laundry machine stands nearby. A cocktail lounge and restaurant is open year round from 11 A.M. until 2 A.M., serving snacks, lunch, and dinner, with live entertainment every night. Another restaurant, separate from the dining room, which is attached to the lounge, operates in simple style from 4:30 A.M. to 9 P.M. weekdays from April to December and is open all day and all night on weekends.

Close to the head of the wharf is a small store carrying a few simple groceries and various nautical novelties, such as T-shirts emblazoned with clever remarks, and the usual array of gifts. If you need more substantial supplies, you can rent an Avis car and drive to Gloucester.

Motel accommodations are available for those who prefer to sleep ashore.

Associated with the marina is Enos Marine. On the same site they have a 20-ton lift, which can be opened to take a masted vessel. They also have a 30-ton Brownell Mobile Lift. This is a heavy trailer with hydraulic arms and elevators. It can be submerged on a ramp, the vessel properly supported; and then it can be towed out by a truck. Your boat can be set up on a cradle in the yard, where you can get at her; or relaunched at once if all you need to do is change a wheel or slap on a coat of copper paint. For extensive repairs, the yard has carpenters and mechanics. Damaged sails can be repaired in Gloucester or Marblehead. Behind the extensive parking lot is a well-appointed marine store selling paint, hardware, and many difficult-to-replace accessories, which are so easily broken or lost overboard.

A charter fishing fleet is based at the Cape Ann Marina to complete the services at a "complete service" establishment. Except that the surrounding marshes provide no very inspiring views, the constant traffic on the canal and the 128 bridge is disturbing, and the whole idea of 300 yachts crowded together is not just what we had in mind, the Cape Ann Marina is one of the best stopping-places on Cape Ann.

South of the marina, one enters the Blynman Canal, a cut through the neck of Cape Ann to Gloucester Harbor. The first bridge is a railroad bridge on a sharp turn in the channel. Approach cautiously, blow the horn vigorously, and keep far to the starboard side of the channel. Trains have the right of way. If the bridge does not open, you can probably turn around in the channel and stem the tide until it does. When the bridge opens, proceed with caution, and continue to sound the horn until you can see around the corner. There really is not room for two vessels to pass in the draw.

The highway bridge is easier, for there is no sharp corner there. However, if traffic is heavy, the bridge does not always open as rapidly as one in a boat might hope. Beyond the bridge in Gloucester Harbor there is shoal water and rocky bottom on both sides of the dredged channel. Run out to the black-and-white buoy and proceed from there.

On approaching the highway bridge from the south with a flood tide, beware of a brisk current running north through the draw. It will affect you at the black-and-white buoy, and with increasing force as you approach the bridge.

The well-known monument to Gloucester fishermen lost at sea faces Gloucester Harbor from the parkway east of the canal. It is a stirring sculpture of a fisherman at the wheel of a schooner, well worth a visit if you have time ashore, and certainly worth a respectful glance through binoculars as you pass.

Note on Leaving Cape Ann Bound East

As one passes the bell outside Annisquam or Thacher Island and the hills of Cape Ann drop astern, the skipper finds himself suddenly alone at sea and on his own. Ahead lie 65 miles of beach, stretching to Cape Elizabeth and the coves of Casco Bay. The only harbors suitable for deep-draft boats in any kind of a sea are Isles of Shoals, Portsmouth, York, and Cape Porpoise. All the others are shoal and have bars at the entrances. Even the harbors mentioned are not easy for the stranger in the fog, and on a foggy night to approach the shore anywhere along here would be foolhardy.

On a hazy day, the landmarks on the shore are difficult for the stranger to pick out. One cupola, water tower, or spire marked on the chart looks much like another. Lights and buoys are far apart. To add to the confusion, fishermen and steamers making for Gloucester, Portsmouth, and Portland traverse these waters at high speed. Their whirling radar antennae are reassuring, but one wonders whether anyone is looking at the screen.

Finally, in the event of an easterly gale, the whole coast becomes a dangerous lee shore.

Nevertheless, if you are to enjoy the bays and islands of Maine, you have to cross this stretch. There are many things in your favor. White Island and Boon Island are prominent landmarks by day and night, the latter marked by a whistle buoy, as well as by a lighthouse and fog signal. There are large whistle buoys off York, Cape Porpoise, and Wood Island. At Whaleback, the Nubble, Goat Island, and Wood Island are lighthouses recognizable by day and prominent at night. The big light on Cape Elizabeth and the bright quick flash on the Large Navigational Buoy (LNB) at Portland provide leading marks. The RDF stations at Eastern Point and on the Portland LNB, picturesquely referred to as the Monster Buoy, are of some help as stations to home in on. To the skipper who has been this way before, the big hotel at Little Boars Head, the great white Wentworth Hotel at Portsmouth, Mount Agamenticus, and the water towers at Cape Porpoise and Fortune's Rocks will be familiar landmarks. Gales are rare in summer and are usually well advertised. There isn't much to hit if you keep well clear of the land, Isles of Shoals, and Boon Island, and you will probably have a fair wind. Be sure of your compass. Lash a big radar reflector in the rigging, and strike out for Maine. You will probably have a lovely sail down east before a summer southwester and see the sun set behind the White Mountains.

Many navigators prefer to head directly for Seguin or Monhegan, making an overnight run of it. It seems that often, when there is a flat calm under the land, the southwesterly breeze airs along offshore at about 10 knots, often working considerably to the west during the night. One yachtsman who has made this run "scores of times" speaks of an easterly set. Between Isles of Shoals and the Monster Buoy, both inside and outside Boon Island, the writer has found a northwesterly set both on flood and ebb. The navigator will do well to check his position frequently. The RDF on Monhegan is very powerful. That line, crossed with bearings on the Portland LNB and Halfway Rock, can be reassuring in thick weather.

Of this run an experienced cruising man writes: "In almost all cases we make the run on a tight schedule and always with a very experienced crew of four or five. In spite of having everything with us, I've run into more bad going in the Cape Ann to Casco Bay stretch than anywhere else, including east of Schoodic, Nova Scotia, or New Brunswick. The notes that follow are not intended to scare the cruising fraternity but I believe the real dangers in this specific 75-mile run should be pointed out.

"1. There is frequently a major weather change along the route. Very often it is fine from Squam to York, but miserable beyond. Two years ago a nice SE breeze turned into a green-water-in-the-cockpit event, beginning at Wood Island. It was so bad that we had to put into the uninhabited islands of Saco Bay for overnight protection.

"2. Really only two harbors on the whole route can be safely entered in a blow, particularly with poor visibility. The most frequently recommended, Cape Porpoise, is probably the worst. In spite of the offshore whistle, inner bell, and Goat Island Light, you need only come on the land 50 yards off course and you are in serious trouble on the ledges. Number one choice by far is Wood Island. Its two approaches always provide a good lee; whether entering from east or west, the light is prominent and on a bold shore. Buoyage is excellent, regardless of the approach. The only precaution one need take is: avoid a southerly sector approach to avoid the ledges off Fletchers Neck. The second reasonably easy entrance is Portsmouth, for obvious reasons. I cannot emphasize too strongly that Newburyport, York, Kennebunkport, Cape Porpoise, and Richmond Island are to be avoided, except under good sailing conditions.

"3. When crossing even small bays along this route the going can be extremely rough even in NW breezes, when you would believe fair protection would be likely. Also, Portland Harbor entrance, including Cape Elizabeth, can be bad. This locale has been consistently the worst we have encountered along this stretch and this includes the Kennebec inside of Seguin.

"4. The on-shore tide set from Portsmouth onward is a major navigation hazard. In spite of the fact that we make a major compensation for this effect we almost always fall inside of the anticipated landfall, particularly at the Cape Porpoise or Wood Island sea buoys.

"Lest you believe I'm being overly pessimistic, I want to reemphasize that I'm talking about making long hauls during the early summer and fall, when poor visibility is the rule. It is also true that we push along in spite of poor going, which would probably discourage the cruising man with time to spare. The point is that weather conditions can change quickly and the casual afternoon sail turns into a situation that makes it necessary to seek shelter in a hurry. Add some fog and darkness and a real party can result."

Essex, Mass. (13279   243). The approach to Essex is marked by a flashing green bell on the edge of the 3-fathom curve. In rough weather, keep well outside it and have nothing to do with any of the harbors in Ipswich Bay. Inside the bell are buoys marking the deepest water over a shallow bar. In 1977, local knowledge promised 5 feet over this bar on anything but a moon low tide. Inside the bar the depths drop off dramatically. The chart shows 56 feet between Castle Neck and Coffins Beach. There is good anchorage along the shore of Conomo Point on the eastern side of the channel or behind the tip of Castle Neck on the western side. In neither place, however, is there a public landing or any of the usual facilities for yachtsmen.

The curious can follow the intricate windings of the Essex River by steep banks of stiff mud and through salt marshes and clam flats to the town of Essex. The passage is buoyed and, on anything but the lowest tides, 5 feet can be carried all the way.

The town of Essex from the water is unprepossessing. There are two boat yards, mostly devoted to hauling and storage, two marinas providing dockage for local boats, three launching ramps, and a fine view of the back doors of several restaurants. There is no town landing and, unless a local boat is away on a cruise, there is unlikely to be a slip open. There are no moorings and the river is too narrow for anchoring. Gasoline and water are available but no Diesel oil. Ice cubes can be provided by the nearby package store. The usual grocery and hardware stores line the main street and antique shops abound.

Back from the shore, however, Essex is a very attractive town. There are several old churches constructed in different styles and many old houses, some doubtless built in Colonial and Federalist times and many built in the days when Essex was a prosperous shipbuilding town. There is a museum, with a variety of tools, photographs, and documents from those days.

Since Colonial times, Essex has been a shipbuilding town. In the hills and on the flat country along the river grew white oak, "blue as a whetstun and tougher'n a b'iled owl," the best of woods for timbers and frames. Chebacco boats were built here and a vast number of pinkies, sloops, brigs, and schooners. In the 1920s, the last of the big, fast Gloucester fishing schooners were built here, among them *Columbia, Henry Ford, Mayflower, Esperanto,* and *Puritan.* Later the yards turned to building draggers. Anyone interested in the history and craft of wooden shipbuilding should seek out Dana Story's *The Building of a Wooden Ship, Frame Up!,* and *Hail Columbia.* Albert Cook Church's *American Fishermen* is a remarkably complete photographic study of the building and operation of the Gloucester schooners, and Howard Chapelle's *American Fishing Schooners* is a thorough and detailed technical study of the vessels.

Now, however, the yards have turned to winter storage. White oak and yellow pine give way to fiberglass. The smell of copper paint and sawdust has fled before monoxide, and the crack of the caulking mallet is heard no more in Essex.

An effort is being made to restore the clam resources. The flats are seeded with baby clams, and nets are erected to protect them from predators, especially green crabs. Just as progress became evident, the "red tide" descended on the clams and the flats were closed.

Plum Island Sound, Mass. (13282   213). For the shoal-draft cruiser, this is an ideal place to explore. Most of the shore is salt marsh or sand dune and much of it, including almost all of Plum Island and some of the western shore, is maintained by the U.S. Fish and Wildlife Service as a refuge. Water birds, particularly, are abundant. Many different species breed here or visit the island on their migrations.

No very satisfactory directions for entering Plum Island Sound can be given, because the bar is constantly changing and the buoys are moved in an effort to keep pace. One local authority states flatly that if you follow the buoys, you are sure to go aground. Another adds that at half-tide or better you can cross the bar anywhere, even where the buoys are. You have to go by the color of the water and the way the seas lump up over the shoal spots. The bottom is all sand, except for one ledge off the end of Plum Island.

Several rivers run into the sound. The Ipswich River is said to be staked out; but as there is almost no water in it at low water and the Town of Ipswich is apparently not going to dredge it, outboard skiffs are about the only traffic on it. Fox Creek is now silted up so as to be virtually no longer navigable.

The Parker River is buoyed out and is navigable to the first bridge, as shown on chart 213. The wooded shores and salt marshes are pretty and abound with bird life. At the bridge are two marinas. The first, below the bridge, is Fernald's Marine. They maintain a marine store and a sales room for canoes and small boats. They do not sell gasoline. Above the bridge, not a drawbridge, is the Parker River Marina, with a store, a Travelift, a small railway, and extensive floats. A snack shop is nearby. From here one can call a taxi from Newburyport, where supplies are available.

Behind Fernald's and slightly east of it is the shop of "Pert" Lowell, who adapted the Swampscott dory to develop the Town Class boats, for many years a popular class all over New England. They are now manufactured in fiberglass. Mr. Lowell is devoting his attention to making wooden mast hoops for gaff-rigged vessels. There is a large demand for these from all over the world. He has leased part of his shop to the Pigeon Hollow Spar Co., formerly of Boston and Quincy. They build and repair wooden spars, hollow and solid, although not on the scale that they once did.

There is a passage, spanned by a drawbridge, from Plum Island Sound through into the Merrimac River. The recently constructed bridge is very narrow and has so altered the tidal currents that new shoals have built up. In 1977, no buoys had yet been established. The view northward from the bridge at low tide in 1977 suggested that any man with a good pair of boots could walk right up the middle of whatever channel he could find. This may be grossly unfair to the place, but the writer's advice would be not to attempt it in anything but a very shoal-draft boat on a rising tide. The bridge is manned at high water only. The channel, such as it is, turns sharply to the west to the north of the bridge and skirts the eastern side of Woodbridge Island. Beware of a ruined breakwater abreast the northern part of the island.

The northern part of Plum Island is thickly settled, mostly with summer beach cottages. The southern part is included in the Parker River Wildlife Refuge and is populated mostly by muskrats, foxes, ducks, geese, and a wealth of other birds. The eastern side is all beach, backed by sand dunes overgrown with coarse grass, beach plum, and wild rosebushes. There is a rough road down the western side on the edge of the marsh, which is a little easier walking than the soft sand of the beach. The Puritan judge, Samuel Sewall, reflected on the natural wealth and beauty of Plum Island about 1650:

And as long as Plum Island shall faithfully keep the commanded post, notwithstanding all the hectoring words and hard blows of the proud and boisterous ocean; as long as any salmon or sturgeon shall swim in the streams of Merrimac, or any perch or pickerel in Crane Pond; as long as the sea-fowl shall know the time of their coming, and not neglect seasonably to visit the places of their acquaintance; as long as any cattle shall be fed with the grass growing in the meadows which do humbly bow down themselves before Turkey Hill; as long as any sheep shall walk upon Old Town Hill, and shall from thence pleasantly look down upon the river Parker and the fruitful marshes lying beneath; as long as any free and harmless doves shall find a white oak or other tree within the township to perch or feed or build a careless nest upon, and shall voluntarily present themselves to perform the office of gleaners after barley harvest; as long as nature shall not grow old and dote, but shall constantly remember to give the rows of Indian corn their education by pairs: so long shall Christians be born there, and being first made meet, shall from thence be translated, to be made partakers of the Inheritance of the saints in light.

Newburyport, Mass. (13282   213). This harbor, at the mouth of the Merrimac River, is an interesting place to visit but can in no sense be regarded as easy of access or as a peaceful anchorage. On approaching from the Isles of Shoals or Cape Ann, you will see a low, featureless shore, with several water towers standing out against the horizon. It is not at all clear which is the "tank" shown on the chart. As you approach, you will strain your binoculars looking for the roller coaster on Salisbury Beach and the cross on the northern end of Plum Island. The roller coaster is a spidery tangle, not nearly as big as you expect, and not at all prominent until you have once seen it. The cross surmounts a small, almost cubical building, probably built of dark stone. It looks much darker than the other buildings on Plum Island and is quite well down the shore from the entrance. The towers of the power lines, which cross the Merrimac River at Newburyport, can be picked out with binoculars, but they do not show up well on a hazy day. The jetties are very hard to find until you are close in. The outer buoy is a black-and-white whistle, a full mile off shore. You will be in no trouble until you pass that.

Just inside the two bells there is a very considerable bar built up by the Merrimac River, which drains most of central New Hampshire and dumps its silt, mud, and sand where it enters the ocean. Frequent dredging is required to maintain the charted depth. The channel was dredged in the summer of 1977. Nevertheless, with a sea running, especially on the ebb tide, this can be a dangerous place indeed. The Coast Guard, the Commonwealth of Massachusetts, and the City of Newburyport have joined to set up a big sign with a brilliantly flashing light on the boathouse of the old Coast Guard station on the south side of the entrance. It is supposed to flash when the bar has 2-foot breaking seas or greater. However, after several days' sojourn in Newburyport, the writer believes it flashes on almost every ebb tide. Nevertheless, if the light is flashing, approach the bar with caution, remembering that dangerous seas look much less dangerous than they really are from seaward and more dangerous from the landward side. The best water appeared to be on the northerly side of the entrance in 1975. One local yachtsman advised approaching the northerly jetty from the north, nipping around the end of it very close in, and following it closely until well inside the nun.

The channel between the jetties can be a very rough place for a small boat on the ebb tide. The whole rush of the Merrimac River, plus the weight of the tide taken up the estuary on the flood, pours through the narrow channel between the jetties. Annually, fishermen are lost here and others are capsized or swamped and rescued. The place is to be treated with profound respect but not with terror.

Just inside the entrance on the port side is a cove by the old Coast Guard station, usually crowded with local boats. The Coast Guard headquarters has been moved up to Newburyport and the boats are usually kept there. However, the wharf and boathouse still stand and are occasionally used.

The channel up the river to Newburyport is well marked and should cause no great perplexity. The current runs hard, so it is well to plan your arrival for a flood tide. Resist the temptation to turn in toward the American Yacht Club, shown in chart 213, until you are well by the rocks marked by can 13A.

Anchorage is difficult in the Merrimac River. The bottom is said to be gravel, well scoured by the swift current. The best bet is the American Yacht Club, surely one of the most hospitable on the coast. Hail the float. The steward may be able to let you use the mooring of an absent member or to direct you to a town mooring above the club. As a last resort, anchor above the bridge where the bottom is said to be mud. Even should you be on a mooring, if it comes to blow hard from the northwest or northeast, you may drag.

Rowing ashore is no easy matter at the strength of the tide. Get close under the shore and work your way up against the current in the comparatively slack water. Also remember that anything you drop overboard will disappear astern at a rate of about 3 knots. If your yacht has a tendency to yaw and swing about her mooring in a tideway, experiment with turning the rudder just enough to balance her weight against the rush of the tide. You may be able to get her to fly like a kite.

Gas and water are available at the yacht club float at certain hours.

Above the yacht club and the power station is the Coast Guard base, and a short distance above that is Hilton's Fishing Dock, a sport-fishing center. Gasoline, Diesel oil, ice, and water are available here, and there is a restaurant on the wharf. Above Hilton's is Windward Yacht Yard with slips occasionally open for transients, the possibility of a mooring, and gasoline, Diesel fuel, ice, and water. Butch Fraxigipane, who runs the yard, has a railway and a lift capable of hauling any vessel that can get into Newburyport. He can effect repairs to hull, spars, and rigging. Sails can be sent to Nat Snow's loft in nearby Georgetown for speedy repair.

Groceries and hardware are available in the town. A resident of Newburyport writes: "A new pier has just been constructed in Newburyport in the Redevelopment Area downtown. This area is well worth a visit. In this area also is a marine museum, which is housed in the old Customs House close to the public wharf. Newburyport waterfront is in constant flux and will be a very exciting place."

It is possible, although perilous, to carry 6 feet of draft inside Plum Island on the high water. It is also possible to push upstream all the way to Haverhill. There are some very pretty stretches of river, but the water is dirty and is spread rather thinly in some places.

Newburyport people have developed a well-deserved reputation for ingenuity. In 1928, when local clam flats were found to be polluted, Newburyport built a chlorinating plant for clams. The costs were assessed on towns bordering the river that contributed to the pollution. In 1961, Massachusetts took over the plant and charged shellfish owners by the bushel. Clams dug in Chelsea Creek are said to be rendered pure and healthful after a dip in Newburyport chlorine.

Interesting and original as this Newburyport project is, it will be hard in any century to top the record of "Lord" Timothy Dexter, merchant, author, and self-styled nobleman, who flourished in Newburyport's days as a prosperous trading center. One of those men who couldn't fail at anything, he shipped a load of warming pans to the West Indies. Contrary to the gloomy predictions of the more conservative merchants of Newburyport, he made a handsome profit. The warming pans were in great demand to dip molasses out of vats into hogsheads. A load of fur mittens in the same port netted a handsome profit when his ship encountered a Russian making up a cargo for home, with iron and flax to trade.

This eccentric gentleman wanted to be called "Lord" Timothy Dexter in defiance of the Constitution, and he offered to pave the main street of Newburyport in return for the handle to his name. Newburyport turned him down, but Danvers said that at that price he could call himself anything he wanted, and he moved to that town.

In his declining years he published a book, *A Pickle for the Knowing Ones.* The spelling and punctuation in the first edition were so unusual that he was much criticized. The second edition appeared with several pages of assorted punctuation and the advice, "Reader may pepper and salt to taste."

Almost any citizen of Newburyport can direct you to Timothy Dexter's house and add more legends to the sample above. The late John P. Marquand, himself a citizen of Newburyport, wrote a delightful book on his unusual fellow citizen.

Another authority is quoted as having said, "The story of Timothy Dexter is the story of Newburyport rum inside a fool."

Hampton, N.H. (13278   1206 inset). This harbor is not of much use to the cruising man. The entrance is shoal and the bridge is manned only at half tide or better. The first wharves are reserved primarily for partyboats and fishermen. A visiting yacht should bear around to starboard, following the channel, which is marked by local buoys if at all, to Hampton Beach Marina. The marina is crowded with local boats but will find room for transients if possible. There are no moorings available and anchorage space is severely limited. However, gasoline, Diesel oil, water, ice, and marine supplies are available. A lift and a launching ramp are located at the marina.

As a refuge in bad weather Hampton is useless because of the shoal and difficult entrance. In good weather, there are better places.

The town is jammed into a narrow space between marsh and beach, traversed by Route 1A. It supports the usual grocery stores, a large

number of restaurants, and a great many summer cottages, built upon
the sand as close to high water as winter gales permit.

Rye, N.H. (13283   211). Rye is marked by a flashing whistle about
¾ of a mile off the entrance and by a can on a 5-foot rock just outside
the south jetty. The harbor is reported to have been dredged to a depth
of 8 feet. Anchoring is difficult in this crowded harbor. Land at one of
the floats on the west side and inquire for the Harbor Master, John
Widen, owner of Ray's Restaurant. He will do his best to find a berth
for you, and he declared to a visitor in 1977 that he had never turned
anyone away.

There is a grocery store about a mile to the south on the state road.
Rye Harbor Bait and Tackle Shop on the wharf serves coffee, dough-
nuts, and other snacks early and late. Ray's Restaurant and Saunders
Restaurant are reported excellent.

Rye is the first harbor north of Cape Ann without a bar at the entrance
and is a good refuge in anything but a full-grown easterly gale.

Portsmouth, N.H.   (13283   211). Portsmouth, easy of entrance in
almost any weather, is well marked by a lighted bell on Gunboat Shoal
and a lighted whistle on Kitts Rocks. Inside is the powerful light on
Whaleback. Two range lights, the northerly one fixed red, the southerly
one flashing red, are located on the Kittery shore behind Pepperell
Cove so as to lead one up the middle of the deep channel off the Coast
Guard base. Here the green range lights on Pierces Island lead on up
the river.

Portsmouth is a busy commercial harbor. Steamers carrying gypsum,
wire, oil, and liquefied natural gas (LNG) move in and out frequently.
The Navy maintains a repair base for submarines on Seavey Island, and
there is a Coast Guard base at Fort Constitution on the northeast point
of Newcastle Island. Therefore, the yachtsman will do well to hang up
a large radar reflector and keep a sharp lookout.

If you want to check the accuracy of your compass, note that the range
lights for the entrance to the river lie on a course of 189°–009° magnetic
and the face of the Coast Guard wharf lies due east-west magnetic. It
is best to run these ranges at slack water, because the tide runs hard and
makes staying on a range very difficult. Note that the ebb tide sweeps
down the river past Pepperell Cove and then swings almost southwest,
setting a vessel in on the shore near Little Harbor.

There are six possible anchorages at Portsmouth:

Little Harbor. This is in some ways the best shelter in the area. It is
close to the route alongshore, so one need not go up into the river, a

slow business against the tide. It is well protected in anything but a heavy easterly, and there is likely to be room to anchor. However, there are few facilities ashore except those provided by the Wentworth Hotel, a huge white structure visible from far at sea and clearly marked on the chart. In entering, keep well clear of the ledges behind nun 4 and beware of a shoal inside the southern breakwater marked as a 3-foot spot on chart 13283 (211). In seeking an anchorage, follow the advice of a skipper who visited Little Harbor in a brisk SE breeze: "We realized that the trick is to find a mooring alongside the channel that leads to the bridge and beyond. Then the boat lies with the tidal current, which is perpendicular to the swell coming in through the opening between the breakwaters. If one tries to avoid the swell by moving off to the side, the current is less and the boat swings with the wind. With a southerly wind, as there was that night, that puts you broadside to the swell."

The new Wentworth Yacht Club, established in 1976, has a landing in the northwest corner of the harbor just inside nun 10. It has three guest moorings, block ice, water, and showers but no fuel or launch service. Dredging and expansion are planned.

The Wentworth Hotel can provide meals and rooms ashore and can arrange for transportation by bus to Boston or Portland.

The bridge over Sagamore Creek can be opened on four hours' notice. Monday through Friday, 8 A.M. to 4 P.M., call the State Public Works office, 436-6748; at other times call Bradley Pike, 436-1860; or Lou Wallingford, 436-2700. One can, by observing due caution, circumnavigate Newcastle Island and come out in the river opposite Seavey Island. This requires passing under a fixed bridge, with a clearance of 14 feet above high water.

Pepperell Cove. This is an open bight in the northeast corner of the harbor opposite Fort Constitution. There is ample depth here, but it is crowded with moorings. If you want to lie here, edge up to the float and search out Frank Frisbee at the store. If there is a vacant mooring, he will know of it. Do not lie on the front of the float except in very quiet weather. The roll is devastating. Lie bow to the southward on the west end. There is water enough to allow you to swing around and come alongside.

On ordinary nights this anchorage is safe enough, but uneasy. Most of the moored yachts are small boats with aluminum masts and wire halyards. When they all get rolling and jingling their halyards more or less in concert, the effect is far from soporific.

Frisbee's store is very well equipped. Gasoline, Diesel oil, water, and ice are available at the float. Captain Simeon's Galley is a small restaurant of high quality, located over the Pepperell Cove Yacht Club in a small building near the wharf. One can dine on lobster and supervise the waterfront activities below.

The yacht club is open on weekends and provides launch service from Friday night to Sunday night. The launch driver may know of a vacant mooring. Toilet, shower, and sometimes coffee and doughnuts are available here to cruising people.

There are excellent eating places within short taxi rides. Warren's Lobster House at the Kittery end of the first bridge has a good reputation for seafood.

In a southerly or easterly gale, Pepperell Cove is impossible. Otherwise it is an acceptable, if not particularly desirable, anchorage.

Portsmouth Yacht Club. This hospitable yacht club is located just west of Salamander Point. The shoal water drops off steeply into the tide-scoured channel, making anchoring difficult. However, the club maintains two guest moorings and may have room to lie alongside. At the clubhouse there is a snack bar open at strategic times, and gasoline, Diesel oil, and water are available from 8 A.M. to 8 P.M. until Labor Day.

Kittery Point Yacht Club. This club is developing a clubhouse and float on Goat Island, southwest of black flasher 9. No anchorage has been developed yet and no moorings have been established. There may, however, be a chance to lie alongside. Plans are being made to lengthen the float and set out moorings. The clubhouse provides showers. Members from Kittery get to the club via launch from Pepperell Cove, although this service may not be continued another year.

Back Channel. This passage north of Seavey Island provides the best protection in Portsmouth, although it is quite a way from open water. In any kind of bad weather it is much to be preferred.

Pass Pepperell Cove and the high land west of it. Leave nun 6 and the beacon on Hicks Rocks to starboard and cans 1 and 3 to port. Bear around to port. Dion's yard will be right ahead. Stop here and inquire for a mooring or slip. Dion's is a well-equipped yard, possessing, among other things, a sort of portable dry dock, a hydraulic trailer onto which a boat can be floated, supported by hydraulically controlled arms, and towed to wherever the owner would like it. There is a good marine store here, and Dion's crew can effect any repair a yacht is likely to require.

A short distance above Dion's, lives Capt. Frederick S. Brown, a former Merchant Marine officer, an experienced yachtsman, and a skillful compass adjuster.

Prescott Park. Just east of the first bridge is a small complex of piers and floats owned by the city of Portsmouth. There is ample depth here and room for several yachts to lie overnight. Rumor had it that in 1977 one could lie here for one night without charge. Fisherman's Pier restaurant is close by and the Boston-Portland bus stop is opposite the church spire shown on the chart in Portsmouth.

Near Prescott Park and below the first bridge is Strawbery Banke. (Note that *Strawbery* is spelled with only one *r* in the last syllable.) This is a developing preservation project and a museum showing Portsmouth as it was in the early days of the nineteenth century when the city was a center for shipbuilding, overseas trade, and inland distribution. A lagoon, then known as Puddle Dock, permitted vessels to lie out of the tide. Various trades flourished around the wharves. Buildings have been rehabilitated, and in them people again practice these trades. A silversmith, a leather worker, a potter, a harpsichord maker and a blacksmith can be seen at work with old-time tools. In another shop, a boatbuilder and a group of apprentices turn out Grand Banks dories, such as were used for offshore fishing. A lawyer practices in a house once lived in by Daniel Webster. Guided tours are available from May 1 through October 31 by means of a tape cassette. This project is well worth a visit and the yachtsman's support.

One can continue up the river, through the two drawbridges for which the signals are precisely set forth in chapter 2 of *Coast Pilot 1.* The tenders of both bridges monitor channel 13 VHF. The signal for the first bridge, the highway bridge, is four blasts on the horn. If the bridge is to be opened at once, the tender replies with three blasts. If, for some reason, this is impossible, he will reply with five blasts, repeated until answered with five blasts by the approaching vessel. The second bridge responds to two short blasts and two long ones. The tender responds, if all is well, with two blasts. If it cannot be opened or is open and must be closed immediately, the tender replies with five blasts, which the yacht should answer with five. In the cases of both bridges, keep back until the signal to proceed is given, for the tide runs hard. It may be necessary to turn around and stem it if the reverse gear is not sufficiently powerful.

A gauge showing the height under the lowest projection of each bridge is installed on one of the abutments of each.

Above the bridges one can proceed as far as draft and inclination dictate. At Dover Point, where Great Bay opens up to port, there are two bridges with a vertical clearance of 46 feet. Great Bay and the rivers that flow into it are inhabited by many kinds of birds and wind through the pleasant New Hampshire countryside. One can ascend the Squam-scott all the way to Exeter.

Isles of Shoals, N.H.   (13283   211). This group of islands affords the first taste of Down East for the eastbound yachtsman. Well offshore, unfrequented except by fishermen, scientists, and the residents at the Star Island Hotel, the archipelago has a bleak, rugged appearance.

It was first inhabited by fishing companies from England in the early seventeenth century. To the Isles of Shoals came the distressed Pilgrims from Plymouth in 1621, and to those islands they sent the godless Thomas Morton of Merrymount, who corrupted Indians by destroying the Pilgrim monopoly on the fur trade and interfered with the Kingdom of God in the Wilderness by dancing, singing, and wild weekend parties.

Gosport Harbor. This harbor, formed by Star, Cedar, Smuttynose and Appledore Islands, is appealing in ordinary weather. It has all the atmosphere of an offshore harbor: rocky treeless shores, deep cold water, gulls, seals, and always a little motion to remind you that you are at sea. You really appreciate the shelter of the breakwater. It was built early in the last century, financed by a cache of silver bars, which Captain Haley found on Smuttynose while digging a well. It was destroyed by a great gale in the winter of 1971–72 and the government declined to rebuild it, claiming that no vessels were registered with Gosport as a home port and that modern weather forecasting and high-speed boats made a harbor of refuge unnecessary. Concerted pressure from local people, fishermen, and yachtsmen at last changed the bureaucratic mind and the breakwater stands today.

In a strong northwester, or in a real easterly gale, the harbor is practically untenable. The bottom is ledge, boulders, and kelp and the water is deep. If the weather deteriorates, there are several choices open to you. If it blows from the northwest, go around Smuttynose and anchor in the lee of the breakwater. Another alternative is to ask permission to lie on the big mooring off the marine biology lab on Appledore. It will be rough, but safe enough. Your third alternative is to run for Cape Ann.

In anchoring in Gosport Harbor, try to land your anchor on the soft bottom, well up in the cove between Cedar Island and Star Island. If you don't get in far enough, your anchor will land on a stretch of smooth ledge. You might as well try to anchor over a parking lot. If there is any wind at all, you will drag until your anchor fetches up in the deep water.

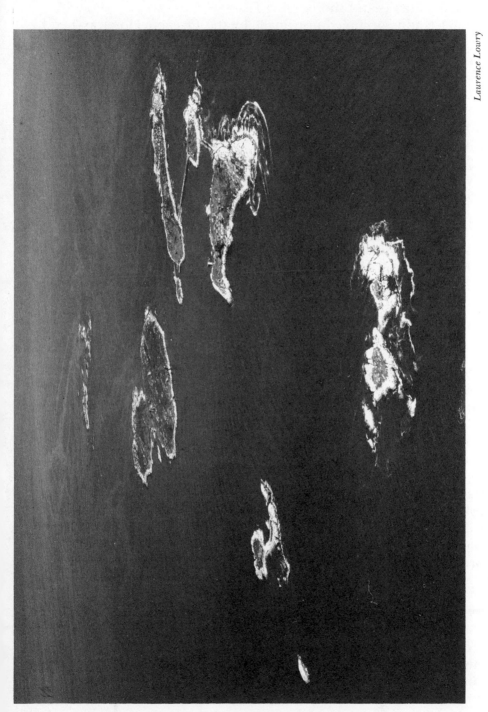

Laurence Lowry

The Isles of Shoals. The anchorage between Star and Cedar Islands is easily seen. This photograph was taken before the Cornell laboratory was established on Appledore Island.

If you cannot anchor on the mud, rig a trip line and anchor close up under the Star Island shore.

Star Island is occupied principally by the Oceanic Hotel, owned by the Star Island Corporation and used by Unitarian-Universalist and Congregationalist groups for religious conferences. Yachtsmen are not unwelcome ashore, but it is urged that they not bring dogs ashore because of the large populations of nesting gulls and young children. Also, do not bring your trash ashore here, for the island produces all the trash it can handle. When you tie your skiff to the float, keep it clear of the buoyed swimming area.

There are several monuments on the island, and there is a candlelight service in the chapel to which visitors are welcome.

Do not count on eating at the hotel. However, if times are slack, you may succeed in making a reservation.

There is no store, no marina, no provision at all for yachtsmen, yet on a pleasant Friday or Saturday night you may see fifty yachts at anchor here. If it comes on to blow in the night, the scene becomes quite exciting as boats swing on the long scope necessary in deep water and drag anchors, which were never firmly set but merely entangled in kelp.

A husky Diesel passenger vessel makes daily trips to Portsmouth in the summer from the hotel wharf.

Appledore Island. The most prominent feature of Appledore is the observation tower on the summit, built during World War II but abandoned since. In the early sixties the island was practically covered by breast-high poison ivy, relieved by a few cottages on the south side and ruined buildings elsewhere.

Professor John M. Kingsbury of Cornell University had the vision to see the possibilities of a marine biology station here and the energy to establish, finance, and construct it. He generously contributed the following account of Appledore's history. He is the author of several professional works, but of particular interest to yachtsmen are *The Rocky Shore* and *Oil and Water.* The latter discusses the impossibility of an oil port at the Shoals and deals with the effects of oil on the marine environment. Mr. Kingsbury's account follows:

Appledore Island. Appledore is the site of the earliest settlement at the Shoals, one of the earliest in America. In the 1600s and early 1700s, cod and other species of fish were landed from the surrounding fertile waters, dried or salted, and prepared for shipment throughout the civilized world. *Shoals,* in fact, refers to schools of fish and not shoal water, which is rare around the islands. During the American

Revolution, colonial authorities made the island population go to the mainland. This evacuation signaled the end of the major fishing and trading era at the Shoals.

In 1839, Thomas B. Laighton, a rising influence in the political and economic life of Portsmouth, accepted the position of lighthouse keeper on White Island, to the surprise of many. He had in mind developing the waning fishing or trading possibilities at the Shoals, at a profit to himself, and he bought up much of the nearly abandoned land of the islands. In 1847, Thomas Laighton constructed a major resort hotel on Appledore, one of the first in New England, and destined to become one of the most famous. His daughter Celia, brought out to barren White Island as a toddler, moved with her family to their new quarters on Appledore at the age of twelve. Here she and her two brothers, Cedric and Oscar, found a whole new world of plants and animals. After Celia's marriage to Levi Thaxter and her removal each winter to the mainland, she expressed some of her longing for the natural beauty of the islands in poetry, which, although from the pen of a person entirely lacking a schoolroom education, found its way to the editor of the *Atlantic Monthly,* who published it. Celia Thaxter soon became one of the better-known authors of her time among those of conservative tradition and, as hostess during the summer seasons at the Appledore House, she attracted the literary and artistic great of New England to this summer resort. Many famous persons signed the hotel register, including Nathaniel Hawthorne, James Russell Lowell, Richard Henry Dana, Franklin Pierce, Harriet Beecher Stowe, Samuel Longfellow, and John Greenleaf Whittier. Celia died in 1894 and the Appledore House, already fallen on hard times, burned to the ground in 1914. Celia, her two brothers (Oscar lived to his one-hundredth year), and her mother and father are buried in the Laighton Cemetery on Appledore.

The most recent development in the history of Appledore has been that of education. Professor C. Floyd Jackson, of the University of New Hampshire, established a field marine station on Appledore in the late 1920s, occupying several of the cottages, dating from the hotel times, that had not been consumed in the fire. This effort prospered, but was brought to an untimely halt after little more than a decade by the advent of the Second World War. Again, the islands had to be vacated for military purposes, and the UNH Zoological Laboratory was abandoned. In 1966, a group from Cornell University, attracted to the islands by their biological richness and freedom from pollution, offered a limited summer course in marine science for undergraduates at the conference center facilities on Star Island. To expand this program, volunteer students, working on a financial shoestring, began reconstruction of some of the hotel cottages on Appledore, which had been abandoned and vandalized for more than twenty years subsequent to the Second World War. As funds became available from private donors and foundations, more old buildings were renovated, and new buildings, roads, and docks were built, much of the labor still being supplied by students, under the direction of a local contractor. Serious construction commenced on Appledore in 1971. The new facilities were first occupied by a class in 1973, and the Shoals Marine Laboratory, operated by Cornell University and the University of New Hampshire, formally came into being.

The Maine Isles of Shoals are a Registered National Historic Site. A large part of Appledore Island has been designated a critical natural area as a heron rookery by the State of Maine. Bird species nesting on the island, beside the thousands of gulls, include Black-Crowned Night Herons, Little Blue Herons, Snowy Egrets, and Glossy Ibis. Black Guillemots and Eider Ducks nest on other islands of the Shoals. For several of these species, this represents an extremely wide range in America. A portion of the magnificent rocky shoreline of Appledore is being considered also as a critical natural area by the State of Maine, and the surrounding waters have been nominated as a federal marine sanctuary by Senator Durkin.

Yachtsmen are welcome to visit Appledore from May to September. Academic visitors and contributors to the Shoals Marine Laboratory are especially welcome. Visitors should land at the dock on the west side of the island (behind Babb's Rock). Here they will find handouts including a map of the island and a self-guiding tour. To protect the natural resources of the islands, open fires are not allowed, all litter brought ashore must be removed with the visitor, and pets may not be brought ashore, even on leash.

The main function of the Shoals Marine Laboratory is education, although some research projects are undertaken as well. Its principal course, Introduction to Marine Science, is being taken by undergraduates from all over the United States and Canada. Advanced courses in marine subjects, adult education programs, and special courses for teachers are also presented each summer.

In the last year of her life, Celia Thaxter wrote a book about the garden in front of her cottage on Appledore, which had become nearly as famous as her literary salon within. With the help of the Rye Beach–Little Boar's Head Garden Club, the Shoals Marine Laboratory and Cornell Plantations are reconstructing Celia's 1893 garden on the same spot, with the same botanical materials.

A picnic table is provided near the garden for visitors.

The vegetation of Appledore, despite the centuries of human occupation, has now reverted to approximately what Capt. John Smith described in 1614. Publications on the flora of Appledore, the marine organisms of the Shoals, a checklist of the flora and fauna (including birds), prepared by personnel of the Shoals Marine Laboratory, and a reprinted edition of Celia Thaxter's *An Island Garden* (with illustrations by Childe Hassam) are available in the bookstore on Star Island, or by writing to Shoals Marine Laboratory, Cornell University, Ithaca, N.Y. 14853.

We regret to report that Professor Kingsbury has resigned as director of the project, but rejoice that it will continue nevertheless.

Smuttynose Island. Smuttynose is interesting because of old Captain Haley. In the early days of the nineteenth century he had a mill and a ropewalk on the little island. He made a practice of keeping a lighted lamp in the window. One February night, in 1813, a Spanish vessel, *Sagunto,* went ashore on the eastern side of the island, and in the morning sixteen bodies were recovered. Three of the men had survived the wreck, but died trying to reach Captain Haley's light. The Spaniards were buried in a small enclosure still visible on Smuttynose, and easily identified by one of Captain Haley's millstones.

In 1820, the captain, while digging rocks for a well, found a cache of silver bars. He used the fortune thus realized to build the breakwater from Smuttynose around to Star Island. In the 1850s, not counting the guests at the Appledore House, there were about 1000 people living on the islands—mostly fishermen.

In March 1873, one Louis Wagner, hearing that Smuttynose was deserted except for three women, and believing that there was money hidden in the house, rowed out from Portsmouth at night, killed two of the women with an axe, and rowed back. The grisly story is recounted by Lyman V. Rutledge, in a pamphlet entitled *Moonlight Murder at Smuttynose.* The island is owned today by Thaxter descendants.

Lunging Island, or Londoners. On this island, west of Star Island, formerly owned by Oscar Laighton, the late Rev. Frank B. Crandall of Salem, Massachusetts, maintained a summer home. The cottage was kept supplied with food and clothing throughout the year for the relief of people marooned or shipwrecked on the island.

Mr. Crandall, one of the individual owners of a part of the Shoals, generously contributed the following:

The Isles of Shoals, as an abode of white men, is older than Plymouth. From 1615 on, it was a fishing base of British companies. My island was the base of the London Company. The word *Lunging* is said to be a sailor's corruption of "London." The other name, "Londoners," confirms this tradition. So my island has this bit of historic interest, it is the first "London" in the New World. The venerable Oscar Laighton used to tell me that the first general store at the Isles of Shoals was located on my island, as it was one place where a landing was possible in almost any weather. The old foundations still remain. My island also happens to be the location of the somewhat famous Honeymoon Cottage, so named because various notables in the past, such as Professor Forbes of Harvard, had their honeymoons in this secluded and idyllic spot.

The year before I was called to the colors as an Army chaplain in World War II, we discovered the evidence of a considerable excavation at the dead-low water line, when we arrived in late May to do some gardening work. The excavation was nearly filled in with sand, but a ring of boulders around the edge indicated that it was not the result of a sea action or tide force.

Later I learned that a company of divers, equipped with some really scientific metal finders, working on the radar principle, had come out to explore for bronze or treasure in our waters. Their report was that they located a quantity of bronze in the deep mud of Gosport harbor, probably bronze cannon from some of the old pirate craft sunk in the harbor. In two places they located a cache of gold, buried cleverly in the sand at a point somewhat below low water. One of these was at the spot where they dug on my beach within the harbor but were frustrated by finding that so much sand had washed in that, 11 feet down, the sea water pushed in through the sand faster than their pumps could take it out. They gave up the quest for the bronze also because of the accumulation of mud on the bottom. They were not equipped to go through this depth. In both cases they realized that it was an engineering operation and were not inclined to make the necessary investment.

York, Me.   (13283   211). This is a well-protected harbor, easy of access under most conditions, whose only drawback is the considerable number of people who know about it and the strong tide in the York River.

The outer mark is a big offshore lighted whistle. However, note that a direct course from the whistle to the bell off York Harbor will take you right across York Ledge, marked with a nun and a spindle. For years that spindle, marked "pile" on the chart, has leaned at a precarious angle. Do not depend on its presence.

When you make the bell, however, entrance is easy. A course for the light on Stage Neck (286° mag.) will take you in, leaving the nuns to starboard and the cans to port. The light has a high-intensity beam on this bearing. Pass about halfway between can 7 and Stage Neck. Then, especially if the tide is running out, keep to the starboard side of the channel close to nun 8 to prevent being swept across on to the ledge marked by the beacon on the port side. The western side of Stage Neck is a steep gravel beach, of which one should be respectful.

There is no room to anchor in York, so thickly are the moorings planted. The Agamenticus Yacht Club on the eastern shore has one guest mooring but the others are all privately owned. Approach the float of York Harbor Marine Service in the cove to port between Harris Island and Bragdon Island, being sure to keep well clear of the spindle off Harris Island, especially on the ebb. Gordon Robins, the manager of the yard, may know of a vacant mooring or may have dock space for the night at a reasonable fee. Showers and laundry facilities are available here around the clock and the yard can effect repairs to hull, spars, or engine. The office listens to channel 16 VHF, so one can call ahead if in need of service.

Another resource is Donnell's, clearly labeled, near the head of the harbor. Inquire here for Thomas Fawcett, the Harbor Master, who may know of a mooring. He is officially responsible for assigning moorings, regardless of who owns the anchor and chain.

The former site of the well-known Marshall House on Stage Neck is occupied by a dressy restaurant, the Stage Neck Inn, and a condominium development. On Stage Neck, too, is the float of the Agamenticus Yacht Club. Visitors are welcome to land here but are urged to leave the dinghy for no more than thirty minutes as the float is crowded. The club runs a launch service, which it is hoped will be continued.

If you are in need of supplies, tie your skiff to the back of the float at Donnell's or Capt'n Dan's and walk the ¼ mile up town to the post office and grocery store. Along the street you will find also various antique and gift shops.

Up the bank from York Harbor Marine Service is the Dockside Dining Room, owned by David Lusty and managed by Steve Roeder. It is a pleasant place to relax over a meal ashore, with a fine view of the harbor. Behind the restaurant is a big farmhouse, now operated as Dockside Guest Quarters, providing accommodations for those who prefer to sleep ashore. It is run by David and Harriette Lusty, the entrepreneurs of the whole operation on Harris Island and reliable sources of local information. Through Mr. Lusty one can rent a car, arrange for limousine service to Logan Airport in Boston, or find out anything from bus schedules to the historic background of York County.

There is a hospital in York, should anyone be so unfortunate as to need it.

Cape Neddick Harbor, Me.   (13283   211). With increasing pressure on York and Kennebunk, Cape Neddick Harbor may be worth considering. Formerly described by the *Coast Pilot* as a "foul bight" and unworthy of consideration, it has now been buoyed and well charted. In ordinary summer weather it is an acceptable anchorage, without the heavy tide of York.

The entrance is well marked by the light on the Nubble off Cape Neddick, clearly visible by day or night and equipped with a strong fog signal. On entering the harbor, give nun 2 a generous berth, as a shoal makes off from the ledge on Weare Point to starboard. Seek an anchorage in the western or southwestern part of the harbor.

Cape Neddick Harbor offers little in the way of facilities. One can land on the beach at the head of the harbor and walk to the village of York Beach for minor supplies but, if it is used at all, Cape Neddick Harbor is useful as an overnight stop for one who does not care to face the last 4 miles to York at the end of a long day pushing into the southwest wind. In a heavy easterly, it might look like a trap.

Perkins Cove, Me.   (13286   1205 inset). Well marked with a black-and-white bell offshore and a nun and can in the entrance, Perkins Cove is nevertheless of little use to the cruising yachtsman. With any kind of a sea running, the seas cock up steeply or actually break in the entrance. Just inside, there is a footbridge, which the Harbor Master, Roy Perkins, has said, will be opened, "on request." If he is not immediately in evidence, land at the float to starboard and open the bridge yourself. Inside there is no room to anchor and there it is most unlikely that a mooring will be vacant. No guest moorings are maintained. The cove is shallow and is constantly being silted up by the river running into its head.

There is a restaurant on the east side of the harbor and there are the usual facilities in nearby Ogunquit.

Wells, Me.   (13286   1205 inset). This harbor is a prolonged disaster. It was first dredged out from the sandy estuary of the Webhannet River in 1962, and two jetties were built to keep the sand from washing in again. Year by year the jetties were extended and the channel re-dredged. Not only were the jetties ineffective, but they seem to have upset the currents, which shift sand along the beaches from Cape Ned-dick to Cape Porpoise, so that some beaches are eroding seriously and shoals build up elsewhere. In 1977, it was being proposed to dredge the harbor and channel again and install sand pumps in the channel to keep pumping out sand as it washes in.

It was proposed originally to dispose of the sand by filling salt marshes around the edge of the harbor, thus opening land for develop-ment. However, disturbance to the ecology led to the abandonment of this scheme, and the persisting sand made waterside lots less desirable than they would have been had the harbor been truly navigable.

At present (1977) the harbor is useless to cruising men, despite its breakwaters, light, and dredging. A local observer writes, "Waves crest and break between the jetties in even a moderate sea." The project is deadlocked between those who think it is the greatest disaster ever perpetrated by the Corps of Engineers and those who see in it still a great opportunity for the town. One can do little but watch it with interest—from well offshore.

The town was confronted with a serious mosquito problem, for the insects bred enthusiastically in the marshes. It was proposed to spray the marshes by airplane, but an opposition party persuaded the town to buy large numbers of dragonflies and release them in the marshes to feed on the mosquito eggs. This method proved to be remarkably successful.

Kennebunkport, Me.   (13286   1205 inset). Since the Kennebunk River was dredged in 1975–76, this is now a good alternative to Cape Porpoise. The outer mark is a flashing bell outside Fishing Rocks. The best course leaves the bell, the rock, and can 3 to port and the light on the jetty close to starboard. Proceed up the river, keeping pretty much in the middle and following the buoys. A short distance inside the entrance is the Kennebunk River Yacht Club, its anchorage protected by a jetty with a pylon on each end.

Just above can 13 on the east side of the river is Chick's Marina, usually with a slip open for a visiting yacht. It is wise to call on channel 16 VHF to be sure of space. He has electricity and water on the floats, and gasoline, Diesel fuel, ice, and water. On the wharf nearby are showers, a laundromat, a telephone, and a store selling marine supplies.

Near the bridge on the west side of the river is Reid's yard, with a marine railway and crew to make any necessary repairs. Below Reid's is the marina of Brendze and Wester. Here one may rent a slip or mooring and find showers, laundry, telephone, and a marine store. Gasoline, Diesel fuel, ice, water, and electricity are available on the float. There is a mechanic on duty most of the time and a Travelift is available here. Dockside Restaurant, well spoken of by cruising people, is nearby, and there are accommodations ashore at the Nonantum Hotel, Yachtsman's Motel, and the Village Cove Inn.

Surrounding Dock Square, near the bridge, are shops specializing in arts and crafts, in some of which a visitor can see the artist at work. If historic houses with an early nineteenth-century flavor interest you, inquire your way to the Nathaniel Lord house. About 3 miles out of town is a unique Trolley Museum, preserving a number of ancient cars that used to traverse city streets or travel crosscountry, their tracks linking cities and providing rapid and dependable mass transit. You can ride in one of these cars, traveling through the countryside in a manner remembered only by a few of us. The trip makes a worthwhile and pleasant variation from cruising.

Those of a nostalgic turn of mind might also enjoy Booth Tarkington's *Mary's Neck,* a look at Kennebunkport in the twenties, at which time Tarkington lived in the town.

Cape Porpoise, Me.   (13286   1205 inset). There is a tank marked on the chart in the midst of the town. It has a rather unusual flattened spherical shape and can be seen from far offshore. The spire is not obvious until one closes with the shore. A big, lighted whistle lies offshore, there is a bell on Old Prince Ledge further in, and a can and a nun inside that. A powerful light on Goat Island, equipped with a fog signal, makes Cape Porpoise look easy. However, there are two serious drawbacks. One is that the ledges on Goat Island and Folly Island project a long way into the channel and are submerged much of the time. Goat Island light is not on the edge of the channel but well to the north of it. One cannot head for it from the bell. There are day beacons on the edges of the channel, but in thick weather, especially at night, they would be hard to find. The *Coast Pilot* recommends giving the southerly beacon a berth of 250 feet and the northerly one a berth of 150 feet! Two yachts, one following the other, were lost on Folly Island trying to get into the harbor in an early morning fog. The writer, arriving at the whistle at 9 P.M. on a foggy night, elected to keep on for Portland lightship rather than try the entrance.

The other problem, a traditional one at Cape Porpoise, is the astronomical number of lobster traps set in the channel. On a smooth, clear day, one can pick his way through, occasionally slipping the engine into neutral to slide by a buoy too close to dodge, but under power at night, in thick weather, or on a rough day, the chances of getting through unharmed are dim. Even the Coast Guard gets wound up. The local fishermen have cages around their propellers to protect them from pot warps. The menace is so bad and the fishermen are so committed to fishing in the channel that no one would take the job of Harbor Master in 1976 because he would have to clear the traps out. Also he would have to remove all unlighted boats, even those on moorings, a Herculean task, which makes the Augean stables look easy. By 1977, a Harbor Master had been appointed, but had made no progress whatever.

After you have negotiated the ledges and the traps, anchor where there is swinging room inside the thickest of the lobster buoys. There is little to be gained by pushing up the harbor. It will be a long row to the wharf anyway and the fishermen leaving early in the morning will roll you around wherever you are.

You can land in a dinghy at a float on the far (north) side of the wharf; but it is crowded with punts and skiffs, so you may have to climb over several of them to get ashore.

There is a pay telephone on the south side of a building on the wharf.

Adjacent to the wharf are a snack shop and Spicer's Galley. This used to be a rather quick, simple, and inexpensive restaurant but has now added tablecloths, dim lights, uniformed waitresses, a bar, and considerable elegance. It is no longer inexpensive.

Gasoline and Diesel fuel can be purchased at the wharf, but one is allowed to lie alongside only long enough to fuel, as the wharf is in constant use by lobstermen and draggers. *In coming alongside be very careful of a steel "I" beam projecting over the water about 10 feet above the wharf.* Its purpose is to lower bait barrels and hoist out fish, but it will surely damage a yacht's rigging. There is room to lie clear of it.

About a mile up the road is a country grocery store, which can supply all the necessities and some luxuries. A restaurant, less elegant than Spicer's, is across the street from it.

There is no boat yard at Cape Porpoise, but help can be summoned from Reid's or Brendze & Wester in Kennebunkport.

Cape Porpoise fishermen have a reputation of being unfriendly to yachtsmen. The writer's conversations with them suggest that they are not unfriendly but are preoccupied. Their business is fishing and it keeps them busy. They have little patience with the yachtsman who lies abed until seven o'clock and interferes with their landing at the wharf at ten.

Note on Tides. Between Cape Porpoise and Cape Elizabeth, indeed all along this shore, there seems to be a current setting to the northwest on both flood and ebb. The following note, received from a correspondent many years ago, seems significant, for the tides change little over the years:

> Too much caution cannot be used when proceeding from Cape Porpoise to Portland Harbor in a fog, especially during spring tides with an easterly wind. Last summer, when lying at Wood Island waiting for a fog to clear, we saw a large schooner under a competent skipper almost bring up dead on Wood Island. The schooner had left Portland Harbor and laid out a course for Boon Island. The following day, when proceeding from Wood Island to Casco Bay, we saw a schooner high and dry on Shooting Rocks. It had come up in the fog the day before from Cape Porpoise and was putting into Portland Harbor. When these courses are laid out on the chart, it is hard to believe that such things can happen, but unfortunately these are facts of incidents that occurred in August, 1936.

The writer, as late as 1977, experienced the same set and has felt it nearly every time he has passed this way. Another correspondent, quoted on pp. 372–73, reports the same effect. This current seems to be significant even well outside the Boon Island whistle and, on the run from Cape Porpoise to the buoys off Cape Elizabeth, it is often quite strong.

Wood Island, Biddeford Pool, Me.   (13286   1205). This harbor is one to remember in a hard chance. It is marked by a powerful light, visible for many miles offshore and has a good fog signal. If approached from north of east, the water around it is quite bold. There is a black-and-white lighted whistle about 2 miles eastward of the light and a bell about ½ mile north of Wood Island. In bad weather, one would do well to make the whistle, run for the light, and follow the shore of Wood Island around the north side, keeping between the island and Negro Island Ledge. Give Negro Island a good berth and pass between it and Stage Island, on which stands a lofty pyramidal monument. Leave can 7 and the beacon on Halftide Rock to port and anchor just out of the tide to the west of the channel.

If you have a powerful engine and don't draw much over 5 feet, push up into the pool and hail Mr. Andrew Lindsay at the yacht club float on the port side. He may be able to accommodate you with a mooring, or at least show you where to anchor. The area around the yacht club was dredged in 1977 and new stone riprap installed to protect the basin from silting.

Keep clear of the big granite piers in the pool. They are icebreakers.

Ashore are a good grocery store, a fish market, and a gas station whence you can lug gasoline in cans. If you have special needs, consult with Mr. Lindsay, who is a very capable deep-water seaman and who knows the area intimately.

The Coast Guard maintains a station at Fletcher Neck.

Bus connections can be made at Biddeford for Portland and Boston. One gets to Biddeford by taxi.

The community ashore is a rather simple summer community, with some local people staying for the winter. The inhabitants of Fletcher Neck value their privacy. Consequently, when the mayor of Biddeford, in whose domain the Neck lies, came down to inspect the beach one day on legitimate business and was kicked off as a trespasser, an awkward push-pull conflict ensued. It revolved around the city's desire for a public beach. It took some Biddeford Pool Association land by eminent domain but was reluctant to pay the high price the court assigned. Just then a girls' Catholic school, right on the beach, came on the market. One plan was for the state and federal governments to buy it and lease it to the city. The city could then relinquish the association land. An educator, Elaine Crosby, who had a small school of her own, undertook to buy the Catholic school, hoping for support of the summer people, who wanted to prevent its becoming a public park. However, the whole thing fell through in the fall of 1977 and the outcome is uncertain.

Two jetties project into the Saco River from Hills Beach and Ferry Beach to keep a bar from building up. Because they are not easily visible at high water, the Coast Guard has undertaken to have a flashing red light established on the northern one and a daybeacon on the southern one. These are to be operating in 1978.

Prouts Neck, Me. (13287 231). Unless he has a particular reason for visiting Prouts Neck, the cruising man will probably pass it by. Located behind a small breakwater on the west side of the neck, it is open to a wash from Saco Bay. The yacht club is said to have a powerful mooring and to be hospitable to visitors.

Up the road a good ½ mile is the well-known Black Point Inn, where he who remembered to make a reservation and to wear coat and tie can dine in style.

A considerable walk beyond the Inn is a small store and post office.

There is a path around the neck called the Marginal Way, from which Winslow Homer painted a number of his well-known pictures. His studio is open from ten to four in the summer and is well worth a visit to one who admires his work.

Richmond Island Harbor, Me. (13287   231). This is a rather uneasy shelter west of the breakwater from Richmond Island to the shore. Because the breakwater is partly submerged at high water and because a wash works in around Richmond Island, there is usually some motion here. The best place to lie is close to the island and west of the breakwater.

One can use Seal Cove to the east of the breakwater in northerly and easterly weather, but the holding ground is said to be poor.

Richmond Island was a trading and fishing station in the earliest years of the seventeenth century.

CHAPTER X

Portland to Rockland

From gray sea fog, from icy drift,
  From peril and from pain
The home-bound fisher greets thy lights
  O hundred-harbored Maine!

General Conditions: At Cape Elizabeth, the nature of the coast changes radically. You find yourself steering east and a little north, even east and a little south, instead of northerly. The beaches of Wells and Old Orchard give way to a succession of long, rocky peninsulas, which run out underwater for miles, showing themselves again as rocky islands and breaking ledges or just as shallower readings on the fathometer.

The deep bays thus formed are peppered with ledges and studded with islands, most of them heavily wooded, and many of them uninhabited. While the North Atlantic breaks heavily on the outer islands, the inner ones form many protected harbors. In Casco, Muscongus, and Penobscot bays, most of these harbors are inhabited in the winter by lobstermen and overlaid in the summer by a heavy population of vacationists, many of them transient but many, too, who own cottages scattered along the shore. Almost every one of these small towns has a town wharf, a lobster car, and a gas pump. Some have Diesel oil. Don't plan to leave your boat alongside a lobster car any longer than necessary to fill your tank, for you will be interfering with those who come to sell lobsters, buy bait, and gas up.

Up the road you will probably find a grocery store with the necessities of life and some of the luxuries. Larger towns are likely to have hardware stores and drug stores, and the yachtier places may have a store selling marine hardware. Hard liquor is sold only in state liquor stores, found only in the larger coastal towns like Boothbay and Rockland. Beer and wine are sold in many grocery stores.

The blight of suburban yachting is spreading up the coast, but thus far you will find few marinas with acres of finger piers, few places to lie alongside and plug in your 120-volt system and your water hose. The farther east you go, the fewer of these you will find. Yacht clubs de-

399

crease in number and have simpler facilities. Rental moorings are scarcer. Land transportation is more difficult as the highways cross bridges far up the rivers and skirt the heads of the bays.

Boat yards are less frequent and major repair facilities are scattered rather thinly. However, unless you are in very serious trouble indeed, you can get help in a hurry almost anywhere between Portland and Rockland. Many lobstermen and many of the mechanics in small garages are excellent engine doctors.

The principal dangers in this area are well buoyed, and the offshore marks are big and loud. However, the less-frequented coves and reaches have many unmarked shoals and the navigator must keep constant run of his position on a large-scale chart.

Fog is more frequent as one goes eastward, developing as saturated air from offshore is cooled when it meets the colder tidal waters near the coast. It may last a week or more, but often there will be a scale-up during the middle of the day, especially up the bays and behind the islands. An accurate compass is a sine qua non. With that and a watch, one can do very well by sailing short courses for bold shores. A depth finder is an additional aid of great value and, of course, radar and loran, when they work, make practically a sure thing of fog navigation. On a foggy morning, make a leisurely start and get in two or three hours before sunset. Be very careful, and you will probably be all right. If you try to wait it out, you will probably ground on your own beer cans, for the fog will hang in and out, off and on, until the wind gets into the north and west.

This may come with a line squall or thunderstorm. The former is usually indicated by a whitish arch of cloud advancing swiftly from the northwest. It is well to reduce sail at once, tie everything down, and be sure there is no danger to leeward. It won't last long, but it can blow unbelievably hard. However, it may amount to little more than a capful of wind, a dash of rain, a bumble of thunder to the north, and the sun shining through beneath the squall.

The ensuing northwester will be cool, puffy, and clear. If the barometer has been low and a major front is coming through, it can blow hard for two or even three days with great green-and-white puffs rushing off the land and the horizon sharp as a knife. Usually, however, the northwester will begin to ease off around noon, the islands to seaward will turn from sharp green to a dusty powder blue, puffy little clouds will build over the land and the wind will die out. You may see someone up the bay still doing very well with the last of the old wind and someone offshore bending to the new. The hot calm hangs over you. Soon, however, you see a blue line of wind approaching from the southward.

The burgee lifts, you feel a cool breath, and in five minutes the sails are full and you have a jacket on.

The unstable air following a front can sometimes breed savage white squalls, which come with no warning cloud. The water to windward looks white, and in seconds the wind is up to 50 knots and you are flat on your side. These don't come often, but are worth watching for. One is enough.

Two or three times during the summer this regular rhythm of northwest followed by a southerly shift, increasing humidity, fog, and a new front is broken up by an easterly. Sometimes it is a cool, clear "dry easterly," a gift from the gods for the westward-bound skipper. It may last all day—once lasted for three days of clear southeasterly. Usually, however, the sky will cloud up, the wind may pick up to 25 knots or even more, the clouds will thicken and it will rain for twelve hours. Seldom do these summer easterlies work up any real power, but in May, June, September, and October they may land pretty hard. It is well, then, to be in a snug harbor.

Once every decade, and sometimes more frequently, a West Indian hurricane breaks out of its usual path and sweeps up the New England coast, usually in late August or September. These ladies are now forecast well in advance and their courses predicted. One first hears of their approach to the coast of Florida and need have no concern. If the hurricane passes Hatteras without recurving to the eastward, especially if there is a trough of low pressure along the New England coast, it is well to seek a landlocked anchorage. If it continues through New Jersey and hits Long Island, get all your ground tackle on the bottom, protecting yourself against the shift of wind from easterly to the north if the storm is to pass to seaward and to the south if it is to go over the land to the westward. Unbend whatever sails come easily, especially jibs, for they have a way of climbing the stay. Be sure the engine and pumps are in order, get the dinghy aboard if you can and lash it down firmly, and be ready. The capricious lady may still change course, split in half, or expire suddenly, but you will probably get six to twelve hours of a heavy wind and rain in buckets. It will be pleasant to talk about afterwards.

The uninhabited islands of Maine all belong to someone. Some are the property of The Nature Conservancy or the Audubon Society or The Friends of Nature, but except for such as are in Acadia National Park, none are public property. Therefore, they must be treated with respect. If the owner is not present, and if there are no threatening "Keep Off" signs, it is probably all right to land on an island. However, do not smoke ashore. If you build a fire, build it on the lee side below high water mark, keep it small, and douse it thoroughly. Of course, you will leave no trash around and will not disturb such local inhabitants as ospreys, herons, eider ducks, or terns.

Sometimes fishermen camp on islands in the summer to be near the lobstering. Do not judge them by the state of the camp, for these are temporary shelters only. It is well to introduce yourself when you come ashore and to make clear your intentions, for sometimes such an island is invaded by unpleasant and even destructive parties, so that the inhabitants become quite surly toward visitors.

On the whole, the local residents you meet will be pleasant and helpful people and they will keep an eye on you. Just look around carefully on any clear day and see how many lobster boats you can see. They see you and they communicate with each other on CB radio. If you need help suddenly, burn a flare and call on the CB radio.

Portland, Me. (13292   325). Approaching from the southwest under ordinary conditions, one would run for the whistle on Old Anthony Rock. In thick weather the powerful horn on Cape Elizabeth and the radio beacon and horn on the big horn buoy offshore provide cross bearings. The experience of many coastwise navigators suggests that one is likely to be set up into Saco Bay.

From Old Anthony, make the gong on Willard Rock and follow the main ship channel up the harbor.

Although Portland Harbor is a busy commercial harbor, much used by large steamers and busy fishermen, it has some advantages for the cruising yachtsman. It is easy to make in fog, bad weather, or at night. There are reasonably quiet berths at the Centerboard Yacht Club or at Marineast, to be described later. Supplies are conveniently available at supermarket prices, and the proximity to air and bus terminals makes Portland a good place at which to change crews. Some people, too, after a week or so on the boat, enjoy getting ashore to a restaurant, a movie, or a shopping center.

If you do decide to visit Portland, lie on the east side of the harbor, either off the hospitable Centerboard Yacht Club, just beyond several large oil tanks, or at Marineast. A 1977 visitor contributes the following note:

Ron Maguire's South Portland marina, Marineast, offers a very convenient central location for cruisers who wish to buy food at supermarket prices without adding an astronomical taxi fare. Within walking distance there is a large and very complete shopping center containing a Shaw's, a liquor store, hardware, and much else. Nearby are two excellent restaurants and a well-equipped, efficient camera and film processing firm. A bus stop right outside the marina puts the city of Portland very close, with its stores, theaters, and a large and growing variety of restaurants. It's a short taxi run to Portland International Jetport, which offers connections for everywhere, as does the Greyhound Bus terminal in town. Canadian and foreign charts are available at Chase, Leavitt, just off Commercial Street.

Marineast itself has a twenty-ton Travelift, which will handle boats up to 40 feet, and Pete Kellogg will work on either gas or Diesel engines. At dockside slips are hookups for electricity and water; ice, gas, Diesel fuel, and chandlery are also available. The marina monitors VHF channel 16 and works channel 9.

Entering, do not take any short cuts. After passing the South Portland Coast Guard wharf, follow carefully the instructions on charts 315 or 325 (respectively 13290 and 13292, after simplification by the Coast Guard). Stay out in the harbor till nearly abeam of the power station. Then enter the channel whose mouth is between two day beacons, and which runs parallel to the power station itself and is marked by day beacons and cans. The controlling depth is 6 feet, but the water in the marina itself, in the lagoon behind the power station, is deeper. Slips are available, but Marineast does not have moorings.

A 1976 visitor to Portland writes:

For easy access to the Portland bus station there is a Portland Town Landing on the Portland waterfront just east of the easternmost pier (not counting the abandoned piers). It has a float about 20 by 40 feet in deep water. The neighborhood is not very elegant, but it is within walking distance (if your duffle is not too heavy) of the bus station. We tied alongside briefly.

Little Diamond Island, Me. (13292   325). On this well-populated island, connected with Portland by ferry service, is the marina of Ted Rand. He maintains guest moorings, and at his wharf one can buy gasoline, Diesel fuel, water, ice, groceries, and lobsters. While not one of the most picturesque anchorages, it is a convenient place from which to start a cruise in Casco Bay.

Falmouth Foreside, Me.   (13290   315). This is the principal yachting center in Casco Bay. It is a large and rather exposed anchorage west of Clapboard Island, the site of the Portland Yacht Club and Handy Boat Service. During a brisk afternoon southwester the anchorage is choppy for a small boat, but as the wind dies late in the day, the chop dies with it. The anchorage is well protected from easterlies and north-westers, which can sometimes blow hard.

In entering south of Clapboard Island, pay careful attention to the buoys, particularly to the nuns south of Clapboard Island and to cans 15 and 17. Especially at night one is tempted to run in for the lights on the shore before clearing York Ledge, an invitation to disaster.

Hail the float at Handy's or at the Portland Yacht Club for a mooring. Except during the weekend of the Monhegan Race early in August, there is likely to be one available. If you must anchor, avoid the channel running in to Handy's float.

Both Handy's and the yacht club operate launch services. It is well to use them, as the facilities for tying dinghies are limited.

Handy's provides almost any service you can imagine. Gasoline, water, Diesel fuel, and ice are available on the wharf. Showers for yachtsmen are near the head of the wharf. There are several slips where one can lie alongside and plug in an electrical system. Two lifts, one of six-ton and one of twenty-ton capacity, facilitate any kind of repair. Carpenters, mechanics, and an electronics expert are available. Merle Hallett, the owner of the yard, also operates a sail loft, which can repair a sail on the spot or build a new one.

The Riodale Shop, also at the yard, supplies gifts, marine clothing, hardware, some books, and miscellaneous gear valuable to the cruising man. There is also a restaurant on the premises.

Up the driveway and about ½ mile to the right is a small grocery store. More extensive provisioning can be done by calling a taxi and going to Portland or to a nearby shopping center and laundromat. Portland's jetport and bus terminals are a short taxi ride away.

The yachtsman with only weekends available can leave his yacht at Handy's and commute. It is only a two-hour drive to Boston via the Maine Turnpike and by airplane one could leave New York or Washington on Friday after work and sleep aboard in Portland.

Do not try to walk across lots from Handy's to the yacht club. There is a steep and bosky gully between them, well sprinkled with poison ivy. Either walk up the driveway, to the right along the road, and down the yacht club drive, or row.

The yacht club supports a busy summer program, its most hectic weekend being that of the Monhegan Race. There are a bar and snack bar at the club, open to cruising members of other yacht clubs, and a public telephone is on a small building near the foot of the driveway.

In the main room of the clubhouse is a coffee table made from the wheel of *America* and given to the club in 1869. The way the spokes are worn on one side suggests that she had a tendency to drag to port.

The anchorage at Falmouth Foreside is a good place from which to start an exploration of Casco Bay, either sailing up the bay toward South Freeport, or east toward Jewell Island, and then up the long sounds between the points.

Yarmouth, Me. (13290 315). It is a pleasant trip up the Royal River to a basin just below the bridge at the Yarmouth Boat Yard. There used to be a sardine factory and then a clam factory just below the yard. In the event of an approaching hurricane, there is no more secure anchorage on the coast. The controlling depth is about 6 feet at mean low water.

The yard offers gasoline, Diesel fuel, ice, and water, as well as extensive repair and storage facilities. Buses to and from Boston and Portland stop at Yarmouth.

South Freeport, Me. (13290 315). This quite large and perfectly protected harbor lies nearly at the head of Casco Bay. It is the center for considerable summer activity on the mainland and on nearby Bustins Island and Mosier Island. The chief landmark for the harbor is an imitation of a medieval castle tower on the shore to the west of the harbor. Casco Castle was part of a summer hotel built in 1903 by Amos F. Gerald, a trolley car magnate, as an inducement for people to ride his trolley line from Portland. He had built and promoted a dozen such railways in Maine and was known as "the electric railroad king." In 1914 the wooden hotel burned, leaving only the tower.

There is a strong tide at the entrance to the harbor and through the anchorage. Follow the buoys carefully and avoid being set to one side or the other, even on the short runs between the inner cans. Although local boats cut Pound of Tea Island, the preferred channel leaves it to starboard. Once inside the harbor, favor the westerly side, as flats extend from the Wolfs Neck shore.

This lovely protected harbor, formed by the Harraseeket River, has become a major boating center. More than three-hundred boats are moored here in the summer. The Harraseeket Yacht Club is on your port hand after entering the harbor. The club has two guest moorings marked H.Y.C. Go in to the floats and inquire their location. Water (of excellent quality), is available at the floats and there is a phone in the clubhouse. Because the tide runs swiftly, it is advisable to pick up a mooring if possible. The club sponsors a junior sailing program in which fifty to sixty young sailors participate each summer. The program is conducted by a sailing instructor and two assistants. Formal series racing is in Lasers, Rhodes 19's and Ensigns.

As you proceed into the harbor, you will pass Ring's Marine, the Town Landing and Harraseeket Marine Service. Ring's Marine has electricity, water, fuel, and ice at the floats, plus mooring service and a recently installed Travelift. Ring's also services inboard and outboard motors.

An experienced yachtsman of many years' standing on the coast slipped alongside Ring's float. One of the Ring brothers asked,

"Have you been around the Bay before?"

"I've sailed this coast for thirty-six years," announced the skipper proudly.

"You're learnin,' " was the laconic reply.

The town landing is not a good place to tie up for long, because of commercial traffic.

Harraseeket Marine Service (beyond the town landing), is a full-service marina having fuel, water, ice, and electricity available at the floats. Available on shore are a Travelift, a mechanic for engine service, a new laundromat and shower building, as well as a fully stocked chandlery, with everything from charts and foul-weather gear to Evinrudes and radio telephones. They rent moorings and charter small sail- and powerboats.

Harraseeket Lunch, located at the Town Landing, serves hamburgers, lobster, seafood platters, and the best chocolate cream pie on the coast. Food is served takeout style and there are tables inside as well as out.

Up the hill from the town landing ¼ mile is the village grocery store and the post office.

Should one wish to visit the famous L.L. Bean's sporting goods store, call their sales room (865-3111) for a lift up and back. The store is always open and is a center for clothes, camping equipment, canoes, boots, hunting and fishing gear, and outdoor equipment of all kinds. The prices are high but the quality is usually outstanding.

The Harbor Master is David Shorey.

If one has to lie over in South Freeport, he can take the ferry to the summer colony on Bustins Island for a pleasant boat ride and a good walk ashore.

Mere Point, Me. (13290 315). There is a small marina and boat yard on the west side of Mere Point. Gasoline, ice, and water are available but no Diesel fuel. The float is a high-water proposition for most boats, since there are only a couple of feet alongside at low water. A marine railway accommodating boats up to about 40 feet affords repairs.

The Goslings, Me. (13290 315). For a good anchorage when in the area of Upper and Lower Goose Islands, run in between Irony Island and Grassy Ledge and anchor between the Goslings and Lower Goose Island. This is well protected and the holding ground is good. The Northeast end of Irony Island makes out quite a way, so give it plenty of room.

Jewell Island, Me. (13290 315). Between the northern point of this island and a small island to the west of it is a well-protected anchorage. This harbor is the nearest to the direct route across the bay, and to the westward-bound yachtsman it means losing the least possible distance to windward in return for a quiet night. The cove is often crowded on summer weekends.

From the west, make the bell off Cliff Island and follow the shore of Jewell Island, keeping far enough offshore to avoid the ledges south of the old wharf. This structure is now so decayed as to be unsafe. Picnic parties still use its pilings as moorings, but one certainly should not try to land on it. Continue off the west shore of Jewell Island and the west shore of the little island with the house on it. This island makes off a long way to the northeast. Do not turn in until you can see the big square boulder on West Brown Cow. If it is hazy, you will have to go by the lobster traps, the fathometer, and a good lookout.

Run up the middle of the cove, favoring the bold eastern shore. There is about 10 feet of water abreast the house on the little island and a little above it. There are several pilings in the mud toward the head of the cove. The first of these is covered at high water and the other is dry at low water. Stay well to the north of them.

From the east, pass between Halfway Rock and the nun on Drunkers Ledge, working far enough to the north as you approach to see the southeast corner of Cliff Island. Do not overdo it, as West Brown Cow makes out a long way. Continue past the end of Jewell Island and turn up the cove. In coming from the east in thick weather, be particularly careful of the ledges on the east side of the island. They make out a long way and are usually submerged. The writer has left some red paint here.

From the anchorage at Jewell Island, walk across the northern point to the Punchbowl. At low tide the water is trapped here and tempered somewhat by the sun. There is a nice beach, too. From the southern end of this cove, next to a large white rose bush, runs a well-defined trail, once a Jeep road, to the lookout towers at the southern end of the island. From the concrete towers on a clear day one can see all of Casco Bay, a view well worth the walk and climb. These towers were built during World War II as part of a coast defense battery to protect

Portland. Bring a flashlight and explore the tunnels in the gun positions beyond the towers, but beware of open manholes.

The southern end of the island is steep, and in some places there are caves and cliffs of rather loose, rotten rock. It is overgrown with juniper, wild roses, raspberry bushes, and other prickly vegetation, so don't try it in short pants.

Mr. W.S. Carter and several friends visited Jewell Island in a fishing sloop in 1858. He wrote:

> As cooked by the Pilot, we pronounced the haddock excellent; and after dinner we raised the anchor, hoisted sail, and cruised idly among the islands till near sunset, when we put into a delicious little cove—narrow, deep, and shady—on Jewell's Island. As we glided in, an old fisherman who resided on the island came alongside in his dory to have a little chat, and gave us a magnificent lobster, which went immediately into the pot for supper. After coming to anchor, we all went ashore in our boat, except the Pilot, who was detained on board by his duties as cook, to explore the island, witness the sunset, and get milk, eggs, and butter from a farmhouse near our landing-place.
>
> The island, which lies about ten miles east of Portland, seemed to be fertile and well cultivated. The farmhouse was built on elevated ground and the view of the sunset and of the island-studded bay was superb. Fresh and sweet were the eggs and milk and butter with which we returned to our sloop and very jolly the supper we had in the little cabin. The evening was pleasantly cool, and the Assyrian, remarking that boiled lobster was not wholesome unless well qualified with something acid, availed himself of the Pilot's steaming teakettle and brewed a pitcher of hot lemonade with a strong infusion of whiskey which he administered to each of us in proper doses, as a sure preventive against any ill effects from our supper.

Great Chebeague Island, Me. (13290   315). One fairly good anchorage is off the "Lobster Beach" west of the northeastern end of the island. There is a picturesque group of fishermen's shacks on the beach, but it's a bit rough for bathing. There is a better bathing beach on the east side of the island near its northeast end, which is known as Hamilton Beach. A path leads southeast from the "Lobster Beach" to the island's main road.

If seeking supplies or communications, anchor off the stone wharf, but watch the depth, as it is shallow there.

The social center for this part of the island is at Riddle's store at the head of the wharf and at the Hillcrest Hotel, up a hill a couple of hundred yards from the store. The hotel, an ancient hostelry, is well spoken of. It is the only hotel on the island. A sporty nine-hole golf course is close by the stone wharf. There is a public telephone on the wharf, and water, oil, and gasoline are available. The post office is nearby to the south. The store is open from 8 A.M. to 5:30 P.M. Monday through Saturday, and from 10:30 A.M. to 12:30 P.M. on Sunday. Taxi service is available there.

A ferry, the *Polly Lin,* runs frequently to Cousins Island, the quickest access to the mainland and transportation. Another ferry takes automobiles back and forth to Cousins Island but can land at Chebeague at high tide only. The Casco Bay Line steamer to and from Portland calls at Chandler Cove at the island's western end four times a day.

At Rose's Point, on the eastern shore near the island's center and behind Crow Island, there is a small boat yard with only 2 feet of water at low tide.

Chebeague Island, the largest in Casco Bay, like many attractive Maine vacation spots, now harbors retired families, who are winterizing their summer cottages and living there the year round.

South Harpswell, Potts Harbor, Me. (13290   315). This is a large harbor and at high water it gives the impression of being rather unprotected. However, when the tide goes and the ledges bare out, it is doubtful if a dangerous or even unpleasant sea would make into the anchorage.

From the west, enter between Upper Flag Island and Horse Island. From the east, follow the chain of buoys from Merriconeag Sound. Note that the channel lies *close* to the east of cans 1A and 3.

On the west shore of the harbor is Dolphin Marina, operated by Mel Saxton. Gas and Diesel oil are available at his float. There is a restaurant nearby, and a marine supply store. Ice can be provided with a little advance notice. A mooring will likely be available.

Harpswell Harbor, West Harpswell, Me. (13290   315). This is a well-protected anchorage on the eastern shore of Harpswell Neck. In anything but a northeaster it affords good protection. There is a depth of about 12 feet at the town float, but there are no facilities for yachtsmen. The Merriconeag Yachting Association, which formerly had its headquarters here, has sold its property to private parties. The association will continue to run a racing program but can offer no facilities for visitors. A local resident writes: ". . . the people are friendly, so I am sure that if a visiting yacht needed to use a phone, the new owner of the MYA property and others who have docks would be glad to have them come ashore."

Mackerel Cove, Bailey Island, Me. (13290   315). This is a comparatively easy harbor to make at night, with lights on Halfway Rock and Little Mark Island, a lighted gong on Turnip Ledge, and a diminutive flasher in the harbor mouth. Watch for the two peaks of Drunkers Ledges, one marked by a beacon and the other by a nun. In clear weather the most useful mark for the entrance is a pair of Coast Artillery observation towers. These are shown on chart 13288 (1204) but not on 13290 (315). However, they are close behind the house, which is shown on the latter chart. The harbor is open to the southwest and any southerly tends to make the anchorage uneasy. The further in you go, the less swell you feel. But the anchorage is crowded, especially at the time of the "Annual Bailey Island Tuna Tournament," held the last full week in July. The holding ground is good.

On the west side of the cove is Dockside, formerly Merrill's Wharf. Dockside is a marina and restaurant, with overnight cabins owned by Stewart Place. Fuel, water, and ice are available at the floats. Marine hardware and charts are sold at the Ships Stores.

Ask Mr. Place about a vacant mooring.

The best place for repairs is Skillings's Boat Yard, next to Dockside. Bill Skillings is an accomplished mechanic.

In the past, Casco Bay Lines has provided regular steamer service from Portland to Mackerel Cove and other Casco Bay landings. In 1977, it was expected that this service would continue, but the operation is marginal and the future of the service is in doubt.

Mackerel Cove has been the headquarters of an annual Tuna Tournament. Charter boats are available and, if you are rigged for tuna, a guide can be found to go with you.

The Orrs-Bailey Yacht Club located behind Cooks Point in the cove west of Wills Gut can, in a pinch, offer gasoline and a mooring to a member of a recognized yacht club, but its facilities are strained by its own membership. Ex-Commodore George Fisher recommends Long Cove at the north end of Orrs Island as a snug anchorage. The upper ⅔ of it is bare at low water but local fishermen use it as a hurricane hole. The entrance is starred with ledges, so proceed with caution.

Quahog Bay, Me. (13290   315). This is a lovely spot to spend a day, especially if you have children aboard. Enter either from Ridley Cove north of Yarmouth Island or from the south. Avoid the ledges north of Pole Island and south of Center Island. An easterly course, leading to a point between Snow Island and the point south of it, carried the writer safely in. Anchor either north or south of Snow Island. The holding ground is good, the protection excellent. The swimming has none of the numbing, breathless quality of the offshore islands. There are flounders to be caught, and there are beautiful protected coves to explore with an outboard or sailing dinghy. Although there have been ugly rumors of an impending development, in 1971, there were only a few scattered cottages on the western shore.

Cundys Harbor, Me. (13290   315). This is a small harbor, well protected in anything but a heavy easterly, and devoted mostly to local lobstering and to summer cottages, rather than the transient trade. There is a store where limited supplies are available, but there is no gas, water, or Diesel oil on the wharves. Local fishermen lug their gas in cans.

The Basin, Me. (13290   315). This is an attractive anchorage off the eastern side of the New Meadows River and a favorite with many. A frequent visitor warns that one should keep to the *outside* of the bends on entering, where the tide scours the channel. Also he warns of a rock almost in the middle of the anchorage. Although this is shown on the chart, it has picked up yachts in the past.

A visitor to The Basin in 1974 contributes the following description of the rock in the entrance:

> On entering The Basin from the New Meadows River, I found that the rock which is marked on the chart was above water, in fact had a seagull on it. This seemed to offer an opportunity to look it over for future reference. About 75 feet north of the rock the bottom came up rather suddenly and I decorated the granite with red bottom paint and a bit of lead. The rock, which is marked with a single asterisk is, I would estimate, over 100 feet long, extending roughly north-south. It appears to be a continuation of the two nearest points of land. Later the tide went down further and a second part of the rock, about 40-50 feet north of the one which appeared first, also showed above water, in fact, a couple of seals indicated its location before it broke the surface.

Sebasco, Me. (13290 315). Here is a good anchorage behind Harbor Island and its outlying ledges, although on a heavy southerly it might be uncomfortable. In entering, keep in the middle. Both shores are studded with ledges, the ones on Harbor Island making out much farther than one might expect from looking at the chart. One of the outer rocks has a locally maintained spindle on it. It is difficult to find at high water, but when you do find it, give it a good berth.

Sebasco Lodge, the prominent hotel on the eastern shore, maintains guest moorings. These are heavy white spars. The ones in front of the float on the east side are more convenient, but if there is any chop running in the harbor, one can be secure and comfortable on one of the western ones. They are 5000-pound granite blocks. Consult the Harbor Master.

Although Sebasco is far from the direct course across Casco Bay, one who takes the time to run up the bay will find a float with 6 feet at mean low water. Gasoline is piped to it. Water is available in an emergency. Just up the shore from the float is a snack bar open from 10 A.M. to 11:30 P.M., at which anything short of a full-course dinner is available. The hotel will supply the latter. Adjacent to the snack bar is a comfortable lounge for visiting cruisers, with a telephone booth, laundromat, and luxurious showers opening off it.

One could lie here a week without exhausting the possibilities for entertainment and diversion, all of which are available to visitors by arrangement. Off the float lies a fleet of Tech. dinghies for sailing around the harbor. Ashore there are a swimming pool, a nine-hole golf course, tennis courts, and bowling alleys. Movies and dances, both square and otherwise, are frequently scheduled.

If you are in need of supplies, consult the Harbor Master. The hotel sends a station wagon to Bath to meet guests known to be arriving on buses.

Alvin Brewer has a small boat shop at Sebasco and can take care of ordinary repairs.

If possible, leave Sebasco on the first of the ebb, keep to the eastern shore down to Cape Small, and get a fine lift to windward from the tide. It runs briskly down the New Meadows River and faster than that out of the Kennebec (see note on the entrance to the Kennebec). Across Sheepscot Bay the ebb tide sets to the south or southeast and is less important to the eastward-bound yacht.

Attractive as Sebasco is in moderate weather, in a strong southerly it is likely to be rough. Although you are probably safe enough on one of the big moorings, you will be much more comfortable in the Basin, Cundy's Harbor, or the pond at Small Point.

Small Point Harbor, Me.   (13290   315). This harbor is the first in Casco Bay for the westward-bound navigator and requires giving up the least distance to windward of any shelter in the bay. Also it is the first

The entrance to Cape Small Point pond at high water. Goose Rock is in the lower center. Notice the sea making into the outer harbor.

shelter west of Boothbay, unless you want to lie in the tide of the Kennebec. Otherwise, it has little to recommend it. The outer harbor is a roll-hole, as the aerial photo shows. The best place to anchor is off the beach northeast of Goose Rock, but that is not really very quiet. The coves on the north shore are no better.

Local boats and cruising men of courage follow the channel east of Goose Rock up into the pond, a perfectly protected anchorage. A glance at the chart and the aerial photograph makes the entrance look worse than it is. The writer sounded it out at low water in 1977 and developed the following directions, which he believes to be reliable. Try to make the trip on a coming tide. The first part is the worst.

Head southerly between Goose Rock and the eastern shore, keeping about in the middle. There are numerous small racing boats moored on both sides of the channel, helping to define it. When you get about abreast of the southernmost white rocks on Goose Rock, and the first white rocks on the shore, swing sharply to the eastward, heading for a windblown pine tree in a patch of bushes just to the southward of a big white house with three dormers. Thus you avoid first a sandbar, which comes out from the eastern side, and then a long gravel bar extending almost from Goose Rock to the shore. Follow the eastern shore, keeping just outside the lobster traps, by the wharf, by a little gray house with a single-pitched roof, to the speed-limit sign at the end of the trees. Then ease out into the middle and keep in the more-or-less straight channel limited by anchored boats. Anchor where the channel widens out into the pond.

The pond is perfectly protected, exposed only to attacks of voracious mosquitoes, which breed in the extensive marshes on Cape Small.

Do not count on supplies at this anchorage. In an emergency, no doubt someone would give you a lift to the store.

Other Anchorages in Casco Bay. There are many other anchorages in Casco Bay, which the adventurous explorer can find for himself, and which he would thank the writers to leave unmentioned. However, we might point out a few in passing.

Winnegance Bay in the New Meadows River; Ridley Cove, the cove east of Wills Gut; Reed Cove on the west side of Orrs Island; Waquoit Bay; and Chandler Cove on Chebeague Island.

The Kennebec River
(13293   314)

Inside or Outside Seguin: When the eastward-bound mariner passes Cape Small and leaves Casco Bay, he must decide whether to go inside Fuller Rock, along the Cape Small shore, across the mouth of the Kennebec, and eastward through the passage between the Sisters and the Black Rocks, or whether to go outside Fuller Rock, outside Mile Ledge and Seguin, and across to the Cuckolds. The decision must be made largely on the basis of local conditions.

The inside route is shorter, and one is likely to find smoother water and more wind under the land. Under ordinary conditions, the inside route is preferable. However, if a strong ebb tide is running and the usual gentle southwester has worked itself up into a real breeze of wind, the tremendous rush of water pouring out of the river against the wind and sea can raise a short, high chop between Jackknife Ledge and the Sisters, which can be dangerous to a small yacht. It would be wise to go well outside Seguin under these conditions.

Also, if the weather is thick, there is a good deal to be said for keeping offshore. There is a magnetic disturbance for a mile or so around Ellingwood Rock, just north of Seguin, a disturbance which may not be evident at all, but which may set the compass off as much as a point (11°). The tide in the mouth of the river runs hard enough to set a yacht running for the lighted bell right down on Seguin Ledges. The flood tide could set one up on Whaleback or the Black Rocks. Allowance for the tide is guesswork at best. It is much easier and safer to make Fuller Rock and run for Mile Ledge bell, with the horn on Seguin for a guide, and then to square away for the Cuckolds. Its horn is not much good to windward, but there is a radio beacon on the light, which is very helpful, and a bell outside the light. Tom Rock is the only obstruction, and except on a very heavy flood tide and light air, it should cause no trouble. The writer once passed north of the Sisters and between Ellingwood Rock and Seguin in a breeze in which he should have been reefed. Even with a strong ebb tide, the situation was manageable. However, another yachtsman in similar circumstances twisted off his rudder post, went ashore on Whaleback, and lost his boat in a smoky sou'wester.

The following account from Carter's *New England Coast* describes a squall off Seguin in 1858:

The mouth of the Kennebec River. The best channel is east of Pond Island at the lower right and thence close by the old fort.

We made sail at once in the direction of Boothbay, but in the course of a couple of hours the wind rose to a gale. The sea grew very rough, and almost every minute a wave would break over our vessel and, sweeping along the deck, deluge the cockpit with water. We closed the cabin to keep it dry, and, gathering at the stern, watched the sea, not without anxiety. The air was so thick with mist that we could see nothing but the raging waves around us, and could not tell where we were going, though the sloop was plunging along at a fearful rate, her bows almost continually under water and her mast opening wide cracks at every tug of the sails. There was considerable danger of the mast's going overboard. In that case we should have been completely at the mercy of the waves, on a coast every inch of which was rock-bound, so that, if our vessel struck, she would be pounded to pieces in ten minutes.

We drove madly along, the grim old Pilot at the helm, and the anxious Skipper, arrayed in oilskin to shed the wet, clinging to the mast and keeping a sharp lookout ahead. Suddenly the mist rose and rolled away before a sweeping blast, and then we saw Seguin light-house, and knew where we were. It was a superb and terrible sight —these wild reefs with the waves foaming and flashing over them, directly in our course. It was growing late, and the gale was on the increase. The sea was white with foam on the surface, but the great waves, as they came leaping and roaring at us, had a black and angry look not pleasant to behold. Our aged Pilot, as he sat clutching the helm, his hat drawn tightly over his brows to keep it from blowing off, glanced uneasily from time to time at the laboring and groaning mast, whose wide seams were alternately opening and shutting, but he said nothing. He had weathered many a harder gale, though never in so poor a craft. The Assyrian, clinging to the cover of the cabin for support, and with strong symptoms of seasickness in his face, at length broke out as a whooping billow swept over us, soaking him from head to foot:

"I say, Skipper, this is coming rather strong. Can't we put in some-where?"

The Skipper had been for some minutes watching a large schooner about a mile ahead of us, and coming aft, said that it was hardly possible to weather Cape Newagin in such a storm, even if our mast held, about which he had great doubts. The schooner ahead of us was running for shelter into Sheepscut Bay, where there was an excellent harbor, and we could easily follow her in. The Pilot, after an emphatic reference to "that damned old stick," as he called the mast, assented to this opinion, and our course was accordingly changed to the north-ward.

Following the lead of the schooner for several miles, we reached about nightfall a beautiful and perfectly sheltered harbor, which the Skipper called sometimes Southport and sometimes Abenacook.

For a lighter view of this desperate passage we add the following yarn (the source is unknown to the writer):

An old gentleman, who had been fishing all his life and who had wrung more water out of the cuffs of his pants than most of us have ever sailed over, made a little money in the summer taking summer boarders sailing in his sloop.

One day it breezed up southwest near Seguin and got pretty choppy. Spray was flying and she began to take water into the cockpit. The passengers were frightened, and finally one said, "Cap'n, we think you ought to offer prayer for our safety."

"I don't b'lieve that'll be necessary," answered the skipper, easing her over a sea.

"Well, we feel that it is your duty as captain of this boat to ask for Divine help and guidance in this emergency."

"All right," answered the skipper, "I'll do what I can if it'll ease you any." So with both hands on the tiller and the passengers kneeling around him, the captain prayed,

"Lord, I never have interfered in your affairs and you have always used me right. But these people have asked me to speak with you. Now I know we'll get in all right, but if you would like to make these people feel a lot better, you can go ahead and calm the waters. But just remember, Lord, this isn't the Sea of Galilee. This is the North Atlantic Ocean."

Our considered advice to those passing Seguin is to go inside unless a considerable sea is running or visibility is bad.

Seguin Island, Me. (13293   314). Seguin Island is the outer mark for the Kennebec. It is surmounted by a powerful fixed white light, easily visible from the deck of a small boat soon after one passes the Portland horn buoy. The island itself is well worth a visit. The cove on the northern side is satisfactory protection on a moderate day. There is a heavy Coast Guard mooring to which a visitor may make fast, although the tide is likely to set you up against the post. Anchoring is possible, although the water is deep and the bottom rocky. Give the point on the eastern side of the cove a generous berth. Shoal water extends north and east.

There is a rough beach at the head of the cove and a boathouse with skids running down into the water. Landing on the beach is probably easier than trying to get a dinghy onto skids made for a Coast Guard peapod. A railway and walk runs up the island, ending at the light. From here, one can see from Monhegan to Cape Elizabeth; and on a clear day, the White Mountains stand up grandly. There are spectacular cliffs on the west side and from the grassy knoll on the north end of the island, poets, painters, and philosophers can contemplate a remarkably sane portion of what, from other points of view, may seem a mad world.

Fort Popham. Although it is possible to enter the river west of Pond Island and the aerial photograph makes this course appear logical, the better passage is east of the island. Practically speaking, you must have either a fair wind or a fair tide to get into the river under sail. With both, you will be hurried by Popham Beach, the fort, and the abandoned Coast Guard station. The grim-looking fort was built during the Civil War to protect the river, Bath in particular, from attack by the South. It has been called facetiously Maine's greatest compliment to the Confederate Navy.

However, it should be remembered that a Confederate naval vessel seized several vessels off the Maine coast, and in one of them a crew slipped into Portland harbor and cut out the fast revenue cutter *Caleb Cushing.* After a spectacular chase, the Confederates were at length defeated, but there certainly was reason to be concerned about Confederate forces at one time.

The Sabino peninsula appears in the early history of our country several times. In 1582, one David Ingram was interviewed by Sir Humphrey Gilbert, then interested in establishing a colony in New England. Ingram had been with Hawkins at the battle of San Juan d'Ulloa near Vera Cruz in 1568. Having been very roughly handled in the battle, Hawkins had neither vessels nor stores sufficient to take his entire expedition to England. Ingram preferred to be set ashore rather than attempt the passage. He walked all the way to St. John, New Brunswick, where he was picked up by a French vessel and taken home. The stenographic account of his conversation with Gilbert, printed in Hakluyt's first edition and reprinted in Ida Sedgwick Proper's *Monhegan, Cradle of New England,* contains the following:

> Taking me into his canoe, we paddled across eastward from the place which he called Sabino to a peninsula which he called Pemcuit

[Pemaquid] and where we rested over that night. When the morning broke, I saw not far to seaward, a great island that was backed like a whale.

Although Hakluyt dropped Ingram's account from later editions as "a tissue of lies," there can be little doubt that he visited Sabino, Pemaquid, and New Harbor, and that he saw Monhegan.

In 1605, Champlain visited Sabino twice, once ascending the Kennebec and descending the Sasanoa and Sheepscot. He named Seguin "La Tortue" because of its resemblance to a tortoise.

In 1605 Waymouth and Rosier were on the coast (see Georges Harbor, page 471). They kidnapped five Indians, who, with Rosier, recommended to Gorges and Popham of the Plymouth Company a site on the St. George River for a permanent colony. But in 1606 Martin Pring visited the coast and wrote what must have been a glowing account of the Kennebec. Unfortunately Pring's account is lost, but we know that it caused Gorges and Popham to send to Sabino, in the spring of 1607, two ships and 120 men, led by Ralegh Gilbert, Sir Humphrey's son, and old John Popham, who was eighty years old.

The colony was well equipped and provisioned. It was going to a site well known. The natives were friendly and anxious to trade. The economic basis of the colony, salt cod, furs, and spar timber, was sound. The expedition was well financed, well manned, and well led. During the summer a number of houses were built and the *Virginia,* the first vessel built in New England, was launched and sent out to explore Penobscot and Casco bays. The winter was hard, but far from intolerable, in spite of the loss by fire of a storehouse. Old John Popham died, to be sure, but young in heart as he was, it is not surprising, in view of his age. Even in Maine a man of eighty can succumb. In the spring a vessel arrived from England with more men and supplies, but with the sad news that Ralegh Gilbert's half brother had died. Gilbert decided to return to England to take care of his inheritance. Popham was dead. Without leadership the colony disintegrated, some returning to England and others going south to Jamestown in the *Virginia.* It seems ironic that the English colony with the best chance of survival did not last, while Jamestown, badly led, badly manned, starved and diseased, and with no strong economic resources, survived and eventually prospered.

Apparently the colony was not a complete failure, however, for Humphrey Damerill, one of the colonists, soon after established a store and fishing station at Damariscove. To Damariscove came the distressed Pilgrims in 1621 and received open-handed help.

The best anchorage at Fort Popham is behind the fort in the mouth of Atkins Bay. Get in behind the hook just enough to get out of the tide. The place has silted up badly, so proceed with caution. Land on the beach. On the ebb tide the swimming is good on Popham Beach below the fort. If the bluefish are running, they can sometimes be caught off the beach.

The River to Bath. The big white house on Gilbert Head, the southern extremity of Long Island, was inhabited at one time by the Etniers: Elizabeth, the author, and Stephen, the painter.

From here the passage up the river is clearly marked and picturesque. The high wooded banks, open farm lands and pretty villages make it something out of a picture book. To sail up here with a fair wind and a flood tide is about as pleasant a way to spend a summer afternoon as has been conceived by the mind of man.

Above the high land of Parker Head is Parker Flats, where schooners used to anchor, waiting for a fair wind and a fair tide to get out of the river. Below Fiddler Reach, on the western shore, is Morse's Cove, where Benedict Arnold's fleet lay in 1775 with the soldiers and supplies for his assault on Quebec via the Kennebec and Chaudiere. The cove today is still the best anchorage below Bath, although the tide circles around the shore. The southwest corner of the cove is the best place, and a second anchor, even a small kedge, is advisable to prevent ranging all over the cove as the tide turns.

Bath, Me. (13296   230). At Bath you will see the Bath Iron Works on the western shore. This yard built naval vessels, mostly cruisers and destroyers, during both world wars and also J.P. Morgan's steam yacht *Corsair* and Harold Vanderbilt's *Ranger,* the last of the J-class defenders of the America's Cup. Recently the yard has built a series of huge container ships.

During the war, when the present writer was working at the Iron Works building destroyers, a naval expediter arrived to inspect the yard. From one of the tall crane towers he and the yard superintendent surveyed the busy scene below.

"And how many men are working here?" asked the expediter.

"About half of them," replied the dour down-caster.

Long before the Iron Works was established, vessels were built at Bath, one of the most famous being the six-masted schooner *Wyoming.* She was the largest wooden vessel ever constructed. Bound east from Norfolk with about 5000 tons of coal, she was lost in a gale in Nantucket Sound. It was thought that, lying to her anchors, her bow was torn off by the strain. Either that or she was run down by a steamer.

The Bath Marine Museum has documents and artifacts chronicling the history of shipbuilding at Bath and is well worth a half-day's investigation. The Apprenticeshop, under the leadership of Lance Lee, is teaching modern boys and girls to build wooden vessels with hand tools, and is turning out some admirable work, both educationally and in other respects. The Muscongus Bay sloop *Charity,* built at the Apprenticeshop, won the Friendship Sloop Regatta in 1977. Her skipper, David Tew, is in charge of the newly established Restoration Shop.

There is a small yard and marina below the Iron Works and Percy & Small's, on the west bank, marked by a large orange Gulf sign. It is operated by Bob Mansfield, a former dissatisfied resident of New York City. The yard has moorings and doubtless, by 1978, will have slips where transients can lie alongside. Fuel and ice are available at the floats, and boats can be hauled for repair. A large steel building has been erected for winter storage and an office-showroom-chandlery is being built adjoining the storage building. Rental moorings and guest moorings are available; however, pick up a mooring as close to shore as possible to avoid the current.

Above the Carlton bridge, for which the signal is a long blast and a short one, is Longreach, another marina run by very accommodating people. They maintain several moorings and often have a slip vacant. They provide gasoline, Diesel fuel, ice, and water on the wharf, have a marine store and sales room for boats and trailers, and are only steps from supermarket, hardware store, laundry, Sears-Roebuck, and all the delights of the city of Bath. Note that Bath is a Customs Port of Entry.

Above Bath the river runs rapidly between high banks. There is a narrow place at Thorne Head where the tide is really inspiring. There are several anchorages among the little islands below Lines Island where one can get out of the tide to some extent. However, after passing The Chops, the tide becomes much less, the banks become lower, and the river widens out into the broad and shallow Merrymeeting Bay formed by the confluence of the Kennebec and the Androscoggin. This bay is inhabited by ducks and geese of many species. In the fall, when the migrants from further north come through, the bay and the marshes are positively crowded. It is a delightful place.

Above the bay, behind Pork Point, is another possible anchorage in lovely surroundings and there is another behind Carney Point on the east side. The preferred passage lies east of Swan Island. This large and lovely island is a game preserve. Deer can frequently be seen as one penetrates further and further into rural Maine.

At the head of Swan Island is an anchorage at the town of Richmond, just below the bridge. The town is a quiet spot, even in the summer time. There is a landing and the usual supplies are available.

If you are not planning to stop here and the bridge does not open on the usual signal of three blasts of the horn, land at Richmond and look up the bridge tender. You will find it an interesting experience.

At Pittston, on the east bank, just below South Gardiner, is a landing and a red house high on the hill overlooking it. This is Colburn's yard, the place where Arnold's soldiers were put ashore, where they picked up bateaux, and whence they plunged into the wilderness in the fall of 1775. The house on the hill is the headquarters of the Arnold Expedition Historical Society, whose enthusiastic president is White Nichols. The house is becoming a good museum and the people in charge are well worth visiting.

The river winds on past Gardiner and Farmingdale to Augusta, the head of navigation. If you feel that you are a long way from salt water here, take the first of the ebb and, with a northerly breeze or a modest engine, you can be off Seguin or the Cuckolds in six hours.

Harmon Harbor, Me. (13295 238) (13293 314). This is a pleasantly neglected cove on the western shore of the Sheepscot River above Griffith Head. The entrance is narrow, between a nun and a bare rock. However, there is plenty of water and there is room enough inside for a yacht to round up and anchor. There are a few small boats and a float near the head of the harbor. The big hotel was not operating at last reports. It is a short walk to the store at Five Islands. There is a little motion in the anchorage at high water but the further up the harbor you go, the less there is.

Five Islands, Me. (13293 314) (13295 238). The easiest entrance to this pleasant and picturesque harbor is north of Malden Island, which has a prominent high white rock on its northeastern side. There is a red-and-black horizontally striped buoy in the entrance that, contrary to the usual custom, should be passed close to on either side. It marks a rock that the *Coast Pilot* declares has 11 feet over it at low water, so for most cruising boats the matter is academic anyway. The old *Coast Pilot* claimed 8 feet, and at a really low moon tide one might bounce.

An alternate entrance is from the north, leaving the red beacon on Crow Island close to port as a ledge makes out from the Georgetown shore.

Inside there is a considerable fleet of small yachts and lobstermen, but there is room to anchor. In the past, the local yacht club has maintained two guest moorings marked FIYC. In 1977, the letters were obliterated but the buoys, red balloons, remained. In ordinary summer conditions the harbor provides excellent protection, although a heavy southerly sends in a roll.

A local yachtsman contributed the following note in 1976:

> There is a town landing on the west shore with 10 feet at low water. The town float is at the south side of the wharf, the float further south being private. At the head of the wharf is the general store, operated by Ray and Alice Grover. Here groceries, provisions, gas, ice, mail, and telephone service are available. Ray will also obtain supplies from Bath if they are not available at the store. On the wharf itself, Maynard and Eleanore Thibodeau provide cooked or live lobsters and clams. The next wharf to the north is that of the Sheepscott Boat Company. Here Billy Plummer provides gas, moorings, repairs, and marine supplies. His lift will accommodate boats up to 4000 pounds.

Many older cruising men well remember Five Islands as the home port of the big Friendship sloop *Sky Pilot,* sailed for many years by the late Rev. Nehemiah Boynton and his family. She was built in 1909 by Jean McClain at Round Pond and was used by the Boyntons until World War II. She sank, then, in the Little Sheepscot behind MacMahan Island. Mason Carter raised her, and Frank L. Sample, Jr. ballasted her with 9000 axe heads, and sold her to Richard Swanson of Rockport, Massachusetts. She was renamed *Jolly Buccaneer* and was one of the most beautiful and picturesque in the fleet at the annual homecoming of the Friendship Sloop Society.

She was sold in 1966 to a group who used her to smuggle narcotics from Cuba. She was captured and attached by the government and sank at her wharf. She is a total loss.

Because the locale of the story is off the mouth of the Sheepscot River, this is as good a place as any to insert a yarn spun to the authors by Rev. Edward Boynton of Essex, Connecticut, a son of the late Dr. Boynton.

> You see, it was this way:
> One day last summer [1945] Al Gould came over in his sloop *Curlew* and was seated on my porch at Five Islands and we were talking of those matters of important and mutual interest which always come to mind when sailor friends of many years get together, where they can look at the rocks and the skies and the running waters of the Maine coast. He said: "Did you ever hear about Captain John Snow of

Rockland and the time he moved the old house from Phippsburg on the Kennebec around outside and up to Rockport?" I had never heard about that time, and even if I had, I would have shamelessly feigned ignorance. For *any* story which Al tells is worth repeating. And this was no exception! So he went on:

"There was a summer fellow up at Rockport who bought a beautiful lot of land on the shore a few years ago. Down in Phippsburg he saw an old colonial house which he thought would look well on his place on Beauchamp Point in Rockport. So he went to Captain John Snow, who is in the towage and lighterage business in Rockland and an expert in salvage and all maritime affairs, and asked him to go and look at the house and see whether he thought he could move it around for him.

"John went and looked at it, and thought he could. 'How much will it be to move it?' the man asked John. 'Well,' replied the captain, 'for a long time I have wanted one of those car floats they have in New York Harbor for my business down here. I know where there is one, secondhand, which can be bought cheap. I'll go and get it; move the house; set it up down to Rockport. When I've got it set up, you come down and look at it. If the job is satisfactory, you pay for the float and it belongs to me; and if you don't like the job, you can keep the car float and we'll forget all about any charge.' So the deal was made. John got the float, skidded the house in Phippsburg down onto it; towed it around outside and up Penobscot Bay; skidded it ashore and into place. Then the owner came down to look at it. The job was perfect. Not even a crack in the plaster.

"One day in Rockport I met John," Al continued, "and asked him about it. John did not have much to say, as he is a very modest man. 'Wasn't there any particularly interesting thing on the way down?' I asked. 'Well,' said John, 'there was one. The fog shut in thick when we got out by Popham. I had the tug out ahead, and she was blowing one long and two short. And to make sure, I had a man up in the cupola of the house with a fish horn, and he was blowing one long and two short too. When we got about off Seguin and were about to make the turn, I heard a jangle of engine bells close aboard to starboard through the fog. A moment afterwards the white hull of a steam yacht broke out of the fog. She had her engines going full speed astern with a jingle. You see, her skipper had got a glint in the fog and saw the house looming up dead ahead and thought he was right in on the beach, though there was not less than forty fathoms all around.' "

Cozy Harbor, Me. (13293 314). This little harbor is cozy indeed, crowded in summer with local craft, but it is completely landlocked and much used in winter for wet storage as drift ice does not pack in.

Leave the red beacon at least 20 yards to starboard, pass close to the south of the can, leaving it to port, and about 10 yards south of the diminutive inner beacon. You may well see bottom in the entrance at low water on a sunny day, but that is no cause for alarm.

Once inside, inquire from anyone on the float or a boat for a vacant mooring. Anchoring will be difficult, but in searching for a berth, do not go to the north of the yacht club flagpole as the harbor shoals up rapidly toward the head.

There are a small restaurant, a snack bar, a bowling alley, and a store on the east side, run by Mr. E.W. Pratt. He is a reliable source of local information if not run ragged by the youthful members of the yacht club. For more extensive supplies, walk up the road, turn left at the main road, and you will find a well-supplied general store.

The active and hospitable Southport Yacht Club stands on a knoll overlooking the harbor. It runs an active sailing and racing program for young people and annually runs a one-day "ocean" race.

If you need help with engine, spars, or rigging, look up Cliff Brewer, who has a small yard at the head of the harbor.

The story is told of a certain lady who, having visited this section of Maine for many years, finally purchased a year-round cottage. Announcing the fact with enthusiasm one day to the local storekeeper, she added, "But you've certainly got some queer people around here." "Yes we have," replied the storekeeper, "but they'll all be gone by Labor Day."

Note on the Inside Passage from Boothbay Harbor to Bath. Strangers with no more than 8 feet draft can, with the aid of chart 230, continue through Townsend Gut and Goose Rock Passage to the Kennebec River and Bath. This entire inside passage from Boothbay Harbor to Bath, though narrow, crooked, and with strong tidal currents, is one of the most delightful trips on the coast. Roughly, the route is about 11 miles, and it is well worth the time required, especially if the weather at sea is uncomfortable. But larger yachts should take a pilot, procurable at either end.

The Sasanoa River, leading from the Sheepscot River to the Kennebec River north of Georgetown and Arrowsic Islands, can be made under sail with a breeze from east around to southwest, and is more fun that way than under power. But one would do well to use the top half of the flood tide, when the current is not quite so swift. Note that at the strength of the current in the narrow places the buoys are often run under for short periods.

The tide is not easily predictable in this passage, but works on the following general principle:

Hockamock Bay is a large body of water, so the flooding tide cannot fill it by the time of high water at Boothbay Harbor. Consequently, for nearly three hours after high water, the tide continues to run up the Sasanoa River from the Sheepscot River and down the Sasanoa River from the Kennebec River, of course with diminishing force, depending on the wind, the height of the tide, and doubtless many more obscure forces. When the level of water in Hockamock Bay approximates that in the Kennebec and Sheepscot rivers, there is a brief period of slack water. Then the tide begins to run out of Hockamock Bay and so continues until about three hours after low water on the coast.

The Sasanoa River is not a pipe line and there is a lot of friction delaying the flow of water, particularly at Boiler Rock and the two Hell Gates. Consequently, the time of slack water at any spot on the river is difficult to estimate. However, the best move is to start from Boothbay Harbor about two hours before high water. This would give something like slack water approaching Hockamock Bay and a fair current to the Kennebec River and down to Fort Popham.

Particular warning should be given of the two Hell Gates, particularly of the ledge above the Lower Hell Gate. An auxiliary cannot buck the tide through here, although a motor cruiser probably could do it. Coming down with the tide, one might think one was entering Niagara Gorge, but keep the power going and the clear channel will appear as you get closer. It is not a difficult place to negotiate, but is very awesome, especially for the first time. The late Captain Wade of the *Balmy Days* (Boothbay Harbor-Monhegan and return) said that this is a really dangerous place for a small boat.

Aside from being a handy passage to the Kennebec River, this is a beautiful trip. There are dozens of secluded anchorages in the ragged shores. The water is ideal for swimming. Clamming and fishing are possible in some places. But rig your mosquito defenses early.

Robinhood, Me. (13293   314) (13296   230). This quiet cove in the Sasanoa River is just below Knubble Bay. The entrance is clear from the chart, but is complicated by a powerful tidal current at Boiler Rock. The buoy is often towed under, and entrance against the tide is almost impossible without power. The tide at Goose Rocks Passage looks worse than it is. Favor the bold southern shore on approaching the cove and take advantage of back eddies under the shore.

Once in out of the tide, the skipper will find a large, well-protected harbor off a good marina. Robinhood is a small Maine village still largely "undeveloped" by summer interests.

The Kennebec Yacht Building Co. will take care of ordinary repairs. The yard has a twenty-five-ton Travelift, which can handle almost any yacht. The yard operates the Robinhood Marina. Here there is usually a vacant mooring or a berth alongside. Gas, water, ice, and Diesel oil are available. An adequate general store is just up the bank. For more elaborate supplies, take a taxi to Bath, only 8 miles away. Buses to Portland and Boston stop at Bath.

Up the cove near the abandoned coasting schooner is a beautiful and secluded anchorage.

A local correspondent writes:

. . . The vessel grounded in the cove is a large Dering five-master, which was towed here and abandoned in the '20's. Opposite the schooner is the summer residence of the late William Zorach, internationally known sculptor. Near the water is one of his statues, a bronze replica of one of his aluminum statues in the Radio City Music Hall in New York.

Wiscasset, Me. (13293   314). For one interested in old houses and shaded streets, this is one of the most attractive towns in Maine. The houses were built in the days when Wiscasset throve on shipbuilding and seaborne trade. At one time the government considered building a Navy yard at Wiscasset.

The trip up the river on the tide is well worth while, but difficult without power. It is 14 miles from the entrance of the Sheepscot to Wiscasset.

The anchorage is south of the wharf just off the swimming club pier and float, where a southerly breeze gets quite a rake. There are two guest moorings.

Yachts up to 30 feet can dock at the town landing (a few hundred yards south of the derelict schooners) for supplies, which are available at any one of the several excellent stores; gas, water, and 110-volt current are available at the yacht club. Haggett's Garage will make engine repairs. "Nick" Roth's small boat yard is on the bend of the river east of Wiscasset. There is launching ramp for boats up to 18 feet by the public landing.

The best place to spend the night ashore and get a meal is either the Wiscasset Inn or The Ledges. Information relating to points of interest to visiting yachtsmen may be obtained at the Wiscasset library.

The Old Jail is now an interesting historical museum. Artists should not miss the collection at the Maine Art Gallery. The Nickels-Sortwell House is the architectural attraction at Wiscasset.

The Central Maine Power Co. operates an electric power plant just south of Wiscasset. Large tankers bring fuel about once a month. It is worth coming a long way to see Captain Eliot Winslow, the local pilot from Boothbay, work one of these enormous vessels around the tight bend just below the town. It must be done on the top of the tide, too, so any miscalculation would have almost disastrous results.

In addition to its lovely old residences and beautifully shaded streets, Wiscasset is notable for the hulks of two four-masted schooners rotting slowly away on the shore just south of Route 1. They are the *Hesper* and the *Luther P. Little.* Dick Vennerbeck tells their story in the *Maine Coast Fisherman* of July, 1950:

> With their appearance of great age it is surprising to learn that they were built not so very long ago at the time of the First World War. For some time during and after the war they sailed out of Boston in the coastal trade; but about 1930, their usefulness diminished, they became the property of the Federal Government, and were tied up in Portland. At that time they were sold to a Mr. Winter at the U.S. Marshal's sale. How the *Hesper* and the *Luther P. Little* came to rest in Wiscasset is involved with the story of the old Wiscasset narrow gauge railroad, since it was to serve this railroad that they were brought from Portland by Mr. Winter.
>
> As early as 1836 it was proposed that a rail line be built from Wiscasset to Canada in order to make Wiscasset the winter port of the St. Lawrence. Had this plan been successful, Wiscasset might well have become one of the East's most important seaports, shipping Canadian timber and food. Misfortune dogged the plan for many years, however, until finally in 1892 a two-foot gauge railroad was begun from Wiscasset. The line was to have been extended only as far as the Canadian border at this later time, but even this modified plan proved too difficult for the owners. The track was extended only as far as Albion, near Waterville, Maine. The railroad had varying fortunes during the 40 years of its existence, but its revenue steadily decreased. In the latter years of its operation the road was owned by Mr. Frank W. Winter, who bought the *Hesper* and the *Luther P. Little.*
>
> Mr. Winter's plan was to use the two schooners as coal carriers for his railroad. When the vessels were towed to Wiscasset one did actually carry a load of coal, but not long afterwards, due to increased

competition from other transportation systems, the narrow gauge at Wiscasset was forced to close. With no job to do, and having no prospective buyers, the two schooners were scuttled and left at the wharf where they rest today.

So ended the life of a gallant little railroad, and with it the active careers of the *Hesper* and the *Luther P. Little.* Its right of way and rotting piles may still be seen near the northern end of the Maine Central Railroad station platform.

An atomic powerplant, Maine Yankee, has been built on Back River just below Cowseagan narrows. To increase the flow of water by the plant, the old Westport bridge and causeway were removed and a new bridge with a clearance of 100 feet was built across to Westport Island. It is now possible once again to circumnavigate Westport Island in a masted vessel and one can approach Wiscasset either up the Sheepscot or from the Sasanoa River up Montsweag Bay and the Back River. The Back River is a most attractive and secluded spot, but the tide runs hard through the narrow channel.

MacMahan Island, Me. (13296 230). In approaching the island, beware of Bull Ledge, a half-tide rock well out in the river. It is marked by a red-and-black nun, but the nun is a considerable distance from the ledge.

One can enter between Turnip Island and Georgetown Island at the south end of MacMahon Island or from the north through Goose Rock Passage. The former passage is clear of dangers but the tide runs hard. After the narrow part, as the passage begins to open out, there is a rock on each side. The one to starboard is marked by a nun and the other usually shows.

The entrance via Goose Rocks Passage is marked by a beacon off Northeast Point and a can off the northwest point of the island. There are several small and peaceful coves along the northern shore of the island, but the land is privately owned and there is no public landing.

Ebenecook Harbor, Me.   (13296 230). This is a large and well-protected harbor on the western side of Southport Island and is part of the passage from the Sheepscot to Boothbay Harbor. The easiest entrance is south of the Green Islands, between them and Dogfish Head. One can also enter north of the Green Islands, between them and the bare ledge to the north. Watch chart 230 closely and move cautiously here. A half-tide rock is reported north of the 6 behind nun 10. Or one can squeeze up close to the north side of Boston Island between it and another ledge north of it. Either side of the Isle of Springs is a safe, if somewhat roundabout and tortuous, channel.

A large vessel can anchor almost anywhere in the harbor. A smaller one will want to lie in one of the protected coves on the south side. Brewer's Boatyard occupies the head of the western cove. To enter, leave nun 2 to *port.* It is a mark for vessels entering Ebenecook from the Sheepscot. The western shore of the cove is quite bold and the ledges on the east side almost always show. Give them a good berth at high water as they are extensive.

Land at Brewer's float and inquire for a slip or a mooring. Gasoline, Diesel fuel, ice, and water can be purchased on the wharf. The yard has a 20-ton Travelift, carpenters, mechanics, and painters. Damaged sails can be repaired by Nathaniel Wilson, whose loft is in East Boothbay. A telephone call will bring him.

The yard store supplies a great variety of marine items and gifts. A general store is about ½ mile away. Turn right where the road from the yard joins the main road.

The middle cove is smaller and shallower. A rock near the western shore has been traditionally marked by a cider jug painted red.

The easterly cove, Love Cove, has a float and house belonging to Capt. Eliot Winslow, skipper of USS *Argo* in World War II. In her he received the surrender of a German submarine. He now is owner and skipper of a large excursion boat named *Argo.* He also is a pilot for the Sheepscot and Kennebec rivers and is owner and skipper of the powerful tug *Alice M. Winslow,* which he uses to dock steamers at Wiscasset and Bath. Love Cove is big enough and deep enough to provide excellent yacht anchorage. The cable shown on the chart is close to the entrance and need cause no concern.

Townsend Gut, Me. (13296 230). This is the passage from Ebenecook Harbor to Boothbay Harbor. It is spanned by a swing bridge and at the southern end is too narrow to beat through against the tide. With a fair wind, however, it can be easily negotiated under sail.

In approaching the Gut from Ebenecook Harbor, you will see nun 4 and will experience a strong inclination to leave it to starboard, for it appears to lie very close to the western shore. Do not do so! *Leave it to port.* A ledge runs from the buoy northward to the end of Indiantown Island, a ledge on which someone lands about once a week in the summertime.

Keep clear of the ledge to starboard at the edge of the cove above Cameron's Point and continue up the middle of the channel. Hodgdon Cove is a well-protected anchorage, although shoal near the shores and noisy in the daytime from the traffic in the Gut.

Blow three blasts for the bridge as you approach. The bridge tenders are alert and open the bridge promptly. As you pass through, you will be asked the name of the yacht and her owner. This is said to be the result of an incident that occurred just after the bridge was built. Some people were skylarking about, going back and forth through the draw for the fun of seeing the machinery in action. However, their foolishness stalled a fire engine at a critical moment and a house was lost on Southport.

Dekker Cove, just south of the bridge, is another good anchorage. There are a seafood store and restaurant here. Across the road is another store; and an excellent inn, *Lawnmeer,* is a short walk to the west on the main road.

South of Dekker Cove is the narrowest part of the passage. Favor the west shore. It is very steep-to beyond the point where a picturesque oak tree grows. There is a ledge on the east side that makes out just north of Juniper Point. It looks dangerous with the tide running madly over it. Nun 2 should also be left to port. Now head for the white church in Boothbay Harbor and run across.

If these narrow places make you chew your gum fast or smoke cigarettes in quick succession or shout at your crew, it may calm you to know that Captain Boyd Guild sailed the coaster *Alice Wentworth* through the gut, and more recently he has sailed the three-masted schooner *Victory Chimes* through.

Newagen, Me. (13293 314). This small but well-protected harbor is useful to the westward-bound mariner because it is close to his route and is well to windward. The cautious navigator will make the bell off the Cuckolds and then swing out to the westward of the course to nun 2 to avoid a 4-foot spot almost directly on the course. When the nun shows east of Mark Island, run for it. It is possible, however, to pass between the Cuckolds and Cape Island. It is likely to be smoother in here and there is likely to be more wind than outside by the bell. Go close to the light and leave the Coast Guard mooring buoy, a white nun, very close to port. Keep away from the western of the two Cuckolds, enough to keep a couple of pot buoys between you and the shore. At low water you can see bottom where the ledge runs out underwater. Once by that obstruction, keep well off the tip of Cape Island. The chart shows two rocks here. They seem to be in line with the point rather than side by side as the chart shows them. They break at low water. The outer one is flat and quite big but the inner one is well in under the point. Then give nun 2 a berth of perhaps 30 yards, for the ledge running in

Newagen Harbor. The picture was taken on a rough day whe the sea appeared to be breaking across the wastern entrance. The eastern entrance is clearly visible.

from it to Hunting Island is quite wide and a direct course to the nun comes very close to it. The writer nearly lost his sloop there and left a good swatch of red paint.

Round the nun and head for the outer white cottage on the northern point of the entrance. This will take you clear of a flat kelp ledge just outside the western end of Hunting Island. Pass between the red beacon and the northern side of the passage. There is plenty of water here, but a ledge runs from the beacon to Hunting Island. About 50 yards inside the beacon is a rock with at least 8 feet over it. No one has hit it, but some have seen the kelp at low water and been alarmed by it. Entering from the west, make the deep-toned red bell SR in the middle of the Sheepscot and run for the houses at the head of Newagen harbor until you see the nun.

Anchor wherever you can find room in the western part of the harbor or hail a fisherman on the town wharf at the head of the harbor. There may well be a vacant mooring.

The Newagen Inn overlooks the harbor from the north and maintains a float for the use of its guests. Do not lie alongside this float for long, as excursion boats stop here. The inn provides rooms and meals and has a bar and cocktail lounge. Consult the hostess for information on use of the tempered swimming pool, the tennis court, and other facilities. There is a post office up the road from the town wharf but no store. Gasoline and lobsters are sold from a float near by.

Ordinarily Newagen is a quiet anchorage, but in a brisk southerly at high water a roll makes in between Hunting Island and Cape Island. If the weather is thick, a powerful horn on the Cuckolds will let you know it.

There is an eastern entrance to Newagen between the southern end of Southport and the first islet in the ring surrounding the harbor. While it is possible to describe this channel, one is advised to take the dinghy and investigate for oneself. The shoalest part is a mud bar at the head of the harbor, before the passage is reached at all. The passage is narrow but deep enough to carry 5 or 6 feet through at half tide or better and the shores are quite bold. Quite large yachts have been known to beat in or out through both eastern and western entrances.

On a rock at the head of the path from the Inn float is a bronze table reading:

NEWAGEN
The Earliest Locality

Visited and Named by
English Explorers
In the Boothbay Region

Here
Capt. Christopher Levett
And the Indian Sagamores
Menawarmet, Samoset
and Cogawesco
Met for Four Days in
December, 1623

Captain Levett was in New England in 1623 and 1624 to establish the fur trade. He built a house on House Island in Casco Bay, ranged from Boston to Newagen at least, visiting the Isles of Shoals and the coast near York. He had a lengthy discussion with Gorges at Little Harbor near Portsmouth and then disappeared. The purpose of the meeting at Newagen was to explain to the Sagamores that exchange of presents and socializing were all very well, but that he wished to establish a commercial relationship.

At the eastern end of the harbor is the town landing with a depth of 3 to 4 feet at low water. There is also a lobster car. In recent years gas was sold here, but the January gale of 1978 demolished the wharf. It will doubtless be rebuilt.

Indicative of the climate on the Maine coast are these temperatures taken with a laboratory thermometer on a pleasant day in early August with a light southerly breeze: air, 70°; Newagen harbor sea water, 61°; Newagen pool, 67°.

That the land and waters of the Sheepscot have changed little in 175 years is clear from the following account of a cruise written by Jacob Bailey in *The Frontier Missionary,* edited by William S. Bartlett (Boston, 1853).

June 9, 1779. About nine we got underway with a gentle breeze from the south-west, and fell down between Parker's island and Jeremisquam into Sheepscot River. The country hereabouts made a romantic appearance; fine groves of trees, shrubby evergreens, craggy rocks, cultivated fields and human habitations, alternately presented themselves to view, and yielded a profusion of pleasure to the imagination.

As night approached it grew perfectly calm, and we were obliged to anchor in Cape Newaggen harbour, a little to the west of Booth

Bay. This is an excellent station for small shipping. The land rises with an easy slope from the water's edge on the north and partly on the east, while the remainder is surrounded with islands on which were erected fishermen's huts. Between these islands you pass into the harbour through very small inlets.

The origin of the name Newagen is obscure, but earliest references call it Capmanweggan, possibly an Indian word, later corrupted to Cape Manwegan and then Cape Newagen.

Boothbay Harbor, Me. (13296 230). This is an easy harbor to make in any weather, by day or night, and is large, well protected, and well supplied. It is a convenient place to fit out or stock up. There are several boat yards with facilities for repairs of every kind. The writer has entered it with anticipation and departed with enthusiasm.

From the west the leading mark is the brilliant flashing light on the Cuckolds, easily visible from far offshore. The horn is powerful and easily heard for miles to leeward, but does not carry very well to windward. Don't count on it. Also it is said to be activated in thick weather by the Coast Guard in Boothbay Harbor. While it is true that they tend to be conservative and start it often before fog or rain shuts down, they sometimes are too late. A low-power radio beacon on the light is very helpful.

From the Cuckolds run for the flashing red light on Burnt Island. Note that this light has a white sector showing to the south toward the Cuckolds and to the southeast toward Ram Island. It shows more orange than white, but it will keep you off of Squirrel Island and the ledge north of it, marked by a red flasher. About halfway from the flasher to Squirrel Island is a big flat white ledge with about ten feet over it. On a sunny day at low water you can see your shadow cross it as you sail over it.

Inside Burnt Island, leave the flasher off Tumbler Island to starboard and run up the inner harbor to the northeast.

From the east, make the black-and-white bell HL off the Hypocrites Ledge. This ledge has no connection whatever with hypocrisy. In early Colonial days, the islands of Boothbay were inhabited by fishermen who salted and dried fish for the European market. Salting fish is thirsty business. They consumed large quantities of hippocras, a cheap Spanish wine. Hence the islands were called the Hippocras Islands. When each island later was given its own name, the original name was corrupted by a later generation, which knew more of hypocrisy than it did of wine and the name stuck to the ledge.

Anyway, make the bell. Leave the two cans, 1A and 1, to port. Three nuns follow. In ordinary moderate summer weather, with a draft of 5 or 6 feet, one can ignore the first two, but the third one, Card Ledge, must be respected for there is a 2-foot rock inside it, between it and the ledge. There is a small red light on Ram Island and a thin bleat of a horn. The Coast Guard proposed to tear down the light, but inhabitants of Ocean Point were outraged and insisted on keeping it.

From Card Ledge, run for Burnt Island at night or simply run up the harbor, keeping clear of Spruce Point Ledge on your starboard side. The ledge makes out to the westward of the line between the nun and the can, which mark the ends of it. The pot buoys are a useful guide. Keep a number of them between you and the rock. Leave to starboard nun 6 off Spruce Point and the flasher off Tumbler Island and run in as before.

Anchor wherever you can find room inside Harbor Island or hail the wharf of the Clipper Inn on the western side of the harbor, or Pierce's on the eastern side, for a mooring or a berth alongside. Gasoline, Diesel fuel, ice, and water may be available at the Gulf wharf near the head of the harbor on the west side, as well as at Pierce's and the Clipper Inn.

There is a town wharf just south of the big white motel, where the excursion boats dock, near the foot of the old square brick chimney, which was part of a pogy factory for trying out the oil in menhaden, called "pogies" Down East.

The best time to shop is between 8 and 9 A.M. After that, the streets and stores of Boothbay Harbor are crowded with sauntering vacationists. The Boothbay Fruit Company stands at the widest part of the main street and carries all that a grocery store should. It is open until 10 P.M. For more modest prices, walk ½ mile north on the main street, over the hill, to a First National. A state liquor store is in the shopping center across the road from the First National. There are two drug stores and a hardware store on the main street. In addition, there are countless little shops purveying all manner of trinkets, clothes, jewelry, antiques, art and photographic supplies, and "gifts." There are restaurants, a great motel, and every kind of service imaginable.

Pierce's Marine in the southeast corner of the harbor is easily identified by a huge blue building used for "in and out" boat storage. Pierce has mechanics skilled in working on both inboard and outboard motors and a forklift that can lift a small boat or step a spar. Pierce sells gasoline, Diesel fuel, and ice in cubes or blocks, and has a water hose on the float. There is a well-equipped marine store at Pierce's, where one can buy anything from a new dinghy to a galvanized split thimble to charts and government publications.

Next to Pierce's is Brown Brothers, a motel and excellent shore-dinner restaurant. Further north on the east side is Bob Fish's Atlantic

Boat Works, where boats can be hauled, stored, and repaired. Beyond that is the wharf of the Rock Tide restaurant, another motel and shore-dinner place with live entertainment. Above this is the well-supplied hardware store and lumber yard of Pierce & Hartung. Beyond the footbridge is another small yard, Rittal's.

On the west side of the harbor are the Gulf wharf and Fisherman's wharf, where numerous excursion boats berth. Then comes the town wharf and another excursion boat wharf. The Clipper Inn, with its extensive marina, motel, restaurant, and bar, is right against the Tug-boat Inn, which has the pilot house of a tugboat next to the main street for an eye-catcher.

Around the corner, behind Harbor Island, lies the *Sherman Zwicker*, a Nova Scotia salt-bank schooner, fitted up as a museum by the enter-prising Mr. McEvoy. He also runs a railway museum a short taxi-ride up the Wiscasset road. He has a narrow gauge locomotive and several cars from the old Wiscasset, Waterville & Farmington line, and runs excursions around a track through the woods and fields. There are also a gift shop, a museum, and numerous artifacts from the steam train days.

Beyond the *Zwicker* is the yard of the late Frank L. Sample, Jr., with a railway capable of hauling any yacht or fishing vessel on the coast. This yard has had a reputation for fine workmanship for many years. Any conceivable repair can be made here. The yard also has a number of moorings, where yachts may be left under the yard's supervision if the owner must be away.

In Mill Cove, at the head of Booth Bay, Eastern Shipbuilding Corpo-ration is building steel excursion and cargo vessels.

When your tanks are full and your shopping done, leave others to rock in the wash of excursion boats and go over to the West Harbor behind McKown Point. Here is the well-appointed Boothbay Harbor Yacht Club, with moorings to rent and launch service. It is a far more peaceful spot than the Inner Harbor and, in a southerly blow, a lot smoother. However, there is no fuel supply or grocery store in the West Harbor. There are a post office and a public telephone. In the event of a really serious gale or hurricane, withdraw to the cove, making in to the south, and anchor behind the big ledge at its mouth.

The dammed-up pond behind the yacht club was once used as an ice pond. The ice was cut in the winter, skidded up ramps into big ice-houses, and packed in sawdust. It was later slid down chutes into the holds of four-masted schooners and carried to the West Indies and India to cool the drinks of sahibs before the days of electric refrigera-tion. One can swim in the pond now and wash off some of the salt.

On the south side of the harbor is the Bigelow Laboratory, which does research in oceanography and marine biology. The Coast Guard base is next to it, with several boats ready to respond quickly to radio calls.

If one must lay over in Boothbay Harbor, there are a number of resources. Beside the restaurants and gift shops, the *Zwicker* and the Railway Museum, there is a movie house on the main street. An excursion boat, *Balmy Days,* runs to Monhegan. This is an all day trip, with about three hours on that very picturesque island. Take a lunch so you will not spend your three hours waiting in line at the crowded restaurant. On certain days of the week, Captain Eliot Winslow's *Argo* runs up the Sasanoa River to Bath and down the Kennebec, a beautiful trip. The way the tide pulls through the Hell Gates is inspiring. *Linekin III* offers a boat ride and a clambake on Cabbage Island in Linekin Bay. A number of boats take fishing parties by the head and smaller sport fishing boats may be chartered. Captain Ben Lewis's *Capella* is known to be a comfortable boat and Captain Lewis is a deep-sea skipper of broad experience, who has taken a steamer around the world. He is also an expert compass adjuster.

Taxi service is available to meet buses for Portland and Boston in Wiscasset.

In one of the Boothbay barber shops a distinguished member of the Phillips Exeter Academy faculty waited his turn, watching with interest the barber wielding an ancient pair of wooden-handled clippers. When he took the chair the barber asked, "How do you want it cut?"

"Short," answered the pedagogue laconically.

"Don't make no sense. She won't lay down," responded the barber.

"Never has," replied the schoolmaster. When the time came for clippers, the barber started to cut quite a swath. The schoolmaster remarked that his barber at home used scissors principally and clippers only around the edges.

"That's where him and me differs," replied the barber unabashed.

The Penobscot Expedition at Boothbay Harbor

Boothbay Harbor has had two minor brushes with war, in addition to sending troops to wars away from home.

In 1779, General McLean of the British Army landed a small garrison at Castine. His commission was to establish a naval base from which British ships could harass American privateersmen and French warships and merchantmen.

Massachusetts, which then included Maine, reacted quickly and organized a large expedition to dislodge him. General Lovell commanded 1200 militiamen; Dudley Saltonstall commanded a "very mixed fleet." Colonel Paul Revere commanded a small band of artillerymen. Esther Forbes in *Paul Revere and the World He Lived In* (Houghton Mifflin Company, Boston, 1942) writes that organizing the expedition "was about like harnessing so many seagulls."

The expedition, with 2000 men and 1200 gallons of rum in 19 armed ships and 21 transports, reached Townsend (Boothbay Harbor) on July 21, 1779. Miss Forbes writes that "The Reverend Mr. Murray entertained the General and his officers in a 'much Genteeler seat than was by most persons expected in that part of the country,' for the coast of Maine was indeed wild enough in those days. Only at Townsend did General Lovell call for a review of his troops and there came off the ships (which were smart enough) and lined up on shore such a collection of 'scare crows' as even the American Revolution in its fourth year rarely brought together."

The Penobscot Expedition ended in disaster, as related under Penobscot Bay, below.

Linekin Bay, Me. (13293   314). This pleasant and protected bay lies east of Boothbay, between Spruce Point and Ocean Point. Its mouth is protected by Spruce Point Ledge, marked with a nun on its northern end and a can on its southern end. These buoys are supposed to tell you *not* to go between them but to leave the nun to starboard or the can to port on entering the bay. At low water there is no doubt.

On an ordinary summer evening there is good anchorage along either shore, although the water is very deep along the eastern side. In really bad weather, Lobster Cove in the northwest corner is a quiet and secure anchorage and is only a short walk from Boothbay Harbor. A large motel and restaurant on the east side of the cove owns a lovely old Alden schooner, which lies on a mooring in the cove and sails parties from the motel. The northeast corner, which backs up to the store, post office, and shipyards in East Boothbay, is also a snug spot, especially in an easterly. A pretty little cove, protected by a ledge and an island on the eastern shore, is good except in a heavy southwester and is not bad then. About where chart 314 shows a cable area coming in on the eastern shore is the yard of Paul E. Luke, easily recognized by his shop with a big white door. For years, Mr. Luke was renowned as a builder of the best in wooden yachts. His crew were craftsmen and his boats were solidly constructed and elegantly finished. When wooden boats became prohibitively expensive, rather than turn to fiberglass, he turned to aluminum. He learned the complex techniques of forming and welding this active metal and overcame the serious problems of galvanic action. He retrained his crew and is now one of the nation's busiest and best builders of aluminum yachts. He has also invented a very efficient and good-looking stove and has developed an anchor that can be taken apart and stowed in three pieces. It looks like a Herreshoff yachtsman's anchor in action, but the flukes are fitted to the shank, like the head on a pickaxe, and the stock slides out. There is a very well equipped machine shop at the yard. Repair work is not sought, as the yard is very busy with new construction, but in an emergency one might inquire.

The writer of this section of the *Guide* inhabits the first house on the shore north of the yard.

At The Elbow, the first cove south of the yard, is Smugglers Cove Motel, with restaurant facilities.

Behind Negro Island is an exposed anchorage, a wharf, and the Ocean Point Motel. There is a ledge south of the wharf that demands serious attention. One can pass through a hole in the ledges east and north of Negro Island, but it is a "local knowledge" job. Excursion boats use the passage regularly.

There are no public landings in Linekin Bay, but it is a pleasant and quiet place to spend the night, and easy of access.

Damariscove Island, Me. (13293 314). In any kind of settled summer weather, Damariscove is a good stopping place. It is well to windward of the course to the westward. Given a fair slant, a close-winded yacht can fetch the passage inside of Seguin in one tack. The harbor is unlikely to be crowded at night as the island is frequented mostly by picnic parties from Boothbay. Lobstermen sometimes occupy camps near the head of the cove. It is a quiet and secluded spot, preferred by some to the busy waters of Boothbay Harbor far to leeward.

In entering from the west, be sure to locate Bantam Rock, a half-tide ledge about a mile south of the island. It is marked by a lighted bell, but this buoy sometimes gets adrift and can confuse the navigator.

The waters to the south and east are full of ledges and unmarked rocks. On a smooth, clear day there is little trouble, but in heavy weather seas cock up and break in unexpected places. From the black-and-white gong on the Motions, run up the middle of the cove, keeping about halfway between the steep shore on the east and the breaking ledges on the west. Just before you come to dry land on the west, bear over to port to avoid a flat ledge making off the eastern shore. On most days when you would want to enter, it will not break, but it would surely trip up a yacht drawing 4 or 5 feet if the tide was down.

Then go back in the middle and anchor off the abandoned Coast

Damariscove Island.

Guard wharf in about 10 feet at low water. You will be able to see the bright sandy bottom.

Flounders are caught here in great numbers.

Another anchorage is off the eastern side of the island's narrowest point. A trip-line is a wise precaution here. The beach is stony, but a pleasant place to swim or picnic. Picnic parties often anchor off the northern end also. Great numbers of birds nest here, so in the early summer it is a foul and noisy spot.

The island is owned by the Nature Conservancy, and visitors are urged not to disturb any form of wildlife, although the writer has heard no objection to landing and exploring around.

The tower on the eastern ridge was built during World War II so Coast Guardsmen could listen for German submarines charging their batteries at night. Several were heard and attacked by planes from Brunswick.

This island, inhabited by white men for well over 350 years, was at last abandoned in 1959 when the Coast Guard moved to manned moorings in Boothbay Harbor. Late in the sixteenth or early in the seventeenth century English fishermen who came in the summer to fish offshore and dry their catch on the island must have built camps to live in and buildings substantial enough in which to store gear that they did not wish to take home and carry back again. Because the first vessels to arrive in the spring would appropriate the best sites, it seems likely that small parties would remain all winter to protect property and to fish. It is not surprising that we read little of this in published accounts, for most of these men were illiterate; and furthermore, no fisherman, having discovered a good place to fish, is eager to advertise it to others.

In 1608, a Captain Dameril, who was a member of the Gorges and Popham colony at the mouth of the Kennebec, established a store at Damariscove, which became known as Dameril's Isle. The Pilgrims at Plymouth, in distress for food in the spring of 1621, sent Edward Winslow to Damariscove for help. He was generously assisted. Of the settlement Charles K. Bolton writes in *The Real Founders of New England*:

It is not too much to affirm that Damariscove was, from 1608, let us say, to about 1625, the chief maritime port of New England. Here was the rendezvous for English, French and Dutch ships crossing the Atlantic, and for trade between Damariscove and New Netherland as well as Virginia to the south. Here men bartered with one another and with Indians, drank, gambled, quarreled, and sold indentured servants. In other words, the harbor which a Captain Damerill is assumed to have picked out years before had by the year 1622 become a typical commercial seaport on a miniature scale. In that year thirty ships rode in the harbor during the fishing season.

A century ago the island was covered with a dense growth of evergreens. Now only a few gnarled and picturesque trees cling to the patches of soil, the sheep having made great havoc with vegetation. The northern half of the island, called Wood End, had trees as late as 1870. In some places the land is suitable for tillage. There are two weatherworn houses, a dozen shacks and a few sheep sheds near the head of the harbor. Two hundred yards away lies a fresh-water pond bright in summer with yellow "cow" lilies and a resort for sea gulls in stormy weather. Here Captain Kidd is said to have sunk his treasure, but Dixey Bull the pirate is a more likely aspirant for the honor. Off the shore, two hundred years after Captain John Smith's visit, the American brig *Enterprise* and the British brig *Boxer* fought their famous half-hour battle.

The late Captain Edward A. McFarland of New Harbor used to tell of meeting Joshua Slocum and his fifteen-year-old son aboard the *Spray* in Damariscove after the ship had returned from her round-the-world cruise. The *Spray* went ashore on the ledges east of the entrance, but all hands turned to and got her off without serious damage.

This island is linked with the famous naval battle of the War of 1812 to which Mr. Bolton refers and which is described under New Harbor, below. One of the spars of the defeated *Boxer* is said to have floated ashore on Damariscove Island and to have been used there for many years as a flagpole. But there is some difference of opinion as to its location.

Little River, Me. (13293 314). This is a snug little cove on the west shore of the Damariscotta River behind Reeds Island. The best landmark is a large new house with a white roof. To enter, make the red-and-black gong in the river. Head for the chimney of the house on the point, leaving the red-and-black spindle to port. After you pass the spindle, continue on the same course until within 40 yards of the steep rock on the western shore. Then run up the middle of the cove between the large bare ledge to the east and the shelving western shore. Anchor anywhere inside the ledge where the depth is adequate. There may be a little motion at high water but nothing to bother a salt-water man. In any case, proceed with great caution here and don't try the entrance under any circumstances if there is a heavy sea. It breaks across the whole entrance.

When you do get in, there is a quiet, secure, and lovely anchorage.

The writer saw a four-masted schooner in here many years ago.

On the east shore above the island with the low house on it, called by its owners Treasure Island, is a wharf and float where lobsters are sold, live or boiled. Cottages have been built along the shores in the woods but are not obtrusive. Wharves used by fishermen line the western shore. On the hill behind them lies the road to East Boothbay, about a forty-five-minute walk to a small store and post office.

The low building on Reeds Island used to be a shore-dinner restaurant, but in 1977 was dormant.

Christmas Cove, Me. (13293 314). This picturesque and landlocked harbor has long been a favorite with cruising men. The origin of its name is confused. Some claim that John Smith lay here on Christmas Day, but the only year he was on the coast was 1614, and his was a summer trip.

The entrance is easy enough from the west. Pass between the nun north of Inner Heron Island and the tiny can off Foster Point. Former visitors will miss the big white pyramidal beacon, which used to stand on the ledge in the middle of the entrance. It has been replaced by a miserable iron spindle with a little red dayboard, quite invisible against the shore behind it from a distance of ¼ mile. However, you will see it before you hit it and the shores are bold. Leave it to starboard and the spindle inside it to port.

From the east, round Thrumcap and run up the river, favoring the eastern shore so as to avoid the Washbowl, a shelving ledge to the east of Inner Heron. It always breaks. Shoal water extends to the south and east. Continue up the river and enter as above.

Or come through the Thread of Life, less perilous than the name suggests. The entrance is buoyed. The southwest wind blows steadily through it, often quite freshly. The shores are bold, and the middle of the passage is deep. In general, tack when you have two or three pot buoys between you and the shore. Be sure to go *south* of Turnip Island. The writer's entire yachting career was nearly ignominiously ended before it began when his father, sailing the new family sloop on her maiden voyage from East Boothbay to New Harbor, neglected this precaution and saw boulders racing by very close to the keel. The old *Dorothy* was always a lucky vessel.

There are several guest moorings in Christmas Cove. Either hail the float at Coveside Marina on the north shore or pick one up and row ashore to consult with Mr. Mitchell, the proprietor. He is a most helpful and hospitable gentleman, who exercises a great deal of authority over activities in Christmas Cove because his is the only gasoline pump on the shore. Hence rowdy people who speed about and disturb the peace of this pleasant anchorage soon run out of fuel.

Mr. Mitchell is the proprietor of the Coveside Inn, Motel, Marina, Restaurant, and Gift Shop. In former editions of this *Guide* the author reflected his pleasant visits to the restaurant in extravagant terms. In one week in 1973 he received two letters from cruising people. One thanked him in enthusiastic language for recommending Coveside and the other reported profound dissatisfaction. Returning to check several times in recent years, the writer votes heavily in favor of Coveside's quality in bar, restaurant, and bakery. Don't miss the homemade pies.

Gasoline, Diesel fuel, water, and ice are available at the float. There is a grocery store about a mile away in South Bristol. If you have special problems, consult with Mr. Mitchell.

There is an active yacht club on the southern side of the harbor that runs small boat races and maintains an active social program.

If you have to anchor in Christmas Cove, beware of what looks like a good open place north of the casino wharf. It is a bare smooth ledge over which your anchor will bounce along until it fetches up in the mud beyond the ledge.

The short walk to the top of the ridge overlooking the harbor and Johns Bay is well worthwhile. Look over the Thread of Life, across Johns Bay to the fort at Pemaquid Harbor and the light on Pemaquid Point. Far offshore lies Monhegan Island.

There is a casino and swimming pool in the southwest corner of the harbor. Movies are shown several times a week.

Minor repairs can be made by Pete McFarland, who has a small yard up the northern cove. Anything he cannot handle can be done by the Harvey Gamage yard in South Bristol, or by Goudy & Stevens in East Boothbay.

Christmas Cove has always been popular with yacht clubs. If you happen to anchor in the cove when a rendezvous is in progress, with all moorings taken, large numbers of yachts rafted together, and the water vibrating with outboards, flee to Farnum's Cove. The writer spent a busy hour between two and three one morning when a northwest squall swept down on the anchored fleet in Christmas Cove. The commodore went ashore on a ledge, and the whole affair was more fun than a clambake.

South Bristol, Me. (13293 314). This harbor is essentially a passage separating Rutherford's Island from the mainland. The narrowest part of the passage is spanned by a drawbridge at the Gut.

West of the bridge is a fairly well protected anchorage dominated by the Harvey Gamage boat yard. This is probably the largest yard in Maine building wooden vessels. It has earned a fine reputation supplying draggers for the Gloucester, Boston, and New Bedford fleets. The yard has built a number of big sailing vessels, including the schooner *Mary Day* for Captain Hawkins, the square topsail schooner *Shenandoah* for Captain Douglas, the Hudson River sloop, *Clearwater,* and the gaff topsail schooner, *Bill of Rights. Harvey Gamage* and *Appledore* were also built here. Almost nowhere else can you see a large wooden vessel being built with sawed frames and heavy 2-inch planking caulked with oakum.

There is a town landing on the southeast side of the harbor.

Under the bridge there is about 5 feet of water at low tide, although shoaling to as little as 2½ feet has been reported. There is a big rock easily visible at half tide on the west side of the bridge. Bound east, head about for the town landing at first and then swing around for the opening to leave the rock to port. The bridge is manned and usually opens promptly, but the tide runs hard and there is little room to maneuver, so wait until the passage is clear. Watch for signals from the bridge, for if someone is coming the other way just as you arrive at the narrow part, there is going to be a collision.

Note that there is a power and telephone cable suspended over the opening at a height of 60 feet.

Despite the complexities described above, at half tide or better there really is little difficulty in negotiating this passage.

East of the bridge is a good anchorage basin, entirely landlocked and perfectly sheltered from every wind. It is much used as a winter mooring area because the swift tide prevents the build-up of heavy ice and helps to keep a boat's bottom clean.

From here a winding passage leads into Johns Bay north of Witch Island.

Gas and Diesel oil can be purchased at Gamage's yard west of the bridge or at a wharf east of the bridge on the north side.

Mr. Harvey Gamage, founder of the yard, died in 1977.

East Boothbay, Maine (13293 314). This indentation in the west shore of the Damariscotta River provides better shelter than the chart suggests. An easterly or northeasterly wind gets enough rake to build a chop in the anchorage, but very seldom does this happen in the summer.

There are several moorings usually vacant belonging to Goudy & Stevens or to John Alden of Boothbay, the two yacht yards at East Boothbay. Pick one up and row ashore to discuss it. If you have to anchor, drop your hook as close to the shore as you can get to the north of the fleet, to keep out of the tide.

There are three yards at East Boothbay. The southern one is Gamage and Stevens, devoted mostly to the construction of large commercial and fishing vessels. The middle one is Goudy & Stevens, builders of the replica of the *America,* among other vessels. Here are a large railway, a well-appointed machine shop and foundry, and numerous carpenters, painters, and mechanics. Any kind of repair can be effected here, or at what is called Hodgdon Brothers north of it. The yard is owned now by John G. Alden, Inc., and is devoted partly to finishing fiberglass hulls for Alden and partly to storage and repair. Nathaniel Wilson, who learned his trade aboard USCGS *Eagle,* runs a sail loft here. He can mend or make a sail of either natural or synthetic fiber. He is also a capable rigger and a most accommodating and knowledgeable person. Electronic work can be done by Whitcomb Radar, also located at the Alden Yard.

Behind Alden's are the telephone and post office, and up the hill to the left is Murray Hill Market, where your grocery needs can be met.

Up the hill to the right is the studio and shop of Andersen's Ceramics, carrying some very attractive and unique creations. Just beyond Andersen's is the studio of Earle Barlow, a talented marine painter and a seaman himself. He built his own ketch and sailed her to Europe and back. His pictures show not only a feeling for salt water but an accuracy about boats that is most satisfying. The peak halyard is rigged properly and leads to the right pin.

Lobsterman's Wharf serves good shore dinners either in a dining room or out on the wharf, where one can oversee activities afloat. The establishment is built around the deckhouse of a small wooden wartime troop transport, built in East Boothbay.

Damariscotta River, Me. (13293 314). The following account of the river and its attractions was provided by Edward A. Myers, founder of Saltwater Farm, now operating under Maine Aquacultural License #1 in the cultivation of mussels in Clarks Cove, and for many years a resident of Lincoln County.

A man with an occasional liking for quiet water and poking about could do worse than spend some time on the Damariscotta River. As in so many other places, he'd better hurry, because the developers have found the Damariscotta. The long, bold shore at the river entrance, uninhabited only a couple of decades ago from Reeds Island to Farnham Point, is now a proliferating line of cabins, with one real beauty—a dock, float, and runway, all painted bile green and covered with spotlights that wipe your night vision when you're trying to sail up at night. The river is a 15-mile estuary, which can accommodate 25 feet of draft as far as Prentiss Cove, 2 miles below the Damariscotta-Newcastle Bridge, and 10 feet of draft the rest of the way. Give little heed to the *Coast Pilot,* which grimly suggests the need for local knowledge above East Boothbay. Anyone with chart 314 can do it handily. There are supplies, a town dinghy landing, and an available mooring or two in Damariscotta.

If fogged in in Christmas Cove or Little River, creep out to the west shore of the Damariscotta River, which is bold enough to let you see the surf well before running out of water, and follow it north. It may be a beautiful summer's day a mile or so upriver, and there's a pleasant day's sail ahead of you in the bights and coves of the river.

Above East Boothbay and South Bristol (described elsewhere), there is an anchorage at least every mile, and scarcely a place where a fresh breeze can get enough fetch to bother your night's sleep.

1. Meadow Cove. About ½ mile above East Boothbay, anchor near the 27-foot spot on the chart. Meadow Cove was featured in the fall of 1977, when a 61-foot steel ketch selected it as the place to unload a million bucks worth of marijuana. It turned out to be an unwise choice.

2. The Back Narrows. Run right up the middle between can 9 and the Boothbay shore. (The overhead cable used to have an authorized clearance of 46 feet; the chart now says 40 feet, but they haven't touched the cable.) Continue to the 13-foot sounding, after which favor the mainland shore for anchoring in the little cove to the west. Those with raw courage, mean low-water slack, 3½-feet of draft or less, and a liking for such adventure may make the passage around the north end of Fort Island as follows: Put the beat-up wharf that's at the southwest end of the cove on your stern and head for the opening (on the chart is a rock and a 2-foot spot) on about 58 degrees mag. The leading mark is a dead spruce tree at a little hole in the woods, but it may not always be there. After passing between the two rocks previously referred to, shape around the Fort Island shore, return to soundings, get your heart out of your boots and return it to its usual position, and sail on someplace where you can tell somebody you've done it.

Both Meadow Cove and Back Narrows are good places to await a fair tide through the regular narrows. When entering at Fort Point, leave nun 10 to starboard; give it a modest berth if the tide is running hard.

On the flood, you will be set to the east as you pass the nun anyway. This buoy can be pulled under on spring tides and has been timed as out of sight for three or four seconds. There isn't enough room on the chart to tell you this, but the 2-footer marked by the nun is about 50 yards southeast of it; east of that, there is a clear passage right up the east shore, where, on repeated runs, soundings have never been less than 14 feet. This is the route used by the locals if they want to get up through the narrows on the ebb. The 4-foot spot on the east side of the narrows above the point is definitely there; someone who denied its existence cleaned the kelp off last summer.

3. Seal Cove. More than a mile in length, this deep cove is a secluded spot in which to spend the night or to explore with the dinghy. Coming upriver, round Hodgsons Island and head right up the middle between the islands into the passage between the two bits of mainland that form the cove. The overhead power line has an authorized clearance of 40 feet above high water. If your vessel can get under, you can go quite a distance on into the cove and anchor near the 14-foot spot. If not going so far, find good bottom about 100 yards north of the telephone line. When uncovered, the ledges around the 14-foot spot well in are generally covered with seals, young and mature. They are always fun to watch as they slither overboard at your approach. When the ledges are covered, the seals can be found out in the river, usually around the ledges west of Hodgsons Island.

4. High Head is ⅝ mile to the north on the same shore. It is not identified on the chart, but one can get in behind the head with 5 or 6 feet. The shore is bold, except for the head of the cove, which can be a good place to gather mussels for a chowder. As you approach High Head from the southwest, you may see a startlingly accurate granite profile of Richard Nixon, if you happen to like stone profiles of Richard Nixon.

5. Carlisle Island is directly across ½ mile of river from High Head. In entering from the south, watch out for the 2-foot spot near the mainland. It is easier to enter from the north. The island and Carlisle Point are at present uninhabited. Be sure to have a trip line on the anchor, as the bottom is rocky and the tide busy.

On your way up, watch that 3-foot sounding on the shoulder of Pleasant Point. The print is tucked under the shore, but the shoal itself seems to be able to reach out 50 yards and catch you.

6. *Pleasant Cove* is around Carlisle Point to the west. As the chart indicates, favor the southerly shore on entering. The bottom is good mud holding ground. Land on the north shore near the road. A lot more people are using Pleasant Cove, I notice. There are now five moorings, where there used to be just the one for years. No outboard menace yet, and water skiing not observed.

7. *Clark Cove* lies on the east side of the river, about 1 mile northeast of the Pleasant Cove anchorage. This was once an extremely active spot, with a brickyard, weir, and the wharf of the American Ice Company. Less than a century ago, vessels cleared from the wharf directly for London, South America, and such thirsty spots as Savannah, Charleston, and New Orleans. The kitchen of one of the houses is floored with South Carolina hard pine, swapped for bricks wanted by the Charleston-born mate of one of the ice schooners. The few pilings that marked the old ice wharf have been taken by the ice, which snapped them off well under low water.

At the end of the long wharf is a pump house that used to supply the lobsters of Saltwater Farm and is now feeding Class A salt water to a number of mussel-growth experiments in the old lobster shop. The east float has six feet at low water; the west float has five. Proceed with some caution once inside the large AF buoy marking the outer edge of the aquaculture lease. There are usually several moorings unoccupied, but inquire ashore first lest you pick up an experimental buoy with a single cinder block on the bottom.

Clams, quahaugs, oysters, and scallops are planted experimentally on both sides of the wharf, so the owner respectfully requests that you do not disturb the laboratory.

On clear northwest days it is possible to see Mount Washington from the Town House on the hilltop, ten minutes' walk from the cove. It makes quite a sight as it rears up 90 miles away.

8. *Wadsworth Cove, Poole's Landing, and Salt Marsh Cove* are on the west side of the river to the north of Clark Cove. Wadsworth is a cozy spot, although big enough to have held a Cruising Club rendezvous some years ago. When rounding the can to enter, hold on to the westward for a bit; the pair of Cruising Club yachts that didn't were lucky enough to have the *Sunbeam* handy to haul them off the ledge. You may not be so lucky.

9. *Poole's Landing*, which once enjoyed a steamboat wharf over which feldspar and bricks were loaded, is a good little anchorage in a northerly, and is within a mile of a 321-foot hill, which commands a good view of the surrounding land and water.

10. Salt Marsh Cove drains out pretty dry, but there is plenty of water and good bottom at its entrance. On Kelsey Point opposite begins the back nine of the Wawenock Golf Club, which is about ½ mile east through the brush. The back nine is still on the architect's board, however, and only the most tenacious golfers should attempt to make their way from the river bank to the front nine. If you must play golf, the best place to land is Clark Cove.

11. Lowes Cove, across the river from Wadsworth, now has four or five moorings at its entrance, and they hold the various research craft of the University of Maine's Graduate Department of Oceanography. The cove drains out but is sometimes worth a dinghy exploration at high water to its very head if you'd like to see the complete spectrum of spring, brook, marsh, wetland, mud flat, shingle, and granite transition from the land to navigable water. Two-thirds of the way in, there is an abandoned brickyard, one of eighteen that flourished on the river in the days when Back Bay Boston needed Maine brick. Interesting to conjure how the old-timers worked brick schooners in and out of such a bight.

Lowes Cove's north shore is formed by Wentworth Point, a gift of 130 acres to the University of Maine from the late Ira C. Darling. There is well over a mile of shoreline on the property. The oceanographic faculty there now numbers ten, and the year round population of students, graduate assistants, and staff is usually over fifty. There are more than thirty marine research projects underway, including a sea grant on oysters, mussels, crabs, and scallops, and one on the thermal effects of nuclear power plants, funded by the Maine Yankee Atomic Power Company.

There is a substantial steel-and-concrete pier, with various floats and runways attached, and at its head is the center's aquacultural laboratory. Interested visitors are encouraged—by appointment, if possible—and if coming by water, use the dinghy float on the north side of Lowes Cove, which has six feet at low water. It is a pleasant ½-mile stroll by an unpaved road to the center's main buildings. Picknicking, camping, and hunting are understandably prohibited.

12. Dodge Lower Cove. Follow the chart and notice that the red spindle on Glidden Ledge is not at the westernmost edge. After coming up with the spindle, hold to the channel along the westerly shore until the ledges are abeam to starboard; then lay your course for can 13. (This amendment is suggested because two men, both of Damariscotta, came up through at night, held to the westerly shore, and found a ledge. The fact that it was well above the ledges and actually part of the shore just shows how careful you have to be in the writing.)

Dodge Lower Cove has become a popular spot for culturing the European flat oyster—three proprietors now have buoyed plantings there; and in Fitch Cove across the river are usually to be seen the rafts of the Aquacultural Development Workshop, a federally supported school in Damariscotta.

Dodge Lower Cove has a shingle beach and a tidal island, where a deer can occasionally be started. On the way up, notice the broken ground between the Fitch Points below Glidden Ledge on the east shore. This is apparently a seal-whelping area—if that's what seals do —and your boat's arrival will usually send twelve to twenty seals splashing into the water.

Continuing upriver, one passes Wiley Point on the east shore, the landing place of a punitive expedition sent from Boston by Governor Andros of Massachusetts around the turn of the eighteenth century. The splenetic governor sent the task force to punish the wrong Indians, in this case the peaceful Wawenocks. The latter rose to the occasion, however, and massacred most of the force in what is now a suburban development of Damariscotta seen as one turns can 13.

13. Prentiss Cove, 1 mile above Wiley Point, is a good place to stop for a swim. The tidal flats tend to warm the water. Pull in just north of the island.

Unless it's the top of the tide, run the buoys carefully from here to the head of navigation. Be sure to locate can 13 and head for it, as it always appears to be east of where the chart says it should be. You cannot lay a course from nun 14 to can 15 unless your boat is amphibious. Favor the west shore a bit, give the long Goose Rocks a berth, and when you are well up with Hall Point, lay for C15.

Between C17 and N18, opposite the Riverside Boat Yard, there are a number of moorings set down by the yard or by local yachtsmen. There are generally no lobster or crab pots this far upriver, so the small buoys you see in this area are moorings, most of them on fairly long pennants because of the tide. *Caveat,* powerboats.

14. Damariscotta and Newcastle. These twin villages lie on each side of the fixed bridge over the Damariscotta River. Both have post offices; the larger trading center is at Damariscotta, on the east side; the bus station (Bangor, Boston, Rockland) is right in the center of town at a drugstore.

After passing nun 18, favor the Newcastle side of the river until up with the small-boat anchorage north of Jacks Point. Then cross the river to the pier, with 6 feet of water on either side of its floats. The tide floods from east to west across the end of the pier, and some allowance should be made for it in landing. It would be possible, by a combination of carelessness and bad luck, to be carried up under the bridge by a flood tide (which overruns the book by about an hour), the last such mishap being recorded in 1918. There is a quiet back eddy on the western side of the pier. The Pier offers a couple of moorings and a small float, as well as the predictable amenities of a waterfront restaurant and bar seven days a week during the summer and six days after Labor Day (the exception is Tuesday). There is entertainment on weekends, and those seeking an early quiet night had best drop down off Riverside Boat. Chasse's Marina is above the bridge, but maintains moorings below; Nick Chasse is willing to send to the pier for your outboard if you need service; you may also rent a small outboard for the trip to the oyster shell heaps and Salt Bay. A natural food store, Margo Moore's gourmet shop, the Yellow-front Grocery, and the First National are all on the main street of town from the head of the pier eastward. The Old Maine Shop is the local chart agency. The state liquor store and laundromat are half a block off Main Street, and on the way, if you'd like to escape reality, you can pick up *The New York Times* or the *Wall Street Journal* at Clark's. The Damariscotta Information Bureau is at the head of Main Street; just opposite is the Chapman House, restored as a museum of local and county history. Striped bass are to be caught in the river, either from a boat or from the bridge, the largest recent catch being thirty-five pounds. Bob Gilliam's fresh-fish market is at the head of the pier. If the pier is crowded, there is a long float for dinghies alongside the launching ramp at the Damariscotta town parking lot, just east of the gulch where the ancient coaster *Lois M. Candage* is dying by inches.

Anchorage, in the event there are no moorings available, is in the channel in good mud bottom. If you are lucky with a patent anchor, you may bring up a bit of brain coral dumped there by sailing vessels returning in ballast from alewife voyages to the West Indies. Hang a bucket over the stern to help lying with the tide, but don't forget to take it in in the morning.

Below the red brick Congregational Church on the Newcastle side are the bedding logs of a shipyard where the *Wild Rover* was constructed over a century ago. This ship rescued a Japanese castaway from the China Coast, returned him to Boston, and sponsored his religious education at Amherst. He returned to his home country to establish the first Christian college in Japan. The great-grandson of *Wild Rover*'s owner attended the centenary of Doshisha University and found a bas relief of the ship over the doorway of the college's oldest building.

A mile north of the Twin Villages, on both sides of the river, are enormous mounds of oyster shells left by feasting Indians many centuries ago. One estimate places the Newcastle shell heap at twelve million bushels. They are indicated on chart 314 at Glidden Point. Go up in the dinghy to be there at slack water, at that point about eighty-five minutes after the book tide at Portland, unless you like to run the rapids under the highway bridge on the way out. Kayakers seem to like it at the full ebb, but you will find it just a nice paddle at slack water.

(Here Mr. Myers's account ends.)

McFarlands Cove, Me. (13293   314). This is a delightful secluded anchorage on the west side of Johns Bay northward and northwestward of Davis Point. A steep hill about 150 feet high rises from its western shore. Anchor about halfway between Witch Island and the shore to the westward in 3 to 4 fathoms. Watch out for the rock (awash at low water) 200 feet off the northwest point of Davis Point.

There are no supplies here, the nearest being at the South Bristol bridge, less than a mile to the southwest.

Pemaquid Harbor, Me. (13293   314). From the south, enter close to the east shore of Johns Island. The ledge to starboard is really a small island and always shows. Swing to the east and pass halfway between the wharf in front of the restored stone tower of Old Fort William Henry and Beaver Island. Anchor east of Beaver Island out of the tide. This cove shoals up quite far out from the shore but affords good anchorage. However, if you find it rolly here, go up the Pemaquid River beyond the shore-dinner wharf, cross the bar above the nun buoy, and anchor in a perfectly protected basin behind the ledges. This is something of a gunk-holing operation, but there is a channel. If you wish to compromise, anchor in the tide off the wharf. However, excursion boats use the float frequently, so allow them room.

This harbor was one of the first places on the coast occupied by white men; and before that, it was one of the principal Indian settlements. In 1605 Waymouth found a large Indian town here. He kidnapped one of its leaders, Skidwarres, who was returned in 1607 by Gilbert on his expedition to establish a colony at the mouth of the Kennebec. Samoset, the chief who welcomed the Englishmen to Plymouth, lived here and at New Harbor.

The English established themselves at Pemaquid early in the seventeenth century, about the same time the French occupied Castine. Raids and counterraids succeeded each other through that century, interrupted by Indian attacks and by pirates. Until the French finally abandoned their ambitions in Maine in the middle of the eighteenth century, Pemaquid was the British outpost.

On the night of September 4, 1813, the British brig *Boxer* lay off the fort and sailed out to be defeated by the American *Enterprise* the next day.

Inside the tower of the old fort is an interesting exhibit of artifacts recovered from the harbor and the site of the old fort. In the summer of 1965, Mrs. Helen Blakemore Camp commenced archaeological exploration of the area west of the old clam factory and shore-dinner wharf. There is now a museum displaying many of the relics uncovered, and the work is still in progress.

The village of Pemaquid Beach, just behind the stone tower, has a small store. It is a pleasant walk across to New Harbor. Meals, snacks, and shore dinners are available either at Gilbert's lobster pound on the wharf or one of the many motels nearby.

There are two beaches close to the anchorage, a rarity on this rocky coast. The larger is south of the village facing south to Johns Bay and the open sea. The breakers can be big enough here to tumble a swimmer about, but seldom is swimming dangerous. The other beach faces west toward Johns Island. It is well protected and the water is warmer than at the other beach.

Pemaquid Point, Me. (13293 314). Pemaquid Point is forked with a wide-open rocky cove between the two parts. The eastern promontory is a high ledge of dark rock with a conspicuous dike of white granite running its length. There is an automatic light on the top of this dike and a state park nearby. The rocks are likely to be black with tourists watching the spectacular surf. The western point is longer than the eastern one and of low shelving rock. From it a ledge runs off more than a mile to a red-and-black can buoy. In really heavy weather, such as occurs after a hurricane or a prolonged northeast gale, the sea breaks all the way from the point to a rock outside the can. In ordinary summer weather, however, it is perfectly safe to leave the unlighted gong off the point close to port bound east.

On an ordinary summer day the wind is quite likely to be soft between the gong and the light and for some little distance east. It is often quicker and more comfortable, particularly if bound west under sail, to stand well offshore. The breeze seems to pick up along the east shore of the point once you are well by the light, so anyone bound up Muscongus Bay from the west can weigh the advantages of slopping through the soft spot to pick up the fresher breeze under the shore. On a rough day, beware of Pumpkin Cove Ledge, an unmarked rock with about 20 feet of water a mile northeast of the light.

Mackerel often are plentiful off Pemaquid Point, and the writer has many times jigged up a codfish on the edge of the ridge between the gong and the can.

Pemaquid Point has had its tragedies. The *Angel Gabriel* struck near the location of the present lighthouse in the August hurricane of 1635; five lives and the possessions of a hundred passengers were lost. In the storm of September 16 and 17, 1903, the coaster *Sadie and Lillie* and the fishing schooner *George F. Edmunds* were lost. The crew of one of these was saved by a man's swimming ashore through the breakers with a lead line and hauling the others through the surf one by one. Vessels were sometimes lost by skippers' neglecting the western point and turning the corner after passing the light.

Muscongus Bay, Me. (13301   313). This is one of the most beautiful and least-publicized parts of the coast west of Mt. Desert. Many yachtsmen cross directly from Pemaquid Point to Old Man whistle and go on to the Penobscot or follow the inside course from Pemaquid Point to the bell off Eastern Egg Rock and thence through Davis Strait to Port Clyde.

For anyone bound from New Harbor to Port Clyde, it is not necessary to go out to the Eastern Egg Rock bell and up through Davis Straits. Leave Haddock Island close to port, Franklin Island to starboard, and Gangway Ledge to starboard. Then pass between Barter Island to the north and Thompson Island to the south. Hug the Barter Island shore as close as 50 yards until you come to the southeast point.

Then leave Old Horse Ledge Beacon to port, Hooper Rocks nun 6 to port, and black can 3 to *starboard.* This route is the shortest possible between New Harbor and Port Clyde—with good shelter at both places.

However, one with a little more time to spend will do well to explore Muscongus Sound, the villages of New Harbor, Round Pond, and Friendship, and to look in at some of the quiet and little-frequented coves mentioned at the end of our account of the bay.

The presence of Franklin Island Light, deserted quarries, and well-buoyed channels to Waldoboro and Thomaston remind the cruiser casually crossing the bay that fifty to one hundred years ago here was the scene of much commercial activity. Schooners as well as a few square-riggers were built at Thomaston and Waldoboro. The *Governor Ames,* first five-master ever built and a huge vessel, was launched at Waldoboro with all her spars stepped, rigging set up, and sails bent.

She was taken down on the tide at once and finished fitting out at Round Pond.

How so small a river floated so big a vessel is a source of wonder today. Sloops and small schooners were built at Bremen on Bremen Long Island, at Friendship, Round Pond, New Harbor, and wherever a good stand of oak and pine was near the water. Considerable lobstering and inshore fishing was done from dories and sloops. There were quarries at Round Pond and Tenants Harbor, and fortunes were made by Muscongus Bay men hauling ice, lime, coal, wood, salt, granite, molasses, rum, and fish. Many of the solid old houses at Round Pond, Wiscasset, Damariscotta, Waldoboro, and Thomaston were built by skippers and owners of ocean-going vessels. Forty years ago, a passing schooner on the horizon was not uncommon. In 1938, several of us boarded the three-master *Thomas H. Lawrence* off Pemaquid Point with a cargo of pilings to keep the New York World's Fair out of Flushing mud. Since then I can remember having seen only two commercial sailing vessels on the coast—except for party boats.

New Harbor, Me. (13301 313). This is a busy commercial harbor, devoted mostly to fishing and lobstering. It is a small harbor, at best, and is crowded with local boats. However, the cruising man will find it useful, as it is the nearest harbor to Pemaquid Point, a promontory one must somehow round.

Approaching from the west, follow the bold shore of Pemaquid Point to Yellow Head. This is composed of faintly yellowish-white granite and is very prominent. This course should take you west of Pumpkin Cove Ledge, a 19-foot spot, which breaks in heavy weather but of no concern on a summer day.

At Yellow Head, stand offshore about ¼ mile to clear the New Harbor Dry Ledges. The southern ledge extends southward for some distance, and there is a rock that breaks in rough weather just north of Yellow Head. It is not prudent to pass between the Dry Ledges and the shore, but the eastern sides of the ledges are quite bold. If it is thick, run for the bell off New Harbor. If not, one can simply give Little Island a reasonable berth of about 100 yards and haul up for the harbor entrance. The southern point makes out only a little, but nun 4 appears to be much too far south. However, it should be left to starboard and the beacon to port. Anchor anywhere inside the beacon, or hail the second float on the north side and inquire for a vacant mooring.

Gasoline, water, and Diesel fuel are available at the floats. Do not plan to lie alongside for long, as fishermen are constantly using these floats. They buy fuel and sell lobsters and ground fish for shipment in trucks to Boston. They may have little patience with yachtsmen who obstruct them.

There is a restaurant and fish market, run by the Fishermen's Co-operative, on one of the wharves, but there is no store close by. The nearest is "on the hill," a walk of about a mile west on the tar road. There is a garage near the store, where a taxi can be engaged to meet the bus in Damariscotta. For a meal ashore, try the Fisher-men's Cooperative. For a more formal occasion, try the Thompson House. Land on the stony beach on the south side of the harbor, follow a path across the field to a road. Turn right and climb a short, steep hill. About 200 yards beyond the summit on the left is the Thompson House.

The Gosnold Arms overlooks the harbor on the north, just behind the first stone wharf. For years it had an excellent reputation but in 1978 its future was in doubt.

There are many attractions nearby. The view from Pemaquid Point, comprising the whole coast from Seguin to Monhegan and nearly to Port Clyde, is well worth the hour's walk. If there has been a heavy southerly or southeasterly, the surf there is a thrilling sight.

There are two good beaches. One is Pemaquid Beach, about a mile to the west of the hill. Leave the garage to port and bear left on entering Pemaquid Beach, a village about a mile west of New Harbor on Johns Bay. Or walk about a mile east from the harbor on the road that runs along the north side to Long Cove. Here is a sand spit, bare at low tide. Although small, it is an attractive little beach and nearer than Pema-quid. At low tide, after a southerly breeze, the water is warmer here than anywhere else.

One John Brown was a landowner in New Harbor in 1625, and as of that date increased his estate by the purchase of Muscongus Island. He must have been pretty well established by that time. A stone marker to the west on the road along the north side of the harbor relates the story of his deed to the property.

The late Mr. Harold Castner of Damariscotta, an authority on local history, wrote of this transaction:

John Brown and his son-in-law John Pierce bought the entire John Brown Tract in 1625 for 50 beaver skins and the very first deed in America was executed, which is recorded in Wiscasset even now. . . . Because of the phraseology of that deed it has been used ever since in America; and Abraham Shurt, the chief magis-trate who did it, has been called "The Father of American Con-veyances."

One could not close an account on New Harbor without relating an incident that occurred many years ago at Penniman's Store on the hill.

A local workman, well known for his conservative approach to financial matters, drove up to the gasoline pump at the store. The proprietor's son, a youngster of some fourteen summers, promptly appeared and grasped the pump hose.

"Shall I fill her up?" piped the boy.

"No, no, just one gallon," quickly replied the owner of the car.

"What you tryin' to do, Gilbert, wean 'er?" was the prompt and fitting rejoinder.

The *Enterprise* and the *Boxer*

Because the surrender in this famous battle was "at a point some four or five miles east from Pemaquid Point, four miles southwest of East Egg Rock at the mouth of the Georges River and about seven miles west northwest of Monhegan," it is appropriate to mention it here.

The full story of the action between the British *Boxer* and the American *Enterprise* off Pemaquid Point on September 5, 1813, is a commentary on the economic, political, and military background of both nations at that confusing juncture in their histories.

In the spring of 1813, a Mr. Tappan of Portland headed a syndicate to buy woolen cloth for the American Army. The army desperately needed the cloth for uniforms and blankets, so was not overly particular about where it came from. Tappan found a supply in St. John, N.B., part of the British dominions with which his country was at war. Nevertheless, it was cloth and was available if the syndicate would see to its delivery at Bath. So the Tappan syndicate chartered the neutral Swedish brig *Margaretta* and sent her to St. John for the cloth. The British were willing to sell the cloth to anyone, even their enemies, because they were badly impoverished by the heavy expenses of the Napoleonic wars and wanted money more than they wanted the American Army to go without blankets. Consequently, *Margaretta* loaded British cloth in St. John for Bath, while H.M.S. *Boxer* was fitting out in the same harbor to cruise against U.S.S. *Enterprise* and American privateers.

As both vessels were ready to leave at about the same time, Tappan suggested to Captain Blyth of *Boxer* that, in exchange for a draft of £100 on a London bank, he convoy *Margaretta* to Bath as, loaded with British goods and bound for an American port, she was susceptible to capture by privateers from either country. Blyth accepted and left St. John in company with the neutral Swedish brig, under charter to his enemy, loaded with British cloth to warm his enemy's army!

Off West Quoddy Head in the fog he even took *Margaretta* in tow.

The comic-opera quality of the whole incident is emphasized by a capture *Boxer* made off Campobello, a small boat with a picnic party led by the wife of the American commanding officer at Eastport. Blyth released the ladies and the American officer wrote him a gracious letter of appreciation through the press.

On September 4, early in the morning, *Boxer* and *Margaretta* were off Monhegan. A small boat came off to her asking for medical help, as a fisherman on the island had been hurt. *Boxer*'s surgeon went ashore with the fisherman, accompanied by two midshipmen and a British Army lieutenant, who was taking the cruise on *Boxer* for his health. They carried fowling pieces with the intention of shooting pigeons.

At eleven o'clock that morning, *Enterprise,* under Lieutenant Burrows, was sweeping out of Portland in a flat calm. A light southerly air came in during the afternoon. As *Boxer* and *Margaretta* parted company near Seguin about 3 P.M., Blyth fired a few guns after his convoy, "should any idle folks be looking on."

Enterprise, slowly crossing Casco Bay, heard the firing but in the haze could see nothing. *Boxer* turned east and lay that night behind Johns Island in Pemaquid Harbor. *Enterprise,* almost becalmed, jogged eastward during the night. Dawn found her off Pumpkin Rock with a light northerly air.

Burrows saw *Boxer*'s spars over Johns Island, recognized her, and hauled on the wind. About seven o'clock *Boxer* made sail and stood down Johns Bay, firing three guns as a signal to the party ashore on Monhegan. About eight-thirty, off Pemaquid Point, *Boxer* broke out her colors and fired a gun. Burrows, to leeward in the light northerly air, figured that the wind would come southerly later in the day and kept offshore.

At eleven, both vessels lay becalmed about 5 miles west of Monhegan. The pigeon-shooting party appeared in a rowboat, heading for *Boxer*. The breeze came in SSW, however; both brigs stood off to the southeast on the starboard tack, and the rowboat returned to Monhegan.

Burrows was now to windward and found that his vessel was faster than *Boxer* on any point of sailing. Accordingly, at three o'clock, he put his helm up, ran down to *Boxer,* and, broadside to broadside, both vessels fired away. Captain Blyth was killed at the first broadside. Burrows was mortally wounded by a musket ball very soon after but lay propped up on deck and encouraged his officers. Lieutenant McCall took command.

Enterprise's main braces were shot away and the sails on her mainmast swung aback. But McCall set foresail and jib, ranged ahead of *Boxer,* and swung across her bow, coming so close that both vessels prepared to board. However, they did not strike. As *Enterprise* crossed *Boxer*'s bow, McCall himself sighted a long nine that had been moved aft to the port quarter and struck *Boxer*'s main topmast just above the cap of the lower mast. Her main topmast and topgallant carried away and dragged overside to leeward.

McCall then took in foresail and jib, luffed across *Boxer*'s bows, and raked her with four broadsides.

Enterprise ceased fire and called, "Have you struck?"

Boxer replied, "We will never strike to any damned shingle jack!"

Enterprise repeated the question and received an affirmative answer.

"Then haul down your colors," hailed *Enterprise.*

"We can't. They're nailed aloft," was the answer.

Enterprise withheld her fire while the colors were lowered.

Both vessels returned to Portland. Before the funerals of the two captains were held, a Mr. Kinsman, representing Mr. Tappan, asked McCall for permission to examine Captain Blyth's effects. McCall refused and Kinsman explained the "deal" Tappan had had with Blyth. McCall, realizing the embarrassment to Tappan and to Blyth's family, not to mention the confused international repercussions, found the draft for £100 in Blyth's pocket, signed by Tappan, and permitted Kinsman to exchange it for $500 in specie.

An armed sloop was sent to capture the party on Monhegan, and a magnificent funeral was conducted for both captains in Portland.

As evidence of the good sportsmanship with which the whole affair was conducted, I quote a paragraph from Captain Sherwood Picking's *Sea Fight off Monhegan:*

—the two crews fought with equal bravery. James, historian of the British Navy, who rarely has a good word to say of Americans, is forced to the damaging admission that "—upon the whole, the action of the *Boxer* and the *Enterprise* was a very creditable affair to the Americans." On the American part this equality of courage was freely admitted. At a naval dinner given in New York shortly after the battle, one of the toasts offered was, "to the crew of the *Boxer:* enemies by law, but by gallantry, brothers."

Many a yacht race is fought with more acerbity than was this important naval engagement.

The ensign of the *Boxer* is among the trophies of the Naval Academy at Annapolis, and the tattered folds of the *Enterprise* are close by those of the *Bonhomme Richard* in the National Museum, Washington, D.C.

The sternboard of the *Boxer,* about 10 feet long, beautifully painted, hangs on the south wall of the George B. Wendell Collection in Mystic Seaport, Mystic, Connecticut. There is a local tradition about Boothbay that a long spar buried in the grass at the north end of Damariscove Island is the *Boxer*'s maintopmast. Rumor has it that the spar floated ashore at Damariscove and was erected at the north end of the island as a flagpole, where it stood for many years toward the end of the last century.

The source for this very circumstantial account is Captain Sherwood Picking's *Sea Fight off Monhegan,* published in 1941 by the Marchigonne Press in Portland. Captain Picking, a Portland man himself, was a naval officer, a seaman, and a yachtsman. He had access not only to McCall's report of the battle and to the British Admiralty's minutes of the court-martial conducted later but to letters and memoirs of many of the participants. The account is admirably documented and most interestingly written. Captain Picking was, unfortunately, killed in an airplane crash in 1941, while on his way to England to serve as a liaison officer with the British Navy.

Round Pond, Me. (13301 313). This is a quiet and well-protected harbor, halfway up Muscongus Sound. Far to leeward of the direct route alongshore, it is only occasionally visited by the high-pressure cruisers in a hurry to "get there."

The entrance is perfectly clear from the chart. Anchor wherever inclination dictates. If a heavy easterly is expected, get up under the northeast point as far as you can. There may be a guest mooring available. Inquire at the town wharf.

This is the most prominent wharf and float on the west side of the harbor. It has a squared-off deck on it, from which the gangway leads down to a float crowded with skiffs. The *Coast Pilot* rather tentatively estimates 6 feet at low water alongside. Local advice suggests less.

Behind the town landing is the Anchor Inn, a simple restaurant but serving excellent food at reasonable prices and with acceptable speed. It is a pleasant place, likely to be crowded at suppertime with local people and summer residents. Arrive early.

One can continue up the road to its junction with route 32, the state road. To the left and up the hill is Bill Russell's King Row Market, a well-equipped grocery. To the right is Martin's grocery. Besides groceries, Mr. Martin sells a mackerel lure that has the reputation of being infallible. If there are any mackerel around, this lure will catch them. If not, it will catch something else. The writer has seen it catch pollock, lobster traps, and even a seagull.

North of the town wharf and the Anchor Inn is the yard of Bruce Cunningham. He is an experienced builder of wooden boats, both lobster boats and yachts. In the winter of 1976–77, he built a 35-foot shoal-draft ketch from a Pete Culler design, a lovely piece of work. He does all kinds of maintenance and repair work and hauls and stores many boats that sail from Muscongus Bay harbors. Consult with him about any problems of repair or maintenance.

During the last century, Round Pond was a busy commercial port, building boats and vessels, shipping fish and granite, and engaging in overseas trade. Captain Joshua Slocum put in here in *Spray* after leaving Gloucester on his famous trip alone around the world.

Muscongus Bar, Me. (13301   313). This boulder-strewn bar between Muscongus Island and Hog Island can be crossed at half tide or better with a draft of 4 or 5 feet by crossing close to a bush stake on the southern part of the bar. This is the shoalest place, but there are no boulders here. At this place there is about a foot of water at a "low dreen" tide, so half tide would provide better than 4 feet. This crossing can save considerable time for one bound east from Round Pond.

For a picnic ashore and a swim, try the beach on the north end of Muscongus Island, but anchor well off, at least 100 yards, as the beach shelves very gradually and there are boulders near the southern end.

Muscongus, Me. (13301 313). This is a shallow bight in the west shore of Muscongus Sound above Round Pond. Protection is better than it looks to be, but a northeaster could be uncomfortable here.

The cove is dominated by the marina of Mr. and Mrs. Nelson Webber, who live in the house on the rise to the north. They maintain a few guest moorings, sell gasoline and Diesel fuel, and maintain a wharf and launching ramp. There is no store closer than Round Pond. Mr. Webber is a capable carpenter and mechanic, but for major repairs one must look to Bruce Cunningham's yard in Round Pond.

Friendship, Me. (13301   313). This harbor, near the head of Muscongus Bay, is well protected in anything short of a southwest gale of wind and is an interesting place to visit. Entrance from the west is easy. Simply follow the bold shores of Harbor, Black, and Friendship islands, running short courses from point to point in thick weather. You will probably get a scale-up as you approach the harbor.

From the east, make nun 2 off the western point of Gay Island and run up the middle of Morse Bay, favoring the bold western shore. The tide runs hard through here, and there is a string of ledges up the eastern shore, with one half-tide rock well out in the middle. You cannot run a direct course from nun 2 to the can off the northern end of Morse Island without hitting this ledge. You will find the can much farther around to the east than you expect.

From the can, run down to the two nuns and through the passage west of Garrison Island into Friendship Harbor. Respect the can at the north end of this passage. A bar runs from it to the south and forms the west side of the channel. The writer saw a husky schooner high and dry on this bar. She struck on a falling tide and lay right down on her side.

Do not ignore the 5-foot sounding on the north side of the harbor off a prominent shell heap. A rock is really there and yachts have bounced on it.

Anchor east of the beacon with the square day board and as close to the shore as your draft will permit. There are six guest moorings on this side of the harbor, maintained by Mr. Albert Roberts, whose wharf, the third from the mouth of the harbor on the north side, is clearly labeled. Pick up a mooring and pay him when you get ashore. If you can't find him, send him a check. Mr. Roberts sells gasoline, has a water hose on his float and can provide a shower at nominal cost.

The next float westward belongs to Maine Coast Seafoods. That and Wallace's to the east of Al's are essentially for the buying of lobsters, and yachts are for their idle times.

In the event of accident to hull, spars, or engine, consult Mr. Roberts. Lester Black is an accomplished mechanic and the Lash Brothers' yard in Hatchet Cove can make repairs.

There is no store near the shore, but a twenty minutes' pleasant walk up the road to the right will bring you to the village of Friendship, where there are a good market and a hardware store.

Should one have compass problems, there are two ranges that may prove useful. To head north magnetic, line up the red spindle on the north side of the harbor with the inner edge of the outer stone pier on a wharf behind it. To head west magnetic, line up the beacon with the tallest tree on Ram Island. It is about ¾ of the length of the island from south to north.

On most summer nights, Friendship is a peaceful and idyllic anchorage, but Wednesday preceding the last weekend in July, it becomes very active indeed until the following Sunday noon. On this weekend is held the annual regatta of the Friendship Sloop Society.

Friendship Sloops and the Friendship Sloop Society

During the latter part of the nineteenth century, the Muscongus Bay sloop was evolved for fishing and hauling lobster traps in Muscongus Bay. Seldom over 28 feet long, either lapstreak or carvel planked and usually built with a centerboard, she was well adapted for working among the ledges and up the rivers. In the eighties the need for bigger, faster fishing schooners for the Boston and Gloucester fleets led to the development of the clipper fisherman. This model was adapted in smaller scale to the Gloucester sloops that fished inshore. Muscongus Bay builders combined characteristics of these new sloops with those of the boats their fathers had developed to produce what came to be known as the Friendship sloop.

Wilbur A. Morse of Friendship probably built more Friendship sloops than any other one man. For most of the first two decades of the century he ran a yard on the north shore of the harbor, in which half a dozen sloops might be under construction at the same time. He had a basic model, now owned by Winfield Lash, which he modified according to the needs and desires of the purchaser.

These sloops were admirably adapted to their use. They varied in length from about 22 feet to over 45 feet, the latter being used for offshore trawling and handlining and for carrying freight. They had high, sharp clipper bows with hollow waterlines to keep the crew relatively dry. Aft, they were wide and low to the water to provide ample working space and to facilitate lifting traps and fish aboard. The cockpit floor was usually of loose boards, so water could drain into the bilge and be pumped out. The stern was a rounded transom, neatly tucked up. The run was quite flat. This, combined with a large sail plan and ample ballast of beach rocks, made a stiff and fast boat.

The mast was well forward so she could be used to haul traps among the ledges under mainsail alone. Yet with a staysail and jib set on her long bowsprit, she could slash through a chop with real authority. Auxiliary power consisted of a long oar and a thole pin on the lee side. A man could steer with one hand and give his sloop steerage way in a calm with the other. In light summer weather, the larger sloops often carried tremendous gaff-and-jib topsails over a sail plan generously conceived to begin with. In winter, topmasts were struck and smaller, heavier lower sails were bent.

Construction was inexpensive. A finished sloop ready to take to sea, except for ballast, which could be picked up in any rocky cove, cost between $600 and $1,000.

Of course, many besides Wilbur Morse built Friendship sloops and adapted them to their own needs. Other members of the Morse family, as well as Carters, McClains, and many more, contributed to the evolution of the type.

With the advent of gasoline engines, sloops became obsolete for fishing, and the Morse yard turned to building draggers. Some of the sloops had been used as yachts, but summer sailors were afraid of the topsails and large mainsails so cut them down to make them easier to handle. Then they complained that Friendship sloops were slow and clumsy, and yachtsmen moved on to the Bermuda mainsail and Genoa jib. Very few Friendship sloops were built until after 1960.

The Friendship Sloop Society. In the fall of 1960, Bernard MacKenzie entered his old cut-down Morsebuilt Friendship sloop *Voyager* in the Boston Power Squadron's Bang-and-go-Back race. The idea was that all boats would start together. When the first one reached the outer mark, a gun would be fired and all boats would tack and head for the finish line, thus each establishing her own handicap. *Voyager,* perhaps a bit logy on the outward trip in the gentle breeze, stood up to it like a lady as the wind increased on the way home and crossed the finish line in the smoke of the gun.

MacKenzie was so pleased with his vessel that he traveled to Friendship and enlisted the enthusiastic support of Herald Jones, the Lash brothers, Carlton Simmons, and the Robertses. With publicity in the Boston *Globe,* through Earl Banner, the Friendship Sloop Society was started to preserve and perpetuate the type. With this purpose in mind, about fifteen sloops gathered at Friendship in 1961 to hold a regatta. Since then a considerable number of new sloops has been built, many by the Lash Brothers in Friendship, but also by other builders up and down the coast. Recently two builders have developed fiberglass sloops. Bruno & Stillman in Newfields, New Hampshire, are building a 30-footer designed especially for them. She carries a topsail and jib topsail and has been "raised up" in her topsides to give headroom below. Jarvis Newman of Southwest Harbor, Maine, used *Old Baldy,* built by James Rockefeller, as a "plug." She is only 25 feet long, but rigged with a gaff topsail she is a fast and beautiful little vessel.

Encouraged by this success, Mr. Newman rebuilt the old *Dictator,* an original sloop well known around Deer Isle but sadly deteriorated. In her he won the regatta, so he used her for a plug to turn out a 31-foot model that when sailing under topsail, is a slippery ship indeed. *Anna B,* one of these, has been a consistent winner.

On the Tuesday or Wednesday before the last full weekend in July,

The Friendship Museum

A Friendship sloop photographed in her working rig in the early years of the century.

gaff-headed sails begin to show up off Pemaquid Point and Monhegan. Al Roberts, Cannoneer to the Society, unlimbers his huge brass cannon, half-size replica of an 1812 naval gun, and salutes each sloop as she comes up the harbor. One by one they round the point of Friendship Island or slip by Garrison Island, until as many as half a hundred line both shores. Spectator craft, Coast Guard vessels, and innumerable outboards crowd in. On Thursday, Friday, and Saturday they race and rejoice. By Sunday night, only the lobster boats and one or two lingering sloops are left.

Almost the only point on which the members of the society fail to find friendly agreement is a definition of a Friendship Sloop. From their most recent book, *Enduring Friendships,* we quote:

A Friendship Sloop is a gaff-rigged sloop with a fisherman look about her. A Friendship Sloop is a beautiful fusion of form and function. A Friendship Sloop is a state of mind composed of independence, tradition, resourcefulness, and a most fortuitous combination of geography and language in the name Friendship.

THE FRIENDSHIP MUSEUM

Under the leadership of Mr. and Mrs. Roberts, the Friendship Museum has been incorporated to preserve records and relics of the old days in Friendship. The town gave the museum the old brick schoolhouse and generous people have contributed tools, pictures, artifacts, and records.

Harbor Island, Me. (13301   313). This is a well protected harbor, little used by yachts. The dangers are unmarked but not difficult to avoid.

The north ends of both Harbor and Hall islands are shoal. If entering from the west, keep far enough off the Harbor Island point to see the south end of Davis Island (grassy) over the north end of Hall Island. When Franklin Island Light shows over the grassy southern end of Hall, run up for it until well by the first trees on Hall Island. From there, follow the Hall Island shore closely. You can go as far up as the fishermen's camps on Hall Island and anchor in 4 fathoms with mud bottom.

A Muscongus Bay resident comments: "Use the entering ranges mentioned in the *Guide,* but do so with caution, as they bring you close to shoal areas. These areas are well delineated by the pot buoys, however, and water unoccupied by these is probably quite safe."

If entering from the east, give the north point of Hall Island a very

Stephen Rubicam photo

A Modern Friendship sloop.

good berth at high water and a generous berth at low water. Continue across the harbor to pick up the Franklin Island range as noted above.

Do not go above the first wharf on Hall Island as the cove above that is foul and the flats make out. There is a rock that has tripped many a yacht just off the second wharf on Hall Island.

There is no permanent settlement here. Fishermen camp on Hall Island in the summer for the lobstering. There is an old stone house on Harbor Island now used as a summer home. It is a short walk across to the west side of the island where there are some impressive cliffs and caves.

Harbor Island is clean, quiet, well sheltered and right on the direct course from Port Clyde to New Harbor, Pemaquid, and the west, via the Thompson-Barter Passage. Also, it is a good base from which to explore the beautiful islands of Muscongus Bay.

Georges Harbor, Me. (13301 313). This convenient and little-used anchorage lies between Allen and Benner islands on the south and Davis Island on the north. The snuggest anchorage is between Allen and Benner islands. In entering from the south, hug the Allen Island shore to avoid a ledge in mid-channel making off the Benner Island shore. Anchor wherever you can find swinging room. One correspondent writes: "There really is a wire (as indicated on the chart) on the bottom—somewhat off a shack on the west shore—wire runs east and west."

If the tide sets against the wind, you may lie broadside and roll uncomfortably. A line to a tree ashore will straighten you out.

The writer once saw a little two-masted coaster moored to trees ashore and loading pulpwood through a chute.

A quieter berth is off the cove in the north end of Allen Island. Work in as close as your draft will permit and anchor off the stony beach.

Fishermen camp on Allen Island in the summer for the lobstering.

One of the old aphorisms of cruising used to be that if you own a boat, you own all the islands. This is no longer true. All the islands are owned. Many are protected by The Nature Conservancy or The Audubon Society. Some are covered by conservation easements. All must be treated with the respect due to someone else's property.

The owner of Allen Island urged us to caution visitors to be very careful with fire. When you realize that there are neither facilities nor manpower to extinguish a fire and that a careless match or the heel of a pipe could transform a lovely island into an ash heap in an hour, your zeal for smoking ashore may be cooled. If you must build a fire, do it below high-water mark with an offshore wind and drown it thoroughly before you leave.

Rosier and Waymouth Visit Allen Island in 1605

The granite cross on the shore of Allen Island overlooking the harbor was set up in 1905 to celebrate the 300th anniversary of George Waymouth's visit. An account of that visit and its connection with early efforts at colonization is extracted from a research paper written in 1962. Anyone seeking the full account with the academic paraphernalia of supporting references may communicate with the writer.

In 1605, the year of Champlain's second Maine cruise, George Waymouth in *Archangel* sailed from Plymouth, England, under the orders of Lord Thomas Arundel and Ferdinando Gorges with the mission of locating a site for a permanent colony in New England.

His Maine landfall was Monhegan. Like other visitors before and after he found plenty of codfish, wood, water, and wild roses, but a wretched anchorage. From the anchorage, writes James Rosier, historian of the expedition,

> we might discern the mainland from the west-southwest to the east-northeast, and a great way, (as it then seemed and we afterward found it) up into the main we might discern very high mountains, though the main seemed but low land . . .

These mountains were the Camden Hills. Proponents of the White Mountains do not realize how dimly the White Mountains are visible on the clearest days and how boldly the Camden Hills stand up on any but the haziest days.

Finding Monhegan to be as uneasy an anchorage as it is to this day,

> we weighed anchor about twelve o'clock, and came to the other islands more adjoining to the main, and in the road directly with the mountains, about three leagues from the island where we had anchored.

North of Allen Island, possibly in the same spot where Champlain had spent a night in 1604,

> he found a convenient harbor; which it pleased God to send us far beyond our expectation, in a most safe berth defended from all

winds, in an excellent depth of water for ships of any burthen in six, seven, eight, nine, and ten fathoms, upon a clay ooze, very tough.

The new anchorage was unquestionably Georges Harbor north of Allen Island and protected by Burnt, Davis, Allen, and Benner islands. Waymouth named it Pentecost Harbor. Rosier describes the scene in delightful and delighted language. He describes scenes of aboriginal picnics and mentions the "cranes" we see today, called Great Blue Herons by the ornithologists, but still "blue cranes" by the fishermen.

The crew, led by Captain Waymouth, turned to energetically to put together a small boat they had brought with them, the boat later referred to as the "light horseman." They dug a well and sank a barrel in it, sent a boat's crew fishing for cod, haddock, and "thorneback" (which may be dogfish), explored the islands, cut firewood, and made several spare spars. They picked up great blue mussels with pearls in them and marveled at "the shells all glittering with mother of Pearle." Meanwhile, they lived like kings on lobsters, flounders, lumpfish, and strawberries. Of American strawberries one of England's noted doctors of the time wrote, "God could have made, but never did make a better Berry." They found even the spruce gum as sweet as frankincense. What an Eden it was that they had found! And Rosier describes it with the ecstasy of one set down in Paradise.

Then natives appeared with brilliantly painted faces, dressed in skins. Of course they had seen Europeans before, and friendly relations were at once established. Knives, rings, tobacco pipes, peacock feathers were offered, and the Indians responded with beaver skins. One afternoon all hands had a lobster bake on the shore and lay around afterward smoking tobacco through the broken large claws of lobsters. Rosier writes of his Indian friends:

> They all seemed very civil and merry: shewing tokens of much thankfulness, for those things which we gave them. We found them then (as after) a people of exceeding good invention, quick understanding, and ready capacity.

He admired their women and little children:

> They [the women] were very well favored in proportion of countenance, though colored black, low of stature, and fat, bareheaded as the men, wearing their hair long; they had two little male children of a year and a half old as we judged, very fat and of good countenances, which they love tenderly.

The savages had good table manners, he records, and showed proper respect for Christian services:

> . . . they behaved themselves very civilly, neither laughing nor talking all the time, and at supper fed not like men of rude education, neither would they eat or drink more than seemed to content nature; they desired pease to carry ashore to their women, which we gave them with fish and bread, and lent them pewter dishes which they carefully brought again.

On June 3 they visited the Indian camp at New Harbor, going in their "light-horseman," surrounded by a fleet of canoes. Although they feared treachery at first, the trip turned out to be a great success, with trading and feasting. But the worm at the bud of this rose shows in a sentence of Rosier's: "Thus because we found the place answerable to the intent of our discovery, namely, fit for any nation to inhabit, we used the people with as great kindness as we could devise, or found them capable of."

One day, five or six Englishmen jumped two Indians with whom they were sitting around ashore eating peas. They had a hard time to subdue the Indians, but they did it at last and tied them up below with three others. Rosier shows little regret and no guilt at this betrayal of trust. He writes:

> . . . we would have been very loth to have done them any hurt, which of necessity we would have been constrained to have done if we had attempted them in a multitude, which we must and would, rather than have wanted them, being a matter of great importance for the full accomplishment of our voyage.

Having seized five Indians and two canoes and having set up a cross on the shore, Waymouth left Pentecost Harbor behind. .

After pausing on Cashes Ledge to catch some more codfish, they returned to England to report their success and prepare a new expedition.

The captured Indians soon regained their good dispositions. They shared everything they had with one another, were friendly and merry. When they had acquired some command of English, they described with appropriate gesture and enthusiasm their method of killing, cutting up, and eating whales. Rosier lists their names as Tahanedo, Amoret, Skicowaros, Maneddo, and Saffacomoit.

When Waymouth arrived in England, Gorges and his associate, Pop-

Georges Harbor at high water. Benner Island is in the foreground and Davis Island lies to the left. A favorite anchorage is off the cove on Allen Island to the right.

ham, were delighted with the report. The Indians were well treated, questioned, and found to be truthful, friendly, intelligent, and naturally enthusiastic about their country. These, of course, have always been characteristics of Maine men.

We know that Tahanedo, *alias* Nahanada, was taken back to Pemaquid by Pring in 1606, and that Skicowaros, or Skidwarres, returned in *Mary and John* in 1607 as a guide for the Kennebec expedition. Maneddo probably died in Spain, for there is no record of his return to England after his capture by the Spanish with Challons in 1606. Saffacomoit, returned from Spain after Challons' disastrous voyage, was sent home by Gorges in 1614 with Captain Hobson and apparently died soon after. The remaining Indian, called by Rosier "Amoret," was really Tisquantum, as this is the name Gorges gives him. He was sent home by Captain John Smith in 1614 when Smith visited Monhegan and then coasted south to Cape Cod. Tisquantum was left on the Cape, as his home had been at Plymouth. But before he could get to Plymouth, a Captain Hunt, who had been left in Maine by Smith to complete a cargo, stopped at the Cape. Tisquantum, who had been well treated by Smith's party, came aboard Hunt's vessel with sixteen other Indians. They were at once clapped under hatches; and Hunt sailed for Málaga, where he sold them as slaves. However, the Spanish recognized that they would not make good slaves, and they were released and taken care of by some monks near Málaga. An English vessel, loading wine at Málaga for thirsty Newfoundland fishermen, took Tisquantum to Newfoundland, where he met Captain Mason, the Governor. He introduced him to Captain Dermer, who was much interested in New England and wanted to start a colony. He took Tisquantum back to England to talk with Gorges again, and then to Monhegan and south to the Cape. Here at last Tisquantum was free to go home. He returned to Plymouth in the fall of 1620 just ahead of the Pilgrims, to find his village wiped out by disease. He spent the winter with the Wampanoags on the Cape and in the spring stepped out of the woods with his friend Samoset to greet the Pilgrims with his famous words, "Welcome, Englishmen"— the only man in the world acquainted with Indian ways and English people, the only man in the world who could have saved the Plymouth plantation.

Other Anchorages in Muscongus Bay.

For the information of the leisurely cruiser, there are a number of attractive out-of-the-way anchorages in this bay, some of them of no value as shelter in a storm and most of them inaccessible from the mainland and without supplies.

Marsh Harbor. This lies between Louds Island and Marsh Island. The anchorage is at the northeast end of the passage close to Marsh Island and off a small beach that faces south. It is good shelter on a quiet night and a good place to picnic.

Greenland Cove. This lies at the north end of Muscongus Sound and is completely sheltered. Anchor under the lee of Ram Island in a southerly.

Louds Island East Cove. Here is a sweet anchorage off a beach; but it is rather open to the southeast, where chart 313 shows 9 feet at the northeast corner of the island. Enter cautiously. For shoal-draft boats only.

Louds (Muscongus) Island (Loudville). The landing for the island is a wharf in a cove nearly bare at low water northwest of the north end of Marsh Island. A few fishing boats are usually moored off the cove in summer.

Of chief interest in this island are the many stories, most of them exaggerated, to the effect that at the time of the Civil War, Louds (Muscongus) refused the draft and became independent territory. In order to get the record straight for cruisers in these waters, a local authority furnishes the following article:

Muscongus or Louds Island was formerly known as Samoset's Island. The noted Indian chief, Samoset, is said to have had his headquarters here and to be buried in the early Indian cemetery on the northern end of the island.

Most of the inhabitants—now 17 families—are fishermen, and there are some good farms.

Alexander Gould was probably the first white settler, coming to the island in 1650. William Loud, an English naval officer, settled there in the middle of the eighteenth century. One son, Roberts, stayed on the island. The Louds who now live there are his descendants. The Carters are of Scottish descent and have long been active in island affairs.

The Polands are of English ancestry. Lemard Poland, who came from Massachusetts, is said to be the only man from the island who saw service in the Revolution.

The political history of the island is unique. It is classified as a part of Lincoln County and has always been true to the United States *when properly approached.* The people pay taxes to the State. For many years they had no voting privileges. At the time of Lincoln's first election they voted with Bristol. Due to a controversy the vote was thrown out.

Up to that time, taxes had been paid to the Town of Bristol. The only local expense was for support of the school, which was met by receipts from fishing privileges bought by New London fishermen. After the loss of voting privileges, the islanders, on advice of several lawyers, refused to pay taxes to the town, saying, "We are willing to support the United States but refuse to help Bristol."

When a draft of soldiers for the Civil War was made, the island was included with Bristol, and by some accident an unequally large percentage fell to the islanders. The men refused to honor the draft. They sent a lawyer to Augusta to learn their rights and were told that Bristol had no right to draft them. They then made a proportional draft and bought substitutes. No citizen enlisted.

Some years ago, a law passed at Augusta, with regard to unorganized territories, provided that residents of such places obtain a certificate from the State Assessor to whom they pay taxes. They then pay poll taxes in the nearest town. In the case of Loudville this is Bristol. The citizens now may vote in state and national elections under these conditions, either by coming to the mainland or by absentee ballot. All legal business such as certificates of birth, death, or marriage and licenses are obtained by the islanders from the Town of Bristol.

The families now living on the island for the most part are descendants of the early settlers and the names Poland, Loud, and Carter are common.

Hog Island. North of Muscongus Island lies Hog Island, "330 acres of untouched wilderness," probably the only mature and unspoiled forest the cruising man will find. The story of the establishment of this island as a sanctuary begins in 1910, when Mabel Loomis Todd, on a cruise in Muscongus Bay, learned of the imminent destruction of Hog Island's forest by a lumber company. She bought the island at once, except for the peninsula at the north end, where a hotel stood, and it was untouched for decades.

Then, in 1935, Dr. James Todd, no relation to Mabel Loomis Todd, bought the peninsula on the north end and gave it to the National Audubon Society. In 1936, a summer camp was started here to interpret to adults the local ecosystem through trips dealing with marine life, bird life, plant and animal life, geology, soil, water, and weather. Over half the participants are teachers and youth leaders, although every other profession and interest group is represented. Fifty-five campers participate in each of the four two-week sessions each summer. An average of thirty-three states, two Canadian Provinces and one foreign country are represented each year. In 1960, Mrs. Walter V. Bingham, the owner of Mabel Loomis Todd's part of the island, gave her part to the Audubon Society. Henceforth, the entire island will be maintained as The Todd Wildlife Sanctuary.

If not occupied by the camp boats, two moorings are available for overnight use. They are located in the cove at the north end of the island off the floats and are identified by N.A.S. on each. If you anchor, be certain you are south enough to get out of the tide, but move cautiously, as the cove shoals up rapidly. It is essential that you are well south of the white cable-crossing signs. The camp's electric and water supply crosses from the mainland to the island at this point. A Visitor Center (small natural-history bookstore and exhibit area) is located on the mainland opposite the camp in the left-hand red barn. It is open from 2:30 P.M. to 5:00 P.M. Tuesday to Saturday, from June 25 to August 20 each year. There is a self-guiding nature trail starting at the Visitor Center and winding $6/10$ of a mile through the field and spruce woods of Hockomock Point. Due to the intensity of the camp program and the unavailability of staff, it is preferred that you visit the mainland portion of the sanctuary. For more information, write Director, Information and Education Department, National Audubon Society, 950 Third Avenue, New York, N.Y. 10022.

No supplies are available, although "Bun" Zahn has a lobster pound and float to which gas is piped behind Oar Island near the beached coaster *Cora Cressy*. This vessel was once in the coasting trade. She was bought by Levaggi, the famous restauranteur of Boston, and tied up to a Boston pier for use as a floating nightclub. This proved unprofitable, so she was sold to Mr. Zahn and towed to Bremen about 1936. He started to drill holes in her to use her as a floating lobster pound, but she was so heavily constructed that he couldn't make enough holes to provide sufficient circulation to keep the lobsters alive. She now forms one side of his pound and seems unlikely ever to move from her present berth. Gas is available here.

Cranberry Island. There is a good summer anchorage in the northeast cove between Cranberry and Friendship islands. Anchor among the lobster boats or just outside. There are no supplies, but there is a small settlement of fishermen who come in the summer for the lobstering.

Otter Island. There is a deep, narrow cove in the southern end of the island that makes a good anchorage on an ordinary summer night. The west shore of the cove is very bold. There is room for a handy sloop to round to and anchor. Across the ridge to the west is a pleasant beach. The island is heavily wooded, but a passable trail leads from the ridge east of the anchorage down the length of the island. Blue herons nest near the middle on the east side. There is a house on the north end.

Oar Island. There is an anchorage north of the island off the Lusty Lobster plant. Gasoline and, of course, lobsters are available here and also at Zahn's lobster pound behind Oar Island, where the hulk of the five-master *Cora F. Cressy* lies. There are launching ramps at Waldoboro and Dutch Neck. There is a store at Medomak.

Burnt Island. This large and heavily wooded island has now been abandoned by the Coast Guard. However, the substantial wharf on the west side still stands. One can anchor off the wharf, although it is rather an uneasy berth. The cable area on chart 313 appears to fill the entire area, but the old cable, if it is still there, actually comes ashore on the south side of the cove south of the wharf. Look sharp and you will probably see it and can avoid anchoring on top of it. If you do hook it with an anchor, you can probably haul it up enough with a winch to get clear, and of course it is no longer in use.

An alternate anchorage is in the cove north of the bar between Burnt and Little Burnt. This is ordinarily a quieter anchorage. On his way to establish the colony at the mouth of the Kennebec, Raleigh Gilbert lay here in 1607 for one night but soon moved over to Georges Harbor, a procedure that the writer heartily recommends. In mid-July Little Burnt is a good place to pick raspberries.

The island is now occupied by an outpost of *Outward Bound,* which is further described under Hurricane Island in Penobscot Bay. One can land at the wharf or on the beach and walk to the top of the island or follow as much of the path around the island as is still visible.

Monhegan Island, Me. (13301   313). This is a foreign country to the cruising man bound east from Falmouth Foreside, Sebasco, Boothbay Harbor, and "civilized" mainland ports. High, rocky, unprotected, and alone, Monhegan lies 9 miles to the south and east of Pemaquid in an atmosphere all its own.

In approaching from the west, make for the middle of the island until the light-green shape of Manana is distinguishable from the dark green of Monhegan. Run in to the north of Manana, being respectful of a black can marking a half-tide rock northwest of Manana. Leave this can to *starboard;* that is, go to the *north* of it. The shores of Manana, Smuttynose (which closes the north end of the harbor), and Monhegan are quite bold and the water is very clear.

The northeast corner of Smuttynose makes out a little. The writer stubbed his toe on this ledge pretty hard. Enter between Smuttynose and Monhegan. Hail the wharf for the Harbor Master. If he is not there, try the pilot boat, easily identified by the word PILOT in big letters on her house. If you still cannot find him, take a mooring with no skiff on it, leave a responsible person aboard, and go ashore and find him. Start inquiries on the wharf.

If there is no mooring without a skiff, you will have to anchor, a messy business at Monhegan. The bottom in the harbor is sandy and is encumbered with chains. One can anchor south of the moorings but the bottom is rocky. A better alternative is north of Smuttynose between Nigh Duck Rock and the shore. The water is deep here and the bottom rocky and it is quite a pull to the wharf. Wherever you anchor, be sure to use a trip line. There is a mooring east of Nigh Duck used by the excursion boat *Balmy Days* from Boothbay. She will be using it from about eleven to three. With permission, you can move to it after she leaves.

Few yachts spend the night at Monhegan, so you can probably get a mooring for the night, but it is a miserable place to lie, for the ebb tide running out of the St. George River swings you broadside to the swell and you roll to the jingle and clink of every spare shackle in every locker aboard. One would do well to run for New Harbor, Christmas Cove, Georges Harbor, or Port Clyde.

It is possible, of course, to pass south of Manana and run down into the harbor. If there is much wind and sea, this can be exciting, especially as there is scant room to round to among the moorings. One yachtsman caught in this predicament had to run right out the northern entrance and round to outside. If there is little wind, it is likely to be soft to the south and southwest of Manana. The breeze draws nicely through the harbor and up the Monhegan shore, so the northern entrance is preferable. One can spend a most uncomfortable half hour slopping around in the tide and chop to the south. In thick weather the horn and radio beacon on Manana make approach from the west simple enough. From the east one loses the horn near the cliffs, but there are several bells, gongs, and whistles.

The tide runs quite hard in and out of the St. George River and will set you north on the flood and south on the ebb. Two wrecks on the southern end of Monhegan are reminders of this.

A yacht can lie alongside the wharf at Monhegan, but this has disadvantages. The tide runs hard by the front of the wharf and is likely to set one off to the westward. Unless there is someone on the wharf to catch a line—and there often is—making fast to a piling calls for an agile hand on the foredeck. And once made fast, you will soon have to move for the mail boat from Port Clyde or the *Balmy Days,* an excursion boat that runs daily from Boothbay Harbor. One can slide in on the north side of the wharf and tie up with long lines to allow for the tide. The only "out" about this is that others do the same and tramp back and forth across one's boat, scrub off topside paint, and bump interminably alongside.

Overlooking the harbor is the Island Inn, an old-fashioned resort hotel with wide veranda, long steps, and a fancy cupola. Rooms and meals are obtainable here. The Trailing Yew serves meals in less formal style.

Climb the steep little dirt road by the inn and look back over the harbor. The bleak, treeless bulk of Manana, the restless harbor, the fishhouses at your feet suggest Newfoundland, Labrador, or the islands west and north of Scotland.

At the crossroads beyond, turn left and climb the hill to the lighthouse, now unwatched. Pass north of the buildings and follow a path through the woods to the east. The ledges jab through the thin soil, and old twisty trees cling to the rocky ridge of the island, and even down in the valley where the woods are tall and quiet, one can hear the surf on the shore. In a few minutes you will come out on the 120-foot cliff at Whitehead, from which, on a clear day, you can see Matinicus Rock, Isle au Haut, the Camden Hills, and the islands at the entrance to Penobscot Bay.

Don't climb down the cliffs. It is perfectly possible, but the rock is "rotten" and a chunk of it may break off in your hand or under your foot. There have been a number of tragic accidents here in recent years in which someone has fallen overboard and others have drowned attempting a rescue. The water off the cliffs is deep and there is always a sea running here. The "suds" around the rocks consist of so much air and so little water that it is too thin to support a swimmer but too wet to breathe.

Continue around the island to the south. Notice the dead trees behind Burnt Head, killed one winter when an easterly gale piled *solid green water* over the cliff.

On the southern end of the island lie two wrecks. The larger is that of the tug *D. T. Sheridan,* which went ashore in heavy snow early one February morning in 1950. She was bound east, towing a barge, and in

Monhegan Harbor. The best entrance lies close to the stone wharf.

due course made Manana Whistle. She laid a course to clear the south end of Monhegan and was running on the fathometer. A strong flood tide set her so far to the north that she struck the Washerwoman, a rock on the southern extremity of the island. The shore was so steep that the fathometer gave no warning. The barge was cast off and later picked up. Efforts to get the tug off failed, and a gale broke her in two and scattered her all over the southern end of the island. Even now the wreckage is impressive. The other wreck is a little white yawl that struck in the same place under almost identical circumstances on a foggy morning in June 1956. Little is left of her now.

After leaving the wrecks, follow the path up the hill, by several quaint cottages with carefully tended gardens, and continue down the road by the Monhegan House and the Trailing Yew to the Monhegan Store. Here is a generous variety of canned goods, meat, fruit, and frozen foods. There is a pay phone here and another on the porch of the Monhegan House. The post office is on the road just before you turn left up the hill.

Many of the summer inhabitants of Monhegan are artists, a fact said to account for unusual costumes, hats, beards, and footgear. A well-known artist to frequent Monhegan was Rockwell Kent, whose view of Manana in winter hangs in the Metropolitan Museum of Art in New York. James Wyeth has a cottage on the island.

You may be fortunate enough to meet one of the year-round Monhegan residents. They are rugged and sensible people. On January 1, they load up their fast, able power boats with traps and bait and go lobstering in the deep water around the island. Fog, snow, heavy winter winds, and those biting winter northwesters that make the sea smoke with vapor—all this they endure to haul and bait and set again. But the lobsters are plentiful and hard in winter and the price is high. On June 1, they take up again, and there is no lobstering around Monhegan for six months. They believe that they can catch all the lobsters there are while the price is high. In the summer they go trawling, or seining, or they take jobs "ashore."

Go ashore on Manana and visit the fog signal station and radio beacon. Perhaps one of the crew will show you the Viking runes carved in a ledge in a gully. These marks have been the subject of much controversy, some claiming them to be runes and disbelievers challenging the believers to translate them. Recently Professor Barry Till, in his book *America B.C.* (Quadrangle Books, 3 Park Ave., New York, N.Y. 10016.) makes an interesting case for the inscription's being Ogam, a Bronze Age language, of which he has found many other examples in America and from which he deduces a considerable European presence on this continent long before historic times. He translates the inscription "Ships from Phoenicia, Cargo platform," a reference to Manana as a place to exchange cargoes.

If you like codfish, run off to the bell on Gull Rock Shoal and head due east until the lighthouse drops into the trees. The writer has done well here.

Monhegan is historic ground, as a plaque near the schoolhouse will testify. From about 1610 on it was the base for English fishermen on the coast. In 1614, Captain John Smith of Pocahontas fame tried to organize an expedition to New England. As there seemed to be no prospect of loot, gold mines, or a northwest passage, he got no backers. However, when he began to hint at the possibility of an Eldorado in Maine, and when he guaranteed to bring home a load of fish, in case the gold was not easy to get at, he was swamped with investors.

He arrived in May 1614, set his crew to fishing at once, and built a small boat. In this he and a few chosen friends explored the coast from the Penobscot River to Cape Cod, making an excellent chart. They returned to Monhegan to find one ship loaded with cod and the other nearly so. Smith sailed for Spain with the loaded vessel, sold the codfish there to a population who had had enough of herring and sardines, and returned to England with a very handsome profit.

The next year Smith sailed with a fleet of seventeen sail, intending to plant a permanent colony in Maine; but storms, privateers, and pirates broke up the expedition.

A correspondent, steeped in the lore of the coast, contributes the following:

Be sure to mention old John Smith, who spent the summer of 1614 at Monhegan, gave the name to New England at that time, cruised all summer in a small boat from Mt. Desert to Cape Cod, and left the finest chart of the coast that had been done up to that time. As a chart of Penobscot Bay you could almost navigate by it today; it covers all of the coast and islands. I can almost see the place where my house is located on it. But the strange thing about this chart is that, although it is so remarkably complete, it has no record of Castine Harbor at all. He evidently went down the bay at a time of fog or haze, and missed Castine altogether. It is not a prominent entrance from the outside, anyway.

Note on Approaching the Coast from Nova Scotia. Matinicus Rock is a better point to head for than Monhegan in coming to the Maine coast from Nova Scotia. While the light on Monhegan is excellent, fog conditions make the approach to Matinicus preferable.

Matinicus has a powerful horn, audible from the east and south. Monhegan's foghorn, situated on Manana Island to the west of the southern part of the larger island, is frequently inaudible from the east. Monhegan's east shore is high bold cliffs, while Matinicus Rock is a small place with a horn that can be heard long before a vessel, under normal conditions, could strike the shore.

Fog along the Maine coast tends to pile up on the windward side of the islands; it is often clear on the leeward side. For example, in approaching Monhegan Island in the fog from the east, head a mile or two off the southern end for the lighted whistle to the southwest of the island, so as to open up the Manana fog signal. Avoid Gull Rock Shoal, marked by a bell, where the sea breaks in heavy weather.

The authors found that, on approaching Monhegan Island in fog from the eastward, the breakers were plainly heard on the northern part of the easterly shore well before the cliffs were visible. They were not audible on the southern part of the shore until after the cliffs hove into sight.

Port Clyde, Me. (13301   313). This is a large and convenient harbor, well sheltered and easy of access, but not very inspiring ashore. It was once much used by coasters and mackerel seiners.

From the west, leave Gig Rock bell and the Sisters to starboard and the nun off Hooper Island to port. Can 3 on the northern end of Hart Bar must be left to *starboard.* It is not a mark for the entrance to Port Clyde but for passage alongshore. From here, run up the harbor, leaving nuns to starboard and cans to port. Marshall Point Light is so situated that by keeping it fine on your starboard bow you can run in from Davis Strait, picking up the buoys as you come along.

From the east, a course from Mosquito Island bell to Marshall Point Light clears all dangers except to the deepest yachts.

On a quiet night, anchor off the wharves. If it looks rolly there, move over under the Hooper Island shore. If really heavy weather is expected, go through the passage north of Raspberry Island and anchor north of Hooper Island. Anchorage off the fish plant at the entrance to the inside passage is possible, but it is likely to be a noisy berth and troubled by tide.

There are six guest moorings off the wharves on the east side of the harbor, marked by red plastic balls. Each consists of a one-ton block of granite with 1½″ and ½″ chain. These are maintained by Mr. Bruce Waters at the store. In 1976 the fee was $3.00 per night.

Land at the middle wharf where there is 10 feet at the end of the float at low water. Here is available gasoline, Diesel fuel, ice, and water. In the store at the head of the wharf is an excellent stock of meats and groceries, beer and wine, charts, clothing, and marine hardware. A shower is available for the use of cruising people. Mr. Waters purchased the store about 1971, renovated and expanded it, and extended the wharf. He is a man of energy and imagination and is taking every possible step to provide services for transients as well as local people. He will put on a lobster bake, for instance, for a visiting yacht club with a little advance notice.

The story goes that the Conservation Commission, of which he is a member, vainly sought to persuade the town to limit the uses of islands under the town's jurisdiction. Some sort of zoning ordinance was sought. As a persuasive gesture, the commission and the owner of Allen Island invited influential members of the town to Boston, provided a magnificent banquet, and showed plans for developing Allen Island into a high-rise-motel-centered vacation community in the worst possible taste. The citizens returned home and enacted the zoning ordinance. The story came from a source usually reliable and always interesting and may possibly be apocryphal; if it turns out to be such, the writer will be sorry.

George Davis, whose number is in the telephone book, is an acknowledged expert with a recalcitrant engine. Lehtinen's yard in Tenant's Harbor is the nearest place for repairs to hull or spars.

It is a long taxi ride to the bus station in Thomaston.

Port Clyde is supported by fishing and lobstering, an uncertain business. The fish go fresh to New York in trucks. Hake and sole go for 8¢ a pound more in New York than in Boston, so it is worth the extra distance.

A restaurant, Driftwood, is just up the hill. Here also are a gift shop, a small variety store, a garage, and a post office. There used to be a sardine factory on the cove to the east of the landing, but it burned in 1971. It is a pleasant walk to Marshall Point. A loran station was established there in 1971.

The passage back of Raspberry Island can be negotiated at almost any tide by anyone drawing less than 6 feet. Enter between the fish-packing wharf and Raspberry Island, keeping well to the eastward to avoid a kelp ledge in midchannel. Continue around the bend, favoring the outside or starboard side. Just beyond a dammed-up cove is a ledge that usually shows. In 1970 it had an iron spike in the top. Leave this to starboard and continue in the middle. Coming in from the river, stay between the rock with the iron in it and two ledges off the end of Raspberry Island. This is a convenient way to get from the upper part of Muscongus Bay to the eastward, particularly for one in need of fuel or supplies.

On a flat ledge, about 20 yards south of the silver oil tanks at the head of the ferry wharf, are deep grooves gouged by rocks driven along by the glacier during the ice age.

St. George River, Me. (13301   313). This broad and beautiful river was selected by Waymouth and Rosier in 1605 as the best place at which to establish a permanent English colony in Maine. Rosier wrote:

"I will not prefer it before our river Thames, because it is England's richest treasure," and then added that he wished that the Thames had all the desirable features of the St. George. He left for England with this sentence of regret: ". . . the river . . . did so ravish us with all variety of pleasantness, as we could not tell what to commend, but only admired: . . . and we all concluded . . . that we should never see the like river in every degree equal until it pleased God we beheld the same again."

The river is remarkably free of navigational hazards, the most dangerous being an unmarked ledge west of Hooper Island in the mouth of the river. Keep well on the western side of the river to avoid this. Other dangers are marked.

There are several attractive coves along the shores, especially Turkey Cove, Maplejuice Cove, and Broad Cove. All are well charted and none have public landings or any facilities whatever. There are said to be striped bass in the river in a good year.

One can follow the channel between the flats to a tight **S** turn and then to Thomaston, site of the state prison and an active cement factory.

In the old days of the nineteenth century Thomaston was a very prosperous town. Thousand-ton ships were built and launched into the St. George River with sails bent and every spar in place. Blacksmiths, sailmakers, and others associated with the yards were busy here. Granite and limestone were quarried, the limestone to be burned into lime and shipped out in the schooners that brought in firewood for the kilns. Ice was cut on the ponds and shipped to tropical countries, and the profit from all these projects went into the solid four-square high-ceilinged mansions that now border the quiet streets. Just east of Thomaston lived General Henry Knox, artillery officer for George Washington during the Revolution. His house still stands as a museum.

Two shipyards are still in operation, in one of which was being built, in 1978, a coasting schooner. She is to be christened *John W. Leavitt,* in honor of the artist and author of *The Wake of the Coasters,* and she is going to try to make an economic success out of cargo-carrying under sail.

The back entrance to Port Clyde from the St. George River. Leave the round wooded island and the tiny islet in front of it to starboard in entering from the river.

Pleasant Point Gut, Me. (13301   313). This gut forms a bottle-tight anchorage between Gay Island and the mainland. Entrance is easy. In running up the river, be very generous to the half-tide ledge to the west of Hooper Island. It extends far out into the river. Favor the western shore. The lobster traps around it are very helpful. Leave the can outside the gut to *starboard.* It is placed for vessels entering the river. Favor the northern shore. Ledges make out northward from Flea Island at high water, but at low water everything is exposed. Once inside, continue close to the mainland shore among the anchored lobster boats. There is an extensive mud flat behind Flea Island, on which the writer spent an ignominious hour or two. Deep-draft boats can anchor in the bight of the northern shore just inside Flea Island. Those of shoal draft can go on up the harbor. Just south of the wharf is a half-tide rock. The rest of the harbor is soft bottom.

A correspondent familiar with the harbor writes: "Go well inside—there is a ledge on the south side of the entrance, which at low water will catch a keel 6-feet deep. This ledge may be—but probably is *not*—the star under the *t* in *Gut* (on the old chart). "My" ledge, which does not bare, is east of Flea Island, generally between the 16 and the 9.

At half tide or better a boat drawing 4 feet can easily go through behind Gay Island into Davis Cove and Friendship Harbor, but the channel is tortuous. Directions for it are picturesque but confusing. Take a local pilot for best results. The Harbor Master is a good one to ask.

There is a wharf with a gas pump and a lobster car on the north shore. At the head of the wharf is a small store selling fishermen's supplies, candy, and tobacco, but no food. The nearest grocery store is 4 miles up the road. Next to the wharf is a lobster pound, now abandoned because the lobsters somehow found a way out unknown to the owner.

Pleasant Point Gut is much used for winter moorings. It is perfectly protected and the swift tide prevents the formation of really heavy ice. In the event of really heavy weather, there is no better place to hole up.

Turkey Cove and Maplejuice Cove, Me. (13301   313). These are quiet and unfrequented anchorages with nothing much to offer but peace and scenery. One cannot easily land at either, as the flats make out. Maplejuice Cove borders on the farm where Andrew Wyeth did much of his best work. There was a plan to restore the place and to collect here a museum of Wyeth memorabilia. However, even before the project got under way, so many visitors thronged into town that the roads were torn up, parking became a problem, and all the difficulties connected with crowds of people proved too much for the town to handle. The project has been abandoned, at least temporarily, and rumor has it that the property has been given to the state.

Tenants Harbor, Me. (13301   313). In anything but an easterly gale, Tenants Harbor affords a quiet anchorage. Marked by the conspicuous abandoned white lighthouse on Southern Island and by a lighted bell with an unusually deep and rich tone, Tenants Harbor is easy of access at any time. In entering, keep more or less in the middle. If anything, favor the northern shore. Anchor where draft and inclination dictate. There is plenty of room.

On the north shore is the small but efficient Lehtinen's boat yard, capable of making all ordinary repairs. Next to it is Cod End, a wharf operated by Red and Anne Miller. Here one may get gasoline, Diesel fuel, ice, and water at the float. A marine store provides charts and other marine supplies. Consult with the Millers about rental moorings. Their specialty is fresh fish and lobster caught from their own boats, either cooked or as it comes. One of their boys will dive to clear a fouled propeller or do other underwater work. They have plans for continued expansion.

The next wharf to the west is the town landing, used almost exclusively by fishermen.

Up the shore is the old East Wind Inn, now entirely remodeled and up to date. Rooms, meals, showers, and even a beauty shop are available here. Meals are served seven to nine, twelve to two, and five to eight. Seafood, steaks, and homemade bread and pies are featured.

Up the road, less than a quarter of a mile from Cod End, is a good grocery store. Outside is a public telephone. To the west, along the street, are a garage and an ice cream and variety store. East of the grocery are a laundromat and the post office.

If you are not in need of shore facilities, Long Cove to the north of the entrance to Tenants Harbor makes a quiet and secluded anchorage.

Alternate Courses:
Muscle Ridge Channel or Two-Bush Channel

The navigator may be in doubt whether to work his way through the islands and ledges of the Muscle Ridges or to take the longer and easier course outside.

Bound East. In most cases, especially if the tide is fair, the best course is inside. The run from Mosquito Island to Whitehead is less than 6 miles, a good deal shorter than the run to Two-Bush. If you change your mind on the way, Tenants Harbor is close to leeward. At Whitehead you can run on up the channel if the tide is fair or wait out a foul tide in Seal Harbor. If the weather is thick, you may have some trouble making Whitehead, because the sound of the fog signal does not seem to carry well against the wind. However, before you can get into any trouble, you will be able to hear it. There is a bell on Southeast Breaker and a good horn on Two-Bush.

The course up the channel is easy, even in thick weather. However, on most days there will be a scale-up in the channel. The islands to the south seem to dry up the fog and stimulate the wind. The tide runs hard but pretty much along the course. One can usually get an echo with the horn off the high land at Sprucehead. The fathometer provides a safe way to prevent wandering to either side of the channel. There are several shelters easily available should the tide turn. Best of all, perhaps, the sea is smooth and the traffic is not likely to be dangerous.

Outside, the breeze may be lighter, the sea rougher, the runs between buoys longer, and the traffic perilous indeed. A 100,000-ton tanker cannot maneuver with agility. The tide seems to run to the west with greater strength and for a longer time than it runs east. The only possible shelter on the outside course is Home Harbor, and that is difficult in the fog.

Bound West. With the wind northwest, particularly if it is early in the day, the inside passage is much to be preferred, for it keeps one to windward, and the northerly is likely to hold longer and blow harder under the land than it does offshore. However, if it gets to be midmorning, the outside course may be a good gamble, for the wind may very well shift southerly within a few hours, and distance down the bay becomes distance to windward. If the northwester holds long enough to get you by the Two-Bush gong, you can probably fetch right into Port Clyde on the southerly. If the wind does not shift, Monhegan or Georges Harbor is a realistic shelter.

If the wind is southerly, the beat down the Muscle Ridges with a fair tide is pretty and provides an active day for all hands on sheets and backstays. The wind will be fresher under the islands than it will outside. However, the beat down the bay has its pleasures, too, and one who likes being to windward can be happy off Two-Bush, where he can fetch a long way to the westward. The beat from Whitehead around Mosquito Bell can be a long pull.

If it is thick and calm, you might as well motor outside, where the buoys are loud and the navigation easy. Be sure to hang up a radar reflector.

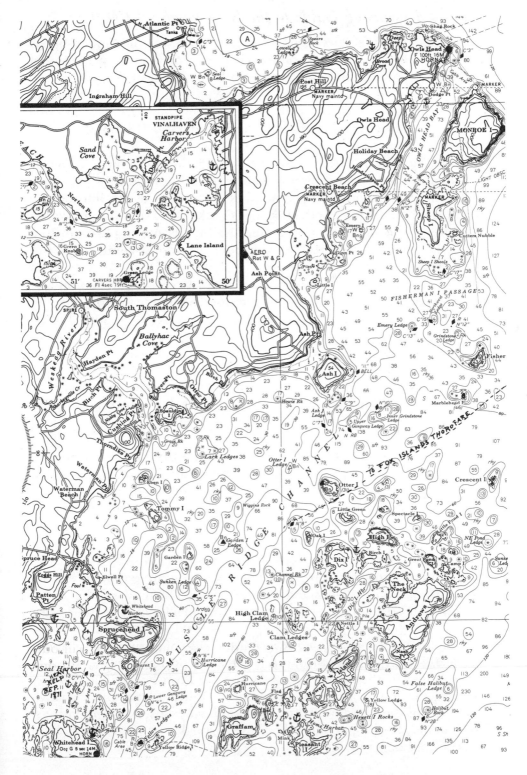

Anchorages in the Muscle Ridge Channel (refer to Chart 310).

At night, the outside route is to be preferred, for the lighted buoys are a great help. The only drawback is the occasional presence of supertankers, which must be treated with the greatest respect.

Shelters between Whitehead and Rockland (13303 322)

Whitehead Island. There is a cove behind the lighthouse, formerly used by the Coast Guard; unfortunately their big moorings have now been removed. The holding ground is good, but a trip line on the anchor is not amiss here as the bottom is rocky. A wash works in around the point of the island, but on a quiet night it is not unpleasant. In a southerly blow it would roll a small boat around uncomfortably but would probably not be dangerous.

It is a pleasant walk down around the old Coast Guard station and the light. An inventive lightkeeper developed a scheme for compressing air for the fog signal by the action of the waves. It was reported to be quite successful until it was carried away in a gale. You may be able to find the irons in the rock where the floats were attached.

Seal Harbor. This harbor was once much used by coasters waiting out a foul tide but is little used by anyone today except lobstermen out of Sprucehead. You will not be crowded here as you might be at Tenants Harbor.

Enter between can 1A and can 3. When Burnt Island is abeam, cross to can 1. Run up the harbor, keeping the lobster boats in the *far* anchorage fine on the starboard bow. Keep well off the 2-foot spot inside of nun 2. The buoy marks a patch of boulders, which breaks at low water and extends west of the line between can 3 and nun 2.

The anchorage behind the jetty is safe enough, but rolly. Unless you need supplies, continue up the harbor, keeping an eye open for the ledge off the unnamed island to the west. The end of the ledge is exposed one hour after high water but makes out to the northeast.

When the lobster wharf on the northeast side of Sprucehead is about 150 yards abeam to starboard, turn sharply to port and run up the line of moorings for the fishing boats south of Patton Point. The channel is *narrow,* but it will take 8 feet at any tide. Do not go beyond the small beach east of the wharf on Patton Point and stay close to the moorings. The channel shoals up to mussel beds very quickly on both sides. There is good holding ground here.

One can anchor north of Long Ledge to avoid going all the way in to the anchorage described above, but the bottom, once stiff mud, is reported to be foul with kelp and eel grass.

Dix Island. The place labeled Dix Island Harbor is a secure anchorage, though not a snug one. Entrance is among unmarked ledges, but most of them show at high water, and all of them are evident at low water. A preferable anchorage for a small yacht is in the cove between Dix Island and Birch Island north of the bar. Enter either side of Oak Island, follow the north shore of Dix Island, and anchor northwest of the tip of Birch Island.

Dix Island is now owned by an association, whose intention it is to allow visitors on the island but not to encourage them. The president of the association writes:

Dix Island was once the site of a big quarry operation, with schooners and barges loading at the dock and gangs of stonecutters living ashore. The island is now owned by the members of the Dix Island Association (President, Sharon M. Lawrence, Yarmouth, Maine), who have an interest in the preservation of the rich natural beauty, the historic significance, and a simple primitive life-style. Visitors may enjoy the shores; however, no fires or camping are allowed. The interior of the island is restricted to the private use of owners.

False Whitehead Harbor. This is a quiet cove. There is no problem in entering except for the possible presence of old weir stakes. It is not a long walk to the store at Sprucehead.

Home Harbor. This is a handy little place to know about, as it is well to windward in the prevailing southwester. It is between Pleasant and Hewett islands (the latter misspelled *Hewell* on the chart) just inside Two-Bush Island. From Home Harbor it is easy to get around Two-Bush and then fetch well down the coast. It is also a good place from which to take off for Matinicus. There are no supplies or facilities of any kind, but in past years there has been a settlement of fishermen who come out with their families from Rockland for the summer lobstering.

To enter from the east, go either side of Yellow Ledge, which is high, bold, and really yellow. Be sure to pick up Hewett Island Rocks and then follow the Hewett Island shore, giving the Pleasant Island shore a good berth off the high bluff. Anchor north of the fishing boats near the weir, where chart 322 shows 16 feet. To get out of the tide, creep with the lead as far south as possible. There is some scour of tide, but it is not uncomfortable.

To enter from Muscle Ridge Channel, run for the small prominent house on Flag Island until you lose Whitehead Light. Then go right up the middle of a hole west of Flag Island. Keep in the middle and look out for a cross tide. You will see bottom, but the writer has carried 5 feet through at low water. When you are through the narrow passage, follow the shore around to the east until well clear of ledges to the south. This is a real piece of gunk-holing, but it is done frequently by the fishermen.

Rockland, Me. (13307   209) (13305   310). The chief advantages of Rockland are its ease of access and its proximity to coastal bus lines, which run far inland from most ports both east and west of Rockland. It is also a good place to stock up on supplies.

With a light on Owls Head and a light and horn on the end of the breakwater, Rockland is easy to make from any navigable direction. In thick weather especially, be alert for big fishermen and for the island ferries based at Rockland, which serve North Haven, Vinalhaven, and Matinicus.

In an easterly, anchor under the lee of the breakwater. Under ordinary conditions, follow the buoyed, dredged channel to the yacht anchorage in the southwest part of the harbor. The seven red balls labeled City of Rockland are guest moorings. The Rockland Yacht Club is located in the Chamber of Commerce building at the head of the wharf. George Burr is in charge.

The next wharf to the north is used by the Down East Packet & Trading Co. The handsome cruise schooner *Harvey Gamage* ties up here. The Black Pearl Restaurant is on the wharf.

In Lermond Cove behind Crockett Point is the Maine State Ferry wharf and next to that the wharf of Knights' Marine, run by Horatio Knight. This is the best facility in Rockland for yachtsmen. Knight has gasoline, Diesel fuel, ice, water, showers, and a laundromat on his wharf. A mechanic is in attendance, and there is a marine hardware store nearby. Here, too, is the safest berth in Rockland, if it really comes on to blow.

Ashore, the city of Rockland affords almost anything the yachtsman might want. Air and bus service are quickly available. Grocery, drug, liquor, and department stores are but a short walk from the shore. Several hotels and motels provide rooms, meals, and cocktails. There is a movie theater nearby. Books, charts, and other government publications can be purchased at Huston-Tuttles on School Street. Skin divers may have air bottles filled within twenty-four hours at Morris Gordon & Son.

The Harbor Master is Leroy Benner. He can usually be reached at the police station.

Repairs of all kinds can be effected at Rockland. Consult the Harbor Master or George Burr.

The Farnsworth Museum, with some remarkable exhibits of local artists as well as those of wider reputation, is well worth while. A walk to it leads through a more gracious part of Rockland than you might otherwise see.

But, at best, Rockland is a city and the waterfront has a commercial air. For peace and quiet, withdraw to Broad Cove for a protected anchorage from the prevailing southerly wash and a lovely view of the Camden Hills.

CHAPTER XI

Rockland to Schoodic Point

General Conditions: This region is the goal of many cruising men. The bays are broken up by hundreds of islands and inlets. The shores are usually bold and of clean pink or yellowish granite. The islands are overgrown with dark spruce trees interspersed with fields of grass and raspberry bushes. Among the rocks are smooth, sandy beaches.

The harbors are many and vary from "live" yachting centers like Camden to uninhabited coves like Buckle Harbor and Webb Cove. The fishing is good almost anywhere. The local people are friendly and willing to help the stranger.

The weather is variable and interesting. It may be thick fog all day with nothing to be seen but an occasional buoy and the loom of spruce trees. Or it may "scale up" into a smoky sou'wester with a chop running up the bays and even the nearby shores a hazy blue-green. The next day it may come off a slashing northwester with the puffs off the hills and islands turning the water green and white, and with every tree standing out clearly. On such a day the mountains of Mt. Desert, Blue Hill, or Camden are sharp cut against the horizon. Whatever the weather, there is always a sheltered harbor to run for at night.

Fog. Don't worry about it. The frequency of fog and its dangers are vastly overrated. No one likes it. Dangerous situations can arise quickly. Carelessness brings its punishment swiftly. But for generations people have navigated Penobscot Bay in the fog and never before with such good equipment as we have today.

In general, the principles of navigating in the fog are applied common sense. Granted a reliable compass, a watch, an engine or a fair wind, a sounding lead or Fathometer, and a chart, one simply lays a course, takes one's departure, and writes the time in the log. The fog shuts down. The world consists of the crests of two waves and the trough between. A lookout is posted to watch, listen, and blow the horn. A reliable helmsman keeps his eyes on the compass and devotes his attention to nothing else. The skipper stands aft, watch in hand, alert for what may befall. Everything has some meaning. A lobster trap will suggest shoal water and will indicate the direction and force of the tide. Gulls screaming will indicate the presence of an island or ledge. The smell of spruce trees, the swash of water on the shore, the distant hoot of a horn, or the muffled tinkle of a bell—all are to be fitted into the pattern.

As time runs out and the mark is near, it is well to stop and listen for a bit. Or take a sounding. Something will turn up. If it doesn't, make a square, timing each side and recording each course. As a last resource, anchor. But fully half the time the fog will scale up in the course of the run, giving you first a wider view of the water and then a dim view of the nearest land. Or you may sail right out of the fog as you would step out of a door.

I remember hunting around for Kimball Island one foggy afternoon and being startled by the sight of Isle au Haut right over me. In seconds the whole northern end of the island was sparkling in bright sun, while behind, still shrouding Kimball Head, was the heavy white mass of the fog.

The odds are against fog, but if it does shut in, make a start, be extra careful in your navigation and extra watchful for unforeseen error, and you will probably "make" all right. Lay your courses for bells, whistles, bold shores, or the lee sides of islands.

Islands. Don't miss landing on an uninhabited island. If possible, bring a bucket of lobsters and something to go with them. If you anchor off the lee side and explore the shore in the dinghy, you will probably find a little beach to land on. You may startle some crows off the seaweed as you land. The rocks are usually steep, clean granite and the water so clear that you can see bottom in two fathoms. Build your fire on the lee side close to high-water mark. While you wait for the lobsters to boil, take a swim, or put on a mask and explore the ledges close to the shore. After the lobsters are dispatched, put out the fire thoroughly and strike inland. You will find thick spruce brush. The blowdowns are usually grown up to raspberry or blackberry bushes. In mid-July or late August the sun-warmed berries are food for the gods—but don't go berrying in short pants!

On the seaward end of the island, if it is seldom visited, you may find the messy nests of gulls and shags with eggs or young birds in early July. Eiders and terns are less common but they do nest on Maine islands. Work back along the shore. You may find a lobster buoy or net float among the debris at high-water mark—or a bait box or a watch; you never know. A blue heron may fly up as you round a point.

There are caves in some islands and cliffs, great smooth ledges, or rough beaches. Ospreys often nest in trees near the shore. Climbing the tree is doubtful procedure. The birds resent your intrusion, the trees are often dead and the branches brittle, and the nest is so big and rough that you can't climb out around the edge anyway. Better not molest the local residents.

When you are ready to leave, check the fire again to be sure it is cold. Whether you return aboard loaded with plunder or not, your trip ashore will be one of the pleasantest parts of the cruise to remember during a long, dreary February.

Lobstering. You will see lobster traps wherever the water is shoal and the bottom is rocky. A clump of lobster traps will often indicate a shoal or a ledge in the middle of a bay or will define the edge of a channel. If you come on lobster traps in the fog, proceed with great care unless you are sure of your location.

In the summer, lobsters are more active, particularly in the warmer, shallower waters where they shed their shells and grow new ones. A "shedder's" shell feels like thin cardboard. Shedders are cheaper and have less meat in proportion to the size of the shell, but probably no less per pound. Opinion is divided. Some people abhor them; others prefer them.

Diving for lobsters is against the law. They can be taken only in conventional traps. These are wooden crates about 2 by 3 feet, built either of spruce bows and laths or of oak frames and laths. They are ballasted with flat rocks or cement, and baited with herring, alewives, redfish, or whatever comes to hand. The bait is salted and allowed to age a little to work the oil out of it and make it attractive to a lobster a little way off. On a warm, still day it makes itself known.

The trap is baited and dropped overboard in shoal water. A ¼-inch nylon line leads from the trap to a bottle, called a toggle, and onto the buoy. Each man paints his buoys a characteristic color. The toggle is attached to help float the line so that weed and other debris doesn't collect on it and drag the buoy under in the tidal current. Sometimes several traps are set in tandem with a buoy at each end of the line. This buoy will probably be a gallon jug in a cage of laths with a flag on top. With a winch geared to the engine, a man can haul the string of traps so that he has one trap on the davit, another halfway up, and the third on the bottom. In the days of hauling from a dory or sloop, a man could haul only one trap at a time, and that was hard work. In a sloop the trick was to pick up the buoy and sail gently off with it, thus towing the trap to the surface. Then it was necessary only to haul it alongside, not to lift it from the bottom.

Under sail, one very seldom fouls a trap, but under power it is well to avoid crossing between the toggle and the buoy. The line is likely to lie slack just below the surface and may be sucked in by your propeller. Half a dozen turns of nylon line hauled tight and twisted hard around your shaft can present a very difficult problem. If you have to cut the line, try to save the buoy and tie it on again. Your thoughtfulness will be appreciated.

A lobsterman is an independent entrepreneur with a considerable investment at stake. He may fish 400 traps, although some far exceed that figure. A trap, line, and buoys cost between $20.00 and $30.00 His boat, with the necessary electronic depth sounder and radio telephone, will cost perhaps $20,000. Then he must have a shore privilege and some sort of fish house. He must buy bait, gasoline, and replacements. He may well have $50,000 tied up in his business. A single winter gale can wipe him out. Do you wonder that lobsters are expensive?

Although there have been violent disagreements among lobstermen, sometimes amounting to "trap wars," in general they respect each other's gear and watch out for each other's safety. Poachers are dealt with roughly. Nothing could make a yachtsman so unwelcome in a fishing community as to be seen hauling traps. A resident of Maine who is both a lobsterman and a yachtsman has this to say on the subject:

> I have heard a good deal in legislative hearings and elsewhere of hauling traps by yachtsmen, and I don't believe it. In the first place, it's hard work to haul by hand and it's wet and dirty if you're not dressed for it. In the second place, most of the dinghys you see behind yachts couldn't take a trap aboard without tipping over. In the third place, if you haul from the yacht itself, it's practically impossible to get a trap aboard without scraping it up the side and taking aboard a quantity of mud, kelp, bait drainings, and all the rest of it. When you consider that the average haul in the summer of 1966 was about a quarter of a pound per trap, the odds against getting something to eat out of a trap make the procedure pretty ridiculous. I doubt that it's much done.

With over 400 traps to pull, a lobsterman is on the water a good part of the day. Wherever you are in Maine, if you look or listen carefully, you are likely to find someone tending traps. A distress signal will bring almost instant help. A flare, a series of shots, or steady blowing of the horn will bring one of these men, who are always watching out for one another and for you, too.

Most lobstermen keep in touch with each other on the CB radio, often running it at absolutely top volume. If you are in trouble, a call on CB will bring rapid response. These people are able and helpful.

You can best repay their help by giving of your friendship in return. A drink in your cockpit and a carton of cigarettes will be much appreciated. Anything else you care to do will probably be appreciated too. These men are not "quaint characters" but are often well informed, intelligent, and independent businessmen engaged in a hazardous occupation that sometimes demands all the courage, endurance, and intelligence a man can call upon. Many of them have wrung more water out of their socks than most summer sailors ever see.

Supplies and Repairs. As you go farther east, you are increasingly on your own. Between Rockland and Schoodic, major repairs can be made at Rockland, Camden, Stonington, and Southwest Harbor. Ordinary supplies are available at most villages, but it is well to be stocked up for several days ahead, so that your itinerary will not be governed by your need for supplies. The towns mentioned above can provide almost anything you will need. Liquor stores are infrequent in this area. They are run as a state monopoly. Rockland, Camden, Stonington, Northeast Harbor, and Bar Harbor have liquor stores and many grocery stores carry wine and beer.

Suggested Courses

Eggemoggin Reach. This is a pretty and usually unexciting sail through protected waters and is to be chosen if the fog is thick offshore. Eastbound, you will have a fair wind up West Penobscot Bay past the dramatic hill of Great Sprucehead, where Eliot Porter took the photographs for the Sierra Club's *Summer Island,* and among the smaller and equally beautiful islands of the upper bay. Bucks Harbor at the west end of the reach is a good anchorage. Thence the course is about southeast down the reach between Deer Isle and the shore, a pleasant sail with the wind abeam in an ordinary southwester. You are unlikely to encounter fog in the reach, as the mass of Deer Isle dries it up. The wind often dies off the mouth of the Benjamin River but, after a short drift, it comes in again. In general, favor the southerly side of the passage for a fresher breeze.

Once out by the bell at Devils Head, cross Jericho Bay, pass through Casco Passage, and head for Bass Harbor Head on Mt. Desert.

Westbound it is a pleasant relief from beating, but of course you will pay for it on the western end; for unless you can arrange a northwester or a dry easterly, you will have a long dead beat down Penobscot Bay. Still, it may be preferable to navigating the Thorofares in the fog.

The Thorofares. This route crosses West Penobscot Bay to Stand In Point, passes through Fox Islands Thorofare between North Haven Island and Vinalhaven past the village of North Haven. It then crosses East Penobscot Bay, leaving Mark Island to starboard bound east and through the well-buoyed passage between Deer Isle and the islands south of it. The course then passes north of Eastern Mark Island, across Jericho Bay to York Narrows, and on to Mt. Desert.

This course is more difficult in the fog than the course through Eggemoggin Reach, but as the tide runs pretty much along your course through the Thorofares, it does not set you off to either side in the tricky parts. The runs across the bays have noisy marks to run for.

This course keeps you to windward bound west. With luck and a close-winded boat, you can fetch the course with only a hitch to windward now and then. Certainly there is greater variety in the scenery.

A variation on this course is to sail from the eastern end of Fox Islands Thorofare to the whistle on the Brown Cow and then thread your way through the islands, coming out either side of Saddleback Island and running across to York Narrows. This is by far the most interesting course although, for the stranger who would not recognize the islands, it can be a horror show in the fog. Still, on a sunny day you are likely to get a scale-up under Isle au Haut.

Outside. Another alternative is to go south of Vinalhaven, through the broken country to the southeast, past Otter and Brimstone Islands, south of Saddleback Ledge and Roaring Bull, south of Long Island, and then up the Western Way. Or you can go through Burnt Coat Harbor, pass west of Long Island, and run up the Western Way by Black Island. A very attractive feature of the outside passage is the approach to the Mt. Desert hills on a fair afternoon, with the shadows changing as the sun swings west. In the fog, one misses this feature and must navigate among the offshore islands and ledges south of Vinalhaven and Swans Island, where there are few buoys and those, for the most part, rather silent. It is no place to be lost.

Rockport, Maine (13307   209) (13305   310). Located 6 miles by water north of Rockland, this is a good anchorage, sheltered from all but heavy southerly and southwesterly winds, and easy of access. The best landmark is Indian Island, with the white light structure. The light is now discontinued, but there is a flashing white-lighted beacon (ten seconds) at the south end of Lowell Rock.

The harbor is perfectly clear, except for the stone pier on Porterfield Ledge marked by a beacon. There is an old weir on the west shore. Anchor well up in the harbor near the mouth of Goose River.

The public landing is at the head of the harbor on the east side of Goose River, with 3 feet or less at low water. Here also is the yard of Rockport Marine, Inc., operated by Lucian Allen. It was on Mr. Allen's Travelift that James Rockefeller launched his Friendship sloops. They were built near the top of Bald Mountain, hauled to the yard on a lowbed trailer by oxen, and launched by machine. The centuries mix picturesquely.

Rockport Marine has gas, ice, water, and the Travelift mentioned above. A mechanic is usually in attendance. Next to it is a restaurant, The Sail Loft, also run by Mr. Allen. It has a very pleasant atmosphere, no small part of which is due to the presence of the Allens; and the quality of the food is second only to the atmosphere.

Supplies are available just up the hill from the landing, on the main street. There is a post office here, and there is a bus stop, where connections can be made for Rockland, Portland, and Boston.

Repairs can be made at Rockport Marine or nearby in Camden. Henry Bohndell, a sailmaker and rigger of wide reputation, lives in Rockport.

Jay Hanna lives on the hill on the east side of the harbor. His principal occupation is building models and making ship carvings. Six of his models are in the Smithsonian Institution. The schooners *Mary Day* and *Bill of Rights* carry trail boards carved in his shop. His work is a beautiful example of what a real craftsman can accomplish with skill and study. A visit to his shop is an inspiration. He has written a book, published by International Marine in Camden, entitled *Marine Carving Handbook,* available at the Owl and Turtle Bookstore in Camden.

On the west side of the harbor is the Penobscot Boat Works, founded by Carl D. Lane and now owned by André Rheault. The yard is building traditional wooden boats by modern methods. There are three basic hull forms: the 26-foot Lubec Boat, the 32-foot Quoddy Pilot, and the 45-foot pinkie from the *Dove* model designed by Ted Brewer. The hulls are strip built and sealed with polypropylene cloth and epoxy, to make a strong and rigid structure. Penobscot also builds custom racing boats by the WEST system of saturating wood with a thin epoxy. If you can stand the vapors, the yard is well worth a visit.

André the seal, a harbor seal adopted when a pup by Harry Goodridge and now the subject of a book, may be seen around Allen's yard. He can no longer be kept in captivity according to the mammal protection act, but he enjoys Rockport in the summer and the Aquarium in Boston in the winter. His trip east in the spring is usually followed in the press.

On Friday nights in the summer, cruise schooners due in Camden on Saturday morning often lie in Rockport. It makes for a lively evening. There are as many as a dozen of these vessels sailing from Camden and Rockland, although only one, *Timberwind,* formerly the Portland pilot boat, hails from Rockport.

If there is a southerly chop running up the bay, Rockport can be uncomfortable on the ebb tide, but it is seldom dangerous in the summer. For well over a century, vessels lay here winter and summer, loading lime, ice, lumber, and lobsters. Ruins of the old lime kilns are still visible on the west side of the harbor, and Rockport ice was said to be so clear you could read a book through it. Half a million tons a year were shipped to the southern states and the West Indies before the invention of mechanical refrigeration.

Camden, Maine   (13307   209) (13305   310). There are many reasons to visit Camden. It is easy of access under almost any conditions, with a light on the Graves and a bell outside it. Curtis Island shows a light and its shore is bold. A lighted beacon is on the ledge at the eastern entrance.

Camden is on the bus line to Portland and Boston. It has good stores, and a first-class boat yard, which can repair any damage to hull, spars, or engine. An excellent sailmaker, Henry Bohndell, lives nearby. Camden's stores can supply whatever you need, from charts and books to groceries and marine hardware. The town, back from the shore, has a quiet and dignified nineteenth-century air. The cruise schooner fleet sails from Camden on Monday mornings and returns Saturday noons, providing a great deal of picturesque activity. Finally, there are the Camden Hills, providing trails for a good walk ashore. As a place to change crews, stock up, or effect repairs, Camden is one of the best on the coast.

However, as a quiet place to spend a night in the course of a cruise down east, it is a dead loss. The anchorage is crowded, so it is almost imperative to get a yacht-club mooring, for which one hails the yacht-club float. The building is made conspicuous by its lawn and flagpole on the west side of the inner harbor. The fee was $2.50 per night in 1976. There are several town moorings for visitors. Consult Harbor Master Rusty Robbins, who may be found on the town wharf. Then one does well to use the launch service at $1.00 per trip for the boat's full capacity of six people. The launch runs from 8:30 A.M. until sunset.

There is not much space to tie a dinghy at the floats in the inner harbor. Even on a mooring there is likely to be a good deal of motion in the harbor, as the roll that runs up the bay all summer agitates the outer harbor. Anchorage is forbidden in the inner harbor. In short, unless some of the material in the following paragraphs attracts you, pass up Camden for more attractive ports in Penobscot Bay.

The Camden Yacht Club, whose headquarters was the gift of the late Cyrus H. K. Curtis, is a gracious and hospitable club but, like many other yacht clubs, its facilities are under heavy pressure from its own members and from increasing numbers of cruising people. You can lie alongside the club float for a few minutes to ask questions or to make a phone call, but be brief and do not leave your yacht unattended. She may have to be moved. Do not plan to change crews or stock up at this float.

The club has a snack bar, open Monday through Saturday from 11:30 A.M. until 2:00 P.M. and on Sunday from 11 A.M. to 1 P.M. There is a telephone on the porch at the north side of the building. The steward will hold mail for cruising people.

Further up the west shore of the harbor are commercial floats, where gasoline, Diesel fuel, water, ice, and marine hardware are conveniently available. Grocery and hardware stores are a short walk up the street. If you have time, stop at the Owl and Turtle Book Shop. There one can purchase a wide variety of books on marine subjects published by the International Marine Publishing Co. of Camden, as well as books by other publishers.

The Lok Marina is an interesting concept, which never became very popular. The idea was to provide a boat basin above the level of the harbor, to be reached by a lock. Boats could lie alongside with perfect protection and all imaginable facilities.

The idea was conceived by the ingenious Dr. Tibbetts about 1952 in the course of a trip abroad. Before he invented the marina he had done very well with crystal microphones for hearing aids. He is credited with inventions ranging from electric refrigerators, hydraulic airplane controls, and a skate sharpener, to a hot-air balloon, which, bearing a cat triumphantly aloft on a windy day, bilged on the cupola of a livery stable and burned it down. The Camden post office now occupies the site.

Across the harbor is the flourishing establishment of Wayfarer Marine, which arose from the wreckage of the old Camden Shipbuilding Corporation. Any and all services, from major repair to filling the water tank are available here. However, the place is likely to be crowded. One correspondent writes, "Wayfarer Marine wonderfully helpful in every way, but prepare for an hour or so of seemingly endless maneuvering and skillful boat handling to get anywhere near its docks." Another adds, referring to our 1972 edition:

Wayfarer Marine warrants more notice. It is a first-rate operation in every way and is patronized by a salty group. . . . It is an experience just to call there. Boats, predominantly sail, are usually racked two to four deep. What one loses in solitude is more than made up by the company of knowledgeable cruising people. Two seasons ago we tried Wayfarer as a place to leave our boat temporarily on the way back from Nova Scotia. We liked it so much that we used it as our base for the rest of the summer, did the same this past season, and plan to do so again this year. The president and active manager is Charles E. MacMullen. Graham Barlow is responsible for yard operations. His principal assistant is named Brewer.

This was written in 1973, but another correspondent in 1976 writes, "In Camden, Wayfarer is every bit as nice as people say, and competent."

Camden has a well-deserved reputation for fine yacht building. The late Elmer Collamore was a one-man yard. He rebuilt John Alden's old *Malabar II,* putting in new backbone, frames, planking, and deck, but using the old ballast keel, spars, and even the old interior cabinetwork. When he finished, she started right off on a transatlantic voyage. He also built *Heritage,* a 28-foot replica of a Rockport stone sloop. She is a piece of cabinetwork from truck to keel.

Jim Rockefeller, in a "yard" near the top of Bald Mountain, built several Friendship sloops of the *Pemaquid* type. One of these, *Old Baldy,* was used as a "plug" for Jarvis Newman's fiberglass sloops, built at Southwest Harbor. Rockefeller also completely rebuilt the 36-foot Friendship *Sazerac.* He built powerboats and gunning boats, and now has established The Great Eastern Flying Boat Company.

Malcolm Brewer, formerly the superintendent at Camden Shipbuilding and Drydock, has built several beautiful yachts modeled on coasting-schooner lines designed by Murray Peterson, as well as a Friendship sloop, *Patience.*

Geerd Hendel, well-known designer, has an office in Camden.

A project originating in Camden is the marine equivalent of the western dude ranch: the schooner cruise. In the late thirties, Captain Frank Swift bought the little coaster *Clinton* and fitted her out to carry passengers under rather Spartan conditions. He had a mate and a cook, and the passengers did all the work.

The idea caught on, so he bought a number of other ancient vessels, including *Annie K. Kimball, Lois M. Candage, Eva S. Cullison, Mattie, Mercantile, Stephen Taber,* and the newer *Endeavor* and *Enterprise.* No doubt there were others, and before long there was an impressive fleet. As the vessels got older and the Coast Guard regulations grew more stringent, many of the old vessels were squeezed out. Captain Swift sold out to Les Bex, who kept several of the old vessels going. Havilah Hawkins sold the famous old *Alice Wentworth* and had a new vessel built especially for the trade, *Mary Day.* Others followed and several much bigger old vessels were brought back. Captain Boyd Guild sails *Victory Chimes,* a three-masted vessel in spit-and-polish condition. Captain Jim Sharpe has *Adventure,* a Gloucester fishing schooner used in the television version of *Captains Courageous,* which incidentally, was filmed in Camden. *Roseway* and *Timberwind* were pilot schooners, and several yachts have joined the fleet. Anyone in Camden on Saturday morning, when the fleet returns from its week's sojourn between Mt. Desert and Boothbay, will agree that schooner cruises are big business.

In need of a word to describe these vessels, the generic term "windjammer," originally applied scornfully by steamboat men to all sailing vessels, has now been applied specifically to cruise schooners. On the coast, these and none other are called windjammers. They are also known by less lovely names. All of these vessels operate under sail alone, except for such help as they get in calm weather from a yawl boat with a powerful Diesel engine lashed under the stern. Were it not for these vessels and for the others sailing out of Rockport, there would be no sailing vessels on the coast to remind us of what the old-timers were like.

In the literary line, Camden excels, too. On the shore behind Lok Marina are the offices of *Down East,* a monthly magazine devoted to the most colorful aspects of coastal, inland, and mountain Maine. The magazine's brilliant color photographs brighten some of the year's darkest days. *National Fisherman,* on the main street, is the breath of life to those suffocating in suburbia in the winter months. It is primarily a trade paper for fishermen but carries news of coastal towns, the homely recollections of Captain Perc Sane, and advertisements as fascinating as the news. These two, with the *Maine Times,* published weekly in Topsham, help us to keep in touch. Close to the lower end of Elm Street is the office of the International Marine Publishing Company, an institution devoted to printing some of the most interesting of marine literature and not tied to authors of brilliant reputation only. Its publications can be purchased at the office or at the Owl and Turtle Bookshop on the principal street. The bookshop has on display a wide variety of prints and posters of interest to yachtsmen. The shop is called the Owl and Turtle because it is about halfway between Owl's Head outside Rockland and Turtle Head on the north end of Islesboro.

If you have to be fogbound sometime, arrange to have it happen in Camden. The shady streets are lined by beautiful old houses, built by shipmasters and merchants when Penobscot Bay granite, lime, fish, ice, and lumber were well known in the world's ports. Often, when it is thick in Camden Harbor, the sun will be shining warmly on the tops of the mountains.

The trail up Mt. Battie starts from the end of Megunticook Street. It is a brisk twenty-minute climb, with a rewarding view—if you don't mind discovering when you arrive breathless at the top that others have driven up in automobiles. Mt. Megunticook, the highest of the Camden Hills, is more challenging, but it is overgrown on the top, so the view from the summit is obstructed. However, Ocean View Lookout and Bald Rock on the sides of Megunticook afford magnificent prospects of the coast. On a clear day one can see from Monhegan to Mt. Desert and north to Blue Hill.

Don't miss the opportunity to visit Admiral Donald B. MacMillan's *Bowdoin,* built by Hodgdon Brothers in East Boothbay in the early twenties for arctic exploration. Admiral MacMillan, a member of Peary's expedition to the North Pole, and a seaman, explorer, scientist, and educator in the broadest senses of the words, took the vessel north twenty-six times. At last she was given to Mystic Seaport in 1959. That institution, unable to maintain her properly, returned her to Maine in 1968 in the care of the Schooner Bowdoin Association, composed of former members of *Bowdoin*'s crews. She is being fitted out as a museum of arctic lore, but several times a year sets her sails and cruises the coast.

From Camden to Upper Penobscot Bay

Vessels bound for Eggemoggin Reach and the islands up the bay need not go around the whistle on Robinson Rock. Many yachts of moderate draft cross Job Island Bar between Job Island and Lime Island. Cross on a southeast course about 600 yards north of Little Bermuda, the grassy island on the bar. You will be nearer Little Bermuda than you are to Job Island, for you will notice that a long ledge makes out from the southern point of Job Island. The stranger making the passage for the first time would do well to choose a rising tide and to move cautiously.

A slightly longer but easier course is to run south of Lasell Island and then northward between Lime Island and Mouse Island. When leaving

Camden, head for the high northern part of Lasell Island, a course that will carry you well clear of East Goose Rock. This rock is said to be inhabited by seals, but if you are close enough to see them, you will soon have more than seals to think about. Note that two unmarked half-tide rocks lie to the northeast of East Goose Rock.

The south end of Lasell Island is bold and picturesque. Follow it around and run up the east side. If you are bound for Pulpit Harbor, go south of Goose Island and keep well away from can 1A to avoid the rock west of it. Those bound up the bay will give can 3 off Mouse Island a good berth to starboard.

In navigating the waters between Islesboro and the mainland west of it, keep an eye out for tankers. They make bell 9 off Great Spruce Head on the way to oil and potato wharves at Searsport.

Gilkey Harbor, Islesboro, Maine (13309 311) (13305 310). This is a large but protected harbor, affording access to several summer communities and with impressive views of the Camden Hills. There are several small coves in which snug anchorage can be found for small boats. This was once a very fashionable summer community, but it has become somewhat less formal in the latter half of the century. In the thirties the writer saw J.P. Morgan's *Corsair* at anchor here.

The easiest entrance, negotiable in almost any weather, is between Job Island and Seven Hundred Acre Island. A lighted bell marks the southern end of the latter island and a nun marks the only outlying danger in the channel. The northern entrance between Grindle Point and Warren Island is also marked by a lighted bell and by a small flashing light on the ferry wharf at Grindle Point, where the ferry from Lincolnville Beach lands several times a day. There is another entrance from the south and east through Bracketts Channel, east of Job Island. This is a tortuous route marked by local buoys. However, one yachtsman, negotiating it on June 27, found no local buoys. They doubtless appeared, he speculates, by July 4, but be prepared to work your way in without them early or late in the season.

There is good anchorage in Ames Cove but proceed cautiously, for it is shoal. The Tarratine Yacht Club maintains a float here, with only about 3 feet at low water. Guest moorings are said to be available, but our visitor on June 27 found none. There is a store ashore.

The Islesboro Inn overlooks the scene. Rooms and meals are available here, and the inn maintains a float for the benefit of its guests.

Cradle Cove, opposite Ames Cove to the west, is a snug anchorage, with guest moorings owned by the Dark Harbor Boat Yard. There is a depth of about 10 feet at low water in the cove. At the boat-yard float is gasoline, Diesel fuel, water, and ice. The yard can make ordinary repairs and has a marine supply store. In the usual southerly breeze, Cradle Cove affords better protection than Ames Cove.

The cove between Warren and Spruce Islands, across from Grindle Point, is a snug spot, perhaps less frequented than Cradle Cove. Warren Island is a state park, with shelters and fireplaces. The state maintains a wharf here and three guest moorings. In entering, favor the Warren Island shore and do not go in beyond the moorings, for the cove shoals up to flats. Parties from cruise schooners occasionally land here for cookouts, but the vessels anchor far enough to the north to cause little disturbance.

There are several other coves around the shore of Islesboro, each well protected from one direction or another and none very heavily used. The skipper will select the one best suited for the day's conditions.

The sail up the Western Bay on a clear day is delightful, with the Camden Hills providing a backdrop to the west. The southwest wind usually draws briskly up this bay. However, there are few attractive harbors on the way.

Lincolnville Beach, Me. (13309   311). There is an anchorage here, rather exposed to easterly and northeasterly weather but quite good on an ordinary summer night. There is a guest mooring. The *Governor Muskie* runs frequently from here to Grindle Point on Islesboro. The Lincolnville Lobster Pound and Hemingway's Lobster Pound are well recommended shore-dinner places. There is a small village with a grocery store, garage, and the usual antique and variety stores. Route 1 goes right through the town and adds nothing to the sense of seclusion. There is a beach, best at high water.

Continuing up the bay, you come to Spruce Head and Great Spruce Head (not to be confused with Spruce Head Island in the Muscle Ridges, nor again with Great Spruce Head Island, which is not more than 7 miles distant in a straight line, in West Penobscot Bay). Lighted bell 9 is a buoy that is religiously made by all commercial traffic passing up and down Penobscot Bay. If you have no radar, you may avoid an unpleasant rendezvous with a supertanker by hugging the shore, which is bold here. From bell 9, it is nearly a straight run to Fort Point or Searsport, and a straight line leads southerly from bell 9 to Owls Head.

A correspondent, in a 25-footer and in a dense fog, mistook the bow wave of a Spanish freighter, bound down the bay, for breakers on the shore and, in avoiding the supposed breakers, passed actually under the bow of the freighter.

The large house opposite bell 9 has a beautifully toned bell on the porch, which is often rung in answer to salutes from passing boats.

Saturday Cove, Me. (13309 311). is exposed to the east and dominated by the summer home of Horace Hildreth, former governor of Maine and U.S. Ambassador to Pakistan.

Bayside, Me. (13309 311). If you follow the mainland shore northward from Saturday Cove you will come to the popular summer colony of Bayside. Here is located the Northport Yacht Club, a good wharf and a float with 6 feet at low water. A guest mooring is available, for the use of which you should see Mr. Al Keith, who lives near the wharf and is the most accommodating type of ingenious Yankee. He is, among other things, the Harbor Master. There is a very well organized and popular summer sailing program here for the young people.

The anchorage looks exposed, and it is to the east, but the usual summer southwester blows from over the land, making a fine lee, and you will imagine yourself moored off the shore of a large lake, because there is no ground swell, and unless the wind is dead on shore, Bayside is a most attractive place.

Belfast, Me. (13309 311). This harbor has been cleaned up radically in the last five years, so, while still not one of the most picturesque ports on the coast, it is not at all the unpleasant place that it was. It has the advantage of being on Route 1, although a bypass avoids the town itself, so that bus transportation to Bangor and the westward is convenient. The usual stores are found in town.

Entrance is easy, as the harbor is wide open to the east and southeast, and the only obstruction, Steels Ledge, is clearly marked. There is a city boat landing and marina on the west shore below where the tugs of the Eastern Maine Towage Company lie. There is 6 feet of water at the float, where gasoline, Diesel fuel, ice, water, and marine hardware are available. There were no guest moorings in 1976, but slips were available at $2.00 per night at the marina.

Young's Lobster Restaurant is said to be a good shore-dinner place and Mr. Young, a former member of the city council, is a most helpful source of local information. He tells, too, of plans to dredge the harbor and to make Belfast and the head of Penobscot Bay more attractive to summer people, cruise schooners, and yachts. Chicken processing is now the principal support of the city.

Searsport, Me.   (13309   311). This is a pleasant anchorage on a summer night, although it would be rolly if the afternoon southerly persisted into the evening. There is a new wharf at Searsport with about 10 feet of water on its outside face, alongside which cruise schooners often spend the night. Inside the wharf is a float with about 4 feet at low water. No fuel or water is available here.

Up the hill from the harbor, in the town of Searsport, is the Penobscot Marine Museum, which now includes the original town hall of Searsport and three large homes of former sea captains. There is a stirring diorama of the Penobscot Expedition of 1779 and there are a large number of log books, documents, pictures, and artifacts associated with the history of Penobscot Bay during the eighteenth and nineteenth centuries. The curator, Mr. Gardner Lane, is a well informed and enthusiastic authority.

At Macks Point is a steamer wharf used by tankers. Their oil is piped to Montreal from here, but the pipeline is now much less used as supplies from the west and from Saint John, New Brunswick, are coming into Canada. Vessels also load potatoes from Aroostook here during the fall and early winter. The *Coast Pilot* adds cargoes of fertilizer, paper, scrap iron, bauxite, sulfur, and salt. It is said to be Maine's second most important seaport.

There was talk at one time of an oil refinery and then of an atomic power plant on Sears Island, but they seem now to be dead issues. Some prospect of a coal-fired plant is still discussed but to the yachtsman, at least, there appears to be no immediate peril.

Stockton Harbor, Me.   (13309   311). This is a well-protected anchorage, little used by yachts. Landing is awkward, as the wharves are in ruins, and there are no nearby facilities of interest to yachtsman. Steamers tie to dolphins to discharge chemicals through a pipeline. However, Stockton affords by far the best protection of any harbor at the head of the bay west of the Penobscot River.

The Penobscot River, Me.   (13309   311). This great river rises near Mt. Katahdin and drains much of central Maine. The stream comes down a narrow, deep channel between mountainous banks and rushes out into Penobscot Bay at Fort Point through a space less than 1 mile wide and 50 feet deep. Unlike many great rivers, it has built up no bar at its entrance. The rush of fresh water sometimes rides over the salt water, even with a coming tide, so the ebb tide appears to be more persistent than the flood. This is especially true after rainy spells.

The trip up the river as far as Winterport is a lovely sail between high wooded banks. Especially if the fog is lying down the bay, it makes a pleasant variation in a cruise. The wind usually draws up the river during the afternoon and frequently one finds a northerly in the morning. It is well to plan the trip for a fair tide.

If it is necessary to anchor in the river overnight, get as close under the shore as possible, and hang up a radar reflector and a brilliant anchor light. Oil tankers supplying Bangor come down the river when they have pumped out their cargoes, be it day or night.

Bucksport, Me. (13309   311). As one might expect, the tide runs hard by Fort Point. Above it one sees the graceful span of the Waldo-Hancock bridge, sweeping from Mt. Waldo to Verona Island. Behind Verona Island is Bucksport. It has a municipal wharf but no facilities whatever for yachtsmen, except for the usual stores in town. There is a launching ramp on the northeast corner of Verona Island. The channel east of Verona Island is narrow and shoal. The clearance under the bridge from Verona Island to the eastern shore is only 17 feet and there is an overhead power cable east of the bridge with a clearance of 42 feet.

Winterport, Me. (13309   311). Here is the Winterport Marina and Boat Yard, the only convenient port on the river for a yacht. There are guest moorings and floats with gasoline and Diesel fuel. Boats up to 20 tons can be hauled for repair. The yard is run by Lieutenant Commander Raymond E. Dillon, USN (ret), who will personally attend to your wants.

Bangor, Me. (13309   311). Once the world's greatest lumber shipping port, whence in one year 3500 vessels cleared, where schooners lay so thick that one could cross the river from deck to deck, Bangor scarcely deserves the name of seaport except for the tankers that supply it with oil. There is no proper place to anchor. The only float is above the first fixed bridge and it is in bad repair. Almost the only thing to recommend Bangor to the yachtsman is its airport, to which planes come from Boston, New York, and elsewhere. If meeting crew members in Bangor, lie at Winterport and taxi to the airport.

Castine, Me. (13309   311). With the prominent abandoned light tower on Dice Head and the new light on a skeleton tower below it and with a bell outside, Castine is easy to make, in spite of the rush of tide in and out of the Bagaduce River. As you enter, you will see the breastworks of former forts on the northerly side of the channel. They fly the flags of those who built them.

Continue past the Maine Maritime Academy's steamer and land at the town wharf or at the Castine Yacht Club east of the commercial wharves. There was, in 1976, a guest mooring off the yacht club, but anchorage here is difficult because of the deep water, fast current, and gravelly bottom. One can telephone at the yacht club and a shower is available for visitors. Macomber's Market nearby can supply provisions. Do not lie at this float longer than necessary. Consult the club's sailing master about moorings.

The wharf west of the yacht club belongs to Alonzo Eaton, a boat builder, seaman, and local authority on Penobscot Bay. His knowledge, wisdom, and picturesque qualities are almost legendary. Beside these valuable commodities, Mr. Eaton sells gasoline, Diesel fuel, and marine hardware. Next is the wharf and parking lot of Captain John's Restaurant and then the town wharf.

The Maine Maritime Academy is situated in Castine. Their classes are conducted aboard their vessel and in their brick buildings, formerly part of Castine Academy. Their recreation facilities are said to be available to local people and visitors for a nominal fee. The academy trains officers for the Merchant Marine and gives them practical experience cruising on their vessel. The vessel is open to inspection by visitors at stated times.

Numerous signs relating to the colorful and significant part Castine played in the early history of the country have been erected around the town.

In colonial days Castine was the advance base for French domination of the coast, as Pemaquid was for the English. The two nations, with varying assistance and opposition from the local Indians, mounted raids against each other's forts and settlements, engaging in mutual and reciprocal massacre.

In 1779, the British General McLean landed with a small force at Castine to fortify it and establish a naval base from which British vessels could cruise against American and French privateers and merchantmen. He was an energetic commander and, by the time the Americans reacted with a force of 40 vessels and 1200 troops, he had built and armed a fort commanding the entrance to the river.

General Lovell commanded the American infantry, Dudley Saltonstall the fleet, and Paul Revere the artillery. The fleet arrived early in August and anchored outside. Nautilus Island was seized and fortified. Indecisive attacks were made against the fort. A colonel tried to persuade Saltonstall to take his fleet into the Bagaduce River to provide cover for the landing force and to capture two British sloops inside. In reply, Saltonstall "hove up his long chin and said, 'You seem to be dam' knowing about the matter. I am not going to risk my shipping in that dam' hole'."

While the American army, the navy, and artillery disagreed and skirmished about, McLean strengthened his fortifications and at the same time prepared to retreat. At last, on August 13 the American attack was coordinated; but before it reached a climax, seven British men-of-war under Admiral Collyer came up the bay, led by a 74-gun ship. This was too much for the Americans. Perhaps, under John Paul Jones or Benedict Arnold, a fleet of small vessels could have successfully engaged 74s, but Saltonstall was no such commander. The Americans fled up the Penobscot River and across the bay. By nightfall every American vessel was run ashore and destroyed and the entire force took to the woods.

Paul Revere, in a towering rage, walked back to Boston and demanded a court martial to clear his reputation. The story is told in circumstantial detail in Esther Forbes's *Paul Revere and the World He Lived In.*

In 1971, David Wyman, an ocean-engineering professor at Maine Maritime Academy, was instructing his students on the techniques of underwater search. They decided to look for the wreck of the 16-gun privateer *Defence,* a member of Saltonstall's force said to have been sunk in Stockton Cove. Wyman had no idea that they would actually find her, but two lumps in the muddy bottom turned out to be her cookstove and two cannon. The vessel, buried in mud, which effectively excluded oxygen, has been remarkably well preserved. Her whole port side is intact. A great many artifacts have been recovered in an excellent state of preservation. Not only have cannonballs, muskets, spoons, and mugs come to light but even articles made of wood, leather, and cloth have been preserved under the mud. They are treated with chemicals to prevent their rapid disintegration in air. Many details of the vessel's gear and construction have been recorded and her lines have been taken off. Much of what has been recovered is on display in the Maine State Museum in Augusta.

The British occupied Castine again in the War of 1812 and the proceeds of customs collected there were used to found Dalhousie University in Halifax, now the largest and most important institution of higher learning in the Maritime Provinces.

Castine was fortified against Confederates in the Civil War, but no attack was made against it. The history of the town since then has been commercial rather than military. Recently the fort on the top of the hill has been restored as have some of the breastworks along the shore. Numerous signs indicate points of interest, and the Wilson Museum has relics from three hundred years of the town's history.

Castine has Roman Catholic and Protestant churches, one of the most interesting being the Unitarian, with a Bulfinch tower, Paul Revere bell, and original box pews.

All the anchorages at Castine are south of the Bagaduce River.

Hospital Island. A number of local yachts, including the fleet belonging to the Maritime Academy, lie in the cove east of Hospital Island. It is out of the tide but is likely to be crowded.

Smith Cove. Large vessels lie in the mouth of Smith Cove, favoring the west shore. A more picturesque and better-protected anchorage is at the head of Smith Cove south of Sheep Island. In approaching this, beware of a rock marked by a nun, just inside the mouth of the cove, and of another rock west of Sheep Island. This is indicated on the chart by a cross, which means it shows at high water, but don't count on it. Close under the western shore opposite Sheep Island is another half-tide rock, but one is unlikely to push in that far.

Holbrook Island. There is excellent shelter south and east of Holbrook Island. The usual course is to enter south of the island. The channel is narrow and deep, with bold water on both sides. Just beyond Goose Falls, site of an early tide mill, swing south into the first cove. One can continue east of Ram Island and anchor anywhere in the well-protected water inside, but be sure to locate the rock in the middle of the channel south of the long ledge making off from Ram Island. The best water appears to be north of the rock.

Ten years or more ago a copper mine was established in Goose Pond. The pond was drained and a considerable amount of ore removed. The agreement was that, after the mine was exhausted, the pond would be allowed to fill again and the area be allowed to return to its wild state. The agreement is reported to have been scrupulously kept.

Weir Cove, Cape Rosier, Me. (13309   311). This is a quiet anchorage on an ordinary summer night, but it would be rough in a heavy southerly. In entering from the southwest, leave Buck Island to starboard, giving the mainland a generous berth. The chart does not show all the ledges here, but if you keep clear of shaded areas you will be all right. After passing Buck Island, head straight up the cove and anchor just south of a small island with a house on it, connected to the mainland by a footbridge.

There are several private floats on the west side of the cove. One may land at F.F. Clifford's float, off his boardinghouse, Cedar Cottage. This is the only wharf on the west side and is just above the small island.

From here it is a pleasant walk north on the road to a country store where ordinary groceries are available.

Weir Cove is usually a placid and unfrequented anchorage, but should the weather look ugly, go into Horseshoe Cove, Orcutt's Harbor, or Bucks Harbor.

Horseshoe Cove, Me. (13309   311). This is an easy harbor to enter for the second time, but the writer got cold feet the first time he entered, on finding himself rushing up a narrowing inlet studded with ledges before a smoky sou'wester, with a green crew adorning the foredeck. However, it is such a good place when you are in and it is really so easy to make that it is well worth the few nervous moments you may have at the start. Seal Cove Boat Yard maintains aids to navigation in this cove.

The first marks at the entrance are Dog Island to port and a privately maintained beacon on a ledge making out south from Howard's Point, the eastern point of the cove. This is on station from June 1 to September 15, or later. Continue up the cove, favoring the eastern shore. Pass a wharf and float with several boats moored off it and continue up the eastern shore. Keep Eagle Island Light to the east of Dog Island. Near another clump of moorings you will see a red cask on an iron pole on the southern end of Cowpens Ledge. Pass between the beacon and the black spars, keeping away from the beacon and close to the spars. Run up the cove, parallel to the ledge, *keeping at least 75 yards west of it.* About halfway up the ledge there is a rock awash at low water, which extends somewhat to the westward. As you converge with the high shore to the west, you will see several moorings. All but the outer one belong to the Seal Cove Boat Yard. Take one of these and prepare to spend the night in quiet comfort. Nothing can touch you here, as has been amply demonstrated in recent hurricanes.

Note that the buoys and beacons are privately maintained, but they are indicated on recent charts. Mr. Robert Vaughan, owner of the Seal Cove Boat Yard, who maintains these marks, has asked the Coast Guard to replace spar 3 with a beacon showing a square dayboard.

If you are in need of boatyard assistance *row in your dinghy* further up the cove to Mr. Vaughan's yard. Mr. Vaughan writes, "Some people have, on the strength of the *Cruising Guide*'s information, attempted to get to the yard itself in large boats; about one in five makes it. It should be emphasized that passage beyond our outer moorings is not recommended in a large boat." Mr. Vaughan refers to an earlier edition of the *Guide.*

The yard, despite its tortuous approach, is a busy place. There is a

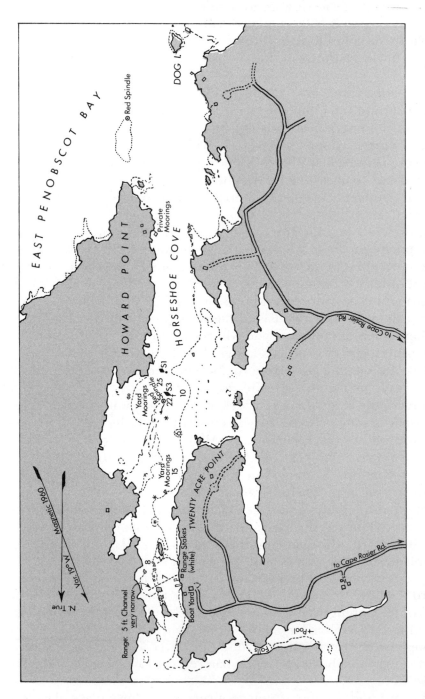

Principal aids and obstructions, Horseshoe Cove, E. Penobscot Bay, Maine. From air photo, 1" to 400'. Note: observe channel marks. It is not recommended to go beyond 15 ft. anchorage without local pilot except in tender.

12-ton lift and a 20-ton railway for repair or storage of yachts. General maintenance and repair work is done and there is limited inside winter storage. The yard finishes fiberglass hulls, builds wooden boats, and makes a specialty of restoring old vessels.

If no one is at the yard, walk up the dirt road to the first house. Mr. Vaughan, whose father established the yard, is an energetic, ingenious, and most interesting authority on all aspects of boating and local conditions.

There is another 1½ miles of wild, unspoiled cove beyond the yard, with 2 feet of water as far as the "lower falls," which drop 4 feet to tide water at low tide but can be shot as rapids one-and-one-half hours before and one hour after the flood.

Take the dinghy, with oars or outboard, and run up the creek about one and one-half hours before flood. You will have an utterly wild 2-mile prowl between clean granite shores, with the trees almost meeting overhead, and the fun of shooting small rapids. Have a warm swim on the rocks of the little lake at the head. Then follow the tide out about an hour after flood.

Orcutt Harbor, Me. (13309 311). This harbor between Bucks Harbor and Horseshoe Cove is not as snug as either of its neighbors but is a quiet and attractive anchorage. It would be well for the stranger to move carefully in here. The upper part of the harbor is studded with ledges.

There are two small boat yards here. Both do hauling, storage, and maintenance work. Steve Bridges is renowned locally as a mechanic and is equipped to do welding. Robert Condon builds small boats, both sail and power.

It is a short walk from this attractive anchorage to the four corners at South Brooksville, where most supplies can be purchased.

Bucks Harbor, Me. (13309 311). This well-protected anchorage lies in a bight behind Harbor Island, at the northwestern end of Eggemoggin Reach. Enter either side of Harbor Island but avoid the area just south of it, a notorious dead spot. The eastern entrance seems to afford the best breeze on a light day. There are several guest moorings, marked with orange balls maintained by the Bucks Harbor Yacht Club. If these are taken, anchor on either side of the buoy in the harbor. This marks a ledge running out from the island. Yachtsmen who frequent Bucks Harbor favor the cove to the east of the main harbor as an anchorage. There are three guest moorings here marked with white posts. When the cruise schooners come in—sometimes seven on a single night—and tune up for a dance, a little distance is very welcome.

Land at the yacht club and walk less than ¼ mile to the four corners, which is the heart of South Brooksville. To your right is the post office and Condon's Garage—another source of help for the ailing engine. Straight ahead is the remarkable store of the remarkable Eddie Noessel. He runs a down east cross between a country store and a supermarket. He stocks the finest of S.S. Pierce groceries and is renowned for his skill as a meatcutter. He has his finger on the public pulse. One winter, contemplating his empty freezer cabinet, it occurred to him to fill it with snowballs. He accordingly laid in a large stock of snowballs, put up by the dozen in cellophane bags. In July they found a ready market at 69¢ a bag. "People said I was crazy," remarked Eddie, "but they keep coming back for more." One winter there was very little snow. During the subsequent summer, customers noted a decline in the quality of the product, a certain iciness, suggesting frozen slush. Eddie explained to the writer that the snow was so cold and dry that it wouldn't pack into snowballs, so he had to shovel it into a box and set it behind the stove to warm up a bit. Some of it got overdone, but none burned.

Mr. Noessel's store was formerly owned by Ray C. Gray, a man much beloved by a former generation of yachtsmen. He was renowned for his delicious homemade ice cream. When President Roosevelt passed through Eggemoggin Reach in a cruiser on his way home from signing the Atlantic Charter in 1941, he sent a boat ashore for a supply of Mr. Gray's ice cream.

"If I'd have known who those sailors were getting it for, I'd have given it to them," I heard him say the next day. Mr. Roosevelt, of course, was an experienced cruising man, and Mr. Gray was almost the only Democrat in the county.

Gasoline, Diesel fuel, water, ice, stove fuel, and a few items of marine hardware are sold at Clifford Leach's granite wharf east of the Yacht Club. There is a depth of 6 feet alongside at low water.

The Yacht Club is a pleasant place, hospitable to cruising people within the limits imposed by an active racing and cruising program. The club hosts an occasional dance and maintains a tennis court.

Repairs to hull, spars, and rigging can be effected by Robert Vaughan at Seal Cove Boatyard in Horseshoe Cove. Steve Bridges in Orcutt's Harbor can attend to an indisposed engine. Donald Hale in nearby Sargentville can mend damaged sails. His loft is in a former schoolhouse close to the northern end of the Deer Isle bridge.

From the top of Caterpillar Hill, reached by following the road to the right at the four corners, the whole of Penobscot Bay lies spread before you. It is well worth the walk.

Note on the Sequence of Harbors

Having been up the west side of the bay and the Penobscot River and down the east side to Cape Rosier, we now take the reader down the bay to North Haven, Vinalhaven, and off to Matinicus. Thence we proceed to Isle au Haut and up East Penobscot Bay to Eggemoggin Reach.

As one goes down the bay from Cape Rosier, he passes a number of islands, most of them uninhabited, where reasonable shelter and a degree of privacy is possible. Hog, Pickering, Bradbury, and Butter are examples. Beach Island and Eagle Island are inhabited. Great Sprucehead has a summer place on it as does the largest of the Barred Islands. Of course one can anchor in any cove he chooses. However, all the islands, whether inhabited or not, are private property and must be treated with respect. Most of Bradbury Island is the property of The Nature Conservancy.

Barred Islands, Me.   (13305   310). There is a quiet and snug anchorage in the midst of the archipelago between Butter and Great Sprucehead islands. Enter from the northwest, passing between the high peak of the northernmost island and a privately maintained beacon off a ledge on the southern side of the entrance. Follow the shore of the peaked island, giving it 150 yards berth, and swing to starboard, keeping about halfway between the big island to port and the smaller one to starboard. Ledges make out from both islands, and there is a 5-foot spot to be avoided. This is usually well marked with lobster buoys. Proceed with care and keep a good eye out for bottom.

Once up to the middle of the big island, you are in about 3 fathoms, with mud, clay, and gravel bottom. Anchor anywhere short of the bar.

The big island is inhabited in summer by the Schauffler family. Their house is on the southern end of the island but out of sight of the anchorage. They are glad to have you explore the island but are justly concerned about fire. Light no fires ashore and do not smoke in the woods.

Great Sprucehead, Me.   (13305   310). This island is owned by the Porter family and is the source of many of Eliot K. Porter's magnificent photographs in *Summer Island*, published by the Sierra Club. There is fair anchorage off the Porter's float, but of course the island is private property and one should not land without permission.

Butter Island, Me. (13305 310). There is an anchorage off the beach on the north side of the island, but be sure your anchor is well set. There have been reports of weed and kelp on the bottom.

The beach is quite smooth for a Maine beach, and the water temperate if not warm. It is a short climb to the grassy peak of the island, which affords a grand view of Upper Penobscot Bay.

There used to be a town, Dirigo, on Butter Island, with a post office, summer hotel, and other evidences of civilization. Gradually it shrank and at length was abandoned, and one winter the whole village was removed. Only cellar holes remain.

The western slope of the island may still abound with wild raspberries in late July. Don't go for them in short pants. If you hear a boiling sound near your feet, run as fast as you can for the shore. Yellow jackets in defense of hearth and household gods show no mercy. Butter Island, like others in Penobscot Bay, is privately owned. The owner is glad to have cruising men visit it but requests that they build no fires and leave it cleaner than they found it.

For a lunch stop one can anchor north of the southeast or southwest tip of the island. There is a steep bluff on the south side and a fairly good beach in front of it. Note that the bar on the northwest corner of the island dries out at low water. At high water one can creep through the passage north of the largest of the Barred Islands into the harbor. Depending on the draft of one's boat, it might be a good idea to view the scene from the dinghy at low water before making the attempt.

Pulpit Harbor, Me.   (13305   310). This harbor is the goal of many a cruising man. Like Northeast Harbor, Roque Island, Cutler, Grand Manan, and Saint John, it is one of those places at which one feels "we have arrived." It is justly popular—large, well protected, easy of access, in a lovely Maine setting with the Camden Hills to the west. The principal problem is to find it.

Running northeastward up the shore from Stand-In Point on a hazy afternoon, it is nearly impossible to pick out Pulpit Rock. However, after you pass a prominent point with a cove behind it, look carefully along the shore. Pulpit Rock looks like a big boulder on the end of a rather insignificant ledge, and both ledge and boulder blend into the shore. Maybe you will see spars of anchored yachts in the harbor.

If you miss the harbor, well before you come to Egg Rock you will see a large house high on the North Haven shore. It has a gable on each end facing the water, and between the gables, three dormer windows. Run in on the bold shore and work back, staying close in, and you will run right into the harbor, for the ledge on which Pulpit Rock sits does not run parallel to the shore but makes off to the north. Once inside, with that rock against the sunset, you will wonder how you could ever have missed such an obvious landmark.

Inside, keep well away from the stony point on the north side, ringed with birch trees. The writer had shoal water here called to his attention by the presence of a large motor sailer high and dry.

The usual anchorage is in the mouth of the cove, which makes in to the northeast. Up this cove is a wharf with a water hose and a telephone. There are no gasoline, no store, no marina, no repair facilities. If you are in need of provisions, you will find it a pleasant half hour's walk through the Maine countryside to North Haven, where there are a store, a ferry landing, and a boat yard.

It is possible to anchor in Ministers Creek, the narrow inlet running in to the southwest just inside the entrance. On the shore is the residence of the Cabot family and their fleet lies in the cove. It is a pretty spot, but it may be somewhat crowded.

Pulpit Rock may be inhabited by a family of ospreys, as it has been at various times for the last 50 years—some say 300 years. They were there in 1973. If they have been induced to return, do not land on the rock or molest them in any way.

As you contemplate the rock and the Camden Hills against a summer sunset, take pains to remember the scene, for your memories will last long after the color photographs are faded and torn.

Fox Islands Thorofare, Me. (13308 235) (13305 310). This deep and narrow thoroughfare lies between North Haven and Vinalhaven Islands and is the shortest route east from Rockland to the harbors on Mt. Desert. Consequently, in fair weather or fog it is constantly agitated by coastal traffic of all kinds, from bouncy Boston whalers to heavy Diesel sardine carriers. One must be especially vigilant in the fog when making a buoy. One thick summer morning the writer encountered, off the black-and-white bell outside the western end of the Thorofare, a small sloop, a lobster boat, a motorsailer, and the North Haven ferry.

The principal marks for approaching the Thorofare from the west are the square granite monument with a pointed top on Fiddler Ledge off Stand-In Point and the cylindrical standpipe on the hill behind North Haven. Note that there is a string of ledges running southward from the bell. They are marked by nuns and must be treated with respect. In running up the bay from Marblehead Island or Fisherman Island Passage, the tide will set you somewhat. On the shorter course from Owls Head, it will set you more, but you will not be in it so long as the course is shorter. On the flood tide, run for the bell and on the ebb run for the gong. In either case, you will be set into the channel. If you miss to the north, you will see the Drunkard or the Fiddler before you hit it. If you miss to the south, you will see a nun or at least a big clump of lobster traps.

In the Thorofare the tide sets east on the flood and west on the ebb.

From the bell or the gong, run for Browns Head Light. With reasonable visibility, the white tower and buildings are very obvious. In the fog, be particularly alert. The wind will breeze up as you come in on the shore and the thin bleat of the horn does not carry well to windward. Thence follow the shore, east of the Sugar Loaves, around the corner into the Thorofare off North Haven.

Beyond North Haven there is a narrow spot between Iron Point and a black beacon. Leave the beacon to starboard bound east and the nuns to port. The dangers are well buoyed past Calderwood Point, Goose Rocks, Widow Island, and Channel Rock. From the bell on Channel Rock you can set a course for Mark Island and Deer Island Thorofare.

Coming in from the east on a clear day, there will be no trouble in finding the entrance. Goose Rock Light is quite prominent and there is nowhere else to go but up the Thorofare. In the fog, you can expect a scale-up as you get in by Calderwood Neck on any except the darkest days.

There are several anchorages in the Thorofare.

Southern Harbor is open to the southwest and on a rough day would be uncomfortable, but it is so narrow that in ordinary conditions it is quiet enough. You are unlikely to find much company here. The head of the harbor is shoal and there is no public landing.

Good anchorage can be found on the south side of the Thorofare opposite North Haven, although passing vessels create an occasional wash. Be sure to anchor clear of the ferry slip, where cars are loaded on a scow for transportation to North Haven.

North Haven. This is a convenient place at which to stop for supplies, water, and fuel as it is on the direct route east and west. Anchor anywhere off the town except in front of the steamer wharf, identified by a small house high in the air over the slip.

The yacht club on the second wharf west of the ferry slip maintains guest moorings marked with orange buoys. One may land at the club wharf, but note that the buildings along the sides of the wharf are private residences. This club is one of the oldest in Maine and originated what is said to be the oldest racing class in America, the North

Haven Dinghy. You will see them sailing and racing in the Thorofare, their colored sails and brightly varnished hulls giving a summery air to the scene.

East of the steamer wharf are landings for Waterman's store and Brown's boat yard. Gasoline, water, and block ice are available here as is an able mechanic, who can attend to the ills of your engine. There are a post office and telephone across the street and a community hall with a snack shop a hundred yards to the east.

North Haven is a quiet community, disinclined to make a stir about visitors. The king of Thailand dropped in one summer not long ago and was delighted that no one paid the slightest attention to him. The people you will see on the street are mostly summer people in from their cottages on the shore to shop or to meet the steamer. There is little night life at North Haven.

When your shopping is finished, it is well to move along to one of the anchorages mentioned previously and leave the North Haven fleet to roll in the wash of skylarking outboards and passing sardiners.

A story is told of a distinguished Harvard professor, long a summer resident of North Haven. Two fishermen were watching him sail a small boat in the Thorofare. The professor was having a good deal of trouble keeping clear of anchored yachts. Said one to the other, "Old Professor ————*knows* an awful lot, but he don't *re-al-ize* nothin'."

The sign on the shore advising of the presence of a water pipe crossing the Thorofare should be taken literally. The writer anchored in a state of excitement one day and fouled it. Gentle twitching, brute strength, and deep diving failed to dislodge the anchor. A passing fisherman tried his hand, with no better success. Finally exercising a "kill or cure or break the water pipe" philosophy, he let out the entire scope of the line and calling on every ounce of horsepower his boat possessed, described huge circles around the anchor at high speed. Just before we got seasick from our own wash, the anchor broke the surface. We hastily gathered in the line and departed, leaving the pipe intact, I am told.

This pipe was laid under unusual circumstances. The residents on the south side of the Thorofare live too far from Vinalhaven to be on town water. In dry summers, they eyed the North Haven standpipe with longing. At last, money was raised to lay a water pipe under the Thorofare. Several mainland contractors and one North Haven resident bid on the job. The latter's bid was much the lowest. The committee raised grave doubts as to whether the job could be done at the bid price, and asked the local man how he proposed to do it so much more cheaply than experienced contractors who owned barges, derricks, and heavy equipment. He refused to tell, but the contract was awarded him, as it appeared that he knew what he was doing.

During the winter he laid the pipe across the Thorofare on the ice and made up the connections. Then he sawed a trench in the ice and lowered the pipe safely to the bottom.

One of the hardest tasks for the yachtsman coming from the west, unable to go farther east than North Haven, is to turn back at that point. To the east and north of North Haven lies the eastern Paradise: Isle au Haut, Eggemoggin Reach, Blue Hill Bay, and the waters about Mt. Desert. Not until he has pushed the prow of his boat to the head of Somes Sound or dropped anchor in Northeast Harbor can any yachtsman say he has seen the best of the coast of Maine. But West Penobscot Bay is a good start, and will only increase his determination to return down east another year.

Perry Creek. This is a small cove in the shore of Vinalhaven Island, making out of the west side of Seal Cove. It is perfectly protected, quiet, and likely to remain so, as the shores are privately owned. There are no facilities for visitors and no public landing.

Round the small island off Hopkins Point, giving it what berth you can, for it makes out some. The ledge on the south side is marked by a pipe on its north end. Favor the southern side of the cove. The 2-foot spot shown on chart 310 *does* exist.

Do not expect to be alone in Perry Creek. If you find it crowded, satisfactory anchorage can be found just outside.

Seal Cove. If you can avoid the deep hole in the entrance and the shoal in the middle, Seal Cove is a good anchorage. Press well up into the head of the cove as far as your draft permits. Do not count on going ashore here as there is no landing and the shore is privately owned.

Waterman Cove. This will get you out of the tide; it is well protected, but not particularly attractive. Take the dinghy and explore the Cubby Hole at the head of the cove.

Kent Cove. This is not as well protected as some of the other coves described above, but on a quiet night is entirely satisfactory, especially if it blows from the north or east.

Carver Cove. This snug shelter behind Widow Island is probably the most attractive anchorage in the Thorofare. It is well protected, quiet, usually secluded, and the surrounding open fields and woods are pleasant indeed to contemplate at sunset. There is no landing, and if there were, there is no source of supplies near by. However, for an overnight anchorage far from the outboard menace of North Haven or the wash of passing power boats, it is superb.

Note that when fog is thick in Eastern Penobscot Bay, it often scales up north of Calderwood Neck as one approaches Channel Rock.

Little Thorofare. Although the tide runs through this passage north of Stimpson's Island, and although the western end is obstructed by ledges, this is an attractive anchorage and a short cut to islands up the bay. Pass north of Goose Rocks Light, close to Indian Point, to avoid the ledges in the middle, one of which usually shows, and cut back into the middle again before reaching the next projection of Indian Point.

Vinalhaven Island, Me. (13290   310). This large island is so cut up with inlets, channels, and ponds, that one is seldom more than a short distance from the water. Vinalhaven was settled before the Revolution and has had an eventful history, involving lumber, fish, and granite, with occasional excursions into privateering. This story is told in *Fish Scales and Stone Chips,* by Sidney L. Winslow. The chapters on the granite boom are most interesting. The pillars for the Cathedral of St. John the Divine in New York were quarried in Vinalhaven. It was intended that each pillar should be cut from one piece of granite. After three had broken on the lathe or in transport, the idea was abandoned and the pillars were made in sections. But the broken pieces of the huge monoliths still lie in a Vinalhaven quarry. The old granite quarries on Hurricane Island are conspicuous. Fifty years ago, a thousand men were working in them, and it was a wild place; Hurricane Island granite was known everywhere. The waters around Vinalhaven abound in unusual tales, too.

The full-rigged ship *Hualco,* 1086 tons, had been launched in Belfast in 1856, just as the 1857 depression was coming on. She lay at anchor in Belfast harbor for six months, unable to get a charter. Then she sailed, ostensibly for New Orleans, but no one knew her business. She was heavily insured.

She sailed from Belfast one morning, and ran down the Eastern Bay with all sail set before a northwest breeze. Approaching Saddleback Shoal, the story goes, the helmsman, a young fellow who had just been fishing off Saddleback, protested to the captain. "You are heading right for Saddleback Shoal, Captain!" "Mind your business, damn you, and I'll mind mine!" roared the captain, who evidently had an insurance job to do.

The *Hualco* struck the needlepoint of Saddleback Shoal going about 8 knots, knocked her bottom out, went over the shoal, and sank in twenty minutes in deep water. Within half an hour the crew, all natives of Belfast, were in the longboat heading for home, and the ship had disappeared.

More recently, the mail boat from Rockland to Vinalhaven was lost. One February day in 1946 she left Vinalhaven for Rockland. Apparently her forward hatches were not tightly secured, for when a heavy north-west squall struck, she took water over the bow and filled her foc'sle and forehold. Down by the bow, she could not be steered; and as the squall developed into a full gale, she filled and sank, leaving three men adrift on a raft in subzero cold. They made Leadbetter's Island at last and attracted the attention of people on Vinalhaven and so were rescued.

Little do we realize, as we run up the bay before a 20-knot south-wester, what double the velocity and winter cold can do to Penobscot Bay. Every winter Maine men are lost at sea.

Vinalhaven is a week's cruise in itself. Hoping not to dim the joy of such a cruise, the editor lists a few shelters on Vinalhaven. Let us start from the western end of Fox Islands Thorofare and circumnavigate the island.

Crockett Cove. A possible anchorage on the way into Fox Islands Thorofare is in Crockett Cove, just eastward of Crockett Point, the southeastern point at the entrance of the Thorofare on Vinalhaven Island. A mooring is occasionally available. There is 6 feet of water at the float at low tide.

The following advice is taken from the yearbook of the Cruising Club of America:

Stand for the end of Crockett Point with North Haven Monument (square stone beacon off Crabtree Point) astern. Keep a distance of about 100 feet off Crockett Point and head for a small red house on the opposite side of the cove until the center of the cove is opened, then head straight up the center until abeam of the float on the port hand. Least depth entering: 18 feet at low water. There is excellent holding ground.

The nearest supplies are at North Haven, 3½ miles away. There is no telephone connection at the cove.

The Basin. This is a dramatic spot and well worth a visit. But anchor outside. All correspondents and advisers with whom the writer has talked warn against going inside. A large proportion of yachts trying this passage fail to make it successfully.

Cedar Island. There is a snug little anchorage between Cedar and Laireys islands. Enter from the south and proceed cautiously. The writer found Irving Johnson's old *Yankee* in here once, but another time he found bottom startlingly close. Laireys Island is clean, smooth, white granite and affords what Samuel Johnson, in his *Journey to the Hebrides,* called "wild and noble prospects."

Hurricane Island, Me. (13305   310). This account of the Outward Bound School was contributed by Mr. Peter O. Willauer, the director.

The island, formerly the scene of a profitable granite quarry, is now the site of the Hurricane Island Outward Bound School.

The first Outward Bound School was established at Aberdovey in Wales in 1941 to help reduce the alarming loss of young British sailors on merchant ships following sinkings by German U-boats. Lawrence Holt, head of the Blue Funnel Line, had noted that, while younger and physically better-equipped men succumbed, the older and more experienced officers survived. He reasoned that success in meeting severe challenge depends more on attitude than on physical prowess. He turned to Dr. Kurt Hahn, headmaster and founder of the Gordonstoun School, who had succeeded in putting physical challenge into his curriculum as a means of developing character in his students. Together, Mr. Holt and Dr. Hahn organized the first four-week course for young seamen, "Outward Bound," for the fleet and for life. The Aberdovey Sea School more than fulfilled the hopes of its founders in developing an individual's initiative, resourcefulness, and individuality. It was apparent by the end of the war that supervised exposure to a series of testing and hostile situations was indeed a successful approach to the difficult transition from youth to manhood.

The idea spread rapidly, and there are now thirty-four Outward Bound Schools . . . the one at Hurricane Island being the only Outward Bound sea school in the Western Hemisphere.

During the months of May through October, hundreds of young men and women aged sixteen-and-one-half and older, are exposed to a program of increasing challenges for twenty-six days at Hurricane Island. Over 30 percent are on scholarship, assuring a variety of cultural and economic backgrounds. The students are divided into watches of twelve, each with two instructors: a watch officer and an assistant. The watch officers are mature men and women and technically proficient. All possess U.S. Coast Guard sailing licenses and are skilled in other areas, such as ecology, rock-climbing, fire-fighting, and emergency medical care. Their extraordinary experience assures a higher standard of instruction and safety.

The Hurricane Island program is not limited to young people. In 1977, over four-hundred adults participated in courses varying in length from five to twenty-six days. Specific courses are designed for businessmen, teachers, and college students (both graduates and undergraduates, with credit available), women over thirty, men over forty, and community and youth workers.

One of the most important components of an Outward Bound School is its Rescue Services. There is always a watch of twelve students on duty at the island. They monitor the Citizens Band Radio (KEK–2392, Channel 4) and VHF radio (Channel 16) twenty-four hours a day, and are also in telephone communication with the Coast Guard and the hospital in Rockland. The school is well equipped to perform search and rescue services in the Penobscot Bay area, as well as fire-fighting aid and emergency medical care. Three power boats (*MV Hurricane, Reliance,* and *Vigilant*) are completely outfitted with radar, radiotelephone, CB, and VHF radios, fire-fighting equipment, diving gear, and first-aid materials. A doctor is usually in residence on the island.

The school also has sixteen 30-foot, open, ketch-rigged pulling boats. These wooden strip-built craft are light enough and long enough to be rowed by twelve students, but also go well to windward under sail. Early training includes a capsizing and righting drill, and the whaleboats, full of water, and with twelve students on board, still have 6 inches of freeboard due to the 32 cubic feet of styrofoam floatation. Basic instruction in these boats emphasizes navigation, sail-handling and, above all, safety. The instructors are on board at all times, but students soon learn to handle the boats by themselves. They take long cruises under a variety of conditions, including fog and night running, and you may see them as far east as Cutler.

About halfway through the course, and after several ecology lessons, the students are each placed on an uninhabited island for three days and three nights. Equipped with a line and hook, sleeping bag, eight matches, a 9-foot-square plastic sheet, a Hibachi stove fashioned from a #10 can, a first-aid kit, two quarts of water, a knife, and a journal, every student has his hours of self-appraisal, of seeing himself in unique perspective. With a little ingenuity, one can eat well on the Maine islands, but who has ever been really alone for three days? The solo is a test of the mind and the spirit of each individual in relation to his environment. If you come across one of these students on solo, he or she would prefer to be left alone!

By all means pick up the guest mooring off the old granite wharf next to the large mess hall on the east side of the island; or anchor, being careful to avoid the half-tide ledges just east of the anchorage. A member of the Duty Watch is available at the Rescue Station on the main pier to show visitors around.

For those returning to the mainland, you are also welcome at the school's headquarters along Rockland's waterfront located just west of Atlantic Point in the southern end of Rockland Harbor adjacent to the National Sea Products Shipyard. Mooring, docking, water, telephone, and other facilities are available.

(Here Mr. Willauer's account ends.)

A local authority claims that the ball bearing was invented on Hurricane Island. A derrick was being built to handle heavy blocks of granite. The boom had to turn in order to swing the blocks off the wharf to the holds of vessels alongside. The ingenious foreman had the plate at the base of the derrick grooved to form a raceway, set several iron cannonballs in the groove, clapped a similar plate on top, and erected the spar on the upper plate. When the cannonballs were well slushed with grease, the derrick operated with great ease and precision.

There is much abandoned and rusted machinery on the island, including the remains of huge stationary steam engines. There is also considerable beautifully fashioned cut stone abandoned near the wharf. The scenery is magnificent, and the view from the cliff overlooking the southern end of the island is particularly superb. Should you want a good idea of what Hurricane Island must have been like when the quarries were running, read Ruth Moore's *Speak to the Winds.*

Old Harbor. This harbor is well protected but it is shoal and the bottom is rocky. There are no convenient facilities ashore.

Green Island Cove. There is a nicely protected cove in Green Island. It is best approached from the southeast. The island is sparsely inhabited if inhabited at all. The lighthouse at Heron Neck on the southern point of the island was manned in 1977.

Carvers Harbor, Me. (13305   310). When anyone says he is going to Vinalhaven, he usually means Carvers Harbor. It is one of the few places on the coast, like Cape Porpoise and New Harbor, where commercial fishing has not been eclipsed by tourism.

The waters to the southwest, south, and southeast of Carvers Harbor are extremely dangerous. The tide runs swiftly between rugged and unmarked ledges and the whole area is wide open to the sweep of the North Atlantic. If one gets ashore in this area, one might well lose his boat.

However, the entrance to Vinalhaven is well marked. Note the white sector in Heron Neck Light, which leads one by James and Willies Ledge. The lighthouse has a powerful horn replacing the former siren. But even the horn is reported unreliable at certain spots. Use great caution in approaching it in thick fog. Once inside the cordon of ledges, follow Heron Neck and Green Island around to the east, pass between Folly Rocks and Green Island, and run up the harbor by the lighted beacon on Green Ledge.

From Deer Island Thorofare or anywhere up East Penobscot Bay, first make Triangle Ledge. This is not always easy, especially in the afternoon with the sun in your eyes. The buoy appears to be very small indeed and seems a long way off shore. Then simply follow the string of nuns around to the south and southwest, by Point Ledge beacon and in to Green Ledge light. Against the very considerable tidal current, this can be a slow process, especially in the late afternoon.

In clear weather there is no very serious problem, but a boat without power in the fog can have a miserable time out there where no buoy has any noise-making machinery and the tide runs very hard.

From the southeast one would make Saddleback Ledge, and leave Diamond Rock to port. It is a very large rock standing well above high water. Then pass between nun 2 and Carvers Island and leave nun 4, Point Ledge, and Green Island Ledge to starboard. This is extremely perilous in the fog.

Inside Green Ledge the channel is clearly marked. Be sure to give nun 4 a good berth to avoid the half-tide rock between it and Green Ledge. Round Potato Island and anchor in the cove to the east and opposite the wharves in the town.

A correspondent reports a bed of kelp in the southeast part of the harbor. Kelp is poor holding ground. If the weather is quiet, you think your anchor has a good bite, but if it comes on to blow, you drift off to leeward with a great ball of vegetation on the anchor.

Hail the lobster car just inside the entrance and inquire about a mooring. The Harbor Master, John Chilles, is likely to be aboard. If he is not, ask for Clarence Bennett.

There is a notorious abandoned mooring lying on bottom to the north of the lobster car and east of the ferry slip.

The main street of the town, with post office, restaurants, stores, and a movie house with street telephone opposite, runs around the head of the harbor. Just west of the Williams Yard is the town landing, with a large parking area. A channel with 6 feet at low tide has been dredged to this point.

Along the main street to the west is the Gulf Wharf, operated by James L. Calderwood, who sells gasoline, water, and Diesel fuel. Ice can be had at Bickford's Fish Wharf. There is a boat yard run by Quinn and Hopkins farther up the harbor, which can haul and repair most yachts. The Islander, close to the main street, provides rooms and excellent meals. A few houses take roomers.

There is no yacht club at Carvers Harbor and no provision for tying up boats for any length of time. The business of Vinalhaven is lobsters and fish. If you obstruct a wharf any longer than necessary, you may become unpopular.

If one has any leisure time at Carvers Harbor, one should walk up the hill to the standpipe. It is possible to climb the ladder of this tank (keeping on the inside of the ladder) and on a clear day obtain a splendid view around the southern and western horizon from Isle au Haut to the Camden Hills. The top of the tank is reported to be open, so be careful!

For many years Vinalhaven derived much prosperity from the many granite quarries in the neighborhood. This stone was shipped in barges to Boston, New York, and Philadelphia. Much of it was for paving blocks in New York, but it had other uses. The huge pillars on three sides of the altar of the choir of the Cathedral of St. John the Divine in New York, each more than 54 feet in height and weighing approximately 120 tons, came from Vinalhaven. Likewise, the massive stone eagles adorning the post office in Buffalo, the granite of the State Capitol in Albany, Grant's Tomb, the Philadelphia Mint, and several large government buildings in Washington and Annapolis all came from Vinalhaven. One could spend an interesting day roaming over the quarries of this section, especially on nearby Hurricane Island.

On the main street at Vinalhaven is a granite eagle said to have adorned Pennsylvania Station in New York. The local resident who discussed it with me was very doubtful that it had come from Vinalhaven in the first place. A dedication ceremony was to have been held on Labor Day, 1966. The same resident doubted that the ceremony would be unduly crowded. The eagle is unquestionably a most evil-tempered fowl, who is determined to take no backwash. He fiercely turns his back on the harbor to face the monoxide fumes to which he is accustomed.

About a mile and a half from the harbor is an airstrip with air taxi service to Rockland, where one can connect with planes to Boston and Bar Harbor.

A community hospital has been established in Vinalhaven. Medical help is quickly available here through the clinic.

Now Vinalhaven is a fish town. The people who live here are busy catching, selling, packing, and shipping fish as well as building fishing boats. Like New Harbor, this is a modern, unspoiled Maine town. It has not gone to sleep on its memories of the 1880s, but its people are vigorously making a living with the best facilities our century has to offer. The big, comfortable, able boats are powered with the best and most reliable engines. They have power winches, fathometers, radio direction finders, and short-wave radios. Their owners are alert, intelligent, energetic people, untouched by the sometimes patronizing attitude of summer visitors.

There are two active fish wharves at Vinalhaven. In the one next to Calderwood's, Burnham & Morrill, fish is processed and sent to Machias, where it is canned as fish flakes. At Bickford's, herring are frozen in very cold brine and shipped frozen to the West Coast, where they are used very successfully as tuna bait. The frozen herring are most lifelike and stay on the hook without falling apart.

The Diesel generator on the western shore provides current for Vinalhaven Island. It went into receivership in 1918, when the father of the present owner took it over. With the heavy demands of increasing summer population, its ancient generators are no longer equal to their task. Vigorous efforts have been made by this one-man utility company to keep the island's current flowing, but shutdowns lasting from an hour to as much as two days are not unknown. Vinalhaven takes it pretty well. "There have been no marches on City Hall," says the selectman. Another resident, commenting on the unreliability of electric clocks, remarked, "They won't even give you the time of day." A yachtsman, speaking to the harassed baron of industry who owns the plant, observed that the noise of the generator was annoying. "It's dammed annoying when you don't hear it," was the answer. By the time you arrive, Vinalhaven's electric utility problem may be solved, but at present (1976) the situation is serious.

Vinalhaven's East Side. There are several coves and harbors in this broken coast, none of which the writer has visited and on which no cruising man has contributed information. Roberts Harbor, Arey Cove, and Smith Cove are challenges to the explorer. However, inside Coombs Hill, there are two very attractive bodies of water, Winter Harbor and Seal Bay.

Winter Harbor is entered between the high, bold Hen Islands and Calderwood Neck. Proceed up the middle of the harbor. Note that opposite Starboard Rock there is a 2-foot spot. Contrary to earlier reports, it is indeed there. The deepest water is reported to be between the 2-foot spot and the ledge southeast of it.

The little cove right under Starboard Rock may be no longer navigable. The chart shows a 1-foot sounding. However, the writer spent a very quiet night lying to an anchor here with a line out to a tree at the base of Starboard Rock. The view from Starboard Rock, extending from Mt. Desert to the Camden Hills and including Isle au Haut and the islands of East Penobscot Bay, is well worth the scramble to get to the top.

The following directions contributed by a daring correspondent, suggest an interesting exploration.

1. From Starboard Rock follow close along northern shore. Give point at creek moderate berth. Bear toward islet west of creek.

2. From islet, southwesterly, leaving mid-channel ledge *close* to port.

3. From high point of ledge, west by south, favoring southerly side of channel.

4. From NW point of Penobscot Island head for bridge on Calderwood Neck until quarry derrick passes out of sight.

5. Turn gradually to port, passing between ledge and point where chart shows 15 feet.

6. Run WSW ½ W for high ledge off cove on starboard hand (in direction of derrick). Leave ledge close to starboard.

7. Veer to mid-channel and anchor SSW of ledge where chart shows 10 feet.

8. Pass north of old weir, holding to mid-channel. Anchor between old weir and old quarry derrick.

Seal Bay. One can enter this large and well-protected bay between the Hen Islands and Penobscot Island. Favor the Hen Island shore to avoid the ledges in mid-channel, which are submerged at high water. Another entrance can be found between Bluff Head and the Hen Islands. Bluff Head is bold except for a rock on its northwest corner, which is usually visible. Steer very close to the Bluff Head shore, particularly near the southern end of Bluff Head Island, to avoid a long ledge making out southeasterly from the Hen Island shore.

The section of this *Guide* on Fox Islands Thorofare deals with the anchorages between Calderwood Neck and Browns Head. We now take the reader offshore to the Green Islands and Matinicus.

Green Islands, Me. (13303   322). These two low, grassy islands lie east of Metinic and south of the Northern Triangles. If you are approaching from the west, keep well away from the Southern Triangles. Note that most of the ledges lie NNW from the can and at a considerable distance, but that one lone rock lies half a mile to the westward of the buoy and is otherwise unmarked. The Northern Triangles have no buoy on their eastern end. Little Green, the westernmost of the two, appears to be uninhabited, although there are a few shacks on it. Large Green has a cove on the northern side, with several large winter moorings described as "piles" on the chart. Pass a line to one. On any day on which you might be likely to visit, the mooring should hold you.

Residents of the island are lobstermen who come out from Sprucehead or Rockland for the summer's fishing. Unfortunately, some visitors to the island have wantonly damaged houses and fishing gear. You may get a cool reception, but it is important to stop in at one of the houses and make clear your purposes before exploring around.

The middle of the island is grass, eaten quite smooth by sheep. All around the shore is a windrow of driftwood composed of odd boards, pulpwood, and the drifting detritus of modern civilization. In amongst it all, though, you may find a treasure.

The island is a nesting place for gulls, terns, petrels, and other sea birds. Be careful not to disturb them or tread on their eggs.

There isn't much on the Green Islands; and in the fog, the whole area is very dangerous, with the perils badly marked. However, on a warm summer day they are a pleasant place from which to contemplate the Camden Hills.

It is a short run to Matinicus or Home Harbor for the night.

Matinicus, Me. (13303   322). The islands in this group are well worth a special trip, but the region should be approached with caution. There are no really snug harbors, supplies are limited, unmarked dangers are frequent, and tides are swift. In fog or storm the careless or inexperienced can get into real trouble.

Matinicus is low and cannot be seen from the deck of a small boat at 10 miles. Just set your course from Vinalhaven, Two Bush, or Isle au Haut and you will raise the islands.

In clear weather there is little difficulty in making Matinicus from the north. From Bay Ledge Whistle or the black-and-white bell south of it, leave the can on Zephyr Rock well to starboard to clear Zephyr Ledges. Leave No Mans Land to starboard and head for West Black Ledge until you are past the Barrel. This is a high rock and breaks, except in the very quietest weather, at high water. Give the red-and-black bell on

Harbor Ledge a good berth and run in north of Wheaton Island.

In thick weather the job is not so easy. The tide runs about NNW on the flood around No Mans Land and SSE on the ebb. Further north, it runs more NW and SE. A shoal-draft boat on a quiet day can make the lighted bell 5 MI north of Matinicus, pass between Two Bush Island and Matinicus, run off to Two Bush Ledge, leave Beach Ledges nun to starboard, and follow the shore in. In a larger boat or in rough weather, from bell 5 MI pass *close* northward of No Mans Land; run up toward the Barrel until you hear it break, and then make the bell and run in. The ledges to the east of the island stand up quite prominently at low water and break heavily. They are easy to hear in the fog and in most cases are quite bold. The radio beacon on Matinicus Rock may be some help too. Nevertheless, it is wild country in bad weather. A friend of the writer, running in for Matinicus Harbor at night in a building easterly, had the fog shut down on him suddenly and ran his yacht ashore on Mackerel Ledge. She was stove in almost immediately. He and his crew hauled the dinghy over the top of the ledge, launched it in the lee, and tried to make Matinicus but were carried off to the north. They spent all night in the boat and in the morning made Isle au Haut. The cautious mariner will pick his chance to visit these dramatic islands.

Inside Wheaton Island to starboard lies the inner harbor protected by a breakwater and obstructed by a big ledge with a pipe driven into its southwest end. The harbor is shallow, with scattered boulders in the western part, and crowded with local boats. The only place for a visitor is the cove between Wheaton Island and Matinicus. Inquire for a vacant mooring, but don't just pick one up and go ashore; for these moorings are much used by seiners, who come and go at all hours and can be understandably impatient to find their mooring occupied by a yacht. If you must anchor, a likely possibility, keep north of a green house with a chimney on its north end to avoid heavy chains to which fishermen are moored. Have a short piece of chain between anchor and rode and rig a trip line on your anchor, for the bottom is rocky.

Row up the inner harbor and land at the stone wharf. You will have to climb a ladder, as there is no float here (1976). At the head of the wharf are the post office, the store, and a telephone, which connects with the mainland by microwave. The hours for the store are irregular. Its new owner, Bill Moody, flies mail and supplies from Rockland in his own plane.

Do not count on buying fuel here except in an emergency. If you are hard pressed, inquire at the store and plan to come alongside at high water or to lug your fuel in cans. There is a well near the store, but water is not piped to the wharf.

A dirt road, little used and pleasant walking, runs up the island from the store. Matinicus's two schools show something of the changes taking place on the island. The old one is a somewhat bleak rectangle, a considerable part of which is occupied by a huge furnace. Several years ago the teacher went on strike because the toilet facilities interrupted learning when the wind was northwesterly, and heat was a problem. A new teacher took over, but in about 1973 a new school was built, triangular in shape, with electric heat, a stage, and a small organ. The walls are brightly decorated and there are no carvings or graffiti on desk or walls. Two teachers work together to educate about fifteen children in grades one through eight. The school is funded partly by the state and partly by the people of the island.

The church, too, is well worth a visit. The pews are beautifully designed and constructed. The World War II Honor Roll shows that twenty-four men went from this small town and that all returned safely. The bell in the church is no longer used. There is no resident minister in the winter, but the Maine Sea Coast Mission boat *Sunbeam* brings a clergyman to conduct services once a month.

Stop at the first house, on your left as you walk south from the corner of Broadway and 42nd St., clearly labeled, and see Jessie Philbrook for a copy of the Matinicus Cook Book.

From the north end of the island the view at sunset of the Camden Hills and the outlying islands of Penobscot Bay is well worth the walk.

Matinicus, like many isolated communities, is undergoing profound changes caused by the pressures of the rest of the world. At least 60 percent of the island is now owned by summer people. Cottages are springing up. A generating plant provides electricity for the island, and telephone service is clear and regular. Prices of food and supplies from ashore keep going up. Lobster prices don't keep up with them. The herring have not been plentiful. The inshore fishing grounds, where trawling and handlining used to be profitable, are nearly fished out and are infested with dogfish. Foreign imports depress fish and lobster prices. Young people are leaving the island, first to go to high school and then to find careers ashore. This writer, in talking with a few residents, felt a sense of desperation, a desire to close ranks against the outside. For instance, there is no float. The mail boat, when it comes at low water, must land passengers on the beach from a dory. Gas is difficult to buy. The fishermen-owners of shore property on the harbor are holding it tightly, refusing to admit outsiders lest the familiar scene be changed.

Of course every inhabitant of the island cannot be thus categorized, and many of the people we met were most hospitable and helpful. Yet here is an island town with its own fragile atmosphere and character, unable to resist the pressure of a pragmatic machine age. Unlike Cuttyhunk, Matinicus is not recognized and appreciated for this, and the inevitable is happening too rapidly.

Still, to the cruising man, Matinicus is unique. The fog sifts through the spruce trees, the dark weed swings in the tide, the distant surf on the ledges underlies every sound. The gentle motion in the harbor is never quite lost. Especially at night you feel you are far offshore, just on the edge of a life beyond your own.

Criehaven, Ragged Island, Me. (13303   322). The anchorage behind the breakwater on the northwest side of the island is small and shoal and should not be attempted except in reasonably settled weather. If caught in a northwester, go over to Matinicus or around Ragged Island to Seal Cove.

Approach to the harbor at Criehaven is not difficult with the nun on Harbor Ledge and the light on the breakwater. Harbor Ledge usually breaks and should be located by the careful navigator. It appears from the chart that a direct course from the nun to the light will lead unduly close to the ledge.

Enter cautiously and anchor or lie alongside a lobster boat temporarily. Go ashore and inquire for a mooring. Picking one up at random is a little dangerous because the mooring buoys are just like lobster buoys. If you can't get a mooring, anchor just inside the breakwater in about 2 fathoms. The best water appears to be on the northern side of the harbor. The water is very clear, so you will see bottom before you hit anything.

Criehaven used to be a year-round town, busy with lobstering, trawling, and handlining. There were a church, a school, a store, a post office, a lobster buyer who sold gas and marine supplies, and daily communication with Matinicus and Rockland via mail boat. Now the island is inhabited only in the summer by lobstermen from Rockland, who go to Matinicus for supplies. None of the above-named symbols of civilization are apparent. Much of the southern part of the island has been bought up by outsiders, who wish to keep it in its present wild state.

Walk across the narrow isthmus to Camp Cove and follow the trail down the eastern part of the island. It is badly overgrown and you may get lost, but you can't be very seriously lost. You can hear the surf on the shore from anywhere on the island. The southern end is bare heath, with a view south, east, and west to unbroken horizon, notched only by the twin towers of Matinicus Rock.

A walk around the southern shore of the harbor is eerie. The abandoned houses, store, and community center of what was once a live and active community are silent, neglected, and overgrown with brush, and the young spruce trees press in upon them.

Ragged Island was called Racketash by the Indians. White men mispronounced it "Ragged Arse," and it was so called for years. Our respectable government, unwilling to print such words on a chart, now labels it Ragged Island.

Matinicus Rock, Me. (13303   322). The short trip from Matinicus or Criehaven to the rock on a calm day is well worth the time. There is a heavy mooring on the western side and a skidway on which to land. However, if there is any sea running, do not attempt to land in a light cockleshell of a yacht tender.

Matinicus Rock is being automated and resident Coast Guard personnel are leaving, so a visit to the tower for a view of the surrounding islands may no longer be possible. Still, there is much to be seen ashore.

Among frequent visitors to the rock are ornithologists interested in the unusual bird life. Arctic terns nest in the grassy meadow on the northwest part of the island. Leach's petrels, guillemots, and the rare Atlantic puffins nest among the boulders. There is a small camp occupied by Audubon Society parties during the nesting season. In response to an inquiry about bird life on the rock, the writer received the following letter from Mr. Carl W. Bucheister, president of the National Audubon Society.

Now in connection with your description of Matinicus Rock, may I urge you to recommend to your readers that the rare Atlantic puffin, which in summer is found nesting only on that rock within the United States, can actually best be seen by cruising around the island. I know from many visits to the rock that one can approach the puffins on the water quite closely, and also see them perching on the island itself to better advantage from a boat.

I ask that you make this recommendation in your text because the constantly increasing numbers of visitors to Matinicus Rock in the summertime constitute a real threat to the Arctic terns, puffins, and Leach's petrels. Many individuals who know nothing about birds and their habits walk right into the tern colonies, causing the adults to fly up, leaving eggs and young. Frequently visitors, completely innocently, walk on eggs and young. Often I have seen visitors stand for hours in the area of big boulders of rocks under which the puffins nest, and they keep the birds from returning to their young with food. The Leach's petrels nest in burrows in the turf between the rocks, and people walking on these turf areas cave in the nesting burrows. This, as you will understand, causes the death of the adult and/or young in the burrow.

At the urging of the Society, the U.S. Coast Guard, in cooperation with the Bureau of Sport Fisheries & Wildlife of the Department of the Interior, has put up signs on the rock with legends asking people not to go beyond certain points.

Our Society can have no objection to a person landing on Matinicus Rock in order to see the lighthouse. We are concerned, as is the Coast Guard and the Bureau of Sport Fisheries & Wildlife, over people going right in to the areas where the birds nest.

Seal Island and Wooden Ball Island, Me.   (13303   322). Seal Island was formerly used as a target for naval gunnery practice but is now attacked by aircraft only. No bombing exercises will be conducted after 5 P.M., on Sundays, or in bad weather. Vessels in the danger zone will be "buzzed" in warning before exercises are held. No live ammunition will be used. These conditions, of course, are subject to change. See the most recent edition of the *Coast Pilot.*

There is no good landing place on Seal Island and very little reason to seek one.

Beware of Malcolm Ledge, between Seal and Wooden Ball islands. It is unmarked and is bare at low water.

Wooden Ball, so named, perhaps, for the eminence on the northeast end, is a barren white rock, tinged faintly green with grass and, at the writer's last visit, supervised by a few lonely and scraggy sheep. Another visitor reported a group of plastic lawn chairs outside one of the camps near the middle of the island.

There are several coves on the southeast side of the island, but only in the quietest weather could one land. Beware of a 1-foot spot off the northeast end of the island. It is unmarked and often does not break.

Isle au Haut, Me. (13303   310) (13313   308). No Maine cruise can ignore Isle au Haut. High, wooded, and touched only on the edges by the twentieth century, it is one of the most dramatic and attractive of Maine islands.

Provide for all your needs before visiting Isle au Haut.

Isle au Haut was named by Champlain in 1604 and means, of course, High Island. The pronunciation of the name, however, is not as obvious as its meaning. On the lobster cars in Stonington you will hear it called "Aisle au Holt" by fishermen, and so it was written in early deeds. Summer people, masters of high-school French, favor "Eel-a-Ho." One fisherman, in an effort to please, called it "Eely-Oley." The late Dr. Howard Sprague, who lived for many summers near Point Lookout, contributed the following authoritative information:

I have just been looking over my 1961 edition of the *Cruising Guide* and want to give you some definitive information about the naming of Isle au Haut, based on some research I did a couple of years ago in Houghton Library. I wanted to find out what name appeared in Champlain's original accounts and on his early maps. (I suppose one calls them "maps" rather than "charts.") The corruption Isle *au* Haut comes from the carry-over of the accenting of the "e" in *Isle* in Isle Haulte and its transformation into a separate and meaningless extra word "au." This was pointed out some years ago by Mrs. Bowditch. The "au" is meaningless in this context. Champlain called it the "high island" and the translation of Isle au Haut would, of course, be "The island of high."

On page 86 of volume I of *The Voyages and Explorations of Samuel de Champlain,* translated by Bourne-Allerton Book Co. in 1922, it says "and nearly in the middle of the sea there is another island which is so high and striking that I named it Isle Haute."

These spellings of Haute and Haulte appear in the original French accounts.

The earliest Champlain map, of which I have a Xerox copy, shows the island with a key reference letter F and the key shows the spelling *Ille haulte.* Mount Desert is *Ille des mont desertz.* This map has the title "Carte Geographique De La Nouvelle Franse Faiette Par Le Sieur De Champlain Saint Tongor's Capitaine Ordinaire Pour Le Roy En La Marine" (all capital letters), published in 1612.

Nowhere in Champlain's accounts have I found the corruption *Isle au Hault.* Mrs. Sprague tells me the accenting or stressing of the final "e" is common in Southern France and Canada and the development of this "au" must have come about from the pronunciation by those who were ignorant of French.

Much of the island is now part of Acadia National Park. In 1878 or 1879, Mr. Ernest W. Bowditch of Boston first visited the island. In 1880, with some of his friends, he formed the Isle au Haut Company and bought a house at Point Lookout. No women, no children, no dogs were the cardinal rules. Since then the rules have been relaxed. At the time of his death, Mr. Bowditch owned almost half the island.

In 1945 and 1946, his children gave most of this land to Acadia National Park. It is preserved nearly in its wild state, modified only by several trails and a road for fire-control purposes down the west side of the island.

The navigation of this area in the fog is chancy business. The tide runs hard and there are few bells and whistles. One Isle au Haut fisherman, with wry understatements adds, "and them spar buoys are awful dam' quiet."

Head Harbor. Coming up from seaward, this is the first anchorage at Isle au Haut. It is wide open to the south, and Roaring Bull Ledge, despite its whistle, is a dangerous obstruction. The bottom in the harbor is rocky and there is a weir. After several days of a winter northeaster, bore tides have been reported in Head Harbor, which make it untenable, but these almost never occur in the summer, and anchorage in the cove at the head of the harbor is entirely satisfactory on a summer night.

There used to be a little village here, and several substantial houses still stand, but the place is largely deserted now, and there will probably be no one to disturb you.

There is a jeep road around the island that passes by the head of the harbor. It is a pleasant walk to Duck Harbor to the westward and a good climb up Duck Mountain on a trail leaving the left-hand side of the road. It is marked by red plastic ribbons on trees and bushes and by yellow blazes.

Duck Harbor. This narrow slit on the southwest side of Isle au Haut is well protected, but it is shoal and has room for only two or three yachts. Plan to get in early. To enter Duck Harbor, stand up the Eastern Bay, east of Saddleback Light, until you find the Brandies, a group of large tawny rocks usually bare at low water. Work your way around to the west of them until you can see right up into Duck Harbor. Then run in on a course about ESE, being very careful to locate Duck Island Ledge and leave it to port.

There are said to be several moorings in Duck Harbor maintained by Acadia National Park and one mooring maintained by a fisherman. If you must anchor, do not go as far up the harbor as the great knob on the southern shore.

Ashore there are three shelters with room for six campers in each. Reservations for the use of these open on December 31 and are filled on that day. Write early if you plan to camp ashore.

Campers and visitors to the park land from the mail boat at the Thorofare and walk down the jeep road to Duck Harbor. It was hoped that arrangements could be made to have the ferry take them directly to Duck Harbor.

There is a well near the campsite, but campers are advised to boil the water thoroughly before drinking it. Build no fires on Isle au Haut except below high-water mark.

An inspiring view of Penobscot Bay is gained from Duck Harbor Mountain. Follow the jeep road east from the head of Duck Harbor for about ½ mile. The trail leads up to the right and is marked, but it is a rough climb.

There is no dump on Isle au Haut. Take your trash with you. The island cannot cope with it.

If you find Duck Harbor crowded and plan to go on to Moore Harbor, simply follow the shore instead of trying to go outside the ledges and half-tide rocks that infest the Eastern Bay.

Moore Harbor. This harbor does not appear to be so well protected as others on Isle au Haut, but it is perfectly good under summer conditions and is actually a lot better than it looks. Enter close to Moore Head on a course about east magnetic to avoid Rock T and a long ledge off Trial Point. Go south of the weir, avoiding the prominent ledge in the middle of the harbor, and anchor east of the weir. In 1970 there was a vacant mooring in here. There is no settlement here and there are no supplies. A correspondent adds:

Last summer we found ourselves trapped behind the weir, along with the fish—nets had been set from both sides of the weir to the shore. The fishermen were most considerate. They checked with us before going off to "lunch" at 9 A.M. (they had been out since 2 A.M.), then weighted down a portion of the net to let us out after we had had our breakfast.

Seal Trap. This is an interesting bit of gunk-holing to try on a rising tide in a shoal-draft boat. The swimming inside is reported to be warmer than elsewhere. One correspondent suggests that the name has nothing to do with seals but is a corruption of the French *ciel,* meaning sky or heaven. A bit of one or the other is trapped here between the wooded shores.

Isle au Haut Thorofare. This is the harbor with the best protection and the site of the island's principal settlement. The store and church are here too.

In entering the Thorofare from the west, first make Kimball Rock, which lies about a mile to the westward of Kimball Head. It is awash at high water and stands up boldly at low water. Then make the can on Marsh Cove Ledge. Give this corner of the island a good berth, for it is a savage lee shore. A course for Robinson Point light will clear the outlying dangers on the Kimball Island shore. They deserve plenty of room. Note that Robinson Point does not have a fog signal but shows a white sector to the southwest, which will lead one safely into the Thorofare at night.

Anchor as much out of the tide as possible on the Kimball Island shore but beware of ledges and boulders. One of the biggest is marked with a black-and-white barrel on a pipe. There is another ledge southeast of Moxie Island. It drops off and then rises up again as a flat rock with about 3 feet at low water.

There is an anchorage for one boat, about halfway between can 5 and the fish house on Moxie Island, in about 1 fathom at low water.

At the northern end of the harbor is a mussel bar with a dredged channel through it. It was dredged with a suction hose, so the boulders never were taken out. The edges have sagged in a bit. It is best negotiated on the high side of half tide. There is a beacon on a rock at the southeast edge of the dredged channel. Give it a good berth. The rock makes out. Keep in the middle of the narrow channel. One correspondent recommends keeping the light on Robinson Point in range with the rockweed line on the point on the east shore next to the 15-foot sounding on the chart. On coming out the northeastern end of the channel, bear a bit to the westward to avoid Eustis's Rock.

There is about 5 feet at the wharf at high water. Gas, Diesel oil, and kerosene are available here. It is well to check out the wharf first in the skiff, for there are boulders, which dry out at low water, both north and south of the wharf and at no great distance from it.

The square building at the head of the wharf is the island's generating plant.

The store is along the road to the north of the wharf. It is easier to land on the beach behind it than to land at the wharf. The store in 1976 was a cooperative started by the summer people and was well stocked with groceries, meat, and some simple hardware. It was open then from nine to four.

The path to the church leaves the road not far from the store. It is all an island church should be. Its steeple, white against the dark slope, is visible far offshore.

Also on the road north of the store is the post office, presided over for sixty-seven years, until October 1976, by Miss Lizzie Rich. She resigned at the age of eighty-three in order to travel. A cruising guide is no place for an essay on this remarkable lady, but one can observe that they named the mail boat for her. There never was a pleasanter or more helpful postmistress.

Point Lookout. In entering from the west, be very careful of the ledges off Flake Island and Kimball Island. They both seem to extend farther than the chart suggests. In the fog, expect a scale-up under Kimball Island. You may find a vacant mooring off the stone wharf. Hail the wharf, unless the one labeled "Guest" is free.

The land at Point Lookout is all privately owned. However, you can land at the float and walk up the road. Bear right at the first fork and you will come out at the Thorofare. You will see a trail up Champlain Mountain, but resist it. The top is overgrown and, although it is a pleasant walk to the summit, there is no view.

The large building above the wharf used to be the Point Lookout Club, established by Mr. Bowditch and his friends in 1880 but now is privately owned.

Burnt Island Thorofare. This narrow and tortuous channel is not difficult at half tide or less, when the dangers are exposed, but at high water it is considerably more difficult. Entering from the west, make the shore of Burnt Island at a stony beach near the west end, and hug this shore until you are up to the peak of the island in order to pass north of the half-tide rock shown between the figures 12 and 16 on chart 308. Then line up the northeast corner of a wharf on Isle au Haut with the south corner of the house behind it. When just west of a line between the wharf on Burnt Island and the wharf on Isle au Haut, drop the hook and snug down to enjoy a beautiful and secluded anchorage. One cruising man, on attaining this goal, was moved to quote the following devout prayer of thanksgiving:

> Lord, we thank thee that thy Grace
> Has brought us to this pleasant place,
> And most earnestly we pray
> That other folk will stay away.

To continue to the eastward, head for the big rock blocking the opening. When less than 100 yards from it, turn south and round the south end of it. If the tide is high and the ledge is covered, edge up to it very cautiously until you see it. It is dangerous to proceed without locating this mark. Once by this ledge, proceed to the eastward, favoring the Isle au Haut shore heavily. Move slowly and watch for bottom.

East Side of Isle au Haut. There is excellent protection in anything but a northeast gale behind York Island. There is an old wharf on the island and a good well. Entrance is complex, and the ledges are said to be covered with kelp. Proceed with care on a rising tide. From an earlier *Guide,* we add, do not go between Dolliver Island and Rabbits Ear. Enter between the two rocks southwest of Rabbits Ear.

Anyone who cruises these waters without George Wasson's *Sailing Days on the Penobscot* (W.W. Norton, New York) is missing much of the excitement of the place. In the last century there was a year-round population of about three-hundred people who subsisted by fishing, lobstering, farming, sheep raising, and wood cutting. The mackerel fleet used to seek shelter in the Thorofare. There was a lobster factory there, too, and vessels were built on Isle au Haut, one of which struck out for the gold fields around Cape Horn in 1850. A schooner rigged up as a floating department store called more or less regularly. Hordes of "plummers," blueberry pickers from the mainland, descended on Isle au Haut in the early fall and once started a fire that burned over a large part of the island.

Now the population is about sixty. With the advent of fast motorboats, there is little advantage in being near the fishing. The people who live on the island live here because they like it.

About half the island is owned by Acadia National Park. Ever since the days of the "plummers," the residents have not been enthusiastic about visitors. The summer people who built cottages and really lived on the island for half the year were different. When the children of Ernest W. Bowditch gave a large part of the island to the park, the problem of visitors arose again.

The park wants to preserve the wilderness nature of the land for people to enjoy. To the islanders this was a contradiction in terms, for campers and day trippers swarmed over the island, trespassing on private land, leaving trash about, camping wherever they liked, and threatening the island with another devastating fire. The park wanted to solve the problem by taking more land by eminent domain. The islanders strongly objected. The matter is not fully settled yet, but the shelters at Duck Harbor and the plan to land campers there rather than at the Thorofare is of some help. Limiting the number of visitors will help, too; but giving up the idea of adding to the park by eminent domain would be a long step in the right direction.

The cruising man may sense a coolness in his reception ashore, especially if he looks and acts like a "plummer." He can help by bringing no trash ashore, by respecting private property, and by appreciating the fragile and beautiful atmosphere of the island.

Pell Island Passage. If Burnt Island Thorofare sounds too tricky, or if it is blowing hard so that moving slowly is impossible, pass between Pell Island and Burnt Island. From the west, go close to the north of Mouse Island and head for the beach on the southwest end of Wheat Island. When about 100 yards off it, swing to the north and follow the Wheat Island shore. Keep away from Pell Island. Keep an eye for Channel Rock to the eastward. It is unmarked but usually shows and always breaks. Still, at high water on a quiet day, it could be a menace.

Great Spoon Island, easily identified by its shape, is now a bird refuge owned by the Audubon Society. In July there are flocks of guillemots and sea ducks around the island. Several ravens preside over the scene.

Black Horse and White Horse are as radically different, as their names suggest. There must be an interesting geological explanation to their differences and their propinquity.

The region to the east of Isle au Haut is no place to be in rough or thick weather. The ledges are unmarked, the tide runs swiftly, and the offshore seas pile in here unobstructed. They seem to crest up wherever you look and break tremendously on half-tide ledges. If the Isle au Haut shore is obscured, it is easy to get confused out here.

Isle au Haut to Stonington. This part of Maine is excelled by none and equaled only by the country between Mistake Island and Jonesport. Here are bold shores, deep channels, and uninhabited islands covered with spruce, balsam, and sweet fern. The shores are smooth, clean granite ledges, easy to walk on and delightful to swim from. Among the ledges are hidden sandy beaches. Many of the islands have been used to run sheep and are criss-crossed with deeply worn sheep runs. Don't follow these into the woods unless you enjoy walking like a sheep. The fishing is usually good. There are a few clams still, and when the herring or mackerel are running and the weirs are fishing, one may get a chance to watch the fishermen pump one out and get a few really fresh fish. Lobstermen fish this region extensively and are most friendly and stimulating people if they are approached with the esteem and respect that they deserve.

There are so many beautiful coves among these islands that it would swell this book to undue proportions to include all of them. Also the writers would incur the undying enmity of yachtsmen who want to meet here only those who have the interest and enterprise to explore for themselves.

We might, however, make a few casual suggestions. Merchants Island has a good harbor and was inhabited in Revolutionary times. There is a cove between McGlathery and Round Island. Enter it from the north. The grave of Peter Eaton overlooks the harbor and is all that remains of a once-busy community. Hearing that the island was to be "pulped" in 1954, Martin R. Haase, a summer resident of South Brooksville, whose *Diablesse* is often seen in these waters, organized Friends of Nature to purchase and preserve it in a wild state. He writes:

We let nature maintain the island and are happy to have people enjoy it properly by appreciating its beauty. Incidentally, we pay about $150 a year taxes on the island and would gratefully accept contributions (tax deductible) from those who like the island to be preserved in its wilderness state.

Look in at the cove north of Spruce Island. There is a summer place on Devils Island and a good anchorage. Anchor north of Saddleback and enjoy a swim on the southern beach. It is shark-proof. There is no better place for a bucket of lobsters and a bottle of beer. There is an *uncharted* and unmarked rock between Enchanted Island and Saddleback between the 12- and 18-foot soundings. The cruise schooners often put on a clambake in the cove southwest of Russ Island.

It was on one of these islands that I stood with a lobsterman looking into the thick fog. As the sun broke through, I observed hopefully, "It's clear overhead."

"Yes," he answered deliberately, "but the hell of it is, Roge, we ain't bound that way."

Air view looking southeast with Stonington in the foreground.

Stonington, Me. (13315 227). The approach to Stonington from the west is easy. Mark Island is prominent in clear weather, but in the fog its feeble bleat does not carry far; and when you are right under it, it sounds a mile away. As the tide ebbs to the west and floods to the east pretty much along your course, little allowance need be made for it. Dangers are well buoyed. Yellow Rock is very obvious at any tide, and one usually finds a scale-up under Crotch Island. Hail the wharf on Staples Point for advice on a mooring. There is perfectly good anchorage off the wharves and out of the tide.

From the east a close-winded yacht can usually fetch all the way in from Long Ledge on one tack. Again, the dangers are well marked and those which are not marked are bold and obvious. Note, however, that the tide in Jericho Bay does not run east and west as it does in the Thorofare, but at different stages of the tide it sets in different directions, perhaps moving in a rotary way like the tides in the Bay of Fundy. Watch the buoys and lobster traps for indications of how things are at the moment.

Stonington started as a fishing town, became a granite town, a ship-building town, and has now reverted to a fishing town, with one or two stonecutters still and a shipyard at Moose Island largely devoted to storage and repair. Stonington has one of the state's most successful fishermen's cooperatives, which deals not only in lobsters but also in scallops, clams, mussels, and groundfish. Having seen what happened to Boothbay Harbor and Camden, Stonington people are in no hurry to promote tourism. There are few motels, only two simple restaurants, two grocery stores, and an extensive hardware store. Summer residents are slowly buying up Deer Isle property and certainly the summer population is greater than it was, but Stonington is no carnival, protected from megalopolis as it is by distance and poor roads.

Gasoline, water and Diesel fuel are available at the principal wharf and within 100 yards are Atlantic Hardware and Bartlett's Market. There is a liquor store on the main street.

Repairs to hull, spars, and engine can be arranged at the Moose Island yard west of the town. Donald Hale, whose loft is just across the bridge in Sargentville, can repair sails.

A walk along the road westward to Green Head gives some feel for the history and background of the town, when the quarries on Crotch Island, George Head, St. Helena, and other islands were loading schooners with granite for Boston, New York, and Philadelphia. The Boston Museum of Fine Arts is built of Stonington granite. One resident of Stonington told me of a voyage east from Boston in the old *Annie & Reuben.* She was a schooner with a huge foresail, her foremast being stepped far forward and her mainmast far aft to accommodate long pieces of stone amidships. The crew ate breakfast at first light under Charlestown bridge in Boston, ran wing-and-wing even with the Boston-Portland steamer at midday, and ate dinner after sunset under Green Head. I last saw the vessel at a coal wharf next to the subway bridge in Cambridge. As I sculled around her stern in a fragile single shell, I asked a man aboard how she was going.

"When she goes, she'll go fast," he answered, referring less to her speed through the water than to her heavy cargoes of coal and stone.

It is interesting to remember, too, that Deer Isle was the home of Charlie Barr, who was sailing master of America's Cup yachts, and many of his crew hailed from Deer Isle.

During World War II, the Billings Brothers' Moose Island yard, which had built the last commercial coaster in 1938, turned to transports, crash boats, and PT boats, producing a real business boom in Stonington. One resident is quoted as wanting to see no repetition of it. "Too many people didn't come back from that boom."

Webb Cove, Me.   (13315   227). Should the weather look threatening, retreat to Webb Cove. The outer part of the cove is well enough protected against anything but a heavy southeaster. The little mudhole inside the inner point is tight as a bottle. However, the shores are muddy and there is no landing here. There is some old quarry machinery rusting on the hill on the eastern side of the entrance.

Sylvester Cove, Deer Isle, Me.   (13305   310). This cove, south of Dunham's Point, and open to the west when the tide is high, is not much to look at on the chart, but is a good anchorage in this beautiful region. Pigeon Island Reef makes a natural breakwater. The reef at the entrance is marked by a nun. Anchor in among the fleet. There is a landing float on the north side of the cove, maintained by the Deer Isle Yacht Club, and a 250-pound mushroom mooring available for visitors. Minor supplies can be had at a store about a mile from the anchorage. The Camden Hills are seen to great advantage at sunset on a clear night. There is an interesting summer colony at Dunham's Point.

In a brisk southwester, it can be uncomfortable, but after the tide is halfway out, the reef provides good shelter.

Northwest Harbor   (13305   310). This harbor, well protected in anything but a northwest gale, is easy of access and comparatively unfrequented. On the northerly shore are a long wharf and a float, privately owned. About 100–150 feet southeast of the float is a ledge, which bares only at moon low tides. It is unmarked and is not shown on the chart. Anchor well to the south of the float or out to the west of it.

The only public landing is in the cove at the head of the harbor, which bares out at low tide. Row up in the dinghy. Here is the village of Deer Isle, with a bank, hardware store, grocery store, post office, and telephone. A local resident writes: "Northwest Harbor is a quiet anchorage averaging about one cruising boat each night and we welcome visitors."

In the days of sail, Northwest Harbor had a ropewalk and sail loft. Vessels wintered here and fitted out in the spring. Now it is quiet and almost deserted, except for an eagle that the writer observed one night, presiding over ospreys, gulls, and a few cottages tucked among the trees.

Billings Cove, Sargentville, Me. (13316 307). This cove affords adequate shelter and greater seclusion than can be expected in Bucks Harbor. If it blows, one can work well up into the cove for protection, but anchorage off the old clam factory ex-blueberry factory is good on a quiet night.

Land at the town wharf or on the beach next to it. It is a pleasant walk up the road to a country grocery in Sargentville. Or one can land on the western shore, climb to the road where it comes off the bridge, and walk a short distance north on the road to an old schoolhouse, now the Hale sail loft. It was founded by Clarence Hale, who still works there in an advisory capacity, and who went to sea in schooners, sloops, and yachts. His son Donald has learned the trade and operates the business with skill and efficiency. It is a place worth seeing. I saw Clarence sitting on a new sailmaker's bench. That is an act of faith in an age when sailmakers' benches are seldom seen except in antique shops.

Deer Isle—Sedgewick Bridge (13316 307). On the Deer Isle end of the bridge at the west side is the Bridge Marina and Motel. There is a float here with 2 feet at low water for the convenience of restaurant patrons and, in 1976, gas, Diesel fuel, and deep-water moorings were promised for ensuing years. However, most of the restaurant's customers appear to arrive over the road, so it would be well to check by telephone before counting on the facilities.

The bridge appears to be broken-backed. The story goes that, after it was started, they found it necessary to increase the clearance so they shortened up on the cables. It swings violently in heavy winds and is said to be the last bridge still standing of several that were built from the same design. However, if it stood the Ground Hog Day gale of 1976, and the winter gales of 1978, it may be good for a while yet.

It was said that there were no skunks on Deer Isle until the bridge was built. Can you imagine two skunks, paw in paw, setting out across that bridge to a new land?

Benjamin River, Me. (13316   307). This is one of those places, like Burnt Island Thorofare, that is much easier at half tide or less, when the dangers are exposed. On entering, favor the eastern shore a little, as both shores consist of flats studded with boulders, but the channel is not quite in the middle. From the big field with the church at the head of it, marked "spire" on chart 307, a long bar makes out with a big boulder almost on the end of it. A locally maintained spindle has been sighted here, but don't count on it. Give the whole concern a generous berth to starboard. Anchorage is off the east shore, near the buildings of the Benjamin River Boatyard. This yard was bought from Frank Day and his son when Webbers Cove Boatyard in East Blue Hill gave up storage and repairs to build fiberglass lobster-boat hulls. The Days planned to build a new shed and to continue to build boats.

No supplies are available here.

The afternoon southwester is often very light off the mouth of the Benjamin River. The alert skipper will keep to the Deer Isle shore.

The yard, of which Mike Bullard was part owner and foreman in 1976, does repair and engine work and hauls boats up to about 40 feet. Most of the yard's work is storage and maintenance but occasionally it finishes out a fiberglass hull.

Center Harbor, Brooklin, Me. (13316   307). This is a convenient harbor on the north shore of the reach just east of the Benjamin River. The chart makes clear the approach from the westward. Anchor about abreast the cove in Chatto Island, if there is room. The bottom is mud. If the wind comes hard northwest, this anchorage can become uneasy, but it would be easy to run over under the lee of the eastern Torry Island.

One can approach Chatto Island nun 2 from the east by passing between the eastern Torry Island and High Head. By doing so, one can save more than a mile and avoid going out into the tide around Torry Castle. It is an easier passage in the fog also.

At Center Harbor is a small boat yard run by Joel White. He hauls, stores, maintains, and repairs local boats and finishes glass hulls. He is renowned for fine work in wood. He has built some small boats for Mystic Seaport, yawl boats for cruise schooners, and some really beautiful sloops and ketches. Nowhere will you find more expert craftsmen.

Consult Mr. White on any matter of repair. Donald Hale in Sargentville will attend to repair of sails. The yard does not sell gas or Diesel fuel and is in no sense a marina as the term is understood to the westward.

About ½ mile up the road from the yard is The Brooklin General Store, owned by Mr. Al Ormondroyd, a very accommodating gentleman, who will deliver purchases to the float if business is not too pressing.

The Center Harbor Yacht Club is on the north shore near the harbor entrance. There is about 4 feet of water at the float at low water. This is a hospitable club, with an active program. Water is piped to the float. Note that nun 2 in the harbor mouth and nun 10 on Torry Ledge lie exactly east-west should one need a compass check. However, as the buoys are quite close together and, as the buoy boat could be off the charted position by a few yards, one should not be extremely fussy about it.

Naskeag, Me. (13316   307). A gravel bar divides this harbor into an eastern and western part. Most boats lie in the eastern part, which is easily entered from the east. The passage between the two anchorages is extremely narrow and should not be attempted at low tide without local knowledge. The western half of the harbor is rather well filled with ledges; caution is advised. The Triangles do not show, even at low water.

The village is on the north side, but there is no dock. There is a public beach, approached by a road running north.

Hog Island is an attractive island with a few small beaches. Devils Head at its southern end affords a good view to the eastward.

A good anchorage is north of the middle of Hog Island.

Southeast Harbor, Deer Isle, Me. (13313   308) (13315   227). Note that the entire harbor is shown on chart 308; the entrance and eastern part are shown on chart 227. This is an excellent harbor and most convenient for boats using Deer Island Thorofare or Eggemoggin Reach.

A correspondent sends in the following:

> If one is looking for extreme privacy, a way can be found south of Stinson's Neck (via Southeast Harbor and on) into Long Cove, in the very heart of the island. Here, completely surrounded by land, is a pool with a depth in the middle variously estimated at from 20 to 30 fathoms. But the channel in had best be negotiated at the top of the tide.

The anchorage is described as Hawley's Deep Hole, with a depth of 102 feet. Don't enter here, unless prepared for adventure. There are many boulders.

Swans Island, Me.   (13313   308). This island, not to be confused with Swan Island in the Kennebec, was named for Colonel James Swan. He was born in Scotland, emigrated to Boston at the age of eleven, and became a clerk in the office of Thaxter and Son. He wrote a book on the African slave trade, assisted at the Boston Tea Party, was wounded at Bunker Hill, and advanced in the Continental Army to become a major in the cavalry. He became secretary to the Massachusetts Board of War and adjutant-general of the state. He speculated in land in Virginia and Kentucky and became a wealthy man. In 1784, he bought Burnt Coat Island, gave it his name, established sawmills, encouraged settlers, and was on his way to establishing a feudal empire. However, he happened to be in France at the time of the French Revolution and devoted his energies to saving his friends, among them Marie Antoinette. He loaded their property aboard a vessel in charge of Stephen Clough of Wiscasset. At the last minute, however, the aristocrats, including the queen, were arrested and guillotined. Captain Clough brought the furnishings and clothes to Wiscasset, where some of them still may be seen. Colonel Swan was accused of owing a debt of two million francs, which he denied, and he was jailed. Being a man of principle, he refused to pay, although he could have raised the money. He was released in 1830 by Louis Philippe and died very soon after.

The island, bereft of its squire, grew in a more democratic way and became prosperous through the sale of lumber, fish, and, finally, lobsters. Now there is a growing income from summer people. The island has a population of 500 in the winter and 5000 in the summer.

There are four good harbors on the island.

Mackerel Cove. There is no difficulty in entering, as the dangers are well marked. However, there are two confusing places. One is the deep passage south of Orono Island. Note that nun 4 is *south* of the rock it marks and must be left to *port.* Then beware of the 3-foot spot to the northeast. The other bad spot is the long ledge outside Roderick Head. This is completely submerged at high water, extends far out into the harbor to the eastward, and the top, which uncovers first as the tide goes, is on the western side. If you seek shelter in the snug cove east of Roderick Head, be very careful of this menace.

The steamer from Bass Harbor lands behind can 3. If you anchor off the wharf, leave her generous room to turn. There used to be a store here, but it was reported closed in 1977. There is a post office at the village of Atlantic.

Buckle Harbor. This is a secure and pleasant anchorage between Swans Island and Buckle Island, but there are no facilities and no landing. Extensive mud flats fringe the Swans Island shore and Buckle Island is occupied by summer people. However, there are three guest moorings in the harbor.

Enter between can 5 and can 7 and favor the Buckle Island shore.

Seal Cove. This large, shallow cove offers good protection and a chance of solitude. Enter close to the ledges off Swans Island Head, between them and the half-tide rock in the middle of the entrance. As you get into shoal water, you will notice clumps of rockweed. Keep away from them. The weed is growing on boulders. The shores are muddy, there are no facilities, and there is little point in going ashore.

Burnt Coat Harbor. When Champlain sailed west from Passama-quoddy Bay in 1604, he named Swans Island Brûle Côte, translated freely as Burnt Hill. The old French name, garbled by generations of English-speaking people, clings still as the name of the harbor.

There is no great difficulty in entering in clear weather. The abandoned lighthouse on Hockamock Head is prominent and there is an automated light on a little beacon below it. In thick weather, however, it is more difficult. The tide in Jericho Bay, confused by currents running in and out of Blue Hill Bay, Eggemoggin Reach, Deer Island Thorofare, Merchants Row and Toothacher Bay, seems to run in different ways at different times of the tide. Fortunately, however, most of the shores are bold and most of the dangers marked. If you can find the bell on Halibut Rocks, you will be by the worst of it. There is usually a good breeze and a scale-up under Marshall Island, and in Toothacher Bay the tide runs pretty much along your course. You can miss nun 4 without worry, for you will surely see High Sherriff if you are to the eastward. The white bell off Hockamock Point is noisy and easy to find. From there the mouth of the harbor is wide open, but notice that since the lighthouse was abandoned, there is no fog signal. There is a gong in the harbor entrance, but it is in so far and in such quiet water that it rings in a most subdued manner, if at all. The best anchorage is north of Harbor Island, but the island is privately owned and is entirely without supplies, facilities, or a public landing.

If you need fuel or supplies, run up the harbor and anchor to the southward of the wharves. The holding ground here is not reliable.

Several cruising men have reported anchors fouled in kelp or weed.

George Tainter, who lives just beyond a Quonset hut on the road north of the harbor, does engine work. Russell Burns has a railway, which can haul lobster boats and small yachts.

Gas, Diesel fuel, and marine supplies are available at the wharf with the red fish houses, the fishermen's cooperative. Further in is another wharf selling fuel, lobsters, and some marine supplies. Up the hill behind the wharves is the Harbor Cash Market. This store occasionally has ice. A mile up the road near the head of the harbor is The General Store run by Terry and Trudy Lunt. This store is open on Sundays in the summer. The Lunts are most obliging people and, if business is not heavy, will drive you back to the shore with your purchases. They have a good selection of meats, groceries, canned goods, and produce but no beer or wine, as the island is dry. There is a prospect for ice in bags in 1977.

A correspondent recommends the fresh-water swimming in an old quarry on the east side of the harbor. "Someone has rigged a line with floating buoys across the center to aid less able swimmers. When we stopped there in August the water was warm, wonderfully clear, and devoid of other swimmers."

The eastern entrance to Burnt Coat Harbor, between Harbor Island and Swans Island, looks perilous on the chart but is quite practicable. Given any wind at all, an able vessel can beat through, although near can 3 the wind may be fluky. The tide does not run hard and the shores are quite bold. Bound east, leave the two cans close to starboard and favor the Swans Island shore slightly after you pass can 3. Out in the Southwest Passage, though, between Swans Island and Long Island, the tide runs vigorously.

Passages from Jericho Bay to Blue Hill Bay

Casco Passage and York Narrows. These are the most commonly used passages north of Swan's Island. One would use Casco Passage going to and from Eggemoggin Reach and York Narrows in connection with Deer Island Thorofare. Both are deep enough for most yachts and clearly marked with buoys. The tide runs pretty hard to the east on the flood and west on the ebb. Approach to Casco Passage from the west is marked only by a nun, but York Narrows has a lighted bell. At the eastern end, the two passages join at can 1 and the black-and-white bell outside it. On the ordinary southwest breeze, one can usually fetch through Casco Passage. York Narrows is wide enough to beat through.

There is excellent shelter at Buckle Harbor and Mackerel Cove on the south, and between Black and Opechee islands on the north.

Pond Island Passage. This is an easy and well-buoyed passage north of Pond Island. It might be more favorable than Casco Passage if one were bound east on an ebb tide.

Outside. Go down Toothacher Bay, between John Island and Swan's Island and east of the Sisters, Black Island, and Great Gott. This route has the advantage of avoiding Bass Harbor Bar and of a dramatic approach to the hills of Mt. Desert, but it is not recommended in thick weather. Note that the ebb tide sets to the southeast out of Blue Hill Bay, making real dangers of the Drums, Horseshoe Ledge, and South Bunker Ledge. Watch the way the tide sets by pot buoys.

As a commentary on the run of tide, consider the course of a skiff lost in a brisk southerly and thick fog somewhere south of Drum Island. It turned up twenty-four hours later, bobbing around under a wharf in Bass Harbor—a journey of 6 miles across Bass Harbor Bar.

Lunt Harbor, Frenchboro Long Island, Me. (13313 308). Dredged out in 1977, Frenchboro is now a very attractive anchorage for those who like offshore islands. With a lighted bell to the northeast and another bell west of Harbor Island, it should not be hard to find. Most of the shores are bold, although at high water the ledges north of Crow Island are a menace.

There is a large winter mooring off the steamer wharf, but the tide runs hard between Harbor Island and Long Island so it is an uneasy berth. The intention was to dredge to a depth of 10 feet up to the wharf on the west side, then to a depth of 6 feet up inside the ledges with a 6-foot turning basin. In 1976, before the dredging, a pole on the western extremity of the ledge had been painted with a red primer, luring several unfortunates to leave it to starboard. Favor the western shore.

There are a small restaurant on the wharf, on the western side, and a float with gas and Diesel fuel. There is a store nearby.

A ferry from Bass Harbor calls twice a week at Frenchboro. In 1976, the days were Wednesday and Thursday.

A visitor in 1973 wrote ". . . and ashore I found it depressing, fierce dogs, and unfriendly. If I had gone to see the Pogonia, I might have changed my mind."

The writer found Frenchboro an interesting and friendly place on the few occasions on which he has been able to visit it. It is well worth a try. There is a tar road running along the east shore, with dirt roads dwindling to paths running off it. These paths make easy and pleasant walking. The island is said to be inhabited by deer, pheasants and beaver released by the State Game Commission.

The population of the island, like that of Matinicus and Isle au Haut, is dwindling, but it has had a recent increase. In the fall of 1969, the Department of Education in Augusta declared that there were so few children on the island that no teacher would be sent to teach such a small school. The children would have to board on Mt. Desert for the winter. The people of Frenchboro at once set about increasing the number of children on the island by taking into their homes fifteen state wards. This swelled the school to the required number, a teacher was sent, and the arrangement worked out well. All but a very few of the children adjusted happily to island life and to their new families. As of 1976 all of the children had moved ashore to go to high school. The elementary school was still flourishing, with seven scholars.

Anyone who drops in here should read what *Sailing Days on the Penobscot* has to say about Outer Long Island. Some fifty years ago, Lunt Harbor had a bad reputation along the coast as a rendezvous for pirates and rough characters. The offshore fishing fleet is reported to have put in there often for a wild night ashore, but now one will find there the usual Maine fishermen, quite ready and willing to be cordial and helpful to visiting yachtsmen.

Regarding the island, a correspondent writes:

The most important thing I know of about Outer Long Island is that on the southwest side there is a bog of several acres in extent, which in early August is completely filled with blossoms of Pogonia! Now, Pogonia is one of our relatively rare New England orchids, with a lovely purple or mauve color, a very delicate and beautiful flower. When I find a single blossom near some inland lake, I rejoice. I'll never forget the first time I came around the point there and saw several acres of solid Pogonia in bloom. It took me quite a while to believe what I saw.

The foregoing paragraph was written in 1936. In 1970 they were still blooming. Enjoy them where they are. They will not stand transplanting.

Blue Hill Bay, Me. (13316   307). This long, deep bay is bounded on the west by the mountains of Mt. Desert and on the north by Blue Hill. Swan's Placentia, Black, and Gott's islands protect it from the open Atlantic on the south. Its shores are bold, for the most part heavily wooded, and sparsely inhabited. Its harbors, though few, are clean and well protected. Often when it is thick outside, Blue Hill Bay will be only hazy.

The best way to get a quick look at the bay is to enter on a coming tide through Flye Island Narrows and run up the bay west of Long Island to Blue Hill. The next day, cross north of Long Island, beat down through Bartlett Narrows, go west of Hardwood Island toward Tinker Island; and if you have an ebb tide with you and the wind to the west a bit, you should be able to fetch Lopaus Point and Bass Harbor Bar. The views of the Mt. Desert hills from the west are magnificent. Should the breeze die or the tide turn foul, there are numerous coves in which to seek shelter.

Allen Cove, Me. (13316 307). This is a big, open cove well protected from west, south, and east with good holding ground. It is surrounded by farms and hayfields. The Northeast Harbor fleet often uses it as a rendezvous on club cruises. There is no landing place and nothing ashore for which to land.

Blue Hill, Me. (13316 307). Entrance in clear weather is quite obvious from the chart. In thick weather—and it is seldom thick up the bay—one might follow the 5-fathom curve to the westward along the shore of Woods Point and make can 1. Inside, the Kollegewidgwok Yacht Club maintains two guest moorings. They are wooden poles with orange pick-up buoys marked KYC. If these are occupied, slip alongside the club float, where there is 10 feet at low water, and speak with the steward. He is there from eight to six daily and on Sunday mornings. Anchorage is good anywhere in the triangle indicated by nun 6, can 7, and the club float.

This is a secure anchorage, even in a hurricane, but should you seek something better, continue up the harbor between can 7 and nun 8 and anchor in the inner pool. You can go all the way to the village in the dinghy on the tide.

Gas, water, and ice are available at the yacht club. Diesel fuel can be ordered by tank truck. The ice is cut by hand in the winter and packed in sawdust near the house of Newt Grindle, about halfway to the village on the right. The usual grocery stores are to be found in the village. It is quite a walk from the yacht club.

Blue Hill Yacht Sales in the village has a mechanic and a small railway that will haul boats up to about 30 feet.

The Kollegewidgwok Yacht Club runs an active racing program. Perhaps its best-known race is the Danforth Cup race from Blue Hill to

Schoodic whistle to Mt. Desert Rock and return.

The yacht club is open from June 15 to September 15, and a steward is in attendance from July 4 to Labor Day. It is a station of The Cruising Club of America. There is a telephone at the club, and one can order groceries delivered from Blue Hill. The steward can be consulted concerning repairs to hull, spars, or engines. Donald Hale in Sargentville is an expert sailmaker and rigger. Captain Walter K. Carter is a compass adjuster of wide reputation living nearby.

It is about a 2-mile walk to Blue Hill, most of it along a rather uninspiring tar road. However, the village is quite interesting. There is a blacksmith on the main street, an artist in black iron. Further up the street are the Cranberry House and Blue Hill Inn, most attractive places to dine. Beyond the inn is the well-known Rowantrees Pottery, started by two ladies in the 1930s as an educational venture. The manganese deposits found on the slopes of Blue Hill are used to make the lavender and black glaze characteristic of Rowantrees products.

The Blue Hill Historical Society has acquired the Jonathan Fisher house and keeps it open to the public in the summer. The Reverend Fisher was an eighteenth-century graduate of Harvard who took his bride to Blue Hill and served there as a very active minister for the rest of his long life. His biography has been written by his descendent, Mary Ellen Chase. Her own autobiography, *Windswept,* tells of her early life in and near Blue Hill.

Also in Blue Hill are the Kniesel Hall Music School and a golf course.

Blue Hill itself, 560 feet high, dominates every view of the town. If you want to climb it because it's there, take Route 15 north from the town for about a mile and turn right on a road to the east, which in 1970 bore a sign: Mountain Shop. The trail leaves the left (north) side of the road at a yellow sign: Trail to Lookout Tower. It is a steep trail through the woods and up the shoulder of the mountain. About halfway up, it is joined by an old jeep road. This is the easier and longer way; but a short, steep path cuts off to the right.

Near the top, the blueberries are magnificent. The view from the tower on a clear day stretches from Rockland to the Mt. Desert hills and south to Isle au Haut and the islands down the bay.

If it is a dry time, there may be a watchman on duty keeping an eye open for forest fires and helping to triangulate them.

The Gazetteer of Maine states:

> The name Blue Hill comes from a commanding elevation of land near the center of the town. It was formerly covered with trees—principally evergreens—which, at a distance, gave a very dark blue tint—whence its name.

East Blue Hill, Me. (13316   307). This little bight is the home of Webbers Cove Boat Yard, operated by John Cousins. The yard builds a basic fiberglass powerboat hull and will finish it or ship it for the owner to finish up. The yard also does repair, maintenance, and storage work. The yard has a 12-ton railway and a lift.

The upper parts of Blue Hill Bay, Morgan Bay, Patten Bay, and Union River Bay are well protected, free of dangers, and afford beautiful prospects, pleasant sailing, and little fog.

Mt. Desert Narrows. It is no longer possible for masted vessels of much draft to pass from Blue Hill Bay into Frenchman's Bay under the bridge at Mt. Desert Narrows. Since the late eighteenth century a drawbridge has spanned the narrows. However, in 1957 a fixed bridge with a clearance of 25 feet above high water was built, and Mr. K.K. Thompson, bridge keeper and descendant of Cornelius Thompson, who built the first bridge on this site, was retired.

Prettymarsh, Me. (13316   307). This is a large harbor, but it affords good protection, for one can anchor under whatever shore is to windward. Somes Cove offers very good shelter in a heavy southwesterly. There was a large white mooring in the western part of the harbor in 1969 that had every appearance of a guest mooring.

The shores are privately owned. There are no facilities whatever, and even the road out is not easy to find.

Prettymarsh is clean and quiet and affords a delightful place in which to be alone.

Bartlett Narrows, Me. (13316   307). This is a deep and easily negotiated passage of surpassing beauty. There is good shelter in Great Cove. Many projects have been proposed for Bartlett Island, but the last time the writer was there the island appeared to be uninhabited.

There are several shelters on the west side of Mt. Desert Island. The best is probably the cove north of the bar behind Moose Island. Seal Cove, Goose Cove, and Duck Cove all have small settlements of summer people and are pleasant places from which to view the sunset on a summer evening. Do not count on them for protection in a storm or for extensive supplies.

Bass Harbor, Me.   (13316   307). This is rather a wide-open harbor, likely to have a bit of a roll making in, and uncomfortable in a heavy southerly. However, there are those who prefer it to being stuffed into Southwest or Northeast Harbor to the snarl of outboards and the constant jangling of wire halyards on aluminum masts.

There are two "marinas" here. The word is in quotation marks, for it should not imply what Cape Cod means by the term. The outer one is just south of the ferry terminal and is run by Mr. and Mrs. Bauer. They provide guest moorings, gas, Diesel fuel, water, ice, and marine supplies. Ashore are a grocery and a restaurant serving cocktails, wines, and beer. Mr. and Mrs. Bauer are most hospitable people and glad to be of service.

Inside, above can 5, where the harbor narrows, a channel has been dredged up to Rich's Bass Harbor Boat Shop and Marina. Favor the western side of the channel. Mr. Robert Rich has gas, Diesel fuel, ice, and water at his float. If no mooring is available, he may be able to find you a place at his float. He has a boat shop where he builds several wooden boats every year and cannot keep up with the demand. If he isn't too pressed, he may let you visit the shop and see how wooden boats are built. It is worth half a day to see these men at work. He also does welding and electrical work, has a marine railway, and can make any kind of repair to hull, spars, or engine. The protection is better here than in the outer harbor, but the crowd is denser.

The ferry to Swans Island and Frenchboro runs from the terminal on the eastern shore outside the sardine factory.

The town of Bernard has all necessary food supplies.

Bass Harbor, unlike other towns on Mt. Desert, subsists more on fish, lobsters, and boat building than it does on tourists. Consequently, there is a less hurried, less sophisticated, and more independent attitude evident.

Bass Harbor Bar, Me. (13318   306). The rocky bar, strewn with boulders, can be crossed under ordinary conditions anywhere north of the middle, but the best water is close to the channel can. In the fog, it is possible to go close enough to Bass Harbor Head to pick up the sound of the fog bell.

The tide runs hard across the bar and reverses the usual rule for Maine passages. It floods west into Blue Hill Bay and ebbs east. With the tide ebbing south in the Western Way and flooding north, it seems likely you will have to buck it one place or the other unless you can hit slack water and have the best of both tides. Bound west, one may do well to avoid the bar altogether and use the ebb tide to beat down to Burnt Coat Harbor, thus getting well to windward. Bound east, it is much more important to have a fair tide through the Thorofares and in the Western Way than it is across the bar.

Bound east from Bass Harbor for Petit Manan and the Bay of Fundy, you would do well to start on the ebb, have a fair tide across the bar, be set to windward as you cross Frenchman's Bay, and have the full strength of the powerful flood beyond Schoodic, where it really counts.

When the wind is blowing hard against the tide, the rip on the bar can become very unpleasant and even dangerous for a small boat. Under these circumstances, wait in Bass Harbor or go out around Placentia and Gott's islands. A hard southerly and an ebb tide in the Western Way can build up a dangerous rip between the nun and the can.

Under most conditions, however, there is no problem in crossing the bar, finding the gong on Long Ledge, and running up the Western Way. The first real view of the hills as you come by Long Ledge on a summer afternoon is one you will long remember.

Mt. Desert Island, Me. **(13318   306) (13316   307).** Mt. Desert Island is the culmination of many a cruise. After a day among the granite and spruce islands to the westward, to round Long Ledge and see the panorama of the Mt. Desert hills in the afternoon sun is breathtaking. As you sail up the Western Way, they grow higher, more distinct, and more impressive until you tuck into Northeast Harbor at night, with the hills rising steeply around you.

The island was rediscovered in 1604 by Champlain on his cruise westward from St. Croix Island. He named it *L'isle des Monts Désert,* the island of the barren mountains. To be logical, one should pronounce the name of the island in French, with the accent on the last syllable, or in English with the accent on the first syllable. But to mix the two and call it Mt. De*sert* suggests the last course at a banquet. There is nothing logical about the English pronunciation of foreign words, however, so do as you like. Most local people refer to their home as Mt. *Des*ert, in spite of the late President Eliot of Harvard.

The island affords excellent anchorages, better than adequate shore facilities, and good communication. There are miles of sailing in protected waters with superb mountain views. The trip up Somes Sound is an example of this. Here is the only fjord on the Atlantic coast of the United States. The mountains drop sharply into the sea, just as they do in Norway. And at the head, the mountains give way to a lovely valley with a snug harbor at the foot of it.

Do not neglect the trails. Most of the island is now part of Acadia National Park. The park maintains trails and carriage roads and publishes a map, available at the stationery store on the west side of the main street in Northeast Harbor or through the Mt. Desert Chamber of Commerce. The trails are, on the whole, well marked, but some of them are very rugged indeed, leading up over almost vertical ledges by means of iron ladders set into the rock. A good day's walk is from Northeast Harbor, by the Asticou Inn, and up the trail toward Jordan Pond. Swing left up the south shoulder of Jordan Mountain. The trail soon comes out on bare ledge, so that as you climb, you gain changing views of Sargent, Pemetic, Jordan Pond, and the islands to the south. From the top of Jordan on a clear day one can see Mt. Desert Rock to the south and Mt. Katahdin to the north.

Cross over to the top of Sargent Mountain, stopping for a quick dip in Sargent Pond. Then return down the south side of Sargent to the Jordan Pond trail. The writers have seldom made this trip without seeing deer in the woods and a variety of birds, including ravens and eagles, on the upper slopes.

One might vary the trip by stopping at the Jordan Pond House at the south end of the pond, widely renowned for delicious popovers.

Do not leave Mt. Desert without hiring a car and driving to the top of Cadillac (locally, Green) Mountain at sunset. From Rockland to beyond Petit Manan the coast lies at your feet, fading in outline as the lights wink on.

History is all around you here, too. Champlain writes of seeing the island in 1604. The Jesuits visited the island in 1613 and settled at the foot of the field on Fernald's Point. Here they found a spring between high and low water that runs freely today. East of Bass Harbor Head is Ship Harbor, dry at low water, where an American privateer is said to have escaped a British warship during the Revolution. In Somes Sound at the foot of Acadia Mountain is a brook where French naval vessels used to fill water casks. Whether Norsemen actually lay alongside the cliffs of Flying Mountain and fought the Indians coming down the sound in canoes is doubtful, but the scene is not hard to imagine. Indians, Frenchmen, and Englishmen; fishermen, seamen, pirates, farmers have rowed and sailed these waters for centuries. Only recently has it become a "vacationland." Still in the recollection of many are the days of steam yachts and great schooners at Seal Harbor, fifty-room "cottages" with formal gardens, stables, and battalions of servants at Bar Harbor, and ladies of leisure with parasols and flowered sun hats enjoying it all. A minor theme was the plain living and high thinking of President Eliot of Harvard and a number of his modest and distinguished colleagues. Characteristic of him is the story told of one of his journeys from Rockland to Northeast Harbor on the steamer *J. T. Morse:*

As the President was leaning on the rail, contemplating the unfolding beauties of Blue Hill Bay, a member of the crew stood beside him a moment and said, "We've been talking about who was the smartest man that travels on this boat. We concluded it was you, but what we don't know is—if you're so smart, why ain't you rich?" To which Mr. Eliot responded with a characteristic blend of wisdom, modesty, and wit, "I guess I never had time."

Visit the Sawtelle Museum on Cranberry Island for more detailed information on the island's history.

For more modern developments, visit the Jackson Laboratory south of Bar Harbor, where continuing work is done on hereditary aspects of cancer. The College of the Atlantic, a new institution in Bar Harbor, is doing advanced ecological studies. The Maine Sea Coast Missionary Society's *Sunbeam* is based on Northeast Harbor and is busy helping people in isolated communities to live richer and better lives. There is a great deal to see and do on Mt. Desert, and a summer is not time enough in which to do it.

The Great Harbor of Mt. Desert, Me. (13318   306). This is the name given to the confluence of the Eastern Way, the Western Way, and Somes Sound. It is a well-protected anchorage for large vessels and a good place to sail small boats. It has two entrances.

The Western Way is marked by a lighted gong on Long Ledge and a beacon on South Bunker Ledge. The tide runs briskly along this course from the gong to the black-and-white bell, northeast on the flood and southwest on the ebb, but seems to set one to the side very little. There is a bar between Seawall Point and Great Cranberry Island, with a passage marked by a can and a nun. The tide runs harder here— perhaps 3 knots—and in the shoal water, with the wind against the tide, it can get quite lumpy. Once over the bar, however, conditions improve, and one can follow the shore right into Southwest Harbor.

The Eastern Way is marked by a lighted gong and a beacon on East Bunker Ledge. The beacon is a squatty pyramid painted white with a red-and-white checkered day board on it. It has been the writer's experience that when approaching the Eastern Way from Schoodic toward the end of the day, it is well to get to windward and come in south of East Bunker Ledge under the Cranberry Island shore. There is likely to be a fresh little breeze under the shore when it is calm and rolly off Otter Cove. The passage south of Sutton Island is to be preferred.

Southwest Harbor, Me. (13318   306). This is a large harbor, open eastward and devoted to sardines, lobsters, groundfish, the Coast Guard Base, and yacht building, as well as to transient yachts. It is not surprising to find the latter coming last. It is an easy harbor to make

A. D. Phillips

The Great Harbor of Mt. Desert looking east from Southwest Harbor across the entrance to Somes Sound and out the Eastern way. Northeast Harbor and Seal Harbor are just above the middle of the picture.

from east or west in the fog or at night, and although it is open east-
wards, there is seldom any concern in summer weather. There are two
principal anchorages.

Manset. This is on the south side of the harbor near its mouth off the
yard of Henry R. Hinckley, which was clearly labeled. Two successive
winters of heavy easterly gales rather tore up Mr. Hinckley's wharf and
floats. It is expected that he will rebuild and will again sell gasoline,
Diesel fuel, water, ice, stove fuel, and ship chandlery and will have
moorings to rent. Yet the writer hesitates to describe facilities that, as
he writes, are in ruins.

The only objection to visiting Hinckley's for fuel and supplies in the
past has been the congestion at the floats. With new boats fitting out,
charter boats coming in or taking on supplies to leave, and considerable
transient business, yachts were stacked all around the floats three deep.

The yard has a name for building the best in fiberglass yachts. Ask
at the office for permission to visit the shop.

To the west of the yard a road runs up the hill to Smith's store on
the first corner. The Smith ladies run a small and crowded shop with
the best of everything, and they are most accommodating people. If
press of business permits, they will give you a ride to the shore with your
groceries.

The post office is a bit further west on the shore road. There is a
public telephone between Hinckley's shop and his wharf.

Mr. Jarvis Newman has a shop a bit west of the post office. He
has developed a fiberglass dinghy that can be rowed, sailed, or pro-
pelled with an outboard. It is a handsome model and beautifully
finished. He builds two models of Friendship sloops in fiberglass.
One is a twenty-five-foot hull from the famous *Pemaquid* model, first
built by Abdon Carter, pictured in Howard Chapelle's *American Sailing Craft,* and built again by James Rockefeller in Camden from the
lines Chapelle took off. Mr. Newman polished up Rockefeller's *Old
Baldy,* used her for a plug, and has made a number of handsome little vessels. The other is a 31-footer made from the hull of *Dictator,* a
sloop Mr. Newman bought on Deer Isle and rebuilt. This model has
the reputation for being very fast. He also builds lobster boats. He
and Ralph Stanley have collaborated on rebuilding some really de-
crepit craft and restoring them to life, although there may be but little of the original wood left in them.

Next to Hinckley's on the east is The Moorings, a pleasant place to
eat ashore; and further down the road to the east toward Seawall is the
Sea Wall Restaurant, which had an excellent reputation prior to the

gales of 1978. If it is rebuilt, as planned, it will no doubt maintain its quality.

On the west of Hinckley's is The Boathouse, which sells gas, small boats, and marine supplies. It may be less crowded than Hinckley's.

Southwest Harbor. The town is at the head of the harbor. There is good anchorage off Harvard Beal's fish and lobster wharf or off the Southwest Boat Corporation wharf. There may be a vacant mooring available here.

This is a busy place, with excursion boats and fishermen constantly coming and going. However, it quiets down at night. Gas, Diesel fuel, water, ice, and, of course, lobsters are available at Harvard Beal's wharf.

Repairs of all kinds can be made and some marine supplies can be purchased at Southwest Boat Corporation. This yard can haul and repair any vessel on the coast. A lot of heavy commercial work on seiners, draggers, and sardine carriers is done here, as well as yacht work.

It is quite a walk up town, but the chances of getting a ride are better than even. In town there are grocery stores, drug stores, a movie theater, a laundromat, and a restaurant.

On the main street, between the library and a delicatessen, is The Live Yankee, run by Joan and Reg Hudson. They can sew up a sail, provide material and sewing equipment, games, books, and gifts.

A taxi can be hired to go to the airport at Trenton or to connect with the bus at Bar Harbor for Ellsworth, Portland, and Boston. A correspondent adds the following notes regarding nearby attractions:

The best mountain accessible from "Southwest" is, of course, Western; but unless you are a confirmed hiker and know the way to it, take a car. The others are Dog (renamed Saint Sauveur), Robinson (Acadia), and Flying Mountain. These may be reached by anchoring in Valley Cove (a good place to picnic); or Norwood Cove, where it is simpler to ask directions of the first person you see. There are two lakes: Long Pond and Echo Lake; the latter is fine for those who like fresh-water swimming. Jesuit Springs in Fernald's Cove is worth looking at. This is a fresh-water spring below the high-tide mark, famous for its clear and sweet water. As soon as the tide has gone out halfway, the water is fresh, and the spring may be distinguished on the beach. The Jesuits, who settled on the point above it, used the spring in the seventeenth century. On a clear day one would do well to take a car from Southwest Harbor to the south end of Long Pond and climb some of the trails on Western Mountain.

A channel has been dredged up the north side of the harbor to the town wharf. There is no room here to anchor, but the trip in the dinghy will save more than half of the walk from Beal's.

Somes Sound, Me. (13318   306). The sail from Northeast or Southwest Harbor up this fjord is a truly inspiring experience. Plan to have a fair tide through the narrows. As you approach, you will see to the west a long field on Fernald's Point. At the foot of it is Jesuit Spring, referred to above, where the first settlers got water in 1613. Leave can 7 to port and keep in the middle.

Valley Cove is the first indentation on the west side. Here the mountains rise almost sheer from deep water, leaving only a narrow strip of beach at the foot of the cliff. Acadia Park maintains four heavy moorings here for visitors. Except in heavy weather, it is a good place to spend an afternoon and evening. There is a trail from the beach across the foot of the slide and up the sound to the Man of War Brook, where it branches, one branch going up Robinson Mountain and the other across to Echo Lake. The latter makes a pleasant walk with a welcome swim in fresh water at the end of it. Robinson Mountain is a steep but short climb, affording a good view of the sound.

About halfway up the sound on the western side is Hall's Quarry, now a small settlement. Williams's boat yard is opposite on the east shore, with a small railway and repair facilities for hull, spars, and engines.

Then the mountains step back from the water and the entrance to Somes Harbor appears behind Bar Island. The entrance is narrow but well buoyed and the park maintains several guest moorings here.

There is a public landing with 4 feet at low water, whence it is a short walk to the store and post office. There is an outdoor telephone in front of the store and the store is open on Sundays in the summer.

Across the sound in the northeast corner is Mt. Desert Yacht Yard, with several guest moorings, a railway, and a reputation for the highest quality of work.

Northeast Harbor, Me. (13318   306). From the water, Northeast Harbor is attractive indeed. It is easy of access, perfectly protected, and surrounded by spectacular views. The light and fog bell on Bear Island make entrance easy at night or in thick weather. Be careful to avoid a ledge just off the entrance between nun 2 and can 1. There is a notorious dead spot off Sargent Head. Keep to the eastward as much as possible to avoid it.

Seek a berth on the east side of the harbor, as there is considerable motorboat traffic to and from the wharves and the marina at the foot of Sea Street.

The town maintains a number of guest moorings. They are marked by white posts, with red copper paint at the waterline. Others have pink balloons with no name or number. There is a marina in the cove on the west side of the harbor, with slips for those who want to use them. The Harbor Master, Mr. Dodge, inhabits an open shed between the marina and the big town wharf. Do not anchor in the channel delineated by black-and-red plastic buoys.

Anything you need ashore is quickly obtained. The Clifton Dock on the west side of the harbor near the entrance carries gas, Diesel fuel, water, ice, stove fuel, and a limited inventory of marine supplies. A grocery order may be telephoned to the Pine Tree Market or Small's Market.

If you wish to go uptown, land at the float moored to the big wharf on the southerly side of the cove. On the wharf is a telephone and a huge steel bucket as big as a truck body, which is filled with trash daily. Adjacent to the parking lot on a knoll is the Chamber of Commerce information center, with showers and toilets at a nominal fee. Thence walk up Sea Street toward town. On your right is Flick Flye's little restaurant, which specializes in lobsters, either live or cooked in any way you want. On the corner of the main street is a garage where you can hire a taxi.

To the right is F.T. Brown's well-equipped hardware store, specializing in marine items and charts both American and Canadian. Beyond that are the post office and laundromat, a busy place in midmorning.

To the left stretches the main street of Northeast Harbor, with several markets, a drug store, fancy clothing stores, a stationery store for trail maps of the island, and numerous expensive shops purveying knick-knacks of every conceivable variety. There are two restaurants where one can get a drink and a meal, The Towne House at the far end of the main street and The Mast and Rudder near Kimball Terraces Motel.

Straight ahead, as you come up Sea Street, is a road continuing up the hill, with a liquor store on the left.

There is a medical center in Northeast Harbor.

It is a good walk on a well-traveled trail to the Jordan Pond House. The trail starts behind the Asticou Inn at the head of the harbor.

On the east side of the harbor, almost exactly opposite the foot of Sea Street, is the Asticou Terraces Dock, the approach to the Asticou Terraces, a unique memorial park left to the town by the late Joseph H. Curtis of Boston. The trip ashore, with a short walk to the top of Asticou Hill, is one of the most rewarding side jaunts of a cruise to Maine. Take it at sunset, or by moonlight. At the top is Thuya Lodge, the old Curtis house, containing the noted Curtis collection of botanical books, open 10 A.M. to 6 P.M. daily. A famous botanical collection has recently been transplanted to the Terraces. At the Asticou Inn, Charles Savage has developed a beautiful Japanese garden.

The Northeast Harbor Fleet has its clubhouse and dock at Gilpatrick's Cove, just west of Northeast Harbor. Don't try to get to the club by water! The anchorage is small and very poor. Cruising yachts are extended a cordial invitation to join the fleet's numerous special races and cruises.

The road skirting the eastern shore of the harbor has been named Peabody Drive in honor of the late Dr. Francis Greenwood Peabody of Harvard University, who, throughout a long life, cruised these waters. Once, when asked his occupation, Dr. Peabody replied, "I stay ashore winters"—a sentiment that cruising men will appreciate.

The authors are indebted to the late Mr. W. Rodman Peabody of Boston, son of Dr. Peabody, for the following story concerning President Eliot of Harvard University:

There is a crop of interesting stories about President Eliot, who, you may know, was a very skillful sailor and who sailed the Maine coast with a good deal of regularity from the end of the 1860s to the time of his death. For many years after his first wife died his summer home was a little sloop called the *Sunshine* and his headquarters were at Calf Island in Frenchman Bay.

President Eliot was, as you may guess, an imperturbable person even when fate was against him. I remember once as a small boy sailing from Bar Harbor to Northeast Harbor with my father, who was preaching at Northeast Harbor. We lunched with President Eliot and then started home for Bar Harbor. You may recall that at the mouth of Northeast Harbor there is a ledge with a high rock at each end. It is now protected by red and black buoys, so that there are two entrances to the harbor. In those days the ledge was unbuoyed.

As the President walked with us to the float, my father asked him for the bearings of the ledge which was directly in front of his house and dead to windward. He immediately got in his rowboat and said: "I will sail you out until you are clear and then row home."

We got under way in a stiff southwester and were swinging to it well when we came up with a crash. The boat stopped, slid off, hit again, and went free. The President, who was steering, without a gesture of concern, then turned the wheel over to my father and said: "Those were the two high points of the ledge. If you will take a careful bearing, you will always know their exact location in the future. Good-by. You preached a good sermon." Without another word he hauled in his painter and rowed away.

Seal Harbor, Me. (13318   306). This harbor offers adequate protection on an ordinary summer night. There will be just enough motion to rock you to sleep. But in a heavy southerly or southeaster, Seal Harbor can be very unpleasant.

Gas and water are available at the town landing. Whether you need supplies or not, take the short and pretty walk to the village. There is a thoroughly adequate store.

The summer homes of Fords and Rockefellers overlook the harbor. The late Mr. John D. Rockefeller was glad to make available to horseback riders and hikers the carriage roads and trails on his extensive estate. The family continues this hospitable tradition.

Seal Harbor is the home port of the *Sunbeam,* the Maine Seacoast Mission boat that serves the inhabitants of Maine's most isolated island communities. (See the article about the mission under Bar Harbor, below.)

Great Cranberry Island, Me. (13318   306). Spurling Cove on the north side is a good anchorage in southerly weather. For those passing through, it saves time. The island is not particularly interesting, though the view is superb.

The Pool, entered from the northeast side, is an excellent anchorage for shoal-draft boats. With a draft of more than 3 feet, it is necessary to leave and enter with half tide or more. When entering, follow the southeast side of the channel and, while rounding the little point, keep only a few yards off the beach. Anchor where the fishing boats are moored; there is about 6 feet at mean low water and a soft mud bottom.

Great Cranberry Island has claim to fame as the birthplace on February 22, 1822, of John Gilley, Maine farmer and fisherman, immortalized in "John Gilley" by Charles W. Eliot, available in his *The Durable Satisfactions of Life,* Thomas Y. Crowell & Co., New York, 1910. Everyone sailing these waters should read this short but moving account of the life and death by drowning of a native and lifelong resident of the islands of Mt. Desert.

Islesford, Little Cranberry Island, Me. (13318   306). This is a great place from which to jump off for down east. Stock up in Manset or Southwest Harbor and sail over to Islesford. Anchor off the wharves and row ashore for a visit to the Sawtelle Museum. This has a number of old charts and many relics of the French days. A walk across the island to the abandoned Coast Guard station, marked Tower on the chart, is a refreshing change from the carefully cultivated paths around Northeast Harbor. You are again on a Maine island, with granite ledge, huckleberry, and sweet fern giving way to a stony beach, a view of Bakers Island, and the sea breaking heavily on the offshore ledges.

Get back aboard in time to enjoy the sunset behind the mountains. This is the best place from which to see it.

Frenchman Bay, Me. (13318   306). This large bay is wide open to the sea at its mouth, but the upper part is well protected by the Porcupines, Ironbound Island, and the northern part of Mt. Desert Island. There are several excellent harbors around its edges, and with the mountains of Mt. Desert in changing perspective, it is a dramatic place in which to sail.

A skipper bound east from Mt. Desert does well to start on the last half of the ebb tide, thus being set to windward as he crosses the bay. Off Schoodic the flood should begin to make, giving him a fine lift to Petit Manan, past that desolate and distant shore east of Prospect Harbor. On a good day, one can ride the flood all the way to Trafton Island, Cape Split, the Cow Yard, or Roque Island.

The vessel bound up the bay along the Mt. Desert shore can expect gentle winds off Otter Cliff, but beyond Great Head and Schooner Head the afternoon southwester sometimes builds into very sharp puffs and lasts well into the evening in the upper bay.

The sail up the eastern side of the bay between Turtle Island and Grindstone Neck, by the cliffs of Ironbound Island and into Stave Island Harbor is easy and pleasant. One can continue around Mt. Desert Island almost to the narrows in protected waters with dramatic views and a selection of nearby shelters.

Bar Harbor, Me. (13318   306). One may enter this famous harbor from the south either by rounding Bald Porcupine or by creeping up close along the Mt. Desert shore and passing between it and the breakwater. There is a beacon on the westerly end of the breakwater, which should be left to starboard on entering. From the east, one simply keeps his bowsprit out of the bushes and runs in. There are no submerged dangers. From the north, leave the bell off Sheep Porcupine to starboard. There is an entrance between Sheep Porcupine and a ledge halfway between it and Bar Island. It is a bit shallower than the others, but practical. Large vessels sometimes anchor north of Bar Island.

The water in Bar Harbor is deep and the holding ground poor.

Therefore, try for a town mooring west of the municipal pier. You can go alongside the pier, where there is 6 feet at low water, and hail the Harbor Master in the information center nearby or simply pick up a mooring and see him when you row ashore. He is a most accommodating gentleman, seeking information only for the visitor's convenience.

At the wharf west of the municipal pier, gas, Diesel fuel, water, and ice are available. There is 6 feet of water at low tide here.

Ashore there are stores of all kinds. Groceries, hardware, and marine supplies are within a few steps of the shore. There are a movie theater, an assortment of restaurants, a liquor store, and numerous motels. The information center on the wharf is staffed by pleasant, hard-working ladies of incredible patience. Bus tours, taxis, excursion boats, and fishing trips are purveyed and promoted up and down the shore. A bus tour will take you to "all points of interest" around the island.

However, the mystique of Bar Harbor is clouded over. What looks like an old mansion on the shore is a motel with an electric sign. Others on back streets are rooming houses, and others were burned in the great fire of 1947. The streets are lined with campers and stationwagons. The visitors are a strangely mixed lot of a variety of physiques and attires, most of them pale and dyspeptic, after a week of driving, and mildly disappointed. It seems a long way from the days of steam yachts, tall schooners, naptha launches, and receptions beneath crystal chandeliers.

There are compensations, however. The view of the mountains is inspiring, and one of the nearest, Dorr Mountain, is within walking distance. The back streets have a delightful atmosphere. There are bus and plane connections for Boston and New York. Furthermore, the easy motion in the harbor keeps many yachts away, so the harbor and marine facilities are uncrowded. The entire upper bay, a lovely and unfrequented cruising ground, is under your lee; and, in the usual southwester, one or two tacks will carry you by Schoodic whistle and on your way east.

North of the harbor is the conspicuous landing of the ferry *Bluenose*, which makes daily trips to Yarmouth, Nova Scotia, leaving about 8 A.M. and returning around 9:30 P.M. Her route runs by Egg Rock and then about southeast by east for Yarmouth. She moves at an uncompromising speed.

The Roscoe B. Jackson Memorial Laboratory, located about a mile south of Bar Harbor on the Seal Harbor Road, is the largest center of mammalian genetics research in the world. Its scientists carry on full-time basic research in genetics and diseases in which heredity is a factor, such as cancer, mental illness, muscular dystrophy, neuromuscular defects, and radiation-induced sickness. The laboratory maintains a colony of 500,000 experimental mice of some 60 different inbred strains. About 2,000,000 animals are produced each year, a third used by Jackson Lab scientists, the rest shipped to researchers all over the world. If you're in any of the island harbors, call the laboratory and inquire about their programs for visitors.

During the early part of the century, Bar Harbor was a glittering social center. Enormous Victorian cottages on huge estates overlooked Frenchman Bay. Steam yachts and even an occasional square-rigged yacht anchored in the harbor. Social distinctions were very significant.

But with changing times this grandeur faded; and the 1947 fire, which destroyed most of the mansions and much of the town, ended the period dramatically.

Bar Harbor is now quite a different place. Six to seven thousand tourists spend the night in Bar Harbor and nearby campsites almost every night during the summer. They swarm on the shores, stand about on the wharf, and jostle on the streets and in the restaurants. The atmosphere at Bar Harbor today is much more like that of tourist centers to the westward than it is like a Maine town or an old-time "resort."

The National Park facilities attract many campers and hikers. The Park Service makes a great effort to keep the camp grounds neat and clean and to provide programs for interested visitors. Lectures on history and on the birds, animals, and plants of the region are given frequently.

"God's Tugboat," a unique vessel, which may be seen in almost any harbor of the Maine coast, is the Diesel motorship *Sunbeam,* owned and operated by The Maine Sea Coast Missionary Society of Bar Harbor. The *Sunbeam* is easily distinguishable because of the white cross on either side of her bow, denoting the practical Christian service in which she is engaged.

The *Sunbeam* is 65 feet long, powered by a 225 h.p. Diesel engine, and draws 7 feet. The vessel is built of steel, and the bow section is reinforced with extra-heavy steel plate and frames for ice-breaking purposes.

The *Sunbeam* was built in Warren, Rhode Island, in 1964, and is the sixth in the succession of vessels that have served the mission since it was founded in 1905. The mission's work is interdenominational, with the objective of providing Christian leadership and pastoral care along the coast and on the islands of the Maine coast, and to engage in all efforts that are calculated to contribute to the moral and spiritual welfare of the inhabitants. The *Sunbeam* is used as transportation for mission workers, and as a lifeline for isolated families and communities, especially in frigid winter weather. This splendidly equipped small ship symbolizes in its ready and able service the total program of the mission, which comprises Christian work in uncounted practical ways—preaching, teaching, aid to the sick and unfortunate, encouragement of young people, visitation and ministry to the lonely, and much more. The mission has an embrace large enough to take in all members of its widespread parish, regardless of their estate, whether clean and scrubbed or spattered with mud from the flats, yet intimate enough to call each one by name. At present, mission workers are stationed either full- or part-time in the following places: Lubec, Jonesport, South Addison, Cherryfield, Milbridge, West Gouldsboro, Swans Island, Frenchboro, Matinicus, Monhegan, Loudville, and Bar Harbor. In addition, services are held either regularly or on a seasonal or itinerant basis in the following: Mason Bay, Cape Split, Wyman, and Islesford. Visitors are always welcome at the mission stations and churches as well as on board the *Sunbeam* and at the headquarters, 24 Ledgelawn Avenue, Bar Harbor, where, since 1970, items relating to the history of the mission have been on display in a small museum.

The mission's annual reports and bulletins constitute an offshore saga full of salty incident and color. Any yachtsman interested in keeping in touch with the Maine coast throughout the year would do well to subscribe to the mission and receive its unique publications.

These, plus the newsy monthly *National Fisherman,* published at Camden and more fully described under that harbor, serve to brighten the long months of those who, like the late Dr. Francis Greenwood Peabody of Harvard, "stay ashore winters."

Sullivan, Me. (13318   306). The Sullivan anchorage is exposed to the south. There is a strong tide in the river, and there is a narrow and rocky place that forms rapids. It is not recommended for strangers.

Sullivan is a small village on the north side of the harbor, 3½ miles above the entrance. There is a privately owned wharf that bares at extreme low tides.

It was on the western side of Hancock Point that a German submarine landed three spies on a late autumn morning in World War II. As they walked up the road, the sheriff's son noticed them, lightly clad in city clothes. He became suspicious, followed their tracks, and notified the F.B.I. They were located in Bangor and followed until they revealed their "contacts" and then were arrested.

On the eastern side of Hancock Point is a dock with about 6 feet at low water and a guest mooring. It is a pleasant place to spend a night in quiet weather.

Between Hancock Point and Sullivan, the Taunton-Sullivan river flows into Frenchmans Bay and near its outlet, on the side toward Hancock Point, is the former site of Mt. Desert Ferry, the busy terminus of the Maine Central Railroad. Here passengers and freight were transferred to three ferry steamers for points inside the bay and to Bar Harbor and other harbors along the ocean side of Mt. Desert Island. The amount of traffic can be visualized if one remembers that at that time there was only a clay-and-dirt road from the mainland, over a bridge, to the island, and almost everything that went onto and from the island went by boat, either from Mt. Desert Ferry or from Rockland. Mr. Dean K. Worcester describes the scene in the early days of this century as follows, in the *National Fisherman:*

> Mount Desert Ferry, of which no trace remains, was a place on the mainland where the railroad track came down alongside deep water, so that the Bar Harbor Express, with its dozen or more sleeping cars, could lie at one side of the dock, while Norumbega lay at the other, rising and falling in the 10′ tide.
>
> The train used to arrive about 7 AM and when the passengers and their baggage had been put aboard, Norumbega would shove off for Bar Harbor, nearly an hour's journey. There was a restaurant in the forward deckhouse, where you could have breakfast and at the same time see where you were going. The course lay nearly due south, and since Mount Desert Island's abrupt mountain ranges and valleys, carved by glaciers, also run more or less north and south, their endwise profile as seen from the steamer was particularly dramatic. After having left New York on a hot summer evening, it was a pleasure to watch the island approaching in the clear cool morning light, gently suffused with eggs and bacon and coffee.
>
> At least that's how I remember it, 50-odd years later.

Sorrento, Me. (13318   306). With a magnificent view of Mt. Cadillac across Frenchman Bay, Sorrento is one of the most beautiful harbors on the coast. It offers good shelter, as one can duck behind Dram or Preble Island, depending on the direction of the wind.

In entering Sorrento from the south, favor the westerly side of the entrance between those two islands. The *Coast Pilot* reports reefs extending 100 yards from Preble Island and 50 yards from Dram Island. The entrance from the westward is narrowed by a reef, partly showing at high water, which extends 175 yards from the north side.

There are two visitors' moorings in Sorrento. The inner one is maintained by the Sorrento Yacht Club, founded in 1925. The second carries the legend:

                    In Memory of
                    Robert M. Lewis
                    1886–1957
                    He Cruised

Captain Lewis was a New Haven doctor who served with the Grenfell Mission in Labrador and cruised the New England coast extensively.

There is a summer resort, but no hotel or eating place within 5 or 6 miles. The Sorrento Yacht Club uses the town wharf with a float where there is 6 feet at low water. Stop there for local information. Water is obtainable at the float. Gasoline can be had in cans from a garage ⅛ mile away, if you have your own cans. Ice is not obtainable. There is a public golf course a mile away. Limited supplies may be obtained 3 miles away at the corner of Route 1. Sorrento is a yachting center for this part of the bay—a quiet, attractive place to visit.

There is a good anchorage in Eastern Point Harbor to the east.

Stave Island, Me. (13318   306). A good but large harbor. In southerly weather, anchor close under the high slopes of Jordan Island. Foss Cove, back of the spar buoy, is small, shoal, and unattractive.

Winter Harbor, Me. (13318   306). Easy of access, deep, and clearly marked, Winter Harbor is an excellent place to spend the night for yachtsmen bound east or west. Bound east, it cuts the run from Mt. Desert to Mistake Island enough to make it an easy day's run even in a modest breeze. Bound west, it postpones until next day what can be a long beat across Frenchman Bay in the chill of a late afternoon.

Entrance from the south is easy with the obvious abandoned lighthouse on Mark Island and the lighted bell off it.

Entrance from up Frenchman Bay is much easier than it looks, but the buoyage is confusing. Leave can 5 to starboard and follow the bold picturesque shore of Grindstone Neck. Leave can 3 and the beacon next to it to starboard, too. It seems an unlikely scheme and the can appears to be right on the shore, but, in fact, there is plenty of room. Then leave can 1 to port and nun 2 to starboard. There are three anchorages in Winter Harbor.

Sand Cove. This is a deep cove on the western side of the harbor under Grindstone Neck. Near the head of the cove on the west side is the Winter Harbor Yacht Club, which maintains a float and guest moorings. A steward is in attendance and glad to be of help insofar as his duties permit. You may telephone a grocery order to Winter Harbor

Food Service for delivery at the float. A tempered salt-water pool and shower can be used by cruising people. See the steward about lunches and dinners. Water and ice are available at the float.

From the south end of the porch a path leads up the hill to the site of the old Grindstone Inn, a symbol of post-Victorian elegance that burned in 1956. The view across to the Mt. Desert hills remains, however, and is worth the walk. There are a number of cottages along the road on the ridge. With their carefully tended lawns and shrubbery, wide porches, and graveled drives, they maintain a dignity and hint at an attitude toward vacations of which but a memory remains.

The Fisherman's Inn and Chase's Restaurant are in the town of Winter Harbor, a pleasant walk from the yacht club, and are reported to serve attractive meals. Chase's is open year round.

Inner Winter Harbor. This narrow cove is much better protected than Sand Cove, and although it is crowded with fishermen and local yachts, you may find a vacant mooring. Hail a fisherman and inquire. The cove has been dredged to a depth of 10 feet as far as the Co-op wharf, where gas and Diesel fuel are available.

Land at the heavy float on the east side. It is a pleasant walk through the eastern Maine countryside to Winter Harbor. There is a telephone on the corner of the main street. Turn right for the store, post office, laundry, and restaurants. The atmosphere of the road, fields, town, and harbor provides a refreshing change from the harbors of Mt. Desert.

The cove may be noisy in the early morning with departing fishermen, but you will want to get along anyway.

It was here that I first heard of fishing for herring with piano wire. One man rows a dory or pea-pod quietly up a cove. Another drags over the side a length of piano wire too short to reach bottom. There is a weight on the end of the wire. If herring are in the cove, they will brush against the thin wire and their number can be estimated by the frequency of the jiggles on the wire. If there are enough, the cove is stopped off and seined.

Henry Cove. This is a shallow cove east of Inner Winter Harbor, rather open to the south but affording good anchorage in summer weather. On the eastern shore is the Winter Harbor Marine Trading Corporation run by Cameron Bradley. He has a small marina and several guest moorings. Gas, ice, and water can be purchased at the float and there are showers for visitors. He can effect ordinary repairs. It is only a short walk to Winter Harbor.

The Grindstone Neck development was laid out about 1892 by the late John Moore, a native of nearby Steuben, who did business in New York and owned the neck and the Schoodic Peninsula. Before his death he presented the latter to the federal government as part of Acadia National Park.

The view of Mt. Desert and the islands of Frenchman Bay on a clear morning from the Winter Harbor entrance, with the sun shining on the cliffs of Cadillac Mountain, is worth going a long way to see.

The easternmost outpost of the Mt. Desert Region, Winter Harbor is one of the most attractive points in this picturesque section of Maine. Bound east, it is the last summer resort settlement until one reaches St. Andrews, N.B.

CHAPTER XII

Schoodic Point to West Quoddy Head

General Conditions. To be headed east by Schoodic whistle before a summer sou'wester with Mt. Desert fading astern and the lonely spike of Petit Manan Light just visible on the port bow is about as close to perfection as a man can expect to come on this imperfect earth.

Astern lie supermarkets, yacht clubs, water skiers, high-charged power cruisers, the pageantry associated with racing and day sailing. Ahead lie cold waters, racing tides, the probability of thick fogs and delightful scale-ups. The islands and most of the mainland shores are uninhabited except for small communities of lobstermen. The long, low, wooded promontories keep one well offshore in rounding them, but between, once east of Petit Manan, are islands, coves, and quiet creeks. You won't go swimming much. The water is fiercely cold. But the fishing is good and there are still clams in some places.

For the experienced navigator with a touch of the explorer, this country is the Promised Land, and for the "cricker" it is a happy hunting ground. The gregarious, the inexperienced navigators, and those who like to dress up and go ashore for dinner at the yacht club every evening will be happier west of Schoodic.

There are a few cautions to bear in mind. Perhaps the first is to be sure that you have proper charts. Charts 303, 304, 305, and 1201 are essential. An accurate compass in which the navigator can have implicit confidence is necessary. Log, lead, and look-out are never to be neglected.

Next, *be careful.* Careless errors may exact their price very quickly on this lonesome coast.

Thirdly, be prepared to stay a while. You may be fogbound or windbound, but be sure that you will have to wait out tides. A tide setting against the wind on this coast can raise a dangerous sea in short order. To beat against a Fundy tide in a light breeze is a losing battle.

Alternate Routes. On this coast there is usually a choice between an inside and an outside passage. From Schoodic one can head well outside Petit Manan, leaving the bell to port in ordinary weather. If a big sea is running, it may be wise to go outside the whistle off Southeast Rock. Or one may go inside, across Petit Manan Bar in smooth weather.

One going inside must be wary of a string of ledges just inside the course, Old Man and the Black Ledges, and of Moulton's Ledge and Stone Horse Ledge just east of them. Petit Manan Bar itself is a dangerous place in rough or thick weather. It is a shallow, boulder-strewn bar across which the tide runs heavily. The buoys, nearly a mile from either shore, are small and hard to find.

The coast between Schoodic Point and the bar looks desolate in the extreme. The harbors are some distance from the course and are either tricky to enter, like Corea, or exposed, like Prospect Harbor. The mouths of Dyer and Gouldsboro Bay are obstructed by ledges and islands. When a heavy sea is running, this is an awesome piece of coast. In thick weather, with a strong and unpredictable tide running, it can be a horror. For instance, the tides here appear to change direction during the ebb or flood. I have noticed the ebb tide still running west at the first of the flood and well around the southwest a few hours later.

Once across the bar, however, one can run up Pigeon Hill Bay or, by using the bold shores, work through the Douglas Islands to a secure and beautiful anchorage behind Trafton Island.

The run offshore, outside Petit Manan Light, is much easier. Although the horn on the light is very hard to hear to the westward, one could scarcely hit any of the dangers outside without hearing the bell or the whistle. Thence the run to Nash Island whistle is not difficult, as the tide affects the course but little. Cape Split is just beyond.

Or one can run outside to Seahorse Rock, the bleak dramatic cliff of Crumple Island, and the powerful horn on Mistake Island. There is good shelter in the Cow Yard or back of Knight Island. The outside route continues outside the Libby Islands, Cross Island, and up Grand Manan Channel to Quoddy Head. Cutler is the best shelter and indeed nearly the only one on this route, and Cutler is easy to make with the help of the whistle outside.

If one has a short enough mast, one may run up Moosabec Reach by Jonesport. The chart claims 39 feet clearance under the bridge at high water. From Jonesport through Roque Island Thorofare, Roque Island Harbor, Foster Channel, Machias Bay, and Cross Island Narrows is a quiet and delightful sail among some of the wildest and most attractive scenery on the coast, spoiled only by four unsightly radar towers behind Bucks Harbor and the huge low-frequency radio towers on Thornton Point back of Cross Island. After passing through Cross Island Narrows, one enters the Bay of Fundy dramatically as one passes Old Man and

Cape Wash. Cutler is the nearest and best port at which to stop and draw breath before making the crossing to Grand Manan or the run up Lubec Narrows.

Fish Weirs. Among the islands down east where the tide runs hard and the waters are well protected, herring are trapped by means of weirs (pronounced "wares"). A weir consists essentially of a circular fence of brush supported by poles four to six inches thick driven into the mud. The fence has an opening on the side facing the ebb tide. From this opening one or two or sometimes three leaders or wings run off at a broad angle to each other. Each wing extends a few yards inside the weir.

The herring run up the bay with the tide and on the ebb "settle back" between the wings and work into the trap. At low water a day or so later, when they have "worked the feed out of them," the fish are seined; and if the haul is good, a carrier is called. This big vessel, perhaps 70 feet long, is equipped with a powerful pump. This sucks the fish out of the seine, scales them, and dumps them into the hold. They are lightly salted and rushed to the factory to be canned as sardines. The scales are sold for "pearl essence," for shirt buttons, for making fire-extinguisher foam, and—it is said—for clearing beer.

The weir is usually built in about 7 feet of water. One wing runs into the shore, where room enough is left for a dory to squeeze by. The outer end is run into deep water. It is usually safe to go close to the outer wing of a weir. The law requires a white light on the outer end of the outer wing, but this law frequently is not observed.

In the winter, ice freezes around the stakes and sometimes breaks them off. This leaves a dangerous stub submerged at high water. If a weir has been abandoned for some time, such stakes can be a dangerous menace. It is well to mark all weirs on your chart as you see them. It is now the practice to locate schools of herring from the air and talk the seiner to them. Consequently weirs are being abandoned and their broken and unmarked stakes remain.

Never miss a chance to watch a carrier pump out a seine. It is exciting to see the men "drying in" the net into dories, forcing the fish into a tight pocket. The pump throws an acre of suds, the fish flip madly on deck, everyone runs around in rubber boots, up to his knees in fish. The radio will probably be squawking over it all at full power, and everyone is enjoying the party and getting richer by the minute. The writer saw two men make $15,000 in half a day out of one weir. All kinds of fish are likely to shoot out of the pump, including mackerel and flounder. And fresh herring make a first-class supper.

After the carrier leaves and the excitement subsides, you may hear some good yarns and—if the ladies are not in evidence—some salty ·singing.

Schoodic Harbor, Me. (13324   305). Known locally as One Squeak, this is not a desirable anchorage. A considerable roll makes in.

Bunker Harbor, Me. (13324   305). Closer than Winter Harbor or Prospect Harbor to the straight course down east, Bunker Harbor is a good shelter and a very pleasant place. Entrance, however, especially for the skipper who is making it for the first time, can be tense.

From Schoodic whistle follow the bold shore of Schoodic Island. The part of the island shown green on chart 305 almost always breaks. Thence make the short run to the lighted bell off Brown Cow. Then follow the shore down to Bunker Harbor and run up the middle. Between the point and the outlying ledge is a shoal with about 7 feet at low water. You may see kelp. Of course, if a heavy sea is running, the entrance is impossible.

If you are coming in from the east, you will see a high pyramidal rock just south of the entrance. This is on the base of the southern point of the harbor and is indicated as a tiny circle on charge 305. The half-tide rock east of it and the ledge colored green on the chart are submerged about half tide. However, they usually break. Halfway between them and the pyramidal rock is about right. If it is high water and you can't see the ledge, give the pyramidal rock a good 50 yards berth. Move slowly and watch for bottom.

Entrance from the north is only for the luckiest of strangers.

On a quiet night, anchorage in the outer harbor is entirely satisfactory, although a slight roll makes in. If conditions are threatening, go into the inner harbor. Stay close to the anchored boats, as the west side of the harbor has a number of ledges. The cove was dredged to 10 feet a few years ago. Inquire for a mooring or a chance to lie alongside a fisherman if you can't find swinging room.

There are two gas wharves with 2 feet at the first and 8 to 10 feet at the second.

It is a pleasant walk of about a mile up the road to Chipman's Grocery and gas station at Birch Harbor, if you can stand the cars whizzing by on the way to or from the park at Schoodic Point.

Birch Harbor, Me. (13324   305). Avoid this harbor. It is open to the south and east and most of it dries out at low water.

Prospect Harbor, Me. (13324 305). This is an easy harbor to make under any reasonable conditons. From Schoodic whistle follow the shore of Schoodic Island. The area shown in green on chart 305 is almost always out of water and breaks except on the calmest days. Run for bell 2 off the Old Woman and then for the gong in the entrance to the harbor. Anchor off the wharves unless the weather looks threatening. Then get in behind the Stinson sardine factory as far as your draft permits. Beware of a 4-foot rock in here, a possible danger if the wind comes to the north. The factory, which used to smell pretty bad, is less offensive than it was and the effluent from it is no longer dumped into the harbor.

Ashore you will find a clean and pleasant eastern Maine town. Stinson's grocery store is said to be closed on weekends.

Be sure your riding light burns brightly and your radar reflector hangs in the rigging, for sardiners often come in at night with fish for the factory.

Corea, Me. (13324 305). This is better sheltered than Prospect Harbor, closer to Petit Manan, and about the same distance as Prospect Harbor from Schoodic whistle. From the west, work your way from bell 2 around Old Woman and find the bell off Cranberry Point. Thence run for Western Island, round the western end of it, and follow its northern shore until well up to its eastern end. Then, and not until then, head for a gray cottage among the trees on a conspicuous yellow ledge on Youngs Point. Favor the easterly side of the entrance and look for the big winter mooring reportedly usually vacant. If it is occupied, slide up to the Co-op float with 9 feet on the west side and inquire. There is only about 6 feet of water in the harbor and yachts have grounded in the mud at low water.

Gasoline and Diesel fuel are available at the Co-op wharf.

It is a very pleasant walk from the Co-op wharf around the head of the harbor to the Harbor Grocery, run by Dorothy Kempski and Jean Symonds. The shop is well supplied with home-baked pies by Mrs. Gerish of Winter Harbor. Correspondents recommend apple and blueberry. Lobster, either live or cooked, is a specialty.

Ice is available, it is reported, next to the grocery and at the Co-op wharf.

A correspondent writes: "Corea seems very crowded, although a mooring was available. A lobsterman, whose boat was the first fiberglass model in Corea, took one of our crew out for six hours lobstering; our man returned, somewhat green, deafened, but happy he had gone."

Gouldsboro Bay, Me. (13324   305). This is a large, protected body of water, which can be entered either through the Western Passage or through Eastern Way. It is far from the direct route but a pleasant place to explore.

Dyer Bay, Me.   (13324   305). Of this bay, a correspondent writes, "I went in there prepared to spend the night and ended up in Prospect. Bay full of weirs and pots. Over Cove a rolly place. I sought an anchorage north and east of Sheep Island—much tide—not good holding—full of pots—anchor came up with a lot of old pot line on it—I departed."

Note on Petit Manan, Me. (13324   305). Petit Manan Point makes out in a long bar to Petit Manan Island and continues underwater, as soundings indicate, for a long way offshore. This place can be very dangerous. Fishermen treat it with respect.

The difficulties are produced by three factors. The tide offshore runs east on the flood and west on the ebb and does so with considerably more vigor than it does farther west. Also, however, the tide runs in and out of Pigeon Hill, Pleasant, and Narraguagus bays to the east, and of Dyer and Gouldsboro bays to the west of Petit Manan. Consequently three different tidal currents meet off the light. This confuses the sea and sets one off one's course unpredictably.

The second difficulty is the exposed position of Petit Manan. It is a long way from a secure harbor and open to the full sweep of the Atlantic. In addition, the bottom is very uneven. The chart shows pinnacles rising 150 feet off an apparently smooth bottom. The consequence is that the sea is always rough and can be confused and dangerous. It is particularly dangerous when the ebb tide meets a brisk southerly wind. A cruiser drawing little water and sporting a hurricane deck and flying bridge could get in serious trouble here very quickly. The motion would find weak spots, too, in a sailing yacht's rigging. The safest course is to pass outside the bell under any conditions and to stay outside the whistle if the sea is heavy.

The third problem is fog. Petit Manan holds the record for maximum number of hours of fog-signal operation for any one year between 1950 and 1963—over 2000 hours. When the fog drops over the rough and tide-scoured waters off Petit Manan, the difficulties are vastly increased. No fog signal is very effective to windward. Anyone running east on a foggy afternoon is very unlikely to hear the Petit Manan horn far to windward. As one approaches, it is the part of discretion to shut off the engine—not just put it in neutral—and drift for a few minutes until the boat loses way. Really listen intently for a solid minute at the very least.

In addition to aberrations of the fog signal, remember that the island is low and that one cannot approach it closely from any direction. One would not even see the loom of the shore before striking.

Plan, then, to pass well outside the light and count on hearing the fog signal, the bell buoy, or the whistle *after* passing the island. Once by the light, it is a long haul to the Nash Island whistle, but the tide will set you off your course little, if any, and the Nash Island whistle seems to be one of the best on the coast. Whether it is the particular buoy or has to do with conditions around Nash Island, we don't know, but you can hear it all over the bay. From Nash Island whistle, run for Pot Rock, The Ladle, and Cape Split. The rock east of The Ladle *almost* always breaks.

Petit Manan Bar has been discussed above under Alternate Routes. On no condition should one try this in the fog. The chances of finding those little buoys are dim indeed.

The following is an account of Petit Manan Bar by a correspondent who was there in 1977 in a power boat:

I have always known about the Petit Manan Bar problem, but on a strong southwest day, perhaps a 25-knot breeze and with a strong ebb against the breeze, I went across it, to my strong regret. I examined it closely first from the east side, looked at the rows of whitecaps in the standing waves just west of the bar, and thought they could be negotiated as they appeared about one foot high with whitecaps. We were tired (always a bad time to make decisions) and did not want to go all the way around the lighthouse. When we crossed the bar, we were all right until we had passed the shallowest spot. Then we met the standing waves. Their height was deceptive and the 1-foot whitecaps were concealing 4-foot troughs between them. The whitecaps were perhaps 30 feet apart measured against our 29-foot boat. While she never buried her bow, being somewhat bluff, she pitched to the extent that the coiled anchor line strapped down on the foredeck was standing straight up in the air and the rowboat on the stern was pitched off its chocks into the cockpit, being tied down only on the inboard side. A thoroughly uncomfortable and undesirable experience. I guess my point is that the waves are so close together as to be deceptive and look smaller than they really are.

Because it is occasionally pleasant to have the rocks and shoals of the coast peopled by figures of the past, the authors venture to repeat here a story told by the late W. Rodman Peabody of Boston, son of Dr. Francis Greenwood Peabody of Harvard University, regarding Petit Manan Bar. Having to do with the nautical adventures of the late President Eliot of Harvard, this story may be put down as a companion piece to another yarn related by Mr. Peabody and included under Northeast Harbor:

I shall always remember another fresh southwest afternoon when, although he was of advanced age, the President had gone cruising with us as far east as Cutler. We were standing across Tit Manan Bar heading for the opening which was marked only by a fisherman's buoy. It was blowing freshly and as we approached the Bar there was a heavy rip. My father, whose boat was one which was characterized by a friend as having "rather long spars for a parson," stood in the companionway watching his whipping topmast with grave concern. Forty years of deference, however, left him tongue-tied. From my position by the mainsheet I recognized that he was praying for the best but without much hope. Obviously the topsail ought to have come in. Not a word came from the President, but I saw him glance at my father, take in the situation and give one long and careful look at the whipping spar and then I thought I saw a slight wink from an almost imperturbable face.

We came through whole and the President remarked casually: "If you don't mind taking the helm now, Frank, I think I will take my afternoon nap." No reference to the sea, the wind or the spars was ever made by either of them, but the younger generation clinging to the weather rail had a thoroughly enjoyable fifteen minutes.

Narraguagus Bay and Pleasant Bay, Me.   (13324   305). The following account of a two-day sail through this region was written by Mr. Arthur F. Chase, Jr. after an exploration in 1973.

Last July 24 *Wild Hunter* crossed Tit Manan Bar in pleasant weather and beat up between the Douglas Islands to Trafton Island where we spent the night in the cove on the north side. The next day, in variable winds, we took a brief look at Narraguagus Bay, passed south of Foster Island and reached up the Harrington River against the ebb past Five Islands. The wind freshened a bit and veered giving us a beat coming down river. At low water there are lots of clam flats and low woodlands with nothing to spoil the low countryside. The water is very muddy and the mud line in the water shifts with the current as do the lobster pots which caused us to think we were further off the rock north of Ripley Island than a couple of cuts would have told us. As it was, hugging the 13-foot line on the depth finder, we scraped our keel as we went by.

We went around Ripley Neck and up the Pleasant River leaving

Bunker Ledge to port and Birch and Mink Islands to starboard. We sailed all the way up the river to anchor across from the town of Addison. It was a lovely sail through very pleasant country with little civilization and practically no waterborne activity. The channel is marked fairly well and a little care and common sense is all that is needed to stay out of trouble. We were told by a clam digger in a skiff, however, to hug the starboard (southern) shore to avoid an unmarked submerged tank with only three feet of water over it, which is just below the town but above the point where the river turns east. There was a lot of water coming down, about two knots in many places, and both at full ebb and full flood it sets you over towards the southern bank across from the town. We used a bow and a stern anchor and recommend getting them well out onto the northern side of the channel to avoid being set too far to the south when the water level drops.

Addison is a pleasant friendly town with a good store and telephone service, seemingly bypassed by the highways as well as marine traffic.

In the morning we started down on the ebb just after the tide turned and found things a bit demanding when the fog shut in. We anchored for breakfast off #6 and found that the holding ground there was rather slippery for the current. After breakfast, the fog lifted and we went on down under sail in light airs around Gibbs Island and up the cove behind it as far as we dared on a falling tide with our 6-foot draft. The shape of the 10-foot shoal suggests how this spot got its name. It is a dramatic cove above water and would make an attractive anchorage with the possibility of exploration ashore, the only building we saw being a neat but simple camp on the little inlet south of Tumbledown Dick.

We stood on down river and stuck our nose into Ports Harbor, which is too shallow for us but a beautiful spot for someone with shoal draft. We then sailed down the eastern shore but passed to port of Norton Island and went across to beat through Flint Island Narrows in freshening winds. We then went around to the west of Shipstern Island to proceed on our way to the Cow Yard.

Our conclusion is that Pleasant Bay and the Pleasant River as far as Addison are distinctly worth a visit. If I were grading charm, I would give Harrington River a C+ and Pleasant River A+ keeping in mind that all Eastern Maine is very good when you can see it and pretty good in thick fog.

Another correspondent adds:

> We went up into Pleasant Bay this year, thinking we would spend the night between the Birch Islands or between the northern Birch Island and Raspberry. These places seemed more open and unprotected than we expected, so we went into Ports Harbor, which proved very attractive and snug . . .

Trafton Island, Me. (13324   305). This is one of the most attractive islands on the coast. The easiest approach is from the east. Round the northeast point and work up the west side of the point by the cliff to a big white rock. Anyone drawing under 6 feet can anchor here.

The island is wooded, but there are open glades in the woods, patches of birch, and thickets of alder. The woods are grown up enough so that walking is not difficult. The south end of the island is covered with huge boulders of white granite, which lie in confused masses, making caves and passages among them. There is a rocky beach in the southern cove. At high water on a warm day the swimming on the beach in the northern cove is good and there may still be some clams on the flats. There are two unobtrusive cottages owned by Mrs. James Ray behind the little island west of the anchorage. The anchorage is quiet and protected. It is supervised during the absence of Mrs. Ray by the owners: an osprey, a family of seals, and a supercilious shag. It was much used years ago by coasters waiting for a "good chance" down the bay.

Before landing to explore the island, stop at one of the cottages overlooking the western cove, make yourself known, and ask permission. The owners are quite properly sensitive about people who invade their property uninvited and leave it less attractive than they found it. Perhaps such advice is unnecessary, but inasmuch as many islands in eastern Maine are wild and uninhabited, it may be helpful to point out that this one is an exception.

Dyer Island, Me. (13324   305). There are two coves on the west side and one on the east that are picturesque and quiet anchorages for small boats on a calm night. None would be much good in a blow. Apparently Northeast Cove is the best. A correspondent reports 8 feet in the middle and 5 feet near the shores. The bottom is mud. A small ledge makes out from the south side about halfway in. The tide runs about ½ knot through this anchorage. Beware of mosquitoes.

There is a camp for underprivileged children on the island.

Flint Island, Me. (13324   305). One can anchor with safety in Flint Island Narrows. The tide runs vigorously. Flint Island itself is a delightful island, much like Trafton. Notice the cliff on the southwest corner of Shipstern Island. The rock looks strikingly like the stern of an eighteenth-century warship.

Cape Split, Me. (13324   305). This harbor is accessible from the sea and easy to make. If coming from the west in thick weather, make for the lighted whistle to the west of Nash Island. After passing the island to starboard, The Ladle offers an easily recognized landmark for the entrance to Cape Split, as the rock to the east almost always breaks. Regarding this rock, a local fisherman writes, "The sunken rock to the east of The Ladle does not always break. If the sea is calm and no roll and high tide, it is just a very dangerous ledge."

Another approach is first to pick up Pot Rock and leave The Ladle to starboard. If coming from the east, note that one cannot run directly from Tibbett Narrows for nun 2 off Wright Point. Bear off to the south and then north. Note that the rocks off the entrance bare at a third from high tide.

Favor the east side of the harbor to avoid an old weir that runs far out into the harbor from the long point on the west shore just south of the wharves. There is good anchorage off the wharves. A quieter berth is to be found in Otter Cove, which indents the east shore of the harbor before you come to the wharves.

Gasoline and simple provisions can be obtained at the well-stocked store of D.H. Look & Sons at the head of the wharf. There is a through bus connection at Columbia Falls. One can hire a car at Cape Split to meet this bus.

Local fishermen consider Cape Split "the best harbor between Northeast Harbor and Canada—better than Cutler, where there is said to be an undertow." Be careful if running in in thick weather, for Cape Split fogs are more numerous and denser than fogs almost anywhere else except in Machias Bay.

A correspondent reports having the fog come down on him from above in less than ten minutes after it touched the top of Jordans Delight. A visitor to Cape Split contributed the following note nearly fifty years ago. It is still pertinent:

There is a general store near the fishing dock on the east side, which has many fine groceries, also rigging and simple boatswain supplies. Letters to be mailed can be left with the storekeeper. There is a spring almost in front of the store.

The country up here is indescribably beautiful: very small fishing villages—excellent harbors; saw only one summer place—at Tibbett Narrows. The natives at Cape Split are very helpful people, who evinced quite an interest in our cruise (which may have been only because we were boys, in a small boat, in September). . . . Their houses are beautifully kept up, with delightful gardens. A walk over to Tibbett Narrows requires about 15 minutes each way and gives a view up Moosabec Reach to Jonesport. Cape Split has an atmosphere about it which I've never experienced before and which I like to think is common to all points to the east of it.

This correspondent recommends that boats drawing 5 or 6 feet anchor well up the harbor among the fishing boats. The harbor shoals up fast to the east of the channel. The tide runs in the channel and there is a slight roll. The holding ground is good, being sticky mud.

The late Mr. Delbert Look of Cape Split was a man of energy and vision. It was he who, back in the thirties, developed the method of transporting lobsters in crates. It had been the practice to dump lobsters into the hold of a smack, which was bulkheaded off and bored with holes to provide circulation. The motion of the vessel killed some lobsters and broke claws off others. However, if the lobsters were crated, there was insufficient circulation of water and they died from lack of oxygen. Mr. Look bought an old schooner, *Verna G.,* lined her hold with cement, and installed powerful pumps so that water could be circulated under pressure. Then he loaded her with crated lobsters and, with pumps running constantly, shipped lobsters to Boston with very low mortality. The method was soon imitated and prevailed until it became cheaper to ship by truck. The wreck of *Verna G.* is rotting on the beach at Cape Split.

During World War II, Delbert's son Oscar was reported missing after Bataan. The father believed firmly that nothing serious had happened to his son and refused to shave his beard in token of it until his son's safe return.

Oscar survives his father and today operates a tremendous lobster pound just above the wharf. The project involves hundreds of thousands of dollars and great risk. The idea is to hold lobsters over a period of low price until the price rises. The difficulty is that lobsters are delicate creatures. If it rains heavily so that the salinity of the water is affected, they will die. If they are fed too much, the food will rot and poison them. If fed too little, they will cannibalize each other. They do not eat with their claws but with very hard "teeth" in the mouth under the proboscis. These teeth can easily grind up another lobster's shell. Of course, if the price fails to rise, the whole scheme is a failure.

However, it is difficult indeed to make a living in Cape Split. Oscar is buying lobsters and taking this risk in order to do what he can to support the economy of this small town.

A correspondent who visited Cape Split in 1974 writes:

> I was there on a good minus tide. On the east side of the entrance are more abandoned weirs than I earlier knew about, so keep to the west side after you make the entrance.
>
> Oscar Look and his wife are in great shape. The store is somewhat bigger and better than it used to be.

Moosabec Reach, Me. (13326   304). Until 1959, Moosabec Reach was the common way for yachts to go east and west along the coast. With the construction of the Beals Island Bridge, with a clearance of 39 feet above high water, only the smaller yachts, sardiners, and old-fashioned gaff-rigged boats can use the reach. The bridge has speeded up the tide by ½ knot and formed a powerful back eddy on the north side west of the bridge during the ebb tide. Do your calculating on the bridge in advance. If the tide is running with you, it is difficult to change your mind at the last minute. The tide in the reach is said to turn about 1½ hours before high and low water.

The approach to Jonesport from the west is easy. Tibbett (usually called "Tabbott") Narrows is buoyed. The tide runs right along the channel, except between Shabbit Island Ledge and Fessenden Ledge. Here there seems to be a cross tide. Allow for it.

Jonesport, Me.   (13326   304). This formerly prosperous fishing and boat-building town has lost a great deal of its character with the departure of the herring that supplied the sardine factories and with the declining market for wooden boats. Clams and lobsters are now the principal resources.

West of the bridge is a Coast Guard station, whose crew are more than traditionally helpful. There is a water hose on their wharf, but it is a hard place for a yacht to get close to. The usual yacht anchorage is in Sawyer Cove at the east end of the town.

From the west the approach is easy. Simply follow up the Reach, keeping well off the northern shore. From the east, the easiest approach is to make Mark Island. It is high, bold, and wooded and there is a bell northeast of it. From here, run up the line of nuns. The tide runs either with you or against you about parallel to your course so will set you off very little, but it runs hard and it pays to have it running your way. If you miss a nun and get into the shoal water to the north, you will probably find The Virgin before you find bottom. If you are set off to the south, you will find Gilchrist's Rock, The Nipple, or can 3. As you approach the light on Nova Rock, you will find the tide running with increasing force. Once by Nova Rock, conditions are much easier. Off the points there are shelving gravel beaches, so keep out in the middle of the channel until you are up to Sawyer Cove. In thick weather there is often a scale-up west of Nova Rocks as you get into the lee of Great Wass Island.

Sawyer Cove is shallow in its upper part. Anchor inside its mouth, just far enough in to get out of the tide. The long wharf with the *T* on the end was used by tankers, which brought gasoline and heating oil to be stored ashore and distributed throughout eastern Maine. However, it is no longer used. There is said to be a dredged channel to the state marina on the westerly side of the cove, but it was dredged only to 6 feet and may very well have silted up some. However, as the range of tide is of the order of 12 to 14 feet, one can approach the marina at ⅓ tide or better, regardless of silt.

An attendant is on duty at the marina from 9 A.M. to 9 P.M. There is a water hose on the float and in the building at the head of the wharf are showers, laundry machines, and a telephone. A launching ramp good at any tide is close to the north. This is not, however, a marina in the sense that Massachusetts yachtsmen use the term. Do not plan to lie alongside for an extended period.

Gasoline and Diesel oil are available at the wharf of OS and BS Look south of the marina. Approach this float with great caution. There is only about 3 feet of water alongside at low tide and a big ledge, which begins to bare out at half tide, extends far out into the harbor along the west shore of the cove. If you line up with the building and the end of the wharf and come straight in, very slowly, at half tide or better, you can make it.

It is a healthy walk of a little less than a mile to the post office, IGA store, Ginny's Restaurant, the hardware store, and the ice machine in the middle of Jonesport. The Sunoco station sells beer, but the market does not.

In the event that repairs are needed, you will find a number of men good with tools in Jonesport. Inquire at the marina. Fred Linfesty has a good small yard and railway on the cove just below the little bridge you cross as you walk up town from the marina. Hans Taubenberger has a machine shop and small railway. He is well spoken of.

An alternative to Sawyer Cove is the Lobster Co-op wharf just east of the bridge. It is a busy commercial place, but gas and Diesel oil are available here. You will have to climb a ladder, but it is a little nearer the store and the ice machine than Sawyer Cove is.

There is no bus to the main bus line at Columbia Falls, but one could hire a car. Consult the attendant at the marina.

Beals, Me. **(13326   304).** This town is on Beals Island, just west of the bridge. Gas and Diesel fuel are available at a lobster car. The hose for the Diesel oil just reaches the north side of the car, which is difficult to approach in a northerly wind. Several heavy iron hoops project from the west side of the car. They could damage a yacht's topsides seriously.

Anchor wherever you can get out of the worst of the tide. Note that on the ebb a back eddy builds behind the causeway to the bridge. Here are several boat shops building various kinds of small boats but specializing in "Jonesport" boats. These are very narrow, sharp boats with a high bow and steep sheer. They have much less flare than boats used farther west. A spray hood or house covers the forward half, and aft is a long, narrow cockpit. The stern is cut off square and the run is flat. The propeller is often well forward of the stern to keep it clear of pot warps and is driven by as powerful an automobile engine as the owner can find. One of these boats, "trying her out" wide open, flinging spray for yards to port and starboard and dragging a huge wake, is a dramatic sight.

Annually, about July 4, there is a great celebration at Jonesport at which the main event is a race to determine whose is the fastest lobster boat in Maine. Another feature is a two-man dory race.

In case of emergency, repairs can be made at one of the yards at Beals.

Eastern Bay, Me. (13326   304). This is fascinating country to the explorer. One of the most interesting things about it is the contrast between high and low water. The mean tidal difference is 11 to 12 feet. The most interesting way to approach this region from the west is outside, direct from Petit Manan.

When you leave the bell at Petit Manan, on a compass course for Seahorse Rock bell, you will see nothing at all ahead. Shortly after you pass Tibbett Rock you will pick up the great white cliff of Crumple Island. Nash Island Light and the stacks at Jonesport will show up inshore. As you approach Seahorse Rock, it will be breaking heavily here and on Seal Ledges. The abandoned Coast Guard station on Great Wass Island only emphasizes the bleak dramatic quality of this country.

Crumple Island and Freeman Rock are great fissured domes of granite with little or no vegetation, bold shores, and tremendous surf breaking on them. As you round Red Head, if the day is clear, you will pick out four great mushrooms on the hill behind Bucks Harbor. It is not

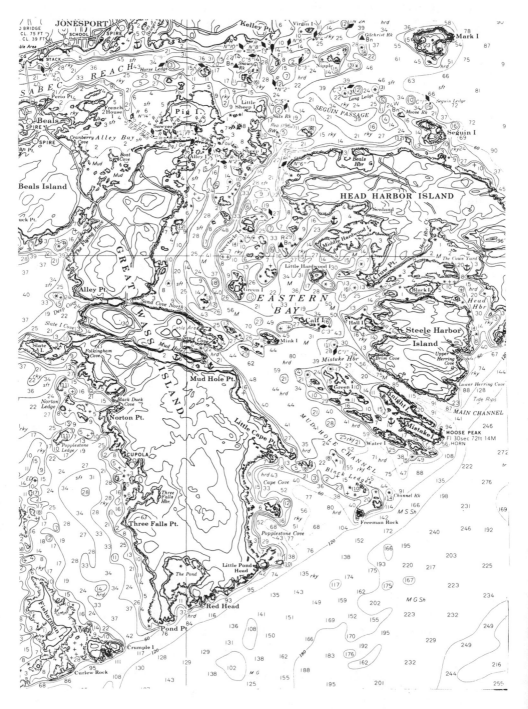

Anchorages between Mistake Island and Jonesport (refer to Chart 304).

an interplanetary landing site, but a radar station. Moose Peak Light is on the southern end of Mistake Island. From here one can continue to Head Harbor and the Cow Yard or run up Mudhole Channel.

However, if the visibility is poor, the trip is a lot less fun and harder on the nerves. If there is not a heavy sea running, from the bell off Petit Manan, lay a course to pass between Tibbett Rock and the nun south of it and on to clear Crumple Island. Allow for a tide running across your course for the first part of the run to the nuns. If you don't see either nun, you can tell when you pass between them by the way the water shoals up.

Continue on the course to clear Crumple Island. The tide will be on your starboard quarter on the flood and your port bow on the ebb. Very little if any allowance is necessary, because if you are set to the north, you will see pot buoys and hear Sea Horse Rock bell; and if you are set to the south, you will see nothing and hear nothing until you bring Moose Peak horn out by Red Head. Note that there is a shoal outside Sea Horse Rock, which you will pick up on the fathometer.

The cliffs are very bold on the end of Curlew Rock, Crumple Island, and Great Wass Island. There is always a big roll, so you will hear the surf and notice the backwash off the cliffs before you get too close.

Keep Moose Peak on your port bow and work eastward until it is abeam. The easiest thing to do is to run up the Main Channel Way, round the northerly end of Knight Island, and anchor in Mistake Island Harbor. A bold alternative is to try for Head Harbor and the Cow Yard, but running in on that shore before the wind and sea in a thick fog is not appealing to many, especially as the eastern shore of Steele Harbor Island is irregular and fringed with outlying rocks. If the day is not too far advanced, you can follow the sound of the surf on Head Harbor Island to Black Head. Do not get in too close if the fog is very thick, for while the cliffs are steep and the water deep close to the shore, there is a fringe of ledge at the foot of the cliff that makes out in dangerous irregular jags. From Black Head run for the gong on Little Breaking Ledge. The sea will be much smoother and the fog might scale up a bit. Thence, run for the bell off Mark Island and then for the entrance to Roque Island Thorofare. The tide will cause little trouble, for it is more or less parallel to your course.

In clear weather, an alternative is to round Freeman Rock and Channel Rock, pass northeast of Black Ledges, and run up Mudhole Channel. There is a snug anchorage behind Mudhole Point behind a weir. If the tide serves, go right up into The Mudhole (see specific directions). In clear weather, one can run northeast of Mink Island, west of Green Island and Spectacle Island, between Head Harbor Island and

Sheep Island, and out into Seguin Passage. Note that the tide ebbs to the east-southeast and floods to the west-northwest here. This passage, or the buoyed one to the east of Spectacle Island, is beautiful, not too difficult to navigate at half tide or less when the ledges show, and is much more likely to provide a breeze than is the trip around Moose Peak. Two things make it difficult: most of the islands are low and flat, and the fish weirs obstruct one's view and confuse the scenery. In general, bear in mind that the outside wing of the weir, usually with a board nailed to the outer post, is likely to be in deep water. Another helpful hint is that on the course west of Spectacle Island, once you are by the rocks north of Green Island, you can run for The Nipple. Of course the navigator would do well to watch the set of the tide carefully, but the range is a good one, and The Nipple makes an easily identified mark.

Westward-bound navigators sometimes prefer to beat south through the smooth waters rather than slop about in a big chop offshore with, perhaps, not enough wind. In thick weather, however, the Eastern Bay can be a "horror show" for the stranger. Keep outside the powerful horn on Moose Peak and run for the diaphone at Libby Islands. Bound west, follow the 20-fathom curve to Seahorse Rock and take off from there.

There are numerous shelters in this area, several of which are described below.

A correspondent who visited Eastern Bay in 1976 writes:

> In Eastern Bay (off Jonesport), I think there is a 6-foot spot about 50 yards north of the outer end of Middle Hardwood I.; I'll try to check this next year. Once this year we came through Eastern Bay from north to south with visibility about 50 yards, tide three-quarters and falling; and even though I had just been through in clear weather, "horror show" is the right description. Except for my being able to recognize individual islands, we would have been in trouble.

Head Harbor, Me.   (13326   304). This is a wretched anchorage, wide open to the south and with rocky bottom. For practical purposes it is just an anteroom to the Cow Yard. Entrance in clear weather presents no problem. Just keep in the middle. In thick weather, however, to come in before wind and sea with both shores foul may be a bit unnerving. Note in your favor, however, that the outlying ledges on the western shore are quite high and bold and that they usually are well out of water. Even near high tide, they usually break. They appear to be a long way from the shore behind them. No doubt the chart is correct, but the appearance is deceptive.

The Cow Yard, Me.   (13326   304). This is a convenient anchorage, as it is far to windward, close to the direct route along the coast, and is fairly well protected, although not exactly snug. Anchor behind the great black rock, which partly blocks the entrance, but move cautiously and stay pretty much in the middle, for it appears to have silted up some. The bottom is mud and good holding ground.

There is an inside route from the Cow Yard out by Crow Point into Eastern Bay, but it is a local knowledge project unless you care to do extensive exploration in the dinghy.

Mr. Caleb Foote published the following paragraphs in *The New England Yachtsman* in the 1930s. It is interesting to see how little this region has changed in half a century. A visit to the Cow Yard in 1976 corroborates almost everything.

Head Harbor and the Cow Yard beyond it form one of the nicest places to visit on the coast. There is no settlement save a simple summerhouse, built on the point that forms the entrance of the Cow Yard, and one fisherman's shack. To starboard, the meadows alternate with woods and outcroppings of rock on the hills of Head Harbor Island, while the smaller islands to port, too numerous to count, are forest-covered to the water's edge.

In entering, beware of an uncharted 2-foot spot, which lies about 60 yards west of Man Island. This rock is on a line from the south point of Man Island W ½ S to the little point in Upper Herring Cove on Steel Harbor Island (see chart 304). The rock off the Steel Harbor shore (almost) always breaks. The aforementioned summerhouse and white flagpole on the point above the 15-foot spot in the harbor are good landmarks.   .

In a sou'wester, Head Harbor is quite exposed, so it is best to go on into the Cow Yard, perfectly protected from any wind. The big black rock in the middle of the entrance always shows. Sail between this and the little island, where the chart shows 8 feet. A fishing boat is moored in 5 feet very close to shore in the northern part of the Cow Yard, and anchorage can be had just outside her in 8 feet. There is a good spring beyond a rock in the meadow 25 feet east of the fisherman's shack.

While you are stopping here, roam over Head Harbor Island. In September, the crop of lush red mountain cranberries is wonderful to see, while the view from the top of the hills is superb. On a clear day the whole coast from Grand Manan to Mt. Desert lies at your feet. On a calm day, at high water, a deep narrow indentation on the shore of the 10-foot cove inside Black Ledge on the east side of the island forms a swimming hole unsurpassed anywhere.

Head Harbor is one of the choice spots on the coast; but the bay to the west is full of interesting places. While as you stand on Black Head you look inshore to Roque Island, its sand and its near virgin timber, to the east lie Machias Bay, sparkling in the sunshine, Libby Island Lighthouse, the fine, bold cliffs of Cross Island and the dim outline of Grand Manan.

Mistake Island Harbor, Me.   (13326   304). The best way to get in here is to run up the Main Channel Way northeast of Mistake Island. The wind is likely to be light and fluky in here, and the tide runs hard. There are swirls and eddies off the shore, but nothing violent or dangerous. The cliffs on Steel Harbor Island are high, sheer, and bleak, with only grass and gnarled trees near the edge. Knight Island, on the contrary, is heavily wooded and "prettier." *Do not* at any tide go between Knight Island and Mistake Island. This looks tempting at high water.

Round the northeast end of Knight Island and give the western shore a good berth, for there are ugly ledges off it. However, they usually show. There is an abandoned weir inside the end of the island. The outer wing is supposed to have a board on it. If you can find no board, give the whole concern a good berth, for a weir stake in the bilge is a most distressing experience. If the board is still there, go close to it and anchor as far up as you can get between Mistake Island and Knight Island. Some wash makes in here, but it is just enough to rock you to sleep.

The Coast Guard, when Moose Peak was a manned light, erected an iron spindle on a ledge, protecting the approach to where they used to have their moorings on Mistake Island. Leave this beacon to starboard. Land at the old steps on Mistake Island and follow the boardwalk across to the light for a good view and a pleasant walk.

This harbor is much easier to make, especially in thick weather, than the Cow Yard. It is somewhat less rolly and less troubled with tide and is considerably less frequented.

The Mudhole, Me. (13326   304). This is a most attractive cove on the east side of Great Wass Island. There is a satisfactory anchorage between the weir in the entrance and the point to the west of it. However, the bottom is likely to be heavily grown up with kelp and weed, so be sure the anchor really has hold of something before you go ashore.

If the tide is well up—say two hours—go on inside. Hang very close to the southern shore, as the big rock in the middle almost blocks the entrance and is submerged at half tide. Inside is a long, lovely cove with mud flats at the head but with high rocky banks heavily grown up to spruce, birch, and alder. Kingfishers flash from branch to branch. Great blue herons stand pensively knee deep. Ospreys dive, and a bald eagle supervises the entire operation.

Row up to the head of a cove where a road crosses. Go north for a pleasant walk to Beals or south to the abandoned Coast Guard station and the bleak southern end of this island.

There are several other interesting places in the Eastern Bay. Northwest of Crow Point there is a good shelter in ordinary weather. North of Middle Hardwood Island is another. Pig Island Gut is navigable at half tide or better and has been dredged and buoyed out. Behind Seguin Island north of Head Harbor Island there is another anchorage. One must move carefully in this region, but it is indescribably beautiful and sufficiently difficult of access so that it is not yet crowded.

Roque Island, Me. (13326 304). Roque Island is both a symbol and a delightful fact. Situated far east of Schoodic and 'Tit Manan, shrouded by Fundy fogs and scoured by icy Fundy tides, it is the goal of many east coast yachtsmen. To have anchored off the beach at Roque is to be marked as an able saltwater man. Few of the rocking-chair sports get by Schoodic. To clear 'Tit Manan and Moose Peak in a fog choking thick and to make a landfall on the back side of Roque is no feat for a mere church-steeple navigator. Most of the yachts you meet in Lakeman's or Bunker Cove are manned by men whom you can respect.

Equal to the difficulties of getting to Roque are the delights of being there. Roque Island itself and the islands surrounding it are owned by the Gardner family. The Gardners, like the Forbes of Naushon, have owned their island for generations. In 1806, Joseph Peabody and a partner, both of Salem, bought the island and built several vessels near the tidal mill dam at the head of Shorey Cove. In 1864, Peabody's daughter Catherine bought the shares of the other owners and with her husband, John L. Gardner, took title to the entire island. Except for the years 1870 to 1882, when it was owned by Longfellows and Shoreys, it has been in the family ever since. Subsequent generations have added the neighboring islands and have preserved the group as nearly as possible in a natural state. The present owners are glad to have considerate visitors enjoy the islands but ask that they use only the northerly end of the beach and especially that they be very careful with fire. Some years ago a careless visitor gave himself and the owners several very anxious hours before a forest fire was extinguished. When you consider how a fire would change a beautiful wooded island to a smoking ash heap, spiked with charred stumps, you surely can forego the pleasure of a cigarette until you get back aboard.

The authors appeal vigorously to all visitors to leave the islands as beautiful as they find them. Do not smoke or light fires ashore.

The island is crossed and crisscrossed with wood roads that make easy and pleasant walking. It is more difficult to walk along the shores, because promontories make out at intervals, with no beaches at the foot of the cliff. Bushwhacking is a slow and scratchy business.

Of course the great white beach is the central feature at Roque. The sand is soft and fine and in it are to be found large white clams, the pursuit of which, while not always productive, is excellent exercise. In the middle of a sunny summer day, the water is warm enough for a brief ceremonial dip, but few will stay in very long.

Anchorage off the beach is usually satisfactory on a quiet night, but if there is a sea outside, one may roll a bit. There is a cove on the south end of the beach that offers some protection. However, the two best anchorages are in Bunker Cove at the west end of the Thorofare or at Lakeman's Harbor, between Lakeman Island and Roque.

Bunker Cove. There is excellent anchorage just inside the western entrance to the Thorofare in the mouth of Bunker Cove, but there is room for only two or three boats. The entrance to the Thorofare is not easy to see from Mark Island or the end of Moosabec Reach, but it will open up as you approach. The shores are quite bold and the surf makes ample noise to warn you of your approach.

Round the end of Little Spruce Island, keeping far enough off to avoid the 3-foot spot on which many a tired skipper has stubbed his toe at the end of a long day. Bunker Cove opens up to starboard, looking deceptively quiet and attractive, especially at high water. However, it is only about 3 feet deep at low water. If you are the first one in, go close under the cliff on the northerly side of the cove, just far enough in to get out of the tide. If you are second in, you may be able to get your anchor down on the edge of the mud without getting into the shoal water. Those who come later either ground on the mud at low water or anchor on the edge of the channel, where the bottom slopes down steeply in a gravelly bank. It is hard to get a bite in the gravel and you will swing with the tide. However, many yachts so admire the beauty of the spot that they stay anyway. There are several acceptable alternatives.

Roque Island and its anchorages (refer to Chart 304).

Patten Cove. This cove lies north of the entrance to the Thorofare. To avoid old weir stakes in the mouth of the cove, follow the eastern shore just outside the line of lobster traps. When the inner end of the islet protecting the cove bears WNW, you are by the weir. The bottom is mud. There is almost no current and the surroundings are lovely.

Roque Island Thorofare. This is a comparatively shallow passage leading to Roque Island Harbor and the beach. There has been a good deal of controversy about a rock in the middle of the passage marked on chart 304 as "Rep." It certainly has been reported and there can be no doubt that yachts have bumped over it. The evidence, however, suggests that these disasters occur only to fairly deep-draft boats at low water. A sardine-boat skipper told the writer that there is a bar with about 6 feet between the little island off Roque and Great Spruce Island and that he does not use the passage at extreme low water.

Mr. Orin Leach of West Southport, Maine, sent the writer a fathometer tracing of his passage of the Thorofare at two hours and forty-five minutes after low water. It shows a level hard mud or gravel bottom at 14 feet. About 75 yards to the west of where it begins to deepen, a sharp rock rears up to exactly 14 feet, the same level as the gravel bar. So the rock definitely *is* there, but the part of it that Mr. Leach went over is no shoaler than the controlling depth in the passage.

Coming from the east, the Thorofare can be located by a weir just north of the opening.

Roque Island Harbor. The most attractive anchorage here, of course, is off the beach. The owner, Mr. Gardner, asks that visitors use the north end of the beach. In spite of the cold water, the swimming is good. For a pleasant climb, go to the north end of the beach and strike back into the woods. You will soon pick up a trail up the hill. This ascends by a series of steps—as a visitor to Roque you are entitled to form your own opinion of how many there are. A few yards above the top step a trail leads to the right and comes out on a ledge at the top of the hill. From here one can see the harbor, the beach, and the country to the south and east.

Note the 7-foot spot between Double Shot and Great Spruce Islands. This often breaks at low water in rough weather.

Lakeman Harbor. In entering, move very cautiously. The ledges, particularly those on the Roque Island shore, run far out at high water. A correspondent writes:

We stayed between one hundred and one hundred fifty feet from the high water mark on the Lakeman's Island side of the entrance. The depth sounder gave us 20 feet all the way in. It was just above half tide. Less than half the ledge which runs out from the north side was showing.

Inside, the best water seemed to favor the western shore slightly in 1976, but a shoal-draft boat could find good protection on the eastern side of the harbor.

A pleasant trail comes to the shore at a stony beach on the Roque Island shore.

For many years there was a colony of fishermen from Jonesport on Lakeman Island. The Carver family maintained a tattered logbook, a photostat of which is now in the possession of the Cruising Club of America, in which visitors registered, wrote comments, and drew sketches. It is a most interesting memorial, extending over several generations.

Shorey Cove. This is a secluded and well-protected anchorage little used by cruising yachts bound alongshore. On the western side of the cove are the homes and farms of the island's owners. There is no public landing and there are no facilities of any kind. You are on your own in this country.

The letter below was written by the late George P. Gardner of Roque Island in 1969, after he had read an earlier edition of the *Guide.* Mr. Gardner was a distinguished seaman and an author, ranging the coasts of New England and Nova Scotia, about which he wrote several books.

Dear Roger:

I have recently been perusing various pages of my 1955 Cruising Guide which, incidentally, carries a very nice inscription to me by Fess Blanchard. Of course one of the parts I was reading was about Roque Island and vicinity. It is most complimentary, which from my point of view is not unalloyed joy for, as you know, molasses draws the flies. However the cruisers are pretty darn good about littering up the beach, etc.

There are a few comments I would like to make of no great significance. First, I always differentiate between Bunkers Cove, which is so well described, and Bunkers Hole, a small indentation which dries out at low tide and where it seems plausible Capt. Bunker ran his schooner at high tide and chopped down his masts.

Second, my cousin, the late Dr. John P. Monks, and I spent a lot of time on several occasions trying to locate the rock in the Thoroughfare supposedly in the middle of the channel near the eastern end and we became convinced that there "want no such animal" with which conclusion the late Eddy Kelly of Lakemans fully agreed. What he thought, and I agree, is that at dreen low tide there is a bar right across the middle which may have no more than five to six feet of water on it. I remember once in my GLIDE, which drew slightly over seven feet, being unable to get over it. As to the other rock indicated as being right in the middle of the channel on the western end one need have no worries unless one veers well into the Great Spruce shore after passing Bar Island and the little nubbin that sticks out from Great Spruce; even then it would be hard to find. John Monks did locate it once after considerable effort.

Third, "The passage between Double Shot and Great Spruce" shows a seven foot spot almost in the middle on the chart. I have on several occasions seen it breaking all the way across the channel and once, being foolish enough to go through, I looked back after being heaved by a roller and saw the bottom bare of water.

Fourth, I have often wondered why someone looking for something different has not tried anchoring in a sort of pool showing twenty-seven feet close in to the shore of Rogers Island just after passing a sand spit at the entrance to Masons Bay. To be sure much of Masons Bay dries out at low tide but there is plenty of water at the entrance and in the pool. The surroundings are lovely. I have been in on many occasions but have never anchored so do not know what the tide would do. With such a narrow entrance and mud flats and shallow water to the south it should be well protected in any weather.

Sincerely,
G. P. Gardner

The authors of this *Guide* have been cursed on many accounts, one of the most valid of which is that they have "spoiled" Roque Island with their unbounded enthusiasm for it. We regret it if it be true, but we reply that it cannot be spoiled by considerate and appreciative visitors. It can be spoiled, as any place in the world can be spoiled, by selfish, careless, and lazy devils who litter the shores, pollute the water, burn the woods, and assault the sensitivities of others. We believe that if you are seaman enough to bring a boat to Roque, you are sportsman and gentleman enough to preserve it.

Roque Bluffs, Me. (13326   304). This anchorage, exposed to the southeast, is in the bight formed by Shoppee Point and Shoppee Island on the northeast shore of Englishman Bay. There is a small settlement, Roque Bluffs, on the west bank of the small Englishman River at its mouth.

The Watts Brothers, Ralph and Scott, are authorities for this part of the coast. The former, long a boatbuilder, lives in a house on a knoll on the south side of the road on the south side of Shoppee Point. Brother Scott lives further up the road to the northwest on the opposite side.

There are no supplies.

On the north side of the point at the end of the road is a substantial wharf, built and maintained by the owners of Roque Island. It is available for use by visiting yachtsmen.

Anchorage off this wharf would be protected only in winds from the northeast quadrant. In heavy weather it is preferable to lie at nearby Roque Island or in Little Kennebec Bay, less than 4 miles to the east.

Anyone wishing to travel by land east or west from Roque Bluffs can order a car by telephone from Machias, about 7 miles distant, where there is through bus connection in both directions.

Machias Bay, Me. (13326   304). This bay would be crowded with yachts all summer if it lay farther to the westward. The shores are high, for the most part bold, and heavily wooded. The islands are dramatic. The harbors are well protected. The bay is sheltered from the sea by the bulk of Cross Island and the long ridge of Libby Islands. Dangers are well marked. The bay abounds in wild life, from mackerel and codfish to ospreys and eagles. Furthermore, it is frequently clear in the bay when the fog hangs wetly outside.

However, most of those yachtsmen who do see the bay see it only in crossing from Foster Channel to Cross Island Narrows. On this run, notice Stone Island, a lovely wooded, clifty island, on which in 1974 a correspondent counted seven occupied osprey nests. An oil port was projected here but the idea has been abandoned.

The drawbridge above Machiasport has been replaced with a fixed bridge. It has a vertical clearance of 25 feet above high water.

Expect to find the can north of Cross Island much farther off the island than it appears.

Speaking generally, it is better to go inside of Cross Island through the Narrows than it is to go outside. The wind is likely to be light outside and the sea rough. The tide runs hard both inside and outside and there is less likely to be fog inside.

Foster Channel is a little difficult to pick out because all the islands are grassy, with occasional big domes of black rock. Foster Island has a white house and a barn on it and Scabby Island has the highest dome.

Beware of a rock north of Scabby Island. It is about 3 feet under water at low tide. The writer spoke with a man who had sounded it with an oar.

Starboard Cove, Machias Bay, Me. (13326   304). For anyone seeking a quiet overnight anchorage in calm weather, not far from the alongshore course, this is a good spot. There is little shelter in northeast or easterly winds. But the convenient cove between Starboard Island and the mainland is perfectly protected by a bar until two hours from high water. Then a sea might roll in from the south, but the ground is so broken in that direction that it would not be dangerous in the summer.

Just inside the point of Starboard Island is an old weir, and there is another across from it. Beware of old stakes. Anchor near the 6-foot spot as far to the south and east as you can get.

There is no gasoline or store at Starboard.

Starboard Creek dries out at low water. It can then be forded by the few summer residents living at Point of Main, whence there is a gorgeous view on a clear day.

Anyone visiting Starboard Cove should not fail to go ashore to the impressive hogback shown on the chart at the northeast shore of the creek. It is heaped high with small pebbles of jasper, "a compact, opaque, often highly colored, cryptocrystalline variety of quartz, commonly used in decorative carvings." To the layman, jasper is a stone of extraordinary smoothness.

Bucks Harbor, Me. (13326   304). This is a well-protected harbor in delightful surroundings. There is no difficulty about entering. Go right up the middle to avoid old weir stakes. In 1973, the harbor was dredged to a depth of 7 feet and a width of 200 feet to the first wharf and to a width of 100 feet to the next one. Anchor more or less in the middle of the harbor. In the event of really bad weather, go up on the tide to the bridge connecting Bucks Neck to the mainland, tie up to it, and lie in the mud. This is known as "Hurricane Anchorage."

The first wharf west of the gravel beach on the south side of the harbor is that of the ambitious Dana Urquhart. He declared in 1976 that he would have ice, water, showers, gas, and marine supplies the next summer. However, nothing was accomplished. Gas is available at the Co-op. About a mile northwest is a settlement and a mile beyond that is the well-stocked grocery of Herbert Rose. From Urquhart's, or the store, one can telephone for a lift to Machias where the through buses to Boston and New York stop and where there is a 3200-foot grass landing strip.

Urquhart thinks well of Bucks Harbor. He contemplates a development that will make it more convenient than Cutler, with all the facilities mentioned above plus a longer wharf, tie-up space, a store, and a restaurant. As it is, Bucks Harbor is an attractive place. It is to be hoped that it is not killed with improvements.

Machiasport, Me. (13326   304). A spire and a cupola mark this small settlement on the bank of the Machias River about 4 miles below Machias, the head of navigation and the principal town of the region.

It is best to come up the river on the tide. Above Round Island the tide sets northwest across the flats, so it is important to follow the buoys closely to stay in the narrow channel.

Anchor in the stream off Charles Ingalls's Machiasport Boat Shop. Mr. Ingalls can take care of repair work and is a reliable authority on local matters.

Gasoline can be bought at the sardine factory.

On the west shore of the river at Birch Point are the Picture Rocks, said to have been carved by Indians as they passed in their canoes from Quoddy to the Penobscot to let those arriving later know they had passed Machias on their way to and from the two reservations.

The first naval battle of the Revolution was fought at Sanborn Point. Fort O'Brien, named after one of the participants in the battle, is on the west bank just above the point. The following account of the battle by Richard Hallet appeared in the Boothbay *Register* of October 1 and 8, 1959.

Maine on the Warpath; the Battle of Machias

To Machias goes the honor of Maine's first pitched battle with the British in 1776 [1775]. Little Machias, with its 80 families, its 150 fighting males, and its formidable Jerry O'Brien, who had mauled a King's magistrate four years before heading that faction, was "not so peaceable."

Two months after the battle of Lexington, Captain Ichabod Jones came home to Machias in his trading sloop *Unity.* Her hold was full of bread, pork, fish, and beans, without which his fellow-citizens must have starved; but before he would open his hatches for trading purposes, he tried to get the people to sign a paper binding them to let him take lumber back to Boston; lumber to make barracks for the King's troops. Ichabod was a prosperous merchant, and probably not the greatest patriot alive, but yet perhaps he was not altogether on the King's side either. He was neutral, at a moment when neutrality was dangerous—since he who would not take sides had everybody for his enemy.

Yet perhaps he might have won his point and filled the holds of his two sloops, the *Polly* and the *Unity,* with lumber for Boston—his argument being that lumber was their only money and that if they didn't send lumber they must starve to death—but unluckily for him, the citizens had heard of the battle of Lexington. The shot had been fired that had been heard around the world, and Machias had raised a liberty pole.

Captain Moore of the King's tender *Margaretta* ordered them to take it down. They refused. The *Margaretta* was the British fighting ship, armed with 16 swivels, which had convoyed Captain Jones' sloops to Machias. Captain Jones, the neutral, persuaded his British friend to stay his hand until a town meeting could be held and the people induced to reverse their obstinate stand on the liberty pole.

Next day was Sunday and the town seethed with argument. . . . Benjamin Foster, who owned a saw-mill, and as a youth had been a soldier at Louisburg . . . called on all to follow him who wanted to capture the *Margaretta* and the two sloops of Ichabod. The O'Briens were right at his heels and many others.

It was Sunday: but "the better the day, the better the deed" in the opinion of Ben Foster. The English officers would come to church and these "not so peaceable" sons of Machias could seize them at their devotions.

But the plan miscarried. The day was warm, the church windows were open, and the preacher's servant, London Atus . . . from his perch high in the Negro pew saw a band of armed men of Machias approaching, gave a frightened cry, and jumped out of the window.

The two Joneses and Captain Moore followed him through the same window. Captain Jones hid in the woods; Captain Moore got back aboard the *Margaretta* and sent this message on shore: "That he had express orders to protect Captain Jones . . . and that if the people presumed to stop Captain Jones' vessels, he, Captain Moore, would burn the town."

In the teeth of this threat Foster and his men took possession of the two Jones sloops. But the *Margaretta,* as if stupefied by this transaction, lay out in the stream and withheld her fire.

The patriots of Machias lined the shore opposite the *Margaretta* and called out to her to "surrender to America." That was a new sound in the ears of British captains; and the tender's skipper called back, "Fire and be hanged to you."

The people on shore fired, and the tender returned this fire, still not using her cannon, and, slipping her cable, went down-stream, stayed the night lashed to a small sloop commanded by one Captain Toby; and in the morning, taking Toby out of his sloop for pilot, made all sail to get off, as wind and tide favored.

At this inglorious retreat, the Americans were all on fire to give chase. Forty of them, under command of Captain Jeremiah O'Brien, swarmed aboard Ichabod's sloop *Unity.* A few had guns, for which there was only a round or two of ammunition; the rest brought pitchforks and narrow axes. After they were under way, they built breastworks of pine boards, to screen them from the fire of the enemy.

A more unequal fight there could hardly be, than this between the sloop *Unity,* which had no guns, and the schooner *Margaretta,* which had sixteen, between the handful of undisciplined Americans and the schooner's veteran crew. But the sheer courage of the O'Briens was a blaze of fire in which the British were shriveled up.

Captain Moore hailed the *Unity* and told her plainly to keep off or he would fire. It availed him nothing. He cut the boats from his stern but at best the *Margaretta* was a dull sailor and the *Unity* came up with her. He opened fire half-heartedly with his muskets, and killed one of the *Unity's* men. The two vessels came so close that John O'Brien, brother of Jerry, made a great leap and jumped onto the *Margaretta's* quarterdeck. Seven muskets were fired at him; but he bore a charmed life; and when those seven musketeers charged him with fixed bayonets, he gave a wildcat screech to unnerve them, and jumped into the water.

His brother picked him up; and just then the *Margaretta's* helmsman was shot in the heart, the ship broached to, and Captain O'Brien ran the bowsprit of his sloop through her mainsail. His ammunition was all gone; but twenty of his men boarded the King's ship armed with pitchforks. . . . Captain Moore had already fallen, mortally wounded; and the sight of those oncoming pitchforks was too much for the midshipman Stillingfleet, who was second in command. He "abscombed himself away" in the hold of the ship and gave up. Pitchforks in that short terrific battle were more than bayonets; and in no time at all the Americans were ready to secure their prize.

They had lost two men, but they had taken the *Margaretta* captive. This was on June 12, 1775, and was certainly the first naval contest of the Revolution. Only Lexington and Concord had preceded it; Bunker Hill was still to come.

Two weeks later the Provincial Congress passed a vote of thanks to Captain O'Brien, Captain Foster, and their men for this exploit and gave into their keeping the captured vessel and the two sloops, *Unity* and *Polly.* Captain Ichabod Jones' neutrality had lost him these valuable properties.

Machias, Me. (13326   304). Since the swing bridge over the river above Machiasport was changed to a fixed bridge, it has been impossible for masted vessels of any size to go up the river. Also, the river has silted up so badly that only a very shoal-draft yacht could negotiate the channel anyway.

Machias is the commercial and communication center for this area. If you need something you cannot buy in a local store, get a ride to Machias and you have a good chance.

The last vessel to carry out a cargo of long lumber was the *Edward Smith,* a three-master, with more than 500,000 feet, mostly spruce dimension, in the autumn of 1940. The last four-master at Machias was the *Spindrift,* launched there in the early twenties.

The father of Dr. Small, a local dentist and an authority on marine and historical matters, owned the last fleet of three- and four-masters of American registry on the Atlantic coast, and the loss of the *Rebecca R. Douglas* in May 1943 marked the end of commercial sail in Maine.

Captain Moore of the *Margaretta,* who was mortally wounded in the action described under Machiasport, died in the Burnham Tavern (1770), now maintained in its original condition as a museum by the local DAR chapter. There is a display of Revolutionary relics and records.

Northwest Harbor, Cross Island. In anything but really heavy weather, there is good shelter just inside Northwest Head off a steep stony beach. The cove is uninhabited, and the surroundings are lovely. A bald eagle circled overhead as we scouted his domain.

Cross Island Narrows, Me. (13327   303). The argument has almost always favored going through the narrows rather than out around Cross Island. It is harder to buck an ebb tide in the Bay of Fundy than it is in Machias Bay, and the wind is likely to leave you slopping around off the cliffs in a confused sea. With a fair tide, you get a fine boost through the narrows, and the breeze will be better inside. In the fog, Machias Bay is often clear when it is thick outside and there is likely to be a scale-up in the narrows. Beating west with a fair tide it might be better to stay outside and get a powerful lift to windward down Grand Manan Channel. However, stand well off the cliffs to avoid a soft spot that often develops there.

Bound east from Foster Channel, look for can 3 at the entrance to the narrows, much farther off Cross Island than you expect. You will find it nearly in range of the powerhouse on Thornton's Point. It usually appears more white than black, as the gulls and shags seem to give it special attention.

The usual course is north of Mink Island. However, there may be less tide south of the island. The wind in Northeast Harbor may be fluky, but it seems to draw across the channel very nicely. One can usually fetch through either way.

There is good anchorage in Northeast Harbor. Work as far south as your draft will permit and get out of the tide. Do not let the children row around here in the pram. If they get in the tide near Mink Island, you may have a rescue operation in hand.

The anchorage off the old Coast Guard station, now occupied by a detachment from the Outward Bound School, is less sheltered but perfectly satisfactory.

It is possible to enter from the eastward between Scotch Island and the ledges to the north. The new edition of chart 303 makes it look easier than the old one did. The writer carried 5 feet in here and saw a great deal of real estate under the keel, but he proved that it can be done.

Cross Island is a rough island to walk on. It was cut over before World War II and has grown up through the slash into a tangle. However, a walk along the cliffs on the south side is interesting if you can find your way.

The radio towers on Thornton Point can no longer be ignored. There are twenty-odd of them—we couldn't agree how many. Almost

1000 feet in the air, they spread a net of copper wire, so that someone in Washington can talk to someone under water in a submarine in the North Sea. This is an ultra-low-frequency station, so low that it is said to bother the hearing of dogs. No dog is supposed to be able to live within 7 miles of the installation. It is pleasant to remember Thornton Point heavily wooded and to recall the feeling that as one passed through Cross Island Narrows one was way down east in primitive surroundings and a long way from civilization.

On emerging from the narrows and passing the bell, one enters Grand Manan Channel, which is part of the Bay of Fundy. The character of the coast changes abruptly. The shore consists of steep, bold, black cliffs, in places covered with greenish lichen. There are no off-lying islands. The seas roll up from the south, troubled by tides. On several occasions the writer has left the mild sunny waters of Machias Bay with a pleasant southwest breeze, and, in the few minutes it took to traverse Cross Island Narrows, found himself rolling almost becalmed in a confused chop with a graying sky, the feel of fog in the air, and the sea breaking heavily on the forsaken cliffs of the Old Man. It is a short run to Cutler.

Cutler, Me. (13327   303). Cutler is the end of the Maine coast as most cruising men think of it. Eastward, 14 miles of cliffs extend almost unrelieved to West Quoddy Head. Thence the country, although part of it is United States territory, has a strong Canadian flavor. For those bound for Grand Manan or up Grand Manan Channel toward Saint John, Cutler is the last American port and the last shelter before Head Harbor on Campobello or North Head Harbour on Grand Manan. Those returning from the eastward usually stop at Cutler, so you are likely to find half a dozen yachts here on almost any summer night.

From the east, the landmark for the harbor is Long Point, distinguished by a big mowed field. A tide rip usually is found off this point. Notice that in thick weather one can follow the line of 100-foot soundings down the American shore of Grand Manan Channel right to the bell off Cutler harbor. The 100-foot contour turns sharply to the westward after Long Point.

From Cross Island Narrows, pass between Cape Wash Island and The Old Man and follow up the shore. If you have a depth finder, you can do it in the fog by running up the 20-fathom line. You will not hear the horn on Little River Island until you are by Western Head, and maybe not until you pass the end of Little River Island. An alternative is to run off to the whistle and thence come in on the horn. This is longer and easier.

The usual entrance to the harbor is north of the island. However, there is often a dead spot off the light, in which one can roll about for some time. The passage south of the island seems to offer a better breeze. It is not as deep as the other, but one could carry 6 feet through this entrance at anything but the bottom of the tide.

Anchor anywhere off the town and out of the tide. Often there is a vacant mooring. Inquire of Neil Corbett at the wharf, just west of a white cottage standing on pilings over a black rock.

In the event of a really heavy easterly—an unlikely event during the cruising season, snug up under Little River Island or withdraw far up the harbor on the tide and pass between two great boulders. You may lie in the mud here for an hour or so, either side of low water.

Gasoline and Diesel fuel are available at Neil Corbett's wharf and ice frozen in milk cartons. Water is piped to the wharf, but a correspondent writes of it: Cutler water, is extremely hard. If in need of really usable water, get someone to carry you and a few jugs about five minutes' drive up the Machias road, where there's an ever-running roadside spring piped to a spot opposite the old cement plant used for building the naval installation. Really good water is sometimes hard for a cruising boat to find, and this is excellent.

The best place to land from a skiff is on the float in front of the large yellow building. Instead of a gangway, a set of stout steps leads to the top of the wharf, each step covered with hardware cloth to prevent its being slippery. The device works very well.

Across the road from the wharf is the post office and the store of Philip and Margaret Geel. While it is no supermarket, it has all the necessities of life and some of the luxuries. The Geels are very generous about letting cruising people use their telephone for collect calls. The outdoor telephone was removed because it was too frequently vandalized.

There is no boat yard at Cutler. In cases of emergency, consult Mr. Corbett. Rowland Ramsdell and George Farris do engine work.

If you have to lie over a day in Cutler during the blueberry season, you can fill a pail with the best wild blueberries in the state in an hour or two. Or consult Mr. Corbett about a handlining trip to some of the nearby shoals. Perhaps you can arrange a trip to Machias Seal Island, where the variety of bird life is most remarkable.

The path along the northern shore of the harbor and out along the cliffs is now closed because the hospitality of the people who own the land was abused.

Cutler used to be a prosperous town with good business in lobsters, clams, ground fish, herring, pulpwood, and blueberries. Lately, however, the ground fish have been overfished, the clam flats have been polluted or depleted, and the woods have been cut back. There are still blueberries and lobsters. Some income is derived from the radio base, and a few summer people are coming in. Weirs are obsolete. Airplanes spot schools of herring and talk the boats to them. In late July 1976, 800,000 bushels of herring were taken out in one haul. The herring are used for "sardines," fish steaks, smoked herring, and fish meal.

Machias Seal Island, N.B. (13327   303). The following account of a visit to Machias Seal Island by an experienced skipper will give a clear idea of the problems and pleasures involved:

The day planned for the run out from Cutler was one of the few foggy ones of the summer, but we decided to go, regardless. We allowed 15° for the flood tide setting us up into the bay, and that turned out to be about right. The passage was uneventful, although I admit to some uneasiness when we did not hear the horn on the island as soon as I expected. Although I should have known better, I did not allow sufficiently for the directionality of the Canadian horns —this one points SW and we were approaching from the NNW. North Rock, 1.3 miles to the left of the rhumb line and in the direction the tide was setting us, could be a hazard on this run. But that is no serious problem—just set your course so as to be sure that if the island is missed, you are to the south of it. There are no dangers there, and you could hardly miss the strong horn that points in that direction. I may be making too light of the navigation problems: While we were on the island, a commercial boat with passengers (perhaps the Captain Corbett mentioned in the *Guide*) came out, having delayed her departure until the fog lifted.

At the island we picked up the big mooring and soon, like the sloop we had seen there before, the tide had us overrunning it, with the log buoy bumping alongside. The men ashore suggested that we move to another mooring about 25 yards to the NE. This is one the personnel on the island have put out for their own use and is marked by a small buoy, not unlike the multitude of lobster-pot buoys in the area. (These pots are those of lobstermen from Maine. Although these are Canadian waters, it was closed season for the Canadian lobstermen. Although the Canadians we talked with in Seal Cove were good humored about the situation, there seemed to be a natural undercurrent of resentment.) The mooring is a grapnel. Although they had confidence in it, I did not find out how big it is. But no matter—I am sure it is sufficient in good weather, and no matter how big the mooring, it would be a desperate place to lie in heavy weather.

There were three or four men standing by to help us land when we went ashore. While no yacht-club float, there is an inclined concrete boat ramp to bring the dinghy alongside at any tide, and the men are knowledgeable and alert in helping. The welcome was quiet, but warm. Mr. Russell was in charge of the station. I told him that I was thinking of passing on this information to you for possible use in the *Guide*, and he was receptive to the idea. The island is a bird refuge, so there is a resident ornithologist during the summer, in addition to the personnel of the light station.

Although our interest in birds is fairly casual, we were fascinated by the birdlife there—the place is jammed! A steady stream of puffins returning with small fish in their great beaks and making a complete low circle before landing on the rocks and disappearing in the crevices. Razorbills, with their black backs, white fronts, and upright stance, looking like penguins. Terns, both common and arctic, trying to drive us off, while we tried to avoid stepping on the young. Add to this the shore birds, feeding on the wave-washed rocks, and a sprinkling of land birds—swallows were nesting under the porch steps to the keeper's house. There are several observation blinds. The reason for the request that visitors keep to established paths is obvious—there are nests and eggs even on the paths. Pets are forbidden for equally obvious reasons.

Grand Manan Channel, Me. (13327 303). This is a deep and tide-scoured channel between sheer cliffs. There are almost no off-lying dangers on either side, except Sail Rock and Morton Ledge, and there is a good fog signal at each side of the eastern end. The tide runs from 2 to 3 knots and even faster at times. Therefore, it is scarcely worth while beating against it with a gentle breeze. However, as the turn of the tide approaches, back eddies begin to build under both shores, and it is possible to creep along close to the cliffs with a favorable current an hour or two before it turns in the channel.

The time of the moon makes a great deal of difference in the strength of the tidal current and in the duration of slack water. At the time of full moon and new moon, the tide will run at a full 3 knots, with no more than a half hour of slack between tides. At first quarter and last quarter, the tide may run no more than half as hard, with as much as an hour to an hour and a quarter of reasonably slack water.

An experienced correspondent from New Brunswick writes: "When crossing Grand Manan Channel, the tide allowance can be as high as 3+, but the rate is available in the Atlantic Coast tide tables under

'Grand Manan Channel' and gives time of turning and maximum flow. I would never venture across in a fog without consulting it, as there is a difference of from 1 knot to well over 3 from neap to spring tides."

Beware of this stretch of water in a small boat with a heavy south-wester against an ebb tide. It can get dangerous quite quickly, and refuges are not as close as they are among the islands to the westward.

In the fog, navigation is fairly simple because of the steep shores and the fog signals, but be alert for sardiners heading for the factories at Eastport and Lubec. They are big, heavy vessels and can move at a rate to inspire caution in any yachtsman.

A radar reflector is a sensible if not a necessary precaution, as these vessels rely heavily on radar to enable them to keep moving at top speed in thick weather. It is vital to them that they get their fish to the factory as fresh as possible.

Be particularly careful of heavy logs and other debris adrift in this channel. The tide seems to keep it on the move.

Indians from Passamaquoddy Bay were accustomed to paddle down Grand Manan Channel on an ebb tide during the morning calm and cut sweet grass behind Little River Head, where it grows abundantly. Then, with a spruce tree in the bow and a flood tide under them, they sailed back in the afternoon. A fisherman hauling a trawl one blowy day beheld a spruce tree bearing down on him with a great collar of foam below it, nearly obscuring the bow of the canoe in which it stood. The Indian, unable to go forward without swamping the light craft and unable to bring her to the wind with his sail plan so far forward, hunched in the stern, clutching his paddle and baling for his life. As he flashed past, he waved his bale dish, and with the gift for brief and pithy expression for which his people are noted, shouted, "Too much bush!"

Many a racing yachtsman lugging a spinnaker in a squall may have felt that he was carrying "too much bush."

There is no shelter on the Canadian side of the channel and only two possible shelters on the American side: Haycock Harbor and Bailey's Mistake.

Haycock Harbor, Me. (13327   303). This shelter is about 6 miles from West Quoddy Head. The harbor itself is exposed to the south, but there is a small gut leading out of the west side of it opening into a small basin with a few wharves and farmhouses.

The harbor is hard to pick out from offshore, but is marked by a sort of "double shot" headland on its east side. Enter halfway between the "double shot" headland and the one to the west on a northerly course and favor the north and northwest shore until you can see straight up the gut for several hundred yards to where it turns into the basin. Sighting straight up the gut, turn west and place the south end of a small gravel beach dead astern. There is a mess of bad boulders (covered by only 1 foot of water at low tide) before you reach the bar.

If you can clear the boulders, you can make it; but don't forget to allow for the ground swell if any is running. The tide runs strongly over the bar, but there is more water than over the boulders. The only spot inside where there is more than 2 feet of water at low tide is close under the cliffs on the north side. It's a 9-foot hole at low water, but you'll need a bow-and-stern line to keep your keel fitted into it. This is a pleasant and remote little eel rut, where you will not be disturbed by any sounds except the surf on the ledges outside. Those who like to go into small unmarked places should not miss it if the tides are right.

Bailey's Mistake, Me. (13327   303). Marked by a whistle and a can buoy, the harbor is easy to make, but, except on a quiet night, likely to be rolly. Leave the can, the ledges, and an old weir to port. Anchor under the high land on the western side of the harbor where chart 303 shows 16 feet. Beware of old weir stakes.

On the high water, it is possible to penetrate far up into the northwestern cove, but this pretty well dries out at low water.

The picturesque name of this harbor refers to an error in judgment on the part of one Captain Bailey, skipper of a four-masted coaster bound for Lubec before the middle of the last century. He miscalculated the tide, perhaps, and instead of rounding West Quoddy Head and running into Quoddy Roads, he rounded Eastern Head and struck the ledges off Balch's Head. The legend goes that he and his crew were so pleased with the town and surroundings when the fog lifted that they built houses from the schooner's cargo and settled there. The Portland *Press Herald* for September 30, 1966, in commenting on this happy ending, observes: "But lumber to Lubec in the 1830's? Who said coals to Newcastle?"

An earlier shipwreck was said to have been behind the first settlement. Captain Congdon, skipper of a privateer in the War of 1812, ran his vessel ashore here to prevent her seizure by the British. After the war he returned with his bride, settled, and established a profitable lumber mill. He was frozen to death with his two oxen in a blizzard in 1822 on the road to Lubec.

Sail Rock, Me. (13327   303). The easternmost point in the United States, Sail Rock is appropriately named. It is marked by a flashing whistle to the southeast. Here the ebb tide running out of Quoddy

Roads meets the tide running southwest down the channel and creates quite a bobble. To approach it in the fog is unnerving, for it sounds like surf breaking on the shore. As you approach, dimly looming through the fog appears a line of breakers. Sailing vessels do well to stand well clear of the rock in light weather, for the tide could set a vessel ashore here.

The moorings shown on chart 303 behind Quoddy Head have been removed.

One often finds a good breeze under Quoddy Head when it is calm outside.

CHAPTER XIII

Grand Manan

"Everything about Grand Manan was magnificent—
a very moving experience."
A reader of the *Guide*

While not a desperate seafaring adventure, the voyage to Grand Manan can be exciting in itself, and it brings with it all the fun of "going foreign." Foreign charts, foreign money, a different cast to the language, different time (Atlantic), Customs formalities, and the Canadian flag at the starboard spreader give the trip glamor, especially if you are going for the first time.

Preparation. No notice need be given to American Customs of your departure. However, it helps to have positive identification for each member of your crew in anticipation of your return. New and expensive foreign items like cameras might be registered, or a bill of sale by an American firm provided. Very seldom, however, is a yacht questioned, and the writer has checked in by telephone on two occasions.

The navigator should have Canadian charts 4340 and 4342. They are much more detailed than H.O. 1057, the best United States chart available. The Canadian Coast Pilot, *Nova Scotia SE Coast and Bay of Fundy,* is very helpful. These can be obtained from the Canadian Hydrographic Service, Department of Mines and Technical Surveys, in Ottawa. Write for the *Catalogue of Nautical Charts, Sailing Directions and Tidal Information,* order specifically what you want, and include payment, with due regard for the exchange rate. This should be done well in advance, as delays are frequent and the materials are indispensable.

The easiest way to make the crossing is to leave Cutler on the first of the flood tide and steer for the bold west shore of the island south of Dark Harbour. The tide will vary in strength with the phase of the moon, but something like 1½ to 2 knots is about right. It isn't very important anyway, because your course converges with a bold shore and you can't very well miss the whole island. If the weather is clear, there is nothing to be concerned about. If it is thick, beware of sardiners, keep the radar reflector in evidence, and watch the clock. When time runs out, look for the cliffs first, pretty well up off the water. Often on a sunny day the top will be clearly visible when the fog is thick around the bottom. When you make the shore, follow it up at a reasonable distance offshore. There are occasional irregularities, so don't get in too close. If the fathometer reads over 15 fathoms, you are surely safe.

Dark Harbour. This is a dramatic and tempting spot, but the cautious skipper will have no trouble in resisting the temptation. Between a rocky bar, bare at high water, and the cliffs is a deep lagoon. There is a low place in the bar over which a small torrent pours into the sea. As the tide rises in Grand Manan Channel, it reaches the level of the water in the lagoon. At this moment there is said to be 6 feet over the bar so one can nip in. Inside, the lagoon is 10 fathoms deep, is perfectly protected and provided with several moorings. Of course one must watch his chance to get out, and it is possible that gales since 1976 have raised the height of the bar. Dark Harbour is best seen from the land.

The principal occupation at Dark Harbour is raking dulse. Dulse is a seaweed that grows below ordinary low-water mark. At moon tides it is raked up and spread out to dry on flat rocks near the top of the bar. The dried weed is of a dark purplish, leathery consistency, looking and tasting rather like the tongue of an old shoe rescued from a bait barrel. However, it is much esteemed as a delicacy by some, is said to "go good with the beer," and is consumed by health food zealots for the vast quantities of vitamins and minerals stored in it. It is shipped to Saint John, packed in plastic bags, and sold in supermarkets.

When the dulse rakers are not harvesting, spreading, or packing dulse, they are relaxing in the little camps and shacks spread along the bar. Moon tides are a very social time at Dark Harbour.

Unfortunately, the great Ground Hog Day gale of 1976 so rolled about and overturned the rocks on which the dulse grew that in the summer of 1976 the harvest was only 5 percent of normal. As this is written, shortly after the gales of January and February 1978, no report has been received from Dark Harbour, but dulse production may not be back to normal for years.

If you are exploring ashore, do not try to climb the cliffs. They are composed largely of loose rocks and grow steeper as you go higher. Near the top, the climb is precipitous and the footing most unstable.

North Head Harbour, N.B. (4340, 4342). Having found the cliffs near Dark Harbour, follow along the shore. The cliffs become higher and steeper, but a small beach appears at the foot. The shore trends more easterly and you will perhaps begin to hear the horn on Northern Head. Before you get to it you must round Long Eddy Point, a bar which interrupts your procedure of following the shore. Give it a generous berth. An unpleasant rip can build up off this point, especially on the ebb with a southerly breeze. You may see the old fog signal station near the base of the cliff.

After you round Long Eddy, the fog will probably scale up and it will be an easy sail up the shore, by Whale Cove to Swallowtail. In the boiling tide around the northern end of the island you are likely to see porpoises, seals, and many different kinds of birds fishing in the disturbed waters. The writer met a whale here on one occasion. Terns, shearwaters, phalarope and puffins are often seen here. Ashburton Head, where the vessel *Lord Ashburton* was lost in a winter gale many years ago, is a most impressive headland.

Whale Cove is well protected in the usual summer weather, but the wharf here dries out at low water. However, there are several moorings.

Continue around Swallowtail, a picturesque lighthouse held to the rock against the winds of winter by a web of steel cables. If you are coming in from the north, from Saint John or Blacks Harbour, you may have trouble hearing the horn on Swallowtail and Northern Head. The reason is that the horn is started automatically. The mechanism depends on two parallel tubes. In the upper one is a bright light. The lower one has a sensing device. If a certain percentage of the upper light returns through the lower tube, the horn starts. Particles of snow, rain, or fog will produce such reflection. It is sometimes the case that the fog will hang a mile offshore and lie thick all the way to Saint John, but the light doesn't know that and fails to react. If you don't hear the horn as you approach the island, you will probably break into the clear well before you get dangerously close.

In crossing from Blacks Harbour to Grand Manan, leaving Blacks Harbour at full flood, 1½ knots was too much to allow for tide. It was not a moon tide. Little current was noticed at the bell outside Blacks Harbour and we were approaching slack water as we closed on Grand Manan.

From Swallowtail, make Net Point bell and run in for the made harbor at North Head. The lights shown on the chart are no bigger than light bulbs and make very little impression on a foggy night.

One can lie in either of the two basins. Anchorage outside is possible but uneasy. Seek a berth alongside a vessel that appears not to be actively fishing, so you will not have to shift lines at an early hour. The fishermen are, on the whole, very considerate about this and will direct you. If you do get outside a boat that must leave, the crew will usually see that you are properly made fast. If you can get alongside the Canadian fisheries boat *Mace's Bay,* you will be well set. Do not lie alongside the wharf itself, for this means the use of long lines to allow for the 17-foot rise of tide.

In North Head Harbour, the writer was lying alongside a sardiner in a little 28-foot sloop with three boys. It was a black night, thick o' fog. I came on deck in my pajamas about 9:30 to look around before turning in and heard a heavy motor running outside the breakwater and the rush of a bow wave. It came rapidly closer, rushed through the narrow gap. Navigation lights glowed through the fog, the reverse gear roared and ground; the heavy sardiner, still going a good 6 knots, swung, and headed straight for us. I grabbed the boat hook and felt very foolish with it as a head appeared over the bow, now frightfully close, and shouted, "Cut him in half."

More violent reversing churned the water in the little harbor, the great presence swung sideways, and stopped alongside without even squeaking the tire that the fierce character forward dropped over the side as he shouted, in a cheerful New Brunswick burr, "Wouldn't cr-rack an egg, skipper-r. We ain't dr-runk, but we ben drr-rinkin'. "

I put on my pants and found the rest of the evening most instructive.

The ferry from Black's Harbour lands at North Head and brings cars to the island.

At North Head, the writer was cautioned not to sail down the eastern side of the island, even with a fair wind and tide. The bottom is very rough and the tide runs hard. Bulkhead Rip is especially dangerous. In the days of sail, fishermen used to anchor there and fish on the flood tide, where the bottom rises from 40 fathoms to 4 in a very short distance. When the tide began to slack, they left at once, for if caught here in the ebb they would cut an anchor line rather than lie there with the heavy ebb tide pouring over the submerged cliff and backing up against a southerly sea.

A frequent visitor to North Head contributes two notes: "It should be noted there are two extensions to the west wharf at North Head, offering excellent protection on both sides. The north portion of the T is longer; and if the south side is full, there is usually space on the other side.

"The new ferry is a 'drive-on drive-off,' but in 1977 the waiting lines were sometimes *three days* long. A second ferry is now planned and is to go into service in the summer of 1978."

Your first stop ashore must be at the customs office, a neat, bare, official building flying the Canadian flag. Now that customs officers have been discontinued at Seal Cove and Wilson's Beach, North Head is one of the few convenient places at which to enter Canada before Saint John, a very awkward place indeed. The officer will check you into Canadian waters, and issue a cruising permit for as long as you wish to stay. After the official transaction is completed, you will find him a most pleasant and informative gentleman. One of the officers may be Mr. Herbert Macaulay of Castalia, formerly the officer at Seal Cove before the office there was discontinued. He is a gentleman of broad acquaintance and of profound knowledge about Grand Manan and the New Brunswick coast. He sells Canadian charts and is a reliable source of local information.

Near the Custom House are an outdoor telephone, a bank, a store, and a snack shop. Back from the road a step is a well-equipped hardware store, but it is light on marine gear.

Near the shore is the ferry wharf where the modern car ferry from Blacks Harbour lands. She is a convincing argument for a radar reflector and a horn of many decibels.

There used to be a fish-meal plant here, but it is inactive. The inhabitants made it clear that it was unwelcome. Rocks got into the grinders. The building and wharf that burned were used to extract eggs from sea urchins. These are a delicacy in Japan, where they were said to be sold for $18.00 per pound. There is also a plant, which was built to salt fish for the West India trade, but which has been inoperative for some time. As lobstering is off season in Canada during the summer, the principal occupation is seining herring. The use of spotting planes is impractical here because of fog. The seiners use sophisticated sonar gear, which can detect a school as much as half a mile away. They use big purse seines with power haulers, pump the fish into the hold, scaling them on the way, and rush them to factories, where they are made into fish meal for fertilizer. Some of them are taken to Blacks Harbour, where they are smoked and canned, and some to Seal Cove or Blacks Harbour, where they are salted and smoked. Some fishermen supplement lobstering by trawling and handlining for ground fish, and a few draggers work out of Grand Manan.

There is no gas pump on the wharf at North Head. Small quantities of gas can be lugged in a can from the station on the road west of the harbor. Bring your own can. If a sufficient quantity of gasoline or Diesel oil is needed, call Irving Oil Company or Allison Ingalls of Gulf Oil; they will send a tank truck.

There is a hospital at North Head for the afflicted.

The Shore Crest Inn can provide a room ashore and a meal, and the Marathon Hotel serves meals in a unique air of faded Victorian simplicity and elegance. It is a most attractive establishment, with an inspiring view down Long Island Bay. The Mananook Restaurant is well spoken of.

If your stay on Grand Manan must be brief, call Mrs. Ora Dow, 662-3321, or Mrs. Earl Green, 662-8212, for a conducted tour of the island by taxi. You should certainly see Grand Harbour, Seal Cove, Southwest Head, and the museum at Grand Harbour Village. This was built, financed in part by the provincial government, on the occasion of the three hundredth anniversary of the founding and settlement of New Brunswick. The principal exhibit in the museum is a magnificent collection of stuffed birds, gathered by the late Allan Moses from the island and adjacent waters.

In 1913, Mr. Ernest Joy, a naturalist friend of Mr. Moses, saw and shot an albatross in the waters of this northern clime, and Joy gave the rare specimen to Moses, who mounted it. The American Museum of Natural History in New York offered to buy it at a great price but Moses would not sell. However, he traded the bird for a place on an African safari as taxidermist. The expedition was conducted by Sterling Rockefeller to search for the rare green broadbill. After searching for a long time with no success, Moses contracted a fatal case of dysentery. He looked up from his sickbed one day and saw the object of the expedition on a tree overhead. He shot it and as he lay dying himself, with the bird in his arms, Rockefeller promised him anything he wanted. Moses was distressed that so much was spent scouring distant lands for rare specimens while species were becoming extinct in his own country. He asked that Rockefeller purchase Kents Islands off Grand Manan as a sanctuary.

On his return, Rockefeller bought the islands and gave them to Bowdoin College, which now administers them as a sanctuary and research site. Dr. Charles E. Huntington, a Bowdoin professor of biology, is now the director.

It is reported that twenty-one petrels were trapped at this station and taken to England to be released. Nineteen of them showed up back at Kents Island in a short time.

Allan Moses's collection of Grand Manan birds was housed in the schoolhouse and was not easily available to the public, but now they are beautifully displayed in lighted cases. There is a good exhibit of the geology of Grand Manan in the basement and there are interesting displays of tools and of relics from wrecks that have come ashore on the island. In front of the museum is the main yard of a sailing vessel, which gives some notion of how heavy was the gear in commercial sailing ships.

Mr. Eric Allaby is now in charge of the museum. He is a most interesting person, well informed on Grand Manan history, and a remarkably capable artist.

There is an airport with a grass landing strip near Swallowtail for those in a hurry.

The skipper bound for Saint John should plan to leave North Head on the last of the ebb tide, moving in the slack water as he leaves the island. The full force of six hours of flood tide will then boost him up the New Brunswick shore at two knots or better. Grand Manan authorities recommend running across for Lepreau and then running up the shore, rather than going directly for Partridge Island, in order to catch the stronger flood current close to the cliffs. Keep well off Lepreau or else get close under the shore, for a nasty rip develops off the light. The direct course for Partridge Island avoids this but should bring you close enough to the shore to hear the horns at Lepreau and Musquash. Coming west from Saint John, there is a good deal to be said for making North Head rather than Head Harbour, Campobello. Not only are there horns at Swallowtail and Northern Head, but there is a radio direction-finder station at Southwest Head, which is very helpful, even though the signal comes over the land. The RDF at West Quoddy Head is of such low power as to be of little use on this run. Another alternative is Blacks Harbour. If you make Lepreau and the whistle inside the Wolves, it is an easy run to Pea Point, with an excellent horn to run for.

Seal Cove, New Brunswick (4340). Make the whistle off Southwest Head and then the bell east of it. This will take you clear of Buck Rock, marked only by a can. However, it breaks noisily and can usually be identified thus. Do not try to follow the shore inside Buck Rock, because you will run into one of Grand Manan's most productive weirs. Round the breakwater into the made harbor at Seal Cove and tie up to the pile driver used to set weirs. This is unlikely to move at irregular hours and avoids the necessity of long lines to the wharf.

Fishing in recent years has been profitable on Grand Manan. Serious efforts are being made to conserve herring resources with a quota system. Lobsters can be taken only in the winter, when the price is high and the lobsters are hard. One Grand Manan fisherman was reported to the writer as having brought in 3600 pounds of lobsters in one day —an almost incredible catch. The waters around Grand Manan are not easily accessible, are highly productive, and are so rough, tide scoured, and obscured by fog that few but Grand Manan people fish them. One

Grand Manan resident declared flatly, "There are no poor fishermen." Despite this categorical statement, it is worth remembering that a boat rugged enough for these waters is expensive. When one adds to the cost of the hull the cost for a reliable engine, radar, Decca or Loran C, sonar, radio, and all the electric and hydraulic gear necessary for modern fishing, one has a tremendous capital investment. The educational qualifications necessary to operate and maintain it are not inconsiderable and are not all acquired in school. It might not be unfair to refer to a modern fisherman as an engineer in charge of a fish delivery system.

Seal Cove is a delightful town, busy in an unhurried way. There is a store that is a pleasant gathering place as well as a source of food and refreshment. The business of the town is fish—principally herring. There is a sardine factory and there are a number of smokehouses. The latter can be identified at once by the vents along the ridgepole, sheltered by a little roof above them and by the spicy aroma of driftwood smoke and salt herring. The fish are first heavily salted for a week or less according to taste and then strung on sticks run in through the gills and out the mouth. The sticks are hung on racks in the bottom of the smokehouse over a driftwood fire built on the dirt floor. Day by day they are moved to higher racks until they are finished just under the roof. When the fish come out, they are a beautiful red-gold color. To prepare a smoked herring, cut a strip off the belly, remove the head, and wiggle the fish as if it were swimming. This loosens the flesh from the bone. Open the creature up, remove the two sides of meat, peel off the skin and store in sealed Mason jars. Smoked herring can be eaten "as is" with beer or soaked out and either fried or boiled.

Herring is the economic mainstay of the island, and in recent years the herring run has been thin. More visitors have come with the new car ferry, but Grand Manan has had some hard times. One ingenious resident, alongside whom the writer lay in 1968, was doing a profitable business searching for wrecks among the ledges to the southeast of the island. With an electronic device to indicate the presence of metal and with information from draggers who had fouled their gear, he went out and salvaged what he could find by scuba diving. He had just recently found a steamer loaded with copper rods. Only gold could have been more valuable.

The vessels you will see at Grand Manan are heavy Nova Scotia-built craft. The lobstermen and fishermen use a big broad-sterned boat with high bow and low waist, heavily powered and equipped with good electronic gear. Sardine carriers are usually double ended to render them easier to maneuver in the weirs and are equipped with pumps like great vacuum cleaners to suck the fish out of the seines and scale them.

The scales are used for pearl essence, which is used in shirt buttons and fire extinguisher foam, among other things. These vessels are built heavily of knotty spruce and designed to navigate the Bay of Fundy in winter—a rugged assignment.

From Seal Cove it is possible to explore Wood Island and the Kent Islands, where Bowdoin College maintains an ornithological and oceanographic station. Also one can run up the east side of the island on the flood tide to Grand Harbour and on to North Head, but the navigator must be very much alert here. These are dangerous waters, with very uneven bottom, violent tides, and dense and frequent fog. Some of the channels are dry at low water, the buoys lying high and dry.

If your schedule affords a day ashore, Seal Cove is an excellent place to spend it. Walk south on the tar road through pretty rolling country, by snug houses, to the point where the road crosses quite a big brook and turns to gravel. Here there is a wood road to the right that leads across to the cliffs. On the way, it becomes a trail and pretty nearly peters out, but it will get you there. The cliffs are breathtaking, especially with the fog blowing up over them and the black water below. The rock is crumbly and breaks off in long vertical slivers, so take no chances on these cliffs. It is not difficult to follow the shore south toward Southwest Head. You will find a sign marking the spot where William and Lucas Jones were wrecked in February 1963. After a snowstorm they were raking moss off Haycock Harbor when their outboard motor died. The wind came off northwest and bitter cold. In their open skiff they drifted across the channel and struck close to Southwest Head. Their skiff was destroyed, and they were nearly drowned. However, William managed to scale the cliff and get to the lighthouse through the heavy snow, whence help was sent to his brother. Few men wrecked on these cliffs are so lucky.

It is a long walk back to Seal Cove, but you may be fortunate enough to get a ride.

In addition to its natural charm for the casual visitor, the island is of unique interest to the geologist and historian. Grand Manan comprises two great and widely differing sections, dividing it almost from end to end: the western section identified in 1839 by Dr. Abraham Gesner, provincial geologist, as trap rock, and the eastern as schistose rock. The actual contact of the two sections is visible at Red Point, near Seal Cove, but cannot be seen at Whale Cove at the north, as it is buried under the beach. The formations of the eastern section range in age from twice to many times that of the western. The latter is of the Triassic period, extending from 160 to 185 million years ago, while the eastern section is of the Palaeozoic and Pre-Cambrian eras, extending from 360 to perhaps 1500 million years ago. The western section constitutes the only extensive example of Triassic igneous rock in New Brunswick, and Red Point affords one of the few easily accessible views of these geological formations in contact.

To those who know Grand Manan, it is one of the few unspoiled spots on the continent. It has a simple charm unmatched along the coast.

The amateur sailor with a staunch and well-equipped boat and a competent navigator would add great interest to his cruise by spending a few days at Grand Manan.

CHAPTER XIV

West Quoddy Head to Calais, Maine

General Remarks. The waters described in this chapter are shown in detail on chart 801. Starting at West Quoddy Head and running north, they include Lubec Channel, Cobscook Bay west of Eastport, Friar Roads between Eastport and Campobello Island, Western Passage leading from Eastport north into the mouth of the St. Croix River, Head Harbour Passage along the northwest shore of Campobello Island, the two Letite Passages from the Bay of Fundy into Passamaquoddy Bay, that bay itself with two small tributaries, and finally the St. Croix River as far as Calais. Of this country, Campobello Island, Deer Island, the northern and eastern shores of Passamaquoddy Bay and of the St. Croix River are Canadian territory. It is often clear in the bay when the fog lies thick outside. Although it is all interesting country, the best cruising ground is "the blue Passamaquoddy."

This large protected bay is something quite unexpected to one coming in through Lubec Narrows or Letite Passage out of the cold Fundy fog. It is likely to be warm and sunny with much less fog and tidal current. The shores are high and bold with dramatic cliffs, jutting promontories, and steep beaches. There are few yachts, some sardiners, frequent Canadian ferries, and a great deal of bird life. Besides St. Andrews, there are several pleasant anchorages in the bay.

Tidal Conditions. Anyone navigating the waters to the north and west of Campobello Island should realize that the tides in those waters are controlled by the stream that enters and leaves north of Campobello, rather than by that which enters and leaves through Lubec Narrows. This statement should make clear the information contained in the following paragraph.

The flood south of Campobello Island sets to the northeast. In Quoddy Roads and Lubec Narrows the current starts to run south one and one-half hours before high water and north at about low water. It attains a velocity of from 4 to 8 knots. North of Campobello the flood sets in a southwesterly direction and splits, going south of Moose Island into Cobscook Bay and north through the Western Passage. Hence, when bound north from Lubec toward Eastport, after passing Treat Island, head over toward Campobello Island on the flood tide. The flood runs southwest along the eastern side of Deer Island. The floods in the Western Passage are stronger than the ebbs, attaining 6 knots during spring tides. There is a strong whirlpool just southwest of the lower point of Deer Island. The current runs for three-fourths of an hour after the tide table shows high and low water. Through Letite Passage the flood sets to the north, and the ebb the reverse. This current meets the current through Head Harbour Passage about half-way between Head Harbour and the White Horse. There is said to be good fishing in the Head Harbour eddy.

An experienced correspondent writes: "Head Harbour Passage develops into a dangerous breaking inlet off the light during and after northeast storms. I have cruised extensively in both oceans and never seen rougher water for a cruising boat."

In proceeding northward through the Western Passage, one will find that the tide swirls off Eastport. A small boat going north against the tide should stay close to the west shore. There is a swift current on the ebb around Deer Point, making north between Deer and Indian Islands. By going up the west shore one profits by the eddies behind the points. Avoid the old weir off Kendall Head, covered at high water. The best general rule for this passage is to hug the American shore on all tides if bound north, the Deer Island shore if bound south.

If forced to make this passage with an overnight stop, Clam Cove on Deer Island is possible, open only to the south, but there are no supplies. Farther up on the west shore is North Harbour, a good anchorage. Anchor southeast of where chart 801 says 40, southeast of the weir.

The waters of the narrow passage between Moose and Deer Islands are frequently white with thousands of gulls and terns snatching fish from the boiling waters.

Quoddy Roads, Me. (13328   801). Quoddy Roads are open southward and eastward. The best anchorage is northward of Quoddy Head, but this is recommended only if you miss your tide.

Lubec Narrows (13328   801). This narrow and shallow channel, now spanned by a bridge with a vertical clearance of 47 feet at a mean high water, can be a real adventure. The tide at full strength runs 6 knots or better. A correspondent writes:

I would suggest a very strong word of caution to all regarding the tidal current under the Lubec-Campobello bridge. We ran through with the tide behind us and had all we could do to prevent piling up on the supporting piers. The eddies on the bay side are fierce, and even the sardine carriers have difficulty getting through.

There are several things to keep carefully in mind if you are planning to enter Passamaquoddy Bay under the Lubec bridge:

1) Measure accurately the height of your mast *above the water.*

2) Remember that the tidal current ceases to run north and becomes slack half an hour to an hour before high water and shortly begins to run south, even though the tide is still rising. The current is slack again at about the time of low water. Of course these times vary with the phases of the moon and with the wind.

3) Consult the chart below and determine the clearance under the bridge with respect to mean low water.

4) Consult the tide table and correct the clearance for the height of the tide on the date in question.

5) If it is going to be a very near thing, note that the curve gives height under the navigation light, which hangs about 18 inches below the underside of the bridge.

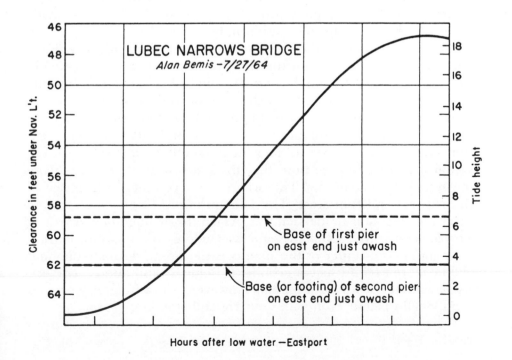

Hours after low water —Eastport

6) Check your arithmetic. If the calculations are all correct and if you have forgotten nothing, you will have an uneventful passage. Good luck.

You may have implicit confidence in the chart. Mr. Alan Bemis constructed it, and his account of its construction is printed below.

With more fixed bridges crossing our waterways every year (and dynamite hard to come by), it is helpful to know their vertical clearance precisely. Published clearance is usually figured at mean high water, and down Fundy way the stage of the tide makes all the difference. We all need to know our exact mast height too. Height above the water seems to be the only parameter not included in the CCA Measurement Rule so many owners don't know it exactly.

Last July *Cirrus,* with Dwight, Helen and Davie Shepler, and myself aboard, decided to determine some of these half-knowns under the new Lubec Narrows bridge, which allows landlubbers to roll on four wheels from Lubec to Campobello Island. Luck made our calibration easy with a 0.0 low tide at Eastport that morning, i.e., mean low water. We ran up a whisker pole on the flag halyard flying 8.4 feet above any more permanent part of the rig and cruised up and down stream under the center span until, as the tide rose, the whisker pole finally struck the green center navigation light.

We kept a log on the time of day; observed various markers awash and such, providing data for the clearance chart submitted herewith; then departed speedily on the flood, to run Cobscook Falls before the puzzled Lubec populace sicked the Harbor Master on us.

The published figure is 47 feet at mean high. Our calibration indicates this is the correct figure for clearance under the green navigation light, which seemed to hang down about 18 inches below the bridge structure. Please note that there are wide departures from mean high and mean low. The bridge has seven piers, three east of the channel and four west. The pair on either side of the channel carry big steel and timber fenders, which throw huge bow waves in the tide and leave turbulence and back eddies below them. Placing your ship in the center of the span is easier going downstream, and will be more exciting as you wonder if Bemis's calibration is correct. (No guarantee made or implied.) However, it is a long way around Campobello Island even with your rig still standing.

Lubec, Me. (13328 801). Lubec is a small town, population 1800, on the northeastern tip of Lubec Neck, a 1½-mile peninsula extending northeast from the mainland toward the New Brunswick island of Campobello. North of the peninsula is Johnson Bay; south of it, Lubec Channel. It is the easternmost town in the United States, of which West Quoddy Head (the easternmost point in the United States) is a part, edging out Eastport, 3 miles to the north, by ¾ of a mile.

A standpipe, 1½ miles west of the town, a church spire, and a stack on the water front are prominent in approaching the town.

The most convenient place to tie up at Lubec is the public marina, north of the town behind a breakwater. A visitor in 1974 reported 8 to 10 feet at low water here. For anchorage, proceed to Johnson Bay to the west of the town, an excellent but large anchorage for small boats. All supplies are available close by the marina. Gasoline and Diesel oil will be delivered by tank truck; water is at Peacock's dock just above the bridge. Groceries may be had at several stores. There are two places to obtain a meal ashore. There are two rooming houses, The Triangle and Stuart's, and a six-unit motel, The Eastland, near the Lubec Airport.

The post office and Customs headquarters are located at the end of the bridge.

Though distant less than 3 miles by water from Lubec, Eastport has no ferry to Lubec. The only alternative is a 40-mile journey by road. See the account of Lubec Narrows, above, for data on the bridge and the current in the narrows.

There is a 2000-foot air strip 2.4 miles west of Lubec. It is lighted upon request.

Mr. Carroll Peacock and his son, Robert S. Peacock, of the R.J. Peacock Canning Company, are authorities for marine information in this section. They are most hospitable to visiting yachtsmen. Don't pass by Lubec without going through one of the sardine canning factories, on which depends much of the prosperity of our easternmost town.

The Washington County Vocational and Technical Institute was started in Lubec, although it is scheduled to be moved soon to Eastport. It is a boat-building school in which forty post-secondary students are taught the exacting skills of building wooden boats.

The two-year course includes all the steps in the construction of a wooden boat, from design consideration through lofting, pattern-making, and actual construction. It also includes a study of costs: time, material and overhead. This involves careful stockroom control, and each student punches the time clock twice daily or more so he will know where his time went. In the course of his first year, each student builds a Whitehall rowboat to demonstrate and make practical his skills. In the summer, between school years, the first-year students go "out on co-op," that is, work at cooperating boat shops in Maine. The second year is spent in building a small Buzzards Bay sloop and a fiberglass peapod.

One may reasonably ask what good can come of teaching hopeful young men a trade that has become obsolete. The answers of some of the instructors are convincing:

Building a wooden boat teaches "working to close dimensions."

"The basic concepts for working in steel, aluminum, or fiberglass are all learned here. For example, a boatbuilder who has his boat-building down pat wouldn't hesitate to tell a welder what to do, but there is no reason why he has to do the welding himself. His job is that of supervisor."

"My major purpose . . . is to make them much more analytic with a lines plan. And my second purpose is to impress on them that boats have balance points."

The director of the whole project is "Junior" Miller, formerly general manager of Southwest Boat Corporation in Southwest Harbor. With the help of his three instructors, he has established a highly effective educational institution to train young men in craftsmanship, design, and business practice. In addition, and far more importantly, he has taught discipline, dedication, imagination, resourcefulness, and self-respect.

Mr. Robert S. Peacock, a citizen of Lubec who has seen the school grow, writes:

This [the school] seems to draw people from Alaska, Oregon, and most all of the other states. They seem to be a pretty dedicated bunch of boys as a whole, one or two being the exception. . . . Most of them go out and work in the shipyards along the coast and it is surprising how many have had families in the shipbuilding industry and have worked around yacht basins etc. and still want to go into the wooden aspects of the yachting field.

Federal Harbor   (13328   801). Those bound up Cobscook Bay or seeking a quieter anchorage than Lubec or Eastport should investigate this harbor on the east side of Denbow Neck below Horan Head. The upper part of the harbor dries out, but there should be good anchorage under Black Head or behind Hog Island or Long Island.

Cobscook Bay, Me. (13328   801). Cobscook is a large bay full of islands and narrow passages, and very pretty. On account of the heavy tides, which in some places attain the force of rapids, it is not much frequented by strangers. But, aside from the falls west of Falls Island, there is nothing that ordinary care cannot overcome.

Note that nun 8 on Birch Point Ledge between Birch Point and Seward Neck usually tows under on every run of tide.

On the high water one can go almost to Dennysville but must anchor 1½ miles below the town to stay afloat at low water.

There is a good anchorage between Birch Islands and Hallowell Island, where chart 801 gives a 9-foot depth. Leighton Point Cove, called Schooner Cove on the chart, is a good anchorage outside the falls. It is said to be quite a trick to get in here at the full force of the tide, for the tide runs by Denbow Point about as hard as it does through Lubec Narrows.

There is said to be good anchorage off Coffins Point, south of Falls Island.

Cobscook Falls, Me. (13328 801). These are reversible falls, located just west of Falls Island, where chart 801 reads 57. They run 10 knots at full run and are something to see. Only crazy men, like the one who provided this data (and who prefers to remain anonymous), run them at full run. He reports that the safest time for sane folk to pass through is at low slack, because all hazards are well above water. The maximum strength of flood current occurs about two hours before high water at Eastport.

The inward run of tide is much more turbulent than the outrun, due to the rock formation. On the inward run the current flows straight past Falls Island to a large ledge, Roaring Bull, which makes out from the western tip of Falls Island. This forces the current violently over toward the north shore, from which it swirls back south to meet the current coming around the south side of the island. This southbound current carries one's boat off Government Rock, located just west of figure 57 on chart 801. Two Hour Rock is just to the southeast, southwest of figure 21 on the same chart. It uncovers two hours after high water. In the lee of Roaring Bull a big whirlpool develops.

On the outward run, however, the current follows a much straighter course.

A more cautious approach is south of Falls Island.

Because of the interest of venturesome cruisers in running the falls, the following is presented from an experienced cruising man, who has been running them for many years in a 45-foot yawl:

Water is swift, with plenty of huge haycocks, and tosses one around plenty. Skipper should proceed up the bay on the rising tide from Eastport. As he approaches the falls, he should place himself in the middle of the stream. The detail chart is quite accurate. Stream will carry one around Roaring Bull, then one must starboard the helm to avoid points of rock to starboard. A large swirl carries one to port after passing Roaring Bull. Beware of the big whirlpool west of the Bull. There are no particular difficulties about going out with the tide if one places oneself in the center of the stream above the rapids. Current runs 10 to 12 knots; should not be attempted in dinghies or small boats, which whirlpools suck down. Dennys River is a charming, isolated spot.

An equally experienced authority adds: "I would discourage this. For anyone unaccustomed to these tides, it's fearsome."

Eastport, Me. (13328   801). Between Eastport and Deer Island is a tidal commotion truly frightening to the skipper unprepared for it. It is caused by the tide coming in north of Campobello meeting the tide running up Lubec Narrows. Huge whirlpools 30 feet in diameter and 3 or 4 feet deep spin even big sardiners halfway around. Great boils rush up, making mounds off which a yacht slides sideways. The whole maelstrom is in constant motion, so passage through it, especially in light weather, can be very exciting. With a fair current and with power or a working breeze, there is no great danger to a seagoing yacht, but a small open boat might find it very dangerous indeed. In rough weather or in a storm, it is too furious to approach, and under any weather conditions it is best taken at slack water.

Eastport now has a heavy wharf and breakwater that provides a protected place to tie up out of the tide. The Customs officer is usually to be found here, and yachts returning from Canada should check in. All members of the crew should be provided with positive identification and proof of citizenship, just to be on the safe side.

In 1976 it was necessary to lug gasoline and fuel oil in cans. Ice can sometimes be bought at a restaurant toward the north end of town. The well-known ship chandlery of S.L. Wadsworth, on the wharf next to the breakwater, was completely destroyed on February 2, 1976, when a heavy gale on the top of a moon tide lifted the building off its piles and dumped it overboard, where it disintegrated into its component planks. The store was reestablished south of the Custom House on the main street and is rebuilding its inventory. For pictures of what happened to Eastport on Ground Hog Day, call at the office of the *Quoddy Times.*

Eastport has stores of all kinds to supply the wants of the cruising man and to restock his lockers. Just above the town, in 1976, was a new marina run by Fred Stinson. He had a wharf and floats, with plans for yachts to tie up alongside, providing water and electricity connections. Ashore he has a restaurant and bar. It is almost the only place of its kind east of Jonesport and promises to provide more services than Jonesport. Mr. Stinson is an imaginative and energetic entrepreneur, most anxious to be of service to yachtsmen.

Eastport is primarily a herring town. 1976 was a good herring year. The sardine factory was busy. The fish-meal plant at Estes Head was spreading its foul effluvium up the bay, people were painting houses, refurbishing stores, and generally looking up. Talk of oil was less strident. Summer people were beginning to discover the region and to enjoy it in spite of, or because of, its distance from megalopolis. It is to be hoped that the good herring years continue.

Eastport has cast longing looks at the oil industry; and although many people quite sincerely oppose it, others wish to bring it in. Consider the plight of a 100,000-ton tanker trying to negotiate the tide between Eastport and Deer Island!

During his administration, Franklin Roosevelt started the Quoddy Project to generate electricity by impounding water in Cobscock Bay at high tide. It was never completed, but is periodically revived and reconsidered.

You will notice on the chart the international boundary line running between Eastport and Deer Island, past Lubec, through Lubec Narrows and Quoddy Roads and then down Grand Manan Channel. The story goes that Daniel Webster and Lord Ashburton, having agreed that the boundary line should follow the main stream of the St. Croix River, met to float down the river and establish the axis of the stream. Mr. Webster enjoyed a good dinner and an excellent rum punch. He lay down for a brief nap, which cost us, if not Deer Island, certainly Campobello and Grand Manan. Just a very little nudge with an oar may have made the difference between Head Harbor Passage and Lubec Narrows.

They say that the fates of nations are decided as often at the cocktail bar as they are at the council table.

Welshpool, Campobello, N.B. (13328 801). This fishing village, across Friar Roads from Eastport, is on the north side of Friar Bay. There is a summer colony, including what was for many years the summer home of the Franklin D. Roosevelt family.

In the summer of 1966, President Johnson and the Prime Minister of

Canada met at the Roosevelt house to dedicate a memorial to the memory of President Roosevelt. The Roosevelt estate is now open to the public and is well worth a visit.

The anchorage is rather exposed, but there is a good wharf. The *Canadian Coast Pilot* states that in westerly weather small craft can find good protection alongside this wharf in 12½ feet.

Harbour de Loutre, Campobello, N.B. (801). Though not so snug or picturesque as Head Harbour on the north end of the island, this anchorage on the northwest side is excellent and well protected. After entering, proceed south, leaving the black-and-red spar buoy to port. Anchor south of the point and weir making out from the west shore, off two houses on the west bank.

Head Harbour, N.B.   (13328   801). One coming east from Cutler will find Head Harbour a convenient stop and a good place from which to take off for Saint John. It is easy of access and perfectly protected. Coming up from Cutler, make Sail Rock whistle and set a course to parallel the Campobello shore. When you think you are by Eastern Head, edge in toward the shore until you hear the surf or see the loom of the cliffs. Beyond Nancy Head, as the shore tends more northward, you are likely to get a scale-up. If you do, pass between Head Harbour Island and the end of Campobello, leave all black spars close to port to avoid old weirs, and run up the harbor. If there is no scale-up, keep off the shore until you hear the siren on East Quoddy Head on a bearing north of west. Then run for it and follow the Campobello shore into the harbor. The entrance is quite narrow. As he followed the procedure above, the writer was once confused by soundings of over 100 feet and found that he was following the outer shore of Head Harbour Island.

On the north side of the harbor is a big government wharf much used in the summer by seiners. The wharf on the south side and the big building behind it were built for a fish-meal plant, which for a few years rendered the region most unattractive. It has now been dismantled. Up the middle of the harbor is a string of moorings, most of them without pennants. Visiting yachts may pass a line through the hole in one of the posts and lie to it, if they wish. Rumor always had it that these were winter moorings for big sardiners and perfectly safe for yachts in summer.

However, some picturesque if unsubstantiated background leads us to take a dimmer view. John and Charles Goodyear were brothers who owned a farm together on the northerly side of the harbor. John disliked Charles extremely. Indeed he disliked him so much that one day he sawed their wharf in half down the middle and bade Charles stay on his own side. Later, incensed at Charles's walking to the shore through a field that John thought was his, John bought a wild bull and pastured it in the field. Charles, by judicious use of apples, sugar, carrots, and a charitable disposition, made friends with the bull, who made no objection to his walking through the field. On one occasion, when John entered the field, the bull nearly killed him. John set out the moorings, planning to rent them out to sardiners for winter lay-up. However, it appeared that under Canadian law this was illegal, for everything below high water is public property. John, accordingly, neglected the moorings.

In due course he died, leaving his property to the church, with the proviso that on no account was Charles ever to get any of it. However, Charles, for reasons not stated, bought the moorings from the church, figuring perhaps that they did not come under the ban. He held them for a while and sold them to one Du Gas, who does not maintain them. Thus the gear may be badly deteriorated. Occasionally, I was told, one lets go and a boat goes adrift; but as there is no sea in Head Harbour and the banks are smooth, no harm is done. The writer, before he heard this story, lay on one through the tail end of the 1976 hurricane without incident.

The story came from Ken McCann, present owner of Charles Goodyear's house, now christened Head Harbour Haven. Mr. McCann is most hospitable, will permit the use of his telephone for collect calls, and has a magnificent and intriguing collection of marine antiques, memorabilia, and artifacts.

It is a pleasant walk from the wharf on the north side to Wilson's Beach. Here there are a store, a fish factory, and a packing plant. There used to be a Customs office here, but in 1977 it was discontinued. Mr. Jack Fitzgerald, who has an office in his house, can enter you, a situation that may not last. However, it is worth trying to get your permit here, for Pugsley Wharf in Saint John is a miserable place to land.

The fish plant will sell you shaved ice and may give you a ride back to Head Harbour. There is a post office at Wilson's Beach but none at Head Harbour.

If opportunity offers, explore the south side of Head Harbour. There are excellent and abundant raspberries around the old fish factory.

From Head Harbour it is about 40 miles to Saint John, a reasonable distance to make in six hours with a 2-knot tide running with you.

Wilson's Beach, Campobello, N.B. **(13328 801).** There is a heavy government wharf affording shelter, where gasoline, Diesel fuel, and water are available. Ashore are a store and a post office. If you can find Jack Fitzgerald here, you can enter Canadian Customs, a far better place to do this than Saint John. Otherwise Wilson's Beach offers little to attract the cruising man.

There is a busy fish-packing operation here, owned by the Jackson brothers. Herring are salted and shipped to canneries, smokehouses, and fertilizer plants. Ground fish go to Portland in ice.

Northwest Harbor, Deer Island, N.B. (801). This is a well-protected and very attractive harbor with high, wooded shores dropping steeply to the water; in places there are impressive cliffs. In clear weather, entrance is easy. Often when it is thick offshore, there will be a scale-up north of Campobello that will carry you all the way to Deer Island. Note that the flood tide runs south around the end of Deer Island. Be sure to give the spar outside the harbor a good berth, as the ledge appears to extend beyond it.

Run up the middle of the harbor. Off the cove on the north shore there is a weir and a big ledge. The writer anchored in front of the ledge on a quiet night and all was well. A later visitor reports the bottom is smooth rock there and suggests going farther up the harbor among the old moorings where the bottom is soft. Beware of old weirs on the south shore. There is one that extends a long way into the harbor just before you get to the mouth of the little cove. There is a small settlement at the head of the harbor, but the nearest store is at Richardson.

In getting out of the harbor, especially in the fog, you may find the tide very confusing. The writer found the first of the ebb setting northeast much earlier than expected.

Lords Cove, Deer Island, N.B.   (13328   801). Although one visitor reported 20 feet between St. Helena Island and Bean Island, the best entrance seems to be up the buoyed channel between St. Helena and Deer Island. When you pick up the range, as shown on the chart, run in. The range is two green lights, but there is a red light on the wharf low down, in front of the other two. The range is marked by day with two white boards. Do not get off the range to port. If you must err, edge to starboard. The range leaves the white beacon close to port and brings you into a bottle-tight little anchorage with 3 fathoms, mud bottom, and several apparently unused moorings. The steamer lands at the wharf under the range lights. There is a landing float at the wharf. The place was deserted when the writer visited. Not a soul was to be seen. However, at steamer time there is more activity.

Coming from the north, the shores are bold and the dangers are exposed at low water. Halibut Rock is big, flat on top, and grassy. There are two weirs on Bean Island, one right under the ledge, which makes out from the easterly point. There is plenty of room to beat in through this entrance and run up the range as described above.

It is a short walk to Richardson, where there are a village and a government wharf with 6 feet at low water.

Saint Andrews, N.B. (13328   801)   (4332). In approaching Saint Andrews from Eastport and the south, stay in the main channel of the Saint Croix River on the flood tide. On the ebb, hold close to the American shore, swinging into the bays to avoid the current and out around the points to avoid the shoals. The easiest entrance is from the western side of Navy Island, identified by whitish sand cliffs. Make the flashing buoy and run in, following the channel as buoyed. The United States yachtsman will be surprised by the small size of Canadian buoys, by the frequency of spar buoys, and by the high numbers they bear.

There may be a spare mooring. Guest moorings are marked with red balloons. If none is available, anchor where inclination dictates.

Entrance from the east is easy after you find Tongue Shoal, which is now much easier than it used to be, for there is a proper light structure on it. Thence, simply follow the line of red buoys. Don't expect anything impressive from the red light on the end of the wharf. It is just a light bulb on a white pole.

Land at the float on the east side of the long easterly wharf. There is said to be 15 feet alongside, but the writer measured 7 feet in 1976. If you have not previously secured a Canadian cruising permit, your first stop is the Custom House at the head of the wharf. Remember that Saint Andrews is on Atlantic Daylight Time, one hour ahead of Eastern Daylight Time. Do not stir up the Customs officers on Sunday as it will cost overtime pay.

Water is piped down the wharf, but unless you have a considerable length of hose, you will have to lug it in buckets to your tank. There is no gas or Diesel oil, but a call to Esso or Imperial Oil Co. will bring a tank truck. Ice is available at a sporting-goods store and there is a gas station to the right on the main street. Also to the right are a good market and a laundry. The liquor store is a short walk down the main street to the left. The Sea Breeze and the Shire-Town Inn are good restaurants.

The town of St. Andrews is essentially one long street, with all necessary and many interesting but unnecessary stores. Besides grocery, meat, liquor, and drug stores, and restaurants, there is a County Crafts shop famous for hand-knit sweaters, each in a unique pattern. There are also china shops carrying all manner of delicate and unusual English china.

There is a large hotel overlooking the town and another on the main street. Train, bus, and air connections are easily made from St. Andrews.

Because cruisers from "the States," having come to St. Andrews, may wish to have some of the historical background of this most attractive region, the following footnote is taken from an article by Earl M. Benson in *The New York Times:*

Among the town's early settlers were Loyalists who came in 1783 in square-rigged vessels from Castine, Me. They thought Castine, on the eastern bank of the Penobscot River, would be in British territory. When they learned that the St. Croix River was to be the boundary line, they sailed farther east to what is now St. Andrews. Some of them even took down their houses in sections and towed them in scows behind the ships. There are still many descendants of these Loyalists living in the town.

These pioneers believed in town-planning. Before building began, the land was surveyed and laid out in squares. The thirteen side-streets, which begin at the water front, were named for King George III and his twelve children.

At the wharf head the visitor will find one of the most rewarding spots in St. Andrews, the County Craft Shop, where the yard is bright with yarns drying in the breeze from the bay. Inside the wide doors are the articles made in local cottages and farmhouses.

There are several shops of interest to the tourist. In one grocery store, established 130 years ago, one can find tempting foods from all parts of the world. Two china shops display sets of Wedgwood, Spode, Chelsea, Royal Doulton and Belleek that are as complete as those in many large cities. Another shop offers the products of various New Brunswick handicrafts—pottery, wooden ware, hand-wrought iron, and homemade jams, jellies, and cheeses.

The story of the building of Greenock Church is a strange one. In the early days there was but one church in the town, the Church of England, and the rector offered his church to the Presbyterians who had no place to worship. At a public meeting a townsman arose and charged the Presbyterians with being "too mean to build a church of their own." This aroused the ire of Christopher Scott, a wealthy sea captain, who came from Greenock, Scotland. He declared that the Presbyterians would have a church like the one in his native town and he would pay for it all himself. He kept his word and the church was built in 1824.

This church, with its Christopher Wren spire, is remarkable for its fine proportions and excellent design. It is unique in that it was constructed without nails or any other metal except that which was used in the locks and door hinges. All woodwork was fastened together by wooden pegs, and today the church appears to be as sturdy as when it was built. Below the steeple clock is a colored bas-relief of a green oak tree, the coat of arms of Greenock. The three-deck pulpit of Honduras mahogany and curly maple, its panels edged with small hand-carved acorns, is a masterpiece.

Guides will take fishing parties for landlocked salmon and lake trout on Chamcook Lake. Small-mouth black bass are found in Wheaton Lake and there is good fly-fishing for speckled trout and Atlantic salmon in the Digdeguash River.

There are two golf courses, one a tricky nine-hole and the other an eighteen-hole course overlooking Passamaquoddy Bay. Greens fees are moderate, and lunches are served at the golf clubhouse.

St. Croix Island, Me. (13328   801). Though there is no harbor here, the island affords an interesting stop on the way upriver. It was on this island that Pierre du Guast (Sieur de Monts) and Champlain and their men celebrated their first Christmas in the New World in 1604.

Of vastly greater historical importance is the fact that this island saw the first European settlement in New England. Here the French first settled in the New World. They remained only one winter, moving on to Nova Scotia, which became a British possession through the Treaty of Utrecht in 1713. Professor W.F. Ganong, who has written the best history of the island, has said, "From the day the keel of her small boat grated on the beach of Dochet [St. Croix] Island, this continent has never been without a population of those races which have made the history of the principal part of America—the French and the English." The island was made a national park in July 1949.

Anchor about 100 yards west of the white conical building on the west shore. The bell on the structure's west side is no longer used. There is no fog signal. But watch for a ledge, covered at high water, just northwest of this spot. Approach cautiously.

In a ledge at the highest spot on the island is a small metal marker with the legend "International Boundary." This may have been true once, but today the boundary between the United States and New Brunswick is in the middle of the river to the east. The United States Government owns part of the island, but not all of it. The light is unwatched.

The only historical marker is a metal plaque on a boulder on the northeast side of the island reading as follows:

> To Commemorate
> The Discovery and Occupation
> of this Island by
> De Monts and Champlain
> Who Naming It
> L'Isle Saincte Croix
> Founded here 26 June 1604
> The French Colony of Acadia
> Then the Only Settlement
> Of Europeans North of Florida
> This Tablet is Erected by
> Residents of the St. Croix Valley
> 1904

The burying ground, where a few skeletons have been unearthed, is in the plateau at the south end of the island. But there are now no traces of it.

Anyone interested in the historical background of this region should read the references to St. Croix Island in *Voyages of Samuel de Champlain* by W.L. Grant (Charles Scribner's Sons, 1907). The island was discovered in 1604 and named by Sieur de Monts "Isle de Saint Croix" (Holy Cross Island) on account of the "cross" formed above the island by the river from the west, Oak Bay from the north, and Warwig Creek from the east. A footnote states that at the celebration of the three-hundredth anniversary of its settlement "it was resolved that it be henceforth called Saint Croix Island." The Maine Historical Society has published a well-illustrated volume, *Tercentenary of De Monts' Settlement at Saint Croix Island, June 25, 1904* (Portland, 1905). The French had a hard winter on the island, thirty-five of the original band of seventy-nine dying of scurvy. The survivors left the following summer for Port Royal, N.S., later renamed by the British Annapolis Royal.

There is an excellent account of the settlement, "The French at Saint Croix Island—the First European Settlement in New England," in a pamphlet entitled *French in New England.* See also *Saint Croix—the Sentinel River,* by Guy Murchie (Duell, Sloan and Pearce, New York, 1947).

A fitting conclusion to any reference to St. Croix Island is a few lines written by Henry Milner Rideout for the Tercentenary of St. Croix:

Into the hill-cleft waterways
With ceaseless ebb and flow astir,
Into the sunset blaze
Craftily steering,
High on her mast
They bore the banner of Old France
To the new Land Acadia, and cast
Their anchor by this island of the bays
At the commandment of Pierre du Gast
And merry, brown Champlain, the King's geographer.

Chamcook, N.B. (13328   801). A correspondent writes:

Chamcook Harbor, N.B. is an excellent though deserted anchorage. It is large but secure, with excellent holding ground. The entrance to the outer harbor, between two buoys, is very narrow, and the tide runs like a trout brook for a few hundred feet, but there is little current inside.

Entrance to the inner harbor is a gap not over 100 feet wide between two sandbars, just as you pass an ancient factory undergoing renovation, and a new shipyard producing trawlers. We draw 4 feet and entered on the bottom of the tide, using the color of the water as a guide. We used the lead to find a sheltered berth at the head of the inner harbor and spent a couple of pleasant hours toward high water watching the automobiles driving across the sand spit to Ministers Island. It was early evening of a very Canadian Sunday, and competition was keen to see which would be the last car that could possibly make it before high tide covered the road.

This is one of the few really secure small-boat anchorages in Passamaquoddy Bay.

Digdeguash Harbour, N.B.   (13328   801). This pleasant anchorage is well protected except in a heavy southerly. It is possible to go up on the tide under the bridge and into the pond, but it is an adventure that demands some advance exploration in the dinghy. It is said to be a beautiful and worthwhile trip. There is a government wharf in Digdeguash Harbour on the west side with a depth of 17 feet at *high* water and a cribwork of timbers on which a vessel can ground out at low water.

Magaguadavic River (4331) (13328   801). This river is easily located by the high land at Midjik Bluff. Here the river is wide and deep, but it quickly narrows. One can go up as far as Saint George on the tide and lie over in a basin there. A correspondent writes:

> Specifically, in terms of the *Guide,* St. George, at the head of the of the Magaguadavic River is one of the most fascinating places I have visited. The run up the river is not difficult. However, it is best to have the Canadian Chart No. 4331. The harbor at St. George is surrounded by high hills and is like a millpond, even in a storm. I recommend spending the night there and probably you will be the only boat there. The pulp mill is now inoperative, except that the generator is operated to generate electricity for the power company. Earlier versions of the *Guide* gave it more space and I feel it deserves it. On August 20 we were told that we were the third "yacht" to be there this year. The Roosevelts used to visit often and I met a former fisherman at Campobello who used to go up in a 70-foot vessel. The dock is now out of commission. When we were there, 2-foot salmon were jumping all around the boat (but alas not biting on *anything*). I would rank the stores as *very* well stocked but Gerry Cans are needed if gas or water is desired. The waterfalls and literal "millpond" are spectacular, to say the very least. The town is close to the harbor and the people most friendly and accommodating.
>
> What the American yachtsman has to get used to is that in Canada many of the buoys are narrow wooden stakes and they are not only hard to see but also they may lie flat at low water. In the latter event, a line of four gulls seemingly standing on the water probably means that that is where the buoy is likely to be. A cautious approach usually is rewarding.

Before anchoring in the basin at Saint George, it is well to sound carefully to be sure you are not lying over a shifting mud bank. A visitor to the harbor speaks of waking up in the night with a strange feeling. His daughter also awoke, got out of her bunk, and the yacht fell over on one side. She had been balancing on her keel, left high and dry by the tide. The slight shift of weight did the business.

Letite Passage, Deer Island, N.B. (801). This is the principal deepwater entrance to Passamaquoddy Bay. The tide runs through here with considerable violence, making swirls, eddies, and boils. However, with power or a fair wind, one can run through with a fair tide. There is no difficulty about making the run at slack water. There are good fog signals on Pea Point and Bliss Island. There is a whistle off Mascabin Point.

The tide runs southeast on the ebb out of Passamaquoddy Bay and then pulls southerly down the Deer Island shore, making it a short beat down to Lord's Cove, Northwest Harbour, or Head Harbour. Mr. Gerry Peer of Saint John, who has cruised this region for many years, writes: "Having used both Letite and Little Letite passages for years as a means to Passamaquoddy Bay, I find they are an interesting and fascinating area to sail, either charging through with the current or plying your wits against it, but it is no place for a vessel with limited navigation equipment in a fog. Mohawk Ledge has had its share of boats and I don't know of any area I treat with more respect in a fog."

Little Letite Passage, Deer Island, N.B. (801). This is a narrow passage from Passamaquoddy Bay, running south of McMasters Island into Letite Passage with 14 feet at low water. It is not recommended for strangers.

A correspondent writes as follows about this district:

I cruised all these waters last summer. Grand and Little Letite Passages are blemished by the new big high-tension line to Deer Island. Do urge all to run Little Letite Passage, which is good fun and perfectly safe on half tide or better. Wonderful climb and view at McMaster Island. Anchor at Red Pebble Beach, west side of island, at the south of Sea Cave.

Another correspondent adds: "Not good fun if the tide is strong."

Another correspondent declares that there is 6 to 8 feet at low water and notes that the ferry runs without reference to tides. He prefers it to Letite because it is so narrow that even in the fog both sides are visible.

CHAPTER XV

The Coast of New Brunswick and the Saint John River

General Conditions. The 40 miles between Head Harbour or Letite and Saint John can assume a variety of disguises according to the conditions. Usually in the summer the trip is a featureless grind, started at an inconvenient hour to catch the tide and completed under the tension of entering a harbor threatened by ocean steamers. If you are lucky enough to catch a northwest breeze, it is a magnificent sail at an incredible speed by a panorama of cliffs, hills, and forests broken by occasional tiny harbors. But run into a head wind, rain, or a real blow and the trip can be an absolute nightmare, especially when the tide turns against you. Shelters are few and widely spaced. In thick weather or heavy seas they are hard to find, and with a 3½-knot tide running, one's reckoning is soon only a little better than guesswork.

The 40 miles is divided in half by Point Lepreau and the halves subdivided, the western half at The Wolves and the eastern at Split Rock. The first 10 miles from Letite or Campobello to The Wolves has three big fog signals—East Quoddy Head, Bliss Island, and Pea Point. The whistle at The Wolves is a good mark. There are several harbors in this part of the run and slightly less tide than one finds farther east.

The second 10 miles, from The Wolves to Lepreau, is dominated by the diaphone and whistle buoy at Lepreau. The armchair navigator, scanning chart 4334, would assume that little difficulty would be encountered here. The diaphone is positively shattering. The point on which it stands is high and bold. The whistle is well offshore and is big enough and loud enough to be worthy of its position. However, bending over the cabin table on a small boat bound E ¾ S from The Wolves, the situation looks very different—what you can see of it. Many cruising men aver that the fog factory, located on Point Lepreau, turns out a concentrated product experienced at its thickest in this region. Many cruising men who have been by Lepreau frequently have never seen it. The tide runs to the eastward in the first part of the course but soon sets heavily to the north into Mace's Bay. Off the point you will find, even on a still day, a very active tide rip, with short breaking seas and vigorous swirling currents. Standing on the plunging bowsprit, choked by fog, blasted by the diaphone blowing from a bearing it should not occupy, looking and listening for an elusive whistle is not quite the same as studying the chart before that comfortable fire at home.

Once well by Lepreau, however, the worst is over. On the course to Split Rock bell the tide will affect you but little and from there to the buoys off Partridge Island you have the powerful horn and the radio beacon to guide you. Of course you must remember that Saint John is a deep-water port frequented by big steamers. You may find them groping for the fairway buoys or anchored awaiting a tide. A radar reflector is a flimsy but valuable means of defense to be seconded by a powerful foghorn.

There is a good deal to be said for breaking the run at Dipper Harbor, which is about halfway, at Chance, or Musquash. If the breeze is light or you don't travel very fast under engine, you may arrive at Saint John with the tide running against you. Getting up the river under these conditions is hard work, especially as that is a likely time for steamers to be coming down. A layover assures arrival with a fair tide and plenty of time to go up the falls the same day.

If you do want to try it in one piece, consider starting from North Head Harbour or Whale Cove on the last of the ebb tide. The distance is a little less than that from Head Harbour, and there are no obstructions on the course at all. One can home in on the Partridge Island radio beacon right from Grand Manan. The big horns at Lepreau and Musquash will give a check on position as you converge with the shore, but you will be well outside the rip at Lepreau. Going west, the Grand Manan alternative is even more favorable, for the radio beacon on Southwest Head is about in line with Swallowtail. Also note that there are big foghorns on Swallowtail and Northern Head.

Once at Saint John, go up the falls as soon as the tide serves. If you have to wait, the best place is at Pier 2 on the west side.

With the falls astern, you have before you many miles of pleasant river, lovely coves, farmland and wooded hills, lakes and pretty towns. Dangers are fairly well marked now—no more of black cows to port and brown cows to starboard. The swimming is warm. Fog is nearly unknown. The people you meet are almost without exception hospitable. It is nearly perfect cruising ground. Only those cussed ones among us who don't like lotus as a steady diet yearn to get back to salt water.

Preparations. The wise skipper will not leave Grand Manan or Passamaquoddy without the basic equipment recommended in chapter II.

Of these, a reliable and accurately compensated compass is a sine qua non.

One should have Canadian Charts Nos. 4334 (Bay of Fundy, Brier Island to Cape Chignecto), 4314 (Plans of Harbors: Chance, Dipper, Musquash, and Lorneville), 4319 (Saint John Harbor), and 4333 (Point Lepreau to Cape Spencer).

One should also have a copy of *Nova Scotia and Bay of Fundy Pilot, Tables of Hourly Direction and Velocity of the Currents and Time of Slack Water in the Bay of Fundy and Its Approaches,* and the *Bay of Fundy Tide and Current Tables.*

All these may be purchased from the Canadian Hydrographic Service, Surveys and Mapping Branch, Department of Mines and Technical Surveys, Ottawa. Write and ask for a catalogue. With your order, send the exact price of your purchase by International Money Order in Canadian money. A recent and indispensable publication is *Small Craft Guide, Saint John River* published by the Department of the Environment, Ottawa, Canada.

Saint John River Weather

One last comment—the weather in the Saint John River Valley and adjacent area is generally fine in the summer months, a fact that may seem unbelievable after what may often be a long run through dungeon fog to get up the coast to Saint John. Once through the falls, even with the most solid fog condition outside and in the harbor, I have never seen a zero visibility condition in the river proper. There are low ceilings and rain occasionally, as anywhere else in the East, but the weather is generally sunny, warm, and dry. Swimming is superb, as the water is considerably warmer in the river and lakes. The winds prevail from the south and west, with occasionally fresh northwesters when a front has gone by. This makes for ideal sailing along close shores with no sea. Nothing is pleasanter than scudding along among verdant farmlands at 7 knots with not a ripple underneath. The height of the river varies from time to time but only through a foot or so, and I have found the soundings on the charts excellent.

L'Etang Harbour, N.B. (4313). This is a fascinating complex of harbors, coves, and sheltered but striking passages, with heavily wooded islands and high black cliffs, often riddled with caves. It is still almost completely wild. In one cove, the arrival of a 24-foot sloop from the States actually brought a couple of carsful of sightseers. This body of water includes Bliss Harbour, Letite Harbour, Blacks Harbour, and possibly Back Bay, as well as many unnamed, uninhabited anchorages. Chart 4313 appears to be an accurate guide, and hazards are few except for countless abandoned weirs. In this area the gunk-holing cruiser will be well advised to reach his anchorage on the bottom of the tide when possible. Otherwise the cockpit conference before supper will be enlivened with the appearance of weir stake after weir stake, each one nearer than the last. Trying to anticipate the pattern is an absorbing pastime.

A fairly recent visitor to L'Etang adds:

This is fascinating, as the *Guide* says, and beautiful. In it, at Crazy Point, is the most lovely anchorage on the whole East coast, beautiful but big enough really only for one boat; two would be crowded; three, impossible. Crazy Point is on the south side of Letang Peninsula.

Crazy Point is named on Chart 4313. Just outside is the anchor symbol. You get to it by sailing generally north between Letang Head and McCann Island and then bearing off to the northeast from Letang Head about a mile.

Do not anchor where the anchor symbol is. Enter straight in from the east, going parallel to the shore, and keeping north of the little ledge on the east end of Crazy Point itself. You will find yourself in a deep, narrow, wooded, rocky cove without a house or a human being anywhere in sight. If the tide is low, you can scratch around and get the world's sweetest quahaugs.

A visitor in 1976 adds:

In L'Etang Harbour one cannot anchor *behind* or at least *inside* Crazy Point. It is essential to note the faint line under the numeral *20* just inside the point on the chart, where it dries out by 20 feet! The anchorage well outside that cove, but inside the line of the point, is OK.

The writer's visit to L'Etang in 1976 confirmed all the observations above. It is a delightful sail by high, wooded, uninhabited shores all the way up the L'Etang River or into Finger Bay. The tide does not run hard, the bottom is good holding ground, and one can anchor almost anywhere under either shore. L'Etang Head and McCann Island would be wonders of the world if they were located in Massachusetts. Crazy Point is as good as the description says it is. When you get there you will know why it is called Crazy Point. There is good anchorage behind Goss Point. Beware of the ledge east of it. It is covered at high water and is a mountain at low water. The only disturbing influence is the fish factory at Blacks Harbour, which spreads a foul stench over the whole neighborhood in an easterly.

Finger Bay (4313) is recommended as a very secure, secluded berth. Anchor just off its mouth. Favor the islands on your starboard hand going in, but not too close. Pick your anchorage with the lead, and remember there is a good 25 feet of tide in these parts. There are a few farms within walking distance of the shore; the dock of an abandoned clam factory makes a good landing place because there is a good gravel road to the main highway between St. George and Back Bay. At any farmhouse with a telephone, supplies may be ordered for delivery right to the old wharf. Call the store of Sylvester Hooper & Sons, 755–3729.

Back Bay (4313) itself appears to be the only protected anchorage with supplies available between Cutler and Saint John. Blacks Harbour is unprotected, busy, and smelly (on an easterly the smell comes to Finger Bay). Head Harbour is without supplies, and the other possibilities are way up in Passamaquoddy. Back Bay is protected by a breakwater built in 1962, and vacant moorings may well be available between it and the government wharf. It's only fair to add that there's a sardine factory here, too; however, the locals point to it as a handy source of fresh water.

An excellent source of local information is Mr. Sylvester Hooper, owner of the store. Gas cans may be filled at the store, but if large amounts of gas are needed, they can easily be delivered by truck from St. George, about 8 miles away. Hooper's store will deliver supplies anywhere between Letite Village and Blacks Harbour, in response to a telephone call.

Bliss Harbour, N.B. (4313). This is a well-protected harbor between Bliss Island and Frye Island, often clear when it is thick outside. There are good anchorages in Fisherman Cove on the southern side and between Fox Island and Frye Island on the north. Explore some of the other coves around McCann Island with which the writer is unacquainted.

Blacks Harbour, N.B. (4313). This harbor has much to recommend it and severe drawbacks for the cruising man in search of the quiet, romantic, and picturesque.

It is nearer to Saint John than any other good harbor west of Lepreau. It is easy of access even under adverse conditions, with a powerful horn on Pea Point, a bell outside, a light on Roaring Bull, and a wide entrance with a bold shore on the northerly side. There are a thoroughly adequate grocery store, a hardware store, a telephone, post office, and laundromat. The town is on the main road from Saint Stephen to Saint John, over which run buses several times a day. The ferry to Grand Manan runs from the first wharf on the south side. Gasoline and Diesel fuel are available at the wharves and ice at a white house on the left as you walk uptown. There is a sign out.

However, you may not want to go in beyond the ferry wharf. There are a few moorings in a cove east of the wharf and a telephone on the wharf. It is about a mile to town, but preferable to pressing further up the harbor by boat. Even here, you will not care to swim.

Above this cove the water is a filthy brownish gray, with a layer of grease on top that prevents a ripple from appearing on its surface. It smells foul. Lie up at the third wharf on the eastern side outside a seiner and row around to the float on the north side. Otherwise you must climb a greasy ladder about 30 feet high at low water.

This is the site of the Connors plant, said to be the world's biggest sardine cannery. Connors also smokes and cans Kipper Snacks and other piscatorial delicacies.

Once you are off the wharf, the stench fades and the country becomes quite attractive. The town is said to be a company town, most of it owned by Connors, not very picturesque but entirely adequate as a supply center. However, once you have seen it and accomplished your purpose, you will do well to depart for one of the lovely anchorages up the L'Etang River or in Bliss Harbor.

Point Lepreau, N.B. This promontory is about halfway between Head Harbour, Campobello, and Saint John on the east side of Mace's Bay. If you start on the beginning of low water slack from Head Harbour, you will be sucked north into Mace's Bay by the flood tide and will soon hear the Lepreau horn to starboard. In heading out again to find the whistle, you will go through the worst of a nasty tide rip. It is much better to pass well outside the whistle. You can't get lost with the Lepreau fog signal and the horn at Musquash. An alternative suggested by some cruising men is to hug the shore at Lepreau and go inside the rip, but local authorities do not think well of the plan. The rip can be really dangerous in the first two hours of the ebb with a brisk southerly wind.

If you are coming to the end of the flood tide, run for the bell off Dipper.

Dipper Harbour, N.B.   **(4314).** After making Fishing Point, run up the harbor, keeping well off the points, where weirs used to stand. Inside the breakwater is a large dredged area with room to anchor or to lie alongside with 10 feet at low water. There may be moorings available. Ashore there are a store, a restaurant, and a very pleasant New Brunswick village.

Chance Harbour, N.B.   **(4314).** Marked with a lighted bell outside and a light on Reef Point, Chance is not really difficult to make and is pretty well protected. In ordinary weather, anchor outside the extension of the government wharf in the cove on the port side as you enter. If it comes on to blow, go inside among the fishing boats, where there is 6 feet at low water. The scenery is spectacular.

Musquash Harbour, N.B.   **(4314).** Again, we have a small dredged harbor marked with a lighted bell and a light ashore. There is also a foghorn on this light. A strong set inshore has been reported off Musquash on the flood tide.

It appears from the chart that one could go all the way up into Five Fathom Hole on the tide, but the writer knows no one who has done it.

Following are some notes on the passage from Passamaquoddy Bay to Saint John, contributed by Mr. Gerry Peer of Saint John. He has cruised widely on this coast and elsewhere and has proved most hospitable to the writer and to many other yachtsmen who visit these waters.

"My Thoughts on Going up the Bay: When I want to go up in one day to Saint John, I usually leave from Blacks or Beaver Harbour. I do not recommend going up to the head of Blacks but behind the Grand Manan Ferry Wharf at the entrance to L'Etang. This is an easy place to get in and out of in a fog and free from the smells and all that goes with the fish plant up at the head of the harbour. There are a number of winter moorings for yachts, which are usually available, and a half-mile walk will give supplies.

"The run from Blacks to Saint John will cut 10 miles off the run from North Head or East Quoddy and many times is the difference in trying to make slack tide at the Reversing Falls.

"Beaver is another 4 miles up the coast and is that much closer, but does have a fish factory in it. It is easy to get in and out of and well marked, but watch the weirs to port on entering. A couple of times I have found them in my way when coming in in a fog or at night. The harbour has provided a surge the odd time, as it is wide open to the southeast.

"The outer part of Blacks is the best and is actually quite a pleasant and well-protected anchorage.

"A good suggestion is to take a day from North Head Harbour or St. Andrews and stop in at the Wolves for a couple of hours, ending up at Blacks or Beaver for the run to Saint John the next day. If beachcombing and remote areas are your thing, the Wolves are a delight. East Wolf has about three or four fishermen shacks, which may or may not be occupied, in a cove on the north side, offering good protection from the prevailing southwester. There are some large rocks well up in this cove, but the water is so clear they can easily be sighted if one proceeds slowly. There is a path from this cove to a pebble beach on the other side, where the beach combing is excellent. The birds, animals, and vegetation are uniquely interesting. The other islands are equally interesting and uninhabited. The light on South Wolf is now unmanned and automatic.

"Pt. Lepreau now has a very conspicuous structure in the reactor building of the new nuclear power plant being built on the point. It is well lighted, with all the obvious heavy construction noises and equipment that go with this type of plant. The other structure that marks the horizon on the way to Saint John is the cove about 3 miles up the bay from Split Rock. One can see the stack and the smoke it spews out from Grand Manan on a clear day.

"It perhaps should be pointed out that to go inside the whistle buoy off Pt. Lepreau with any sea running at all can be a smashing experience. The seas in the rip are as close to being a vertical wall as I have seen, and more water goes over the boat than under it.

"Tiner's Point horn is no more. It is now on Musquash Light around Split Rock Point and is not nearly as good."

There is a new cruising guide, *Small Craft Guide Saint John River,* which is a must for a trip on the river.

Saint John, N.B.   (4319). You must prepare for sudden changes as you approach Saint John Harbour, particularly if the weather is thick. Problems multiply. Finding Partridge Island is easy, for it has a good horn and a radio beacon. As you get close, you can run off to the eastward following the 5-fathom line and run right into the first of a line of black flashing buoys. Be sure to make proper allowance for tide. You will probably arrive close to high water.

The next consideration is the steamer menace. Saint John is a busy seaport; except for Halifax it is the only large ice-free port on Canada's east coast. You may expect steamers to be about at almost any time. The usual defenses of horn and radar reflector are vitally important. In addition, you should have crystals for channel 14 VHF. All conversation among approaching vessels and all information broadcast for their benefit is carried on this channel.

Steamers anchored are required to ring a bell and are a minor menace. Steamers coming in will probably be moving comparatively slowly and will be approaching on a course of about northeast from the Pilot Boarding Station shown on chart 4128. They should be to the east of your course. Remember, however, that at slow speeds a steamer does not respond quickly to her helm and cannot get out of your way. She has the right of way under the new International Rules of the Road, anyway. A steamer coming out on the ebb tide will be on the western side of the channel and may be coming toward you a great deal faster than the incoming vessels. In the fog, especially at high water, there is a good deal to be said for approaching just west of the channel and parallel to it.

The spring range of tide at Saint John may reach 30 feet but the normal range is about 20 feet. Because salt water is heavier than fresh water, one often finds that even on a flood tide, when the water level is rising in the harbor, fresh water from the river will run out vigorously over the top of the salt water, giving the appearance and effect of a head tide to a vessel entering the harbor.

If you have already entered Canadian Customs at North Head or Saint Andrews, you can follow the west side of the channel up Saint John Harbour. If the weather is thick, your course may bring you suddenly on to the stern of the Digby ferry at the first wharf as you approach the city. The wharf is below, southward of, the fog signal on the second wharf. Follow up the ends of the piers and slide in between piers 1 and 2. Here you will probably find a barge or the floating crane *Glen Buckie,* to which you can make fast while waiting for slack water at the falls. There is no really satisfactory berth for a small boat on the east side of the harbor. If you have business in Saint John, wait until you get to Milledgeville and go to town by taxi.

If you have not entered Customs, you will have to cross over to Pugsley Wharf on the west side of Reed's Point. Pugsley Terminal Wharf is a massive concrete wall against which the harbor chop dashes, complicated by wash from hurrying tugboats. If you cannot tie up—and you probably cannot—you will have to jump for a ladder and deal with the Customs officer while your wife keeps the yacht out of trouble and tries to bring her back in range when you have finished. The Customs

Office is a blue building on the south end of the wharf, open from 8 A.M. to midnight Atlantic Time. Atlantic Daylight Time is one hour ahead of Eastern Daylight Time.

A possible alternative is to go up to the Royal Kennebecasis Yacht Club in Milledgeville and call the Customs Office. They will send an officer out to issue a cruising permit, but it is a nuisance to them and you will have to pay the transportation costs.

Just above Saint John Harbour, at the gateway to the river, lie the Reversing Falls. This is a ledge over which the river falls into the harbor at low water. As the tide in the harbor rises, it reaches the level of the water in the river. At this time the current over the falls is more or less slack. As the tide continues to rise, the Bay of Fundy pours up over the ledge into the river. The slack is repeated again as the tide falls. The duration and exact time of the slack varies with the height of the water in the river and the tide in the harbor. With the river low, a spring tide and a southerly wind, for instance, the slack on the rising tide will come early. Normally slack water occurs 3 h 25 m after high water and 3 h 50 m after low water. See Mr. Peer's notes on the falls, below.

If you would like a pilot to take you up the falls, call Mr. Peer at Akatherm Atlantic; Mr. Edward Hartshorn, the Royal Kennebecasis Yacht Club; Mr. Ralph Gates at the Saint John Power Boat Club, or the Rothesay Yacht Club. All are most hospitable to visitors. However, the falls are not really so frightful. Mr. Hartshorn writes:

"No one who is able to get a yacht to Saint John should be at all frightened of the falls—just respect them. And use good common sense. And do not go looking for thrills. But as we are all sailing for fun, it does take some of the worry out of it if you have some help, and that is where we of RKYC love to be of any service."

As slack water approaches, move up the middle of the river under the first bridge; and as you approach the sharp turn by Split Rock and the second bridge, keep over to the right where there is an eddy and slack water. If the tide is running out, wait until the current appears to moderate enough for you, crack the throttle wide open, and try it. If you can get up by Split Rock and under the bridge, you can make it. If you can't, the current will carry you back and you will have to wait. If it is a near thing, drop back and wait.

When the tide looks to be as slack as it is going to be, which is not really slack but an uneasy swirling equilibrium between the river current and the Fundy tide, pass close to Split Rock and under the middle of the bridge. Then edge over close to the pulp mill. You will see a great boiling and swirling to starboard. This is the "pot." Avoid it. Some-times pulp logs, pulled under by whirlpools, are shot up by boils and their own buoyancy with force enough to bend a propeller or start a seam. Also, the surface is often covered with thick suds from a detergent used in the mill, so you can't see the logs. Move cautiously.

Coming down the river, arrive in plenty of time and wait at the Saint John Power Boat Club. Here you will find slips with water and electric-ity, 7 feet of water at low tide, a hospitable welcome and reliable advice. When the time of slack water approaches, edge down the river and wait on the edge of the cove just above the mill until conditions are right.

Remember that, even if the tide in the harbor below the bridge is supposed to be flooding, the fresh water may be running over it. You may be shot down the harbor a lot faster than you intended and plunged from the bright warm sunshine of the river into a choking thick bank of cold Fundy fog.

The following notes were written by Mr. Gerald Peer for the guidance of visitors:

"My Thoughts on the Falls: I have found over the last few years that if one calculates the slack by *Eldridge* it can be as much as 20 minutes out, coupled with a variance of up to 20 minutes either side of the calculated slack. Depending on the height of the river, this could give a run of water that could make passage through either impossible or a bit hair-raising.

"The slack is calculated on the normal summer low. With the advent of the Macdaquack dam above Fredericton and after a heavy rain, the river can be 4 feet above normal summer low in July or August. In May, at the height of the spring runoff or freshet, slack is at high tide if there is one at all. Just keep in mind, if the river is high, the slack is early on a high slack, i.e., 2 hours and 10 or 15 minutes, instead of 2 hours 25 minutes after high tide; and it is late on a low slack, i.e., 4 hours and 5 or 10 minutes after low tide, instead of 3 hours and 50 minutes.

"My boat *Arronta* can do about 6½ knots with the safety valve tied down, and I stand still at 30 minutes after the slack. The fastest run is at the mill, with under the bridge a close second. If I can get by the mill, I can make it.

"If one goes through the falls at dead slack, it is no trick at all. If in doubt about the time, go up about 20 minutes early and keep on the north side next to Ocean Steel. You can proceed right up to a point where you can see Split Rock under the bridge. When the water stops running by the rock, proceed. There is very little current in on that shore on a flood or an ebb. On going out, after passing Kingsville and

Indian Town Harbour, head for the chipping machine on the pulp mill. You can go right up to the mill in quiet water and watch the rip around the mill until it stops. In my own boat I leave the RKYC 1 hour before the slack and do 6 knots. This gives me about 10 minutes to wait for the slack. The run at the mill can be deceiving. It is usually running a little harder than it looks.

"The height under the bridges is inches less than 80 feet at summer low, with the railway bridge the lowest. There is more clearance on a low slack. I took *Running Tide* through last year with a 78-foot mast. During her stay we had a heavy rain, and we went down through early on a low slack so we could make it. The next day the river went up 3 inches, which would have given us problems. That is the highest mast I have put through the falls.

"By giving oneself lots of time and with careful calculations and observation at either end, no one should have any problems with this stretch of water."

Royal Kennebecasis Yacht Club; Milledgeville, N.B. (4319). Once by the falls, continue up the river through the dramatic clefts in the rocky hills, round Boars Head (aptly named), and anchor off the Royal Kennebecasis Yacht Club in Brothers Cove at Milledgeville. There is a buoyed channel up to the club, marked at the outer end with a red spar and a white flasher and from there with red and black spars. Head for the white flasher and then for the red flash on the club. This will take you right up the middle of the channel to the corner of the wharf. Inquire at the club for a mooring or advice on where to anchor. There is about 7 feet at the front of the wharf.

Shortly after rounding Ragged Point, visiting yachts are sometimes confused by an orange racing buoy. It was put out by the Ministry of Transport and does look like a navigation buoy. There is another off the face of Kennebecasis Island in Grand Bay, and a third off McColgan Point.

At the club wharf one can buy gas, Diesel fuel, and ice. There is a water hose available. At the club are a telephone and a substantial bar. There is a small marine railway next to the club. There is a good grocery store just up the road. Saint John is a ten-minute taxi ride away; it has all the facilities of a big city. Investigate the situation on buying bonded liquor. If you agree not to broach it until you leave Canada, there may be a considerable saving.

The members of the Royal Kennebecasis Yacht Club are without doubt the friendliest and most hospitable people in the yachting world. They will do anything they can to make your visit pleasant. There are a few amenities that seem minor, but that the considerate yachtsman will follow. For instance, you should fly the Canadian flag, the maple leaf, at your starboard spreader on entering Canadian waters and the United States ensign at the staff astern or on the leech of the mainsail. When you take the American flag in at night, take in the Canadian one, too. Bring along an extra club burgee, especially if you belong to a club whose members do not often visit Saint John. Perhaps the gentleman who pilots you up the falls would appreciate it. Anyway, be sure to pay his taxi fare back to the city, and don't let him die of thirst on the way. Always write out Saint John—don't abbreviate it. And remember that Saint Johns is in Newfoundland, not New Brunswick.

We who have been treated so hospitably in Canada await the opportunity to return the hospitality at our own yacht clubs and in our own harbors.

The Royal Kennebecasis Yacht Club is a center for yachting on the river, not only for visitors, but for local people as well. On one occasion, the Cruising Club of America, an assemblage of salt-water, stick-and-string gentlemen accustomed to Bermuda and transatlantic passages, visited the club. They proceeded from Massachusetts in a seamanlike manner through all kinds of weather. From Mt. Desert on they had it thick all the way, but being accomplished navigators, they all made it without serious incident, by means of compass, chart, fathometer, RDF, and all the best of equipment and judgment. At Saint John, a local pilot met them. At just the earliest reasonable time they passed the falls and proceeded triumphantly through the last of a sunny summer day to the peaceful anchorage at Milledgeville. As they were snugging down, a power cruiser came roaring in, flying the American yachting ensign and bearing a nondescript pennant at her bow staff. The owner bumped up to the wharf. A member of the Cruising Club, thinking perhaps the new arrival had been a little late for slack water at the falls asked, "How did you make it coming up the falls?"

"What falls?" inquired the new arrival.

He had come all the way from New York on an oil-company chart; and, without any advance planning, or even knowledge of their existence, had hit the falls at exactly slack water.

Kennebecasis Bay. This is a very pleasant and unfrequented cruising ground, at the entrance of which is the hospitable Rothesay Yacht Club. The bay is well worth exploration. Some of the nicer summer homes of Saint John residents are situated in the communities along the shore, and much of the sailing activity of the various clubs is carried on in this area. Forester Cove, at the entrance to the Kennebecasis River, is large and deep but gives good protection. Attractive sand beaches can be found on the north end and in the cove at the south end of Long Island.

The Saint John River. In navigating this very pleasant river, do not neglect a copy of the *Small Craft Guide, Saint John River,* published by the Department of the Environment, P. O. Box 8080, 1675 Russell Rd., Ottawa, Canada. It is a most helpful and comprehensive pilot, perhaps a notch ahead of the charts. Also, of course, one should have charts 4141 and 4142, which are printed in strips to show the course of the river.

No longer are logs brought down to the mill in booms, as they used to be. The logs are now reduced to chips and taken down in a barge. If you meet the barge in a narrow place, you will do well to give it all the room you can.

Do not pass close ahead or astern of ferries. They progress by winching themselves across the river on a cable, which is close to the surface forward and aft.

After leaving Milledgeville, leave Kennebecasis Island to starboard and push on up the river. The shores are mountainous, with beaches at the water's edge, backed by forests and farms. Occasionally one passes small towns with ferry slips or little coves where tributaries enter. Beware of bars off these. The waters are protected enough so no sea ever makes up, and a breeze usually draws up from the south. Fog is almost unknown. An occasional salmon leaps, and local yachts add interest to the scene, especially on weekends.

There is not much shelter until you come to Whelpley Cove at the end of Long Reach, although one could anchor almost anywhere under the shore. There is also a cove at Oak Point. Gasoline is available at the public landing. However, it is not a particularly attractive place to stay because the main road runs close to the shore here and trucks passing in the night do little for the romantic atmosphere.

The writer anchored in a hurry off Oak Point with his broken topmast hanging from the spreaders, while the entire Cruising Club of America sped by. One valued friend in a 40-foot yawl, with only two men and a woman aboard, was jibing an enormous spinnaker with great skill and coolness. He found time in the midst of the evolution to ask if we needed help.

Beyond the dramatic Gorham Bluff, one can follow the chart sharply to the right or proceed north along the river and enter the narrower deeper channel between Pig and Hog islands and get into *Kingston Creek* and Belle Isle Bay, one of the most beautiful and desirable cruising areas on the river.

On the right around Gorham Bluff is **Shamper Cove,** a shoal one with foul bottom. Crossing the head of Shamper Cove and again turning right to the south'ard brings one into **Kingston Creek,** one of my favorite spots. The west side of the cove is bounded by high granite bluffs and, farther in, a steep hillside down which a rocky brook falls with a fine soft music on quiet nights. On the east side the cove is bounded by steep meadows and farmlands, both sides affording fine shelter except in the case of strong winds out of the north. Kingston Creek about ten years ago was navigable for a distance of almost 2 miles, but, due to continued logging operations in the surrounding woods, it is difficult to carry 6 feet more than a mile in. The waterlogged pulpwood has lessened the charted depth considerably, and while we felt our way some distance in carrying 6 feet, an accompanying boat drawing 3 feet struck the foul bottom right next to us. The rest of the cove provides good anchorages along the shores, provides great exploring country, and is quiet and peaceful.

It is reported to be windy in strong southwest weather as the wind funnels through the anchorage.

Belle Isle Bay

From Kingston Creek, exploration of **Belle Isle Bay** is a *must.* It has bold shores, and from our experience it is navigable for a distance of about 5 miles for drafts of up to 10 feet. Several points make out from the shores and small sandbars can be found off these, but they are clearly identifiable. When entering Belle Isle Bay, either enter through Shamper Channel, a route much used by local boats, or continue north past Shamper Cove and make a U-turn to the east at the north end of Belle Isle (Hog Island). (See inset on chart 4344.) At that north end is a red-and-black spar and a red spar. Go between them. Then going south there are two black spars. Leave them close aboard to starboard on your way south into the bay, and, naturally, close aboard to port on your way north, past the island and back into the river. This is the opposite of red right returning. From the more southerly of the two black spars you can lay a course of 138 magnetic, which will take you toward a white target painted by a fisherman on the south shore of the bay. Carry that course until you get in the middle and then turn northeast for **Ghost Island.**

Proceeding up the bay, one comes first to a pretty, wooded, unnamed island (Ghost Island), on the east side of which will be found what appears to be a naturally formed obelisk of rock. The island is steep to, and you can tie right up to the trees on most of it, except where the beach lies on the west side. The scenery at this point is grand, with high granite bluffs giving way to thick woodlands and occasional farm areas. Since Jenkins Cove is no longer uninhabited, many visitors now prefer the anchorage at Ghost Island.

Around the next high bluff on the left lies one of the best coves I have ever been in. It is *Jenkins Cove,* named for the family owning and still operating the farm on the north side. The cove is spacious but well protected, with good holding ground. The real surprise, however, is a hidden secondary cove of minute but deep dimension, found only after completely entering the main cove. This small cove is ideal and completely sheltered, with steep sides of beautiful granite, birch, and spruce. The road passes close to the westward of the cove. The store is a good mile up the road to the north.

Brown's Cove, just beyond Jenkins Cove, is not nearly as scenic and, being a V-shaped cove and open to the south, it does not afford very much protection in strong winds. A little way down the bay on the opposite side is *Erbs Cove,* which we have looked into but never entered. While it appears to be deep, it is another wide-mouth cove with no particular attraction. Another mile up the bay is Long Point, beyond which the depths are in doubt, and local knowledge seems to indicate that 4 feet or less draft may be required for the additional 4 or 5 miles to the end of this beautiful bay.

As you come out of the bay to go on up the river, either course may be used as in entering, but the natural track would be up the Hog Island Channel. The black spar about halfway up the length of Hog Island must be left to starboard and rounded sharply. The channel lies close to the island, as will be seen, until nearing the north end, where it swings over to Pig Island, passing between the island and a red spar as it enters the river proper.

Navigation and Canadian Buoyage

Since we are moving well up the river now, it may be appropriate to have a few remarks on navigation and buoyage from here on. If the river is high, as it sometimes is during the summer months, spars showing on the charts often project above the surface only a little, even 6 inches. These sometimes have to be sought out, but with no tide, smooth water, and only a moderate current, you can usually go right up to where you think something should be and look around. What looks like a dead tree stuck in the bottom should not be disregarded. It may replace a spar buoy.

The channels among the islands are relatively easy to follow, in that most of the islands are low and grassy, and the weeds and aquatic plants seem to grow to the surface up to a depth of almost exactly 5 feet. If uncertain, follow the water clear of growth and it will almost always be deep. A great many cattle, sheep, and some hogs graze on the islands in the river and along the grassy shores. However, the old tale that the brown cows will always be to starboard and the black-and-white ones to port when entering just isn't so.

Things indicated as lights with varying characteristics on the chart may be almost invisible by day because of foliage and location. By night, with a few exceptions, these lights will average what appears to be about 25-watts intensity.

Lastly, we mention the matter of birch and spruce stakes with the foliage still attached. These are easy to follow and should be treated like any other buoyage. The depths may vary somewhat from the charts, but I have found that in most periods when we have visited the river, the charted depths are conservative. As mentioned above, the Canadian authorities have taken definite steps to improve the aids in the river and have done a great deal, particularly in the lower portion. In many places local bush stakes have been replaced with Ottawa valley buoys, i.e., a spar with a metal bottom and wood top.

Tennant Cove to Grand Lake

Tennant Cove, just beyond the entrance to Belle Isle Bay, is a poor one, having a bad entrance and being shoal. Gas may be purchased at *Evandale* at the wharf north of the ferry landing the west bank of the river.

Our next run would be up the right side of the river, passing either side of Spoon Island and bearing right to go up the east side of Long Island. Just before coming to the end of this sizable island, one should enter *Washadamoak Creek,* passing along the east side of Lower Musquash Island until the entrance to Washadamoak Lake appears. It is buoyed and, though narrow, can easily be followed, bringing the cruising man into a lovely, long lake with numerous coves and bays and fine cruising country. This lake is now accurately charted.

Many New Brunswick yachtsmen recommend the anchorage at Colwell's wharf up the Lawson River beyond the entrance to the lake.

A little farther along one comes to *Lewes Cove,* known locally as *Big*

Cove, on the southern shore of the lake about 3 miles from the entrance. Go *well* in, past the little island, and anchor at the end off the last farmhouse to port. Draft of 6 feet is all right, but anchor to starboard and well in. There is a lovely granite bluff and two small wooded islands, Spruce and Birch. It affords protection from all directions and is an excellent spot. About 3 miles beyond is the town of Cambridge, with the village of Narrows on the opposite side of the lake. Here limited supplies may be secured.

The bridge at Narrows blew down in the Ground Hog Day gale. A new bridge is being built with a clearance of 56 feet. A cable ferry is serving in the interim. I am told the lake is navigable for considerable draft as far as Cody, another 10 miles. Though the scenery is not quite as dramatic as Belle Isle Bay, this lake definitely should not be missed, the hills rising to several hundred feet on either side.

Gagetown, N.B.

Leavig Washadamoak Lake and going on north, the narrow, deep channel reminds one of the European canals. On leaving Colwell's Creek, one should be careful not to continue to the north of Upper Musquash Island, as a bar obstructs this channel about halfway out to the river. Rounding Killboy Island, turn south and head for the open river, turning north when in the mainstream. Continuing north, we enter Gagetown Creek and tie up at *Gagetown,* where limited supplies and fuel may be had.

Gagetown is one of the larger towns on the river. Here is Tom Colpitts's General Store, with a float providing gasoline, Diesel fuel, and ice. There is 10 feet of water alongside. The store itself sells groceries and gifts, souvenirs and notions. Colpitts's store will accept credit cards. One can call ahead and supplies will be ready to pick up (506-488-2979). Tom Colpitts has expressed himself as eager to encourage yachtsmen to enjoy the river. One can tie up to the government wharf with 7 feet alongside or anchor in Mount Creek about half a mile above Gagetown on the east side of the river. Anchor about on the U and push ½ mile farther up the creek in the dinghy to the ruins of the oldest house in New Brunswick.

Our plans would now take us south on Gagetown Creek again and up the river proper to the almost invisible entrance to the *Jemseg River,* where one passes between shores about 75 feet apart to enjoy a 3-mile run up to the highway bridge at the village of Jemseg. This is a new high-level bridge with an 75-foot clearance, replacing the old drawbridge. There is a restaurant and store at Jemseg and gasoline stations along the highway.

If the chip barge, which runs between Chipman and Saint John, is in the channel, it is advisable to wait until it clears the channel before proceeding. It is on a tow line and can fishtail and drive you out of the channel when passing. It looks like a hotel going by.

After successfully negotiating the bridge, we make for *Grand Lake,* following the marked channel out of the Jemseg River and across Purdy Shoal at the lower end of the lake. This channel is well marked with both stakes and brush; and, with a few obvious places easily identified on the chart excepted, the whole area of Grand Lake is a fine cruising ground with ample depths, sheltered coves and bays, and fine beaches. The water is generally clear and clean enough to drink, and we have often filled our tanks with it. It is suggested that this be done above Grand Point bar.

Grand Lake, N.B.

The lake averages 3 miles in width and is about 25 miles long. In my opinion, no trip to the Saint John River should fail to include a run into Grand Lake.

In Grand Lake the first important spot is *Douglas Harbor* on the northwest shore. This is a lovely series of coves shown in a detailed insert on the Canadian chart. Straight up the harbor toward the wharf will be found a long sand spit, which serves as a dandy swimming beach. We usually moor about halfway between the spit and the wharf in about 8 or 9 feet.

The cove on the left as one enters the harbor looks fine, but, though deep inside, has a 1-foot bar across the entrance and must be explored only in dinghies. . . . The cove on the right, known as Bedroom Cove, is a beautiful place and usually secluded.

Up the shore from the wharf is a general store, which sells gasoline and ice, among many other things. Across the street is a public telephone.

Mill Cove and White Cove, on the southeast shore of the lake, are perfectly good anchorages, though wide coves and not very snug. The same is true of *Young's Cove* about halfway up the lake, where we have been a couple of times when we wanted to get near the highway from Saint John in order to swap crews. Though we have never used it, the small cove inside Fanjoy Point near the village of Waterborough can also be used for the crew-shift problem. **Cumberland Bay** is a large bay running west-southwest to east-northeast and, having a wide mouth, is likely to be choppy with the prevailing winds.

Entering the northeast arm between Goat Island and Cox Point, there are two coves on the left and one on the right. **Barton Cove,** the latter, is deep, but, again open to the southwest. **Flowers Cove** on the left is interesting and completely snug. Though the inner portion of Flowers Cove is blocked by a power line with a clearance of 38 feet, the outer cove is fine. We anchored in the center of a circle passing through the numerals 11, 14, 12, and 12. Favor the north shore. There was a bar in the middle where the chart shows 12 feet in 1977.

The cove north of Flowers Cove is silted up to about 3 feet north of the point where chart 4362 shows 12 feet. There *may* be a narrow channel, if you hug the north shore, but local knowledge is contradictory and that mud is some sticky. I'd stay away. At **Newcastle Creek** a couple of miles farther up the left side of the lake, there is a small but deep harbor, a large power station, and a small town, the only sign of anything resembling big industry for miles. This is not a good place to lie but can be used for supplies if the charm of Grand Lake extends one's visit.

Into the North Woods

From here we embark on another delightful adventure by following the marked channel around Lead Island and Moray Points into the mouth of the **Salmon River,** a fine north-woods stream in which one can carry 6-foot draft for about 11 miles upriver to the town of Chipman pretty nearly into the deep woods of central New Brunswick.

The banks of the Salmon River are thickly wooded, and when one can make the run upstream under sail, as we did, a sense of departure from the conventional cruising atmosphere is most evident. There is the delicious north woods smell of pine and wild flowers, and the only sound is an occasional bird call, or the scurrying of animals in the woods. There is no sign of civilization, except at Camp Wesegum, a Canadian religious camp about halfway to Chipman.

After this peace and solitude we finally made the turn at Davis Turn, and with some surprise saw three bridges, a dam, a busy sawmill, and log booms filling the river. You can tie up to the wharf at the foot of the bridge or to one of the scows tied along the bulkhead. This is a lumber town and railhead, with both Canadian Pacific and Canadian National railroads crossing the river at this point. All kinds of supplies are available in the town, and the people are most friendly and helpful. Our 40-foot cutter was the first masted vessel they'd seen in town, and we had a large number of visitors, adult and youthful, the latter bearing most welcome gifts of fresh blueberries and home-grown lettuce.

A local authority reports that R.K.Y.C. cruises have been going regularly to this town for the last eighty years, sometimes with yachts up to 65 feet.

However, you can't take a tall-masted vessel all the way to Chipman, as there is a high-voltage line with a clearance of 54 feet just south of Iron Bound Cove, but it was a nice trip to that bend.

Another correspondent notes:

> My experience at Chipman was far from encouraging. What might be referred to as a wharf was in fact used as a platform from which huge trucks were dumping logs into the boom in the river. There was no way to land and we returned downstream. A good anchorage is between the unnamed island and the eastern shore 4,000 feet down river from Davis Turn. Particular attention should be paid to the hazards outlined in the *Small Craft Guide,* especially above Davis Turn.

Another interesting side trip from Grand Lake is described below by Mr. Love in an excerpt from his account of a cruise in these waters in 1965:

> While on this cruise I had occasion at the time of the Douglas Harbor rendezvous to make an investigation of the chain of lakes which run in a westerly direction from the southwest end of Grand Lake. We had towed a Boston Whaler along as a tender, and I was able to make an extensive run in comparatively little time.
>
> The entrance to this fascinating waterway is at Indian Point 2.3 miles northwestward from the mouth of the Jemseg River and is marked by red-and-black spar buoys and bush stakes. One must stay close to in rounding Indian Point, and immediately behind it one finds a very small neat cove with about 9 feet of water. At normal river height, 6 feet can be carried in.
>
> I had a beautiful trip through Maquapit Channel, or thoroughfare, across Maquapit Lake, through French Lake Thoroughfare, across the bottom of French Lake and a short distance up to the Portobello River, a distance of about 10 or 11 miles. What the status of the one highway bridge is I don't know, but it seemed operable, clearance being about 15 feet closed. [The French Lake bridge does not swing, but there is a depth of at least 5 feet for a

considerable distance beyond. Ed.] This is a real gunk-hole trip, but perfectly beautiful.

Note.—A canoe trip of historic interest, one of the favorite water routes of the Indians in the early days, may be had by portaging at Maugerville from the Saint John to the Portobello River, a distance of one to two miles. French Lake is reached by descending the latter river and thence the various water areas just described through a channel to Grand Lake. The shores of the latter may be skirted throughout, if so desired, before rejoining the Saint John river at Lower Jemseg. In very dry seasons sufficient water even for canoes may not be found in some parts of the Portobello River.

The low marshland and numerous ponds surrounding Grand, French, and Maquapit lakes are the feeding grounds for large flocks of black ducks, whistlers, teal, and other water fowl. Each autumn brings numerous hunters to the vicinity for the annual duck shooting.

On to Fredericton, N.B.

This is the story of the "Rhine of North America," and obviously I am enthusiastic about it. The Saint John River, of course, continues in a northerly and westerly direction for many miles. It is navigable from where we left it at Lower Jemseg as far as Fredericton, with drafts as deep as 6 feet. This latter run I have never made because I have felt other parts of the river and area are more attractive. Fredericton itself is a small city bustling with business activity and a very active chamber of commerce, which puts on a prominent outboard and small-boat regatta every year. For the average cruising man I think there are years of more fascinating cruising to do in the area we have described.

APPENDIX A

Birding Under Sail

by

CHRISTOPHER M. PACKARD
Maine Audubon Society

Intrinsically bound with the sound of the sea is the call of the gull. The sea has a birdlife peculiarly its own. It is constantly changing, whether one cruises along the coast or heads offshore; and it also varies from month to month. Whether one is content merely to admire the freedom and grace of a bird's flight over the open sea, or becomes intrigued in identification and behaviorism, birds can provide added pleasure to any cruise. A yachtsman is in a unique position to observe and enjoy some of the choicest birds of New England. The following paragraphs name some of these and suggest avenues of further exploration.

The most common gull along our coast is the herring gull, which takes unusual pleasure in perching on moored craft. How many a yachtsman has forsworn anything to do with birds after such an early and intimate encounter. However, though at times unwanted companions, they do much to keep our harbors clean. Actually there are a number of different kinds of gulls along our coast. The great black-backed is our largest. A little smaller than the herring gull is the ring-billed, especially plentiful in harbors south of Maine. You may occasionally see gulls with black heads and dark backs; these are probably laughing gulls, which breed west of Penobscot Bay. In late summer the Bonapartes appear along the coast. Just slightly larger than a tern, we are more apt to see immatures or non-breeding birds already in their winter plumage. The more you look at gulls, the more different kinds there may appear to be. However, gulls have a number of different plumages for different stages of growth. Fortunately the field guides show these, and with their help, you will soon be able to identify a first-

or third-year gull with hardly a second glance.

"Mackerel gulls" are the name fishermen use for terns. Graceful, swallowlike, plunging into water after small fish, they are a joy to watch. The common tern is probably the most abundant, until you reach a place like Matinicus where several thousand arctics breed. A third species found in New England is the roseate.

Close relatives to the gulls and terns are the shorebirds. Commencing in late July, you are apt to encounter migrating flocks. Many different species occur at this season, such as the black-bellied plover, ruddy turnstone, dowitcher, sanderling, and semipalmated sandpiper. However, the one that breeds on our rockbound islands is the spotted sandpiper. This is the one that wanders over the rocks, frequently stopping and teetering. There are shorebirds, however, that are really a yachtsman's speciality. These are the phalarope. Thousands gather in the Bay of Fundy in August, and often large flocks will be seen resting on the water offshore. Both red and northern species occur at this season, truly pelagic shorebirds that the landbound birder all too seldom sees.

Among the islands from Casco Bay east, you may see some brownish ducks with a flotilla of ducklings. The common eider has been increasing on the Maine coast as a breeding species. As soon as courtship is over and the eggs are hatched, the males usually go off by themselves. However, by late summer small rafts of eiders, both sexes and all ages, will be seen congregating over shoal beds where they feed. Stay clear!

A nonbreeding sea duck that may be found occasionally is the scoter. All three species (black, surf, and white-winged) summer along the coast. Two other species may surprise you. Black ducks (we usually think of them breeding on fresh water) do breed on some offshore islands. They may be seen resting on the ocean, though they do not dive or feed in deep water. The common loon, the bird of Maine's inland lakes, now breeds on islands as far at sea as Matinicus. We think the outboard motoring on inland waters may have been just too much for them to stand.

Superficially similar to the loon is the double-crested cormorant (shag to fishermen). This is the dark-colored bird often seen perching on a nun or can with wings outstretched in a spread-eagle fashion. Colonies nest on islands, sometimes building their nests on the ground, and at other times building in trees. Fishermen long thought the cormorant was a dangerous competitor, but studies seemed to indicate it ate only trash fish. Again the bird is suspect, large numbers of shiny tags having been found in cormorant rookeries; tags used to mark salmon in Maine's restoration program for that fish. Extensive studies will probably again be undertaken to determine this relationship.

Man's interests and those of birds have clashed all too often. The eagle, once seen with regularity along the Maine coast, has within recent years been able to produce less than six young annually in the entire state. The osprey, still nesting on innumerable Maine islands, is also becoming less common. There are more unoccupied nests than occupied. The stately great blue heron, which was a common sight in coves, is no longer producing young in its former numbers. It is in cases such as this that bird counts become important. Unless counts are made this summer, we will have nothing with which to compare a summer hence. Yachtsmen are in a unique position to help determine the magnitude of this changing picture of New England seabirds.

At the turn of the century our seabird colonies were threatened by plume hunters. Protection was provided and gradually colonies of terns, eiders, and gulls increased. Today there is again concern due to visits to offshore islands by people seeking recreation. If you visit a bird colony, bear in mind that your presence may be keeping adult birds from incubating eggs or causing the young needless and often fatal exposure. The greatest care must also be observed not to step on eggs or young, which in the case of seabirds are usually protectively colored. On grassy islands where petrels nest, great danger can be caused by walking across the turf and compressing petrel burrows. The situation has reached such proportions that part of Matinicus Rock is being declared "off bounds" during the breeding season by the U.S. Fish and Wildlife Service and U.S. Coast Guard. On Machias Seal Island the Canadian Wildlife Service requests that you keep to paths and the bird blind. If you do visit a seabird colony, please observe discretion.

It is on Matinicus Rock and Machias Seal Island that the puffin nests, a species that birders will travel miles to see. Matinicus marks the southernmost breeding colony on the Atlantic seaboard and, if cruising Penobscot Bay, swing around Matinicus Rock, especially the cliffs on the eastern side. Here you should get wonderful views of puffins in the water, close to your boat. A few pair of razorbills (auk) may also be found at the Rock, but far more will be seen off Cutler and Machias Seal. The third alcid that breeds in New England is the black guillemot. This is a little black bird with conspicuous, white wing patches, which breeds from Pemaquid east. It is a great diver and upon surfacing small eel-like fish may be seen clutched in its beak. Again nature may trick you. By late summer, many guillemots will already be wearing winter coats of white—back to the field guides!

When the fog rolls in we call it "Shearwater weather." It is at such times that we usually get the largest counts of greater and sooty shearwaters. I have come upon a raft of sixty or more sitting on the water off Matinicus in fog. With the breeze blowing and fair weather, the shearwaters are usually on the wing. They may come soaring in close to your boat, and just as suddenly disappear. These are truly pelagic birds, spending much of their lives over the open ocean, and the manner in which they ride the wind currents is a pleasure to see.

Also spending much of their time at sea are petrels. The Leach's storm petrel breeds on a few of our turf-covered offshore islands in eastern Maine. The Wilson's storm petrel, when encountered in summer off the New England coast, is biologically "wintering." It breeds during our winter months in the Southern Hemisphere. Collectively these birds are called "Mother Carey's Chickens," both by Maine coast fishermen and by mariners for generations. If you see small dark birds, fluttering close to the surface and often acting like swallows, check out the petrels.

While it may seem strange to mention land birds in a cruising guide, they will be encountered frequently. At anchor in the coves along the coast, one is treated to a chorus of bird songs in the evening and early morning. The notes of the hermit thrush, white-throated sparrow, black-throated green warbler, and parulas drifting out across the water add to the tranquillity of the hour and setting.

Many land birds migrate across the Gulf of Maine, some traveling as far as from Nova Scotia to Cape Ann or Cape Cod in a direct line. I have encountered hummingbirds and chimney swifts far at sea. Often warblers and other small birds will alight on your yacht, pausing for a short rest. At such times these birds are extremely tame and may even hop over your body or roost on your head! Occasionally, black-backed gulls will pursue these small migrants. The gulls will swoop down on them, forcing them close to the water, where they become easy prey. On several occasions I have had migrants seek refuge on my boat from marauding gulls.

The fall migration starts in late July off the New England coast and reaches its height in late August and early September. At such times you may even encounter butterflies at sea. While I do not recommend taking a butterfly book aboard, do not overlook taking a book on land birds, for you may have an opportunity to identify a surprising number, even far offshore.

Never before have so many fine books been available to assist in bird identification. The three most useful are: *Birds of North America* by Robbins, Brunn, and Zim (Golden Press, New York), which illustrates all North American birds in color; the *Audubon Water Bird Guide* by Richard H. Pough (Doubleday & Co., Inc.), which has excellent colored illustrations and a text that gives details about the habits of seabirds; and *A Field Guide to the Birds* by Roger Tory Peterson (Houghton Miffin), which has long been a standard identification guide. Any one of these is easily stowed aboard. Another very good and newly published bird book is *The Audubon Society Field Guide to North American Birds: Eastern Region* by John Bull and John Farrand, Jr. (New York: Alfred A. Knopf, 1977). The State Audubon Societies can provide check lists of birds you are likely to encounter in New England waters along the coast and off shore.

The yachtsman who has become proficient in bird identification is in a position to provide extremely valuable information to the State Audubon Societies. These organizations are dependent upon records of seabirds from fishermen or upon their own, all too infrequent, offshore field trips. Concentrations of shearwaters, dates of offshore encounters with land birds, records of migrating waterfowl, etc., are the type of information these societies are anxious to obtain. Do not underestimate the value of your observations. The following would like to hear from you: The Maine Audubon Society, Gilsland Farm, 118, Route 2, Falmouth, Maine 04105; The Audubon Society of New Hampshire, 3 Silk Farm Road, Concord, New Hampshire, 03301; The Massachusetts Audubon Society, South Great Road, Lincoln, Massachusetts 01773; and The Rhode Island Audubon Society, 40 Bowen Street, Providence, Rhode Island 02903.

APPENDIX B

Geology of the Maine Coast

by

OLCOTT GATES

Department of Geology, The Johns Hopkins University
and
Maine Geological Survey

The yachtsman sailing the Coast of Maine is enjoying a cruising paradise (barring a little fog now and then) that was 400 million years in the making. The history of these 400 million years is written in the rocks that frame Maine's green islands and bold headlands. The yachtsman cannot help but notice their great variety, and I hope the following description of the geology of the Maine Coast will heighten both his joy in this pleasant land and his interest in its origin.

Let us begin our geological cruise at West Quoddy Head and work westward. One always sees more of the coast beating back, and besides we will be following in the wake of C. T. Jackson, a Boston physician and Maine's first state geologist, who in 1836 sailed in the Revenue Cutter *Crawford* from West Quoddy Head to begin the first systematic study of the geology of Maine.

From West Quoddy Head to the Cow Yard most of the rocks are dark gray, dark green, black, or dark rusty brown. They are massive and unlayered although commonly highly fractured. These dark, massive rocks are termed *gabbro.* Typical examples can be studied on West Quoddy Head, the shore around Cutler harbor, the bold cliff on the east side of Bunker Cove, and Black Head on Head Harbor Island.

A close look at gabbro—preferably with a magnifying glass—will reveal a mass of interlocking crystals, some of which are white or gray and others black or dark green. The white crystals are of *feldspar,* a mineral composed of oxygen atoms tied together by atoms of calcium, sodium, aluminum, and silicon. The dark mineral is *pyroxene,* also composed largely of oxygen atoms but tied together by atoms of magnesium and iron as well as silicon. Feldspar and pyroxene are two very common minerals in the earth's crust.

On the north side of West Quoddy Head or at Balch Head south of Baileys Mistake the dark gabbro can be seen cutting sharply across a sequence of layered rocks; and *dikes* (narrow tabular bodies) of black gabbro cutting other rocks are numerous along this part of the coast. Chemical analysis indicates that gabbro has the same chemical composition as the basalt that makes up typical lava flows. The massiveness and crystalinity of gabbro, its cross-cutting relation to older rocks, and its chemical similarity to basalt all suggest that gabbro is an *igneous* rock, one that formed by the cooling and crystallizing of hot molten rock— *magma*— like the liquid lavas erupted from volcanoes. However, in the case of gabbro, the magma never reached the surface as lava. Instead it intruded rocks below the surface and cooled slowly at depth so that there was time for large crystals to grow.

At a few places, the observant yachtsman will notice that the rocks are layered, built up bed after bed like a pile of books of different thicknesses. Good examples are on the cliffs between Baileys Mistake and Haycock Harbor, beneath and just east of the steep cliff at the northeast end of the beach at Roque Island, and along the shore below the summer cottage at the Cow Yard. Each layer or bed is an accumulation of mud, limey mud, sand, volcanic ash, or large fragments of volcanic rocks (called *breccia*), which long ago settled as sediment on the sea floor, hence their name—*sedimentary* rocks. Most sedimentary rocks, such as sandstone, shale, or limestone, do not contain volcanic materials, but those of the Maine Coast largely do. Some black basaltic lava flows (on the point beyond the fish weir at Roque Island beach, for instance) are also present on this part of the coast. A third type of rock is a glassy one containing scattered white or pink crystals of feldspar. A good example is the reddish rock on the shore of Bucks Harbor in Machias Bay. Such rocks are called *porphyry*. They generally are volcanic igneous rocks that cooled quickly on or near the surface, so that only a few crystals had time to form. Some of these porphyries have an intricate swirling banding, like ribbon candy, made by the flow of very sticky and stiff lava.

For the sake of simplicity, the sedimentary rocks with ash and volcanic fragments, the basalt flows, and the porphyries will be collectively termed *volcanics*.

Sailing from the Cow Yard on our next run to Mt. Desert, we pass the now familiar gabbro and volcanics along the shore of Head Harbor Island on the port hand, but to starboard on Steel Harbor Island there is a new rock—massive pink *granite.* The granite continues along the shore of Great Wass Island and the chain of small islands to the bell off Egg Rock; and from here to Casco Bay we shall rarely be out of sight of pink granite. Granite, like gabbro, is an igneous rock that rose as magma from deep in the earth and slowly cooled beneath the earth's surface. Thus, like gabbro, it is coarsely crystalline; but the minerals are different, hence the pink color rather than the dark colors of gabbro.

Four minerals can be seen in most of the Maine Coast granites, particularly with a magnifying glass: white calcic and sodic feldspar; pink potassium-rich feldspar; *quartz,* which looks like glass and is composed of oxygen and silicon; and a black mineral, which may be either platey *mica* or fibrous *amphibole,* both of which are made up of oxygen, silicon, magnesium, iron, aluminum, and water.

The most spectacular body of granite on the Maine Coast is that which makes up the mountains of Mt. Desert. This great mass forced its way as magma up through several miles of volcanics. Otter Point is close to the contact between the granite and the host volcanics, and there along the shoreline can be seen huge angular blocks of volcanic and sedimentary rocks shattered where they collapsed into the granite magma. On the shores of Bar Harbor and Northeast Harbor are excellent exposures of bedded volcanic and sedimentary rocks; and the Cranberry Islands and Seawall Point are made up primarily of volcanic breccia carrying numerous large fragments of lava and other volcanic rocks spewed out by volcanoes and spread over the sea floor by submarine landslides.

From Mt. Desert to Islesboro the rocks are dominantly granite, along with a lesser amount of the volcanics and gabbro that the granites intrude. The shores of Deer Island, Merchant Row, and Isle au Haut are largely granite. The Fox Islands are more complex geologically. Most of North Haven Island, including the shore of Pulpit Harbor, is of dark basaltic lava flows and volcanic breccias. The shore of Fox Island Thorofare displays a spectacular array of red, yellow, and purple porphyries, bedded ash, and coarse breccias full of angular rock fragments torn from the throats of volcanoes by violent eruptions and deposited on the sea floor. Most of Vinalhaven Island is of granite, well exposed at Carvers Harbor and in nearby granite quarries.

The Matinicus group of islands is also largely of granite. If fogbound at Criehaven, with time to spare, take a walk along the east shore of Ragged Island for about 100 yards south of Camp Cove to a magnificently exposed contact of granite against bedded rocks. Here is proof that granite is emplaced as a hot liquid. The granite truncates the layers in the bedded sediments along a line as sharp as a pencil line, and small fingers and offshoots of granite extend upward into the host rocks. Clearly, the granite must originally have been a liquid forced into the surrounding rocks. Note that right along the contact and in the off-shoots the granite is somewhat finer grained than elsewhere. The chilling of the magma against the slightly cooler host rocks prevented the growth of large crystals. And the magma must have been hot enough to heat the rocks it intruded, for the latter are very hard and considerably recrystallized.

West of the Fox Islands, the granites continue (the Muscle Ridge is largely in granite) but the rocks the granites intrude are no longer volcanics. The host rocks are now *schists*. We have crossed a contact between volcanics on the east and schists on the west, which extends from Owls Head, south of Islesboro, through Castine, Blue Hill, Bartlett's Island, and then inland to the northeast. This zone of schists intruded by granite continues west along the coast to Cape Elizabeth and beyond. Good exposures of schist are on Hooper Island west of Port Clyde; on Pemaquid Point, where the schists are laced with sinuous granite dikes; and on the islands of Casco Bay, where the north-northeast trend of the islands lines up precisely with the north-northeast trend of the vertical layers in the schist.

Schists are rocks formed by the transformation or metamorphism (hence the term *metamorphic* rock) of older parent rocks, commonly sandstone, shales, and limestones. Although many metamorphic rocks retain the bedding of the parent sedimentary rocks, the original grains of sand, silt, and clay have been completely recrystallized to new minerals, and the rocks have been sheared and very intricately and tightly folded. This recrystallization requires high temperatures and the intricate folding testifies to tremendous pressures. These high temperatures and pressures can only be found deep in the earth's crust; and high-grade metamorphic rocks such as schists probably have at one time been buried to a depth measured in miles.

From West Quoddy Head to Islesboro we have cruised through bays and islands underlain primarily (excluding granite) by gabbro and by volcanic rocks of many kinds. A very few fossils of marine shellfish (brachiopods) found in the volcanics indicate that these rocks date from the Silurian geologic period, some 350 to 3,000 million years ago. Volcanics like these and of approximately the same age extend into New Brunswick to the east and are found near Boston and in the eastern Carolinas to the southwest. Many geologists believe that these volcanic rocks are remnants of a long volcanic island archipelago, much like the present East Indies, which during the Silurian period bordered the North American continent from Georgia into Canada.

The metamorphic schists west of Islesboro represent sedimentary rocks originally deposited on the sea floor, which must have been pushed many miles down into the earth's crust to levels where temperatures are high and pressures tremendous. The only earth forces capable of squeezing rocks once at the surface to great depths are those that also raise mountains. Most of the world's present mountain chains, such as the Alps or Himalayas, are composed of thick sequences of sedimentary rocks that have been pushed together as in a vise between major blocks of the earth's crust. Gravity measurements show that high mountain ranges are underlain by masses of light rock—such as sedimentary rocks are—which extend to depths far deeper than the mountains are high. In other words, most of the sedimentary rock has been folded down and forms a root under the mountain range comparable to the underbody of an iceberg. It is in this root that the temperature and pressures are high enough to metamorphose the original sediments into schists.

Our cruise westward from Islesboro through the schists has thus taken us deep into the depths beneath an ancient mountain chain. Similar metamorphic rocks extend from Georgia to Newfoundland, and geologists interpret this belt as the root of a great mountain chain, which they call the Appalachian mountain system because the finest, most extensive exposures of this metamorphic belt are in the present-day Appalachian Mountains. The Maine part of the ancient mountain chain is clearly younger than the Silurian volcanics, for they too are folded and fractured, although they were not buried as deeply as the schists. Geologic studies of the Appalachian mountain system suggest that this ancient mountain range was built in different places and different times over a period ranging from 300 million to 200 million years ago.

The masses of granite so numerous along the Maine Coast intrude both the volcanics and the schist, and hence must be younger than the volcanic archipelago or the old Appalachian mountain system. Throughout the world, large intrusions of granite are confined to former mountain systems, and commonly the greater the degree of metamorphism in the root rocks, the more abundant the granite. These facts have led some geologists to the conclusion that the temperatures at the roots of mountain systems may become so high that the rocks not only are metamorphosed but actually melt, and this molten rock is granite magma. The magma thus formed then may work its way upward to cooler levels of the crust beneath the mountains where it crystallizes to granite. Hence it is possible that the granite of Mt. Desert may have begun as a sequence of sedimentary rocks on the sea floor. And today the streams on Mt. Desert and the waves beating against its cliffs are eroding the granite and returning it as sand and clay on the ocean bottom.

Today in the place of the ancient volcanic island archipelago and the old Appalachian mountain range there is the happy configuration of bays and islands that makes the Maine Coast such a good cruising ground. Erosion, extending over a period from 200 million to only one million years ago, has reduced the former mountain range to a low rolling upland cut by broad valleys in which slow meandering streams flowed southeast to the sea. These valleys were the forerunners of the great bays, such as Casco, Penobscot, Blue Hill, Frenchman, and Machias. Above this upland stood a few hills of particularly resistant rocks, the granites of Mt. Desert and Isle au Haut and the metamorphic rocks of Blue Hill and the Camden Hills. Geologists call such erosion remnants *monadnocks.* As erosion gradually removed the weight of over-lying rocks, the rocks deep in the roots of the ancient mountains slowly rose so that the volcanics, schists, and granites now at the surface originally were considerably deeper.

Across this rolling upland cut, during millions of years of erosion, spread the Pleistocene continental ice sheets, possibly as far to the southeast as Georges Shoals. The coast of Maine (during the ice age) must have been much like parts of the present coasts of Green-land and Antarctica. Beginning about one million years ago, there were four separate advances and retreats of the ice; and the inter-vals when the land was ice free were probably longer and the weather milder than since retreat of the last ice sheet. In Maine, only the last advance and retreat of the ice has left a record. The advance began about 40 thousand years ago and the last ice disap-peared from Maine only about 10 thousand years ago. Ancient man in Eurasia probably followed the arctic game northward during the last retreat of the ice there.

The glacier, which must have been thousands of feet thick, was armed by innumerable rock fragments imbedded in it and thus was a very effective gigantic file as it moved across the volcanics, schists, and gra-nites. The broad stream valleys were scoured out and deepened to form the present bays; and low hills and knobs were smoothed and polished to make the typical low round Maine island. Close examination of almost any smooth shoreline rocks will show many grooves and stria-tions, generally trending between east and south, made by rocks gripped in the ice at the base of the glacier. The ice was thick enough to bury Mt. Desert and the Camden Hills and locally, on the lee slopes (to the southeast), plucked away large blocks of bedrock to form steep cliffs. Valleys, such as those between the mountains on Mt. Desert, which once were V-shaped, were scoured out to a U-shape. Somes Sound is the most spectacular example of a scoured-out U-shaped glacial valley east of the Rocky Mountains.

As the glacier melted back, it deposited its load of immense boulders, gravel, sand, and fine rock flour in long, looping, morainal ridges marking the front of any particular ice lobe, in outwash plains of sand and gravel where streams poured off the ice front, and in patches of bouldery clay scattered randomly over the bedrock. This glacial garbage is a mixture of rock fragments picked up by the ice sheet both locally and hundreds of miles inland. The sand and pebble beaches of Maine are found where the sea has cut into these unconsolidated deposits of gravel, sand, and clay and then has reworked, resorted, and redeposited this material in the wave zone. The beach at Roque Island is perhaps the finest example. The low cliff behind it exposes the glacial bedded sand and clay from which the beach sands are derived. Many of the bars, like those at Bass Harbor Head and Petit Manan, are of glacial debris eroded from the original glacial deposits by the sea and concentrated in bars by tidal currents.

The yachtsman's most intimate contact with deposits arising from the Ice Age is the black sticky mud, which makes such good holding ground in Maine's harbors, such a mess of his topsides and deck when the anchor comes aboard, and such extensive and uniquely fragrant mud flats at the head of many coves and bays. Mud like this, commonly with clam shells of a more arctic type than found in Maine today, occurs as far as 100 miles up the Penobscot and Kennebec Rivers at an altitude of more than 100 feet. The same type of black clay occurs in places along the coast up to an altitude of 200 feet. Clearly, the Maine Coast must have been flooded by the sea after the ice retreated to a height of almost 200 feet above present sea level.

The submergence and the rise of the land since was caused by two main factors. The weight of thousands of feet of ice depressed the earth's crust; but at the same time there was enough water stored up in the great continental ice sheets to lower sea level even more, so that during maximum glaciation sea level all over the world was probably as much as 300 feet below what it is today. When the ice melted back, the ocean filled much more rapidly than the earth's crust rose in response to unloading of the ice. Consequently the sea flooded far inland, depositing black and brown mud in protected bays. The black mud on the mudhook was originally deposited there and has since been eroded by waves and streams and resedimented on the bottom of Maine's harbors and bays.

Geologists disagree as to whether the sea is still withdrawing from the Maine Coast. If it is doing so, withdrawal is so slow that the Maine Coast will remain a cruising paradise for many future generations of yachtsmen—if we can control the water-skiers and the atom.

APPENDIX C

New York State Pump-out Stations

Here is a selected list of the New York State marinas that, at the time of writing, have pump-out facilities for use by boats equipped with the state's approved marine toilet pollution control devices. Note that this list covers *only* those coastal and inland areas described in this guide and *does not include all* facilities within New York.

A special New York State chart indicating all existing facilities is updated from time to time and may be obtained free by writing the New York State Department of Environmental Conservation, 50 Wolf Road, Albany, N.Y. 12233.

Hudson River

Staatsburg, N.Y.	M.L. Norrie State Park
Poughkeepsie, N.Y.	Poughkeepsie Yacht Club

Long Island Sound

New Rochelle, N.Y.	Municipal Marina (by appointment—tel. 914-632-2032)
Mamaroneck, N.Y.	Nichols Yacht Yard (by appointment—tel. 914-698-6065)
	Mamaroneck Boat and Motor
Rye, N.Y.	Tide Mill Yacht Basin
Cos Cob, Conn.	Harbor Marine Center
	Mianus Marine Corp.
Stamford, Conn.	Stamford Landing Yacht Corp.
Norwalk, Conn.	Rex Marina
Clinton, Conn.	Clinton Harbor
Old Saybrook, Conn.	Black Swan Marina
Oyster Bay, N.Y.	Roosevelt Memorial Park
Glenwood Landing, N.Y.	Tappen Beach Marina
Glen Cove, N.Y.	Glen Cove Yacht Service
Huntington Harbor, N.Y.	Knutson's Marina
	Halesite Marina
	Milldam Marina

Northport Harbor, N.Y.	Woodbine Marina
Port Jefferson, N.Y.	Port Jefferson Marina
Mt. Sinai Harbor, N.Y.	Cedar Beach Marina

Eastern Long Island

Greenport, N.Y.	Mitchel's Sea Resort
New Suffolk, N.Y.	North Fork Shipyard
Dering Harbor, N.Y.	Dering Harbor Marina
Coecles Harbor, N.Y.	Coecles Harbor Marina
Sag Harbor, N.Y.	Baron's Cove Marina
Three Mile Harbor, N.Y.	Three Mile Harbor Boat Yard
	Maidstone Marina
Montauk, N.Y.	Deep Sea Marina
	Montauk Marina Basin

APPENDIX D

Hospitals

Almost every city along the coasts of New York, Connecticut, Rhode Island, and Massachusetts has a hospital. In Maine however, they are less frequent. Hospitals are located in the following towns and cities:

Kittery	Rockland
York Harbor	Camden
York Village	Belfast
Biddeford	Bangor
Saco	Castine
Portland	Blue Hill
Brunswick	Ellsworth
Bath	Bar Harbor
Boothbay Harbor	Eastport
Damariscotta	Calais

APPENDIX E

St. Croix River to Sandy Hook

Chart Number		Title	Scale
Old System	New System		
114–SC	13229	FOLIO SMALL-CRAFT CHART S. Coast of Cape Cod and Buzzards Bay	1:40,000
116–SC	12372	FOLIO SMALL-CRAFT CHART Long I. Sd.–Watch Hill to New Haven	1:40,000
117–SC	12364	FOLIO SMALL-CRAFT CHART Long I. Sd.–New Haven Hbr Ent and Port Jefferson to Throgs Neck	1:40,000
120–SC	12352	FOLIO SMALL-CRAFT CHART Shinnecock B. to E. Rockaway In.	1:40,000; 1:20,000
204	13322	Winter Harbor	1:10,000
205	13323	Bar Harbor	1:10,000
206	13321	Southwestern Hbr. and approaches	1:10,000
209	13307	Camden, Rockport and Rockland Hbrs.	1:20,000
211	13283	Cape Neddick Hbr. to Isles of Shoals	1:20,000
		Portsmouth Harbor	1:10,000
212	13285	Portsmouth to Dover and Exeter	1:20,000
213	13282	Newburyport Hbr. and Plum I. Sound	1:20,000
214	13211	Long I. Sd., N. Shore–Niantic Bay	1:20,000
215	12375	Connecticut R.–Long I. Sd. to Deep R.	1:20,000
		Long Island Sound, North Shore–	
216	12374	Duck Island to Madison Reef	1:20,000
217	12373	Guilford Hbr., to Farm River	1:20,000
218	12371	New Haven Harbor	1:20,000
		New Haven Harbor (Inset)	1:10,000
219	12370	Housatonic R. and Milford Hbr.	1:20,000
220	12369	Stratford to Sherwood Pt.	1:20,000
221	12368	Sherwood Pt. to Stamford Hbr.	1:20,000
222	12367	Greenwich Pt. to New Rochelle	1:20,000
223	12366	Long Island Sound and East River– Hempstead Hbr. to Tallman Island	1:20,000
224	12365	Long Island Sound, South Shore– Oyster and Huntington Bays	1:20,000
226	12339	East R.–Tallman I. to Queensboro Br.	1:10,000
227	13315	Deer I. Thoro. and Casco Passage	1:20,000
230	13296	Boothbay Hbr. to Bath, incl. Kennebec R.	1:15,000

231	13287	Saco Bayhand vicinity	1:20,000
233	13281	Gloucester Hbr. and Annisquam R.	1:10,000
235	13308	Fox Islands Thorofare	1:15,000
236	13223	Narragansett Bay, incl. Newport Hbr.	1:20,000
237	13228	Westport R. and approaches	1:20,000
238	13295	Kennebec and Sheepscot R. Entrances	1:15,000
240	13275	Salem and Lynn Harbors	1:25,000
		Manchester Harbor	1:10,000
241	13276	Salem, Marblehead, & Beverly Hbrs.	1:10,000
243	13279	Ipswich Bay to Gloucester Hbr.	1:20,000
		Rockport Harbor	1:5,000
244	13269	Cohasset and Scituate Harbors	1:10,000
245	13253	Plymouth, Kingston and Duxbury Hbrs.	1:20,000
		Greens Harbor	1:10,000
246	13270	Boston Harbor	1:25,000
246–SC	13271		
248	13272	Boston Inner Harbor	1:10,000
248–SC	13273		
249	13230	Buzzards Bay	1:40,000
250	13244	Eastern ent. to Nantucket Sound	1:40,000
251	13236	Cape Cod Canal and approaches	1:20,000
261	13238	Martha's Vineyard–eastern part	1:20,000
		Oak Bluffs Harbor	1:10,000
		Vineyard Haven Harbor	1:10,000
		Edgartown Harbor	1:10,000
264	13233	Martha's Vineyard	1:40,000
		Menemsha Pond	1:20,000
265	13241	Nantucket Island	1:40,000
		Connecticut River–	
266	12377	Deep River to Bodkin Rock	1:20,000
267	12377	Bodkin Rock to Hartford	1:20,000
268	13219	Point Judith Harbor	1:15,000
269	13217	Block Island	1:15,000
270	13248	Chatham Harbor and Pleasant Bay	1:20,000
271	13215	Block Island Sound	1:40,000
274	12342	Harlem River	1:10,000
275	12338	Newtown Creek, East River	1:5,000
278	13224	Providence R. and Narragansett Bay	1:20,000
		Hudson River–	
282	12343	New York to Wappinger Creek	1:40,000
283	12347	Wappinger Creek to Hudson	1:40,000
284	12348	Coxsackie to Troy	1:40,000
285	12333	Kill Van Kull and northern Arthur Kill	1:15,000
286	12331	Raritan Bay and southern Arthur Kill	1:15,000
287	12337	Passaic and Hackensack Rivers	1:20,000
		Kennebec River–	
288	13298	Bath to Courthouse Point	1:15,000
289	13298	Courthouse Point to Augusta	1:15,000
293	13213	New London Harbor and vicinity	1:10,000

		Bailey Point to Smith Cove	1:5,000
303	13327	West Quoddy Head to Cross Island	1:40,000
304	13326	Machias Bay to Tibbett Narrows	1:40,000
305	13324	Tibbett Narrows to Schoodic Island	1:40,000
306	13318	Frenchman Bay and Mount Desert I.	1:40,000
307	13316	Blue Hill Bay	1:40,000
		Blue Hill Harbor	1:20,000
308	13313	Approaches to Blue Hill Bay	1:40,000
310	13305	Penobscot Bay	1:40,000
310–SC	13306	Carvers Harbor and Approaches	1:20,000
311	13309	Penobscot River	1:40,000
311–SC	13310	Belfast Harbor	1:10,000
313	13301	Muscongus Bay	1:40,000
		New Harbor	1:10,000
314	13293	Damariscotta, Sheepscot & Kennebec Rivers	1:40,000
314–SC	13294	South Bristol Harbor	1:10,000
315	13290	Casco Bay	1:40,000
322	13303	Approaches to Penobscot Bay	1:40,000
325	13292	Portland Harbor	1:20,000
339	13251	Barnstable Harbor	1:20,000
343	13242	Nantucket Harbor	1:10,000
350	13227	Fall River Harbor	1:10,000
		State Pier	1:2,500
352	13225	Providence Harbor	1:10,000
353	13221	Narragansett Bay	1:40,000
353–SC	13222		
358	13214	Fishers Island Sound	1:20,000
359	13212	Thames R.–New London Hbr.,	
		Long Island Sd. to Norwich	1:20,000
361	12362	Port Jefferson & Mount Sinai Hbrs.	1:10,000
362	13209	Block I. Sd. & Gardiners Bay, Long I.	1:40,000
363	12358	Shelter I. Sd. & Peconic Bays, Long I.	1:40,000
		Mattituck Inlet	1:10,000
369	12327	New York Harbor	1:40,000
369–SC	12328		
375	12332	Raritan R.–Raritan B. to New Brunswick	1:20,000
540	12349	New York Hbr.–Gravesend Bay	1:10,000
541	12334	New York Hbr.–Upper B. and Narrows	1:10,000
542	12350	Jamaica Bay and Rockaway Inlet	1:20,000
542–SC	12351		
544	12330	Sandy Hook Bay	1:10,000
580	13249	Provincetown Harbor	1:20,000
581	13250	Wellfleet Harbor	1:40,000
		Sesuit Harbor	1:10,000
613–SC	13274	Portsmouth Harbor to Boston Harbor	1:40,000
		Merrimack River Extension	1:80,000
745	12335	Hudson & E. Rs.–Governors I. to 67 St.	1:10,000
		Hudson River	
746	12341	Days Pt. to George Washington Br.	1:10,000

747	12345	George Washington Br. to Yonkers	1:10,000
748	12346	Yonkers to Piermont	1:10,000
801	13328	Calais to West Quoddy Head	1:40,000
		Eastport Harbor	1:5,000
824–SC	12324	Intracoastal Waterway–	
		Sandy Hook to Little Egg Harbor	1:40,000
‡1201	‡13325	Quoddy Narrows to Petit Manan I.	1:80,000
†1202	†13312	Frenchman & Blue Hill Bays & apprs.	1:80,000
†1203	†13302	Penobscot Bay and approaches	1:80,000
‡1204	‡13288	Monhegan Island to Cape Elizabeth	1:80,000
‡1205	‡13286	Cape Elizabeth to Portsmouth	1:80,000
		Cape Porpoise Harbor	1:10,000
		Wells Harbor	1:20,000
		Kennebunk River	1:10,000
		Perkins Cove	1:10,000
‡1206	‡13278	Portsmouth to Cape Ann	1:80,000
		Hampton Harbor	1:30,000
‡1207	‡13267	Massachusetts Bay	1:80,000
		North River	1:20,000
‡1208	‡13246	Cape Cod Bay	1:80,000
‡1209	‡13237	Nantucket Sound and approaches	1:80,000
‡1210	‡13218	Martha's Vineyard to Block Island	1:80,000
‡1211	‡13205	Block Island Sound and apprs.	1:80,000
†1212	†12354	Long Island Sound–eastern part	1:80,000
†1213	†12363	Long Island Sound–western part	1:80,000
‡1214	‡12353	Shinnecock Light to Fire Island Light	1:80,000
‡1215	‡12326	Approaches to New York	
		Fire I. Light to Sea Girt Light	1:80,000

†Includes Loran-A Lines of Position
†Includes Loran-C Lines of Position
‡Includes Loran-A and Loran-C Lines of Position

INDEX

the COUNSELORS

the COUNSELORS

conversations with 18

courageous women who

have changed the world

ELIZABETH VRATO

RUNNING PRESS

PHILADELPHIA · LONDON

© 2002 by Elizabeth Vrato
Foreword © 2002 by Bill Clinton

9 8 7 6 5 4 3 2
Digit on the right indicates the number of this printing

Library of Congress Cataloging-in-Publication Number 2001098268

ISBN 0-7624-1215-1

Cover design by Whitney Cookman
Interior design by Alicia Freile
Edited by Melissa Wagner
Typography: Adobe Garamond, Trade Gothic, and Trajan

This book may be ordered by mail from the publisher.
Please include $2.50 for postage and handling.
But try your bookstore first!

Running Press Book Publishers
125 South Twenty-second Street
Philadelphia, Pennsylvania 19103-4399

Visit us on the web!
www.runningpress.com

For Gwendolyn

ACKNOWLEDGMENTS

More courageous people, without whom I would have never gotten anywhere—

First and foremost, thanks to Jennifer Worick and Melissa Wagner, my editors at Running Press. Jennifer plucked my proposal out of her mail pile and gave me a call. We met for lunch and went from there. Melissa's work, both as an editor and as a passionate supporter of this project, has been invaluable. Our book designer Alicia Freile, copyeditor Nancy Armstrong, and publicist Jennifer Brunn came on board at a crucial time and threw themselves into making the best product possible. Everyone I have met from Running Press has been terrific in this same way . . .

Special thanks to the American Bar Association Commission on Women in the Profession—especially to former Chair, Karen Mathis; Director, Ellen Mayer; and to Kim Calcagno—for their guidance and assistance in meeting recipients of its coveted Margaret Brent Award . . .

Thanks to the law firm where I practiced while writing this manuscript, Wolf Block Schorr and Solis-Cohen LLP in Philadelphia—for the flexibility and kindness extended to me so I could travel, research, and write—and especially to Mark Alderman, who, as the firm's cochair, was the face behind the flexibility and kindness . . .

Reneé Riebling must be thanked, because despite being extremely busy, she always helps me with at least as much as I ask . . .

Thank you to the best friend anyone could ask for, Michele Patrick, who talked with me that first night over pizza (and later many other nights over many other meals) about how great it would be if we could meet our heroes and ask them to tell us their stories; she provided much help in shaping this project, groundwork, and emotional support . . .

And thanks to a new friend, Kinney Zalesne, who has helped me over and over again. At first I didn't know her very well, and she helped me anyway; somewhere along the way she became a trusted friend and advisor.

*For without belittling the courage with which
men have died, we should not forget those acts of
courage with which men—such as the subjects
of this book—have lived.*

—John F. Kennedy
Profiles in Courage

It is not the critic who counts, not the one who

points out how the strong man stumbled or how

the doer of deeds might have done them better.

The credit belongs to the man who is actually in

the arena, whose face is marred with sweat and

dust and blood; who strives valiantly; who errs

and comes short again and again; who knows

the great enthusiasms, the great devotions, and

spends himself in a worthy cause; and who, if he

fails, at least fails while daring greatly, so that

his place shall never be with those cold and

timid souls who know neither victory or defeat.

—Theodore Roosevelt
"The Man in the Arena"
Address delivered at the Sorbonne, April 23, 1910

O you daughters of the West!

O you younger and elder daughters! O you mothers and you wives!

Never must you be divided, in our ranks you move united,

Pioneers! O pioneers!

—Walt Whitman
"Pioneers! O Pioneers!"

TABLE OF CONTENTS

FOREWORD

During the past four decades, America has made real progress on our journey toward equality and justice for all. American women, who just over eighty years ago were prohibited from voting, now serve at the highest levels of government. Women are also breaking through the glass ceiling of corporate management to lead some of our country's most prominent businesses. And once denied the resources and opportunities to play organized sports, American women today are making sports history.

But this progress has not come easily or without cost. The women profiled in this book—all of whom have received the Margaret Brent Women Lawyers of Achievement Award and three of whom I had the honor of appointing—share personal stories of their struggle to overcome barriers and of the women and men whose guidance, wisdom, and encouragement inspired them to persevere. These are stories of triumph as well. Justice Sandra Day O'Connor, whose grandmother was denied the right to vote, now sits on the highest court in our nation; Herma Hill Kay has seen the percentage of female students at Boalt Hall rise from 3 to 52 percent; Jamie Gorelick was sworn in as Deputy U.S. Attorney General to a female U.S. Attorney General by a female Supreme Court Justice when, just two decades before, not one of those positions had ever been held by a woman.

The accomplishments of the women in *The Counselors* are a testament to the power and promise of the American Dream and are sure to resonate deeply with many young women who have the desire and ability to make their own unique contributions to this legacy of progress. Today, more young women than ever are pursuing careers in law, medicine, government, and business and, like their predecessors, they need guidance to advance and excel. Just as the women in this book were empowered by the efforts and example of those who came before them, a new generation will be inspired and encouraged by the spirit and achievements of this remarkable group. *The Counselors* is a tribute not only to those who have successfully navigated the challenges of the professional world, but also to the mentors who helped them along the journey.

I know from my own experience the difference a strong positive role model can make, beginning with my mother, who, like several of the women profiled in this book, got up early, worked late, and still managed to put her children first. In high school, my band director and principal were role models I had the privilege of knowing personally, while from afar I admired President John F. Kennedy. With his optimism, passion for civil rights, and unshakable belief in America's bright promise, he gave me hope for the future and an insight into its possibilities.

Now a grown man with many, but I hope not all, of my life's accomplishments behind me, I continue to draw strength and motivation from both people I have known personally and those I know only from their stories: from Theodore Roosevelt and Martin Luther King, Jr., to my good friends Daisy Bates and Yitzak Rabin.

As someone who has benefited enormously from the example and counsel of role models like these; as the son and grandson of two women who were mentors in their own right; as the husband of an amazing woman who, with mentors of her own, was recently elected Senator from New York; and as the father of a daughter I hope will always be free to make her own way with inspiration from the women around her, I am proud to introduce you to the extraordinary women in *The Counselors: Conversations with 18 Courageous Women Who Have Changed the World.*

—Bill Clinton

THE
COUNSELORS

INTRODUCTION

Mentors, Role Models

I can personally vouch for the difference mentors and role models make.

I literally became a lawyer because of Jerry Shestack. My mother was a part-time secretary at his law firm while completing her college education. She told him she had a daughter who was going to be a lawyer someday (I was sixteen). Jerry said, "Well, get her in here. Let me see this future lawyer."

My mom took me in to visit his office on a school holiday. I remember the feeling of fear, apprehension, and excitement while she introduced me to him. He questioned me about school, told me about his practice, and took me under his wing. I wanted to be just like him.

Jerry is an internationally recognized lawyer who recently served as the President of the American Bar Association. He is a champion of women, minorities, and international human rights. No one in my family was a lawyer when I was growing up. Jerry's encouragement—as well as his patience and guidance—has shaped my life.

I wanted to become a lawyer in the first place because of my high school English teacher, Mrs. Geruson. She was a retired lawyer. I remember her teaching Shakespeare's *Merchant of Venice* with pleas for our class to consider the questions it raised about the nature of justice. She would have stood on her head to get through to us. I remember her coaching me for speech and debate competitions—tracing with her finger on my desk to show me that arguments need foundation and have to flow in logical sequence. I wanted to be just like her.

I think about Jerry and Mrs. Geruson all the time—things they said, what I think they would say, things they did, how I think they would handle something facing me now. If I leave Jerry a voicemail full of questions, he'll call back the same day (usually after eleven at night)—from wherever he is in the world—to respond to my message. Mrs. Geruson passed away a few years ago, leaving me enough advice to live by that it will still take me years to get to it all.

Why Not Women?

When I was a college student at La Salle University in Philadelphia, I was not too concerned about issues related to my gender. When I graduated from New York University School of Law a few years later, this was still the case.

Yet once I was in the work world for just a short time, my experiences and those of my friends made issues extremely important to me that had been of no concern while I was in school: the gap between women and men in earnings, power, and positions of responsibility; sexual harassment; discrimination; the failure of male-dominated professions and male-dominated institutions to welcome women into their fold.

For the first time, I found myself thinking regularly, "Where are the women?" and "Why not women?" I began to wonder more and more: Why can't there be seven women and two men on the Supreme Court? Why can't Congress be ninety percent women and ten percent men? What if the president were a woman? What if the *Forbes* and *Fortune* lists of wealthy people listed as many wealthy women as wealthy men? And if just some of these things were true, how would this country be different? How would its agenda be different?

I found peace from the demons that were plaguing me when I decided that instead of dwelling on the negatives and becoming disheartened (because for a time I *did* dwell on negatives and *was* disheartened), I would learn about women who overcame obstacles and what their stories teach.

My intention here is to introduce role models who can motivate and teach others, on the plain premise that everybody can use a little help. It doesn't matter who you are, who your family is, how much education, intelligence, or money you have. If you want to pursue a career, you will benefit from the knowledge of those who have gone before you.

The signposts left by other women on their journeys can show you what has been overcome and how far women have progressed—and make it easier for you to start leaving trails for other women to follow. For instance, in England in the 1600s—not so long ago in the timeline of history—if William Shakespeare had a sister named Judith, who was just as gifted and adventurous as he, what would have happened to her? British writer Virginia Woolf contemplated this hypothetical in *A Room of One's Own* (New York: Harcourt Brace, 1989, p. 47). Judith, she concluded, would have been kept at home while William went to school. And Judith's parents would have arranged a marriage for her with the son of a neighbor, while William went to seek his fortune in London and work in the theater.

In Woolf's essay, Judith was forced to scribble pages in a loft and then hide them or set them on fire. Frustrated, she ran away to London. When she stood at the stage door and said she wanted to work in theater, the men who ran the theater laughed in her face. She was tormented by her "poet's heart" that tugged at her without any means of expression. Stifled at every turn, she killed herself, and the world has never seen a sonnet or play of hers.

This is Woolf's rather extreme way of delivering the message that if you were born a female with potential and ambition—and not that long ago—you had no future. I think about "Shakespeare's sister" when a woman of brains and character is unappreciated or hindered.

In 1929, Woolf opined in *A Room of One's Own* that women could not become great writers for "another hundred years' time" because they needed to have a tradition established behind them—as Shakespeare had Marlowe before him, and Marlowe had Chaucer, and Chaucer had those unnamed men who had "tamed the natural savagery of the tongue" (ibid., p. 65). As Woolf goes on to write:

> One could not go to the map and say Columbus discovered America and Columbus was a woman; or take an apple and remark, Newton discovered the laws of gravitation and Newton was a woman; or look into the sky and say aeroplanes are flying overhead and aeroplanes were invented by women. There is no mark on the wall to measure the precise height of women. (ibid., p. 85)

What Woolf had to say about women who aspire to be writers applies equally to women who aspire to succeed in the workplace. In America, women did not customarily work outside the home or pursue professions until a few decades ago. Now, in the early twenty-first century, it seems hard to believe that one hundred years ago, most women were considered the property of their husbands, and women could not vote. Today we are building a new tradition—a tradition of women who pursue careers—made, in part, by the very women in this book.

A New Frontier for American Women

The foreword to this book was written by former President Bill Clinton, whose presidency was uniquely supportive of women's quest to establish a new tradition. He helped to break the glass ceiling for many women as lawyers, as judges, and in government positions. He advanced the opportunities for and status of working women more than any other American president. He appointed the first female U.S. attorney general, Janet Reno. And the first female Secretary of State, Madeleine Albright. Other women who served in the Clinton Cabinet include: Donna Shalala, secretary of Health and Human Services; Alexis Herman, secretary of Labor; Carol Browner, administrator of the Environmental Protection Agency; Aida Alverez, administrator of the Small Business Administration; Charlene Barshefsy, United States trade representative; and Janice La Chance, director of the Office of Personnel Management.

Mr. Clinton appointed more women than any other president. Women made up forty-four percent of Clinton Administration appointees. Thirty percent of the federal judges Clinton nominated are women, including Justice Ruth Bader Ginsburg, the second woman in history to serve on the United States Supreme Court.

President Clinton signed into law the Family & Medical Leave Act (which enables workers to take up to twelve weeks of unpaid leave to care for a new baby or a sick family member), the Violence Against Women Act (which made billions of dollars available to states and national organizations to prevent and prosecute cases of rape, stalking, and domestic violence), and the toughest child support laws in history. His Administration expanded business opportunities for women, including a May 2000 executive order requiring departments and agencies to develop long-term strategies to expand opportunities for women-owned small businesses.

The Clinton Administration increased funding for breast cancer research. He proposed and signed into law legislation requiring insurers to cover at least forty-eight hours of a post-natal hospital stay. He promoted safe reproductive health services for women, including increased funding for quality family planning. He signed the Freedom of Access to Clinic Entrances Act, establishing a safety-zone around women's health clinics. Clinton established the White House Office for Women's Initiatives, to contribute to the development of policy relating to women and families.

Compared to this record, the forty-one previous presidents did precious little to address the needs—and promote the talents—of the female half of the population. Mr. Clinton showed visionary leadership by aiding women in the ground-breaking work of obtaining positions of power and responsibility. Future presidents who now do the same will be viewed as following in his footsteps and fulfilling the promise of the revolutionary quantum leaps his administration took for American working women—as President Kennedy did for civil rights. I cannot thank Mr. Clinton enough for his inspiring foreword here.

Meeting New Mentors

To further the new tradition that Mr. Clinton and so many women have worked to create, I interviewed a number of women whose advice would be valuable to the next generation and others. Each was a recipient of the American Bar Association's Margaret Brent Women Lawyers of Achievement Award. Margaret Brent is the first woman known to have pursued a profession in the United States. She and her brothers arrived in Maryland in 1638 with a family land grant. With her brothers' permission, she represented the family in court on matters concerning family property, and also made other court appearances. Her name appears over a hundred times in Maryland court records—"Margaret Brent, Gentleman." There is no evidence of another female lawyer in the United States until the suffrage movement in the late nineteenth century.

Senator Hillary Rodham Clinton (D-New York) served as the first chair of the ABA Commission on Women in the Profession, from 1987 to 1992, before she served as first lady. She established the Margaret Brent Award in 1991 to recognize women in the legal field who have achieved excellence, influenced other women to pursue careers, and opened doors previously closed to women.

The Margaret Brent honorees were a terrific interview pool for this book for a number of reasons. First, law is a profession with wide application—private practice, government, business, public policy, academia—and it's one into which women have made wide inroads. We live under a rule of law, as opposed to under the rule of king or queen. You need look no further than the number of television shows that are about lawyers, include characters working as lawyers, have real-life judges solving real-life disputes, or are hosted by lawyers, to see that Americans also love the law as a part of our popular culture. Lawyers make our democracy work for justice—revitalizing and reshaping old institutions to contribute to society's needs today.

But *The Counselors* is mostly about mentoring—not about law, lawyers, or the biographies of Margaret Brent honorees. The women whose conversations are shared here have information and insight that is valuable to all women. Over the course of a year and a half, I traveled 25,000 miles and filled many hours spending time with and writing about these women. I thought, if I can gather their stories, and get them to more people than they could ever possibly meet during the course of their busy days, then I would be doing some good.

The wonderful, generous women you are about to meet were willing to talk with me in their offices, their homes, at restaurants, and hotels—then continued chatting with me by telephone and e-mail. Their authentic desire to lend a hand to others was evident in every exchange.

Through the experience of writing this book I learned that there are numerous ways to be the beneficiary of mentoring: counseling from one-on-one exchanges; observing someone who is good at what she does; or being influenced by someone in the public eye whom you'll never meet. While guidance often comes from those who are older, it can also come from peers or those who are much younger. Stories and examples infuse your decisions with context. This can help in choosing a school or a job, accomplishing your goals, balancing your life, and solving problems.

During the summer of 2001, while we were preparing this manuscript for publication, the ABA Commission on Women in the Profession issued a report concluding, in part, that women's opportunities have been limited by inadequate access to mentors and informal networks of support, by traditional stereotypes, by inflexible workplace structures, by sexual harassment, and by other forms of gender bias in the justice system. (You can view the report at www.abanet.org.) I felt very on-topic and current as we wrapped up our editing. That's not to say that I think all the answers are found in this book. But the topics explored here can help you ask some of the right questions for your own journey.

Before reading further, take a moment to think about who has helped you. Would you have been able to get this far without them? And could you perhaps benefit from more help from others? That's what this book is all about.

I.

LYNN HECHT

SCHAFRAN

It was summer 1998, and I was about to have my first meeting with a recipient of the Margaret Brent award. It was Lynn Hecht Schafran, at the NOW Legal Defense and Education Fund. I didn't know much more than that. But I was eager to learn.

In fact, I couldn't wait to talk to her. I wasn't sure what shape my conversations with the women was going to take. I'm an optimist though, and I hoped to have them culminate in a book. But who knew? Nothing's sure for any of us, and it's no small thing to say that you're going to talk to people in order to make a book when you haven't even talked to the first person yet, and when you've never written a book before. There were variables: What would these women say? How able would I be to take this project from an idea to fruition? It was just hard to say. Fear was creeping in, replacing my excitement. I felt scared.

Lynn and I sat in her office, and we started to talk. She told me she had been a charter member of the American Bar Association's Commission on Women in the Profession. She said that when the Commission began giving out the Margaret Brent award to recognize some of the women who were crashing through the glass ceiling and changing the world, some Commission members and staff were concerned that not enough tickets would be sold to fill the room for the award luncheon. But Lynn told them she was sure the luncheon would be a success, because she believed there was a hunger to see this kind of recognition for women. Sure enough, the room sold out, so the next year the Commission booked a bigger room. And they sold out that room, too. The Brent award luncheon now sells more than a thousand tickets every year and is the single biggest event at the ABA annual meeting.

I could relate to a story about the misgivings that can be associated with a new venture! Perhaps I could even draw strength from the fact that this new endeavor had worked out all right in Lynn's account. I began taking notes, saying, "Well, here's chapter one!"

As we parted, I told Lynn I would keep her apprised of developments. She encouraged me to send her any news and volunteered to look at chapters as I wrote them. Whenever I e-mailed Lynn some text for a look, somehow— despite her hectic schedule—it was always faxed back to me within a few days with her suggestions. With this kind of support, is it any wonder that there came a day when I had enough material for a book?

Lynn Hecht Schafran invites: "Draw a circle in your mind. This represents all the people in the world. Divide the circle in half. Mark one half 'women' and one half 'men.' Within the half marked 'men,' draw a line that marks out one-third of the segment. This one-third is all the white men in the world. Now shade a tiny sliver of this one-third. This sliver is all the educated and privileged white men in the western world. This sliver made our history, our literature, our art, and our law." Lynn uses this consciousness-raising exercise to explain that, "this sliver of men is not making all the rules anymore."

Lynn Hecht Schafran

RESIDENCE: New York, New York
BORN: 1941
PERSONAL: Married (2 children)
PROFESSIONAL: Director, National Judicial Education Program to Promote Equality for Women and Men in the Courts, (a project of NOW Legal Defense and Education Fund in cooperation with the National Association of Women Judges)
1996 Recipient of the Margaret Brent Award

Lynn's mother inherited the world of this "sliver" in the 1930s, when she tried to work outside the home at a radio station. A few days after she began working, Lynn's great uncle came to the station, pulled her mother outside, and told her to quit because she was taking a job away from a man. Nonetheless, she eventually became an interior designer and had one of the most beautiful showrooms on Madison Avenue.

By struggling to develop her own business and earn income, Lynn's mother was far in advance of her time. Yet Lynn was always conscious that her mother never had the opportunity to fully realize her potential and high intelligence. She lacked family support, community culture, and a peer group—all critical ingredients to career success not given to women during her mother's prime years.

Lynn remembers feeling that those around her had a very clear sense of how boys and girls should behave. Boys, for example, were given cars, and girls were not. Boys were given good allowances, while girls had paltry ones. Boys could get away with escapades girls could not. It was expected that girls would stay in the house and wait to be telephoned by boys who wanted to take them out (aided by their cars and allowances).

Lynn's father, who was a lawyer, was approached repeatedly by politically active friends to become a judge. He always declined, telling his family he had a dim view of the ability and integrity of many of the judges he knew.

These early influences—her belief that her mother did not have enough opportunities, the expectation that males and females had certain roles to follow, and her father's concerns with the quality of judges—helped shape Lynn into the person most responsible for changing the way the American court system treats women.

Training to Change the World

In autumn 1961, as a senior at Smith College, Lynn planned on applying to Harvard Law School until a fellow student told her Harvard only started accepting female law students in the 1950s. "At that moment," she recalls, "I felt unwelcome in the field of law." Instead, she went to Columbia University for graduate work in art history and then held positions as an art curator, lecturer, and critic.

While working at the Museum of Modern Art ("MOMA") in New York City, Lynn first confronted institutional gender bias. "I learned that you were not allowed to be pregnant as an employee of the MOMA. So I hid my pregnancy with baggy clothes, took a two-week vacation to give birth to my son, and came back to work—a pregnant employee no longer! I was so proud of myself for getting around their rule that it did not even occur to me to challenge the rule as unfair to female employees. As a woman at that time, my conditioning was to outsmart the system to get what I needed, not to change the system." Over time, that would change for Lynn.

Lynn's interest in law persisted. Ten years after she first considered attending law school, she started at Columbia Law School with the goal of becoming a civil rights lawyer. One of her teachers there would change her life. Professor Ruth Bader Ginsburg taught her how the civil rights laws that had helped minorities could advance women as well. She credits Justice

Ginsburg with putting her on the path of women and law. Lynn worked for Ginsburg at the American Civil Liberties Union Women's Rights Project; and after graduation, she was a clerk for the same federal judge for whom Ginsburg had clerked after law school.

Educating the Adjudicators

Several years after graduation, Lynn became founding director of a new organization of female lawyers formed to screen proposed nominees for federal judgeships on their demonstrated commitment to equal justice. Her focus on the judiciary and equal justice led NOW Legal Defense and Education Fund to ask Lynn to assist the sociology professor they had engaged to initiate a new project focused on the way courts treat women: the National Judicial Education Program to Promote Equality for Women and Men in the Courts ("NJEP") (in cooperation with the National Association of Women Judges). Lynn became NJEP's second director in late 1981.

"I learned that you were not allowed to be pregnant as an employee of MOMA. So I hid my pregnancy with baggy clothes, took a two-week vacation to give birth to my son, and came back to work—a pregnant employee no longer! . . . As a woman at that time, my conditioning was to outsmart the system to get what I needed, not to change the system."

Lynn met with tenacious resistance and many barriers when she solicited judges and lawyers to assist in NJEP's mission of eliminating gender bias as an institutional problem in the courts. The principal problems were threefold: First, denial (judges claiming there is no bias in the way women are treated in court); second, the "generational thinking" defense (judges believing that any bias that exists will disappear when the next, more enlightened, generation arrives); and third, the problem of sustaining attention over the long term (courts providing a program on gender bias for their judges once and then believing they don't need to do it again—even though there is constant turnover among judicial and non-judicial court personnel).

She found the "generational thinking" defense particularly objectionable and naïve, because given the dynamic nature of law, openness to change is essential to being an effective lawyer: "When a revised tax code is issued, no one would dream of suggesting that those who were used to the old code—had used it for more than ten years, were comfortable with it—were excused from learning the new tax code, that having the next generation learn it would be enough. . . . The notion that gender bias will automatically disappear when younger women and men become lawyers and judges underestimates the deep-seated and deeply unconscious nature of gender bias, as well as the need to educate both sexes about areas where ignorance about the social and economic realities of women's and men's lives undermines justice. . . . Age is wholly unrelated to knowledge of such critical issues as the counterintuitive fact that being raped by someone you know produces greater and longer-lasting psychological trauma than stranger rape. Judges who don't have that information impose minimal sentences on non-stranger rapists because they do not grasp the profound harm to the victims."

Lynn overcame the resistance she encountered by gathering evidence of bias from the country's courts, in order to make her "case" that there was an immediate need for improvement. "I wanted to make people see women's cases through women's eyes," she remarks. In response to NJEP's judicial education programs which emphasized providing state-specific data to overcome denial, a majority of the state supreme courts and federal judicial circuits created high-level task forces to investigate gender bias in their own court systems and make recommendations to eliminate it. Lynn worked with all these task forces and now works with their implementation committees, making concrete changes in areas ranging from court rules to legislation to codes of conduct for lawyers, judges, and court personnel.

Anecdotes Become Data

The task forces on gender bias in the courts gathered information from trial and appellate judges, court personnel, lawyers, law professors, jurors, sentencing surveys, academic research, and the litigants who use the courts. Interviews with women revealed they often felt ambivalent about turning to the courts because they wondered whether they would be treated fairly or be further victimized.

For instance, in divorce cases, Lynn found a version of the old boys' club. Many judges displayed a protective attitude toward fathers' incomes and lifestyles. Testimony by a father as to his limited ability to pay alimony and child support would be accepted by a judge without question, but a mother would be required to prove all of the expenses related to their children. Courts were unwilling to value a homemaker's non-monetary contribution to the marriage. They also did not recognize that a homemaker who did enter the workplace was unlikely to reach the economic level of her former husband. Studies found women living in economically depressed circumstances after divorce, while their ex-husbands continued to have the same or a higher standard of living.

This lack of knowledge about women's reality, resulting in unfair trials and unfair results, was also apparent in rape cases. That rape is a crime of violence, the seriousness of "date rape," and the long-term mental and emotional injury of rape were not considered.

"The notion that gender bias will automatically disappear when younger women and men become lawyers and judges underestimates the deep-seated and deeply unconscious nature of gender bias, as well as the need to educate both sexes about areas where ignorance about the social and economic realities of women's and men's lives undermines justice."

Some lines of questioning included gender stereotyping or harassment of the victim. For example, a rape victim might be asked if she enjoyed the sex or if she had been wearing something seductive. Some judges categorized a rape as "non-violent" if the victim was not beaten and bruised, not realizing that rape's most profound injuries are inflicted on the psyche and the soul. To counter these manifestations of gender bias, Lynn developed a model judicial education curriculum titled *Understanding Sexual Violence: The Judicial Response to Stranger and Nonstranger Rape and Sexual Assault,* now being used to educate judges, prosecutors, police, rape crisis counselors, and other anti-violence advocates across the country and internationally.

Female lawyers representing clients in our nation's courts did not fare any better than female litigants and witnesses. Lynn was an original member of the American Bar Association Commission on Women in the Profession that was formed in 1987 and chaired by Hillary Rodham Clinton. The Commission's report stated: "Women [lawyers] report that they are often treated with a presumption of incompetence, to be overcome only by flawless performance, whereas they see men attorneys treated with a presumption of competence overcome only after numerous significant mistakes."[1]

A probable explanation for this problem, Lynn comments, was that most judges were men who had few, if any, female colleagues when they were in law school or in practice, and their wives were probably not professionals working outside the home. These judges had limited contact with this "new breed"; as a result, they were not entirely comfortable with young female lawyers. Judges tended to focus on the "femaleness" of the lawyers before them, without realizing this chipped away at those lawyers' credibility and professionalism in front of a jury. For instance, by addressing a male lawyer as "Mr." or "Counselor," and then calling the female lawyer "young lady," "dear," or "Lynn," a judge sends a clear message to the jury as to whom he perceives to be the more competent professional.

---

[1] American Bar Association Commission on Women in the Profession, Resolution and Report to the House of Delegates, Aug. 1988 at 12.

Breaking Stereotypes

Lynn used the information gathered by the gender bias task forces and the ABA Commission to conduct gender fairness seminars for judges all over the country. Most people were responsive to her; she credits this to judges' sincere interest in being impartial and fair. But she still met with periodic resistance. She remembers: "I gave a seminar where three judges were openly contemptuous. When I went around the room and asked the judges why they had chosen to attend, these three said the topic was so ridiculous they had come to laugh! At a sentencing hearing the next year, a female lawyer asked one of these judges what she could do to convince him that her client was an ideal candidate for an alternative sentence. The judge replied, 'You can start by taking off your clothes.' Later—as part of his apology to avoid being reported to the judicial conduct commission—the judge told the lawyer that he had attended a course about this kind of thing, but had not paid enough attention."

Breaking stereotypes wide open was essential to making progress, Lynn believes, because there is a link between female stereotypes and sex discrimination. Many of the custody decisions where mothers were treated unfairly stemmed from the stereotype that mothers are pure, self-sacrificing, and at home full-time. For instance, a mother with a live-in boyfriend would be treated as a bad influence on her children, but a father with a live-in girlfriend was seen as "starting his new life." She also stressed that distorting application of the law to perpetuate male-female stereotypes can harm men as well. In one case, a judge said he would not award custody to a "house-husband" father because he would be a terrible

> *" . . . By addressing a male lawyer as "Mr." or "Counselor," and then calling the female lawyer "young lady," "dear," or "Lynn," a judge sends a clear message to the jury as to who he perceives to be the more competent professional.*

role model for his son.[2] In several cases, judges showed reluctance to give fathers overnight visits with their infants, assuming that a man does not know how to care for a baby.

Because of Lynn's work, the mood and conduct in courtrooms during the last two decades has changed dramatically. Bias and fairness training is now accepted as a component of every judge's orientation to the bench. In divorce cases, an expert may testify that a woman's at-home work has economic value. And in rape cases, a psychologist can testify that the trauma a victim experienced kept her from reporting her rape to the police immediately after it happened. Judges who think a female lawyer is being treated in a condescending manner by a male lawyer are likely to admonish the male lawyer on the record in open court. These were not accepted practices even twenty years ago.

"The concept that 'merit will out' is naïve. . . . There are plenty of qualified and talented women who have not gotten their due because they are women."

Since starting along her path, Lynn has trained thousands of judges, lawyers, and court personnel on how to provide justice without gender bias. She notes, "Now I'll teach a session about the economic consequences of divorce and a judge will come up to me afterward and say, 'When you explained the difficulty for a homemaker rejoining the workforce, I realized I did not give enough alimony to a woman who came before me last week.'" Judges who attend NJEP's course on rape trials often provide feedback, such as "I didn't know what I didn't know!"

Gender Equity Beyond the Courts

Lynn helped prepare opinion pollsters retained by NOW Legal Defense and Education Fund to conduct focus groups to gauge what is important to our

---

[2] *Peterson v. Peterson*, No. 86-0642 (Iowa Ct. of Appeals 1986).

country's girls and women. These focus groups revealed that women all over America care about the same things: equal pay for equal work, prevention of domestic violence and rape, and increasing the respect shown to them both in the workplace and at home. Variables such as the age, race, social background, and economic background of the focus group participants did not change the results.

She tells these girls and women, "The concept that 'merit will out' is naïve. . . . There are plenty of qualified and talented women who have not gotten their due because they are women." Female employees from some of the most prestigious firms and companies have contacted her with complaints that their employer has basically said to them, "We don't want you to succeed here."

Even at the "top," women find gender equity to be a scarce commodity. Lynn places a newspaper article on the table as she speaks: "The insidiousness of gender bias was brilliantly 'outed' by senior women faculty at MIT who, in 1999, reported that despite their lofty professional titles, they experience 'discrimination in areas from hiring, awards, promotions, and inclusion on important committees to allocation of valuable resources like laboratory space and research money.'"[3]

She advises younger women to raise their awareness of gender issues because discrimination has become less blatant than it used to be, though it remains just as destructive. Male supervisors may have learned not to say to a female subordinate, "Have sex with me and you'll get a raise," or "Go on a date with me or you're fired." Yet discrimination and harassment against women is still prevalent in more subtle forms—in fact, Lynn believes this form of prejudice is the last publicly acceptable form of discrimination in the sense of the overtness with which it is expressed. For instance, regardless of a judge's or lawyer's personal prejudices, few will say in open court, "What can you expect from a Jewish lawyer?" or "What can you expect from an Asian lawyer?" But if you substitute the word "woman" for the words "Jewish" or "Asian," this is the kind of incident female lawyers still report over and over again.

---

[3] Carey Goldberg, "M.I.T. Acknowledges Bias Against Female Professors," *The New York Times*, March 23, 1999 at A1.

The huge influx of women into the workplace is slowly chipping away at the traditional workplace model and making it better for women. As a result of this, Lynn points out that women are now less often excluded from formal and informal networks in their companies and communities. Additionally, employers are forced to deal with talented female workers who make important contributions, but who do not have a spouse in the suburbs taking care of their children and running the house. As a result, progressive policies such as parental leave, corporate-sponsored day-care centers, flex-time, and telecommuting—which were championed by women—are being institutionalized, to the benefit of fathers as well as mothers.

"Male supervisors may have learned not to say to a female subordinate, "Have sex with me and you'll get a raise," or "Go on a date with me or you're fired." Yet discrimination and harassment against women are still prevalent in more subtle forms . . ."

On a more personal level, Lynn advises, "If you decide to marry, make sure you marry someone who will be your cheerleader. My husband Larry, who is not a lawyer, is my chief supporter. . . . A few years ago the husband of a judge I know in Pennsylvania told me that whenever he is asked 'What's it like to be married to a feminist?' he smiles thoughtfully, pauses for a few seconds, and replies, 'I don't know. You'll have to ask my wife.' That answer is one Larry could give as well. He is the always-interested first audience and critic for all my speeches . . . the groupie who travels to judicial education programs with me whenever he can . . . and when, as occasionally happens, I wonder if this cause is making progress, stagnating, or even moving backward, he is my major source of encouragement."

Through untiring effort, Lynn Hecht Schafran created a new legal concept called "gender bias in the courts." Judges who exhibit gender bias in the courtroom are now reversed by appellate courts and sanctioned by judicial conduct commissions, and judges sanction lawyers who exhibit this behavior. Thanks to this extraordinary woman, our courts are a fairer place for America's women, and Justice is becoming blindfolded to gender.

II.

PATRICIA

SCHROEDER

In 1991, Anita Hill asked to submit testimony to the Senate Judiciary Committee nomination hearings for Supreme Court Justice Clarence Thomas. She alleged that while working at the Equal Employment Opportunity Commission, Clarence Thomas had sexually harassed her. The committee declined her request to be heard.

The committee later changed its decision and allowed Anita Hill to testify. I was one year out of law school at the time. New to the work world, I was fascinated by the emerging stories of Hill's struggle with office difficulties and dynamics.

Hill's testimony fueled conversation on new topics among friends and coworkers, and it sparked a national dialogue on sexual harassment and gender issues in the workplace. Hill's testimony changed things. After her testimony, the number of sexual harassment complaints increased, and the number of women in Congress doubled in the next election.

How had the committee's initial "no" been turned to a "yes"? Congresswoman Pat Schroeder of Colorado led a group of Democratic congresswomen in approaching Senate Majority Leader George Mitchell (D-Maine) to use his influence to bring Anita Hill before the committee. Nine congresswomen, among them Schroeder, Patsy Mink (D-Hawaii), and Barbara Boxer (D-California), interrupted Mitchell during a Senate luncheon and asked him to meet with them in his office. He did, and with his support Anita Hill testified before the committee.

Without Schroeder's initiative—and willingness to stand up for someone she had never met—Anita Hill probably would not have been heard. Schroeder was accustomed to struggles in politics, however; she was first elected to Congress in 1972, when women were just breaking through the glass ceiling in many professions. She faced struggles large and small, daily and constant, just like millions of other American working women.

It was with great anticipation that I climbed the steps on a busy Washington, D.C., street to Pat Schroeder's office, to learn more about this former congresswoman who has spent so much of her career standing up for herself and for millions of other Americans who've only recently had a voice in politics.

"The White House might as well have a 'No Girls Allowed' sign posted on the door," Pat Schroeder notes. The number of women who have pursued the United States presidency can be counted on one hand. Pat launched her campaign in 1987. Before her were Shirley Chisholm (1972), Belva Lockwood (1884), and Victoria Woodhull (1872), and in 2000 Elizabeth Dole added her name to the list.

Pat has spent her life tearing down "No Girls Allowed" signs. When she began attending Harvard Law School in 1961, there were only fifteen women in her first-year class of more than five hundred. She remembers male students changing their seat assignments in the lecture halls so they would not have to sit next to a female law student. "Infiltrating the boys' club of Harvard prepared me for infiltrating the boys' club of Congress," Pat observes.

Patricia Schroeder

RESIDENCE: Washington, D.C.
HOMETOWN: Denver, Colorado
BORN: 1940
PERSONAL: Married (two children)
PROFESSIONAL: President of the Association of American Publishers, and formerly a twelve-term U.S. Congresswoman
NUMBER OF POLITICAL CONSULTANTS HIRED AND POLLS TAKEN WHILE SERVING TWENTY-FOUR YEARS IN CONGRESS: Zero
1996 Recipient of the Margaret Brent Award

After Pat and her husband, James, graduated from Harvard Law School together in 1964, they settled in Denver, Colorado. Pat practiced and taught law for several years. Then she was approached by a local committee searching for a candidate to run against the Republican incumbent in their district. She won that seat and entered the Ninety-third Congress in 1972.

Sharing a Seat on the Armed Services Committee

Upon her arrival to Congress, Pat faced one of her biggest challenges as a congresswoman—she set out to become the first female member of the prestigious U.S. House of Representatives' Armed Services Committee. The committee was extremely powerful. At that time, it controlled about sixty-five cents of every dollar Congress spent—but no woman had ever breached this sacred male bastion.

Pat's biggest opposition to her appointment was a formidable opponent, the committee's chairman, F. Edward Hebert of Louisiana. He was dead set against women or minorities becoming members of his committee. "When I arrived in Congress, these chairmen were demigods. Younger representatives were expected to be quiet, wait their turn, and hope they could outlive their opposition! Everyone was afraid of Hebert . . . Armed Services was the most powerful committee in Congress during the Vietnam War, and Hebert ran it like a personal fiefdom."

Remarkably, Pat succeeded in her quest for an appointment to the committee. But when she and a fellow representative, Ron Dellums (a Democrat from California and the first African-American to be appointed to the committee) arrived for their first meeting, they found only one open chair in the committee meeting room. Apparently Hebert, furious that his veto of their appointments was ignored, had announced that women and African-Americans were worth only half of one "regular" member, so he allowed only one new chair to be added to the room for his two new "half" members. None of the other forty-two committee members offered to get them another chair—many of them had military bases in their districts, so they felt they had a vested interest "to please the chairman, no matter how outrageous he was!" Pat expounds, "They felt their political careers depended upon their being able to go home and tell their constituents, 'Look how much money I got for you this year for our base.'

"Infiltrating the boys' club of Harvard prepared me for infiltrating the boys' club of Congress."

"Ron and I had two choices over the chair. We could go ballistic or we could hang in there." Pat and Ron decided they did not want to jeopardize their appointment to the most powerful House committee by starting a commotion over the lack of a seat, so they sat together on one chair. "We were 'cheek to cheek,' trying to retain our dignity." Not surprisingly given their close quarters, Pat and Ron became great friends and supporters of each other. "Once, in a heated debate, Ron said to Hebert, 'There are only two of us with the balls to stand up against what we all know is wrong.' I tugged on his arm and suggested 'balls' was not a precisely accurate description of our little coalition of two."

Pat exercised her right as a committee member to attach to the annual defense budget bill her individual views not shared by the committee. She submitted supplemental reports about Pentagon practices. She provided alternative defense budgets, suggesting that NATO allies contribute more money, or pointing out that while some weapon systems worked, others weren't at all reliable. Some colleagues thought her motivation was to goad Hebert, but that was not the case. Pat considered the submission of supplements with alternative views as part of her duty as a free-thinking committee member. She continued to include supplements expressing her views during her entire tenure on the committee, even after Hebert was gone.

Hebert, furious that his veto of their appointments was ignored, had announced that women and African-Americans were worth only half of one "regular" member, so he allowed only one new chair to be added to the room for his two new "half" members.

Repeatedly, she felt committee members were afraid of Hebert and, even more, afraid of vigorous, open debate about the role of the military. When she asserted her views, a frequent refrain from committee members was, "What could she know? She never served in the military." Yet most of them had not served in the military either.

Committee members who criticized Pat were just following the example of their chairman. Hebert continually characterized her efforts in the most denigrating light. "I questioned U.S. bombing raids on Cambodia, and he said, 'I wish you'd support our boys like you support the enemy.' And when I voted to cut off the funds for the continued bombing, he yelled, 'No! That's the dumbest thing I ever heard!'"

Hebert's hold on the Armed Services Committee was finally challenged when the first group of post-Watergate representatives came to Washington in 1974. These representatives had been elected in a wave of voter backlash against the perceived corruption in Washington, D.C. The reform-oriented representatives requested a report from the chairman of each committee on progress and goals. Because of them, chairmanship was changed from an appointed position to an elected one, with a secret ballot every term. "Hebert had been branded as an autocrat, in part because word was getting around about the way he had been treating me and Ron over the past two years. The freshmen decided Hebert should be voted out. He tried to campaign for votes, but it was too late." And with Hebert's replacement, Pat and Ron had chairs of their own. (Ron Dellums would later serve as chair of the committee, from 1992 to 1994.)

Taking a Stand

Pat believes often just the willingness to stand up for yourself—though in her case it was to sit down for herself—and to remain tenacious are the most effective means to an end. She points out that she learned this lesson in part due to a very difficult situation: The second time Pat was pregnant, which was before she entered Congress, she started to bleed in her fourth month. Her obstetrician brushed off her concerns. "He called me high strung, and said that since I was a Harvard lawyer, I must be having trouble adjusting to life as a housewife."

Two months before her due date, she went into labor. In the delivery room, it was discovered that Pat had been carrying twins, a boy and a girl. The girl died early in the pregnancy and had been the cause of the hemorrhaging. The boy was born barely alive, weighing only four and one half pounds, and died by the next morning. Pat explains, "I was angry at the doctor for refusing to listen to me, but I was furious at myself for letting a doctor convince me I had no right to question his judgment." She has never forgotten this lesson brought home in tragedy.

A Pioneering Campaign

Most of the time, Pat has stood up not only for herself, but she has also embraced what some have called "women's issues"—but which she calls "American issues"—involving fairness, equality, and justice. Nowhere was this more evident than in her historic Presidential campaign.

In the spring of 1987, during her tenure as a congresswoman from Denver, Pat cochaired the presidential campaign of Senator Gary Hart of Colorado. The campaign fell on hard times when Hart, who was married, defended himself against accusations of womanizing by daring the press to "go ahead and follow me." Shortly thereafter, the *Miami Herald* obtained photographs of him on a yacht with a woman named Donna Rice on his lap. His campaign dissolved virtually overnight, and Pat's role as cochair came to an abrupt end.

However, Pat's supporters urged her to take a look at joining the presidential race herself. She recollects, "I asked myself, 'Could I raise the necessary money? Build an organization? Be accepted?'" Pat's largest obstacle was time. Seven other Democrats already had been running for some time. Also, there was the issue of her gender—Pat would be the first woman to make an attempt at the presidency since 1972,

> *"I was angry at the doctor for refusing to listen to me, but I was furious at myself for letting a doctor convince me I had no right to question his judgment."*

and though it had been fifteen years since Shirley Chisholm had unsuccessfully given it a go, there were no real indications that mainstream voters were ready to embrace her candidacy.

Pat nonetheless decided to throw her hat in the ring. She knew she could not win, but she also knew she could add something to the candidates' debates that was not being addressed by her male counterparts: a discussion of family issues with the American people. It was an important subject that needed to be addressed, and she felt that she was the person to bring it to the forefront.

As she campaigned, the anticipated focus on her gender began. She found some aspects of it amusing—and some annoying. The press called her "the women's candidate" and measured women's progress in society by her candidacy. At one of her appearances, a state Democratic Party chairman introduced her in glowing terms, then ended with, "Of course I can't vote for her because I have a problem with a man for first lady."

"Can you even imagine a male candidate being asked the outrageous question of whether his wife knows if he is running for president?"

At other events, she was asked, "Does your husband know you're running?" Pat queries, "Can you even imagine a male candidate being asked the outrageous question of whether his wife knows if he is running for president?"

As she campaigned, she was struck by how ready people were to talk candidly about family issues. Audiences of mixed gender asked how she managed to be in Congress, have a spouse, and raise two children. Men had been running for president for generations, and they were never asked these types of questions because it was assumed their wives handled all the domestic responsibilities. Pat found that "men and women, from college students to senior citizens, wanted politicians who understand what is going on in their lives and government policies that reflect that understanding. Americans were desperate for someone to help them juggle all the roles and chores modern life has laid upon them."

Out of this dialogue with the American electorate, Pat became convinced that people needed government policies to help them with burgeoning family and health care issues. As the modern age progressed, more and more families needed two incomes to survive financially, but the government had done little to address this change. Pat explains, "After World War II, America was the world's 911 number. We poured money into providing the world's military defense, while our allies put money into paid health care, free college tuition, and excellent childcare for their citizens. They could afford these programs because we denied them to ourselves in order to provide the world's defense." Pat wanted our government to have more policies to help families.

When August arrived, Pat ranked third for the Democratic nomination in a *Time* magazine poll, but she felt that winning would have taken more money and time than she was able to give. Reluctantly, she decided to withdraw from the race. In the end, finances triumphed. "I just didn't have enough money to be truly competitive," she reflects. "All along, people had been saying, 'It would be really interesting if you ran,' and I thought that meant they would support me. Some did, and some just thought, 'How nice—the race is more interesting.' It was a reality check. I wanted to be president, not interesting! Other politicians were hesitant to put their own careers on the line by actively saying I was a viable candidate."

She began to cry while delivering the farewell speech of her campaign— emotions overwhelmed her as she looked into her parents' eyes, as the audience groaned, as people chanted "Run, Pat, run." The political climate is so different now that it is hard to imagine the response Pat received to her tears. She recounts, "Those seventeen seconds were treated like a total breakdown. . . . I went on with my speech, but it was my tears that got the headlines, not my words."

The media discussed her tears for weeks. "Some writers went so far as to say that my tears had dampened all

"Traditionally, politics has not been a field for women to pursue, but we are just as able and have just as much to offer as men."

hopes for women in presidential politics for the rest of this century," she recalls. The critics who angered her the most were "the ones who said they wouldn't want the person who had their finger on the nuclear button to be someone who cries . . . but I wouldn't want that person to be someone who doesn't cry!" In response to all the media attention, Pat started a "sob sister" file. It included news items on the public tears of Ronald Reagan, George Bush Sr., Margaret Thatcher, and Oliver North. After the media commotion her own tears had caused, Pat got some satisfaction in finding that other political figures also cried in public. She points out, "Now crying is something male politicians need to do to show they're compassionate. . . . Crying came out of the closet."

Pat Schroeder not only brought crying out of the closet, she also showed the nation that traditional feminine qualities can be leadership qualities. In the years following Pat's pioneering campaign, issues important to American families have become a priority in politics. Pat sponsored the Family Leave and Medical Act (1993) and the Violence Against Women and Child Abuse Protection Act (1994). She was instrumental in the passage of the Health Care Equity Act, which guarantees adequate funding for women's health issues, and she served as a cochair of the bipartisan Congressional Women's Caucus.

> *"I'm passing this torch. . . .*
>
> *Come and get it!"*

Today, she characterizes her candidacy as a quest for the answer to the question, "Is America 'man' enough to back a woman?" The answer, she found then, was "No!" It is probably still the answer.

Passing the Torch

When she left Congress in 1996 after serving for twenty-four years—making her the longest sitting female member of Congress—Pat taught at Princeton University's graduate school of public service. She was both amazed and dismayed to discover that most of her students had no intention of ever running for public office. Pat wants young women to aspire to serve in Congress. She believes that only when women reach a critical mass in Congress will they make a real difference. "Traditionally, politics has not been a field for women to pursue, but we are just as able and have just as much to offer as men."

Pat also encourages young women to become comfortable with the term "feminist," as it is a term and philosophy designed to help them. Pat says, "I can't tell you how many girls and young women I have met who insist they are not 'feminists.' . . . I don't know how they came to associate feminism only with mythical acts like bra-burning. But I always think, 'Give it a couple years out in the work world, and then we'll talk.' Sure enough, so many working women came into my congressional office to complain about the unfairness of lower pay or some favoritism shown to male counterparts. . . . And I'd say, 'Welcome to feminism!'"

Seated, Pat sets down her glass of ice water, raises her arm in the air, gives her characteristic Cheshire cat smile, and says, "I'm passing this torch. . . . Come and get it!"

It is time for a new group of American women to pull down some of those "No Girls Allowed" signs.

III.
LOUISE
RAGGIO

Growing up in Philadelphia, the cradle of American liberty, I cannot even count how many times I visited my city's historic sights. Suffice it to say that Independence Hall, the Liberty Bell, Betsy Ross' house, and Benjamin Franklin's house were popular field trips in grade school.

I thought Benjamin Franklin was cool. He tried his hand at so many different things. He conducted experiments with a kite and a key in a storm to prove there is electricity in lightning. He was the author and publisher of Poor Richard's Almanack. *He invented bifocals, signed the Declaration of Independence, and served as United States Ambassador to France. He said many quaint but catchy—and substantive—things like, "Little strokes fell oaks" and "Keep thy shop, and thy shop will keep thee."*

During one of the colonial America tours, I learned Franklin used to start each day by asking himself, "What good shall I do this day?" And at the end of the day, he examined his conduct by asking, "What good have I done this day?"

So from time to time, brushing my teeth or getting ready for school, I used to think of Ben Franklin and label something I was going to do that day as "good." Then I grew up, went to college, left Philly, and didn't think about Ben Franklin while brushing my teeth anymore.

The concept of examination of a day, or a life, came to the forefront again when I met Louise Raggio. This time, I was at an age and a point in my life where I could really appreciate it. Louise is a Texan octogenarian who meets the tests life provides head-on. "What a good person," I said to myself repeatedly as I listened to Louise and thought about her afterward.

I tried to put myself in Louise's shoes. What if I were eighty-something years old and telling someone I had never met before about the way I had been spending decades of time? Just what would I have to say for myself?

I thought about the people I hope will be with me and the work I hope will engross me in the decades to come. Now there is another layer over everything I do, and I know it wasn't there even a few years ago. It's the layer of—no matter what I'm doing—being conscious of the question, "How am I living this life of mine, as I go around doing these things that are important to me?"

Thank you for that, Mr. Franklin and Ms. Raggio.

A t the age of twenty-two, Louise Raggio thought she had an ideal life ahead of her. Her plan was to marry the lawyer she had fallen in love with and then stay home, be a lawyer's wife, and raise their family. She planned on spending spare time volunteering for church and community affairs. With a twinkle in her eye, she says, "If you want to make God laugh, go ahead and make a lot of plans for yourself!"

Louise did do some of what she planned. She married the lawyer. She raised three sons. She was involved in her church and her community. But she never did get to stay home and be a lawyer's wife.

World War II intervened and changed the course of her life. Louise never told close friends and relatives the full story. They saw Louise grow into a feminist lawyer who transformed the face of law for women in Texas. She kept silent in order to protect her husband, and even now she is willing to tell the whole story only because he has passed away. The story involves a slice of World War II history. It tells her answer to the question "What makes a feminist?" and contains lessons in loyalty and strong character.

Louise Raggio

RESIDENCE: Dallas, Texas
BORN: 1919
PERSONAL: Widowed
(Three sons, all practice law with her)
PROFESSIONAL: Partner in the law firm Raggio & Raggio PLLC
1995 Recipient of the Margaret Brent Award

Finest Hours

Louise met her husband, Grier, when they were both working for government agencies in Austin, Texas. On their very first date, he told her they would marry. She remembers, "I just thought he was being a smoothie—he was tall, handsome, personable." But Louise found herself falling for the smoothie lawyer, and Grier's assessment of their compatibility was accurate. In April 1941, after knowing each other just three months, they married.

On December 7, 1941, the Japanese bombed the U.S. naval base at Pearl Harbor, Hawaii, and the United States entered World War II against Japan and Germany. Louise had found out she was pregnant just days before. Grier obtained permission to delay going overseas until their baby was born. When Louise gave birth to Grier Jr., Grier left for the South Pacific. The husband who left Louise to go to war was not the same man who came back.

As part of his military service, Grier was sent to "island hop" in the South Pacific. "Island-hopping" was a military strategy to first invade and liberate the surrounding Japanese-held islands before invading mainland Japan. Month after month, under a hail of bullets and grenades, American soldiers and sailors stormed successive beachheads, where the sands turned red from the blood of dead and mutilated comrades.

The last major battle of World War II was fought on one of these South Pacific islands, Okinawa, which is generally acknowledged to have been the bloodiest battle of the war. The second to last battle of WWII was on the island of Iwo Jima. It is generally acknowledged to have been the second bloodiest battle. Over the course of weeks and months, American soldiers fought to occupy these islands—climbing over bodies of dead soldiers, dodging enemy flame-throwers, mortars, and bullets.

Grier lived in a foxhole and tent on Iwo Jima for five months, as the battle for the island raged and ebbed. He buried the bodies of friends he had fought alongside, handling their severed arms, legs, and heads. After the battles of Iwo Jima and Okinawa, President Truman ended World War II by dropping two atomic bombs on Japan.

When the war was over, after years of separation, Grier returned home to Louise. Louise remembers, "Grier was a changed man. . . . He weighed two hundred pounds when he left, and he weighed one hundred and twenty-nine when he came home. Today we would say he suffered from post-traumatic stress disorder, although nobody called it that back then. . . . He was still a loving person, but he seemed sad a lot of the time. And for the rest of his life, he had flashbacks . . . he would awake in the middle of the night, shaking with nightmares. . . . Of course, I knew I was just lucky he came home alive at all, when so many men had died in the war."

Blacklisted

Trying to resume a normal life in Dallas, Grier started a job with the Veterans' Administration. Then, as Louise tells it, "After serving his country selflessly, his country kicked him in the teeth." Grier was fired because he was labeled a "security risk" and "blacklisted." At the time, Senator Joseph McCarthy of Wisconsin was capitalizing on America's post-war fear of communism by instituting the House Un-American Activities Committee in the U.S. House of Representatives. He recklessly investigated alleged communists and pilloried them in the media and in Senate hearings, so the public could carry out the intention of McCarthy's blacklist by shunning and censuring these people.

A person who was blacklisted was virtually unemployable. In fact, an employer willing to employ a blacklisted person could suffer in the business community. Senator McCarthy's methods were ruthless and vicious. He destroyed peoples' lives and livelihoods with little or no evidence of wrongdoing. With horror, Louise followed news stories of blacklisted people committing suicide because their lives were ruined. She comments, "When you saw the way McCarthy tapped into people's fears, and how people reacted to him and joined the frenzy, you could better understand how someone like a Hitler could ever have come to power. In Dallas, a rabbi and a Unitarian minister spoke out publicly to say that what McCarthy was doing was wrong. They were the only ones. . . . I was so grateful to them— and so impressed by them—that I converted from fundamentalism to the Unitarian church."

Grier was not a communist. Louise believes he was targeted because of some work he was doing with the United Nations, elaborating, "Many people

"I had learned much from that McCarthy nightmare. . . . I learned that innocent people can be accused, and that it is important for some of us to be vigilant about protecting the rights and liberties of the rest of us."

in Dallas in the 1950s considered the U.N. to be a subversive organization. . . .
They thought it was a tool of communist agents or that it was on a mission to
create one world government, destroying individual national sovereignty." As
with most people who were blacklisted, she does not know the actual reason.
She says part of her wants to see the FBI files on herself and her husband, but
she dreads the re-opening of those old wounds.

Mrs. Grier Raggio, Esq.

Louise and Grier challenged Grier's firing, and eventually he was reinstated.
But Louise's dream of being a lawyer's wife and staying home to raise their sons
and being taken care of was now put aside for good. Grier suggested to Louise
that she go to law school so that they could open their own law practice, and
she decided his idea was a good one. "I had learned much from that McCarthy
nightmare. . . . I learned that innocent people can be accused, and that it is
important for some of us to be vigilant about protecting the rights and liberties
of the rest of us."

Additionally, Louise was becoming concerned about her husband's well-
being: "He never admitted he was hurting inside, how ravaged—physically,
mentally, emotionally—he must have been from the war and the blacklisting.
He always put on a brave 'can do' front. . . . That's what men of his generation
did. They thought it was 'weak' to complain. . . . In the back of my mind,
earning the law degree grew in importance because I could see that Grier was
frail. In case he were to become unable to work, I wanted to have a marketable
trade I could use to raise our boys."

She attended Southern Methodist University Law School at night, so her
husband could be at home with the children after work. They could not
afford a babysitter. ("We were dirt poor," she recalls. "We didn't have a
phone, a refrigerator, or a dishwasher.") She recounts, "I was the only woman
in my class. . . . They didn't want me there. . . . People in the admissions
office told me I was taking the place of a man who could use a law degree
to support his family. But that's why I was there! I needed to have a way to
support my family, too."

Five years later, Louise was awarded her law degree. Her degree read "Mrs. Grier Raggio." There were only a handful of women who were lawyers in Dallas, and law firms openly stated that they would not hire female attorneys. Though at first she had a difficult time finding a job, Louise's career got a boost when she befriended U.S. District Judge Sarah T. Hughes (who, years later, swore in Lyndon Johnson as president aboard Air Force One after John F. Kennedy was assassinated in Dallas). Sarah mentored Louise and emboldened her.

Sarah and Louise

Judge Hughes wanted to see a woman as a criminal prosecutor in the all-male district attorney's office, and she wanted it to be Louise. With Sarah's support and assistance, Louise became the first female assistant criminal district attorney in Dallas. "Everyone who ran things thought women couldn't do criminal prosecution," says Louise. "Women were not even allowed to sit on juries, how were they going to argue before them—persuade them? . . . Nonetheless, Sarah called up the district attorney, Henry Wade, and said she was going to keep calling him until he appointed a female prosecutor. He later said he hired me when she asked because he knew you might as well do what Sarah asked you the first time she asked, because she would eventually get her way."

Louise and Judge Sarah Hughes began holding monthly meetings for all the female attorneys practicing in Dallas. The meetings were held in a small room around a table. They encouraged female lawyers to become active in the community, city politics, and bar

"I was the only woman in my class. . . . People in the admissions office told me I was taking the place of a man who could use a law degree to support his family. But that's why I was there! I needed to have a way to support my family, too."

association activities. "If any one of us heard about an opportunity, we called all the others. If any one of us had a problem, we called all the others." She smiles. "Back then it was survival—now it's called mentoring."

The two of them undertook many progressive projects and had many adventures, one of which Louise introduces, with a laugh, as "Our campaign of terror on Republic Bank!" "Sarah called me up and told me to buy stock in Republic Bank," she begins. "I said, 'Yes Ma'am, I'll do it—just tell me now— why am I doing it?' Sarah explained that apparently Republic's president had said there would be no women vice presidents as long as he was there. So we were going to go to the shareholders' meeting to protest. . . . I bought the stock, and six months later, I dressed up, and we went to the meeting. . . . Sarah now owned fifteen shares of Republic stock, and I had twenty-five. . . . We found out they had learned of our plan and appointed two women vice presidents before the meeting . . . so we had to change the plan a bit. . . . I stood up and thanked the bank's officers for appointing the female vice presidents. Then Sarah stood up and said she was furious at them for not having women on the board of directors! Not long after that, Republic and every other bank in the city had a woman vice president or board member."

> "If any one of us heard about an opportunity, we called all the others. If any one of us had a problem, we called all the others. Back then it was survival—now it's called mentoring."

Balancing Act

Shortly after Louise had entered the D.A.'s Office, Grier opened a law firm with the intention that Louise would join him as soon as she gained experience trying cases and established some connections to bring clients to their firm. When she joined Raggio & Raggio, they set up a satisfying professional experience that would serve clients while keeping their children as the top priority.

For instance, in order to make sure they spent time with their sons everyday, one of them tried to get to the office by 7:00 A.M. and leave for home by 4:00 P.M. Sometimes they brought home files to work on after the boys went to bed. Louise still participated in her sons' activities at school and took her turn serving lunches in the school cafeteria with the other mothers. On weekends, she cooked roasts and meatloaf and froze them, to provide home-cooked meals on weeknights. Having her own business gave Louise the flexibility to balance the competing needs of being a competent professional and a good parent.

It was a hard pace, and Louise was making up the rules as she went along. "I was probably one of the first women lawyers to put it together and have a family and a career. . . . Growing up, I could only conceive of three careers for a woman—teacher, nurse, and secretary. I would have loved to have been a journalist, for instance—I took courses and wrote for the high school and college papers—but a woman couldn't get a job in journalism."

"I was probably one of the first women lawyers to put it together and have a family and a career. . . . I used to shudder to think what the local headlines would say if my kids ever got into trouble."

She confesses to having felt great anxiety as a result of her nonconformance with the societal expectations of women at the time: "In the fifties, people said, 'If you're not with your children all day, they'll end up in the detention center.' And I was scared of that. I used to shudder to think what the local headlines would say if my kids ever got into trouble. . . . My own mother used to tell me I was ruining my children by going out to work in an office!

"The only reason I did it is because I felt I had to. . . . Sometimes I used to feel that I had to have Grier in an office with me, where I could watch him and protect him, or he was going to die. I could never say that. . . . I used to just tell people that Grier had been unhappy with government service and we wanted to work together. . . . I still wonder what Grier could have done if he had not been through so much in World War II. He was such a loving husband and father. And he was far ahead of his time where I was concerned. Most men back then didn't want their wives to be 'stars.' . . . But Grier encouraged me in everything I did."

Rewriting the Laws

Although she was licensed to practice law and was a partner in her own law firm, Louise was not allowed to sign a bail bond for a client—Grier would have to sign it for her. Under Texas law, a married woman could not sign a contract on her own, even in the context of professionally representing a client. Additionally, a married woman could not run a business without her husband's consent or control the property she owned before she was married. Louise recalls, "A woman lost her property rights upon marrying. . . . We used to say if you're a minor, a mentally incompetent person, a felon, or a married woman, you have no rights in Texas."

"You can't go through what I've been through and not be a feminist."

Louise vowed to use this frustration as an impetus to change the law for herself and for the women of Texas. "You can't go through what I've been through and not be a feminist," she reasons. She persuaded the president of the state bar association to let her put together a committee to rewrite the law, and then she organized a task force of domestic relations experts who drafted legislation and worked for its passage in the Texas legislature. The new law allowed a wife to run a business and to control her separate property.

Next, Louise spearheaded an effort to write a Texas Family Code pulling together all the various state statutes concerning marriage, custody, family, adoption, and divorce into one cross-referenced source. Contradictory or antiquated statutes were eliminated. It was the first unified domestic relations law code in the world and served as a model for many other jurisdictions that took on the task of writing a unified code. She was the code's principal organizer and drafter; she participated in seminars all over the state to educate lawyers about it.

For the Next Generation

Thinking back, Louise observes, "Being a woman was an advantage when I started practicing law, because everybody underestimated me. . . . But, I was a child of my time. I grew up accepting that girls were not as valuable as boys. I used to 'sweet-talk' to get my way instead of being direct or having a confrontation. I wouldn't do that today though. Girls don't have to do that today."

There is a speech Louise gives when she is invited to speak at schools, which she calls the "I was a nerd" speech. She explains that as a child, "I was heavy and tacky [only wore hand-me-downs] with poor, uneducated, immigrant parents—and lived on a dirt farm in the country." She tells students, "The only way for me to go was *up!*" Then she explains that the only way for her to move up was to get good grades in school. She tells students that doing well in school is the key to having options in your career path. And she stresses, "Don't concentrate on what you don't have. Concentrate on your assets, on your strengths, instead of your disabilities."

Louise believes young women should avoid the kind of piecemeal schooling she received because of her circumstances. She advises female students to focus on their education first, before they consider taking on the roles of wife and mother, saying, "Women in the past didn't accomplish much out in the world when they got married and then had a child every two years."

"We used to say if you're a minor, a mentally incompetent person, a felon, or a married woman, you have no rights in Texas."

She warns young women, "Never think you have it made. That's what the suffragettes thought after they won the right to vote in 1920, and we've had plenty of new battles for equality since that one!" Louise speaks from experience. She was friends with suffragettes Jane McCallum and Minnie Fisher Cunningham, who led Texas' campaign for passage of the Nineteenth Amendment. She met them when she did some volunteer work at the Austin League of Women Voters after college. "I could listen to their stories all day long. . . . I often thought of Jane and Minnie for inspiration during my dark days. . . . They went through a lot . . . they were harassed and insulted for something which seems common sense. Who could doubt today that women have the right to vote?"

"I grew up accepting that girls were not as valuable as boys. I used to 'sweet-talk' to get my way instead of being direct or having a confrontation. I wouldn't do that today though. Girls don't have to do that today."

Louise concludes, "I had some horrible obstacles to overcome, but they made me the person I am today. I have had more than my share of blessings, and I do what I can to help others. . . . As women get more support in their families and communities, get more education, and make more money, things are only getting better for us."

IV.

JAMIE
GORELICK

When Jamie Gorelick told me she has referenced her children's books at meetings, I started thinking about other sources—besides the very desirable advice of a wise parent, teacher, tribal elder, or pioneering woman—from which I draw guidance. And I sheepishly realized I had been doing my friends a disservice by not acknowledging them as the important role models and counselors they are. Here's what I mean:

When I tell a friend I'm upset about something that happened in an important relationship, as we talk over the events involved, I come to realize there is another unarticulated issue brewing underneath the surface that is the real reason for my anger. It would have been much more difficult, if not impossible, for me to dig out of my emotional reaction and clarify the issue on my own.

When I show a draft of some writing to a friend, and she says, "I like it. I remember when that happened," I feel like I'm on the right track. Or when I e-mail a draft to a friend and he replies, "Nope, I don't get it," his fresh set of eyes and honest feedback re-focus me before I proceed.

Those group discussions with ensemble decision-making (which often seem to take place at coffee shops or with take-out food in somebody's living room) help to manage all the different areas of our lives—often with a lot of laughter in the process. Laughter is an important aspect of taking care of each other and helping each other along. Recent topics submitted for deliberation at group functions include: "How can T—— ask for better training at work?" "Do we like Y——'s old boyfriend better than her new boyfriend?" "What the heck is 'success' anyway?" "Should O—— move to London?" "Would M—— like going to law school?" and "What's a good title for that book E—— has been writing about mentoring?"

Jamie Gorelick helped me to realize a broader concept of what comprises mentoring—I hope that you, too, will realize more of the possibilities for inspiration in your own life, just as I've enjoyed discovering some of my own influences.

(Don't forget your friends!)

I t was a first. At Jamie Gorelick's swearing in as deputy U.S. attorney general in 1994 by Supreme Court Justice Ruth Bader Ginsburg, Attorney General Janet Reno commented upon it: "Who would have thought when we graduated law school we would be swearing in a deputy attorney general who is a woman, to serve under an attorney general who is a woman, and sworn in by a Supreme Court justice who is a woman?" Indeed,

Jamie Gorelick

HOMETOWN: Washington, D.C.
BORN: 1950
PERSONAL: Married
(2 children)
PROFESSIONAL: Vice Chair of
Fannie Mae, and formerly
Deputy Attorney General of
the United States
*1997 Recipient of the
Margaret Brent Award*

the appointment of these three women by former President Clinton to such high-powered posts furthered his goal of changing the composition of government to better reflect the composition of American society.

The deputy attorney general is second-ranking only to the attorney general, who leads the Department of Justice. The U.S. Department of Justice (often referred to as "DOJ") represents the United States in legal matters, focusing on law enforcement and crime reduction. With Jamie as Attorney General Reno's deputy, for the first time in our country's 218-year history, women held the two most powerful law enforcement positions and were running "the largest law firm in the world," as the DOJ is sometimes called.

The wall outside Jamie's office at the Justice Department was lined with photographs of her male predecessors. Five former deputy attorney generals became attorney general, two served as secretary of state, and two were appointed to the Supreme Court. These photographs served as constant reminders that Jamie was a trailblazer in a new era for women. They were also reminders that the upper echelons of power are filled with men who may or may not be receptive to women entering their realm.

Jamie's Law

The deputy U.S. attorney general is the day-to-day manager of operations at the Justice Department, which employs over one hundred thousand people.

He or she supervises investigations and litigation in many areas, including civil rights, civil claims, antitrust, tax, immigration, environmental law, and criminal law, as well as law enforcement agencies like the Federal Bureau of Investigation, the Marshals Service, and the Bureau of Prisons. The deputy attorney general also coordinates DOJ relations with Congress, the president, the judiciary, and federal agencies.

When Jamie was first briefed on her new duties, she learned Attorney General Reno was facing a problem inherent in many bureaucracies. The attorney general ("A.G.") was often presented with issues that were not adequately defined, requiring her to spend valuable time gathering background information, asking questions, and analyzing facts before a decision could be made. Jamie remembers, "I called my predecessor, who warned me that Reno wanted her deputy to do a job that can't be done. . . . I decided my first step would be to serve up issues to the A.G. for final decisions in a crisp and clean way. I wanted to enable the A.G. to do her job of making important decisions and representing the DOJ to the public."

"I have a system of lists, detailing what needs to be done at work and at home—and I always have back-up plans. That's what happens when you put a working mom in charge!"

As Attorney General Reno noted, there were immediate changes under Jamie's management: "She swept in here one day, dressed to the nines, took command, ordered people around like she was a general, but did it in such a gracious way, and I kind of sat there and looked and they told me that was a Jamie Gorelick."

The A.G. and Jamie decided to decrease the number of people reporting directly to the Attorney General and had them report to Jamie instead, giving the A.G. more time for policymaking and public duties. Jamie increased the frequency of meetings among the Department's top officials to make the DOJ more responsive to inquiries. She identified unresolved issues, assessed the ramifications of various courses of action, and forwarded her recommendations to the A.G. for resolution. At Jamie's behest, a systematic review of Congressional testimony by DOJ officials was required, to ensure that follow-up promised to Congress was being provided.

Jamie's knack for streamlining to the heart of issues is memorialized in a gift from one of her former law partners. He gave her a gavel inscribed "Because I said so," which rests on a base inscribed "Jamie's Law." Jamie used this gavel to run meetings, rapping the table to bring order to arguments and to cut through emotional exchanges to the bottom line. She elaborates, "At the end of a meeting, I would say what we need, and I would give deadlines. People need to know what you want and when you want it."

She believes the secret to effective management is organizational skills. "I have a system of lists, detailing what needs to be done at work and at home—and I always have back-up plans." She grins and chuckles, "That's what happens when you put a working mom in charge! So many working women I know are great organizers. . . . When the tasks on a list have been accomplished, I toss the list away. . . . I don't hang onto information I don't need going forward."

As deputy attorney general, Jamie faced a mind-boggling array of issues on any given day. "We used to say to each other, 'If you don't like an issue before you, wait fifteen minutes . . . somebody will give you a new one.'" For example, Jamie supervised the first DOJ gathering of intelligence on how to secure our nation's computer infrastructure against "cyber-terrorists." Terrorist on-line attacks in cyberspace could paralyze ground and air transportation, telephone systems, gas and oil pipelines, medical records, banking, financial markets, and police and governmental operations. Jamie warns, "There has to be a structure in place to protect us against a Pearl Harbor-like cyberspace attack."

She also worked extensively on old-fashioned crime prevention. "I love cops," she says, in her straightforward manner. "This may sound corny, but it is so patriotic—people who come to work everyday willing to die for their community. To me, cops are the very models of public service. My father was an immigrant, my mother from an immigrant family, and they were extremely patriotic and hardworking, so I'm very comfortable with those values. . . . Cops I've talked with, cops on the street, the most experienced, know criminal sanctions are not enough to prevent crime. Cops need to know the kids in a community, and the kids need to know the cops. Communities also have to offer alternatives to hanging out on street corners and getting in trouble. . . I grew up that way. In my community, there was plenty for us to do. . . . Communities have to be places where we can make friends, make a difference, and make a home."

Jamie flourished at the DOJ and talks about her tenure there with unbridled enthusiasm. "Government, unlike some places in the private sector, doesn't have the ability to waste human resources. It is lean and mean. A talented woman will have her talents used to the fullest—and with less prejudice about her functioning effectively in any particular role. Government service lets people show their stuff!"

A Zig-Zag Path

Jamie's career path didn't begin in government. After graduating from law school, she started at a small white collar defense firm in Washington, D.C. Soon after President Carter started the Department of Energy, she served on the transition team for the second secretary of energy, under the direction of Colin Powell. Then she returned to the private practice of law. Later, during the Clinton Administration, she served as general counsel of the department of defense, supervising more than six thousand lawyers. After only one year, President Clinton tapped her for service in the Justice Department.

Varied experience in both government service and the private sector has allowed her to pursue different interests and opportunities. "Career paths don't have to go in straight lines. Getting involved outside your organization makes you more valuable to your organization. If the organization you're working for can't accommodate your involvement in outside endeavors, find another place to work." This is part of the reason Jamie never pursued a high-paying job in a large corporate law firm: "I feared I would have been buried and pigeon-holed." Also, she knew she wanted to have a family and wanted an environment that offered flexibility.

To students mapping out careers, she says, "Make sure you will be challenged everyday and will be learning all the time. You don't want to just tread water. . . . Find your own pace—don't be driven by what those around you are doing. . . . Be open and ready for opportunities that arise. . . . You can't fully plan the most interesting careers." She also recommends downplaying other people's anticipation of obstacles. "I've developed a certain lack of awe through the years, and it's been helpful. I am never daunted when people say things can't be done. I recommend a lack of awe . . . it helps you get the job done."

When Jamie left the DOJ to become vice chair of Fannie Mae (the United States' largest source of home mortgages), her transforming work at the DOJ received bipartisan acclaim. With fans ranging from former President Clinton to Secretary of State Colin Powell, she could be selected as attorney general at some point in her career by either a Democratic or a Republican president.

"Career paths don't have to go in straight lines. Getting involved outside your organization makes you more valuable to your organization. If the organization you're working for can't accommodate your involvement in outside endeavors, find another place to work."

Aware of her professional rank, she observes, "There are still not enough women in senior positions to give young women enough different kinds of female role models. . . . I take seriously my own role as a mentor—not so much my giving advice, although I do that—but just my being there as an example."

The Importance of Family

The primary example in Jamie's life has been her parents. "My brother and I grew up feeling our parents would do anything for us. My parents had grown up poor, so they wanted to give us every possible opportunity. I had so many lessons—every lesson under the sun—piano, guitar, clarinet, glockenspiel, tap dancing, jazz, modern dance, French . . ."

Her parents played complimentary roles in her development. "My mother gave me her empathy and caring for people and her commitment to community and friendship. On any given weekend, one day I could be in a parade with my Brownies troop and another day I could attend a civil rights march. . . . My father gave me an enormous curiosity about the world. And virtually every woman of achievement I know had a father who believes girls can do anything."

As much as she learned from her parents, Jamie is also open to learning from her kids. She and her husband have two young children, a boy and a girl. They started a family when Jamie was in her late thirties, after her career was blooming.

"It's great to be at home and have your kids just treat you like a mom. . . . It leavens even the most serious moment." When Jamie began at the DOJ, her five-year-old son was a Power Rangers fan. She recalls, "One night, he answered the phone when the Department's Command Center—which kept us in touch twenty-four hours a day—called, and said, 'This is the Command Center for the deputy attorney general.' Dan brought me the phone with a trembling hand, saying, 'Mom, Zordon [the Power Rangers' controller] is on the phone!'"

Jamie expands on what she has learned from her children. "I have given up my old hobbies, which were gardening and tennis, in order to hang out more with my kids. . . . So I've learned a lot about *their* hobbies—*Star Wars,* insects, bicycling, and building with Lego. . . . I like reading to my kids. . . . Childrens' books have so many nuggets of truth in them. For instance, I like *The Little Prince* by Antoine de Saint-Exupéry, which teaches important lessons about building your community.

"I've caught myself quoting storybooks at big meetings. One night we had a senior staff meeting at the DOJ, and one of the assistant attorney generals said something like, 'Oh, we *can't* get the terrorism bill passed, and the immigration bill is *hung up,* and the nominations are *such a problem,*' and the first thing that came out of my mouth in response was 'Stop it! You sound just like Eeyore!' . . . Eeyore is the pessimistic donkey in *Winnie the Pooh* stories . . . soon everyone was teasing him that he needed more of a Pooh and Piglet attitude."

Finding a Balance

She observes that societal expectations of mothers have reversed. Working mothers used to have to explain away the stigma of working outside the home. Now it is assumed women will work outside the home while raising a family, and they often have to justify to others the choice to stay home to raise children full-time. Jamie does not like either of these assumptions, preferring to believe that women have choices unencumbered by such expectations. She notes, though, that mothers with careers have a difficult balancing act to perform in fulfilling professional and personal responsibilities, and a supportive spouse can make the sometimes precarious balance easier to maintain.

Jamie gives her husband a lot of credit for her ability to have a successful career while raising a family: "He's more than a supportive husband . . . I have a partner. My husband is my best friend. He knows me well. He says that I have only two states of being—bored or overworked."

"Make sure you will be challenged everyday and will be learning all the time. You don't want to just tread water."

Jamie shares some of the details of her own balancing act. "I'm always thinking about how to create a better balance in my life. I try to be home in the evenings. I can work on the computer at home after the kids go to bed if I need to. . . . My view at the Department was that, with over one hundred thousand people working there, another hour from me at the office could not make a difference. . . . And I try to not work on the weekends . . . or be away from home more than one night a week.

"The balance I have come to in my life might be one that other women would not enjoy, but there are so many different balances that can work. Everyone has to make their own decisions about priorities. It is an individual choice. That's what our women's movement has been all about—giving us a choice.

This new world of opportunities for women is chock full of choices. And because Jamie's choices have led to her career advancement and the striking of a personal balance, she is a role model to watch.

V.

SANDRA DAY
O'CONNOR

In the winter of 1990, when I was in my first few months of work after law school graduation, I came across a small item in the newspaper that really shocked me.

It read that Justice Sandra Day O'Connor had participated in a "Women in Power" conference at St. Louis' Washington University, where she had said that the "paucity" of women in executive positions is rooted in "blatant sex discrimination and the widespread belief that women are unfit for power positions." She also noted that, although she was at the top of her graduating class at Stanford Law School in 1952, the only job offer she got was as a legal secretary.

It was news to me that the first woman to sit on the Supreme Court had been treated so disrespectfully by her profession when she first entered it! After all, I was working at a prestigious firm, and I knew I sure wasn't Supreme Court justice material.

At that time, I didn't know Justice O'Connor's background at all, but I had imagined that she had practiced at some "prestigious firm"—maybe after having a prestigious clerkship (the Supreme Court?)—and was treated wonderfully everywhere she went during her professional development, before she blossomed upon being appointed to the Supreme Court. I just didn't know. I hadn't been taught anything about this in school, and I didn't have work experience to speak of. It certainly gave me something to think about.

I photocopied the article ten times and passed it around to the other women who sat near me. Several of their reactions were as strong as my own had been. We talked about the "paucity" of women in power positions—at the firm, at our law schools, in general.

I trimmed the article's edges down to its smallest possible size, covered it with strips of scotch tape (homemade laminating), and put it in my wallet. It stayed there for years. One time a friend putting change back into my wallet saw it and said, "Why don't you throw this away?" But I liked bumping into it from time to time. It was a touchstone of sorts.

Eventually I took the article out of my wallet, but I never lost track of it. I know exactly where that taped-over news item is right this minute— it's paper-clipped to the letter Justice O'Connor sent me after we worked on this chapter.

For most of her life, Sandra Day O'Connor's grandmother could not vote in her home state of Arizona. Women in this country were denied the right to vote on the basis of gender until ratification of the Nineteenth Amendment to the U.S. Constitution in 1920. Today, Justice O'Connor not only votes in national elections with citizens of both sexes, but—as one of nine U.S. Supreme Court justices—she casts votes deciding the most important issues of the day presented to the highest court in the land.

Sandra Day O'Connor

RESIDENCE: Washington, D.C.
BORN: 1930 in Greenlee County, Arizona
PERSONAL: Married (three children)
PROFESSIONAL: Associate Justice, Supreme Court of the United States
2000 Recipient of the Margaret Brent Award

"I have taken voting for granted all my life, but it is something many people's grandmothers never enjoyed," Justice O'Connor reflects. "I have a special interest in the period of women's suffrage and entry into the work-place—the two are intertwined. The amount and the rate of progress is astounding. . . . Even in my own time and in my own life, I have witnessed a revolution."

A Century of Change

In order to understand the extent of the changes that have taken place in the last century, Justice O'Connor believes that first we must have an understanding of the past. "In 1776, Abigail Adams—the wife of future President John Adams—implored her husband, 'Remember the Ladies!' in drafting this nation's new charter. Her plea fell on deaf ears. . . . Our Founding Fathers envisioned no role for women in American government. The Constitution permitted each state to determine the qualifications of its voters, which was essentially the same as denying the vote to women. If the federal Constitution did not give women the right to vote, the states were not going to go out on a limb to provide it."

Justice O'Connor explains that women and men moved in separate spheres in the late eighteenth century, with the commercial, political, and professional realms dominated by men, and the domestic sphere relegated to women. "The two distinct spheres defined by gender were rooted in the belief that women were subordinate to men by nature, almost certainly less intelligent, and biologically less suited to the rigors of business and politics." Women were unable to step outside of their domestic role because of what today's theorists name the "cult of domesticity"—the idealization of a woman's role in the home as wife and mother. It was commonly believed that women's natural character is selfless, gentle, moral, and pure, best suited to art and religion rather than logic. O'Connor continues, "Men, on the other hand, were considered to have been fitted by nature for competition and intellectual discovery out in the world—battle-hardened, shrewd, and authoritative."

> *"Even in my own time and in my own life, I have witnessed a revolution."*

Seneca Falls and the New Women's Movement

The seeds of change were sown in the mid-nineteenth century abolitionist movement, when women took a leading role in northern antislavery communities. O'Connor elaborates, "Women reformers spoke at public meetings, conducted petition campaigns, and sharpened their organizational skills. . . . They eventually used these skills to press for their own rights, especially the right to vote.

"A World Anti-Slavery Convention in London served as a catalyst for the women's movement. . . . The United States' delegation included a number of women, but only the male delegates were allowed to sit on the convention floor. Among the females forced to observe passively from the galleries were Lucretia Mott, founder of the first Female Anti-Slavery Society, and Elizabeth Cady Stanton, wife of abolitionist leader Henry Stanton. . . . Afterward, Lucretia and Elizabeth discussed the irony of women working for the anti-slavery cause, supporting the principle that one man should not be enslaved to another on the basis of his race, yet being denied a voice at the convention because of yet another trait one was born with and did not choose—gender.

"When Lucretia later visited Elizabeth at her home in Seneca Falls, New York, they organized their own convention: a 'women's rights convention.' For two days in July 1848, more than three hundred people gathered—some traveling from as far as fifty miles away, which could be a few days' travel in those days. . . . Elizabeth Cady Stanton inspired lively discussion with her Declaration of Sentiment—eleven points outlining rights for women modeled after the Declaration of Independence. Resolution Nine provided: 'Resolved, that it is the duty of the women of this country to secure to themselves their sacred right to the elective franchise.'"

The women's movement in the United States is commonly dated from the Seneca Falls convention. Word of the convention spread, and women started to organize to overcome their proscribed societal position. "Women had been in agreement about their dissatisfaction with the current state of affairs. Now they developed goals. And they took action to achieve their goals. Additional women's rights conventions followed. . . .

"In 1776, Abigail Adams—the wife of future President John Adams—implored her husband, 'Remember the Ladies!' in drafting this nation's new charter. Her plea fell on deaf ears."

Initially, few women felt as strongly as Elizabeth Cady Stanton about the importance of securing the vote. Issues considered to be more pressing included women's inability to control property and earnings, limited opportunities for higher education and employment, and lack of legal status. . . . Elizabeth won supporters as women realized it would be extremely difficult to correct these iniquities without the right to vote."

Legal Setbacks

The potential for change brought about by the emancipation of former slaves after the Civil War brought the right to vote to the forefront of discussion in parlors and state houses around the country. Justice O'Connor relates, "The suffragettes were hopeful, reasoning, 'If newly-freed black slaves are to be guaranteed the same civil rights as all other citizens, including suffrage, shouldn't women be swept up in the expansion of the right to vote?' Their hopes were dashed, however, when the draft of the Fourteenth Amendment introduced to Congress in 1866 incorporated an explicit gender restriction into the Constitution, saying the vote would not be 'denied to any of the male inhabitants' of a state. Explicitly excluding women from the vote in this amendment meant that another constitutional amendment would be required to explicitly provide women the right to vote."

"Lucretia and Elizabeth discussed the irony of women working for the anti-slavery cause, supporting the principle that one man should not be enslaved to another on the basis of his race, yet being denied a voice at the convention because of yet another trait one was born with and did not choose—gender."

Meanwhile, women trying to enter professions such as law were facing insurmountable obstacles. O'Connor tells of how in 1875, one Wisconsin court ruled that the practice of law was unfit for the female character because exposing women to courtroom life would "shock man's reverence for womanhood and relax the public's sense of decency."[1] She recounts another case of a similar nature that went before an Illinois court in 1869 and eventually all the way to the U.S. Supreme Court

---

[1] *Goodall's Case,* 38 Wis. 232 (1875)

in 1872: "Myra Bradwell of Chicago studied law as an apprentice under her husband and applied to the Illinois bar in 1869. She was refused admission on the basis of her sex. The Illinois Supreme Court reasoned that, as a married woman, her contracts were not binding, and an attorney-client relationship cannot exist without contracts.[2] The U.S. Supreme Court denied Bradwell's claim that this ruling was depriving her the privileges and immunities of U.S. citizenship. . . . In the Court's decision, Justice Bradley wrote, 'Man is, or should be, woman's protector and defender. The natural and proper timidity and delicacy which belongs to the female sex evidently unfits it for many of the occupations of civil life.'"[3]

Winning the Vote

After years of persistence through setbacks and struggle, the suffragettes were eventually successful in their mission to secure the right to vote for American women. "The suffragettes marched. They petitioned. They met with members of state legislatures to line up support for a Constitutional amendment. . . . Some of their opposition disappeared when liquor interests, which had been very hostile to them, needed to re-channel resources to fend off a prohibition amendment. . . . Women won the right to vote on August 20, 1920, when the Nineteenth Amendment was signed into law. . . . Seventy years had passed since the Seneca Falls convention, and it had been a tough row to hoe. Elizabeth Cady Stanton didn't live to see the realization of her dream. She died in 1902. Luckily for us women today, our female predecessors had far more spunk and spirit than they were given credit for . . . I look up to them."

The Justice muses, "Once you get a flavor of the struggle for women's right to vote, think about this: What was it all for? The suffragettes were jailed, attacked, and divorced in their quest for the American Dream of full citizenship. . . . Now, eighty years later, what will you make of their ideals? Do you use your right to vote? What do you think needs to be done for women to

[2] *Bradwell's Case*, 55 Ill. 535 (1869).
[3] *Bradwell v. Illinois*, 16 Wall. 130 (1872).

reach full and equal citizenship in other respects? The suffragettes' concerns are still pertinent today."

Jumping over Professional Hurdles

Gaining the right to vote didn't immediately remove the obstacles still in place for women seeking to be recognized outside the domestic sphere. "Obtaining the right to vote was not a panacea for working women. Society as a whole still accepted the separate and unequal status of women. . . . For instance, a 1936 Gallup Poll found eighty percent of all Americans, men and women, in agreement with the proposition that a wife should stay at home if her husband had a job."

O'Connor cites very personal examples of the gender restrictions that remained in place even decades after the suffragettes won their battle. "Events in my own life illustrate the continuing struggle that remained for women after the right to vote was won. . . . My parents had a ranch on the New Mexico-Arizona border called the 'Lazy B.' My grandfather was a pioneer. He traveled west from Vermont in 1881 to establish the ranch three decades before Arizona became a state. Growing up, I rode horses, drove a tractor, and fixed fences. I played with dolls, too. . . . I thought I could do anything I wanted. After high school, I was even able to fulfill a dream of my father's: to attend Stanford University. My dad had been forced to give up college plans to run the Lazy B when my grandfather died. . . . I stayed on at Stanford for law school.

"Luckily for us women today, our female predecessors had far more spunk and spirit than they were given credit for . . . I look up to them."

"After graduation, I got a dose of women's reality for that era. The world was not going to be my oyster just yet. . . . In 1952, I interviewed with law firms in Los Angeles and San Francisco. None had ever hired a woman as a lawyer, and they weren't ready to start. . . . My husband and I settled in

Phoenix. I held a job in government and then opened my own firm, next to the local supermarket. My clients were generally people who had problems with their bills or leases.

"Then my babysitter moved to California, and I gave up my practice for five years and stayed home. I say 'stayed home,' but I wasn't home all that much! I ran the Junior League, helped the Salvation Army, volunteered at schools. I was so busy that after five years of 'staying home,' I decided a paying job would make my life easier to manage. . . . I became an attorney with the state attorney general's office, which positioned me to be appointed to fill a vacancy in the Arizona State Senate in 1969. I was elected for two more terms, and my colleagues voted me majority leader."

A Woman of Firsts

After finishing her term as the first woman majority leader in a United States legislature, in 1974, Sandra Day O'Connor was elected to the Maricopa County Superior Court. Five years later, she was elevated to Arizona's Court of Appeals. It was during her tenure on the Court of Appeals that President Ronald Reagan became aware of her. In 1981, he nominated Sandra to be this country's first female Supreme Court justice. She says that support by friends Senator Barry Goldwater (R–Arizona) and Senator Dennis DeConcini (D–Arizona) was instrumental in advancing her nomination in the White House.

"The suffragettes were jailed, attacked, and divorced in their quest for the American Dream of full citizenship. . . . Now, eighty years later, what will you make of their ideals?"

"By the mid-seventies, because of the efforts of persevering women and supportive men, I saw a new public awareness of women's potential. For instance, Justice Brennan empathized with what women had been up against, writing in one decision, 'There can be no doubt that our Nation has had a long and unfortunate history of sex discrimination. Traditionally, such discrimination was rationalized by an attitude of "romantic paternalism" which, in practical effect, put women, not on a pedestal, but in a cage.'"[4]

Justice O'Connor provides another example of the changes brought about by the hundred years of challenge to the system. "See the difference from the case of Myra Bradwell. . . . Here, the Supreme Court strikes down a Utah statute providing that child support is required for girls only until their legal majority at eighteen, while support for boys is required until twenty-one. The state justifies the difference by arguing women mature faster, marry earlier, and tend not to require continuing support through higher education, while men usually require this additional support. The Court rejects this argument and concludes, 'a child, male or female, is still a child. No longer is the female destined solely for the home and the rearing of the family, and only the male for the marketplace and the world of ideas. . . . Women's activities and responsibilities are increasing and expanding. Coeducation is a fact, not a rarity. The presence of women in business, in the professions, in government, and, indeed, in all walks of life where education is desirable, if not always a necessity, antecedent is apparent and a proper subject of judicial notice.'"[5]

> *"Growing up, I rode horses, drove a tractor, and fixed fences. I played with dolls, too. . . . I thought I could do anything I wanted."*

Forging Ahead

Justice O'Connor relishes her experience within this new society created by the labors of so many women. "I am thankful for the opportunity to experience a fulfilling career as well as a supportive family life. Lessons I learn in each aid me in the other. I revel both in the latest adventures of my growing granddaughter and in the legal subtleties of the Free Exercise Clause of the

[4] *Frontiero v. Richardson,* 411 U.S. 677, 684 (1973)(plurality opinion).
[5] *Stanton v. Stanton,* 421 U.S. 7, 14–15 (1975).

First Amendment. . . . I pursue—and other women pursue and will pursue—the same goals as men in this society, instead of inhabiting a separate and parallel universe."

Sandra Day O'Connor, the daughter of American pioneers—and a pioneer in her own right—comments, "Some of your paths ahead will be easy to traverse: voting, getting a degree, opportunities for varied careers—this part is well-paved by now, with brick, with stone, or packed, smooth earth. Where this next generation of women will make their mark is in expanding opportunities for women throughout all sectors of the economy and in obtaining more positions of power. Here you will have to start fresh paths, navigate obstacles, sometimes stand your ground.

"Forge ahead!" she laughs, "But—'Remember the Ladies!'"

"Where this next generation of women will make their mark is in expanding opportunities for women throughout all sectors of the economy and in obtaining more positions of power. Here you will have to start fresh paths, navigate obstacles, sometimes stand your ground."

VI.

MAUREEN
KEMPSTON DARKES

After I worked at a job for a while, I was asked to handle projects on my own. Consider the following scenario, representative of some of my experiences.

I am asked to coordinate the preparation of a legal brief for one of the firm's clients. I have a month until the brief is due. I discover, however, a few variables and moving parts, namely:

• The client's employees find documents, in good faith, which I was previously told did not exist; the documents must be incorporated into the brief mid-way through the project.

• The senior partner is a hands-off supervisor. The best time to get more than two minutes of his time is before 9 A.M. (Most of the day he is locked away in meetings or on conference calls.)

• The junior partner has a hair-trigger temper. I brace myself to be yelled at about something whenever we meet, so I choose the time of day accordingly. ("Do I feel like being yelled at before lunch or after lunch today?") Sometimes his response to a question is, "You're a big girl, you figure it out."

• The senior associate is knowledgeable in the areas of law at issue. He provides legal theories to apply to the facts. He promises the junior associates will be able to find cases to cite as precedent for these theories.

Time will prove him correct.

• *The junior associates are spread too thin. Despite this, they are pulled from their regular workload about once a week to spend a day or two on some emergency project that must go out the door. The two who are assigned to do the research on this brief will not truly focus on it until the week before it is due, when they will be told by the assigning partner to work on it to the exclusion of their other cases. The assigning partner will at that time also pull two or three additional associates onto the case to make sure everything gets done in time.*

• *The paralegals and secretaries have a bunch of administrative problems—the copying service, the messenger service, the over-time schedule, vacations that have been planned for a year, the color of the cardstock the court requires for the cover of the brief.*

• *All the people senior to me in the chain of command are male (the client, the senior partner, the junior partner, the senior associate). All the people junior to me in the chain of command are female (the two junior associates, two paralegals, and three secretaries).*

• *Blend all these ingredients together for a brief. Bake and serve.*

This is all by way of saying, school just doesn't teach you about a lot of the real-life issues that come up in the workplace! So imagine (with experiences not dissimilar to the example I played with above) how fantastic it was for me to meet a woman who has broken the mold on managing responsibilities and resources in a large organization. As a result of meeting Maureen Kempston Darkes, my management skills are much improved. I'll be surprised if you don't share with a friend something you read in this chapter. (I'm still telling friends about Maureen's management style!)

"Women buy fifty percent of cars and influence eighty percent of car-buying decisions," Maureen Kempston Darkes asserts. "So why can't a woman run an auto company?"

Maureen Kempston Darkes

RESIDENCE: Oshawa, Ontario, Canada
BORN: 1948
PERSONAL: Married
PROFESSIONAL: President and General Manager of General Motors Canada Ltd., Vice President of General Motors Corporation
1998 Recipient of the Margaret Brent Award

Maureen Kempston Darkes is a leader in the male-dominated automobile industry. In 1994, she became the first female president of General Motors Canada, making her one of Canada's most important business leaders and the highest-ranking woman executive in the history of General Motors ("GM"), one of the world's largest companies.

She learned at a young age that life can bring unexpected change. When she was only twelve, her father died, forcing her mother to work outside the home as a bank secretary to support herself and her three children. "An early lesson was that one needs to prepare for this life because we don't know what it will hold," Maureen shares. Her mother taught her to value independence and education, tools which can help a person succeed no matter what unforeseen obstacles one encounters. Because of advice like this, Maureen credits her mother with the success of her three children—Maureen's brothers both pursued careers in the medical field, while she eventually chose the law.

Maureen attended the University of Toronto, expecting to graduate with a doctorate in history so that she could live the academic life of teaching and researching. As her undergraduate years

"People tell me I have gasoline in my blood!"

progressed, however, she decided that she'd appreciate pursuing a more non-traditional career for women, something which might afford her more of an opportunity to help create history rather than simply learn and write about it. She became interested in the law—she enjoyed its intellectual challenges, and realized that it can be an effective tool for helping others. "I saw lawyers making things happen, creating things of real value. Lawyers are perhaps the most creative group in society—we tend to focus only on the image problem brought about by personal injury lawsuits, but most of the profession is engaged in creating worthwhile projects and opportunities for people." Maureen went to the University of Toronto Law School, and after a brief stint at a law firm, she joined the legal staff of General Motors in 1975.

"There were not very many women in management when I first came to GM," Maureen remembers. "But I think over time people came to respect the fact that I worked hard, I was very serious about my work, and I intended to make a significant contribution to the business." She laughs, "People tell me I have gasoline in my blood! . . . Also, I was fortunate to be noticed by two very progressive senior executives who took a

"One needs to prepare for this life because we don't know what it will hold."

liking to me and took an interest in my career development—Jack Smith (who is now chairman of the board in Detroit) and George Peapples (until recently, vice president of corporate affairs in Washington, D.C.)."

Nontraditional Management

Maureen's pursuit of a career path she considered "nontraditional" seems consistent with her approach to working within her career as well. She practices what she calls "management by walking," which means she strolls frequently through corporate headquarters, talking with employees about the work they are doing. Her office has no leather couches or doors or even walls—it is an open workspace with a desk, found at the end of a row of similar cubicles inhabited by fellow employees. She uses a nearby glass-enclosed conference room for private meetings and phone calls. "I like informality and flexibility . . . they are critically important qualities in business today. . . . Sitting out in the open, I know what's going on here. People stop by to chat with me all the time."

Workplace Diversity

When questioned about her goals for her company, Maureen lists some of the points you would expect to hear from any person in charge of Canada's most profitable company, with $42 billion Canadian (about $28 billion American) in annual revenues: Customer enthusiasm and loyalty, product quality, and value. In addition to those attributes which have traditionally measured the success of a company, Maureen cites workplace diversity as an equally important endeavor. "The inherent importance of diversity has got to be recognized. We need a work culture where different life experiences and different perspectives are appreciated, and everyone makes a contribution. . . . I want employees to come to work at General Motors every day saying, 'I make a difference. I contribute to this business.'"

"Sitting out in the open, I know what's going on here. People stop by to chat with me all the time."

Maureen feels that diversity in the workplace isn't just a social responsibility—it's also smart business. "We should mirror the global mosaic within our own organizations. To do this will give us an enormous competitive advantage globally. Look at the marketplace we serve. It's very diverse. . . . Why wouldn't you want the inside of your company to mirror your consumer marketplace? Because if it does, you'll probably understand your consumers better and will be more successful."

GM includes the goal of workplace diversity in developing business strategies in marketing, community affairs, human resources, and with its suppliers. Maureen explains that GM's television and print media targets women consumers as well as men and depicts women of a variety of ages, lifestyles, professional, and ethnic backgrounds. "I think as more and more business leaders come to realize the absolute importance of diversity, we will see a major cultural change. If I can further that cause, I want to do that."

The Women's Advisory Council

To help encourage diversity within GM Canada, in the early 1980s (while she was still part of the corporation's legal staff) Maureen spearheaded the creation of a very nontraditional sort of entity: the General Motors' Women's Advisory Council. The council is comprised of about twenty employees from all areas of the company, including senior management. Maureen explains that the council was formed because senior management at GM recognized women were facing difficulties in their efforts to become part of the company's mainstream. The council met to identify and to respond to issues women faced in the workplace. Maureen's work on the council brought tangible changes to GM's corporate culture.

"We should mirror the global mosaic within our own organizations. . . . Why wouldn't you want the inside of your company to mirror your consumer marketplace? Because if it does, you'll probably understand your consumers better and will be more successful."

The council identified barriers keeping women from reaching their full potential, including prejudice, lack of effective career path planning, exclusion from networks, and the difficulties associated with career/family balancing. To assist women in overcoming these barriers, the council developed progressive policies for General Motors to adopt, including a mentoring program, job sharing, and telecommuting. These policies have changed the face of the workplace for both women and men.

The Mentoring Program

The mentoring program assigns, upon request, a more senior person with whom an employee can meet regularly to ask questions and to discuss setting and reaching professional goals. Employees appreciate the support they gain from their mentors, and senior employees enjoy the opportunity to share what they've learned. Maureen believes, "Those women in an organization who have met with some success have an obligation to assist other women coming along. . . . They do this directly, by providing mentoring. They are also doing this more generally by helping to lead changes in our corporate culture and practices—to facilitate the fuller participation of women and minorities. Changing the culture of an organization is a long-term activity, but it is happening at GM."

The mentoring program has also proven to make good business sense, as employees who are satisfied with their career development are more likely to remain with a company.

Alternative Work Schedules

The council also assisted with implementing alternative work schedules. In addition to part-time schedules, GM offers "flex-time," which allows employees to choose the start and end of their workday within certain ranges of time. This enables employees to structure a workday that accommodates personal obligations such as sending children off to school each morning.

GM also allows "job sharing," which means that two employees literally share one full-time job. For instance, one employee works Monday, Tuesday, and then Wednesday just until lunchtime. After lunch on Wednesday, a second employee arrives and works Wednesday afternoon, Thursday, and Friday. Both people work at the same desk, computer, and phone extension, and both are responsible for continuing the same projects and completing the same tasks. The two employees essentially function as one. Job sharing allows employees to work a part-time schedule and still affords the company conti-

"I think as more and more business leaders come to realize the absolute importance of diversity, we will see a major cultural change. If I can further that cause, I want to do that."

nuity within the office. A shared job is covered each workday by one of the two employees assigned to it, whereas under the traditional part-time scenario, if an employee is out of the office, a task or request may have to wait until he or she returns. Thus job sharing is an efficient way for a company to accommodate an employee's schedule while still maintaining business as usual.

"Experience has shown that when people are given flexibility, they are generally grateful for it, don't exploit it, and do a better job because they are better able to manage the competing interests in their lives. . . . Jobs can get done without spending ten hours a day of 'face time' at the office. Clients and customers are still satisfied and properly served."

Another of the workplace changes brought about by the council was the implementation of telecommuting. Telecommuting permits employees to perform assignments away from the traditional work site, perhaps assisted by a laptop computer, fax machine, cellular phone, or beeper. The amount of telecommuting an employee can do varies with the amount of responsibilities they have that are transportable. For example, some tasks cannot be performed away from the traditional work site—such as work on a production assembly line.

Of these alternative work arrangements, Maureen observes, "Experience has shown that when people are given flexibility, they are generally grateful for it, don't exploit it, and do a better job because they are better able to manage the competing interests in their lives. . . . They're happier. . . . Productivity and accountability do not suffer. Jobs can get done without spending ten hours a day of 'face time' at the office. Clients and customers are still satisfied and properly served."

Community Outreach

The council also developed outreach programs to the community. For example, after noting that a disproportionate number of young females drop math, science, and technology courses, thus narrowing their future career opportunities, the council paired up with educators to prepare a video-based career counseling program that encourages high school students to continue developing skills in those disciplines.

A Varied Career Path

The council's Targeting Improved Participation Strategy, which allows employees to try a new position at GM for a six-month period while maintaining the option of returning to their previous position, is an initiative of which Maureen is especially proud. She explains, "For instance, a woman might want to try a short-term manufacturing assignment to ascertain her aptitude for the work and to measure her desire to move into the manufacturing area. But if it weren't for this program, she would not otherwise be pursuing her interest."

Maureen anticipates positive long-term effects from assisting women to pursue varied interests in the company: "The number of women in entry-level jobs is impressive, but the number of women decreases as occupational rank increases. . . . Certainly women are breaking through the glass ceiling that shuts them out of top positions, but it needs to happen more."

"For young women to progress in an organization, they have to develop a broad base of experience from a variety of experiences within the organization. That is how you groom yourself for top positions."

Maureen has advice to offer young women who want to reach positions of power in the corporate world. "One thing I've noticed is glass ceilings are often supported by glass walls that are just as detrimental to women's careers.

You'll never break through the glass ceiling until you crash down some glass walls. When I say 'glass walls,' I mean that for young women to progress in an organization, they have to develop a broad base of experience from a variety of experiences within the organization. That is how you groom yourself for top positions.

"For instance, a woman who works first in a company's financial offices ultimately needs experience in marketing. And if it's a manufacturing business, she also needs to learn how the plant operates. If the company has offices overseas, she'll need international experience on her way up. You need the widest exposure possible to all of the key elements of an organization to become a leader in that organization."

"I can't stress enough to young women that they must learn the way decisions are made within their organization. When you understand the decision-making process in your organization, you can then influence the process and the decisions."

An example of varied learning is presented in Maureen's own career. "I went to New York City in 1985 for two years to work on GM's divestiture of its South African operations. General Motors had agreed to divest its operations in South Africa in response to anti-apartheid pressure. My job was to find the most expeditious, least costly approach to do that. It was a huge and very complicated endeavor. And that's when I stopped being perceived in the company as just a lawyer and was seen as someone who could move to higher corporate levels and take on much more."

Maureen also urges women to learn the ins and outs of the organization for which they work. "I can't stress enough to young women that they must learn the way decisions are made within their organization. When you understand the decision-making process in your organization, you can then influence the process and the decisions."

In 2000, Maureen was named an Officer of the Order of Canada (Canada's highest honor for lifetime achievement). And if it is true that imitation is the sincerest form of flattery, then proof that Maureen is affecting a great deal of positive change in the business community may be seen in that competitor Ford Motor Company of Canada appointed its first female president, Bobbie Gaunt, in 1997 (three years after Maureen first took the helm at GM). If Maureen Kempston Darkes has anything to do with it, this is just the beginning of a changing mosaic, inlaid with a lot of shattered glass.

VII.

MARGARET HILARY
MARSHALL

I found myself thinking about the Kennedy family a lot as this manuscript took shape. I had to. The Kennedys' dedication to progressive social policies and public service during a dynamic period in American history inspired many of the women I met, including Margaret Marshall.

As a political science major in college, I used to love learning about the Kennedy Presidency (the touch-football games, the appreciation for the arts, those wonderful Cabinet members!). We used the Cuban Missile Crisis as a model for crisis management and political analysis again and again: JFK ignoring the first letter from Khrushchev (the nasty one) and responding to the other (the cordial one); JFK not pushing his opponent into a corner, and allowing his opponent to save face while retreating from the conflict. (Note: I've found that this approach works in regular life, too.)

Margaret Marshall was a teenager in an apartheid-ruled South Africa during the spring and summer of 1963, when the American Civil Rights Movement gained momentum, as African-Americans demonstrated in the streets, boycotted segregated schools, and stood in long lines to become voters.

In June 1963, President Kennedy federalized the Alabama National Guard and committed to fighting race discrimination. In a nationally televised speech, he endorsed a civil rights agenda including legislation to end segregation in public accommodations and race discrimination in employment. Kennedy challenged, "Now, the time has come for this nation to fulfill its promise . . ."

In 1966, Margaret (by this time an anti-apartheid student leader) sat on a platform with Robert Kennedy as he addressed student audiences. Robert Kennedy told students at the University of Cape Town, "I hope you will often take heart in the knowledge that you are joined with your fellow young people in every land, they struggling with their problems and you with yours, but all joined in a common purpose; that like the young people of my own country and in every country that I have visited you are all in many ways more closely united to the brothers of your time than to the older generation in any of these nations. You are determined to build a better future."

Thirty-five years later, I find his words stirring to read. I can't imagine how thrilling it must have been for Margaret Marshall to hear this kind of rhetoric as a participant in the civil rights movement of her country.

M argaret Hilary Marshall explains that as a 1960s college student in Johannesburg, South Africa, "I majored in art history—minored in student protests." Margaret participated in protests as a member of the National Union of South African Students ("NUSAS"), a twenty-thousand-member group that worked to end racism in a country where government rule was based upon racial segregation and white supremacy.

Margaret Hilary Marshall

RESIDENCE: Cambridge, Massachusetts
BORN: South Africa, 1944
PERSONAL: Married to Anthony Lewis *New York Times* columnist
PROFESSIONAL: Chief Justice of the Supreme Judicial Court of Massachusetts, and formerly Vice President and General Counsel of Harvard University
1994 Recipient of the Margaret Brent Award

She continues, "Prime Minister Balthazar Johannes Vorster considered NUSAS to be radical. . . . He called us a red cancer that should be cut out! His government stifled anyone who opposed apartheid publicly. . . . Nelson Mandela was imprisoned, the African National Congress was banned. South Africa was a fine place to be in the mid-sixties if you were white and supported apartheid. Otherwise, it could be a nightmare."

In 1966, NUSAS president Ian Robertson affronted the apartheid government when he invited New York Senator Robert F. Kennedy to address student audiences. As a result, government officials "banned" Robertson; he could not speak in public, study at a university, or meet with students or friends. "Many of the men in the anti-apartheid movement were in prison, or under some kind of restriction, or in hiding," Margaret says. "When Robertson was banned, I was asked to take over as president of NUSAS."

Despite controversy, Senator Kennedy visited South Africa in June 1966 and addressed hundreds of students. Newspapers carried a photograph showing Kennedy speaking at a podium with Margaret seated behind him, next to an empty chair symbolizing Robertson's forced absence.

"Working with NUSAS broadened my horizons," she reflects. "I grew up in the small village of Newcastle, in what is now the Kwa Zulu province, sheltered from the oppressive reality of apartheid. . . . But once I was exposed to that reality, I dedicated myself to campaigning against the apartheid government. As a consequence of my unanticipated leadership role in student politics, I developed new skills, such as how to talk publicly, how to deal with the media—and how to do both in a politically charged arena."

Discovering America

Margaret broadened her horizons further by coming to the United States to pursue graduate studies after college. In April 1968, shortly after her arrival in America, Martin Luther King Jr. was assassinated. "Dr. King's passionate fight for civil rights, without promoting violence, left such an impression on me," she notes. Then Senator Robert Kennedy was assassinated not long after Dr. King. "I had met him just two years earlier when he visited South Africa, so I also felt a great loss at his death. His genuine dedication to the principles of equality was inspiring. King and Kennedy remain heroes of mine to this day."

Although she was now a student at Harvard—halfway around the world from home—Margaret continued her work against racism in the United States. She realized her experiences under apartheid in South Africa were a powerful resource she could share in America. Margaret traveled across the United States, continuing her campaign against South Africa's government, arguing that the U.S. government should impose economic sanctions against South Africa and should discourage banks from lending money to the South African government.

"Any immigrant can make a difference here. No one in America is born into a situation that it is forbidden by law to change."

She remembers, "I met so many Americans during my travels, from all walks of life. At that time in our history, I found that communities, large and small, were often divided over the great issues of the time: civil rights and Vietnam. I recognized that Americans were conflicted because they were so committed to wanting to do the right thing.

That made a great impact on me. . . . I fell in love with this extraordinary society, a nation that has given me unbelievable opportunities," she smiles, "this society that is in a real sense a society of immigrants. . . . As a result of my protesting activities in America, I could not return to South Africa. At the same time, America opened new paths for me to follow."

"I discovered that in the United States there is a special place for immigrants. Immigrants continue to make the history of this country in new ways and with new energy. Any immigrant can make a difference here. No one in America is born into a situation that it is forbidden by law to change. . . . Once I was committed to staying here, I decided to go to law school. Law plays a central role in this country. We are a nation of laws. . . . Attending law school seemed the best way to learn about American culture and politics."

". . . if you are in the company of people who are good at their jobs, just watch them. . . . Observe how your company's top executives handle themselves in many different ways . . ."

When she graduated from Yale Law School, Margaret began working in a Boston firm. There she discovered that one way to learn new skills was to become a close observer of successful lawyers: "I started to watch lawyers in different situations that were new to me and from which I might learn something. I asked courthouse clerks to telephone and let me know when Boston's best trial lawyers would be giving opening or closing statements in their cases, or cross-examining a key witness. I would then go to the courthouse to watch them.

"More generally, if you are in the company of people who are good at their jobs, just watch them. . . . You don't have to have a relationship with everyone. Observe how your company's top executives handle themselves in many different ways . . . when they interact with the people who work in the cafeteria, or with receptionists; learn from the people who are successful at attracting new clients. . . . Succeeding in your career will go hand in hand with really trying to become the very best you can be."

A Step Forward

After sixteen years in private practice, she returned to help one of the universities she had attended, by becoming the vice president and general counsel of Harvard University—the first woman to hold the post in Harvard's 350-year history. "When I first met with Harvard's president, Neil L. Rudenstine," she recounts, "I did not have any expectation that I would leave my law firm. But, when someone asks you, 'Would you like to walk through this door?' the answer should seldom be 'no.' You take a peek at what it might be like to walk through that door. . . . Take a step or two forward before you decide to reject an invitation. After I learned more about the position, I believed it would be a good one for me. Besides legal issues, the position involved building consensus and reaching compromise on contentious issues—something I've always been good at and I enjoy."

Other factors contributed to Margaret's decision to go to Harvard. "Harvard's president was committed to something I believe in: to excellence and to the university being accessible to the most talented people. If institutions limit or exclude people and their manifold talents, they are weaker institutions. . . . For example, institutional leaders need to focus on how they can bring women along in a way that the women are not constrained by institutional traditions or by their own social conditioning."

She elaborates on her philosophy of how to bring other women along. "Women and others historically excluded from our nation's great institutions of all kinds must be made to feel they now have an interest in contributing to these institutions. One small way that I found was helpful in expanding the numbers of women in civic organizations, such as bar associations, was to take a junior lawyer along to a meeting whenever I could.

"Another thing that helps is to make on-the-job criticism something that is appreciated by the person who receives it, because it allows her to focus on improving some weakness to become stronger. Criticism is often presented in a way that is too personal, and it makes the recipient feel her worth to the institution is diminished or makes her feel isolated from the institution. . . . Whenever I work with more junior women—and men, too!—I am mindful of reflecting on what I've learned in the past and present, and passing those lessons on to them, for better or for worse! I had to learn so much on my own. There is so much to be gained from inclusiveness, and it gives me great pleasure to be part of that."

In 1996, Margaret was appointed to the highest court in Massachusetts, the Supreme Judicial Court, where she now serves as the chief justice. Sitting on the bench is where she feels she belongs: "My respect for an independent judiciary stems from growing up in South Africa, where there was no constitution, no written bill of rights, and where the judiciary could not be counted on to be fair and unbiased. No one thought of going to the courts to redress injustice.

"The Massachusetts Supreme Judicial Court ("SJC") is the oldest court in the United States," she continues. "It pre-dates the Declaration of Independence. The SJC was founded in 1692, but the adoption of the Massachusetts Constitution in 1780 after the war of independence was a key moment in the court's history. It issued the first judgment to end slavery in this country, in 1783, nearly a century before the Civil War. . . . John Adams, who conceptualized the idea of three co-equal branches of government, was a justice on the court. Adams had drafted

". . . when someone asks you, 'Would you like to walk through this door?' the answer should seldom be 'no.' You take a peek at what it might be like to walk through that door. . . . Take a step or two forward before you decide to reject an invitation."

the Massachusetts Constitution, later used as a model for the United States Constitution. I am a great admirer of John Adams. I served as president of the Boston Bar Association, which he founded." As Margaret (the second female to serve on the Supreme Judicial Court and the second female president of the Boston Bar Association) concludes, she starts to grin, "Sometimes I think John Adams is turning in his grave—but Abigail Adams may be dancing."

Sound Advice

Margaret is often approached by girls and young women for counseling on their careers. One piece of advice they seem to find helpful is one she follows herself. "Ask yourself," she begins, "what do you genuinely enjoy doing every single day of your life? Write it all down. What are the things I'm good at? Not good at? What do I enjoy doing? Not enjoy doing? What would I do with my life if there was no pressure from my family or my peers and no need to make money? Ignore the *'shoulds'* of your life . . . the school you *should* attend, the internship or clerkship you *should* pursue. If you read the *Wall Street Journal* or *Barron's* because you should, without any actual interest, you will not be happy as a corporate executive. . . . You don't have to show this list to anyone. Make the list for yourself. Have an honest dialogue with yourself, to begin to think about the kinds of interests you will pursue in your career and your life, and those you will be willing to forego. . . . Re-think and revise the list periodically. You don't have to plot out every move in your career journey by the time you are eighteen or twenty-one or twenty-five years old. . . . Find what resonates within you. The most wonderful thing

> *"Whenever I work with more junior women—and men, too!—I am mindful of reflecting on what I've learned in the past and present, and passing those lessons on to them, for better or for worse! I had to learn so much on my own. There is so much to be gained from inclusiveness, and it gives me great pleasure to be part of that."*

about a career that you find personally satisfying is that your work will be a source of energy for you, not a drain on your energy.

"There are no rules that apply to everyone." Margaret goes on. "Sometimes I advise people to move to a different location to pursue the career they want. For instance, when a young woman tells me she wants to succeed in international affairs, I might advise her to leave Boston and go to New York City or Washington, D.C., where the range of opportunities might be broader. . . . If she tells me she likes the entertainment business, it would probably help if she pursued that in New York City or Los Angeles. If she is interested in the commerce of ideas, she will be happy in Boston—Boston, with its many colleges and universities, is in the business of ideas."

She warns, "Think about the role money will play in your life. When you choose a job, remember that employers paying higher salaries will necessarily make more demands on your time. Usually the equation is 'more money, less control over your time. Less money, more control.' It doesn't take long to learn, but sometimes it does require figuring out . . .

"Sometimes I think John Adams is turning in his grave—but Abigail Adams may be dancing."

"Also, think carefully about the lifestyle you want to have, and balance it against the career choices necessary to support that lifestyle," she recommends. "You may be limiting possible career paths because you are counting on making a certain amount of money. . . . Some people seem to hold on to unfulfilling jobs just to afford the place where they live, or the car they drive, or the watch they wear. Money is not the best measure of satisfaction or success. . . .

"I certainly advise new lawyers to eliminate their student loans and any other debts just as soon as they can—so they can choose from a broader spectrum of career choices, and how they will spend their time, and where they will leave their mark in the world. Some people can't pursue their true passions because they have burdened themselves with far too much debt. . . . I often tease my law clerks about the temptation of money. They know if they come into work wearing too many new outfits when I know they are burdened by debt, they're going to get my lecture on money."

Margaret encourages young women to be honest with themselves about whether they should be in the field they are in, or whether some other calling should be followed. "One of the things I learned about myself by list-making," she says, "is I am more comfortable with the kind of work that resembles a 'chess game,' as opposed to work that requires starting from a 'blank canvas.' Give me a set of rules—say, the applicable state or federal statute—and I'll enjoy working to be as creative as I can within those rules. I'm not an artist or a scientist, with a blank canvas before me, inspired to create from nothing. My way doesn't suit everyone. Some 'blank canvas' people resist the constraints imposed by rules. I thrive in that environment."

"Ask yourself, what do you genuinely enjoy doing every single day of your life? . . . What would I do with my life if there was no pressure from my family or my peers and no need to make money? Ignore the 'shoulds' of your life . . ."

The Question of Gender

To questions about gender in the workplace, Margaret has a sincere response. "I have been noticing gender differences for many years now," she comments. "There are some that you have to fight against—those that involve fairness and equality. Others don't require action. Not every gender difference can be eradicated—or needs to be—to bring equal opportunities in schools and the workplace. But it is always helpful to be aware of differences. . . . For instance, my brother and I were raised together—yet somewhere growing up he learned to do electrical wiring, and I never did. Electrical wiring is not innate knowledge for males. My brother learned to do it along the way perhaps because someone—a parent, teacher, or friend—thought it was important for him to know. No one ever asked me if I would like to learn how to do electrical wiring, but I'm sure I could learn it."

She suggests that there are lots of different ways for women to communicate easily with their male professional counterparts: "I used to be completely out of my depth when men talked about sports. Terms like 'Let's punt!' or 'Monday morning quarterback' used to baffle me. I learned that the sport I called 'football' was 'soccer' to Americans. I wasn't entirely sure who Joe DiMaggio was . . . but I recognized that by talking about sports, colleagues or clients were finding ways to build bridges, common understandings in their work relationship with each other when they talked about things other than work. I looked for other ways to do the same thing. I was comfortable talking about the children in office photographs or travel, books, or movies—and those became my 'small talk' topics.

"I also built confidence in my relationships with colleagues and clients by being accessible to them. I gave people my home phone number. I always inform my secretary about where I can be reached so if anyone is looking for me, she can find me and let me know, wherever I am, at a meeting or having a haircut (and I am confident that she will use her judgment to screen out unnecessary telephone calls)."

> *"When you choose a job, remember that employers paying higher salaries will necessarily make more demands on your time. Usually the equation is 'more money, less control over your time. Less money, more control.'"*

Margaret suggests that it is helpful "to try to make alliances with other women—all women, any woman. Women who advance through levels of power are scrutinized closely. A devastating attack upon a woman's reputation can be the hint or suggestion that other women don't like her or trust her. . . . My generation had to contend with what we called the 'Queen Bee syndrome'— the idea that there is only room for one woman in the group to have any power or position in the whole 'hive' of 'worker bees.' There was always the charge that if a woman is number one, she protects her turf, she won't help other women, and she might even hurt them.

"I have actually never experienced that syndrome. Women ahead of me have always extended a helping hand. But I understand where this perception came from. . . . Women who had careers before my generation achieved remarkable things at tremendous cost to themselves. They were often emotionally spent when they advanced up the ladder—the barriers were so high. They could not possibly have the energy to be supportive of every woman who followed behind. I admire greatly the generations of women ahead of me, and I never experienced them as intentionally exclusive."

"I have been noticing gender differences for many years now. There are some that you have to fight against—those that involve fairness and equality. Others don't require action. Not every gender difference can be eradicated—or needs to be—to bring equal opportunities in schools and the workplace."

She has other observations. "Whenever I'm asked if I'm a feminist, I always answer 'yes,' and then I add, 'I don't know what you mean by that word, and I may not know what I mean.' But I know I cannot disassociate myself from feminism, whatever it may mean. If you are a woman, surely you have to take an interest in issues that concern women in the workplace and in society. If you don't, it will be to all of our detriment."

Women should not think they have to do everything on their own to succeed. She advises, "Reach out for help. You will find that help is there for you. . . . For instance, the first time I needed to prepare a press release, I made a number of telephone calls and asked people to help me until we located one to serve as a model. I've spent a lot of time watching and a lot of time asking. Both are ways to reach out to others for guidance. . . . Asking takes confidence you may have to develop. If you ask, people will help you. If you think asking conveys weakness, you will find it much harder to learn. I have found that if you ask for help and assume people want you to succeed, you will do very well. . . . People will feel included in your progress—they want to see you succeed, not fail."

Margaret recognizes that she is an example to others. She notes, "Anyone can get ahead in this country. I came on my own to the United States with no ties to Boston or to America. I did not come from a home of enormous privilege. I did not know any lawyers here. I was an outsider in every sense. . . . Even if you are an outsider, as I was, with the help of others no barrier is insurmountable. I should know, because so many people helped me!

". . . Try to make alliances with other women—all women, any woman. Women who advance through levels of power are scrutinized closely."

"I hope that I can play the same role for the next generations of women," she states. And she does. A continent away from her days as a South African student leader, Margaret Marshall is still working to tear down the barriers and roadblocks to equality.

VIII.
ELAINE
JONES

As my awareness of gender issues grew, my sensibilities began to change. For instance, I stopped laughing when television or movies exploited stereotypes of women. I began to notice terms like "woman doctor." And notice that you never seem to read of someone being referred to as a "male lawyer," "male executive," or "male basketball coach." This is because in America, the white male is the norm. Given no other information than that someone is "a person," most people think of a white male. So you never seem to hear someone referred to as a "white pilot" or a "white scientist."

It is important to be aware of the way we categorize people. Research has shown that categorizing—things, locations, people—is part of the way our brains process and store information.

I learned that the trick, then, is to be aware of whatever stereotype pops to mind and not to act on it in a way that is biased or unfair. Developing this reaction to stereotypes becomes more important as we become a more diverse, multi-cultural society.

Women of color are twice removed from the white male norm. The intersection of race and gender means that women of color may have experiences similar to white women or to men of color, as well as experiences unique to the group.

On the day I met with Elaine Jones of the NAACP LEGAL DEFENSE FUND, I realized that I had never had the opportunity to have a conversation about career issues with a woman of color who was not one of my peers. (I'll bet this is true for a lot of people.) You might say this is because I don't have enough exposure to diversity in my work experience. You could also say it is because there are just not as many women of color in positions of power and influence as there ought to be.

E laine Jones used public water foun-
tains and bathrooms labeled "colored" during her childhood in the
South, where Jim Crow laws legally
enforced racial segregation everywhere
from buses and trains to hospitals and
the military. Despite the often difficult
environment in which she grew up,
Elaine's parents encouraged her to aim
high and instilled in her a strong sense

Elaine Jones

RESIDENCE: Washington, D.C.
HOMETOWN: Norfolk, Virginia
PROFESSIONAL: President and
Director-Counsel, The NAACP
Legal Defense and
Educational Fund, Inc. (LDF)
*1993 Recipient of the
Margaret Brent Award*

of self-worth. "Our dinner table was a training ground!" she exclaims. Elaine's
father was a member of the United States' first African-American labor union
as a Pullman porter, and Elaine's mother was a public school teacher. They both
experienced their share of racial discrimination and worked hard to prepare
Elaine, her older brother, and younger sister for the realities of the world for
African-Americans. "They led spirited dinner-time conversations on segregation, other racial issues, and current events. . . . My parents made us *think*, and
they let us know they were expecting great things of us."

At an early age, Elaine decided she wanted to be a lawyer. She remembers
that her parents encouraged her, but that other adults reacted differently:
"Relatives and teachers used to look sort of sad when I said I wanted to be a
lawyer. I realized when I got older that they had thought it could never happen
for me because of my gender and race, but they didn't want to discourage
me." But Elaine was inspired by the outstanding contributions of African-
American heroines such as Sojourner Truth, Harriet Tubman, Ida B. Wells,
Mary McLeod Bethune, and Constance Baker Motley, and she refused to be
dissuaded from her goal.

After graduating from Howard University, Elaine served for two years in
the Peace Corps in Turkey. Then she approached the challenge that had produced the sympathetic look from many of her elders years earlier. In 1967,
she became the first African-American woman to attend the University of
Virginia ("UVa") Law School. Three years later, she was its first African-

"Relatives and teachers used to look sort of sad when I said I wanted to be a lawyer. I realized when I got older that they had thought it could never happen for me because of my gender and race, but they didn't want to discourage me."

American female graduate. Recently, nearly three decades after her graduation, the University of Virginia awarded Elaine its highest honor—the Thomas Jefferson medal in law.

The handful of women in Elaine's class used to meet in the lounge attached to the women's restroom to support each other, often talking over how to deal with sexist comments and behavior by students and professors. She recalls, "One day during my first week of law school I was taking a break alone in the lounge. A middle-aged white female came in, looked at me sitting on the sofa, and said, 'I know you're on your lunch break now, but when you finish could you clean out the refrigerator?' Then she left. I didn't respond, but I realized she thought I was the cleaning lady! That was a scenario my white female classmates did not have to face." Elaine later saw the woman again in the dean's office—she was his secretary. The woman never apologized for her mistake, and Elaine never discussed it with her, but Elaine carried the weight of the misunderstanding with her for years. "What's surprising to me from my own experience, as well as from stories I have been told, is how small indignities can be very difficult to shake off. You remember them for years, even if you vow to forget them."

Making Choices

When Elaine started law school, she planned to return to her hometown of Norfolk, Virginia, after graduation, to open a general practice law office to help the members of her community. During her last year of school, however, she joined many of her classmates in interviewing for jobs with the large New York City law firms. She eventually accepted a position with what had been

President Nixon's firm, but as graduation approached, she felt concerned about her decision. She started thinking that sometimes the best job and the job that pays the most money aren't the same thing.

"I was taking the job that paid the most money, and I knew it wasn't the job I wanted," she explains. "I felt I had lost my way." Elaine turned to her law school dean, who had become a proven counselor and friend. He helped her to focus on pursuing the kind of work that would be interesting to Elaine, and he helped her to get through the temptation of money. "I had always known I wanted to use my law degree to address social justice issues, so he assisted me in obtaining a position with the NAACP LEGAL DEFENSE AND EDUCATION FUND, INC. ("LDF"). I knew this job would suit me because of the immediate sense of relief I felt when I accepted it."

Elaine joined the Legal Defense Fund in 1970 and, except for two years at a government post, she has been with LDF ever since. Her first few years at LDF were spent arguing death penalty

> *"One day I was taking a break alone in the lounge. A middle-aged white female came in, looked at me sitting on the sofa, and said, 'I know you're on your lunch break now, but when you finish could you clean out the refrigerator?' Then she left. I didn't respond, but I realized she thought I was the cleaning lady!"*

cases throughout the South. The job was enormously satisfying. She recollects, "I was needed. I made a difference to people who were otherwise having trouble getting quality legal assistance—or any assistance." Her work with the LDF opened her eyes to inequities in the application of the law. She offers an example concerning the use of the death penalty in this country: "Application of the death penalty was—and still is—tainted by race discrimination. This has been shown in study after study. . . . For instance, if you look at two homicides committed under similar circumstances by defendants with similar criminal records, a defendant will be several times more likely to receive the death penalty if the victim was white than if the victim was African-American." Thus, Elaine joined the ranks of civil rights attorneys in this country who have developed a tradition of using community organization strategy in court, and public opinion to serve clients and advance causes.

> *"Decide what you want to accomplish, then work backwards to figure out how to get there. Ask yourself, 'What do I need to accomplish my short-and long-term objectives?' . . . Make six-month goals, one-year goals, five-year goals—and change your goals when what you want changes."*

Role Models

Elaine has been LDF's president and director-counsel since 1993, and she is still inspired by her predecessors at the Fund. "The Legal Defense Fund has a glorious history. I have been honored to throw myself into this work, important work begun by LDF's founder, Thurgood Marshall—an American hero—and continued by his handpicked successor Jack Greenburg, who served LDF ably as director-counsel for twenty-three years. Jack hired me as a young lawyer in 1970. LDF's current board cochair Julius Chambers was my mentor while he served as director-counsel from 1984 to 1995. All of us at LDF work hard to live up to the high standards and ideals established by my three predecessors.

"LDF has changed our history and inspired us with its vision of what America could be. LDF asked this country to make good on its promise of equal justice when it led the crusade to have the 'separate but equal' doctrine (the legal basis for segregation) declared unconstitutional in *Brown v. Board of*

Education, which Thurgood argued and the Legal Defense Fund won before the Supreme Court."

Elaine urges others to draw inspiration from the true meaning of LDF's vision of equal justice under the law. "I always tell people, decide what you want to accomplish, then work backwards to figure out how to get there. Ask yourself, 'What do I need to accomplish my short- and long-term objectives? Knowledge? Skills? Formal education? And how will I measure my progress?' Make six-month goals, one-year goals, five-year goals—and change your goals when what you want changes."

Elaine's comparison of attainment of a life goal by laying the precedent for it to the *Brown* decision is particularly powerful when considered against the impact of *Brown:* "The *Brown* decision laid the foundation for ending racial segregation a generation before Southern state legislatures would ever have enacted desegregation legislation. . . . Courts in this country are extremely important and extremely powerful. Consider just two cases: *Roe v. Wade* and *Brown v. Board of Education.* The first decision legalized a woman's right to choose. The second prohibited legally-sanctioned segregation. And each changed American culture radically." The difference in the lives of people before and after each decision illustrates her point. For instance, before *Roe,* abortion was illegal, and women would show up in our country's emergency rooms from the results of self-abortions or illegal abortions. After *Roe,* abortion was legal, and the number of women performing self-abortions decreased dramatically. Before *Brown,* African-American and white children did not attend the same schools, although they might live in the same neighborhoods and play together. After *Brown,* changes came to pass to

> *"The pursuit of civil rights is not a narrow path to trek,"* she says. *"Anything that improves the quality of lives and lessens discrimination against African-American people helps society as a whole."*

desegregate America's schools. The holding and reasoning of *Brown* and the 1964 Civil Rights Act were later applied to desegregate other public facilities, including parks, libraries, beaches, and buses.

It's All Related

Through the years, Elaine has believed that discrimination against any group of people is related to discrimination against another group—fighting prejudice in any form will help to break down the barriers that separate all people within society. "The pursuit of civil rights is not a narrow path to trek," she says. "Anything that improves the quality of lives and lessens discrimination against African-American people helps society as a whole." In addition to her fight against racial prejudice, Elaine has taken an interest in litigation concerning discrimination of other kinds—including gender, age, ethnicity, religion, or disability. She refers to the laws governing these protected groups as "sister statutes" because of the interrelationship of the issues involved. For instance, a decision on the admissibility of a certain kind of evidence in an age discrimination suit that is harmful to a plaintiff can also be used against plaintiffs who bring race or gender suits. "Any denial of opportunities to one group affects the rights of other groups," Elaine remarks.

"Be aware that we stand on the shoulders of those who came before us. Remembering them and all they endured for us to get here will help us to proceed successfully."

Elaine believes this interconnectedness between minority groups made the legal theories and energy of the civil rights movement in the 1960s extend to the women's movement in the 1970s. "It certainly was not the case that white women couldn't drink at a public water fountain, attend a public school, or eat in a restaurant. They could go almost anywhere and eat almost anywhere. But—like African-Americans—white women did not have opportunities equal to those of white males. They were limited by societal conventions, and they were judged based upon something they were born with (their gender) instead of on their abilities or the contributions they could make."

Things have changed through the years, but there is still a lot of work to do. "When Thurgood Marshall headed the Legal Defense Fund, litigation was his best chance for making progress in the fight for civil rights. This is because, as I was saying, Marshall needed the courts to take steps society wasn't ready to take. . . . We litigate cases when that is the most effective means toward an end. . . . However, we also engage in advocacy in our institutions—social, political, cultural—which can lead to consensus, action, and positive change. . . . As litigators, it is important that we speak before school boards and Senate committees as well as in courtrooms." It is impressive for the leader of a legal organization that has brought landmark litigation to speak of the important role of alternative means of dispute resolution.

"All of us need opportunities that allow us to show the kind of wonderful and competent people we are. My work is to break down some of the barriers that prevent our merit from being noticed and valued."

A Sense of History

"Be aware that we stand on the shoulders of those who came before us. Remembering them and all they endured for us to get here will help us to proceed successfully. . . . I am often reminded of the African-American families who sent their children to desegregated schools after the *Brown* decision. It tugs at my heart to think those families risked their lives because they believed there is no place for segregation in America. They saw some things we'll never see—and that's a good thing. They changed a way of life, moved this country forward, and made us all better people. . . . We cannot afford to take steps backwards now. . . . We've come too far, it's been too painful, and we've made too much progress."

Elaine points out, "I think it's important for young women to be aware that the Constitution our Founding Fathers adopted in 1787 excluded women. African-American women were arguably twice excluded." The ringing rhetoric of our Founding Fathers—"All men are created equal"—excluded everyone except propertied white males. African-Americans were counted as three-fifths of a person for apportioning congressional seats and were considered chattel, not persons. It was not until the Reconstruction Congress (approximately eighty years later) that the states ratified constitutional amendments making African-Americans American citizens and giving African-American men the right to vote. Gender-based discrimination would still be permitted under the Constitution until the early 1970s (when the work of people such as Ruth Bader Ginsburg began to change that).

> *"I advise . . . women to be aware of how far we've come over a difficult road, and to help us all continue moving forward by putting themselves into the fray—to pick an issue and participate in our society's evolution. . . . . Anything you do to improve in some measure the sum total of human dignity is worthwhile. . . ."*

Despite all the positive changes in the last thirty to fifty years, the struggle for equality still has a long way to go. "Few people would argue with me," Elaine states, "when I say that we have not yet fulfilled this nation's promise of equal opportunity and overcome our nation's troubled legacy of discrimination." Elaine sums up her mission: "All of us need opportunities that allow us to show the kind of wonderful and competent people we are. My work is to break down some of the barriers that prevent our merit from being noticed and valued."

Fighting Discrimination One Person at a Time

Young women have approached Elaine with their own tales of workplace discrimination. "Certainly exclusion can be explained by reasons other than race and gender, and I don't want to encourage anyone to be paranoid! On the other hand, discrimination is sometimes only evidenced by things like being denied a mentor or important work assignments, or interpersonal slights. In many cases, we'll never know the reason for the lack of inclusion."

Elaine encourages women seeking guidance to have a sense of their history, and to get involved. "I advise these women to be aware of how far we've come over a difficult road, and to help us all continue moving forward by putting themselves into the fray—to pick an issue and participate in our society's evolution.

"I believe anything you do to improve in some measure the sum total of human dignity is worthwhile. There are enough of us who care about progress that some of us can be working on each issue where help is needed—gender, race, poverty, children, the elderly, health care. Pick your issue, and do something positive related to it. . . . What is of paramount importance is to become involved in some cause you care about and to stretch yourself by working on concerns beyond those of your immediate circle."

Elaine has literally dedicated her life to making life better for the rest of us. And she works with an organization that has a tradition of doing the same thing. There are easier ways to make a living. However, she addresses with a smile the unspoken question hanging in the air about all the hard work and all the tough times: "There is a saying—a Swahili warrior song—that life has meaning only in the struggle. Triumphs and defeats are up to the gods. So let us celebrate the struggle."

IX.
HERMA HILL KAY,
NANCY DAVIS, AND
DRUCILLA RAMEY

*I have coached high school students in moot court a number of times. I enjoy
seeing the students broaden their horizons and develop new skills as they take
on a challenge outside of the usual school day.*

*A few years ago, I walked the halls of the firm where I worked with
one of my students. The firm was laid out in an old-fashioned style,
with secretaries' offices lining the hallways, and lawyers' offices in an
inner layer, virtually hidden, accessible only by first walking through
the secretaries' area.*

*On the way from the conference room to my office, therefore, we
saw about ten women sitting in these assorted little outer offices working on
the computer or talking on the phone.*

*The student interrupted our discussion of trial strategy. She said to me,
"Don't you have any men lawyers here?"*

*She actually thought the entire length of a hallway in one of the largest
law firms in one of America's largest cities could be filled with only female
lawyers! Including women of color!*

It was too funny.

This required some quick processing. She was about sixteen years old and a young woman of color. Who could even foresee all of the possible future injustices she might encounter in the workplace or elsewhere because of her gender or the color of her skin? Someday she would have her spirit crushed. I did the equation in my head. I decided it wouldn't be my doing. At least not that day.

So I replied, "The men are on another floor."

She nodded in a matter-of-fact way, question answered. Information digested. We did our work, and she went home. But I couldn't forget the question and the innocent way it was asked. She assumed—even expected—equality and fair dealing. How terrific that she grew up this way! When I was her age, I am positive I never would have thought all those women were lawyers.

I thought of the exchange with this student during the couple of days I spent meeting Herma Hill Kay, Nancy Davis, and Dru Ramey in northern California. In the bold new world these women are constructing, it is possible for that student to be more right than wrong—it is my old-fashioned assumptions that are out of step.

Herma Hill Kay

Very few of America's top law schools include female deans in their administrations. One of the first women to have such a position was Herma Hill Kay at the University of California, Berkeley (called "Boalt Hall"), who served as dean from July 1992 through June 2000.

On the wall of Herma's office hangs a photograph of her with three other women—all wearing skirts, hats, and gloves—all the females from northern California who passed the California bar exam in 1960. There are also framed crayon drawings done by children whose mothers brought them to Herma's classes when babysitters were not available. There is a framed announcement from 1974 for the publication of Herma's textbook *Sex Discrimination,* the first on the topic. She points out a large pink thank-you card from a group of young women who went on to start a public interest law firm after they graduated from Boalt Hall. The room's atmosphere is warm and supportive, reflecting Herma's personality.

The first thing Herma mentions is that she wanted to be a lawyer since sixth grade. In the mid-1940s, she was the only student in her South Carolina classroom willing to argue in a debate that the Confederacy should not have won the Civil War. "My teacher told me I would make a good lawyer. When I told my mother about it, she said 'Don't be silly, you can't make a living as a lawyer—you'll get married.'"

Women in Academia

"In 1919, Boalt Hall became the first major American law school to have a woman on its faculty," she says. "Her name was Barbara Nachtrieb Armstrong. Barbara became a great mentor and friend. She had earned a Ph.D. in social economics from Berkeley. She taught social economics and law in the graduate

---

Herma Hill Kay

RESIDENCE: San Francisco, California
BORN: 1934
PERSONAL: Married (1 child)
PROFESSIONAL: Law Professor, University of California–Berkeley Law School, Boalt Hall; Dean of Boalt Hall (1992–2000)
1992 Recipient of the Margaret Brent Award

---

school and was eventually invited to come over to lecture at the law school. . . . The law school was comfortable with her lecturing here because first, she was already a Berkeley professor; second, she was viewed as 'Berkeley's own' and a prize scholar. . . . If she hadn't had those two things going for her and had simply applied to the law school to teach, I doubt she would have been hired in that era.

"When I first started at Boalt, there were not even a handful of women in each entering class. Since then, the percentage of female students here has gone from three percent to fifty-two percent."

"Barbara taught family law and authored a treatise on the subject. It was the definitive work on family law at the time—an academic 'bestseller.' Although Barbara had tenure, she had trouble getting promoted as part of the merit reviews. The dean of the law school then, William Lloyd Prosser, an icon of the legal community (and himself the author of a treatise, the classic *Prosser on Torts*), recognized Barbara's brilliance and wanted to help her. . . . An unconfirmed story goes that he walked to the table where the university's chancellor was eating lunch in the faculty dining room and said, 'No one else here has done this for the school' and plopped down in front of the chancellor the two heavy volumes of Barbara's treatise. . . . Prosser had to resort to unbureaucratic channels because the traditional channels were not responsive," she concludes.

Breaking the One-Woman-At-A-Time Rule

"As Barbara neared retirement, she asked that someone be hired to replace her. And she asked that the new professor be female. I tell people that makes me the law school's first 'affirmative action hire!'. . . So, in 1960—a mere forty-one years after Barbara was hired," she smiles, "the powers that be around here decided we could break the 'one-woman-at-a-time rule.' Boalt then had two female professors! There were only about a dozen of us around the whole country. It was at least another decade before law schools started hiring women as a matter of course."

Barbara played a large role in helping Herma begin her career as a law school professor. "Barbara was a terrific hands-on mentor to me. She gave me her notes from the marital property course she taught. In the afternoons, over tea in her office, she taught me the law of community property. . . . Like her, I always took a special interest in the women students. I wanted to encourage them."

And in time, Herma would coauthor an "academic bestseller" of her own on the subject of sex discrimination. "Ruth Bader Ginsburg, then at Columbia, Ken Davidson of the University of Buffalo, and I met each other at a conference at NYU Law School. . . . Ken told us he had drafted a manuscript for a sex discrimination text. It was written from an employment law perspective. I volunteered to add the family law aspects. Ruth volunteered to add constitutional law, education, and comparative law. Our first edition came out in 1974. After Ruth became a judge, and Ken joined the government, I edited the second and third editions. Professor Martha West, of U.C. Davis, became my co-author on the current fourth edition in 1996 and the 1999 supplement."

> *". . . In my mind, I think of affirmative action as finding ways to give opportunities to qualified people who might have been closed out of opportunities in the past."*

Affirmative Action

Herma discusses some of the changes since those afternoon teas in Barbara's office. "It's becoming a different world. . . . When I first started at Boalt, there were not even a handful of women in each entering class. Since then, the percentage of female students here has gone from three percent to fifty-two percent." Herma believes affirmative action efforts, which increased the number of women and minorities in the student body at Boalt and other law schools across the country, have produced beneficial changes. "Technically,

"Once you open the door of opportunity for a woman who might not have had a certain door open to her in the past, what do you do next? Do you walk away, pleased with yourself that you opened this door for her and leave her to fight it out—to succeed or fail—on a path few others have traveled? Do you try to provide some tools that will help on her journey, or do you go along with her for some or part of her way?"

what's called 'affirmative action,'" she explains, "was a series of civil rights laws, governmental programs, and presidential executive orders by Roosevelt, Kennedy, Johnson, Nixon. . . . But in my mind, I think of affirmative action as finding ways to give opportunities to qualified people who might have been closed out of opportunities in the past.

"For instance, Boalt's admissions policy emphasizes students' individual achievements and places less value on their undergraduate grades and LSATs [the standardized law school admissions test]. . . . Boalt sends recruiters to a wide range of undergraduate colleges, without actually targeting students of a particular gender or race. Our recruiters talk to people, tell them about the school, make contacts with college counselors. In past years, we sent a video about the school to admitted students. We attract a more diverse student body with this approach."

Important questions related to affirmative action are raised by Herma: "Once you open the door of opportunity for a woman who might not have had a certain door open to her in the past, what do you do next? Do you walk away, pleased with yourself that you opened this door for her and leave her to fight it out—to succeed or fail—on a path few others have traveled? Do you try to provide some tools that will help on her journey, or do you go along with her for some or part of her way?"

Helping Others on Their Journeys

Herma has helped many women along unchartered paths—those just starting school, as well as working women who may struggle with a different set of concerns. But all the Boalt women benefited from her work to establish support networks for graduates: "I had the idea for a reunion of Boalt's women graduates, and we had one in spring 1998. . . . Someone was here from every class that had graduated a female student, going back to the 1930s, and up to some women who had been admitted to start that upcoming fall. Over one hundred female alums came to campus for a weekend program including keynote speeches, panel discussions on topics like 'managing your life and your law practice' or 'being a woman of color in the profession,' and of course, social events to get to know each other. . . . Participants thought it was a great success and suggested we do it again in five years."

Nancy Davis, Herma's friend and former student, is a perfect example of the results of Herma's good works. "Nancy was my research assistant. From the start, I was impressed with her resourcefulness, her leadership, and her high ideals. . . . I remember she helped write brochures for college career counselors called, "WANTED by The Law: WOMEN." They helped increase applications to law school from women. . . . She and her friends wanted to start a law firm after graduation to advance women's issues. I helped her to accomplish that because I was drawn to Nancy's determination and desire to help people. . . . One day she told me that while growing up, she and her sisters had a sailboat named *Determination*. I was not surprised!"

Nancy Davis

The next morning, at an early lunch, Nancy Davis comments, "I grew up believing the law was an instrument for social change. Herma helped me put that belief into action."

Nancy tells of growing up in a Democratic family in a Republican suburb of Chicago. "An organization called the Young Republicans welcomed people who moved into the neighborhood. Their representative couldn't believe her ears when my mother declined her invitation to join. One of my most memorable moments in high school was wearing a big JFK button on my coat lapel the morning after the 1960 presidential election!"

She recounts, "My dad was a tax lawyer who devoted a third of his time to *pro bono* work and believed deeply in public service. My mother—just about the smartest person I know—was a teacher and homemaker who raised three daughters, all of whom became lawyers. (She would have been the best of all of us!) We all practiced law that reflected their values. My sister Karen, who is deceased, worked with the American Civil Liberties Union in Tennessee and with Legal Aid in Oregon; my sister Linda was chief of the Criminal Section of the Civil Rights Division of the Department of Justice and is now a judge on the Washington, D.C. Superior Court."

In 1965, Nancy went to Mississippi under the sponsorship of the Mississippi Freedom Democratic Party, which was mounting voter registration drives and establishing Freedom Schools in African-American communities throughout the state. "A defining experience for me as a young adult was participating in one of the historic Freedom Summers of the 1960s. . . . I wanted to put my commitment to civil rights into action—I and my sisters, both of whom went to the South in the mid-60s, were acting on the values our parents had taught us. Before we left, our dad sat us down and gave us each a pile of stamped postcards. I remember feeling he was more solemn than usual. He said, 'I know you'll be busy this summer, so don't worry about writing to me and your mother. But drop one of these postcards in the mail to us everyday. If three days go by without our getting a card from you, I'll be on the next plane down there to make sure you're all right.'"

The Influence of Mentors

"Enough about me," Nancy laughs, "let's get to Herma! Herma taught me at Boalt. She was a fabulous role model for women students. She wanted to prepare us for the real world. We started a student group called the Boalt Hall Women's Association after Herma called all the women students together and told us that, given the discrimination we would likely encounter as women lawyers, we had better get to know each other and start working together."

Nancy and two of her classmates wanted to start a "teaching law firm" specializing in sex discrimination law. Nancy recalls, "When we broached the topic with Herma, she took us seriously. . . . Herma began providing guidance, and she never stopped. . . . She helped us obtain grants, establish relationships with Bay Area law schools, develop teaching materials, and set litigation priorities. She chaired the board of directors . . . She put her exemplary reputation behind us to help us do something we never could have accomplished on our own. . . . Herma taught me the law, while encouraging me to work on improving it to make justice a reality for everyone. One of the greatest strokes of good fortune in my life was meeting and being taught, mentored, and befriended by Herma."

Another key player and mentor in this process was Barbara Babcock, the first woman on the faculty of Stanford Law School (and a 1999 recipient of the Margaret Brent Award). She helped develop the concept of the "teaching firm." Once the firm was open for business, Babcock became the first board president and worked full-time with the firm's co-founders until being appointed in 1976 by President Jimmy Carter to head the Civil Division of the United States Department of Justice.

The Firm

In 1974, Nancy and her colleagues Mary Dunlap, Joan Graff, and Wendy Williams fulfilled their dream of opening Equal Rights Advocates ("ERA"), a teaching law firm. "As a law firm, we represented women's interests in a broad range of cases that included challenging pregnancy discrimination, unequal pay for equal work, sexual harassment, women turned away from firefighter and bus driver jobs because employers regarded those positions as 'men's work,' and unequal terms of incarceration for women prisoners. One of ERA's great strengths has been its commitment to enforcing the outcomes of cases (our lawsuit against the United States Forest Service, for example, went on for nineteen years), to assure that our clients and those they represented reaped the benefits of the risks they took in challenging unlawful discrimination."

"My dream is to see a workplace free of intimidation and harassment of women. I want to see anti-discrimination laws on the books enforced. I want our country to develop sound public policies that reflect the needs of women and their families. . ."

The "teaching" part of ERA gave students from Bay Area law schools litigation simulations based on the firm's real cases. Students also assisted with litigation pending in the firm—researching issues, drafting pleadings, analyzing evidence, preparing for trials. Nancy notes, "Students saw busy courts, anxious clients, and a variety of opposing counsel and judges. They learned about sex discrimination law, but they also learned how to function as professionals in the workplace."

Nancy sums up her goals in starting this firm: "There are enormously complex issues related to this country's policies with respect to half its population—the female half! The movement for women's economic, social, and political equality is still a work in progress," she observes. "My dream is to see a workplace free of intimidation and harassment of women. I want to see antidiscrimination laws on the books enforced. I want our country to develop sound public policies that reflect the needs of women and their families. . . . Ideally, I'd love to see Equal Rights Advocates put itself out of business, because there is simply no longer a need for an organization that fights for these things. But I don't think that's going to happen in my lifetime or the lifetimes of my children."

Toward the end of the conversation, Nancy wants to know who else is being interviewed for *The Counselors*—and seems to either be friends with or at least be an acquaintance of all the women interviewed in the book. She comments, "After two decades of school, work, and networking, finally, we're all getting to know each other!"

Drucilla Ramey

Nancy's good friend Drucilla Ramey is a master networker and the executive director and general counsel of the Bar Association of San Francisco (BASF). Dru (as she is called by friends) encourages women and men to help their careers by getting to know people in the community. "Women and minorities too often think that hard work alone will get you where you want to be." Dru smiles and waves her arms through the air: "I tell them, 'Get out

> **Drucilla Ramey**
>
> **RESIDENCE:** San Francisco, California
> **BORN:** 1946
> **PERSONAL:** Married (1 child)
> **PROFESSIONAL:** Executive Director and General Counsel, Bar Association of San Francisco
> *1997 Recipient of the Margaret Brent Award*

of your office! Come to the bar association! Your whole life isn't your computer in the cubbyhole on the thirty-seventh floor!' Bar associations sponsor career-enhancing programs, and you'll meet community leaders. . . . Why, I myself met my husband through a prestigious bar association committee. . . . To sit in an office for long hours working hard is a *sine qua non* to career success, of course. But working for the public good with leaders of the legal community can also provide an essential element and an independent basis for self-esteem."

Dru directs the resources of the BASF towards community equality and service. Under her leadership, this large metropolitan professional association with a 110-person staff has presented programs, lobbied legislatures, and submitted briefs in support of issues important to women—including the right to choose an abortion, equal pay for work of comparable worth, gender discrimination, sexual harassment, and breaking through the glass ceiling. She singles out a couple of BASF projects she believes have had the most far-reaching positive effect: drafting and lobbying for passage of a San Francisco ordinance banning discriminatory clubs; and developing and monitoring the implementation of model policies for area employers to adopt, including a Model Policy on Flexible Worktime Options, Goals and Timetables for Minority Advancement, Model Guidelines on Sexual Harassment Policies, and Model Guidelines for Elimination of Sexual Orientation Discrimination. Additionally, Dru has produced videos for national distribution on eliminating discrimination in the workplace and created a national model for community education on breast cancer prevention and treatment.

"With too few exceptions . . . women are still not running things in business, academia, and government. If you look at the raw power in the professions, we're not there yet."

Achieving Equality in Numbers

In terms of sheer numbers, Dru observes that the position of women in the workplace has never been stronger, then continues, "With too few exceptions, though, women are still not running things in business, academia, and government. If you look at the raw power in the professions, we're not there yet."

Affirmative action was a driving force in assisting women and minorities to gain access to professions that had previously been off limits, but not everyone agrees that affirmative action programs were beneficial. Some question whether affirmative action can produce a mentality where women question themselves and doubt they have the ability to earn things in their own right. Dru views such arguments with asperity: "Some would say I have been the beneficiary of what our society calls affirmative action. People of my gender were completely excluded from this profession, then admitted in carefully limited numbers. . . . But white men benefited for a very long time from legally and illegally denying women access to education, to the professions, and to community power. This country is still righting those wrongs. . . . I never heard of a man named Adams, Cabot, Lodge, or Rockefeller second-guessing that his admission to Harvard or Yale wasn't completely merit-based. . . . Women used to not be hired or admitted because of our gender. Now there are people who say women shouldn't want to be hired or admitted or promoted because of our gender—since we might then feel uncomfortable. I say hire me, admit me, promote me—as long as I'm qualified— and if my gender puts me over the top, I'll deal with the discomfort.

"Yale Law School, where I obtained my law degree, systematically excluded women and people of color from its student body and faculty. After dozens of years of limiting women to four or five a year, in 1968—perhaps not coincidentally a year in the middle of the Vietnam War—Yale suddenly admitted

> *"I never heard of a man named Adams, Cabot, Lodge, or Rockefeller second-guessing that his admission to Harvard or Yale wasn't completely merit-based. . . . I say hire me, admit me, promote me—as long as I'm qualified—and if my gender puts me over the top, I'll deal with the discomfort."*

twenty-five women in one year. One of my classmates the following year was Hillary Rodham—before she married Bill Clinton, who was also there. Another barrier was breached in 1968 for racial minorities, until then limited to a few each year—most of whose fathers were either doctors or lawyers or ambassadors to or from an African or South American country." In this newly diverse environment, Dru and her female classmates successfully lobbied the school administration for a women and law course, the first in the country.

An Accomplished Mother

Dru's willingness to suggest doing things that have never been done before and then enthusiastically throwing herself into their development—evident in her lobbying for a women and law course at Yale and again in her work today—is a trait she attributes to her mother. She shares anecdotes about her mother, who pursued a medical career starting in the 1940s with a commitment and resulting success that were rare for a woman of her day.

"My mom titled herself the 'Feminist Endocrinologist' of Georgetown Medical School. Endocrinologists specialize in hormones, and in the early 1970s she received national attention when she responded to a male surgeon who stated publicly that women couldn't be president because of their raging hormonal imbalances. . . . Mom pointed out to him—and it was published in a bunch of newspapers and magazines—that male hormones rage a lot more than female, which makes the lives of males generally shorter and more stressful. She also noted that President Kennedy had had Addison's Disease, which is a hormonal imbalance, yet he had been, for the most part, a fine president who functioned well in a crisis.

"I know the advice my mother rarely hesitates to pass along. . . . First, to pursue your education as vigorously as possible. . . . Second, don't smoke! If you do smoke, quit! My mother is an indefatigable foe of smoking. As a physiologist, she saw what it does to the heart, the lungs, the body. In fact, she says it's practically the only way to defeat the life-enhancing effects of estrogen. . . . At a dinner where Chief Justice Rehnquist pulled out a cigarette, she told him to put it out. As they were later dancing, she smelled the smoke on him and told him—the chief justice of the Supreme Court—that you have to be a congenital idiot to smoke. Of course, she then went on to say, 'But you know, I wouldn't mind if Jesse Helms smoked.'. . . She told me that, to Justice Rehnquist's credit, he was very polite about all this!"

This example from Dru illustrates how dramatically the world has changed: "A few years ago I introduced a medical luminary as the keynote speaker at an awards luncheon sponsored by a law firm founded by a friend of mine. The keynote speaker was my mother, Dr. Estelle Ramey. The firm was Equal Rights Advocates, founded by Nancy Davis. One of the awardees that day was Dean Herma Hill Kay. It used to be that when the director of a big city bar association introduced a parent—a medical professor—to give a keynote address for a firm founded by a close friend, and honoring the 'big cheese' who supported the firm, you'd be on pretty safe ground assuming all four players in that scenario were men. But in this scenario, all the players were women. That could not have happened a generation ago."

"It used to be that when the director of a big city bar association introduced a parent—a medical professor—to give a keynote address for a firm founded by a close friend, and honoring the 'big cheese' who supported the firm, you'd be on pretty safe ground assuming all four players in that scenario were men. But in this scenario, all the players were women. That could not have happened a generation ago."

Because of Drucilla Ramey (and Dru's mother, Dr. Estelle Ramey), Herma Hill Kay, and Nancy Davis, paths that once were hewn out of unchartered terrain and stood alone are now connecting into the highway of achieving women.

X.

JANET
RENO

*As I was admitted through security at the United States Department of
Justice, I was thinking about when Attorney General Janet Reno first came
on the national scene in 1993.*

*When Reno was nominated to be this country's first female attorney
general, I had no less than twenty conversations that day—in person and
on the phone—with female friends and colleagues. The gist of all the conversations was this: "A woman as attorney general! Do you believe it? WOW!"*

*It was big news. Huge. It may not seem like such a big deal now,
because we've already had a woman serve as attorney general. And as
secretary of state, and in other high-ranking government positions. It's
great that it might not sound like a big deal now, or that it might not be
when it happens again. But at the time, it was big news.*

I was rooting for her.

*In 1995, I went to see Reno speak at my five-year reunion from
New York University Law School. The school's largest auditorium was
packed to capacity. She was a fabulous speaker. I asked her a question
from the audience.*

*And there I was—on my way to ask her a bunch of questions one-on-one.
It was surreal!*

It brought home to me how blessed I had been in this whole exercise. I was meeting incredible woman after incredible woman—not one of whom I had met or known previously—and being received not like a journalist or a member of the press, but as a person who really could be talked to and trusted. During the course of her tenure as attorney general, it had become evident that Reno was a public servant of the highest caliber. I wanted to learn the stories behind what someone might read about her in the headlines, sensing that her background and motivation could encourage others.

Sure, my friends had been feeling sorry for me lately. Writing this book was requiring an awful lot of time and dedication. I needed to announce more and more often that it would be a "lockdown" weekend, which meant I wouldn't make plans to go to the movies or dinner and unplugged the phone. I would stay home, listen to music, read, and write. (I plugged in the phone for pizza orders.) Lockdown weekends are not good exercise for the cardiovascular system or for the social life, but everything I got out of writing this book meant more to me than any sacrifice.

Feeling like the luckiest woman alive, I was escorted into Janet Reno's office.

I t is a few days before Christmas 2000. Janet Reno is sitting in an armchair facing the fireplace in her office at the United States Department of Justice. Above the fireplace hangs an oil painting of Robert Kennedy, wearing a brown leather bomber jacket. In a few weeks, the Clinton Administration will come to a close, and Janet Reno will no longer be attorney general of the United States.

Reno is the first woman to serve as our nation's attorney general. Traditionally, presidents often have reserved the post of attorney general for a close friend. For example, President Kennedy selected his younger brother, Bobby, and President Nixon chose his law partner, John Mitchell. Although President Clinton did not know Janet Reno personally before nominating her for the post, she became one of the most recognized members of the Clinton cabinet. But today is not about name recognition or how beloved she is by the public. Stories of family, work, goals, and obstacles comprise the agenda for this meeting.

Janet Reno

RESIDENCE: Miami, Florida
BORN: 1938
PERSONAL: Single
PROFESSIONAL: Attorney General of the United States (1993–2001); Highest ranking female ever in a presidential line of succession
1993 Recipient of the Margaret Brent Award

What Attorney Generals Are Made of

"My parents were both newspaper reporters," she says. "My father for the *Miami Herald* and my mother for the *Miami News*. . . . I think you could say I had the kind of upbringing that developed a young woman without some of the societal constraints of the time. That was mostly because of my mother. . . . When I was eight, my mother moved the family to twenty acres on the edge of the Everglades in Florida. Our family needed room to grow, and there she built us the cedar log house I lived in until I moved to Washington in 1993. In our yard, at any given time, you could find an assortment of cows, horses, goats, donkeys, snakes, raccoons, pigs, and peacocks. We called all the peacocks 'Horace.' Alligators lived nearby. My mother was known to wrestle with one once in a while." She grins, "I'm not kidding."

She cups her chin in her palm and leans her elbow on the arm of her chair—emanating accessibility, friendliness, and a willingness to chat. "Even more than four decades later," she continues, "my mother had faith in how well she had built that house. When Hurricane Andrew struck the area, I wasn't sure it was completely safe for us to stay there while ferocious storms were raging. But my mother sat at the kitchen table with her hands folded in front of her—by now she was old and sick—and told me she had built the house well, the house could stand adversity, and we would be fine. Needless to say, she was right. There was massive damage to the Miami area, but all that happened at our house was a couple of the window screens blew out. . . . After the hurricane, whenever I would drive down the driveway through the woods toward home—with a problem, or some obstacle to overcome—the house reminded me you can do anything you really want to if you put your mind to it, and that you can prevail against adversity when you are put together well.

"After the hurricane, whenever I would drive down the driveway through the woods toward home—with a problem, or some obstacle to overcome—the house reminded me you can do anything you really want to if you put your mind to it, and that you can prevail against adversity when you are put together well."

"My mother used to take us deep into the Everglades to meet the Native Americans who had lived there for centuries—the Miccosukees and the Seminoles. They were kind to us, even allowing us to attend some of their tribal rituals. . . . She took us canoeing down wild rivers. . . . She herself once walked over one hundred miles up the Florida coast alone and wrote of it in her journal, 'It might be that someday I shall be drowned by the sea or die of pneumonia from sleeping out at night, or be robbed and strangled by strangers. These things happen. Even so, I shall be ahead because of trusting the beach, the night, and strangers.'"

Reno also lists some more traditional pursuits encouraged by her mother: "My interest in books. Also, she taught me about poetry, and expected me to be knowledgeable about world affairs. . . . We never had a television, though. She used to say that television contributed to mind rot. I think today she would also say it contributes to violence."

She speaks of sometimes feeling embarrassed by her mother while growing up: "With her free-spirited ways, she was so different from other people's mothers. . . . As I matured, I learned to appreciate that she was simply who she was, and it was not for me to judge her or to change her. She wasn't hurting anyone. She loved us so completely! That became more important than anything else about her, and I became comfortable with her just the way she was. I think acceptance of parents and family is a challenge a lot of young people can relate to. . . . .

"One of the things I am proudest of in my life is that I lived with my mother, and when she got sick I was able to take care of her."

"In fact, in my mother's old age, I truly enjoyed walking around Miami greeting people with her—she in her floppy sun hat, smiling without any teeth because she didn't want to wear dentures! . . . Whenever I have asked myself what life was for, or what the meaning of life was, I needed only to look over at her, or call her if I was away from her, or in her last days, reach over and hold her old and gnarled hand to know the answer. . . . One of the things I am proudest of in my life is that I lived with my mother, and when she got sick I was able to take care of her. She was able to stay at home and not go to a nursing home. I tried to contribute to giving her a full, wonderful old age— taking her for rides up and down the river in our boat, despite the fact that she was terminally ill and increasingly frail."

Divine Timing

Janet Reno was a high school debating champion, earned a degree in chemistry from Cornell University, then graduated from Harvard Law School in 1963. She recalls, "My mother kept selling acres of land to pay for our tuition. The family land is now one quarter its original size." In the course of her career, Reno worked in private practice (she was one of the first women to be a partner at Miami's largest law firm), served as the staff director for the Judiciary Committee of Florida's House of Representatives, and was elected state attorney for Dade County (which includes Miami) for five terms, totaling fifteen years. She cites Sandy D'Alemberte (a past American Bar Association president) as a mentor and positive influence in her career development.

The telephone call from President Clinton asking her to be his attorney general could be characterised as "divine timing": "The President called six weeks after my mother passed away . . . I would not have left Miami if she was still suffering with lung cancer." Reno had been approached continually to run for governor or to accept an appointment to the Florida Supreme Court during her mother's illness, but she was not willing to leave Miami and the family's log house until her mother's struggle was over.

The Influence of Role Models

In the spring of 1993, as Reno was learning the ropes of her new job as attorney general, a traumatic event occurred. When she was sworn in, the Federal Bureau of Investigation ("FBI") was in the midst of a three-week stand-off with the Branch Davidians in Waco, Texas. The Branch Davidians were a religious cult with an illegal arsenal of weapons to use against citizens or government officials. Reno approved the FBI's plan to end the stand-off by allowing the use of force and refused to attribute responsibility to anyone but herself for the manner in which the attack was conducted or the fire and deaths related to it. She mitigated a situation that was becoming wrought with finger-pointing and assessment of blame when she stood outside her new office in Washington, D.C., and stated, "I made the decision. . . . I'm accountable . . . the buck stops with me."

Janet Reno's declaration "The buck stops with me" echoes the words of one of her heroes, President Harry Truman, who kept a sign on his desk in the Oval Office which proclaimed "The buck stops here." It was a recognition that decision-makers and those with responsibility often "pass the buck" to others, a course eschewed by Truman. She names other heroes—Washington, Lincoln, Franklin Delano Roosevelt—and points to a plaque on the wall adjacent to where the Kennedy oil painting hangs. The plaque is entitled "Duty As Seen by Lincoln." It says, "If I were to try to read, much less answer, all the attacks made on me, this shop would be closed for business. I do the very best I know how—the very best I can; and I mean to keep doing so til the end. If the end brings me out all right, what is said against me won't amount to anything. If the end brings me out wrong, ten angels swearing I was right would make no difference."

It is fitting that Reno chose for inspiration the words of a national leader who was vilified in his own lifetime, but—with the perspective afforded by the passage of time—is now regarded as a great moral hero. Again, these are words applicable to her own life. In 1980, while serving as state attorney for Dade County, Florida, Janet Reno's office tried but failed to convict five police officers in the beating death of an African-American insurance executive. Rioting ensued throughout Miami, during which some people demanded her resignation. In the midst of the riot, she visited a community center and met with citizens to listen to why they were angry. She conducted an ongoing dialogue with the African-American community about the circumstances of the case—accepting invitations to speak and to listen at church halls, community centers, and schools.

"I made myself accessible to the community," she remembers. "I was everywhere . . . I kept the doors of communication open and made efforts to communicate directly with communities before I made a decision and to explain decisions to them afterward." In time, she was invited to march in the Martin Luther King Jr. Day parade with the African-American community, during which she was hailed as a hero. It is no wonder she was re-elected four times to the office of state attorney.

"Justice is not served when prosecutors cut corners"

Reno's sense of responsibility, attention to detail, preparedness, and integrity shine through in every aspect of her life. When she discusses law enforcement and prosecution, these traits come through again. She applies the metaphor discussed earlier with regard to character, drawn from her mother's experience—building a house that is structurally sound. She says, in part, "People always ask why prosecutions take so long. . . . I think building a prosecution is in some ways like building a house. When we build a case, we focus on building the foundation well, starting carefully, building it carefully, making sure that we go from a lower-level person to a higher-level person if they are involved, until we ultimately identify all the people responsible. . . . When a person drives by a construction site where work is being done on the foundation—out of sight—that person might conclude that since they can't see walls or a roof, little progress is being made. But we can't nail on shingles until we've laid a foundation, put up the walls, and added the roof.

> *"If you want to accomplish anything, you must start the day by asking yourself tough questions, and end the day by demanding of yourself real answers."*

"If we don't build the foundation of a case solidly," she goes on to say, "all of our other work will be for naught. We must proceed on a case in an orderly manner, building it like a house that will stand the test of time and—if prosecutions result—will withstand the scrutiny of the courts and be upheld on appeal.

"Justice is not served when prosecutors cut corners," she concludes. "We must probe our cases beyond—and to the exclusion of—reasonable doubt. All the while we continue digging. New evidence and new leads may surface. In the end, we must meet the highest standard of all. We must convince twelve people on a jury that a crime has been committed and that the person charged is guilty of the crime. . . . The legal system's demanding standards of proof prevent us from basing our judgments on information that might satisfy onlookers who consider the issue for a moment."

Reno shares her reasoning: "If you want to accomplish anything, you must start the day by asking yourself tough questions, and end the day by demanding of yourself real answers. . . . You gain nothing by lying to yourself. See things for what they are. Only then can you assess whether they are 'good' or 'bad' or whether you want to do anything to change anything."

Influencing the Law

In a later discussion with Kinney Zalesne, a young attorney who worked for Reno, Zalesne observes, "I never before met a person who is as impressive and intelligent as Attorney General Reno, yet so down-to-earth and unimpressed with herself. She knows herself. She is comfortable with herself. It is something to strive for. She brings that wisdom and fortitude to every issue she addresses. . . . I have seen her willingness to make an unpopular decision because she believes she is doing the right thing. Her commitment to evidence and law helps her to withstand criticism, and in the end she is usually right. On some issues, like the nurturing of children as an aspect of crime prevention—besides its humanitarian aspects—she was ahead of her time."

As attorney general—and previously in Florida—Janet Reno focused on developing systems to strengthen communities and to help children grow up in a healthy and constructive environment. While state attorney for Dade County, she helped restructure the juvenile court system and visited local schools to talk with students, teachers, and parents—answering questions about her job, giving out her home number, and telling the children to call her at home if anyone abused them. She comments, "I would rather prevent crime by reshaping the lives of children than any other way."

Reno considers child development and family responsibility to be a critical aspect of law enforcement. "Today, it is common to hear police chiefs and prosecutors talk about 'starting out early' with kids. Decades ago, prosecutors who talked about helping children would be branded and castigated—it was called 'a female approach' or 'acting like a social worker.' But without question, at many points in a child's life, adults can target issues and make a difference. Risky times in a child's life are windows of opportunity for positive change.

"When I was a prosecutor," she remembers, "I would look at pre-sentence reports over and over for places where somebody could have intervened. Often, there were big red waving flags in a file—for instance, the father went to jail, the child had a fever that went on too long untreated, or there was a shoplifting incident at age eleven. Now this troubled child got older and committed a murder and robbery, and we were going to put him away behind bars—because that is what we do in this country with those who commit murder and robbery. But there would be the feeling that this incarceration could have been prevented. I see no reason to wait for a child to be thirteen and in some sort of trouble before we try to help. . . . Every child development expert I've ever talked to says the most formative time in a child's life is from birth to age three. This makes it so important to reduce teen pregnancy and to improve prenatal and pediatric care. . . . When kids get into trouble with the law, we can't just lock them away with their mistakes. As a community, we must care for them and help them to take their place among us. They can begin again —they can learn and work and grow."

In addition to promoting coherent community planning, Reno urged domestic federal agencies such as Housing and Urban Development, Health and Human Services, and the Department of Education to collaborate with the Department of Justice to support community efforts for children. To this end, she spearheaded the creation of the "Safe Schools/Healthy Students" program in 1999, streamlining funds from the Justice Department, the Department of Health and Human Services, and the Department of Education to communities all over America for youth programs.

Domestic Violence

A similar collaborative approach has been taken with regard to domestic violence. Reno notes: "I worked with the Department of Health and Human Services to develop a comprehensive support network for victims of domestic violence, including shelters and referral systems to protect and provide for battered women and their children." She continues, "Domestic violence used to be a private matter within a family. When it became generally acknowledged as a problem through public awareness, it was only from the criminal standpoint. But now we also look at domestic violence in the way it relates to healthcare, the workplace, and the community. . . . We educate people that beating one's spouse, child, live-in, or parent is not acceptable in a civilized society; that this is not the problem of one race or social class; that the overwhelming majority of the victims are women; that domestic violence is the single major cause of injury to women; that domestic violence is usually the result of a pattern of intimidation and control by the batterer, which also includes threats and coercion; and most importantly, that the victims don't ever deserve this treatment."

In the larger context, Reno believes, "A child who sees his or her mother being beaten is more likely to accept violence as a way of relating to people in life. . . . We can do tremendous amounts of good through conflict resolution programs in schools." She emphasizes, "Most of all, families have to be involved. I find when government approaches citizens and says, 'We want to work with you, we need your input,' a lot more good can evolve from that."

"I would rather prevent crime by reshaping the lives of children than any other way."

Native Americans

While attorney general, Reno employed this approach successfully in initiatives to help Native Americans address and solve problems in their communities. "We issued a policy on American Indian sovereignty and government-to-government relations," she describes, "which means that the Justice Department will respect tribal rights and will consult with tribal leaders whenever appropriate. We held a National American Indian Listening Conference to share ideas on how tribal communities can become safer and healthier. . . . We created the CIRCLE Project [Comprehensive Indian

Resources for Community and Law Enforcement] as a way to assist Native American communities to fight crime, violence, and substance abuse more effectively. The tribes play the lead role in developing and implementing efforts."

Not surprisingly, in light of her childhood experiences in the Everglades, Reno has respect for and an affinity with Native Americans: "I learned growing up that many Native American people had strong, strong democratic traditions that value the wisdom of a tribe's elders, respect women as equal to men, and cherish the children as the future of their nation. . . . Tribal traditions give young people a sense of belonging to something special, a sense of their heritage—the feeling that their ancestors were brave and courageous people from whom they can learn and take inspiration."

Leslie Batchelor, former associate deputy attorney general to Reno, later provides perspective on the groundbreaking work with Native American communities: "This Attorney General has done more to try to improve the lives of Native Americans than any attorney general before her. Not only does she take seriously the federal government's special trust responsibility for Indian tribes, but she has worked to strengthen tribal communities from within. Her respect for tribal sovereignty and her commitment to self-determination have led her to encourage tribal communities to draw upon their own traditions and rely on tribal systems of justice to solve the problems they face. By empowering tribal communities, she increased their ability to improve the well-being of their members into the future. I believe this will be remembered as one of her lasting achievements as attorney general."

> *"I never forget where I'm from and where I'll go back to."*

Looking Back, Looking Forward

Of her tenure in Washington, Ms. Reno reflects, "I have learned how much the work of the Justice Department affects all Americans. . . . Our employees work around the nation and around the world. They catch spies and drug lords and terrorists. They stand guard at our borders. They uphold our liberties.

And around the country, the Justice Department is a full partner with police, mayors, and neighborhoods in the twenty-four-hour world of protecting the public and prosecuting criminals.

"In a wide range of areas, we have made important strides to improve the quality of life for Americans. We have put church-burners behind bars, helped boost minority lending to record levels, and enabled Americans with disabilities to use 911, eat out with their families, and sit next to their friends at movies or stadiums." She laughs, "Can you tell I am very proud of the dedicated women and men I have worked with? One of the things I'd like to do—both while I'm in office and when I leave office—is let the American people know that these people who serve them care passionately about this country, work long hours, and deserve our respect and gratitude."

Janet Reno served as attorney general for nearly eight years—longer than any other attorney general in the previous century. When reminded that President Truman left office and returned to Independence, Missouri, to become "Citizen Truman" again, she remarks, "I never forget where I'm from and where I'll go back to."

XI.
JOAN DEMPSEY
KLEIN

I've been a joiner. In high school, I joined the French club, intramural sports, and the tennis team, among others. I never went home when classes ended at 2:30. In college, I joined the pre-law society, the literary magazine, the speech and debate society, and a few more.

I've also been a leader. I've spearheaded projects or served as an officer in organizations I've joined. And I served as my high school's student council president.

"Relevance, Counselor?" as my friend Jerry says to a lot of my stories. Well, two things.

First, joining and actively participating in organizations is a great way to spend free time, meet other people with common interests, and possibly do some good for others. Organization membership can also help build a résumé or increase career prospects.

And second, while I know what it is to be a joiner and a leader, I have never been a founder. I've never started an organization for other people to join and in which they could become leaders. I have never seen, in my mind's eye, the potential for a group of people to make common cause—and then taken that idea and put it into action, to create an entity that has members and newsletters, officers and conferences, and helps people.

For instance, we all know of those extraordinary people on the evening news who, when they face real tragedy—such as having a child disappear, killed by a drunk driver, or born with autism—address their grief, in part, by starting support groups, advocacy groups, or establishing foundations (The Polly Klaas Foundation, Mothers Against Drunk Drivers, and Cure Autism Now, respectively). And what about those who had the vision and gumption to start Amnesty International, Planned Parenthood, or Greenpeace?

Joan Dempsey Klein has done this "founder" sort of thing three times! Before we met, I spent some time thinking about the attributes I expected such a person to have. She should have a strong intelligence, charisma, and a way of speaking that makes people take note, I thought. In Joan Dempsey Klein, I did find all these things and more.

On June 5, 1968, Joan Dempsey Klein needed to open her courtroom before seven o'clock to perform a gruesome duty. The man to be charged with the murder of presidential candidate Robert Kennedy, Sirhan Sirhan, was about to be brought before her by the district attorney.

The preceding day, Kennedy had been assassinated after delivering his victory speech in the California primary. Some viewed this as an event that altered the course of history, as it appeared he could win the election in November and become president. The country was horrified. His brother, former President John Kennedy, had been assassinated while in office less than

Joan Dempsey Klein

RESIDENCE: Los Angeles, California
BORN: 1929
PERSONAL: Married (five children)
PROFESSIONAL: Presiding Justice of the California Court of Appeals, Founder of three organizations to advance women professionally: The National Association of Women Judges, The California Women Lawyers Association, and The International Association of Women Judges
1997 Recipient of the Margaret Brent Award

five years earlier. The district attorney and several police officers stayed awake through the night to prepare the charges for this arraignment. Members of the Kennedy family were flying in from all over the country to mourn. In this emotionally charged atmosphere, Judge Dempsey Klein presided over the courtroom and set bail at $250,000. She also ruled that Mr. Sirhan would be held in custody in lieu of bail.

Then she had to move on and accomplish other tasks on other cases that day. She says it was difficult, but she did it. Joan Dempsey Klein shares this story in the context of a conversation on how decisions made by judges can change people's lives—affecting their freedom or their pocketbook, among other things. She provides the perspective that no matter how crucial a case is to the parties involved (and it may be the only case in which those parties are ever involved) it is still just one of the cases a busy judge may handle in a week, a year, and a career. Clearly, being a judge is not the sort of job everyone could do. Further, more so in 1968 than today, it was generally not the sort of job that would be done by a woman.

Joan Dempsey Klein has been a judge for more than thirty-five years. The sheer longevity of her career as a female professional is worthy of note. Though it is fairly common to find men who have been judges for thirty-five years, the same is not true for women. It is also fairly common to find men who have had legal careers for more than forty years; again, this is not the case for women. In the future, we know this will not be true. Larger and larger numbers of working women will eventually be judges for more than thirty-five years and will eventually have legal careers for more than forty years. But today, Joan is still a rarity.

Growing Up

Joan came of age during the 1930s, when American societal standards held women to respect and obey their husbands above all others. Joan remembers her mother's relationship with her father: "My mother did not have a say in anything. . . . She had no money of her own—never held a job. . . . I remember grocery shopping with my mother on Saturdays when I was a girl. She and I would go through the market with a cart and select food. After the cashier rung up our total, we would ask the cashier to please wait a moment while we retrieved money to pay the bill. Then we walked outside to the parking lot, where my father was sitting in the car. He doled out the money for the groceries to my mother, then she would walk back into the store to pay the cashier. I used to think, 'Can't he estimate how much money she'll need and give it to her in advance?'"

Joan realized her mother's confidence and self-esteem had been whittled away by ongoing dependence on her father. She observes, "My mother did not have a say in *anything*. She had no money of her own, never held a job. . . . They were not on equal footing in that relationship. My mother essentially took orders from my father."

Not wanting to follow in her mother's footsteps became a motivating force for Joan. "Sometimes a parent can show you precisely the person you don't want to become, the same way a parent can show you precisely the person you aspire to become. . . . Whenever I faced hardship in my education and career, the thought of my mother's life provided me with negative motivation, spurring me onward. I persevered through difficulties because I was scared that if I didn't, I would end up being just like my mother."

Reflecting on it now, Joan acknowledges that it must have been difficult for her parents to raise a daughter who refused to follow the well-established family course of conduct, which included a college education and career for men but not for women. "No woman in our family challenged things the way I did. My parents did not know how to handle a girl like me. . . . My father told me he did not believe in education for women."

So Joan went through college and law school without her parents' financial support, working part-time during school terms and full-time during vacations. On the road to becoming a lawyer, she held jobs as a teacher, a playground director, a lifeguard, a sales clerk, and as a legendary riveter.

"'Rosie the Riveter'—that was me! What a transforming experience. . . . I worked for the Defense Department

"No woman in our family challenged things the way I did. My parents did not know how to handle a girl like me. . . . My father told me he did not believe in education for women."

while the men were away fighting in World War II. I shot rivets into planes. I made my own money, and I made a lot of money. I supported myself. I bought myself a car. When the men came home from the war, all the 'Rosie the Riveters' were sent home. . . . We essentially were told that since the men were home to resume their former place, we should resume our former place."

Joan found giving up a source of her growing independence and self-reliance to be difficult. "With the loss of that job, I lost its financial rewards, certainly. . . . But what is not so easily measured—and is equally important—

is that I lost a source of intellectual stimulation, community recognition of my accomplishments, and personal gratification."

Taking the Road Less Traveled

Joan illustrates with a story of how sometimes what appears to be a detour from a chosen path can turn out to be exactly the sort of course you would have wanted to choose for your development. "While I was a lifeguard at the Y, two girls in the pool asked me to help them practice their swimming strokes because they were preparing to audition for a water show to tour Europe. As I helped them, they explained they had no way of getting to the Hollywood Athletic Club for the audition. They urged me to audition with them, so I volunteered to drive all of us. The way it worked out was a bit awkward! I was chosen to travel with the water show—though both of them were not.

"We presented a large cast of swimmers, divers, and dancers in fabulous costumes, with lively music, just like the MGM extravaganzas starring Olympic swimmer Esther Williams. We traveled with a collapsible pool, diving well, and stage—and lush Hawaiian-style sets. . . . We assembled our trans-portable *Palais de Sports* (Sports Palace) throughout Europe—including Paris, London, Zurich, and Rome. We put on a show each night and went sightseeing during the day."

After traveling with the water show for nearly a year, Joan returned home to continue school. As a result of her experience, she learned a number of things worth sharing with others. "First, I gained an appreciation for physical fitness. You don't have to become an amazing athlete to get benefits from physical fit-ness. It feels great to just take a walk, stretch a little, and take deep breaths. If you participate in team sports, there are additional benefits to be gained. Playing team sports makes you more comfortable competing, which is something with which a lot of females are not so comfortable. Girls are usually raised to get along with others and to bring people together—not to compete. But if you want a career, you'll find it's important to be comfortable with competitive people, with a competitive atmosphere, and to win and lose with grace. People who play team sports know lessons are learned from both winning and losing."

Through her time with the water show, Joan also gained an appreciation for travel. Her confidence increased from getting along day-to-day in different countries—handling different currencies, trying new foods, finding historical sights, and meeting people from varied backgrounds. She advises, "Young people can travel on a shoestring budget, with student train passes and hostel passes, and I encourage it—while you can still stand wearing a backpack and before you acquire a taste for hotels and restaurants!"

Comparing Cultures

Because of her love for travel, Joan eagerly participated in the People-to-People program when she became a judge. People-to-People was started by President Eisenhower to introduce Americans to their counterparts around the world—for instance, American engineers might visit engineers in Scandinavia, or American nurses might travel to meet nurses in Argentina. The first People-to-People excursion for female judges was to China in 1983.

"Playing team sports makes you more comfortable competing . . . If you want a career, you'll find it's important to be comfortable with competitive people, with a competitive atmosphere, and to win and lose with grace. People who play team sports know lessons are learned from both winning and losing."

Joan recalls, "I was struck by the fact that the Chinese government was recruiting citizens to become lawyers. Apparently, when China was ruled by a repressive regime, lawyers and other intellectuals were persecuted—and literally chased away to live in the countryside instead of in the cities. When China began opening itself up to do business with the West, it found that people in government and business from the West expected Chinese lawyers to show up to conduct negotiations and to draft contracts. I learned that lawyers and repressive regimes generally don't mix."

Joan has now traveled all over the world—from Japan to Australia, Scandinavia to Kenya—and she believes that the United States provides the best opportunities for women to succeed. Further, the conditions under which she has seen women living worldwide have convinced her that efforts to advance women will be needed for many years to come.

Organizations for Women

One of the ways in which women have furthered their advancement in this country is by organizing together and making joint efforts. Such organizations can take on issues—supporting candidates for public office, advocating in favor of legislation, or raising funds. They can also provide education and inspiration to members or to the public. They can work to improve conditions or increase opportunities for members, or facilitate professional networking for members. The possibilities are as varied as the different types of people who decide to work together, recognizing that a group working toward a common goal probably has a better chance of success than individual or uncoordinated individual efforts.

Joan knows the value of organizations dedicated to women's advancement and is the founder of three: The National Association of Women Judges, The California Women Lawyers Association, and the International Association of Women Judges.

She was a cofounder of the California Women Lawyers Association ("CWLA") in the 1970s, an organization that, among other things, submitted "friend of the court" briefs in important California cases to support affirmative action and abortion rights, and to criticize discriminatory clubs. Joan worked on the CWLA Judges' Committee. She observed a correlation between women lawyers being in a well-organized group and a rise in the number of women on the bench in California. So she went national, and eventually global. She recalls, "The National Association of Women Judges ("NAWJ") was an idea whose time had come for a number of reasons. . . . Whenever there was a conference for the judges in our state, invariably the ten or so females would get together in a room to compare war stories and search for solutions."

During their gatherings in the mid-1970s, the women discovered they encountered a different set of problems than their male counterparts—problems like male attorneys trying to take charge of their courtroom; male attorneys who insulted female attorneys, clients, and witnesses; and male attorneys who would address female judges as "my dear" rather than with the respectful "your honor." Joan explains, "We reasoned that if we've got so many gender issues to contend with, and we're in California—and California is supposed to be such a progressive place to live—then what must it be like for female judges in other parts of the country?" The group decided to identify female judges throughout the country and invite them to a meeting. Joan volunteered to be in charge of the national outreach.

She hired a couple of interns to locate female judges across the United States. There was no computer database of attorneys, no Internet—not even a directory of judges. The interns were able to identify female judges around the country, with larger numbers in traditionally progressive areas like New York City, Chicago, and Florida. Joan invited all the women they found to a four-day conference in Los Angeles, and more than one hundred women accepted the invitation to a meeting in October 1979.

"Young people can travel on a shoestring budget, with student train passes and hostel passes, and I encourage it—while you can still stand wearing a backpack and before you acquire a taste for hotels and restaurants!"

Telling the story of that first conference, Joan smiles broadly: "Words are not adequate to describe the joy. . . . It was so much fun, such a thrill! We couldn't get enough of each other—sharing our experiences, laughing, crying. Everyone was heard saying to each other, 'How can I help you?' I don't think I slept for four days straight. . . . We had so much to tell each other. We were kindred souls, and we were coming together to form an organization to help each other and to help other women come on board and move forward. As a result of that conference, the NAWJ had one hundred and twenty-five charter members."

Cissie Daughtrey, a long-time friend of Joan's and a charter member of the NAWJ, described the need for the NAWJ and groups like it: "A woman's group has a different set of priorities. We see problems men don't see. And it's hard to get some of these things done through the traditional associations. . . . Joan brings women together. . . . There's security in a network of professional colleagues, and Joan has provided that security to countless women."

> *"Always make time to help another woman along. Even the smallest gestures help those who are finding their way."*

Joan describes some of her activities as a member of the NAWJ. "I was part of the NAWJ delegation to Washington, D.C., to meet with key members of the Reagan administration and endorse the nomination of Sandra Day O'Connor to the Supreme Court. Sandra was one of our charter members. She later asked me to testify before the Senate Judiciary Committee on her behalf. I testified that Sandra was a highly qualified judge and that the step of having a woman on the Supreme Court was long overdue."

Then, in 1989, at the tenth anniversary meeting of NAWJ, it was discovered that there was enough support from women jurists visiting from other countries to form an international group for women judges. In 1991, Joan founded the International Association of Women Judges ("IAWJ")to enable this international community to pursue goals with a unified voice. Presently, the IAWJ has over four thousand members from eighty-five countries.

From advice gathered from her community of female judges, Joan was able to decide upon the following method to deal with male attorneys who called her "my dear" as she sat on the bench presiding over a trial: "I would call the attorney to the sidebar and say, 'You are not displaying respect for this court when you call the judge "dear." You may not respect me, but you must respect the court. There will be no more "my dears" unless you wish to be held in contempt.' Needless to say, no one I said that to ever called me 'dear' instead of 'Your Honor' again."

Joan explains why she found this terminology so offensive: "It's not that I don't ever like to be given compliments or called by endearments. But in a professional context, these things are irrelevant to my competency and can subtract from the image of my competency. The courtroom or a serious professional setting is simply not the place for men to display chivalry to women. . . . Chivalry is about men being the protectors of women. One aspect of sexism is the social domination of women by men. The chivalrous rules of who follows whom or how to address each other reinforce the lesser power of women in society. . . . When I am the judge in a courtroom, the male attorney arguing a case before me is not my protector."

Helping Others

Joan's climb to the top has given her a generous perspective on women just starting out. "Always make time to help another woman along. Even the smallest gestures help those who are finding their way.

"Let me tell you the moment I became a feminist. . . . It was after law school, while serving in the state attorney general's office. I was doing the work of an attorney the next level up, but was not being recognized for it by my job title or by my salary. I had heard people were saying that I did not really need to have my job because I had a husband. One day when the head of the office stopped by, I braced myself, looked him in the eye and explained that I felt my contribution was not being appreciated. I asked for an explanation of why I had not been promoted to reflect the workload I already had. He struggled for words. . . . He did not give me any straight answers. As he left my office, in that instant I knew I had not received the promotion because of my gender. . . . I knew that if I were a man with a wife and children to support, I would have had that promotion already. I pledged to myself to continue to push forward professionally despite unfair roadblocks. And I remember feeling overcome with the awareness that huge improvements were needed in the workplace for all women. . . . So, I promised myself

"I still meet people who feel threatened by strong, intelligent women. But I also meet so many men who have daughters that want careers. This changes the male perspective and the way they see me. We have a common cause. I want great things for their daughters, and so do they."

I would always dedicate some part of my life to helping the women who came behind me."

She points out, "Today, there are more women in college than men. And, it is predicted that in the near future, more women will graduate from college than men. Those college degrees are going to open a lot of professional doors for a lot of young women. . . . It's an exciting time. . . . I still meet people who feel threatened by strong, intelligent women. But I also meet so many men who have daughters that want careers. This changes the male perspective and the way they see me. We have a common cause. I want great things for their daughters, and so do they."

Joan Dempsey Klein, a.k.a. "Rosie the Riveter," is today one of the best justices in California—male or female. Adversity has only made her stronger, and along the way she's helped other women find strength as well. She knows that it's up to the next generation to carry on the work of women's empowerment. "I've come a long way, but we still have a long way to go . . . Get out there and start riveting!"

XII.
PATRICIA WALD AND
JOYCE KENNARD

The strangest part about graduating from law school was the feeling that I could go out into the world and do anything. What I mean is, when I graduated from high school, I didn't feel like I could go out and just do anything. I felt like I had to go to college. And when I was in college, I didn't feel like I should be doing anything except doing everything I could to get into law school.

After law school graduation, I had some freedom in choosing which path to take. A lot of my classmates were making their decisions based on wanting to keep as many options open as possible. This is what I did, too. For me, it was a mistake. I wish I would have based my decision on what would make me happy. But I wasn't courageous enough to do it.

And so I've learned (and the stories of Pat Wald and Joyce Kennard will bear this out) that time and experience can lead you onto a different path—maybe hooking you right back onto one you rejected, lost, or didn't realize existed. For instance, people who think they're finished with formal schooling because they've gotten into the workforce and gotten a little older may come to pursue education again, to help them in the job market or for personal fulfillment. Some people revise their plans by deciding to branch out—going into business for themselves, starting a new career, or delaying retirement.

People say "life is short." But I say life is long. Too many times, I've seen things work out the way they're supposed to—the way that feels right and fits the big picture—only after some time and struggle.

I've always loved the scene at the end of the movie The Natural *where Robert Redford cracks the baseball out of the park—taking the skin right off the ball, as he was meant to do all along. He gets to where he's supposed to be the long way, the hard way, but he's there. And it's a marvelous achievement, made no less marvelous because he didn't get there quickly.*

Pat Wald and Joyce Kennard are absolutely inspirational real-life role models, who remind us that you don't start where you will end up, you might not get to where you want to go on the schedule you set for getting there, and the process of getting there is worthwhile in itself.

Patricia Wald

Patricia Wald relaxes in an armchair in her chambers at the Washington, D.C. Court of Appeals, thinking about her career path. "I was treading a new path, for sure. It included detours, false starts, plenty of bruises along the way—and a few lucky breaks."

She tells of being raised in a Connecticut manufacturing town by her mother, aunts, and grandparents. She does not remember her father, an alcoholic who deserted the family before Pat was two and was not heard from again.

Patricia Wald

RESIDENCE: Washington, D.C.
BORN: 1928
PERSONAL: Married
(5 children)
PROFESSIONAL: Circuit Judge, U.S. Court of Appeals for the D.C. Circuit (Chief Judge, 1986-91), Judge of the International War Crimes Tribunal for the Former Yugoslavia in the Hague
1996 Recipient of the Margaret Brent Award

She recounts, "Being the only child in a household of adults made me mature for my age. And I was always young for my grade in school. I went to first grade at the age of four because there were no daycare centers, and the household relied upon all the adults working. Later, I even skipped from sixth to eighth grades. A fond childhood memory is—you know the way people rent videos today?—I used to go to the drugstore with my aunts on Saturday afternoons to rent a jigsaw puzzle for the family to work on that night. It cost a nickel!"

Pat was an A-student and valedictorian of her high school class. She attended Connecticut College for Women on scholarship. A Pepsi-Cola fellowship enabled her to attend Yale Law School. She graduated in 1951. "In hindsight," she reflects, "it was naive of me and my female classmates at Yale—who never saw a woman faculty member, visiting lawyer, or judge—not to realize the whole professional world would have to change for us to succeed in it."

A Curve in the Road

Only two years after completing her streamlined educational path, Pat put aside the practice of law to start a family. "We had five kids in seven years! . . . In the early sixties, our youngest child went to kindergarten, which meant all five kids were spending some part of the day in school. Then, I slowly began re-entering the work world. Thanks to help from a law school classmate who worked for Robert Kennedy at the Justice Department, I worked part-time with a consultant's contract for the Justice Department. I set up a desk in the den at home and did my work while the children were at school or while they slept. Other projects during that time included President Lyndon Johnson's Commission on Crime in the District of Columbia and the Ford Foundation's Drug Abuse Research Project.

"After a few years," she continues, "I felt the children could manage with my working full-time outside the house. The older children helped take care of the younger ones, and we hired household help. So I got a job in the local Legal Services office. . . . Most of the lawyers handling cases there were ten years younger . . . I was a forty-year-old lawyer, and I had no courtroom expe-rience. This was a big change for me—after always being the youngest one in class and a star pupil. The public interest environment provides tremendous expe-rience very quickly, though. Within a year, I was arguing a case before this Court of Appeals on the right of indigent women to get divorced without paying a fee. . . . Now I should add this. It is a ritual for judges and elders of the bar to lecture those younger that they should devote time to *pro bono* work ('for the good of the public'). But I can personally attest—having done a great deal of work in the public interest, for the poor, the mentally ill, and juveniles—that there is great satisfaction in devoting yourself to causes larger than money and personal reputation."

"People always ask me whether there is a secret spring of sensitivity to the plight of women or of humanity that a woman judge brings to the law. And I always answer that at least in some cases I think there is!"

It was when Jimmy Carter won the 1976 presidential election that a strong focus was placed on making a place for women in a national administration for the first time. As a result of her work with the Justice Department, Pat was appointed assistant attorney general for legislative affairs. Then in the late 1970s, when President Carter announced his intention to increase the number of women on the federal bench, Pat applied and was nominated for a position on the United States Court of Appeals for the District of Columbia.

"An Enemy of the Family"

Pat had a stormy confirmation to the bench in the spring of 1979. She came to see how a candidate's private life is put under a microscope upon nomination for a public post: "My daughter's landlord, my son's high school coach, and my gynecologist were interviewed. . . . I was told by a knowledgeable Senate aide how 'the scandal business' works. . . . Your detractors pin *something* on you . . . just to put your name out there to the public. Then they wait for somebody unknown to come forward with the *real* scandal about you. . . . My detractors could not

"In hindsight, it was naive of me and my female classmates at Yale—who never saw a woman faculty member, visiting lawyer, or judge—not to realize the whole professional world would have to change for us to succeed in it."

find anything in my personal life to criticize and exploit. I was faithful to my marriage, and I didn't do drugs—although I had worked on reports about drug usage. But an article I wrote on the rights of juveniles became a target. In it, I suggested juveniles might have certain legal rights when their interests conflicted with those of their parents. I raised questions, such as 'When can legal status for children begin?' 'When can a child make a decision to choose a school, seek medical or psychiatric help on their own, or make a decision to sign a contract?' and 'Can someone under eighteen be informed enough to vote?'"

"It is a ritual for judges and elders of the bar to lecture those younger that they should devote time to pro bono *work ('for the good of the public'). But I can personally attest—having done a great deal of work in the public interest, for the poor, the mentally ill, and juveniles—that there is great satisfaction in devoting yourself to causes larger than money and personal reputation."*

Much to Pat's surprise, editorials appeared all over the country naming her an "enemy of the family." "A fundamentalist preacher holding a red leather Bible testified against my nomination before the Senate Judiciary Committee, saying I was an instrument of the devil. . . . For those aspiring to public office, I advise limiting youthful indiscretions and to face them head-on when questioned!"

Despite her opponents' search for scandal, Pat's nomination was confirmed, and she was heartened to learn of a hidden ally. She remembers, "Senator Robert Dole (R-Kansas) came up to me after the results of the vote were announced and said, 'My wife [Elizabeth] told me not to come home for dinner unless I voted "yes" for your confirmation today.'" Thus, Senator Dole was able to go home for dinner, and Pat readied herself to take on new challenges as a member of the federal judiciary.

The Nature of Judging

Upon taking the bench, Pat learned things about the nature and power of judges that someone who is not a judge may not realize. "The nature of judging," she explains, "can be isolating and frustrating at times. Judges exercise power, but only within tight limits. You cannot initiate action—only react to what is put before you by litigants. Judges don't reach out and find topics they want to rule on and issue opinions on them. . . . The name of the game in this twelve-member environment is collegiality—creating a smoothly running machine where our differences are tackled on paper. There is no point in showdowns and power struggles with other judges on the court." She smiles broadly, "Judges are like monks—but without the unifying bonds of a common faith! We are consigned to each other's company, with good conscience we address hard questions, and we do not speak about our work outside the walls of this 'monastery.'"

A judge who does not agree with the majority as a participant on a panel of judges may issue their own dissenting opinion to explain differing views. Pat elaborates, "In many countries only one opinion is rendered by a court, whether or not all the judges agree. Minority dissenters are silenced. The rationale for this is that it may be unsettling to citizens and to the development of a stable body of law for judges to disagree with each other publicly. In the United States, however, our practice is different. From the beginning, we have allowed dissenting opinions on the record, to be looked at again with the intelligence of a future day."

Does gender play a role in her decisions? "In most of my cases, my gender does not make a difference . . . but

"A fundamentalist preacher holding a red leather Bible testified against my nomination before the Senate Judiciary Committee, saying I was an instrument of the devil. . . . For those aspiring to public office, I advise limiting youthful indiscretions and to face them head-on when questioned!"

sometimes I see something in a case my male colleagues simply don't get—for instance, my intuitive negative reaction to an asserted, but undocumented, justification that women did not get choice assignments in an agency because they chose not to compete for them. . . . People always ask me whether there is a secret spring of sensitivity to the plight of women or of humanity that a woman judge brings to the law. And I always answer that at least in some cases I think there is!"

Of the present place of women in the workplace, Pat observes, "The majority of women in this country work in gender-segregated jobs without much opportunity for advancement. Sex segregation by occupation is extensive, pervasive, and—it sometimes seems—intractable. Women hold few construction jobs, ninety percent of clerical jobs, and about two-thirds of all the minimum-wage jobs. . . . Women simply have to be given a chance to try their hand at other jobs."

"Young people today are the key players for this country's participation in a global economy. Don't avoid the game. Your work in the several decades when your schooling is over will be the most important part of your life . . . Make it count."

One of the reasons women have been held back from exploring new areas is they are told they don't have "merit" for a job. She asks, "What does it mean to say someone 'has merit' for a particular position? Individual merit is, in the end, a social conclusion—influenced substantially by conventional stereotypes and past traditions. In many cases, only affirmative efforts to assist women—the way President Carter did—can bring equilibrium, so individual merit based on non-gender criteria can prevail over the long run."

Pat suggests investing time in developing oneself as 'human capital.' "In this new millennium," she reasons, "the workplace needs young women with finely-honed skills in marketing, personnel training and management, and computer sciences. And let me toot the horn of the legal profession—lawyers serve as negotiators, dealmakers, advisors, and advocates. . . . Young people today are the key players for this country's participation in a global economy. Don't avoid the game. Your work in the several decades when your schooling is over will be the most important part of your life. . . . Make it count."

Joyce Kennard

A month later, three thousand miles away on the opposite coast of the United States, Joyce Kennard tells a story in her chambers that presents different difficulties than those presented by Pat Wald—yet her story shares the common theme of success borne out of a winding path including obstacles and detours. "I was born during World War II on the island of Java, then a part of the Dutch colonial empire," Joyce starts. "I'm of

Joyce Kennard
RESIDENCE: San Francisco, California
BORN: 1941, island of Java
PERSONAL: Married
PROFESSIONAL: Associate Justice, California Supreme Court
1995 Recipient of the Margaret Brent Award

Indonesian, Dutch, and Chinese descent. My father died in a Japanese concentration camp when I was a year old." She then spent her early childhood in an internment camp with her widowed mother. . . "Shortly after liberation by the Allied troops, when I was about five, a playmate showed me the thickest, most beautiful book I had ever seen. It had thousands of pictures of toys and pretty dresses, things I had never had, things I associated with a fairytale world. It was a Sears catalog!

"Five years later," she continues, "after Indonesia gained its independence from the Dutch, my mother and I left for the last remaining Dutch colony in the East Indies—the western half of New Guinea. My mother found a job as a typist with a Dutch oil company. . . . We lived in a racially segregated area in a small Quonset hut shared with four other families. . . . The bathroom was an outdoor enclosure containing an oil drum filled with water; the toilet was a filthy ditch at the edge of the jungle. . . . I attended a tiny school run by Catholic missionaries. My fellow students were the sons and daughters of natives whose not-too-distant ancestors had been cannibals.

"The school folded when I was thirteen. . . . The only other school was five days' sailing away, so that was where my mother took me," Joyce states simply, as though this remarkable move was the only logical next step. "Then a year later, when I was fourteen, there was no more schooling to be had there. . . . My education had been woefully inadequate, but I had been taught the rudiments of English—and I picked up a lot of simple words related to love and heartbreak by listening to Radio Australia, which regularly played the American top hits. To this day," she smiles, "I can either sing or hum those hits from the early fifties."

Joyce's mother continued to be resourceful in seeking new opportunities to further her daughter's education. "My mother realized that the wild jungles of New Guinea—basically a man's country—was no place for a fourteen-year-old girl. Determined to get me an education, my mother decided we should leave for Holland. . . . In Holland I experienced such wonders as making my very first telephone call and getting my first peek at television. . . . My mother found a job in a restaurant peeling onions. And eventually she talked the director of a high school into accepting me as a student on a trial basis. . . . When the director noted my lack of background in math, my mother pointed out my high grades in whatever subjects the New Guinea missionaries had taught. I was accepted on the condition that I would get special tutoring in math."

But only six months later, Joyce's schooling would come to an abrupt end: "A tumor on my leg led to an operation and then resulted in an amputation above the knee. . . . I knew I could never catch up in school. And there were no second or third chances in Holland at that time." Thus, Joyce learned typing and shorthand and became a secretary at sixteen.

"A couple of years passed. And then around 1960," she relates, "America opened up a special immigration quota for people of Dutch nationality who were displaced from New Guinea when it changed from Dutch to Indonesian rule. My mother and I fell into this category. . . . In those days, it was extremely difficult for anyone born in Asia, as we were, to immigrate to America. So this new quota was great news to us—a door into America—the land of liberty and opportunity, the land of an immigrant's dreams."

The Land of Opportunity

In 1961, Joyce arrived in California alone. "My mother stayed in Holland so that if I could not make it in America, I could return there. . . . America exceeded my wildest expectations. All I had expected was an assembly-line job in a factory. Instead, 'fresh off the boat,' so to speak, I was hired as a secretary at a large insurance company with a salary of $280 a month."

"Today I can truly say that I have lived the impossible dream. My success could have happened only in America."

Six years later, Joyce was able to realize her dream of getting a college education. "My mother passed away and left me her entire life savings of five thousand dollars. I know she had scraped that together for me at great personal sacrifice. . . . I became a college freshman at the age of twenty-seven and completed four years of college coursework in three years, while still working at least twenty hours a week to help pay my expenses." Despite this difficult schedule, Joyce graduated from the University of California *magna cum laude* and Phi Beta Kappa.

Her boss encouraged her to make the transition from working for him as a legal secretary to becoming a lawyer in her own right. Taking the challenge, Joyce pursued a joint degree program in law and public administration at the University of Southern California; her masters' thesis earned the school's "Outstanding Thesis" award.

She gained experience as an attorney for a dozen years, first in the State Attorney General's Office and then as a research attorney in the State Court of Appeal. In the mid-eighties, Governor George Deukmejian appointed her to be a judge on the Municipal Court. He then advanced her over each of the next three years with appointments to the state's Superior Court, Court of Appeal, and Supreme Court. She has been on the California Supreme Court since 1989—only the second woman to serve on the seven-member court.

Joyce has earned a reputation as an independent thinker who does not shirk from disagreeing with her colleagues. She has put her name to numerous dissenting opinions to prove it. Before she was appointed, some people thought she would fit a certain "moderate conservative" role, and she must have disappointed them—and perhaps pleased others—when she did not play out their expectations.

For example, one case in which she may have surprised people is a lead opinion she wrote for a case where the California Supreme Court prohibited school-endorsed prayers in public school graduation ceremonies. The Court advanced the public policy that in a religiously diverse society, religious neutrality must be respected.[1] In the opinion, Joyce wrote, "Respect for the differing religious choices of the people of this country requires that government neither place its stamp of approval on any particular religious practice, nor appear to take a stand on any religious question. In a world frequently torn by religious factionalism and the violence tragically associated with political division along religious lines, our nation's position of governmental neutrality on religious matters stands as an illuminating example of the true meaning of freedom and tolerance."

Only in America

Today Joyce is in a position where she impacts many people's lives. She asserts, "While I was growing up on the Indonesian island of Java, later in the jungles of New Guinea, and then as a teenager in Holland, I never imagined in my wildest dreams that one day I would be lucky enough to live in the United States. I never thought that I would ever be an attorney. I never thought that I would ever be a judge. Today I can truly say that I have lived the impossible dream. My success could have happened only in America.

"I have a deep love for America. America gave me a chance to get an education when I was well beyond normal school age. America gave me a chance to succeed against all odds. And America taught me that the boundaries of achievement are set largely by the individual. As former President Lyndon Johnson said, 'America is the uncrossed desert and the unclimbed

---

[1] *Sands v. Morong Unified School District,* 53 Cal. 863, 884 (1991).

ridge.' There's so much to be gained by setting out to conquer those yet unclimbed ridges."

Joyce has other advice to share. "Have integrity. Temper your drive for success by fair play and fair dealing, which is a concept that has withstood the test of time. . . . The ethical dimensions of life are not incompatible with success. To the contrary! It is only by adhering to the highest standards of ethics and fair play that one can become truly successful and respected. Finally, don't give up on ideals, on dreams. In the words of the poet Langston Hughes, 'Hold fast to dreams, for if dreams die, life is a broken-winged bird that cannot fly.'"

Joyce Kennard followed a curving path to pursue her education and profession and then steered onto a relatively straightforward career course. Pat Wald obtained her education via a direct route and then put aside career to raise a family, later re-entering and advancing in her profession by less direct means. These two complementary tales illustrate the advantage of continuing with education,

"Have integrity. Temper your drive for success by fair play and fair dealing, which is a concept that has withstood the test of time. . . . It is only by adhering to the highest standards of ethics and fair play that one can become truly successful and respected."

career, and self-improvement in the midst of—or in spite of—more pressing life situations, and the value of applying long-term perspective to such efforts.

XIII.
ANTONIA
HERNANDEZ

Spending time with Antonia Hernandez made me think about my teachers.

The first grown-up who wasn't related to me who reached out to start a friendship was Mrs. Geruson, my high school English teacher. I was fourteen years old. She was something between a parent and a friend. The great thing about her was she knew a lot more about a lot of things than my other friends, yet her advice was more fun and hip than listening to my mother.

One day her son, a college student, visited our class. He talked about "college life." I remember he was wearing (and I'm not one to remember what people are wearing) a "fisherman's sweater"—off-white, crew neck, long rows of rope stitching, hanging to his hips—with faded blue jeans and white leather sneakers. And I remember looking at him and thinking, "So that's what a college student looks like."

He told us he had changed his high school study habits and become more self-disciplined because college had fewer day-to-day assignments, more projects and term papers. He explained how he lived within a budget and the expenses of being a college student. He told us he had recently started dating a girl who, when he first asked her out, said, "If you didn't ask me out soon, I was just going to ask you out!" He said he would not have minded if she had asked him out first (and I filed that away as an important thing to know about college boys). Once I made it to college, I can't tell you how many times I remembered things from his conversation with our class that day.

After high school, I stayed friends with Mrs. Geruson. I also got to know her son and her husband. In college, I even became the proud owner of a fisherman's sweater. When I wore my "college student outfit"—which was that sweater with jeans and sneakers—I knew I would be fitting in just fine anywhere around campus.

Mrs. Geruson remained available for advice. My girlfriends and I went to visit her at home for dessert and to talk about college life. She was thrilled when I was admitted to NYU Law School. I remember sitting in my bedroom on the phone with her, the two of us just screaming in delight and celebration. Then when I was a few years out of school, she passed away. I was told she had been sick in the hospital for a few weeks first; if I had known, I would have dropped everything to go and visit her.

I moved back to Philadelphia a few years after that. One day I happened to be in the building where I knew Mrs. Geruson's son worked, so I stopped by. When he walked out to say hello, I saw her face so clearly in his face, and I started to cry. We hugged and cried together.

The conversations in this book are like the conversations I used to have with Mrs. Geruson, like the one her son had with our class that day. They can really make a difference to the person who is there to listen and learn— they are not forgotten; they are drawn from again and again. They are savored and become sweeter with time.

Although there are plenty of differences between myself and Antonia Hernandez, I bonded with her because of something we both have had that is exactly the same: a group of grown-ups who really wanted the best for us and really wanted to help.

A ntonia Hernandez walks through the elegant wood-paneled corridors of the Mexican American Legal Defense and Educational Fund ("MALDEF") in the art deco-era Banks Huntley Building in downtown Los Angeles, explaining some recent endeavors for MALDEF. MALDEF is this country's chief advocacy group for Latino rights, and Antonia is MALDEF's president and general counsel. As she enters her impressive office, and settles in behind her desk, the questions in the air are, "How did she get

Antonia Hernandez

RESIDENCE: Los Angeles, California
BORN: 1948
PROFESSIONAL: President and General Counsel, Mexican American Legal Defense and Educational Fund
PERSONAL: Married (2 children)
1997 Recipient of the Margaret Brent Award

here, and how could someone else get here?" Antonia goes on to share the story of how the support of family and others—combined with her own drive to succeed—brought her from a ranch in Mexico to where she sits today.

"I had a very happy childhood," Antonia begins. "I grew up in the 1950s as a poor girl, but unaware of things other people had that I didn't have. My family lived on an *ejido* [a communal ranch] in Mexico with several hundred other people—many of whom were related to us."

Antonia's family moved to California when she was eight. They lived in an East Los Angeles housing project. She remembers, "My mother used to make us sweep the sidewalk in front of the project. And she would give us Comet cleanser to scrub graffiti off the exterior walls. My mom really believed cleanliness was next to godliness. . . . Used *National Geographic* magazines were always in our house. Although my parents did not read English, the magazines had symbolic value—they meant that we valued increasing our knowledge of the big wide world."

During the summer, the seven children in the family contributed to the household by picking crops with their parents in the San Joaquin Valley. Antonia recollects, "It was hard labor. The four oldest of us were girls. My parents never told me and my sisters that we couldn't do something because we were girls. They needed us to work hard for the family. My sisters and I grew up never shying away from anything.

"When I think back, I can't believe how little my parents had, and yet how much they gave us. My parents' message was simple and never-changing. Sometimes they said it, and sometimes you felt it: 'Work hard at everything you do. . . . Be proud of who you are. . . . You're all that matters to us. We'll make sacrifices for you so that you can be educated and have a better life.'"

The Importance of Teachers

Reflecting upon the role teachers played in her development, Antonia describes how one of her grade-school teachers would ask her to stay after school to assist with organizing the classroom. "She told me she asked me to help her because of how smart I was. That made me want to be smarter. . . . A teacher's perception of a student can help shape that student's development—call it self-fulfilling prophecy. . . . When a student is treated as incompetent, you encourage their incompetence. When a student is treated as competent, you encourage the development of their confidence in their abilities. . . . If you know your teacher thinks you're a smart girl, and you're confronted with a new situation, you'll think, 'How does a smart girl act in this situation?' and that's the way you'll act, striving for smart choices."

Antonia also encountered teachers of the discouraging variety. One of her high school teachers gave a writing assignment on the topic, "What I want to be when I grow up." She wrote an essay about how she wanted to go to college when she grew up. The reaction of Antonia's teacher was very discouraging—and almost unbelievable knowing all that she's since achieved. "He drew a sad face on top of my essay. . . . He wrote next to the sad face, 'Not college material—start thinking about other options.' I couldn't believe a teacher told me I wasn't 'college material' when I was an A-student. What was 'college material' then? I don't know why he discouraged me—my gender? My ethnicity? My lack of intelligence?

"I have since learned that people can harbor beliefs and assumptions that lead to prejudice even when they mean well. . . . It may just be easiest to like and to promote those who most remind us of ourselves. . . . Fortunately, this teacher's mixed message—rejecting my goal without good reason, but couched in a supportive way—did not hurt me. I was mature enough and had received enough positive feedback from my parents and from other teachers to know I was on a course headed for college. Yet his comments still deflated me."

After high school, Antonia attended the college nearest to home—East Los Angeles Junior College. She joined the school's Mexican American Student Association and participated regularly in student protests. Her parents remained protective and supportive: "I remember sitting in the kitchen one night explaining to my father why it was so important for me to participate in a protest against the Safeway supermarket for selling grapes picked by Mexican migrant workers. When I convinced my dad this was a worthwhile and safe activity for me, we chose a nearby landmark for him to drop me off and pick me up from the protest."

"If you know your teacher thinks you're a smart girl, and you're confronted with a new situation, you'll think, 'How does a smart girl act in this situation?' and that's the way you'll act, striving for smart choices."

In college, Antonia met the teacher who did the most to advance her development. She sighs with a smile, "Dr. Helen Bailey, the chair of the History Department of East L.A. College, was the most fascinating person I ever met. . . . She dressed bohemian. . . . She had traveled to China and Tahiti. . . . I wanted to be educated like her. She advised me to expand my course of study by going to the University of California at Los Angeles ("UCLA"). . . . It was on the other side of town, but I didn't even know it existed. It was part of the Anglo world, of which I knew very little. . . . With her encouragement, I applied to UCLA."

A Whole New World

Before she could transfer schools, though, Antonia would have to address her parents' reaction to the news that she had been accepted to UCLA. "I knew the sensitive part would be that it was a far commute, so I would have to live there. For all that my parents gave me free rein when something involved work for the family or for school, I knew in one respect they were extremely traditional: no one in our family left their parents' home until they married. I told my mom Dr. Bailey believed it was the best thing for me professionally. I knew my mother trusted my teachers and would never want to stand in the way. . . . She knew how hard I worked at my schoolwork. . . . As I waited for her reaction, I was so scared she would reject the idea and crush my hopes. Eyeball-to-eyeball, she said to me, 'We're going to have to work on your dad.'"

Antonia's father eventually consented to the transfer, and she began preparing to enter the "Anglo world" of UCLA. Money was put aside for new school clothes. She recounts, "My mother and I went shopping for a suitcase and then filled it with new clothes from Lerner's. . . . The day before the first day of school, my whole family drove me to UCLA in our big beige car—Mom, Dad, six kids, and that suitcase. Before my family left, my father walked all through the dormitory to make sure no boys lived there and to check the security system."

Antonia befriended her roommate, the first Anglo person with whom she had ever spent time outside of school. She elaborates, "My roommate had blonde hair and blue eyes. She wanted to be a historian. She was serious about her schoolwork and was a very positive influence on me."

This time of change and assimilation is remembered fondly. "For me, the process of 'becoming American' was first perfecting the language, then learning the styles, and finally making friends who had been born here. My family retained many Mexican traditions and customs we brought with us, while striving to take advantage of the opportunities this country offered. . . . I had a fire in my belly during those years. I remember feeling it in the morning while I dressed—that I wanted to get out there and accomplish things. I hadn't been integrated enough into the real world yet to know the obstacles that were waiting for me, based upon being a minority twice—as a female and a person of color. Failure was not an option I ever thought about. Looking back, I can see the positive side of that, because when you take the time to very clearly lay out all your limitations, they truly *become* your limitations."

A UCLA professor of history told Antonia he thought she would make a good lawyer, but Antonia had planned to teach after graduation. Her family was expecting her to contribute some of her income to help her sisters and brothers to attend college. Attending law school would mean postponing the earning of income for three more years. But her teacher's advice persuaded her to yet again take the path her parents never expected. "Dr. Bradford knew I wanted to help Latinas, and he told me the law was the best vehicle for change. He challenged me that if I really wanted to help my people, the law was the way to do it.

"I had a fire in my belly during those years. . . . Failure was not an option I ever thought about. Looking back, I can see the positive side of that, because when you take the time to very clearly lay out all your limitations, they truly become your limitations."

"So at home, it was the same procedure again as with the transfer to UCLA. . . . I told my mom about my desire to attend law school before I told my dad. I told her I had the support of my teacher, and she told me, 'We'll work on your dad.' I decided to broach the topic with my father that night. My uncle was visiting. Their first reactions to my going to law school are still vivid. . . . My father said, 'Why do you want to be a lawyer? They're a bunch of thieves.' My uncle said, 'You can't be a lawyer. You're a girl.' . . . My father was predictable, though. After I explained why this would make me happy, he said he would support me."

Career on the Rise

Antonia graduated from UCLA Law School in 1974 and worked as a staff attorney with the Los Angeles Center for Law and Justice and then the Legal Aid Foundation of Los Angeles. In 1979, she was hired as counsel to the United States Senate Judiciary Committee, then chaired by Senator Ted Kennedy (D-Massachusetts), and moved to Washington, D.C. Her family was honored to have her serve Senator Kennedy. Antonia comments, "The Kennedy family was revered by Mexican-Americans for their record of supporting Mexican-Americans on issues important to us. Robert F. Kennedy is especially remembered for his civil rights work. . . . John F. Kennedy was the first Catholic President, and Ethel Kennedy even visited Cesar Chavez when he was imprisoned for trying to unionize the grape-pickers in California. . . . Mexican-Americans from all over the country write to Senator Kennedy with their concerns.

"On my first day, Senator Kennedy called a meeting to welcome the new staff members. He said, 'Always be fair, but always pursue what we want. . . . Represent me well.' The one thing about Senator Kennedy I never stopped appreciating was the direct access he provided to himself. That is a leadership skill I have tried to emulate. Anytime I needed feedback on anything, I just wrote it up in a memo and put it in a pouch kept on his desk. The black bag was sent to wherever the Senator was, and you always had his feedback or approval by phone or by memo within forty-eight hours."

> *"The one thing about Senator Kennedy I never stopped appreciating was the direct access he provided to himself. That is a leadership skill I have tried to emulate."*

When Republicans took control of the Senate in 1981, most of the Kennedy staff had to find new jobs, including Antonia. She became the director of MALDEF's Washington, D.C., office. Since 1985, she has been MALDEF's president and general counsel, working to promote and to protect the civil rights of the tens of millions of American-Latinos in education, employment, immigration, and voting access. MALDEF also has brought many of the lawsuits resulting in greater Hispanic political representation.

She states, "I get paid to do what I love to do. If you can find a job you love to do and it helps humanity, you'll be blessed as I have been. . . . But no matter where you are in life or how you make a living, I suggest seeking variety in your life experiences—and getting to know people of color and the poor."

Antonia leans back in her chair and looks upward, seemingly looking back over the tale of her journey she has shared. "I am the product of the good will of good people who saw something in me and gave me opportunities. I am where I am thanks to Mom and Dad, my brothers and sisters, my teachers, mentors, and colleagues. . . . Each time somebody provided me with a new opportunity, I did my best to produce for them and make them not regret that they had given me the chance to prove myself. And I try to use the position I have as a result of all their good will to do good for others."

"I get paid to do what I love to do. If you can find a job you love to do and it helps humanity, you'll be blessed as I have been."

XIV.
RUTH BADER
GINSBURG

In the days leading up to my meeting with Justice Ruth Bader Ginsburg of
the United States Supreme Court, a piece of striking news footage came to
mind repeatedly: It was Ruth Ginsburg, standing in the Rose Garden of the
White House in 1993, as she accepted President Clinton's Supreme Court
nomination. She evoked the memory of her mother—"the bravest and
strongest person I have ever known, who was taken from me much too soon.
I pray that I may be all that she would have been, had she lived in an age
when women could aspire and achieve and daughters are cherished as much
as sons." President Clinton, standing nearby, was moved to tears.

The poignancy of the new justice's image stemmed from the fact that we
truly live not only in a new age, but in a new world, for women—one that
female ancestors might not recognize, much as they might have dreamed of it.

Ginsburg's words made me think about my mother's life, my grandmoth-
er's life, and everything they did to encourage me in pursuing a career. I
thought about how their lives would be different if they were girls growing
up in America today.

While I was in grade school, my grandmother (who lived with us) was
in charge every afternoon until my mom got home from school or work.
Grandmom, an immigrant who spoke broken English, had not received

much formal education. She was absolutely in awe of school and what it could do for a person. My grandmother's pride in clearing off the kitchen table from 3:00 to 5:00 P.M. so I could spread out my homework was palpable. I knew how pleased she was that I was an A-student who wanted to be a lawyer. I know she would be proud of me today.

There is no doubt that Justice Ginsburg has lived up to her mother's greatest hopes for her—after all, she has done no less than to alter the social and legal status of American women.

Justice Ginsburg is relaxing in a quiet reception room at Atlanta's Ritz-Carlton Hotel, where she will accept the American Bar Association's Thurgood Marshall Award later in the evening. When I explained to her that I've never forgotten her eloquent tribute to her mother in the Rose Garden when she was sworn in, she explains, "My mother influenced my life more than anyone else. She was extremely intelligent, a prolific reader, caring, and resourceful. . . . She completed high school at fifteen, always earning top grades. She got a job and contributed part of her income to support her older brother in college. She never attended college, despite what her dreams for herself may have been. From a young age, I knew she was putting aside part of her 'pin money' for me to go to college. . . . She passed away the day before my high school graduation. It is a comfort she knew I was going to start Cornell University in the fall—the school her brother had attended." The description Ruth provides of her mother is a reminder that even though women in the past were not always in the forefront of the political or business scene, they have long influenced others to achieve their very best.

At Cornell, Ruth met Martin Ginsburg, who was a year ahead of her. They decided to pursue careers in law together. After his graduation, Martin began studying at Harvard Law School. They married shortly after Ruth's graduation from Cornell. Before they could study law together, however, they moved to Fort Sill, Oklahoma, for two years—during which time Martin was in the service and their daughter Jane was born. In 1956, Ruth began her law studies at Harvard and Martin resumed his. When Martin graduated and accepted a position in New York City, Ruth transferred to Columbia Law School for her last year of study. She graduated from Columbia in 1959, tied

---

Ruth Bader Ginsburg

RESIDENCE: Washington, D.C.
HOMETOWN: Brooklyn, New York
BORN: 1933
PERSONAL: Married (two children)
PROFESSIONAL: Associate Justice, Supreme Court of the United States
1993 Recipient of the Margaret Brent Award

---

for first in her class. Because she had completed two years of study at Harvard, Ruth was later offered a Harvard Law School degree, contingent upon her returning her degree from Columbia. She refused to do so.

Ginsburg & Ginsburg

Graduating ranked first in the class from an Ivy League law school such as Columbia can be a stepping stone to a Supreme Court clerkship and job offers from prestigious law firms. In 1959, however, this stepping stone could only be tread upon by males. One of Ruth's professors at Harvard recommended her highly for a Supreme Court clerkship, but reported back to her that Justice Felix Frankfurter had said he "wasn't ready to hire a woman." No prestigious law firms came knocking. "Firms were just starting to turn around on hiring Jews. Here I was, a woman, a Jew, and a mother—it was a bit much for them!" After a lower court federal clerkship and authoring a book on Swedish civil procedure, Ruth began teaching at Rutgers Law School and volunteered to litigate cases with the American Civil Liberties Union ("ACLU"). She later held teaching positions at Columbia and Harvard law schools.

"Firms were just starting to turn around on hiring Jews. Here I was, a woman, a Jew, and a mother—it was a bit much for them!"

"Fortunately, in my marriage I didn't get second-class treatment," she smiles. "My marriage provided an environment of equality, in which I felt respected and cherished. It was a source of strength. . . . Whenever I needed to travel for work, Martin happily took over the primary caretaker role—something few men did at the time. When he tasted my tuna casserole, could not tell what it was, and asked whether I had cooked dinosaur, he decided he would simply take over cooking for the family. He had fun with it—he told me he thought of cooking as mixing things in a chemistry lab and became a really great cook.

"My unconventional husband encouraged my growing interest in women's place in the world and questions of gender equality. And so it was appropriate that my first foray into women and the law was a team effort with him. . . . In 1970, he was flipping through summaries of tax rulings at home and dropped one in my lap, saying, 'You'll find this interesting.' He was right. I found it fascinating.

"A traveling salesman, named Charles Moritz, claimed a dependent care deduction on his taxes for money spent to take care of his eighty-nine-year-old mother while he traveled for business. The Internal Revenue Service ("IRS") disallowed the deduction and ruled it was only for women—or men who were married, divorced, or widowed. Mr. Moritz was single, so the IRS said he could not claim this deduction. Moritz argued *pro se* [he represented himself, with no attorney] before the tax court that he would have been allowed the deduction if he were a dutiful daughter instead of a dutiful son. I read the summary and said, 'Let's take this case!' So my husband called Charles Moritz, and we prepared an appeal brief for him.[1] I provided constitutional law analysis and Marty provided tax analysis. The remedy we sought from the court was not to invalidate the statute, but to apply it equally to both sexes." The Ginsburg team's arguments prevailed. The appeals court reversed the lower court decision and held that the taxpayer (Mr. Moritz) was entitled to the dependent care deduction. Ruth comments, "My husband calls that brief the 'grandmother brief' because it was the first time I thought through the legal analysis for a gender discrimination issue. He jokes that everything I did after that was really just recycling the same brief over and over again. He's not entirely wrong."

Using the Law to Fight Inequality

Soon after her work on the *Moritz* case, Ruth would take that gender discrimination analysis all the way to the United States Supreme Court. She

---

[1] *Moritz v. Commissioner,* 55 T.C. 113, 115 (1970), *rev'd* 469 F.2d 466 (10th Cir. 1972), *cert denied* 412 U.S. 906 (1973).

remembers, "The director of the ACLU's national office asked me to work with him on a case the Supreme Court had just accepted for review. The case was very simple: Sally Reed's teenage son died under tragic circumstances, and she applied to be administrator of his estate. The boy's father—the parents were separated—also applied to be administrator. The state of Idaho had a rule for deciding such cases. The rule was that between persons equally entitled to administer a decedent's estate, males must be preferred to females.[2] . . . I am sure it's astonishing to younger people that laws like that were on the books in the United States in the early 1970s, but they were—and there were many more.

"We urged the Supreme Court to recognize the equal stature of men and women. The Supreme Court had interpreted the Fourteenth Amendment's Equal Protection Clause[3] as prohibiting discrimination based on race and requiring 'strict scrutiny' of any law drawing a race-based distinction. I believed any sex-based distinction warranted the same scrutiny." The Supreme Court found the law at issue in Reed to be unconstitutional. For the first time in the 103-year history of the Fourteenth Amendment, the Supreme Court ruled that the Equal Protection Clause protected women's rights. Following the success in Reed, the ACLU established a Women's Rights Project with Ginsburg as codirector.

But Women Are Treated Better than Men . . .

Ruth saw her role both as an advocate and as a teacher. She explains, "The enormous difference between fighting gender discrimination as opposed to race discrimination is good people immediately perceive race discrimination as evil and intolerable. But when I talked about sex-based discrimination, I got the response, 'What are you talking about? Women are treated ever so much better than men!' They took what I said as criticism of the way they treated their

[2] *Reed v. Reed,* 404 U.S. 71 (1971).

[3] The Fourteenth Amendment to the U.S. Constitution provides, "No state shall make or enforce any law which shall abridge the privileges or immunities of citizens of the United States; nor shall any state deprive any person of life, liberty, or property without due process of law; nor deny to any person within its jurisdiction the equal protection of the laws."

wives, mothers, and daughters. Judges needed to be educated that old notions were limiting the opportunities and aspirations of women in this country.

Justice Ginsburg shares the story of Gwendolyn Hoyt to demonstrate women's place under the law before she applied her considerable talents to changing women's place: "A good example of the starting point from which this process began is a Supreme Court case from the early sixties on whether women should be required to serve on juries or whether, as Florida had it, women who wanted to serve on juries had to sign up in the court's office—with the result that very few did.[4] . . . The facts of the underlying case were these: Gwendolyn Hoyt had a philandering husband who regularly humiliated her to the breaking point. We didn't have terms like 'battered woman' in those days, but she did not have a happy marriage. One day, in a rage at the humiliation to which she was exposed, she turned to the corner of the room and spied an old broken baseball bat. She brought it down on the head of her husband—ending the fight, ending his life, and starting a murder prosecution.

"Gwendolyn was convicted of murder by an all-male jury. . . . Her argument to the Supreme Court was that women on the jury—or at least in the pool from which the jury was picked—would better understand her state

> *"The enormous difference between fighting gender discrimination as opposed to race discrimination is good people immediately perceive race discrimination as evil and intolerable. But when I talked about sex-based discrimination, I got the response, 'What are you talking about? Women are treated ever so much better than men!'"*

[4] *Hoyt v. Florida,* 368 U.S. 57, 61–64 (1961).

of mind, her utter frustration, and would improve her chances of being convicted of something less than murder. . . . The Court found that Gwendolyn Hoyt's not being given a jury pool drawn from a fair cross section of men and women is purely a favor to women. Women have the best of both worlds—they can serve if they want to, and they don't have to serve if they don't want to. In essence, they responded to her plea by saying that women are treated better than men, so there is nothing to complain about. . . . No one riveted attention on her underlying murder conviction, which was left standing." Ruth continues, "The law had been contributing to the perpetuation of gender stereotypes. We now had to use the law to abolish these iniquities."

> *"The law had been contributing to the perpetuation of gender stereotypes. We now had to use the law to abolish these iniquities."*

Women Can Be Independent

Ginsburg then executed a strategy to accomplish this goal: Cases would be chosen for sequential presentations before the Supreme Court to attack the most pervasive stereotype in the law at the time—that men are independent and women are men's dependents.

She describes how the use of a male plaintiff assisted in making a clear, easy-to-understand case of how gender stereotyping harms both men and women: "We had a male client, Stephen Wiesenfeld, who—like Sally Reed—had suffered a tragedy. His wife died while giving birth to their first child. He was given a healthy baby son, and he decided to stay home and raise his child. When he went to the local Social Security office and asked about the benefits a sole surviving parent could get, he was told that benefit is called a 'mother's benefit' and he didn't qualify. . . . He wrote a letter to the editor of the local newspaper. He started his letter, 'I've heard a lot about women's lib. Let me tell you my story.' He explained how his wife had been a wage-earner, paid the same Social Security tax a man would pay, yet he didn't qualify as a care-giving parent who could collect her child protective death benefit because he was male. His letter ended, 'Tell *that* to Gloria Steinem!'"

The Supreme Court rendered a unanimous judgment in favor of Stephen Wiesenfeld's right to collect his wife's death benefit, striking down the gender-based classification.[5] "Wiesenfeld's case shows the irrationality of gender-based classifications," Justice Ginsburg observes. "Consider his wife—she worked as a man did, paid the same Social Security tax as a male wage-earner, but the government would not protect her family the way it protected the family of a male wage-earner. . . . Then there was the husband, Stephen—he wanted to care for his child, but was told there were no benefits to do that because he was a male parent, not a female parent. . . . And there was the baby, Jason: he could not have the opportunity to have the care of his surviving parent, for the sole reason that it was his mother who died instead of his father."

An Impressive Record

Through the seventies, Ginsburg argued six and won five of the first and most important cases regarding equal rights for women and men before the Supreme Court—an amazing record of Supreme Court advocacy.[6] In addition, the Court accepted Ruth's view that challenges to gender-based discrimination deserve heightened scrutiny in *Craig v. Boren*, 429 U.S. 190 (1976) (in which Ruth filed a "friend of the court" brief). Kathleen Peratis, a former codirector of the ACLU Women's Law Project, described what it was like to work with Ruth on gender discrimination cases. "She wasn't just a wonderful lawyer. She was a visionary. . . . When we worked together at the ACLU, I knew Ruth would someday be on the Supreme Court—and we hoped become chief justice. . . . Step-by-step she made things happen that women

---

[5] *Weinberger v. Wiesenfeld,* 420 U.S. 636 (1975).

[6] The six Supreme Court cases Ruth argued, using the Fourteenth Amendment to erase gender discrimination, are: *Frontiero v. Richardson,* 411 U.S. 677 (1973); *Kahn v. Shevin,* 416 U.S. 351 (1974); *Edwards v. Healy,* 421 U.S. 772 (1975); *Weinberger v. Wiesenfeld,* 420 U.S. 636 (1975); *Califano v. Goldfarb,* 430 U.S. 199 (1977); and *Duren v. Missouri,* 439 U.S. 357 (1979).

had been dreaming about for a hundred years. Ruth's work for women is transcendent in the history of this country."

Two presidents confirmed Kathleen's assessment. In 1980, President Carter appointed Ginsburg to the United States Court of Appeals for the D.C. Circuit. In 1993, President Clinton, impressed by her sparkling record on the appellate court and by the significant precedents for women's rights she had set, hailed her as "the Thurgood Marshall of gender-equality law"—and elevated her to the Supreme Court.

Conquering Male Strongholds

In 1996, the Supreme Court decided that the exclusion of women from the Virginia Military Institute ("VMI") violated the Equal Protection Clause of the Fourteenth Amendment. Thus, the Commonwealth of Virginia could not exclude women from attending a public military college (VMI) if they met the entrance requirements. Fittingly, Justice Ginsburg wrote the Court's opinion, noting, "'inherent differences' between men and women, we have come to appreciate, remain cause for celebration, but not for denigration of the members of either sex or for artificial constraints on an individual's opportunity. . . . [S]uch classifications may not be used, as they once were, to create or perpetuate the legal, social, and economic inferiority of women."[7]

Ginsburg tells of a touching letter she received after the VMI decision: "A 1967 graduate of VMI wrote to say he knows a few young women today who are physically, intellectually, and emotionally tougher than he was when he first attended! He said since he made it through, he knew they would make it, too. . . . He wrote again a few months later and enclosed a pin given to the mothers of the graduating cadets at his graduation. His mother is now deceased, and his family decided they wanted me to have her pin—as an adjunct member of the 'VMI family.' . . . In his words, as a 'mother' to VMI's first and succeeding women graduates. . . . It is a gift I treasure."

And "like mother, like daughter" (as the saying will have to become),

---

[7] *United States v. Virginia,* 116 S. Ct. 2264, 2275-76 (1996).

Ruth's daughter Jane has also pursued a profession in law. Ruth speaks of Jane Ginsburg with pride and affection. Jane is an authority on copyright law who teaches at Columbia Law School. They share a love of the law. "We are the first mother-daughter pair to have attended Harvard Law School," Ruth reports, "and the first pair to serve on a law faculty in the United States (Columbia). . . . Consider this—yet another example of how the world has changed since I started on my way. At Harvard Law School in 1956, I was one of nine women in a class of over five hundred. By the time Jane attended in the late seventies, her class had one hundred women. Today there are at least twice that number in every starting class. . . . While I was there, I never imagined females would infiltrate a male bastion like Harvard Law School in those numbers."

The Supreme Court must still be regarded a male bastion, as Ginsburg— the 107th Supreme Court Justice in this country's history—is only the second female to serve. She states, "I am glad to contribute to the end of the days when women, at least half the talent pool in our society, appear in high places as one-at-a-time performers."

" . . . 'Inherent differences' between men and women, we have come to appreciate, remain cause for celebration, but not for denigration of the members of either sex or for artificial constraints on an individual's opportunity. . . . [S]uch classifications may not be used, as they once were, to create or perpetuate the legal, social, and economic inferiority of women."

Sisterhood among the Brethren

Of the first woman appointed to the Court, Justice Sandra Day O'Connor, Ginsburg comments, "Justice O'Connor also met with gender discrimination when she entered the work world. She graduated from Stanford Law School in 1952 at the top of her class. Our Chief Justice, William Rehnquist, was in her class. He also ranked at the top. Rehnquist got a Supreme Court clerkship, a much sought-after job for young lawyers. Not only was that opportunity not available to Sandra Day, but no firm would hire her to do a lawyer's work. She was offered jobs only as a legal secretary.

"I am glad to contribute to the end of the days when women, at least half the talent pool in our society, appear in high places as one-at-a-time performers."

"When I first arrived at the Court, Justice O'Connor was like a big sister—telling me many things to make my life easier. We may be on opposite sides in cases, but we respect each other. . . . For instance, there is a myth that the first opinion assigned to a new justice is a unanimous, easy case. My first assignment was not so easy, and the decision was six to three. Justice O'Connor joined the dissent. As I read a summary of my opinion from the bench, I was passed a note by a messenger. The note said: 'This is your first opinion for the Court. It is a fine opinion. I look forward to many more.' The note was signed 'Sandra.'"

The Thurgood Marshall Award

The American Bar Association's Thurgood Marshall Award recognizes long-term contributions to the advancement of civil rights in the United States. Thurgood Marshall himself received the inaugural award in 1992. When Ginsburg accepted the award a few hours after our conversation, she invoked its namesake—the person with whom she is most often compared—Thurgood Marshall:

> My chambers, some of you may know, are the only Justice's quarters upstairs at the Supreme Court. The rooms were Justice Marshall's from the time of his retirement until his death. Now and again I am

invited to move downstairs, but I am glad to stay in my current space. Across the room where I work, on a bookshelf I can see from my desk, there is a photograph of Justice Marshall, Ninth Circuit Judge Clifford Wallace, and me. . . .

Marshall's advice to his law clerks was in tune with his signal achievement, his careful orchestration of the campaign that culminated after many preparatory years in *Brown v. Board of Education.* He told his clerks that, to avoid exhaustion and burnout, one must carefully choose the battles one will fight. . . .

My advocacy, of course, did not begin to compare with Thurgood Marshall's. My life was never in danger, and the ACLU litigation I superintended was never the only show in town. Unlike the 1940s' and 1950s' efforts to achieve racial justice, controlled by Thurgood Marshall and his colleagues, sex discrimination litigation, from the start, was dispersed, with many, often uncoordinated, players on the scene. But of one thing there is no doubt. I gained courage and inspiration from Marshall's example—his measured step-by-step strategy; his understanding that it was necessary to educate his audience; his provision of that education in ways comprehensible by, and palatable to, the decision-makers.

When Ginsburg stops speaking, a long-lasting applause begins and swells. She remains at the podium and smiles. Her demeanor is modest, gracious. And it is evident that the audience needs to give this outpouring of appreciation and admiration to her much more than she needs to receive it. She has been accustomed to working for so many years in silence, without accolades or recognition. Ruth Bader Ginsburg's work as an advocate, an educator, and a spokesperson has provided women opportunities in a new landscape—to achieve and aspire, to tread upon stepping stones, to climb ridges, and to reach for the stars.

XV.

NORMA

SHAPIRO

Norma Shapiro and I worked about ten blocks from each other in downtown Philadelphia.

I left my office to walk to our meeting and headed toward City Hall—with its statue of William Penn shimmering atop it in the morning sun. Penn founded Philadelphia in 1682. Choosing the name because it means "City of Brother-ly Love," it comported with his goal of establishing a city on the precepts of religious freedom and civil liberty. I wondered what he would think of the changing roles of women in his city.

Then I walked through City Hall and down Market Street toward Independence Hall. There, almost a century after the founding of Philadelphia, a committee comprised of the brightest minds in the Continental Congress—Benjamin Franklin of Philadelphia, John Adams of Massachusetts, and Thomas Jefferson of Virginia—met to draw up the reasons why America should declare its independence from England. This resulted in Jefferson's drafting of the Declaration of Independence, with its assertion "All men are created equal." Likewise, as I walked, I mulled over what the Founding Fathers might have to say about all the women I had been meeting and their efforts on behalf of other women.

Across the street from Independence Hall is the federal courthouse. I entered and looked for Norma, the last "counselor" with whom I would be meeting. By this time I was on part-time status at my law firm, to give me the time to pull together the interviews and produce a manuscript.

And by this time, I had started to think about the path I would take after I made this manuscript as good as I possibly could and left the law firm. All I knew for sure was that, anymore, I didn't think anything was worth dedicating myself to unless I felt it could help those who come behind us and make the world better for them. I decided Penn, Franklin, Adams, and Jefferson would agree with me. That's what they were all about. And I decided the counselors I had met so far would agree with me, as that's what they're all about too.

I would have to put my mind to this and figure it out for myself very soon. For the moment, with a little tug of sadness at my heart, I walked into Norma's chambers for the last of the conversations.

The hallways leading to Norma Shapiro's judicial chambers in the federal courthouse are lined with annual group photographs of the judges who have served there. None of these photos includes a woman's face in the sea of distinguished-looking gentlemen until 1978. Until Norma Shapiro. Norma Shapiro is the first female to be appointed to the federal bench in the Third Circuit, which encompasses the federal courts of Pennsylvania, New Jersey, Delaware, and the Virgin Islands.

Norma Shapiro

RESIDENCE: Philadelphia, Pennsylvania
BORN: 1928
PERSONAL: Married (3 children)
POSITION: U.S. District Court Judge, Eastern District of Pennsylvania
1999 Recipient of the Margaret Brent Award

Seated at the conference table in her chambers, Norma comments on the composition of the photos in the outer hallway. "I certainly was lonely for a time," she says, mildly, but emphatically. "For years I had no one with whom to share feminine insights. I felt left out of informal meetings and socializing among the judges, and I was the only woman at our formal gatherings and meetings. There was hardly ever a woman in the halls. It was sometimes a difficult atmosphere."

It was necessary to become accustomed to being the only woman in the room, however. When she practiced law before becoming a judge, Norma was the first woman admitted to partnership at her firm—one of the largest in the city. In fact, she was one of the first few women to make partner in any of Philadelphia's major law firms. She was the first woman to serve on, and the first woman to chair, the Philadelphia Bar Association's Board of Governors. She is also one of the founders of the Women's Law Project, a coalition of women attorneys dedicated to public policy and education campaigns.

One of only eight women in her starting class at University of Pennsylvania Law School in 1948, a professor predicted this group of female students would "never make it." Norma flourished, however, becoming an editor of the law review and graduating at the top of her class. As law firms were generally unwilling to hire women as attorneys, her law school assisted with placing her as the first female law clerk of a very respected judge on the Pennsylvania Supreme Court. Upon completing the one-year clerkship, she did receive a job offer from a Philadelphia law firm—but as the firm's librarian, not as a lawyer. Instead, she decided to teach legal writing at the University of Pennsylvania Law School. Eventually, she was able to make her way into private practice. After three years of litigating at a firm, she took a leave of absence for nine years (during which time she had her three children and was very active in civic matters); she then came back to the firm in 1967 and was made a partner in 1973. President Jimmy Carter appointed her to the federal bench in 1978.

Lighting the Way

Lifting a piece of paper from her desk, Norma volunteers, "Let me share one of my favorite quotations. This sums up my advice to young women embarking on the journey of a new career. It is from Gaius, an ancient Roman official: 'One who helps the wandering traveler does, as it were, light another's lamp by their own, and it gives no less light because it helped another.'" She then remarks, "When you light the candle in another's lamp with your own, your lamp still shines bright. . . . My lamp has never burned out."

Norma's lamp has, in fact, lit the way for countless travelers, including Phyllis Beck (a Pennsylvania Superior Court judge, the third woman in Pennsylvania to win a state-wide election, and the first to serve on an appellate court). Phyllis recognizes Norma as one of her great supporters. Phyllis, in turn, is a supporter of Norma's. "When I became a judge," Phyllis remembers, "I received a phone call from Norma. She welcomed me to the bench and gave me some advice on getting started. She offered herself as a resource for anything I might need. At professional gatherings, she sought me out. . . . But the wonderful thing about Norma is not that she was nice to me when I was a new judge. It is that I have learned I am not the only new judge to whom she has extended this sort of kindness. So many women who have joined the bench from this area were contacted by Norma. We all think of her as a friend we can call upon. She is the roots of a tree that is growing and blossoming." She smiles, "Just call me Norma's number one fan."

Another traveler Norma helped along her way is United States District Judge Anita Brody. Brody recounts, "After Norma spent fourteen years as the only woman on this bench, I also was appointed to it. . . . She was elated to have me join her. . . . She told me she felt like a child who had been waiting to have a sister—though that did not mean she didn't love her brothers! She provided invaluable guidance. . . . And I have seen her chambers open to young women seeking advice from the student level to those seeking public office. She is dedicated to mentoring."

When asked why she chose to take up a lamp and go out and travel the hard road years ago when there were few other women on the path, Norma responds, "There were a number of influences, but I'll share one early one— a woman I admired but never knew. Florence Allen, a judge of the Ohio Supreme Court, was this country's first female federal judge. I wrote an essay about her in eighth grade. . . . She inspired me, as hope I have encouraged others, to pursue a career in the law."

". . . I recommend not only networking and mentoring, but actually forming a network of mentors."

Constructing a Network

Norma explains how she came to value mentoring. She remembers how, even though she had "been admitted through a door" by being appointed to a federal judgeship, she sometimes felt excluded when she saw what is often called "the old boy network" in action: "I would be in a meeting with male colleagues, and the name of a man in our professional community would come up. Invariably, somebody in the group knew him— from prep school, college, graduate school, sports, military, country clubs, or time spent practicing at firms. I was amazed repeatedly at how many of their colleagues my male colleagues knew or knew of. . . . They used this informal network to move their careers along.

"Women entering the professions lacked this established network—we didn't serve in the military together, we didn't play team sports. We were not made to feel entirely welcome or included by male colleagues. . . . So we tried to reconstruct the dynamic of the old boy network amongst ourselves—in a bit of a contrived way, perhaps. Women had meetings and started organizations with the explicit purpose of career consulting and career enhancement for women. Men didn't do that. They didn't need to. They got to know each other in other ways, and then used those friendships for career advancement. Women had meetings for career advancement, and then became friends and did other things together. . . . Now there's a substantial network out there of women—and men—who are willing and able to help a woman advance after a door has been opened to her."

Mentoring 101

In addition to forming a network of professional friends and acquaintances, Norma recommends cultivating mentor-protége relationships in the workplace. "You learn so much from someone further along in her career who helps you develop your potential," she observes. "It's a nurturing relationship, in which your errors are corrected and your efforts are supported. You learn how to do your job, but you also learn how to fill out the edges of being a professional— how to make decisions that include strategy on the big picture or ethical issues, how to infuse humor into a difficult situation. . . . I also suggest to young women that they find mentors outside of their company or organization to provide career guidance. I even think mentor relationships with people outside your field are helpful. . . . So I guess you could say I recommend not only networking and mentoring, but actually forming a network of mentors."

She describes some of her activities involved in the ongoing business of mentoring: "Some people just need you to listen and provide encouragement. Some ask me a question or two once in a while. Sometimes I sit here coun-seling someone and I think 'Whom do I know? And whom do my friends know?' so I can provide an introduction needed to help achieve a goal. . . . Some people need information from me. Some want to discuss their plans and solicit advice. . . . It is a joy for me to do all of it. I love spotting new talent and vicariously enjoying the successes of others." She smiles, "I make a lot of new friends in the process.

"If a female attorney told me she wanted to establish a professional presence in the community," Norma elaborates, "I would coach her with these suggestions: Branch out and work for some new people in your firm; develop an area of expertise that people in the firm, clients, or the media will come to you about; teach a seminar in the professional community on recent legal issues; publish an article in a trade journal read by clients, lawyers, and potential clients; participate in a local professional committee, perhaps through the bar association; and get involved in a community endeavor. . . . For instance, I have served as an associate trustee of a university, a trustee of a hospital, as well as a school board president. And I am presently serving as the president of the Jewish Publication Society. . . . The people you meet in these sorts of activities are often leaders in the community, and this is a good way to get to know them."

". . . Identify what it is you want to accomplish and what you need from others . . . Then think about who could help you—and be able to tell them why you think this.

List the anticipated obstacles you will face in accomplishing your goal, as well as anything that has prevented you from doing so in the past."

Norma talks about some ways in which a student might augment school experience through volunteer work and be affected by even a small amount of encouragement from a mentor. For example, a college student volunteering to help a lawyer one afternoon a week in a law firm can witness how a lawyer functions, develop various workplace skills, get advice on subjects to study in school, or solicit other career advice. Further, small gestures, such as a mentor adopting language suggested by a student for an article or a speech can have a positive impact on the ego and confidence of the student. Norma comments, "A small thing like that is wonderful, isn't it? Someone sees more in you than you see in yourself and goes out of his or her way to help you. . . . Everyone should take that kind of interest in others."

How to Approach a Mentor

When looking for advice from a mentor, Norma advises that there are a number of things to keep in mind. "First, identify what it is you want to accomplish and what you need from others—training, advice, information, an opportunity, an introduction to someone. Then think about who could help you—and be able to tell them why you think this. List the anticipated obstacles you will face in accomplishing your goal, as well as anything that has prevented you from doing so in the past. . . . Don't define success and achievement strictly in relation to your family or your peers. There are many ways to get to the same place—and there are plenty of great places to go! Think about the paths most suitable for you. . . . Keep in mind you can wander a bit without being lost.

"The helpful role of failure must be recognized." She counsels, "When you experience a failure or a set-back of some kind, assess what went wrong so you can avoid the same problem in the future. . . . Then, when you proceed again, don't proceed in a way designed to protect yourself from other failures. Proceed having learned things about yourself and others or about a situation. . . . Realize that everyone has failures. Not succeeding at something right away—or in the way you want—may cause you to re-examine what is important to you and what your goals will be. Lots of people tell me how a perceived 'failure' helped them to better define their desires and actually assisted them on their way to success. In hindsight, they're happy things did not turn out as they originally hoped and planned. . . . To put today's failure in perspective, write down a few things you've accomplished in the past. Remind yourself of what you had to overcome and how you did it. In the future, today's failure will be a tiny blip on the radar screen."

Norma stresses the importance of being appreciative of those who take the time to help you. "When someone mentors you—and I mean 'mentor' as a person who helps you along your way (he or she doesn't have to be your boss or your teacher . . . it could be a peer)—show your gratitude! Someone has stopped what she was doing to help you with what you're doing. She might have something to gain from it, or she might not. But she extended herself for you just the same. . . . A short note, voicemail, or e-mail from you saying thanks and letting her know what happened as a result of the effort is appropriate— and it keeps the door open for future assistance. . . .

"A caveat! Be considerate of busy schedules. Don't call in the middle of the workday expecting to discuss an issue that will require an hour. . . . I have found there are plenty of women who feel it is their obligation to mentor other women. . . . So I am always surprised at the disbelief a young woman might express to me when we meet somewhere, talk a bit, and I say 'call me for lunch so we can talk some more.' . . . People sometimes seem surprised that there are those of us who offer help—who look for ways to help others along. Yet, the reason I'm at this job is because I believe in the importance of this country's future generations. . . . I support and defend the Constitution of the United States so our children and their children's children will know the blessings of liberty."

"Not succeeding at something right away—or in the way you want—may cause you to re-examine what is important to you and what your goals will be. Lots of people tell me how a perceived 'failure' helped them to better define their desires and actually assisted them on their way to success."

Improving Communication

Norma suggests others could start to be mentors in the same manner she did: "I used to always tell my coworkers things I wished I'd known earlier. From the positive feedback I received, I discovered I enjoyed helping people."

Norma goes on to share something she has learned in her career that she wishes she had known earlier. "You cannot overestimate the importance of communication skills in the workplace—and in life, for that matter. When you interact with a loved one, an adversary, or a colleague, you must understand the other person before you can hope to influence them. Listen attentively. Paraphrasing in your own words what the other person has said to you is a good tool to make sure you understand. Ask follow-up questions. . . . Communication is not successful because of what you're saying—it is successful based upon what the other person is hearing.

"Communication is not successful because of what you're saying—it is successful based upon what the other person is hearing."

"Improve your reading and writing, your speaking and listening skills. Spend time with words. Read books by good writers. Revise your own writing until it says what you want to say—precisely. Edit your writing until it is polished—until it sparkles! . . . In an information society, words are what we exchange—not our handiwork. Make the way you handle words a craft. Choosing the right words to use can clarify issues and bring consensus."

She also considers being able to speak in front of others an essential career skill. "Project confidence—speak up, loudly and clearly. What you have to say is important enough to be heard. . . . Lawyers standing before me in the courtroom to make an oral argument or an opening statement have known the facts and the case law—but mumble. It is hard to believe they are attempting to convince me or the jury of anything. . . . Some ways to improve speaking skills are by reading aloud, by talking into a tape recorder and reviewing the tape, and by practicing presentations in front of others or in front of a mirror. . . . Practice really does make you better at it. When I served as president of the school board, I was often called upon to give off-the-cuff remarks. Now I never need a rehearsed speech."

A Parting Lesson

Norma comes around from behind her desk and sits on its edge: "One more thing . . . As a woman who started a career in the 1950s, let's just say I suffered countless acts of gender discrimination and harassment. It doesn't matter what they were. There's little to be learned from that. But you can learn from the way I dealt with it. I coped by never assuming that any mistreatment resulted from anything I said or did. . . . Discrimination and anti-feminine prejudice is a defect of the discriminator

"Discrimination and anti-feminine prejudice is a defect of the discriminator and a sign of insecurity—not mine, but his. . . . There was something about me he feared. And, as far as I was concerned, he had something to learn."

and a sign of insecurity—not mine, but his. It was a sign that something about me made him uncomfortable. There was something about me he feared. And, as far as I was concerned, he had something to learn."

MARGARET BRENT AWARD RECIPIENTS

Margaret Brent arrived in America in 1638 with a large land grant. As an unmarried property owner, Brent was able to exercise rights of "court-baron" and "court-leet." Maryland court records show that she appeared in over one hundred cases. There is no evidence of another female lawyer in the United States until the suffrage movement in the late nineteenth century.

In 1991, Senator Hillary Rodham Clinton, while serving as chair of the American Bar Association's Commission on Women in the Profession, established the Margaret Brent Women Lawyers of Achievement Award to recognize women who have achieved excellence, influenced other women to pursue careers, and opened doors previously closed to women.

I met with about twice as many Margaret Brent Award recipients as are featured in *The Counselors*. Time and space constraints prevented further conversations from being pursued or presented. It should be noted that all of the recipients I met, as you might imagine, were uniformly impressive, inspirational, and wonderful.

2001 Honorees

Laurel Bellows, Partner, Bellows & Bellows, Chicago, Illinois

Irma Herrera, Executive Director, Equal Rights Advocates, San Francisco, California

Hon. Gabrielle Kirk McDonald, Special Council on Human Rights, Freeport McMoran Copper & Gold, New York, New York

Hon. Mary Schroeder, Chief United States Circuit Judge, United States Court of Appeals for the Ninth Circuit, Phoenix, Arizona

Marna Tucker, Partner, Feldesman Tucker Leifer Fidell & Bank LLP, Washington, D.C.

2000 Honorees

Sheila L. Birnbaum, Partner, Skadden, Arps, Slate, Meagher & Flom, LLP, New York, New York

Shirley M. Hufstedler, Senior Counsel, Morrison & Foerster, LLP, Los Angeles, California

Hon. Judith S. Kaye, Chief Judge, Court of Appeals of the State of New York; New York, New York

Justice Sandra Day O'Connor, Supreme Court of the United States, Washington, D.C.

Dovey L. Roundtree, General Counsel, National Council of Negro Women, Charlotte, North Carolina

1999 Honorees

Prof. Barbara Allen Babcock, Judge John Crown Professor of Law, Stanford Law School, Stanford, California

Carol E. Dinkins, Partner, Vinson & Elkins, LLP, Houston, Texas

Justice Carol W. Hunstein, Supreme Court of Georgia, Atlanta, Georgia

Pauline A. Schneider, Partner, Hunton & Williams, Washington, D.C.

Hon. Norma L. Shapiro, United States District Court for the Eastern District of Pennsylvania, Philadelphia, Pennsylvania

1998 Honorees

Special Award: **Justice Claire L'Heureux-Dubé,** Supreme Court of Canada, Ottawa, Ontario, Canada

Maureen Kempston Darkes, President, General Motors of Canada, Ltd., Oshawa, Ontario, Canada

Justice Bernette Joshua Johnson, Louisiana Supreme Court; New Orleans, Louisiana

Irma L. Rangel, State Representative, Texas House of Representatives, Austin, Texas

Judith Resnik, Arthur Liman Professor of Law, Yale University Law School, New Haven, Connecticut

Judith A. Winston, former Executive Director, The President's Initiative on Race, Washington, D.C.

1997 Honorees

Special Award: **Roberta Cooper Ramo,** Past President, ABA, Albuquerque, New Mexico

Evelyn Gandy, First woman Lieutenant Governor of Mississippi, Hattiesburg, Mississippi

Jamie S. Gorelick, Vice Chair, Fannie Mae and former Deputy Attorney General of the United States, Washington, D.C.

Antonia Hernandez, President and General Counsel, Mexican American Legal Defense and Educational Fund, Los Angeles, Calfornia

Hon. Joan Dempsey Klein, Presiding Justice, California Court of Appeals, Los Angeles, California

Drucilla Stender Ramey, Executive Director and General Counsel, Bar Association of San Francisco, San Francisco, California

1996 Honorees

Hon. Rosemary Barkett, United States Court of Appeals, Eleventh Circuit, Miami, Florida

Justice Beryl Levine, North Dakota Supreme Court, Palo Alto, California (retired)

Nina Miglionico, Partner, Miglionico & Rumore, Birmingham, Alabama

Lynn Hecht Schafran, Director, National Judicial Education Program/NOW Legal Defense and Education Fund, New York, New York

Patricia Schroeder, United States House of Representatives, Denver, Colorado (retired); President of the Association of American Publishers

1995 Honorees

Special Award: **Hon. Bella Abzug,** former Congresswoman & Cochair, Women's Environmental & Development Organization, New York, New York (deceased)

Justice Shirley S. Abrahamson, Wisconsin Supreme Court, Madison, Wisconsin

Mahala Ashley Dickerson, Partner, Dickerson & Gibbons, Anchorage, Alaska

Prof. Lani Guinier, University of Pennsylvania Law School, Philadelphia, Pennsylvania

Louise B. Raggio, President, Raggio & Raggio, Inc., Dallas, Texas

Ada Shen-Jeffe, Director, Evergreen Legal Services, Seattle, Washington

1994 Honorees

Special Award: **Prof. Barbara Jordan,** LBJ School of Public Affairs, University of Texas, Austin, Texas (deceased)

Nancy L. Davis, former Executive Director, cofounder of Equal Rights Advocates, San Francisco, California

Jean E. Dubofsky, Attorney, sole practictioner, Boulder, Colorado

Margaret Hilary Marshall, former Vice President & General Counsel, Harvard University, Cambridge, Massachusetts; Chief Justice of the Supreme Court of Massachusetts

Vilma S. Martinez, Partner, Munger, Tolles & Olson, Los Angeles, California

Hon. Patricia McGowan Wald, United States Court of Appeals, D.C. Circuit, Washington, D.C.

1993 Honorees

Special Award: **Hon. Janet Reno,** former United States Attorney General, Washington, D.C.

Hon. Betty Weinberg Ellerin, Associate Justice, Appellate Division, New York

Justice Ruth Bader Ginsburg, United States Supreme Court, Washington, D.C.

Elaine R. Jones, Director-Counsel, NAACP Legal Defense & Education Fund, New York

Justice Joyce L. Kennard, California Supreme Court, San Francisco, California

Esther R. Rothstein, Partner, McCarthy and Levin, Chicago, Illinois (deceased)

1992 Honorees

Special Award: Anita F. Hill, former Professor, University of Oklahoma College of Law, Norman, Oklahoma

Margaret L. Behm, Partner, Dodson, Parker & Behm, Nashville, Tennessee

Hon. Betty B. Fletcher, United States Court of Appeals, Ninth Circuit, Seattle, Washington

Dean and Prof. Herma Hill Kay, University of California Law School (Boalt Hall), Berkeley, California

Rep. Patsy Takemoto Mink, United States House of Representatives, Honolulu, Hawaii

Justice Leah J. Sears, Supreme Court of Georgia, Atlanta, Georgia

1991 Honorees

Hon. Phyllis A. Kravitch, United States Court of Appeals, Eleventh Circuit, Atlanta, Georgia

Andrea Sheridan Ordin, Attorney, private practice, Los Angeles, California

Justice Rosalie Wahl, Minnesota Supreme Court, St. Paul, Minnesota (retired)

Jeanette Rosner Wolman, Attorney, Baltimore, Maryland (deceased)

Marilyn V. Yarbrough, former Dean, University of Tennessee College of Law, Knoxville, Tennessee

Resources

Here is contact information for organizations and causes related to *The Counselors*. I will be donating some portion of any proceeds I receive from the sale of this book to each of the following.

American Bar Association Commission on Women in the Profession

The Commission on Women assists women in law school, law firms, public interest, academia, and the judiciary. The Commission recognizes trailblazing women with its Margaret Brent Award at the ABA annual meeting every summer. It has a newsletter as well as a number of other publications for sale.

ABA Commission on Women in the Profession
750 North Lakeshore Drive
Chicago, IL 60611
Phone: (312) 988-5715
Email: abacwp@abanet.org
www.abanet.org/women

College Summit

College Summit works to increase the college enrollment rates of low-income, academically mid-tier students by helping students show their whole selves to colleges in the application process and by helping schools and businesses to better identify and prepare these students. I have served as a writing coach at College Summit's workshops on college applications.

College Summit
P.O. Box 9966
Washington, DC 20016
Phone: (202) 966-1222; (866) 266-1100
Email: jharrison@collegesummit.org
www.collegesummit.org

Equal Rights Advocates

Equal Rights Advocates uses litigation and advocacy to work for equal rights and economic opportunities for women and girls. Nancy Davis, interviewed for Chapter IX of *The Counselors,* is ERA's co-founder and former executive director.

Equal Rights Advocates
1663 Mission Street, Suite 250
San Francisco, CA 94103
Phone: (415) 621-0672
Advice and Counseling: (800) 839-4ERA
Email: info@equalrights.org
www.equalrights.org

Families for Freedom Scholarship

Former President Bill Clinton and Former Senate Majority Leader Bob Dole are cochairs of a scholarship fund that will provide educational assistance for the children and spouses of those killed or permanently disabled as a result of the terrorist attack on America on September 11, 2001.

Families of Freedom Scholarship Fund
Citizens' Scholarship Foundation of America
1505 Riverview Road
P.O. Box 297
St. Peter, MN 56082
Phone: (877) 862-0136
Email: freedom@csfa.org
www.familiesoffreedom.org

The International Association of Women Judges

The International Association of Women Judges works to promote the rights of women to equal justice around the world. Joan Dempsey Klein (Chapter XI) is a founder of IAWJ.

The International Association of Women Judges
50 F Street NW, Ste. 8312
Washington, DC 20001
Phone: (202) 393-0955
Email: office@iawj-iwjf.org
www.iawj-iwjf.org

Mexican American Legal Defense and Education Fund

The Mexican American Legal Defense and Education Fund works to promote and protect the civil rights of the tens of millions of American Latinos in education, employment, immigration, and voting access. Antonia Hernandez, the subject of Chapter XII, serves as its president and general counsel.

Mexican American Legal Defense and Education Fund
634 S. Spring Street
Los Angeles, CA 90014
Phone: (213) 629-2512
Email: maldefone@aol.com
www.maldef.org

NAACP Legal Defense and Education Fund

The NAACP Legal Defense and Education Fund, Inc. uses the legal system, public education, and policy research to work for the civil rights of African-Americans and other disenfranchised individuals. Elaine Jones (Chapter VIII) is LDF's president and director-counsel.

NAACP Legal Defense and Education Fund Inc.
99 Hudson Street, 16th Floor
New York, NY 10013
Phone: (212) 965-2200
Email: info@naacpldf.org
www.naacpldf.org

The National Association of Women Judges

The National Association of Women Judges has members who are both female and male judges, from all levels of the judiciary. NAWJ strives to improve the administration of justice by working toward fairness, gender equality, and diversity in America's courts. Joan Dempsey Klein, whose story is shared in Chapter XI, is a founder of NAWJ.

The National Association of Women Judges
1112 16th Street NW, Suite 520
Washington, DC 20036
Phone: (202) 393-0222
Email: nawj@nawj.org
www.nawj.org

NOW Legal Defense and Education Fund, including the National Judicial Education Program

NOW (National Organization for Women) Legal Defense and Education
Fund uses the law to work for women's rights—in courts, Congress, state
legislatures, and the media. I work for the National Judicial Education
Program (a project of NOW LDF in cooperation with the National
Association of Women Judges). Lynn Hecht Schafran, Director of the
National Judicial Education Program and the subject of Chapter I
in *The Counselors,* suggests obtaining the *Gender Fairness Strategies
Implementation Resources Directory* from the NJEP to learn more about
what the gender bias implementation committees have done.

NOW Legal Defense and Education Fund and/or
National Judicial Education Project
395 Hudson Street
New York, NY 10014
Phone: (212) 925-6635
Email Helpline: peo@nowldef.org
Email for NJEP: njep@nowldef.org
www.nowldef.org

The Truman Scholars Program

The Truman Scholarship was established by Congress in 1975 as the official memorial to the United States' 33rd President. The Truman Foundation awards scholarships for college students to attend graduate school and to prepare for careers in government and public service. I'm a 1985 Truman Scholar.

Truman Scholarship Foundation
712 Jackson Place, NW
Washington, DC 20006
Phone: (202) 395-4831
Email: office@truman.gov
www.truman.gov

INDEX

About the Author

Elizabeth Vrato is an attorney practicing with the NOW Legal Defense and Education Fund—she is currently working on an initiative to promote gender equality in the legal system. She earned her law degree from New York University School of Law in 1990, where she was an editor on the Moot Court Board. She was valedictorian of her graduating class from La Salle University in 1987 and a 1985 Truman Scholar from Pennsylvania. As a woman in a traditionally male-dominated profession, Elizabeth has sought out mentors and role models and has seen the difference they can make.